Exploring Direct and Relationship Marketing

Dedication

MJE: Dedicated to the one I love (KAB)

Exploring Direct and Relationship Marketing

Second edition

Martin Evans

Lisa O'Malley

Maurice Patterson

THOMSON

Australia · Canada · Mexico · Singapore · Spain · United Kingdom · United States

THOMSON
™

Exploring Direct and Relationship Marketing

Copyright 2004 Martin Evans, Lisa O'Malley and Maurice Patterson

The Thomson logo is a registered trademark used herein under licence.

For more information, contact Thomson Learning, High Holborn House, 50-51 Bedford Row, London WC1R 4LR or visit us on the World Wide Web at: http://www.thomsonlearning.co.uk

British Library Cataloguing-in-Publication Data
A catalogue record for this book is available from the British Library

ISBN 1-86152-901-5
First edition published 1999 as Exploring Direct Marketing by Thomson Learning.
Reprinted 2001.

Typeset by LaserScript, Mitcham, Surrey

Printed in Croatia by Zrinski

Contents

299 **PART 4** Relational Vehicles and Messages

301 **10** Relational media

Preface

What's it about?

So, what are you expecting? A book that explores 'junk mail'? A book that provides a techie's view of technology-based customer relationship management (CRM)? Or perhaps a book that focuses on media such as the Internet? Well, you have opened a book that is none of these (exclusively) yet is all of them and more!

Many people still receive what they regard as junk mail. This is directly addressed mail but which is not seen to be relevant, accurate or timely. We do indeed explore this (but not only in a 'mail' context) and suggest how the 'junk' can be replaced with 'relational'. CRM has had a somewhat inauspicious life, with many CRM projects failing and practitioners turning away from them. We do explore the technologies that fuel these projects but show how a more strategic and organisation-wide role can lead to mutually satisfying relational interaction between organisations and their various stakeholders. Yes, we do also explore the Internet, but only as one of the interactive communications media that facilitate interactive relational marketing.

But we also explore other issues, such as how marketing is now able to collect and analyse a wide range of market and customer data in order to target more precisely and relevantly than ever. We are critical in that this is often not reflected in practice. We also explore how the new marketing is able to test different approaches, in relatively mechanistic ways, but how this needs to be complemented with insightful understanding of customers and markets.

The fusion of data and insight can extend transactional interaction between organisations and customers to relational interaction. Indeed, a thrust of the entire book is that in order to be effective, marketing should not focus exclusively on transactions with customers but rather it should move further towards greater understanding of customers in order to identify and target those with whom there are more likely to be mutually satisfying relationships.

The synergy of data and new interactive media is leading to new business models. The Internet, for example, allows customers to band together (virtually) in buying cooperatives and, in this way, the customer-to-customer (C2C) model shifts control a little away from the organisation. It is also clear that the new marketing is fuelling organisational alliances both up- and downstream and across partners. The sharing of data via knowledge management approaches is also creating new business models. All in all, we are seeing some of the most significant changes that have ever impacted marketing.

But we do not shy away from a critical analysis of all of this. There are plenty of examples of claimed relational interaction where rhetoric is stronger than reality. We explore customer reactions to direct and interactive relational marketing and provide reviews of data protection legislation.

Approach

We deliberately incorporate substantive conceptual underpinning of the interactive and relational marketing approaches that we discuss (and include 'in theory' boxes in each chapter). There is also substantial referencing to the academic and practitioner literature, so you can delve into topics that are related to, but beyond the scope of, our coverage.

At the same time we use a large number of examples and case studies to illustrate our points. So, essentially our approach is to blend theory and practice.

Structure of the book

Part 1 explores what Direct Relational Marketing actually is and is concerned with the growth of interactive and relational direct marketing. It provides the background to the adoption of data-informed marketing by many organisations and introduces the concept of relationship marketing.

The transition to the new era of relationship marketing is facilitated by the collection and use of 'data'. In Part 2 (Data and Information Drivers) the new 'metrics' such as recency, frequency and monetary value (RFM) and long-time value (LTV) allow companies to identify those customers who are not contributing as much revenue or profit as the company would like.

Sometimes this leads to termination of the relationship by the company by 'deselecting' or excluding these customers. Throughout the book we introduce cautionary notes and there are some at this point. Could some of those deselected now become top-tier customers in the future? Would they actually be very loyal even if they don't contribute much to the bottom line? Does it fit with the marketing concept to set out deliberately not to satisfy some customers? Perhaps this is stated in extremis but the issues are worth considering.

We also explore aspects of market research and testing in Part 2 that are relevant to direct and relational marketing. There is another cautionary note here: customer data such as that concerned with *what* has been purchased, *when*, and *how*, is sometimes taken to be 'the' surrogate for true understanding and insight. What helps to overcome this is research into the psychology of how consumers process information, how they respond to marketing activity and so on. In Part 2 we also explore some dimensions of consumer behaviour within the relational context and how the blend of this and data-informed segmentation can be used in targeting.

Part 3 then explores the nature of relational marketing that the new data-informed marketing brings. The current conceptualisation and normative application of relationship marketing is analysed and evaluated. The recent infatuation with customer relationship management (CRM) is also examined and several reasons are proposed as to why many CRM projects have failed. Not least is the frequent over-focus on technology to analyse data at the expense of a more pervasive paradigm shift in the organisation that recognises the importance of wider marketing networks. This is an approach that moves relationship marketing towards intra- and inter-company networks within what should be a broader CRM paradigm. Our coverage of knowledge management in particular addresses this issue which includes the importance of converting data into knowledge that is shared across functions and partners.

Within our coverage of relational marketing in Part 3, we explore the progression from *acquiring* to *keeping* customers. The logical extension of this progression is to strive for customer loyalty and we provide conceptual and practical manifestations of this, but also introduce cautionary notes, which again concern the oft-seen mismatch of rhetoric and reality.

Part 4 is concerned with media and messages for relational interaction. The new relevance of the Internet is recognised and we explore how this medium can facilitate, enrich (and also damage) relationships. In addition, we draw from the behavioural sciences to suggest how messages that can enhance interactive relationships can be created.

We complete the book with synergistic chapters that are concerned with direct and relational marketing planning, but which position this within a societal context. The wider ramifications of the new data-informed relational direct marketing are explored. A particular focus is that of possible social concerns such as privacy invasion arising from the collection and use (and sometimes abuse) of personal details. The contribution of data protection and other legislation is also summarised, as are possible solutions that marketers and their organisations can implement themselves. We provide a model for relational marketing planning and discuss its elements and stages.

As an overall summary of the book, Exhibit 0.1 shows our view of the relationship between organisations, customers and technology. The dimensions inside the triangle reflect the increasing trend towards data-informed relational interaction between customers and organisations and between organisations. We are less happy with a purely 'data-driven' paradigm. If 'data' is used tactically in a mechanistic way to drive targeting within campaigns, then we feel marketers are in danger of reinforcing customer perceptions of 'junk' targeting. If, however, 'data' leads to real and insightful understanding of customers, often blended with more affective understanding, then the resulting knowledge can be used to inform relational interaction. This is not merely between organisations and customers but increasingly with suppliers and partners, and requires sophisticated and effective management of data across these parties in order for 'knowledge' and insight to be used strategically and tactically.

Learning aids

We provide a variety of aids to student learning both within the text and on the accompanying website.

EXHIBIT 0.1   Relational interactions

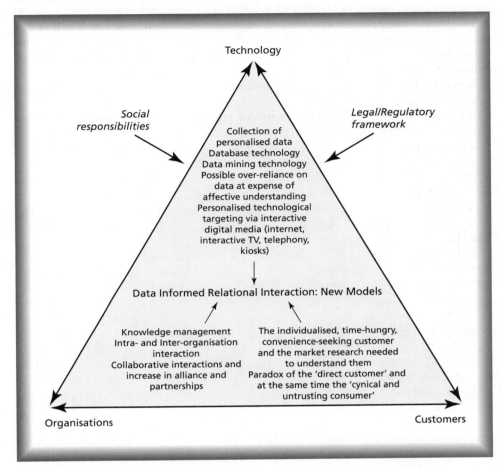

Each chapter includes an 'in theory' box as already mentioned, in which deeper conceptual issues are explored. We also provide a large number of case studies across all chapters and these link our discussion of issues and concepts with the real world. We are very grateful to all who either contributed case material exclusively for this book or who granted permission for us to include their already published material.

We have a range of cases from the Direct Marketing Association (DMA)/Royal Mail Annual Awards of 2001 and 2002. As well as being able to incorporate some of these cases within the text, we are especially grateful to the DMA for allowing us to use our accompanying website as a repository for the full range of cases as published in the annual 'Book of the Night' as it is known. The web-based cases are all in PDF file format and include useful narrative summaries of the cases along with interesting graphic images of the campaigns concerned. We organise these cases within different themes, such as 'CRM' or 'Creative' or 'Door-to-door media' and so on.

We have also been granted permission to incorporate cases and articles from *Marketing Direct, Direct Response* and *Revolution*, all from the Haymarket portfolio of marketing journals. Again, we include some of this material in the text but there is much more on the accompanying website, much of which includes full-colour graphics within the PDF files: www.thomsonlearning.co.uk/marketing/evans.

The website is also home to other material such as a live Access database for you to play with.

In addition, we provide links to useful websites, such as those of Experian, CACI and DunnHumby.

Acknowledgements

We are grateful to many who have helped in the preparation of this book. These include:

Alex Williams, Haymarket Publications
Ross Facer, Experian
Emma Chablo, SmartFocus
Nigel Lawrence, DunnHumby
Nigel Magson, Talking Numbers
Steve Barr, The Values Engine
Sean Moore, DMA

Also to the following companies which granted permission for us to include their material, and cases studies:

Experian
Eurocamp
SmartFocus
Talking Numbers
CACI
DMA
Marlboro Customer services
The Future Foundation
DunnHumby
Values Engine
MVC
Jackson's Stores
Haymarket Publications

We are grateful to the many students and colleagues at several Universities for their feedback on the First Edition and suggestions for this Second Edition.

Thanks also to the students at the University of the West of England for their BMW case solution (web site) and to Jennifer Pegg (Thomson Learning) for her Access database web site. Thanks also to Jennifer for your encouragement and support before, during and after the writing of this book and to all the production people at Thomson Learning.

List of exhibits

List of tables

Foreword

As the authors remind readers in their Preface, to many consumers, 'direct' equates to 'junk' when it comes to marketing through mail, telephone and internet channels. Despite the widespread implementation of data warehouse projects to hold extensive information about customers linked to an increasing range of powerful analytical tools to target marketing to those defined as being prime prospects, anecdotal evidence suggests that the situation has not improved over time. In fact, the application of technology is probably a prime factor in exacerbating the position, making it infinitely easier, and less costly, to implement campaigns and significantly shorten the cycle of development, execution, response and performance analysis. Market sectors have become more competitive leading to the same individuals being selected by the different players, selection probably being based on the application of similar propensity models.

Many of those initiating these campaigns probably believe, or hope, that all this activity will magically create bonds with customers and prospects that will cement or instigate a long and beautiful relationship. The reality is somewhat different. It is not really surprising that data privacy legislation includes special restrictions applying to direct marketing activities, or that 'preference' services are welcomed by the public as a way to control the flow of promotions through the letterbox, telephone and computer.

So why does it seem to go wrong, on so many occasions? This book seeks to provide some of the answers and identify ways in which organizations can use the direct channels responsibly and effectively as routes to develop mutually beneficial relationship with their customers. By tracing the development of direct and relational marketing, and discussing the societal issues, the book also provides a wider perspective on the overall topic, enabling readers to appreciate why they need to take a broader view when assessing the impact of their marketing activities.

In particular, this book tackles the important question as to why amassing customer related data does not necessarily lead to a better understanding of the customer, or their needs, when developing marketing strategy. It also places the role played by technology firmly into context – not 'back in its box', but in a position where investment in IT tools and solutions is soundly based on the need to achieve clearly defined business goals.

And this is rather more than simply a book. Through the accompanying web site and extensive bibliographies, readers can gain access to a rich seam of additional knowledge, including case studies, commentaries by specialist journalists and academic papers on a wide range of related topics.

Overall, this book is aimed at providing students, academics and practitioners with sound advice and guidance to help them build the foundations for developing relationships with customers that deliver real value to both parties.

Peter Mouncey, FMRS, FIDM, Visiting Fellow of Cranfield University School of Management, Associate of the Marketing Best Practice Consultancy and formerly Chairman of the Market Research Society and, at the Automobile Association, responsible for Group Marketing Services and CRM Strategy.

PART 1
What is Direct Relational Marketing?

1 The growth and nature of direct relational marketing

Direct marketing is not new, either conceptually or in practice. In Venice in 1498 Aldus Manutius published a book catalogue and William Lucas published a gardening catalogue in England in 1667. A variety of other mail-order catalogues and clubs appeared, especially in Europe and the USA, through the 18th and 19th centuries and in fact there was a significant growth in the USA in particular during the 1800s because of rising demand for goods from isolated communities which could be serviced by the improving distribution and postal systems (Institute of Direct Marketing, 1995). In these ways, then, 'going direct' has strong origins in distribution and in more recent times there has been significant adoption of 'disintermediation' strategies to bypass wholesalers and/or retailers. There are obvious cost savings to be made in many cases by not having to resource and stock physical premises, perhaps in many different locations. It also allows for direct interaction between supplier and customer rather than the 'knowledge of customer' advantage of this being enjoyed by the intermediary.

The mail-order industry in the UK grew partly on this disintermediation basis, but also from 'savings clubs' (for example, Christmas Clubs) which many retailers used to operate. This was extended to credit availability, so another major motivation in the UK revolved around financial considerations. The development of sophisticated credit referencing can be traced back to this era and is a significant factor in the growth of current direct marketing, because this means there is knowledge not only of what customers have purchased but also of their financial standing.

By analysing customers via their previous purchase patterns and overlaying this with information on their financial and personal characteristics, it has become increasingly possible to develop more personalised understanding of individual customers, even in fast-moving consumer goods (fmcg) markets. This has fuelled the paradigm shift in marketing from transactional marketing, based on the 'marketing mix' approach created by Borden (1964) and popularised into the 4Ps by McCarthy (1960), to the notion of retention strategies within a relationship marketing context.

In addition, we now see a greater range of interactive media for reciprocal communications between organisations and their customers and other stakeholders. These include the Internet, telephony (increasingly of the mobile variety) and interactive television. So as well as direct distribution being a manifestation of much direct relational marketing, so is direct interactive marketing communications. But the new interactive media provide the facilitators of potential relational interaction.

Although later chapters explore details of these and other developments, Part 1 focuses on the nature and development of direct and relational marketing. In short, there is more data to describe customers, a desire to shift to more relational interaction with them and more vehicles for facilitating this.

References

Borden, N.H. (1964) 'The Concept of the Marketing Mix', *Journal of Advertising Research*, 4(June), pp. 2–7.

Institute of Direct Marketing (1995) *Marketing Planning: Strategy, Planning and Analysis*, Module 1, 1-3-05.

McCarthy, E.J. (1960) *Basic Marketing: A Managerial Approach*, Homewood, IL: Irwin.

1 The growth and nature of direct relational marketing

Learning objectives

Having completed this chapter, students should:

- Comprehend how direct relational marketing has evolved from a number of different origins.

- Be able to explain how direct marketing can be manifested in direct distribution and/or direct marketing communications.

- Be able to analyse the drivers of direct interactive marketing.

- Be able to trace the development of the relational approach to direct interactive marketing.

- Understand the nature of direct relational marketing.

Chinese delivery service

In a village in ancient China there was a young rice merchant, Ming Hua. He was one of six rice merchants in that village. He was sitting in his store waiting for customers, but business was not good.

One day Ming Hua realised he had to think more about the villagers and their needs and desires, and not only distribute rice to those who came into his store. He understood that he had to provide the villagers with more value and not only with the same as the other merchants offered them. He decided to develop a record of his customers' eating habits and ordering periods and to start to deliver rice to them.

To begin with, Ming Hua started to walk around the village and knock on the doors of his customers' houses asking how many members there were in the household, how many bowls of rice they cooked on any given day and how big the rice jar of the household was. Then he offered every customer free home delivery and to replenish the household rice jar at regular intervals.

For example, in one household of four persons, on average every person would consume two bowls of rice a day, and therefore the household would need eight bowls of rice every day for their meals. From his records Ming Hua could see that the rice jar of that particular household contained rice for 60 bowls or approximately one bag of rice, and that a full jar would last for 15 days. Consequently, he offered to deliver a bag of rice every 15 days to this house.

By establishing these records and developing these new services, Ming Hua managed to create more and deeper relationships with the villagers, first with his old customers, then with other villagers. Eventually he got more business to take care of and, therefore, had to employ more people: one person to keep records of customers, one to take care of bookkeeping, one to sell over the counter in the store, and two to take care of deliveries. Ming Hua spent his time visiting villagers and handling the contacts with his suppliers, a limited number of rice farmers whom he knew well. Meanwhile his business prospered.

(Source: Grönroos 1996)

Introduction

The opening vignette is a story told to Christian Grönroos by some visiting students from China. This story demonstrates how Ming Hua, the rice merchant, changes his role from a transaction-orientated channel member to a value-enhancing relationship manager. By doing this, he creates an advantage over his competitors who continue to pursue a traditional strategy. This ancient story illustrates that developing and maintaining interactive direct relationships has always been important in doing business.

These and other recent changes in the business, marketing and market environments, together with advances in technology, have led to a renewed focus on relationships as the core of marketing strategy. This chapter explores many of the issues involved with this progression (Exhibit 1.1) and in so doing sets the scene for our coverage of the elements of direct relational marketing in subsequent chapters.

Distribution origins

Contemporary UK direct marketing has evolved from rather humble beginnings in the field of direct distribution. In an effort to reach consumers who were

EXHIBIT 1.1 Origins and concepts

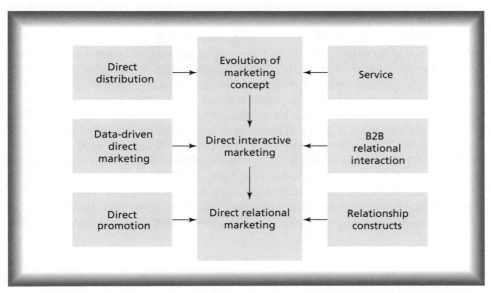

geographically dispersed some companies began to offer direct distribution services. In order to let consumers know the kinds of products they sold, these companies developed lists of products with their associated prices. These lists were then mailed to prospective customers. As competition grew, many of the lists became more detailed. Descriptions and in some cases pictures of the products were included. After choosing from these catalogues, consumers would place an order by mail, and wait until the product was delivered. Thus, the idea of purchasing directly from a company was originally associated with ordering by mail – or mail order. Actually, the Royal Mail originated the Kays catalogue in the UK as far back as 1898 (Carr 1994).

As many readers will know from personal experience, there are now other ways of ordering products and services (such as via telephony and the Internet). The Internet can even 'deliver' some products electronically (such as computer software). Davies (1998) and Dibb *et al.* (2001) even define direct marketing as a 'distribution process'.

In the 'nation of shopkeepers' era, in the UK, before self-service and the abolition of Resale Price Maintenance, retailers operated on a neighbourhood basis, serving customers individually, getting to know them, their families, their interests and buying behaviour. Despite this, it was the manufacturer who held the balance of power in distribution channels. They developed the brands, controlled the advertising and also the pricing (through Resale Price Maintenance). Retailers, despite their lack of control of brands' marketing programmes, achieved an enviable link with their customers: there was personal interaction analogous to being greeted by the landlord of the local pub, not only by name but with the favourite tipple, which might even appear in a personalised glass. 'Ordering' was not necessary.

Then the power-balance in distribution channels shifted with the abolition of Resale Price Maintenance in 1964, which allowed retailers to discount their prices across most product categories. This in turn led to buying groups who negotiated cost reductions based on bulk buying, which meant there were price discounts that could be passed on to consumers. As buying groups became larger and ever more powerful those retailers who couldn't match these prices went out of business; an unstoppable cycle had been set in motion. Retailers became less staff intensive as a result of cost-cutting self-service methods and, with their buying power and resulting price advantage, were even able to undercut wholesaler prices. This process distanced the retailer from consumers until electronic point-of-sale (EPOS) systems allowed them to be very clear about which lines sold well and which didn't. Such information was helpful to retailers who were then in a position to be able to dictate to manufacturers which products should be produced and at which price points. The emergence of retailer 'own brands' was one result and this corresponded with a decline in manufacturer brands in many fmcg markets, and to a relative decline in manufacturer control and power within distribution channels.

Communications origins

Shimp (1992) defines marketing communications as representing 'the collection of all elements in an organisation's marketing mix, that facilitate exchanges by establishing shared meaning with the organisation's customers or clients'. Furthermore, this definition recognises that a marketing organisation is both a sender and a receiver of messages, therefore highlighting the importance and relevance of direct marketing facilitating two-way exchanges of information. This is important because it recognises the progression from outbound communications, that focused on what the organisation wanted to say about itself and its products, to more interactive and reciprocal communications (Kitchen and Schultz 1999). This interaction or dialogue is made possible through a wide range of media, each of which can be utilised on its own or as part of a battery of media. Indeed, a well-explored topic in the marketing literature in recent times is 'integrated marketing communications'. It isn't enough to consider and use a range of communications media but to ensure consistency across all platforms; to ensure the media advertising is not communicating a message inconsistent with that which direct mail or press releases might be conveying. Many marketing communications agencies are claiming to be able to offer integration of different promotional approaches but a somewhat cynical note has to be sounded, because there is little evidence of this being more than rhetoric in many cases. The problem is that many such agencies have 'bought' agencies that specialise in those communications media that they themselves do not. This might lead to 'all under one roof' but it does not necessarily mean that there are not partitions between the departments under that roof.

There is added importance of all of this as the range of communications vehicles increases. Electronic media such as the Internet, digital interactive television and mobile telephony, for example, are providing different forms of marketing communications, based on greater interactivity (Hoffman and Novak 1996) and on greater targeting abilities (Shultz 1999). The two combined is a potentially powerful blend and can lead to the sort of direct relational marketing that is the focus of this book. For instance, as Bezjian-Avery *et al.* (1998) suggest such targeted interactivity is 'the immediate iterative process by which customer needs and desires are uncovered, met, modified and satisfied by the providing firm'. Reciprocal direct communication has therefore been another major driver of modern direct relational marketing and although direct marketing developed from mail order and was thus considered to be a means of direct selling, it is increasingly playing an important role in marketing communications and vice versa.

Direct relational marketing is seen by several marketing textbooks just within a communications context and even some practitioner books reinforce this: Bird (1996), for example, defines Direct Marketing as 'any advertising activity which creates and exploits a direct relationship between you and your prospect or customer as an individual'. Even the American Marketing Association (1996) defines direct marketing as 'an interactive system of marketing which uses one or more advertising media to effect a measurable response and/or transaction at any location'.

We feel this again is rather narrow because of the distribution origins discussed earlier and the 'data' and relational contexts explored next. However, other dimensions are introduced by Bauer and Miglautsch's (1992) definition of direct marketing which has become accepted by the UK Direct Marketing Association: 'Direct marketing is a cybernetic marketing process which uses direct response advertising in prospecting, conversion and maintenance.' Again, 'advertising' is the context. In this case, though, cybernetics adds a dimension related to the AMA's one of being 'measurable': the science of control and communication. A cybernetic system is one in which there is feedback of information on the deviation of output from goal. A cybernetic system contains a control mechanism which compares output (actual result) to system goal (forecast). In direct marketing, micro-control is practised through the use of tracking codes, allowing deviation of actual response from forecast response to be recorded – and allowing the actual response to inform future decisions. The 'data' and relational components of this definition are introduced next.

Data origins

Tempest (1996) states that direct marketing is: 'a marketing technique using a number of different media which involves direct contact between an organisation and an individual consumer or company, and seeking a measurable response'. This extends the distribution and communications origins by introducing 'measurability', which in turn depends upon 'data'.

Information on customers is critical to developing and maintaining customer relationships. While small organisations with very few customers find it relatively easy to collect and use relevant information in building customer relationships, larger organisations find this practically impossible to do. Thus, information technology, initially in the form of the database, was regarded as 'an agent of surrogacy to be enlisted to help marketers to re-create the operating styles of yesterday's merchants' (Sisodia and Wolfe 2000).

Have a look at the following fine case study on Eurocamp by James Lawson, editor of *Database Marketing* magazine (www.dmarket.co.uk). It demonstrates the power of data-driven marketing, especially when there is a richness of in-house transactional data.

CASE STUDY 1.1

Data-driven Eurocamp

Sometimes success brings its own problems. What if you only have a finite number of attractive products to sell and your customers can't get enough of them?

By James Lawson

Eurocamp, the popular continental European self-drive camping and mobile home holiday operator, could sell its peak season holidays two or three times over – what it needed to do was to retain those customers but push their bookings out into the less popular 'shoulder periods' of June and September which lie outside the peak season school holidays.

When Chris Meeke joined the company as customer loyalty manager in August 1997, he had plans to start exploiting the diverse information the firm holds on its customers.

'We are very data rich,' says Meeke, 'and I wanted to look at increasing retention using targeted communications based on what we know about our customers, rather than loyalty cards or points schemes.'

Meeke aimed to build on an already excellent retention rate, and increase the conversion rate of enquiries into actual bookings, as well as promoting the spare capacity in the off-season months. With the popularity of the company's holidays and the knowledge that many customers don't buy on price, Meeke saw no point in offering discounts that might weaken the whole pricing structure.

Eurocamp's established marketing practice has been to mail a brochure or brochure request forms to customers from previous seasons. This direct approach is also backed by an above-the-line campaign in a selection of magazines and newspapers. Chris Meeke says: 'The previous year's customers are the warmest prospects – the holiday is still fresh in their minds. But we wanted to split that down even further.'

The department looked at doing its data analysis in-house by choosing and purchasing the software tools, then recruiting and training the staff to use them. But the figures didn't add up and Meeke decided to outsource the work to Talking Numbers Database Solutions.

'Eurocamp certainly has a lot of information on its customers,' says Nigel Magson, managing director at Talking Numbers. 'It has the transactional holiday booking data, site facility information and attitudinal information, plus much more about the type of holidays they have been on and which regions of Europe they have historically preferred.'

After performing a data audit, merging datasets from different areas and then deduping and post coding the final customer database, Talking Numbers initially performed some RFV (recency, frequency, value) analysis on the last five years of customer data. That is, the recency of the last booking date, how many bookings a family had made (frequency) and the customer's total historical value to Eurocamp in terms of average bookings.

'We built the RFV model after deduplicating the customer file, which also allowed us to identify multiple holiday takers in one season,' says Magson.

Next, the team tagged on codes from Claritas' PRIZM classification to provide extra data on life stage and income, then set bandings for each of the three variables, took counts of how many customers fell into each band and wrote the results back to the database.

'The total value of the holidays wasn't too important in the end as peak season demand is way ahead of capacity anyway,' says Eurocamp's Meeke. 'We concentrated on investigating the profiles of those taking holidays in the shoulder periods of June, early July and September.'

Talking Numbers used standard SPSS statistics software as the main tool for all the analysis work. 'We started doing cross tabs of the RFV data so we could locate those who went twice in 1998 and spent an above-average amount,' says Magson.

The next step was to combine the scores to create 15 groups of customers graded from best to worst – the initial segmentation. The worst would have come once a long time ago and spent little on the holiday, while the top group of loyal customers would come twice annually and spend a fortune. Magson worked out a historic average LTV (lifetime value) for each segment, that is, how much each segment has spent on its holidays on average. 'There was a big difference between the best and the worst group,' he says.

He then assigned an index score of one to the average customers in the middle groups to give a simple measure of their value to Eurocamp; a score of seven would mean seven times more valuable than normal. 'It was a standard transactional RFV,' says Magson. 'A good starting point.'

Next up was a profiled RFV model, which used the PRIZM data, tagged on at the start. According to Magson, 'PRIZM is a good dataset here because it works with life stage, which is a crucial variable for Eurocamp.'

By profiling the existing RFV segments against PRIZM life stage and income bands, a clearer picture of the different groups within Eurocamp's whole customer base appeared. Counts were taken of different PRIZM groups within each segment, which would identify groups of customers by life stage and affluence, for example high-affluence older singles.

Once this work had been done for the whole database, it was linked to the time of booking, giving detailed information which was then available for the marketing department to act on. 'The whole point of profiling is to create differences in the database and exploit those differences,' says Magson.

Chris Meeke says: 'We found that families that went in June had a completely different profile to those going in peak season. We weren't targeting them at all in our advertising.'

Magson then scored the customer base and enquiry file by propensity to go in the shoulder periods. After ranking customers by how likely they were to go in June and other periods outside of the main school holidays, Eurocamp started much more focused activity to achieve the main objectives of getting existing customers to go outside the main season and converting enquirers both to book and go at the 'right' time of year.

To get customers to shift their holiday times, high season bookers and the enquiry file were scored for how likely they were to go off-season, that is, how close their profile was to off-season customers. Likely clients were then targeted for specific mailshots promoting the benefits of changing dates.

Analysing the enquirer's file brought more discoveries; one person had enquired 21 times but had never booked a holiday. Getting rid of timewasters and deduping gave a solid base of actual enquirers to target.

'If we can't move these people, we effectively lose the bookings,' says Meeke. 'So in our mailings, we're emphasising the quieter roads, the great weather and the less crowded campsites, though not the cheaper price. These people can afford peak season.'

The mailshots use the PRIZM household profile to determine both the content of the letter and the artwork. They took a real sample of the target group, looked at the percentage of pre-school families and retired couples and compared it to the PRIZM-derived estimate. Happily, the match was 'very close'. Families with pre-school children get colourful pictures of happy kids on their letter while, on mailings to 'empty nesters', children are notably absent, replaced by active fifty-somethings with a penchant for bicycles and boules.

Chris Meeke says: 'In the letter, we refer to the last area they went to, hoping that it will bring back the memories and they'll turn to that page in the brochure.'

The next operational area to fall under the analytical spotlight was media buying. By linking the percentage of new prospects converted to paying customers and which medium they had initially responded to, a customer profile of each publication was built up (potential customer value and so on) as well a measure of its effectiveness in attracting new bookers.

'We now give this information to our media buyers and they use it to pick the titles we advertise in,' says Meeke.

The media analysis found that broadsheet readers spend more on holidays but book less frequently than tabloid readers who do the reverse, spending less money but going more often – the usual pattern found in newspaper versus broadsheet-reading customers. The higher initial cost of recruitment for broadsheet readers (higher ad rates), who generally tend to be more promiscuous, means that retention became even more important.

'We took this even further,' says Magson, 'looking at which media was best for filling the shoulder periods and which was best for peak season. It's precise actionable marketing information. It doesn't end there. Penetration analysis of postcodes where new or repeat brochures are requested has shown areas of below-average response. By looking at the PRIZM profile of those regions and thinking about why the residents are not attracted to Eurocamp (too far north to drive easily or low affluence), the decision can be made on whether or not to buy local media ads or to send extra mailings to that area.'

Every year, Eurocamp produces a multi-media CD-ROM that customers can use to find out more about the different sites that they can book, a useful and modern marketing medium. But Nigel Magson saw it as yet another rich source of data. 'We know which sites people go to and their profiles. By linking to the campsite database, we can now look at persuading people to go to different, less popular sites at certain times of the year.'

And that brings us up to date. Mailings were sent out in September and November of last year with the most recent one going this March. Response so far has been encouraging but it's too early to tell what the exact results have been as this is the first season that the more targeted campaign has run.

'This project was classic data mining,' says Magson. 'We took completely disparate datasets and uncovered interesting patterns of information.'

Eurocamp's deeper understanding of who its customers are and why they behave in the way they do has certainly brought a new element of science to its marketing activities and the company is very pleased with the way things have gone.

'Our general feeling is that it has been a great thing to do,' says Chris Meeke. 'We're targeting customers personally and have more accurate communications with them. It's relationship marketing, simple as that.'

(Source: Case study reproduced with the kind permission of Eurocamp and Talking Numbers)

Chapter 2 reviews the range of sources of data that can be used to know customers on relatively individual bases. The more technical metrics in this case, such as RFM analysis, are covered in more detail in Chapter 3 but the case does provide a clear example of how direct marketing can be data-driven.

Indeed, the ability to extend customer knowledge and develop successful relationships lies in an organisation's ability to understand its customers, their individual preferences, expectations and changing needs. While today's markets are so complex that such customer intimacy may be precluded (DeTienne and Thompson 1996), the database is perhaps over-employed by contemporary marketers to try to overcome this problem. In the absence of intimate knowledge of individual customers and interpersonal contact, the database promised an opportunity to capture information on customers in a useful and accessible fashion (Shani and Chalasani 1992), enabling them to identify individual customers, monitor their buying behaviour (Blattberg and Deighton 1991), and communicate with them on an individual basis, often with personalised offers. We explore the 'surrogacy' effect in Chapter 6 and suggest that the database cannot really be a full replacement for more affective understanding of customers, but it certainly can be a powerful driver within direct marketing campaigns.

DeTienne and Thompson (1996) provide their definition of database marketing: 'Database marketing is the process of systematically collecting, in electronic or optical form, data about past, current and/or potential customers, maintaining the integrity of the data by continually monitoring customer purchases and/or by inquiring about changing status and using the data to formulate marketing strategy and foster personalized relationships with customers.'

The last point concerning relationships is where data-driven marketing evolves into relational marketing: 'to build a long-term connection between the company and consumer' (Copulsky and Wolf 1990:17).

The creation of a 'special status' between company and customers (Czepiel 1990; Rowe and Barnes 1998) relies on fostering customer intimacy (Jackson 1994). In order to achieve this, data on transactions is held in the customer database and this is overlaid with demographic, geodemographic and lifestyle data and a range of other data sources, including country court judgments (CCJs), electoral register, etc. The data are fused and held in a data warehouse where 'biographic data' (Evans 1999) on individual customers can be viewed. Thus, within an RM strategy, the database becomes a key knowledge tool for the organisation (DeTienne and Thompson 1996; O'Malley et al. 1999b) and is used to simulate indices of intimacy and connectedness. In addition to databases, other technologies have developed that 'can give companies a host of opportunities for communicating with the customer and have information on hand to engage, inform, and direct each customer with complete knowledge as to the customers' preferences and behaviours' (Gordon 2000:512). These developments include the Internet, telecommunications, and computer-telephony in call centres. These technological developments have served to make systems that are supposed to support RM more affordable and, perhaps, more effective for companies operating in mass markets (Rapp and Collins 1990; Sisodia and Wolfe 2000).

Some technologies have opened up new channels of dialogue, which can be customer initiated as well as organisation initiated. This being the case, efforts must be made to capture data at all interactions and make that information available for subsequent conversations. This is possible when technology is used at the customer interface to secure real-time or near real-time interaction (Gordon 2000). This has resulted in a need to move beyond the customer database as the basis of RM and to link the central information centre with call-centre software and Internet systems that allow direct interaction, as well as into other functions that contain histories of customer interaction (such as accounts and product service departments).

The year 1981 was a watershed for UK marketing and heralded a shift in both marketing practice and theory. The 1981 UK Census led to the first geodemographic system but was also a major catalyst in providing alternatives to anonymised (traditional) market research samples of perhaps a thousand respondents, representing the entire population and profiled according to a few demographic descriptors. The new alternative was based on data from all households in terms of dozens of characteristics. The further fusion of geodemographics with personalised data from lifestyle surveys and from transactional data provides what marketers are taking to be a buying 'biography' of customers and from this they think they can develop relationships with customers. We explore data sources and what can be done with the resulting information in later chapters, but the relational paradigm is worth introducing here. By definition, relational constructs provide origins, but so too does 'service', which we explore next.

The service origin

Because there is high variability in the quality of service provision, many customers are likely to seek continuity with the same provider when excellent service is experienced, particularly when that service is important, complex, and/ or when the customer is highly involved (Berry 1995). In this way we can see another of the origins of the relational approach; it is not merely a case of having the right product at the right price in the right place at the right time, but it also requires high-quality service procedures around the various stages, appropriate to the context, such as ordering, delivery, post-purchase support and so on.

One of the consequences of the recent interest in service marketing is the increased recognition of the importance of the person-to-person encounter between buyer and seller – client and provider – to the overall success of the marketing effort (Solomon *et al.* 1985). The 'dyadic interaction between a customer and a service provider' (Surprenant and Solomon 1987) is known as the service encounter. This focuses attention on the interpersonal element of service performance. Customers rely upon employee behaviour to evaluate services because the service itself offers little evidence given its intangibility. Thus, the satisfaction of customers is likely to be influenced by the way service providers perform. More importantly, these service providers are often not marketing personnel as such; rather, they are part-time marketers (Gummesson 1987).

IN THEORY

There have been a number of important developments in the concept of service quality. In the USA, Berry and Parasuraman (1991) made a significant contribution in terms of differentiating between *actual quality* (in terms of how a company might measure it), and the concept of *customer perceived quality* (i.e. how the customer perceives quality). Five independent dimensions (Exhibit 1.2) of service quality were identified (Parasuraman, Zeithaml and Berry (1988).

It is notable that three of these elements focus on the human component of the interaction (Bitner *et al.* 1990). Exhibit 1.3 identifies how the Nordic School of Services Marketing further differentiates quality into *functional quality* (the quality of the interaction) and *technical quality* (the quality of the service outcome) (Grönroos 1983). Functional quality refers to how the service provision and delivery process itself is perceived. Because it is relatively easy for firms to reach an acceptable technical quality, the functional quality has become more important, and in many cases becomes the dominant criterion of customer evaluation. This is not to suggest that technical quality is no longer important, just that 'its part of the total quality perception may even be marginal as long as it remains acceptable' (Grönroos 1995). Thus, the interaction itself becomes an important focus for management research and training.

EXHIBIT 1.2   Dimensions of service quality

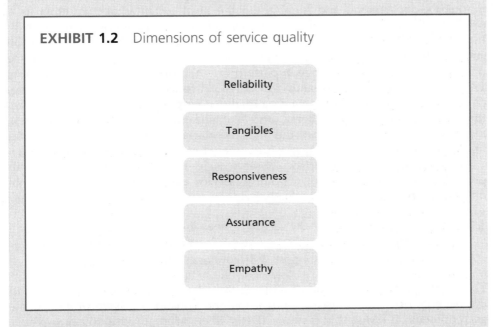

Reliability

Tangibles

Responsiveness

Assurance

Empathy

EXHIBIT 1.3   Functional and technical quality

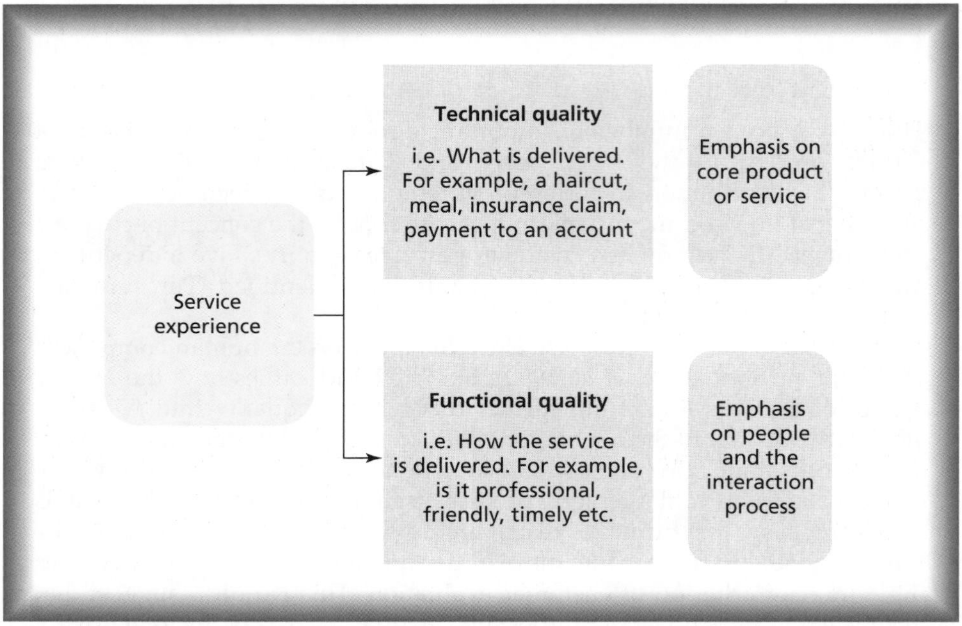

Interestingly, the conclusion that part-time marketers may be vitally important has raised some questions as to the continued relevance of the traditional marketing department, and highlighted the need for internal marketing as a prerequisite for the successful management of external relations (George 1990). Internal marketing reflects the recognition that 'a service must first be successfully marketed to the personnel so that the employees accept the service offering and thoroughly engage in performing their marketing duties' (Grönroos 1978). Internal marketing is similar to the HRM function in terms of 'attracting, developing, motivating, and retaining qualified employees through job-products that satisfy their needs' (Berry and Parasuraman 1991) and the process responsible for ensuring that the firm is market orientated. Thus, internal marketing is integral to the successful management of external relationships.

Given the unique characteristics of services, it was recognised that it was both possible and appropriate to customise service provision. Thus, the idea of developing relationships was already evident:

   ❝ as a marketing strategy, many service businesses seek ways to develop formal, ongoing relations with customers in order to ensure repeat business and/or ongoing financial support. ❞ (Lovelock 1983)

The convergent influences of a maturing industry, technological advances, and the benefits of relationships to both firms and consumers 'have propelled the current focus on RM within services' (Berry 1995). More importantly, however, is the nature of services marketing which forces the buyer into intimate contact with the seller and thereby facilitates the development of relationships. In this way the service encounter, referred to as a moment of truth (Norman 1984), has an important impact on the customer's perception of, and satisfaction with, the service.

It is evident from the services literature that not all service encounters have the potential to be relational (Crosby *et al.* 1990). Indeed, it is only when the service encounter is extended, emotive or intimate (in terms of spatial proximity) that it is likely to lead to 'boundary open transactions ... resembling a meeting between friends' (Price *et al.* 1995). This generates opportunities for customising or personalising the service and developing relationships. The service encounter also facilitates the development of social bonds between the customer and service provider. Social bonds are important in developing customer loyalty, in particular when competitive differences are not strong (Crosby *et al.* 1990). They may also make customers more tolerant of service failure.

In summary, researchers argued that given the unique characteristics of services, mix management offered them little guidance. This led to an emphasis on the dyadic interaction within a service encounter, and the importance of customer-perceived quality. In turn, these research streams have contributed to the relational paradigm within services. These contributions include:

- Service provision can be *customised* to suit the specific customer requirements.
- The development of formal, ongoing relationships is a viable strategy in attempting to engender customer *loyalty*.
- There is a difference between *actual quality* and *customer-perceived quality*.
- Customers assess services on the basis of both *technical* and *functional* quality.
- The importance of *part-time marketers* was recognised and highlighted.
- *Internal marketing* was accepted as an important tool in ensuring service quality and in underpinning relationship management.
- The nature of services forces the buyer into *intimate contact* with the seller.
- The service encounter has an important impact on customers' *perceptions* of, and *satisfaction* with, the service.
- Service encounters facilitate the development of *social bonds*.
- Not all service encounters are necessarily relational, only those which are *extended, emotive* or *intimate*.

B2B interactions

It has long been recognised, in both theory and practice, that the business-to-business (B2B) environment is often heavily dependent upon effective relational interaction between buyer and seller. The Industrial Marketing and Purchasing research group (IMP) took the *relationship* as its unit of analysis, not an individual purchase or the marketing company itself. This approach was not just an academic device, but was based on the belief that the critical task for the business marketer is the development and management of its relationship with its customers (Ford 1997).

IMP researchers also view buyers and sellers as active parties. This view was based on a number of factors, including:

- Each party to a relationship may take the initiative in seeking a partner, or either may attempt to specify, manipulate or control the transaction process. Thus, 'this process is not one of action and reaction: it is one of interaction' (Ford 1997).
- The relationship between buyer and seller is frequently long-term, close and involves complex patterns of interactions.
- The links between buyer and seller often become institutionalised into a set of roles that each party expects the other to perform. Thus, both parties are likely to be involved in adaptations of their own processes or product technologies to accommodate the other, and neither party is likely to make unilateral changes to its activities without consideration of its opposite number.

Because relationships are important in industrial markets, 'the marketer's and buyer's task in this case have more to do with maintaining the relationship than with making a straightforward sale or purchase' (Hàkansson 1982). Therefore, the marketing and purchasing of industrial goods is seen as an interactive process between two parties within a certain environment. Such an interaction cannot be considered in isolation, but must be analysed within the context of the relationship of which it forms a part and within the wider context of the environment in which it operates.

This view is accommodated by the interaction model (Exhibit 1.4) (Turnbull and Valla 1985) which is based upon four groups of variables that describe and influence the interaction process between buying and selling companies. Its basic elements include (Hàkansson, 1982):

1 **The interaction process**: variables describing the elements and processes of interaction. Because of the complexity of buyer–seller relations and the importance of mutual adaptations, the interaction process distinguishes between individual exchange episodes (product/service, information, financial, and social exchange) and the longer-term aspects of the relationship (routines, contact patterns and adaptations made). These exchanges can be viewed as the currency of the interaction between buyer and seller (Wilson and Möller 1991). Each episode affects the overall relationship and a single episode can radically change the relationship.

2 **The participants involved in the interaction**: variables describing the parties involved, both as organisations and individuals. The characteristics of the interacting parties (both at an organisational and individual level) also have an impact on the relationship. The characteristics of the organisation (technology, size, structure, strategy and experience) and the

EXHIBIT 1.4 The interaction model

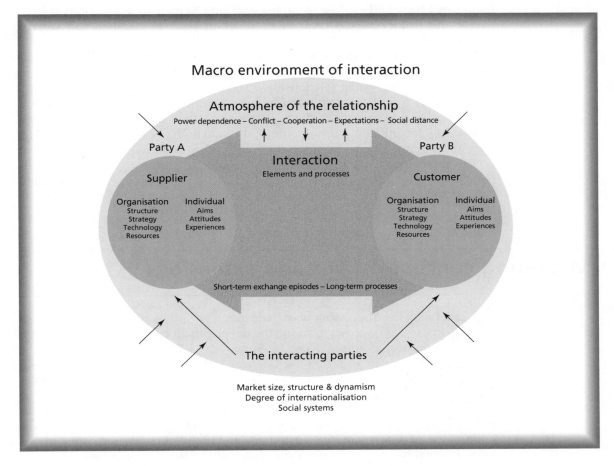

individuals involved (personalities, experience, motivations, role, level and function) both play a part.

3 **The interaction environment**: includes market size and structure (e.g. the extent of buyer or seller concentration), the extent to which the market is international, and the social system (nationalistic buying practices, regulations and business constraints).

4 **Atmosphere**: finally, the atmosphere of the relationship is seen to be both a product of the relationship and also capable of influencing the impact of other variables (e.g. environmental, company-specific and interaction process characteristics). It is described in terms of:

> ❝ … the power-dependence relationship which exists between companies, the state of conflict or co-operation and the overall closeness or distance of the relationship as well as by the company's mutual expectations. ❞
> (Hàkansson 1982)

The relationship between a buyer and seller: '... may be distant and impersonal but is often close, complex and long term. The relationship is built out of the history of the companies' dealings with each other and can be described in terms of adaptations, commitments, trust and conflict' (Ford 1990).

It is clear then that relational approaches in consumer markets also had their origins in the B2B context. Here, marketers and buyers have similar roles in developing and operating relationships. The match between supplier capability and customer need is accomplished by interaction between the two parties, and adaptation by one or both of them. Personal contacts are frequently used as a mechanism for initiating, developing and maintaining relationships (Cunningham and Homse 1986). The interaction with other companies is the force that unifies the company and gives it the capability to perform its activities. This perspective might over-emphasise social interaction compared with what would be expected in consumer markets, where there is also the tremendous use of data and IT to explore and develop interaction and relationship.

Marketing concept origins and extensions

In parallel with the discussions above concerning a variety of origins of the direct relational paradigm, we can examine the development of marketing itself. Many commentators (for example, King 1965) saw the 1950s as the dawning of the marketing concept in so far as the UK was concerned. King plotted the well-rehearsed shift from a production orientation (between 1900 and 1930) to a sales orientation (between 1930 and 1950). The emerging marketing orientation of the 1950s was typified as being concerned with mutually satisfying exchanges between organisations and their customers. The paradigm shift was based on the importance of understanding customers and delivering desired satisfactions more effectively and efficiently than the competition. The paradigm shift was from 'selling things' to 'helping customers buy benefits'. This might not always have been operationalised but the concept itself was generally applauded.

However, there have been concerns that even though markets were segmented there was, relatively speaking, a mass marketing culture and that this precluded much beyond transactional marketing revolving around anonymised one-off purchases or at best a series of anonymised purchases. If organisation–customer interaction focuses on this, there is little recognition of individual customers, their prior history or anticipated future interaction with the organisation. However, the relational approach redresses the balance in these respects and also includes the elements of relationship, network and interaction.

As we have already discussed, the 'service origin' of direct relational marketing is an important one. It extends the 'mix' paradigm of the '4Ps' (product, price, place and promotion) by including 'personnel', 'physical assets' and 'procedures' (Lovelock 1996). A further extension is suggested by Goldsmith (1999), who includes 'personalisation' as an eighth 'P'. It is the blend of these elements that Goldsmith proposes as being important for the new marketing, in order to convert a more personalised service-enhanced marketing mix into mutually beneficial interactions between organisation and customer such that longer-term relational interaction can develop, which in turn has a better chance of leading to customer retention and loyalty.

The 'new' approach also claims to change the paradigm from a focus on one-off exchanges to one in which exchanges trace back to previous interactions and reflect an ongoing process. This in turn can lead to increased satisfaction for the customer as well as facilitating brand loyalty and more accurate sales forecasting for the company.

The main operationalising of relationship marketing is via database marketing, because this provides the means to identify and track individual customers and their buying behaviour, calculate 'lifetime' value, and generate personalised marketing communications. So here we have the synergy of the origins as explored so far.

But the more conceptual underpinning of relationship marketing involves trust, commitment mutual benefit, adaptation and regard for privacy (O'Malley *et al.* 1997). However, there is a degree of theory–practice mismatch here because marketers in practice are not overly concerned with inviting customers to establish mutual relationships. Consider the following advice to business:

> relationship marketing . . . requires a two-way flow of information. This does not mean that the customer has to give you this information willingly, or even knowingly. You can use scanners to capture information, you can gather telephone numbers, conduct surveys, supply warranty cards, and use a data overlay from outside databases to combine factors about lifestyle, demographics, geographics, psychographics, and customer purchases. (Schultz *et al.* 1993)

This, probably commonplace, view would define relationship marketing as an oxymoron.

Also, we can question whether earlier eras were only concerned with one-off transactions. It is interesting to remember that even in the 1960s marketers were not concerned exclusively with these. Retention strategies such as the old Green Shield stamps example, and indeed the entire branding process, are clearly not concerned exclusively with acquisition. It is common sense that marketers want customers to return and spread goodwill about the product, brand or company.

Two points here; first, the 'old' definitions of marketing often do include relational constructs:

> Marketing means customer orientation – a true alliance with the fellow at the other end of the pipeline, but it insists upon a course of action of mutual benefit. (Borch 1957)

Indeed, the relational concept that proposes past, present and future interaction between organisations and customers and wider 'networking' issues was suggested by Wroe Alderson in the 1950s:

> it means creating a pattern for dealing with customers or suppliers which persists because there are advantages in both sides. (Alderson 1958)

Also, the well-established 'adoption' construct within diffusion-adoption theory is concerned with regular committed purchasing.

The second point is the confusion over conceptualising relational approaches. In a recent talk on CRM the practitioner presenter (not disclosed, to save blushes) explored the issues involved and built up to a definition of CRM. This emerged as the management process that 'identifies, anticipates and satisfies customer requirements efficiently and profitably'. This is the Chartered Institute of Marketing's definition of 'marketing' of 30 years ago!

Perhaps the main 'difference' revolves around the synergy of elements and approaches that we have explored so far: the distribution and communications origins and data-informed understanding of individuals which leads to personalised interactive communications via a new and wide range of media. Another difference concerns the concept of 'network' mentioned above. Möller and Wilson (1995), for example, argue that 'Relationship Marketing is about understanding, creating, and managing exchange relationships between economic partners; manufacturers, service providers, various channel members, and final consumers.'

We explore this particular angle in our coverage of knowledge management but it is pertinent here to introduce the notion of relationship marketing going beyond organisation–customer interactions to those with partner organisations and with other organisations up and down the supply chain. As noted above, Alderson had already spotted aspects of this back in 1958.

Perhaps more helpfully, Grönroos (1994) redefines marketing in terms of relationships, arguing that: 'Marketing is to establish, maintain and enhance exchange relationships with customers and other partners, at a profit, so that the objectives of the parties involved are met. This is achieved by mutual exchange and fulfilment of promise.'

Consider the following short case study, which provides a very simple yet powerful demonstration of the combination of relationship building, distribution, service provision, communications and new media.

CASE STUDY 1.2

No more Pot Noodle

In the UK and many other countries there are what are termed 'industrial estates'. These are usually located out of town (or on the edge of towns) and are home to a number of different organisations: manufacturers, distributors, transport companies and so on, and in a previous era many of the larger companies on such estates might have had their own catering facilities for their workforces' lunch and break times.

More recently, however, many canteens have closed to reduce costs and workers have had to resort either to bringing their own sandwiches or pot noodles or travelling off site to a café. It is noticeable, also, that many mobile 'hot-dog' stalls open up at lunchtime on some industrial estates. This is one example of direct distribution but also demonstrates how regular customers become known by the stallholders and perhaps their favourite burger or hot dog will be ready and waiting for them without having to queue. Take this a stage further, e-mail allows a food company to interact directly with workers on an entire industrial estate. The company can arrange to be part of the estate's intranet and e-mail orders can come from workers a couple of hours before lunch. This allows the food company to plan ahead and make only what is ordered, and over time the electronic interaction provides a very useful database which can be analysed for patterns of food preference. This, coupled with direct personal interaction when the food is delivered, can lead to the development of more personalised relationships. A simple idea but potentially effective.

Direct interactive marketing

The strands of argument through this chapter can be contextualised within a dramatic rise to prominence in recent years of what is clearly 'direct' and 'interactive' marketing. This has witnessed impressive growth in terms of both volume and expenditure. Such growth might be taken as proof of direct marketing's current sophistication, its strength as both a communications and distribution medium, and its success in meeting the needs of contemporary markets. The range of companies that now use direct marketing is also expanding, with many fast-moving consumer goods marketers gradually moving into the area. Consider for yourselves the number of companies that now label themselves as 'direct' (Direct Line, First Direct, and so on). Indeed, direct interactive marketing is currently employed in business-to-business and consumer markets, by charities, and even by the government. Such is its flexibility that it also lends itself well to campaigns outside the domestic market. Unsurprisingly, on the back of this recent growth, many industry experts predict continued success for direct marketing in the future (for example, Barwise and Styler 2002).

Having discussed what we mean by direct interactive marketing and some of its origins, it is worth exploring some of the drivers of its relatively recent growth. This growth can be attributed on a general level to a combination of demand- and supply-side factors (Exhibit 1.5) (Evans *et al.* 1996).

Demand-side factors are based on changes in market behaviour and also on changes in the effectiveness of traditional media. In terms of markets, it is clear that fragmentation has taken place. Markets have become demassified and this has been a major trend aiding the growth of direct marketing. This is manifested in greater pluralism within society, evident in the high street where pluralism in clothing styles is observable. The Henley Centre (1978) predicted this trend as far back as the 1970s when they discussed household behaviour as being 'cellular' rather than 'nuclear' – households were beginning to do things together less and less and beginning to behave more independently; families were not eating together as often, having TV and sound systems in their 'own' rooms and, whereas at one time it was typical to have one large 'family sized' packet of Corn

EXHIBIT 1.5   Catalysts of change

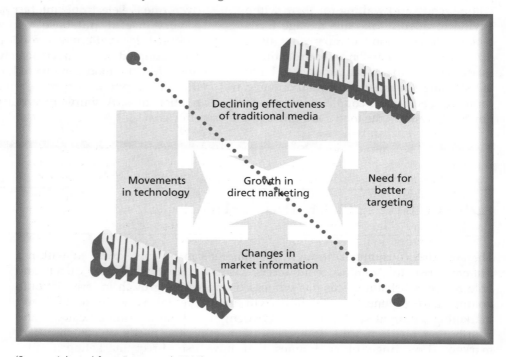

(Source: Adapted from Evans *et al.* 1996)

Flakes in the kitchen, it was becoming more likely that each household member would have a packet of 'their' cereal in the cupboard.

Other changes have seen the increase in the number of working women, many of whom are joining their male counterparts in seeking time-saving purchasing methods, such as direct mail and telemarketing. Working women are also more independent and contribute to the greater number of smaller households which require narrower targeting. The divorce rate has risen and with it the number of small and single households – affecting both sexes. This also means that more men are deciding which washing powder they will buy and more women are buying cars and pensions for themselves. The continuing trend away from cash as the means of payment to credit, debit and smart cards, through the post and over telephone and internet cables, has enabled purchase behaviour to take place when the customer wants it – 24 hours per day and from the armchair, office phone, travelling laptop computer and even mobile phone that can also access the Internet.

Companies have become disillusioned with more traditional promotional media over recent years. Market fragmentation has resulted in diminishing audiences for individual media, media costs have soared and consumers are experiencing clutter. 'Demand' for a different marketing approach also came from perceived problems with traditional, less targeted, media which are sometimes seen to be expensive and less accountable. Expensive, in that a campaign running for not much more than a month, with 30-second TV commercials repeated a few times each evening during peak viewing time, can cost over £6m. In just one quarter of 2000, the ad spend on the Cornetto brand alone was over £9m and Guinness advertising expenditure is often in excess of £16m per year (CreativeClub, 2003). As for being accountable, although the quotation often attributed to Lord Leverhulme, to the effect that he knew half his advertising was wasted but didn't know which half, is not entirely fair on the more sophisticated media evaluation techniques of today, it does point to the general problem that marketers are being pressed to be accountable and direct communications can be 'counted out and counted back in'.

Although above-the-line advertising *is* targeted at specific audiences – the audience for a late-night Friday show on Channel 4 is unlikely to have the same composition as one for a Wednesday afternoon on BBC2 (or if it has, it might not be in the same frame of mind) – the targeting is still of the 'shotgun' variety rather than the 'sniper's rifle' which is possible through direct marketing. Audiences are fragmenting as more TV channels appear (satellite and cable) along with more newspapers and magazines – all with advertising space to fill. Furthermore, consumers are not helping the advertiser by video-recording TV programmes and 'zapping' the commercials (Kitchen 1986). Indeed, the next phase of this behaviour comes with the personal video recorder (PVR) which, amongst other things, allows the viewer to skip the advertisements automatically. Direct marketing is seen to have the potential to overcome the difficulty of this 'clutter' because the message can be personalised and communicated via other direct and interactive media.

Together the trends have created a *demand* for more effective targeting. The *supply* side on the other hand is concerned with changes in information about customers (based on much more sophisticated research) and also on technological improvements which have facilitated the collating and analysis of huge amounts of detailed and personalised information.

In parallel with markets' apparent desire to be treated more as individuals and marketing's desire to find more effective media is the marketer's search for more detailed and personalised information about customers.

This is based, in part, on the relative decline of demographic segmentation variables, due to their lack of explanatory depth and their relatively broad targeting capabilities. The typical market profiling according to age, gender and social grade saw, in the 1980s, parallel profiles in psychographic and geodemographic terms. Indeed, the rise of psychographics and geodemographics has added to demographics' decline because of their potential abilities to understand target customers in great detail, even individually, and to be able to target them equally specifically.

The availability of more individual-specific data, coupled with technological facilitators, is leading to the targeting of individuals based on what we know of their interests and characteristics. The means for storing and retrieving such individual data is the marketing database and it is this that is the driver of much direct marketing. We do not, however, advocate this per se. It is certainly the case that data-based decisions can lead to the identification of better prospects because they possess similar characteristics to our current best customers, and it can suggest future purchase patterns of individuals based on previous patterns, but it does not in itself provide the sort of understanding that would lead to relational interaction.

To summarise some of these drivers, Fletcher *et al.* (1991) states:

> " In the early 1980s, two things began to happen simultaneously. Electronic data processing costs declined and marketing costs climbed, both dramatically. These two curves crossed and this was the catalyst for European direct marketing growth. "

Before we continue the process indicated in Exhibit 1.1, by exploring the transformation of direct interactive marketing into direct *relational* marketing, we need to spend some time delving into the data and informational drivers that facilitate this (Part 2). We return to the conceptual issues involved in the relational paradigm in Chapter 7.

Summary

- This opening chapter has shown how direct marketing and the relational marketing concept have evolved from a variety of origins and via a number of drivers. Direct marketing has its own origins and applications in distribution and marketing communications.
- Databased marketing saw the rise of computer power and had its impact upon data-driven campaigns. Along the way, we saw how the marketing concept itself recognised the importance of being orientated to relationship building rather than just transactions.
- The 'service' dimension is of importance within this, as are lessons transferred from the relational interaction evident in B2B markets. New interactive media have come along to facilitate direct relational marketing.
- Subsequent chapters explore the importance of 'data', affective understanding, the sharing of knowledge across function and partners, and media for implementing direct relational marketing. We also explore approaches to the acquisition of new customers, the retention of existing ones and how loyalty can be encouraged. We draw from the behavioural sciences to suggest how organisations can develop relational messages for customers and we set the above issues within the broader contexts of relational planning which itself is within the wider social environment, with all its concerns over data privacy and legislation.
- The first area we explore concerns the data and informational drivers of direct relational marketing: data sources, data metrics, testing and research and technological targeting.

Review questions

1 What technological developments fuelled the growth of the direct interactive marketing industry over the last 20 years or so?

2 Why have many fmcg manufacturers, who have traditionally been heavy users of mass communications media, recently embraced direct approaches?

3 Industry experts predict that the phenomenal growth currently being experienced by the UK direct marketing industry is likely to continue unchecked into the future. What factors do you think might promote future growth? What factors might have an adverse impact upon future success?

4 'The company wants a relationship with its customers but does each customer want a relationship with the company?' Do you have a mutually beneficial relationship with any company? Why or why not, and how could such interaction be improved?

5 How would you define the differences between direct communication, direct promotion, direct marketing and direct relational marketing?

Further reading

Bauer, C.L. and J. Miglautsch (1992) 'A conceptual definition of direct marketing', *Journal of Direct Marketing*, 6 (Spring), 7–17, as referenced by Scholfield, A. (1995) The definition of direct marketing: A rejoinder to Bauer and Miglautsch, *Journal of Direct Marketing*, 9(2), Spring, pp. 32–8.

Evans, M. (ed.) (1998) Special Issue of *Marketing Intelligence and Planning* on Direct Marketing, 16(1).

Evans, M. and Moutinho, L. (1999) 'Contemporary Issues in Marketing', *The 'New' Marketing'*, Chippenham: Macmillan, Chapter 9.

McCorkell, G. (1997) *Direct and Database Marketing*, London: IDM/Kogan Page.

References

Alderson, W. (1958) 'The Analytical Framework for Marketing', *Conference of Marketing Teachers*, University of California, pp. 15–28.

AMA, cited in Lindgren, J. and Shimp, T. (1996) *Marketing: An Interactive Learning System*, Florida: Harcourt Brace.

Barwise, P. and Styler, A. (2002) *Marketing Expenditure Trends*, London: London Business School.

Bauer, C. and Miglautsch, J. (1992) 'A Conceptual Definition of Direct Marketing', *Journal of Direct Marketing*, 6 (Spring), pp. 7–17, 10–11.

Berry, L.L. (1995) 'Relationship Marketing of Services – Growing Interest, Emerging Perspectives', *Journal of the Academy of Marketing Science*, 23(4), pp. 236–45.

Berry, L.L., and Parasuraman, A. (1991) *Marketing Services – Competition Through Quality*, Free Press: New York, p. 151.

Bezjian-Avery, A., Calder, B. and Lacobucci, D. (1998) 'Interactive Advertising versus Traditional', *Advertising Journal of Advertising Research* 398(4) pp. 23–32.

Bird, D. (1996) *Common-sense direct marketing*, London: Kogan Page.

Bitner, M.J., Booms, B.H. and Stanfield Tetrenault, M. (1990) 'The Service Encounter: Diagnosing Favourable and Unfavourable Incidents', *Journal of Marketing*, 54(January), pp. 71–84.

Blattberg, R.C. and Deighton, J. (1991) 'Interactive Marketing: Exploiting the Age of Addressability', *Sloan Management Review*, Fall, pp. 5–14.

Borch, F.J. (1957) *The Marketing Philosophy as a Way of Business Life*, New York: General Electric.

Carr, M. (1994) 'Database Marketing: Talking Direct to our Listing Customers', *Marketing Intelligence and Planning*, 12(6), pp. 12–14.

Copulsky, J.R. and Wolf, M.J. (1990) 'Relationship Marketing: Positioning for the Future', *The Journal of Business Strategy*, July/August, pp. 16–20.

CreativeClub (2003) *MultiMedia Analysis Report*, 2002–2001, London: Thomson Intermedia plc.

Crosby, L.A., Evans, K.R. and Cowles, D. (1990) 'Relationship Quality in Services Selling: An Interpersonal Influence Perspective', *Journal of Marketing*, 54(July), pp. 68–81.

Cunningham, M.T. and Homse, E. (1986) 'Controlling the Marketing-Purchasing Interface: Resource Development and Organisational Implications', *Industrial Marketing and Purchasing*, 1(2), pp. 3–27.

Czepiel, J.A. (1990) 'Service Encounters and Service Relationships: Implications for Research', *Journal of Business Research*, 20, pp. 13–21.

Davies, M.A. (1998) *Understanding marketing*, Hertfordshire: Prentice Hall.

DeTienne, K.B. and Thompson, J.A. (1996) 'Database Marketing and Organisational Learning Theory: Toward a Research Agenda', *Journal of Consumer Marketing*, 13(5), pp. 12–34.

Dibb, S., Simkin, L., Pride, W.M. and Ferrell, O.C. (2001) *Marketing: Concepts and Strategies*, European Edition, Boston, MA: Houghton Mifflin.

Evans, M. (1999) 'Food Retailing Loyalty Schemes and the Orwellian Millennium?', *British Food Journal*, 101(2), pp. 132–47.

Evans, M.J., O'Malley, L. and Patterson, M. (1995) 'Direct Marketing: Rise and Rise or Rise and Fall?', *Marketing Intelligence and Planning*, 13(6), pp. 16–23.

Evans, M.J., O'Malley, L. and Patterson, M. (1996) 'Direct Marketing Communications in the UK: A Study of Growth, Past, Present and Future', *Journal of Marketing Communications*, 2, pp. 51–65.

Fletcher, D.C., Wheeler and Wright, J. (1991) 'Database Marketing: A Channel, A Medium, Or A Strategic Approach', *International Journal of Advertising*, 10, pp. 117–27.

Ford, D. (1990) *Understanding Business Markets: Interaction, Relationships, Networks*, London: Academic Press, Harcourt Brace and Co. Publishers, p. 1.

Ford, D. (1997) *Understanding Business Markets: Interaction, Relationships, Networks*, 2nd edn, London: Academic Press, Harcourt Brace and Co., p. xi.

George, W.R. (1990) 'Internal Marketing and Organisational Behaviour: A Partnership in Developing Customer-Conscious Employees at Every Level', *Journal of Business Research*, 20, pp. 63–70.

Goldsmith, R.E. (1999) 'The Personalised Marketplace: Beyond the 4Ps', *Marketing Intelligence and Planning*, 17(4), pp. 178–185

Gordon, I. (2000) 'Organising for Relationship Marketing', in J.N. Sheth and A. Parvatiyar (eds) *Handbook of Relationship Marketing*, Thousand Oaks, CA: Sage, p. 512.

Grönroos, C. (1978) 'A Service-Orientated Approach to Marketing of Services', *European Journal of Marketing*, 12(8), p. 594.

Grönroos, C. (1983) *Strategic Management and Marketing in the Service Sector*, Cambridge, MA: Marketing Science Institute.

Grönroos, C. (1994) 'From Marketing Mix to Relationship Marketing: Towards a Paradigm Shift in Marketing', *Management Decision*, 32(2), pp. 4–20.

Grönroos, C. (1995) 'Relationship Marketing: The Strategy Continuum', *Journal of the Academy of Marketing Science*, 23(4), p. 253.

Grönroos, C. (1996) 'Relationship Marketing: Strategic and Tactical Implications', *Management Decisions*, 43(3), 5–14.

Gummesson, E. (1987) 'The New Marketing – Developing Long-Term Interactive Relationships', *Long Range Planning*, 20, pp. 10–20.

Hàkansson, H. (1982) *International Marketing and Purchasing of Industrial Goods*, New York: Wiley, p. 13.

Henley Centre (1978) *Planning Consumer Markets*, London.

Hoffman, D.L. and Novak, T.P. (1996) 'Marketing Hypermedia Computer-Mediated Environments: Conceptual Foundations', *Journal of Marketing*, 12(1), pp. 63–71.

Jackson, D.W. (1994) 'Relationship Selling: The Personalisation of Relationship Marketing', *Asia-Australia Marketing Journal*, 2(1), pp. 34–53.

King, R.L. (1965) 'The Marketing Concept', in G. Schwartz (ed.) *Science in Marketing*, New York: Wiley, pp 70–97.

Kitchen, P. (1986) 'Zipping, Zapping and Nipping', *International Journal of Advertising*, 5, pp. 343–52.

Kitchen, P. and Schultz, D.E. (1999) 'A Multi Country Comparison of the Drive for IMC', *Journal of Advertising Research*, 39(1), pp. 21–38

Lovelock, C.H. (1983) 'Classifying Services to Gain Strategic Marketing Insights', *Journal of Marketing*, 47(Summer), p. 14.

Lovelock, C.H. (1996) *Services Marketing*, Upper Saddle River, NJ: Prentice Hall.

Möller, K. and Wilson, D.T. (1995) 'Introduction: Interaction and Networks in Perspective', in K. Möller and D.T. Wilson (eds) *Business Marketing: An Interaction and Network Perspective*, Norwell, MA: Kluwer Academic Publishers, p. 1.

Norman, R. (1984) *Service Management*, New York: Wiley.

O'Malley, L., Patterson, M. and Evans, M. (1997) 'Intimacy or Intrusion? The Privacy Dilemma for Relationship Marketing in Consumer Markets', *Journal of Marketing Management*, 3(6), pp. 541–59.

O'Malley, L., Patterson, M. and Evans, M. (1999a) 'Data Fusion – Data Control: Privacy Problems – and Solutions?', *Journal of Targeting, Measurement and Analysis for Marketing*, 7(3), pp. 288–302.

O'Malley, L., Patterson, M. and Evans, M. (1999b) *Exploring Direct Marketing*, London: International Thomson Business.

Parasuraman, A., Zeithaml, V.A. and Berry, L.L. (1988) 'SERVQUAL: A Multiple-Item Scale for Measuring Consumer Perceptions of Service Quality', *Journal of Retailing*, 64(1), pp. 12–40.

Price, L.L., Arnould, E.J. and Tierney, P. (1995) 'Going to Extremes: Managing Service Encounters and Assessing Provider Performance', *Journal of Marketing*, 59(April), p. 84.

Rapp, S. and Collins, T. (1987) *Maxi Marketing*, New York: McGraw Hill.

Rapp, S. and Collins, T. (1990) *The Great Marketing Turnaround: The Age of The Individual and How to Profit*, Englewood Cliffs, NJ: Prentice Hall.

Rowe, G.W. and Barnes, J.G. (1998) 'Relationship Marketing and Sustained Competitive Advantage', *Journal of Market Focused Management*, 2, pp. 281–97.

Schultz, D.E. (1999) 'Integrated Marketing Communications and How it Relates to Traditional Media Advertising', in J.P. Jones (ed.) *The Advertising Business: Operations, Creativity, Media Planning, Integrated Communications*, London: Sage, pp. 325–38.

Shani, D. and Chalasani, S. (1992) 'Exploiting Niches Using Relationship Marketing', *Journal of Business Strategy*, 6 (4), pp. 43–52.

Shimp, T.A. (1992) *Promotion Management and Marketing Communications*, 3rd edn, Fort Worth, TX: Dryden.

Schultz, D., Tannenaum, S. and Lauterborn, R. (1993) *The New Marketing Paradigm*, Lincolnwood, IL: NTC Business Books.

Sisodia, R.S. and Wolfe, D.B. (2000) 'Information Technology: Its Role in Building, Maintaining, and Enhancing Relationships', in J.N. Sheth and A. Parvatiyar (eds) *Handbook of Relationship Marketing*, Thousand Oaks, CA: Sage, p. 551.

Solomon, M.R., Suprenant, C., Czepiel, J.A. and Gutman, E.G. (1985) 'A Role Theory Perspective on Dyadic Interactions: The Service Encounter', *Journal of Marketing*, 49(Winter), p. 99.

Surprenant, C.F. and Solomon, M.R. (1987) 'Predictability and Personalisation in the Service Encounter', *Journal of Marketing*, 51(April), p. 87.

Tempest, A. (1996) 'Direct Marketing and its Future', unpublished occasional paper, Federation of European Direct Marketing.

Turnbull, P. and Valla, J.P. (eds) (1985) *Strategies for International Industrial Marketing*, Croom Helm: London.

Wilson, D.T. and Möller, K.E. (1991) 'Buyer–Seller Relationships: Alternative Conceptualisations' in S. Paliwoda (ed.) *New Perspectives in International Marketing*, Routledge: London, p. 87–107.

PART 2
Data and Information Drivers

Part 1 was concerned with setting the scene for our coverage of the elements and implications of direct and relational marketing. One of the facilitators of this is the collection and use of 'data' and a variety of 'information'. This is a major theme of Part 2 of the book. It is clear that technology has had a major impact on the operationalising of relational marketing, so we also explore this in some detail.

The vast range of data sources is explored and contrasted with the relatively simplistic and narrow 'age, gender, social grade' dimensions that were often the primary descriptors of target markets of previous eras. Data sources range from personalised profiling based on, for example, the Census, to more behavioural data from transactional records derived from EPOS or Internet purchase details. A variety of other personalised data can be collected, such as from tracking Internet surfing, credit referencing and so on. We explore these in some detail, together with the technological means for fusing and mining the data.

The new 'metrics' such as RFM and LTVs allow companies to identify those customers who are not contributing as much revenue or profit as the company would like. Although this makes sense when there are clear pressures for marketing activities to be accountable and measurable in times of pressures on budgets and increasingly competitive and dynamic business environments, the result is often the ability to identify segments to target that are more likely to be lucrative. It is with these that marketing will attempt to cultivate relational interaction. Sometimes this leads to a termination of relationship by the company by 'deselecting' or excluding less profitable customers. We continue to offer cautionary notes and provide critical analysis of some of these more recent marketing approaches.

We discuss technological targeting and its underpinning of data-informed market segmentation. We show how personalised profile and behavioural data can be linked or fused together to form 'biographics' (a sort of 'buying biography' of individual customers).

The large datasets that all of this produces allows for sophisticated testing of different approaches: different lists, different creatives and so on. We explore the testing process and provide examples of how this can be implemented.

We are concerned, though, that data should not be used as *the* surrogate for customer understanding. So we explore the nature and role of market research in the relational process. We have a specific concern that some so-called relational programmes tend to be over-reliant upon 'data' – which, admittedly, can provide a wealth of knowledge of customers, but perhaps sometimes at the expense of more insightful understanding. So the final chapters of this part focus on more traditional market research methods that the direct and interactive relational marketer could employ and the more behavioural dimensions that can inform relational interaction.

2 Data sources

Learning objectives

Having completed this chapter, students should:

- Understand the potential role in relational marketing of a variety of sources of personalised data.

- Be able to analyse and evaluate the nature and sources of transactional and profile data.

- Understand how different types of data can be used in relational marketing campaigns.

- Be aware of some of the ethical issues involved with the collection of personalised data.

Dear Mrs Brown . . .

The detail can be profound. With reference to the type of transactional data emerging from EPOS systems linked with individual shopper's loyalty or smart cards, an inspection of a resulting retail loyalty scheme database revealed, for a certain Mrs 'Brown', her address and a variety of behavioural information, including: she shops once per week, usually on a Friday, has a baby (because she buys nappies), spends £90 per week on average and usually buys two bottles of gin every week (Mitchell 1996), perhaps on Thursdays. By knowing what individual consumers buy and the value of their average shopping basket, the retailer might be able to target them with relevant offers while the consumer saves money in the process. Targeting is increasingly at point of sale rather than time-lagged via mailshots. As such, some retailers are working to access customer transactional profiles while the customer is in the store in order to target relevant offers in real time.

(Sources: Authors; Mitchell 1996)

Introduction

The previous chapter explored some of the reasons for the importance of a relational approach. It also introduced the concept of CRM and explained that in practice this is more usually manifested via technology that enables data to help drive relational marketing. Our perspective is that by no means should relational marketing be equated only with data technology, and this theme continues through the book. However, data technology *is* highly relevant because it is this that has operationalised much relational marketing.

This chapter focuses on one of the major facilitators of relational marketing, namely 'data'. There have been technological developments over the past two decades, especially, which have influenced the way in which market information can be collected, stored, analysed and utilised. This chapter focuses on the sources of such data and provides a review of the vast range of different types of data that relational marketers are increasingly collecting.

There is now a proliferation of databases in existence, including geodemographic, lifestyle and purchase data, all of which improve the target ability of relational communications. These developments have been important because 'direct marketing depends on customer information for its effectiveness' (Stone *et al.* 1995). This information needs to be accurate and easily accessible to managers if the benefits are to be maximised: 'very few companies know the real value of their own customer base, but that value is probably the single most direct link to the bottom line. A true customer-focused enterprise increases the long term value of its customers by engaging them in individual, interactive relationships ... through the use of databases that can track the interactions and transactions of individual customers and combining the principles of one-to-one business practices with mass customisation, companies tailor their products and services to meet the needs of each customer' (Peppers 2003).

Sources of data

Preview of data sources

Every contact with the customer can be an opportunity for data-based relational marketing to gather more data (ECHO: Every Contact Has Opportunities). This is manifested in the lists of target prospects that can be purchased from list brokers. A list of, for example, prospects in the gardening market might have been compiled from the following sorts of sources:

- subscribers to gardening magazines;
- purchases of gardening products via mail or via the Internet;

- entrants to competitions for products in this market;
- visitors to certain gardens or 'heritage' sites;
- respondents to lifestyle surveys (see later in this chapter) who claim to have an interest in gardening;
- profile of other interests based on lifestyle survey response;
- profile based on analysis of Census and financial data, via geodemographic profiling (see later in this chapter).

See Exhibit 2.1 for an example of a list and, on reading this, consider the sources from which its components were compiled.

Lists are one of the manifestations of data fusion and data mining, so we explore in this chapter how data is collected and from which sources, and then in Chapter 3, how database technology and management processes it for the creation of various lists, targeting purposes and relational understanding.

There are many sources from which data can be obtained, as outlined in Exhibit 2.2. We shall discuss many of the components in this exhibit in this and subsequent chapters.

We attempt, throughout this book, to provide approaches that move us in the true relational direction but at the same time raise some of the more ethical issues

EXHIBIT 2.1 Lists

LIST DATA-CARD

Welcome to britart.com a brand new list to the market !

britart.com is the UK'S leading online contemporary art gallery.

Innovative and most definately interesting
you can view contemporary art at its best on their
excellent website.

Well educated and affluent buyers, exhibition attendees
and subscribers to britart's news letter, this unique
list can offer you 14000 personalised email addresses.

Prices range from £50.00 making Britart.com a list
well worth testing for your financial, fashion, travel,
wine, books and upmarket offers.

GENERAL INFORMATION	
Total Size	14000
Lead Time	3 Days
Minimum Qty	3000
List Number	22058
List Warranty	TBA
Standard Charge	
Base Rental	£120.00/000
Selections	
Gender	£8.00/000
Format [Delivery Included]	
Disk	£25.00
E Mail	£25.00

New test rates available on request

Enquiries & Orders

Tel:	0870 120 1236	MM Group
Fax:	0117 916 8261	Contact House
Email:	lists@mmgroup.co.uk	Feeder Road
Online	www.listbroker.com	Bristol
Web:	www.mmgroup.co.uk	BS2 0EE

(Source: Data card reproduced with kind permission of MM Group Ltd)

EXHIBIT 2.2 Data sources

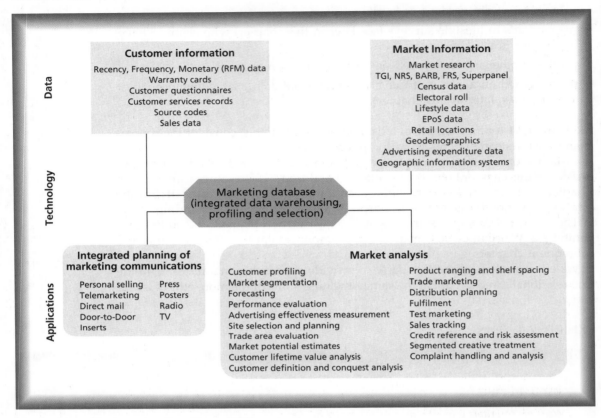

(Source: Adapted by the authors from Patron 1996)

involved in the mechanics of relational marketing. For example, how do you react to the following?

> relationship marketing . . . requires a two-way flow of information. This does not mean that the customer has to give you this information willingly, or even knowingly. You can use scanners to capture information, you can gather telephone numbers, conduct surveys, supply warranty cards, and use a data overlay from outside databases to combine factors about lifestyle, demographics, geographics, psychographics, and customer purchases.
> (Schultz, *et al.* 1993).

This, possibly commonplace, view could philosophically define this sort of relationship marketing implementation as something of an oxymoron and it perhaps raises ethical concerns over the collection and use of personal data. We will not comment much further in this chapter but Chapter 13 explores ethical issues relating to some data sources in more detail. We do, however, suggest that you consider your own perspective on this as we outline some data sources from this point onwards.

In Exhibit 2.3 we provide a framework for fusing data from a variety of sources for data mining purposes. There is a 'non-marketing' term included in this (neuro-biographical clustering). The point here is that there is such a skills shortage of numerate marketers that statisticians and more technical staff are employed to conduct this fusing and mining of data. We therefore use more of a statistical term than, for example, 'segmentation or profiling' in this respect. The issue is explored in greater depth later in this chapter and in our coverage of knowledge management, but is worth introducing here.

There are some 'off-the-shelf' databases which can be purchased, including lifestyle databases (e.g. from Experian and Claritas) and geodemographic databases (e.g. from Experian and CACI). In addition, there are a vast number of lists, thousands in fact. There are also more in-house sources of data from which to populate the database. For example, there are a company's own customer transactional records, results from sales promotion campaigns (coupons, competitions etc.) and also from market research.

In our later coverage of fulfilment, in Chapter 14, we show that there is an iterative process, because data from customer enquiries and orders together with payment details and invoicing data all need to be fed back into the database and overlaid with external profiling data such as geodemographics and lifestyle data, in order to improve subsequent relational interaction.

The data sources shown in Exhibit 2.3 are not necessarily in any specific sequence. Some organisations will naturally start with their own customer data, whether this be basic name and address or more sophisticated recording of each transaction according to date, time and method of payment. Other organisations may start without transactional data, by 'buying-in' lists of a lifestyle or geodemographic nature. These issues are introduced in the following case study.

EXHIBIT 2.3 Data layers

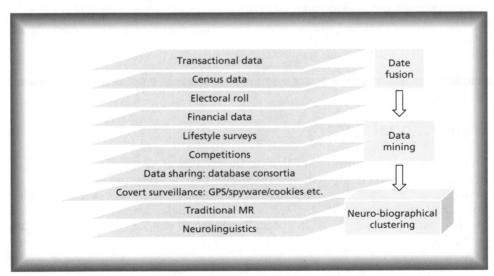

CASE **STUDY** 2.1

DIY data

Sometimes you have to be reminded of the sheer scale of the direct marketing industry. The 4.6 billion items of direct mail that winged their way to doorsteps in the UK last year was up 319 million on the year before, while the 23 billion sent across Europe was four per cent higher than in 1999. To list brokers this has meant just one thing – an upsurge in demand for data. Or has it? Although list brokers have traditionally fed the direct marketer's hunger for data, they aren't the only option anymore. Clients are now turning to a mixture of brokers, data-pooling companies, lifestyle data suppliers and are experimenting with using viral campaigns, promotions and incentives to get the data they need. Companies such as Philips are adopting a do-it-yourself approach to list building which risks cutting list brokers out of the loop. And why not? Like many manufacturers that do not sell their products direct, electrical products company Philips has always suffered from having limited information about its customers. In an attempt to gain more customer feedback but also to add to its customer database with opted-in email addresses, it recently decided to build its own list. Working with Claritas and its

e-registration product, customers who had just bought a Philips product were directed in their product manual to visit the Philips Consumer Communications website. The design of the questionnaire was deliberate to maximise the amount of analysis that could be done. The first and third sections gathered primary data such as name, address and email address, as well as demographic and lifestyle information including age, marital status and number of children. This can be used for segmentation analysis and provides Philips with an understanding of the customer profile of each of its products. The second section also collects data about the motivations behind buying a Philips product. Adeline Perrissin, product manager at Philips Customer Communications, says: 'Suffering from limited visibility, this is a hassle free way to collect information. The data we are now gathering helps us optimise our acquisition and loyalty strategies to improve sales and customer relationships.'

(Source: *DIY Data, Marketing Direct*. Reproduced from *Marketing Direct* magazine with the permission of the copyright owner, Haymarket Business Publications Limited)

Transactional data

The important development facilitating the collection of transactional data has been the installation of point-of-sale (POS) computers. Widespread acceptance by retailers has resulted from technological developments which led to smaller, faster, and more reliable EPOS (Electronic Point of Sale) terminals. Closely allied to this progress has been the development of product codes which are standardised between manufacturers, distributors and retailers (McGoldrick 1990; Shaw 1991). The European Article Number (EAN) is compatible with the

Universal Product Code (UPC) in the USA. This implies that any retailer with an EPOS system can access information. More importantly, this can be downloaded daily – giving rich market information.

The marketing application of bar codes (EAN/UPC) in retailing includes the ability to record who buys what. Products can be matched with customers via credit, debit (Switch) and loyalty card numbers. Retailers will therefore be able to match special offers with individual customers (Shaw 1991).

We are beginning to see the introduction of 'smart' cards (Exhibit 2.4) on which can be stored vast amounts of cardholder information, from age and date of birth to previous purchases and even medical records (Evans *et al.* 1996).

An example would be useful at this point. It is easy for special offers relevant to a shopper's birthday to be made at the right time and for shoppers' new purchases to be added to the bank of information on their previous purchases, and hence the amount and quality of information grows – and so, potentially, might the 'relationship' with individual customers (Foenander 1992). Smart cards may see the end of multiple cards, being able to act as a bank card, credit card, loyalty card, ID card and for medical records. At the time of writing, the UK had

EXHIBIT 2.4   Smart cards

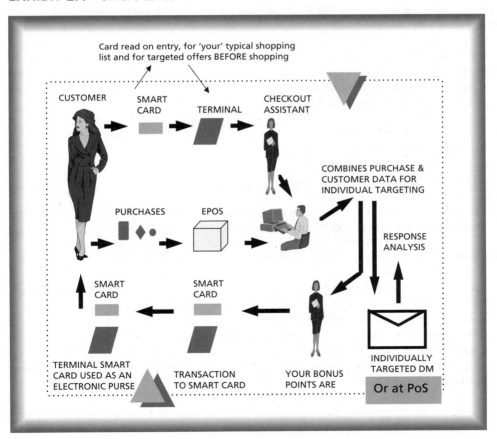

not introduced an identification scheme – many other countries already have 'ID's but it is known that the UK government is seriously considering different models of ID scheme.

Transactional data provides scope for analysing who buys what, when, and through what form of payment. Purchase patterns can be revealed for different geographic locations, store branches, seasons of the year and of course for each customer. This also means that purchase levels and repeat purchase patterns per customer can be analysed and this is something we examine in detail later in this chapter, where the appropriate metrics for determining the more profitable customers are demonstrated. This in turn leads to strategic decisions about which customers to target for relational interaction and which to exclude.

This is fine in itself but transactional data merely provides the behavioural dimensions of purchase, it doesn't shed light on the customers' other interests, their characteristics or other profile dimensions. This is where the fusion of transactional data with other sources of data can lead to enhancement of knowledge about customers.

For example, for business customers, we could add standard industry classification (SIC) codes to their transactional data and details of name, company and nature, value and time of purchase. We could also add Yellow Pages classification; number of employees; telephone number; contact name etc. For customer lists, there are geodemographics and lifestyle profiles that are popular enhancements for additional profiling.

Profiling involves using the data held on one group of customers to identify other potential customers (prospects) with similar characteristics. We provide examples of this in Chapter 9 on 'acquisition' strategies. By profiling existing ('best') customers, the company can draw up a data-based 'identikit' to be used to target 'more of the same'.

Profile data

Census, electoral roll and geodemographics

The use of the national Census in many countries was a watershed for marketing and heralded a shift in both practice and theory. The Census, of course, led to geodemographic systems and was a major catalyst in providing alternatives to anonymised market research samples. Instead, we have data from all households. The further fusion of geodemographics with personalised data from lifestyle surveys and from transactional data provides what marketers are taking to be a buying 'biography' of customers, and from this they think they can develop relationships with customers (Evans 2001). With this as a sort of chronological sequence, we commence our review of data sources with an exploration of geodemographics.

The problem is being addressed by the merging and sharing of data (see case below).

Geodemographics

Reference was made above to the Census as a catalyst. This claim was not made lightly. From 1981 in the UK, the national Census has been available for marketing purposes. Names and addresses from the Census cannot be revealed, but a link via the postal code system with the electoral roll means that it is possible to identify individual households and their characteristics. One of the current debates (at the time of writing) is between the Information Commissioner's position that the electoral role should not be compiled for marketing purposes and should not therefore be used in this way, and on the other hand the argument from the marketing industry for freedom in its use. Although the electoral roll is rarely used as a list in itself, it is used as a base for many targeting tools. One concern of the Information Commissioner is that some people may disenfranchise themselves by not registering for fear of being over-targeted by marketers. A legal case has already brought this to a head. In November 2001 a member of the public won his case against Wakefield Council after that Council had not been able to confirm that his electoral roll data (name and address) would not be supplied to third parties without his consent, such as marketers (Acland 2001). Having said this, an opt-out option has been added to the electoral roll and this should help to alleviate privacy concerns at the same time as shifting relational marketing in yet another direction: 'permission marketing'. Perhaps customers will give permission to specific organisations to use their details for specified purposes. But this means that only a smaller and, by definition, an incomplete electoral register can be used for marketing and one study suggests that a ban on using the full electoral roll data could cost advertisers £55 million per year because 'the cost of not having access to the electoral roll would be five pence per (mail) pack' (Denny 1999).

Within months of the electoral roll 'opt-out' being introduced, over 24% of UK citizens (over 10 million people) had opted out (Larkins 2003). The figure varies across local authorities, partly due to the different way they stated the nature and reason for possible opt-out on their annual electoral register forms. So there are additional problems of lack of uniformity in geographical terms of the size of the population available for commercial purposes. For example, for about 8% of local authorities, over 40% of citizens opted out but for about 16% of authorities, the proportion opting out was less than 10%. The use of the electoral roll specifically for credit referencing was topical at the time of writing and the industry response to a court case that would have contested the legitimate use of the electoral roll for credit referencing but collapsed due to the failure of the complainant to secure legal aid was one of jubilation (Rubach 2003).

Britannia Music

Britannia Music needs to recruit around 750 000 customers a year and does so through direct mail, telesales and press ads. With mailing volumes of around 40 million packs a year, the impact of an edited electoral roll (ER) was always going to hit hard. 'Many of our business plans are built around the availability of the ER,' says Tony Kane, former managing director of Britannia Music and now a Britannia consultant. 'If there's any movement in any one of the routes, we still have to recruit 750 000 customers to cover churn.' As well as prospecting, the company uses the ER in other ways. For instance, Britannia sells certified films for over-18s. 'One strength of the ER was in validation of names for direct mail campaigns,' says Kane. 'We would never knowingly mail contractual information or sell PG films to those under 18 years of age. 'To replace the ER, Britannia is looking at products like Experian's National Canvasse. 'It will act as a clean replacement to the ER, and in an enhanced manner,' says Kane.

(Source: Adapted by the author from Royal Mail (2002) 'Life After the Electoral Roll', in a sponsored supplement to *Marketing Direct*, October, pp. 8–9. Reproduced with the permission of the copyright owner, Haymarket Business Publications Limited)

Electoral roll alternatives
Supplier: Experian
New product: National Canvasse
What's in it: The non-opted-out electoral roll (ER), Experian's Canvasse lifestyle survey data, plus data from two unnamed organisations
Supplier: Claritas
A new product which includes the non-opted-out ER, Claritas lifestyle survey data, including BehaviourBank, Lifestyle Selector and Claritas Interactive data collected via the Intemet
Supplier: CACI
New product which includes the non-opted-out ER, lifestyle data from a joint venture partner, data from shareholders' registers and an additional high-volume data source
Supplier: EuroDirect
Revamped product: Data Exchange
What's in it: The non-opted-out ER, data from the original Data Exchange (a data pool of 22 million people), EuroDirect's UK Lifestyle data and the Investors Database for Footsie 350
Supplier: Acxiom
Product: Infobase UK Marketing File
What's in it: Fifteen data sources, including data from Claritas and EuroDirect.

Data alliances or consortia are discussed later, but along with the extension of lifestyle surveys, these are probably intended to replace missing Census data. In the chapter on loyalty (Chapter 9) we discuss consortia of loyalty scheme data, such as the Nectar Scheme.

The value of the Census and electoral roll was really distilled from the 1981 UK Census, when some forty census variables were cluster analysed and the emerging clusters of households led to the creation of 39 neighbourhood types in the first geodemographic system in the UK (ACORN – A Classification of Residential Neighbourhoods, developed by CACI – Consolidated Analysis Centres Incorporated). Compare this with one of the leading alternatives of the time – social grade – which classifies the entire population into just six groups on the basis of one variable (occupation of the chief income earner in the household). Whereas these profiles are often based on sample surveys of 1 000, the marketing industry then had access to a census of 56 million.

There are 'me-toos' of the original ACORN system. Richard Webber, who created ACORN, set up one of the competitors after he left CACI to join another similar agency, CCN (but now called Experian, following the link with the American company of that name), and developed MOSAIC which analyses the census data in conjunction with a variety of data sources, including CCJs, electoral roll and Royal Mail data. The fusion with financial data is partly based on the origins of CCN as the credit referencing arm of Great Universal Stores (CCN stood for Consumer Credit Nottingham).

The basic rationale behind geodemographics is that 'birds of a feather flock together', making neighbourhoods relatively homogenous. An easy criticism in riposte is that 'I am not like my neighbour'.

Geodemographic systems are not restricted to the UK, and a number of similar systems have been operating around the world for many years. In other European countries similar systems exist and several geodemographic companies now operate throughout many European countries, such as Experian (with its MOSAIC brand).

There are examples on the accompanying website of geodemographic profiles of UK and European cities, but we provide a few examples here. It is straightforward to profile the area around a postcode in terms of geodemographic categories. This could be the catchment area of an existing retail outlet, bank, pub and so on, or it could be the profiling of a 'drive time' area of one of several possible locations to site a new branch of a multiple retailer. It is likely that the retailer (in this case) would know the geodemographic profile of existing best customers (see our coverage of RFM and LTV analysis later in this chapter) and from the geodemographic profile of the new area would be able to purchase (from Experian or CACI, for example) the names and addresses of those who match this profile, with potential for direct mail or telemarketing contact.

Exhibit 2.5 depicts the sort of neighbourhood profiling of geodemographic systems (MOSAIC in this case).

There is now a full geodemographic analysis of the Target Group Index (TGI) (see our coverage of market research in Chapter 6). The TGI is an annual report in 34 volumes of buyer profiles in most product-markets, based on samples of over 20 000. From this, each geodemographic category's interest in the product

EXHIBIT 2.5   Geodemographic groups

concerned can be determined. In fact the TGI sample design is now based on geodemographic categories and so the sample design is an application of geodemographics. In addition, the National Readership Survey is similarly analysed by geodemographics and this can provide readership profiles for media selection purposes.

We introduced the concept of data fusion earlier and there is significant fusion of data from different sources in the current compilation of geodemographic groupings. The TGI is fused with BARB TV panel data (see Chapter 6) in order to estimate the media habits, lifestyle, product purchase and geodemographic profiles of the population. Also, most geodemographic systems are now heavily fused with financial data; remember the origins of Experian outlined above. It is not surprising, therefore, that such marketing data is of interest to government departments. CACI, for example, have an entire department dealing exclusively with government contracts for ACORN and related products. The Inland Revenue would have particular interest in the financial details of households to check financial details and trends against tax returns from those they want to investigate further.

It is interesting to note that for the 2001 Census, the British government, for the first time, 'officially added commercial business to the list of users' of the Census (Exon 1998). New questions potentially relevant to the marketer and market researcher were added, including a clever question revealing the sexuality of partners (Exon 1998; Brindle 1999). The question wording asked for names of partners in the household and presumably marketers will assume same or different sex partners to indicate sexuality, the gay market being an important one for many marketers to target (see our coverage of 'targeting' in Chapter 6).

However extensive the Census becomes, the major limitation of Census data relates to the difficulties associated with updating information, particularly because in the UK the Census is only carried out every ten years. There are also concerns about the quality of the Census data itself: 'The *Financial Times'* findings cast doubt on the reliability of the census and its main conclusion that Britain has been bereft of large numbers of men in their 20s and 30s' (Briscoe 2003). It appears that the wording of the census rubric, whether the respondents saw themselves as being 'usually resident', was not clear enough and some did not, therefore, respond at all. Because of the ten-year intervals, some might have thought that to live here for, say, two years did not qualify them to be residents.

There are suggestions that annual updates might be based on survey research, especially of the 'lifestyle' type which is discussed in the next section.

Another issue concerns the generic nature of geodemographics. These have traditionally been off-the-shelf systems from which we can profile our existing customers according to postcode or select a sample of certain geodemographic clusters for research or testing purposes. But all this is fine as long as the underpinning clustering of the specific data included is relevant to our purposes. If we clustered different census questions and overlaid these with different financial and other details, to form more tailored clusters relevant to our specific operation, then the customised geodemographic system might be even more useful.

As sophisticated as geodemographics might be – certainly compared with the simplicity of age, gender and occupation (the main variables of the demographic alternative) – the approach is essentially the same – that is, it 'profiles' people. It does not in itself explain why people behave as they do and neither does it provide individualised information on what people buy. These issues are, to some extent, addressed by other approaches, outlined in the sections on transactional data, lifestyle and biographics.

Lifestyle data

Lifestyle research is not new, as the discussion of traditional lifestyle approaches in Chapter 6 confirms. However, before exploring that, it is worth turning our attention to the more contemporary lifestyle data that is especially relevant in building databases and lists.

The contemporary 'lifestyle survey' asks respondents to 'tick' those responses that apply in terms of which products and services they claim an interest or actual purchase. Exhibit 2.6 demonstrates some typical questions, some of which will be sponsored by specific companies.

This exhibit reflects just a portion of typical current lifestyle surveys. Many more questions are included, covering claimed buying behaviour across many different product and service categories. Some questions will be sponsored by specific companies – for example, a car insurance company might sponsor a question asking for the month in which the car insurance is renewed. Because these surveys are not anonymised, the data will be filed in a database by name and address of respondent, and it is likely that the month prior to that respondent's renewal date, he or she is very likely to receive direct mailings soliciting defection to the sponsoring company.

A slightly different version of the lifestyle survey is the Postal Preference Survey (PPS). This seeks 'opt-in' by asking consumers which products and services they want to receive communication about. The following case study shows one user's evaluation of this, compared with the less obvious 'opt-in' forms.

EXHIBIT 2.6 Contemporary 'lifestyle' research

Please indicate your marital status:

single

married

divorced/separated

widowed

What is your name and address?

What is your partner's full name?

Holidays:

How much are you likely to spend per person on your next main holiday?

up to £500 ☐   £501–£999 ☐   £1000–£1499 ☐   £1500–£2000 ☐

£2000+ ☐

In which country are you likely to take your next main holiday?....................

In which month are you likely to take your main holiday?..........................

CASE **STUDY** 2.3

Abbey National

Ever since Abbey National launched its retail insurance policy in 1997, direct mail has played a significant part in an integrated marketing strategy to develop its products in a competitive sector. The service provides home or motor insurance direct over the phone or through the Internet. Yet in recent years, Abbey National was finding that the cost effectiveness of traditional lifestyle lists was gradually deteriorating, with response levels consistently falling below the company's target levels. In 2001, John Hawkins, marketing manager of the retain insurance division at Abbey National, decided that he needed to try a different approach. Keen to sell competitive policies to consumers who had other insurance renewals approaching, Hawkins was interested in two questions included in the Postal Preference Service questionnaire: 'Would you like information that can save you money on car insurance?' and 'When do you renew your motor insurance?' If there was a yes answer to the first question and a date was provided for the second, then all these consumers were mailed at the appropriate time before their insurance ran out. Because these two questions were deemed targeted enough, other criteria for targeting did not need to come into play, cutting out the need for any additional profiling. According to Hawkins, the response to the mailings, which targeted people between 25 and 75 years of age, was unprecedented. 'We have used Postal Preference Service data since July 2001,' he says, 'and response rates are up by 25 per cent. This is compared to data bought from other leading lifestyle lists.' He adds: 'PPS data, unlike other sources which rather mechanically supply data, has been one of the best providers of data we have used to date. We will certainly plan to use its data again in the future.'

(Source: *Marketing Direct* (2002) How to Make Opt-In Work, Guide to Data and Permission Marketing Supplement, October pp. 6–7. Reproduced from Marketing Direct magazine with the permission of the copyright owner, Haymarket Business Publications Limited)

Although the industry has claimed that there is now a lifestyle census, the reality is somewhat different. Admittedly, a large number of individuals (around 20 million in the UK) have responded, but the survey is by definition a self-selected sample and it is known that some respondents do not tell the whole truth in completing the questionnaire (Evans *et al.*, 1997). The difference between the more traditional form of lifestyle segmentation discussed earlier and the current approach is that the former builds psychographic profiles of segments from relatively small datasets and expands these to generalise patterns within the larger population. The latter, however, has the ability to list names and addresses of those who claim to be interested in specific products, brands and services and it is this, of course, that contributes to more directed segmenting and targeting of markets. It provides data on what respondents claim they buy but doesn't in itself reveal the same type of *affective* data on opinions and 'outlook on life' that can be derived from traditional lifestyle research as is explored further in Chapter 6.

One topical application is the use of lifestyle data as a sort of surrogate for the missing millions from the electoral register as a result of the new opt-out facility discussed earlier (around a quarter of the UK population and up to 80% in some specific localities). But there are likely to be accuracy and reliability concerns unless the lifestyle survey becomes more precise and useful.

The clustering of lifestyle data and then inferring similar profiles for others in similar postcodes is geo-lifestyle profiling. This is the major approach adopted by Claritas with their PRIZM system.

Competitions

Competitions have long been used not only as a form of sales promotion but also to gather personalised data. It is obvious that those entering a competition could be existing customers but equally they might never have had any contact with the organisation concerned. As a result, the competition is a good way to gather data from prospects as well as to upgrade existing data on customers, depending on the sorts of questions asked. These questions can sometimes be the main purpose of the competition, even if, to the entrant, the competition itself is more clearly *their* intent.

Data consortia

There is clear evidence of a trend towards the creation of strategic alliance *consortia* between companies based on sharing data (Marsh 1998). This is, of course, entirely congruent with relational constructs, notably 'networks'. For example, an insurance company has a ten-year agreement with motor companies, a vehicle breakdown service and a satellite TV company. There is clearly synergy to be had between these, if data is shared, with respect to complementary business (for 'cross-selling') and for advertising purposes. Unilever, Kimberly-Clark and Cadbury have formed the Consumer Needs Consortium (Jigsaw), which aims to reduce research and database costs. 'It is difficult to make the numbers work on expensive database building and relational marketing strategies, which provide the framework for ventures such as direct shopping, when you are churning out low purchase price items' (Richards 1998). An issue that is likely to be raised in the future is how to assess which companies should join such partnerships – corporate culture will be as important as product-market synergy. This is germane to Jigsaw because the consortium initially included Bass but this company left shortly after the consortium was launched. We discussed the PPS 'opt-in' lifestyle survey earlier and it is interesting to note that Jigsaw has appointed PPS to handle its data collection (Borrof 2001): 'the appointment means all PPS packs will contain a Jigsaw questionnaire inviting recipients to answer questions on product areas of Jigsaw Consortium companies (Borrof 2001).

Another significant consortium operates in the financial services sector (Tank!). It involves Royal Bank of Scotland and is backed by the DMA (UK) and IDM. Forty other financial services organisations have pledged support (Kemeny 1998a). Although initially the intention was to pool general relational marketing statistics, it soon progressed to sharing response data (Kemeny 1998b). One of the basic propositions underpinning the sharing of what is perceived to be sensitive competitive data parallels category management – rather than concentrating on discrete brands, the aim is to grow a category. This is reinforced in a database context where it is often found that those interested in one brand or store in a category will also be interested across the category.

Another variation of the sharing theme is provided by Abacus, an American statistical modelling company, and Claritas (the lifestyle and geodemographics provider) which are fusing data from 1 000 mail order companies in the USA. They have now replicated the approach in the UK, with a consortium of over 200 mail-order companies in the UK, and intend to extend this into France and Germany. Again their rationale is that the best customers are those who buy from several catalogues. The data will be used for prospecting new customers (Morris 1998) and for other uses as discussed in Chapter 8.

Interestingly, Abacus was acquired in 1999 by DoubleClick, which recently lost a court case when it illegally sold personalised data on Internet use combined with other private data (Dixon 2000).

The Nectar Scheme is another such consortium and this operates between (at the time of writing, but it was noticeable that new partners joined regularly during the first few months of its operation) Sainsbury's, Barclaycard, Debenhams, BP, Thresher, Adams and Vodafone. The 'small print' of the Nectar Scheme application form mentions other partners needed to operate the scheme but these are not stated in the publicity material. Some customers may be willing to allow their details to be shared amongst these main partners but be more concerned over where else their details might go. So, for some alliances, data might illegally go to countries that are, in data protection terms, outlawed, without customers knowing (see Chapter 13).

Covert surveillance

Another 'layer' being added is derived from observational methods – a DM industry source wishing to remain anonymous revealed that in the USA, redundant *surveillance satellites* are being used to take pictures of households – accurate to within a few feet – to update databases on the ownership of swimming pools, caravans and other items that can be seen outside a household. With SPOT digital imaging these satellites are able to read a car number plate and even newsprint from several miles in space (Webster 1999). In the UK an aerial photographic census is being created (Anon 1999) by Simmons Aerofilms and the National Remote Sensing Centre and will be 'married with other data sets such as Census information and demographic details' (Stannard 1999). Some people might see this as an uncontrollable invasion of privacy. Also, there is the possibility that American surveillance technology in the UK could be used on behalf of American companies for competitor intelligence (BBC 2003).

There is also the covert surveillance of web traffic, via 'cookies', as discussed in Chapters 11 and 13. The 'surfing' behaviour of those visiting websites can provide valuable information about prospects' and customers' behaviour on the Internet.

Market research

Chapter 5 on marketing research explores this area so we will provide only cursory coverage here. However, it is reassuring that some database marketers are incorporating more traditional market research data. Those who do not do so rely very heavily on testing. As we will see in Chapter 5, this is one of the database marketer's tablets of stone. It allows list A to be tested against list B, for copy Y to be tested against copy Z and so on. Response rates are analysed to determine which to roll out. However, it is important to understand 'why' response rates are as found. This only comes from more qualitative research.

The fusion of data from the 'breadth' of databases covering very large numbers of customers and potential customers and the 'depth' of panel data which provides greater richness from a smaller number of market research respondents produces the 'T-Group', as also discussed in the chapter on market research.

Neurolinguistics

Another 'layer' of data comes from the investigation of different information processing styles (Broderick 1999). Some of these might be based on gender because, *neurolinguistically*, male and female brains have been found to process information differently (Nairn *et al.* 1999, Evans *et al.* 2000).

Neurolinguistic programming (NLP) is already being used in practice to target consumers; for example, Tunney (1999) explains the use by Marketing Focus of NLP to identify 14 different types.

Could it also be that there are different cognitive and communication styles of people who are 'first borns'? In research reported by Nancarrow *et al.* (1999) it is shown that first borns tend to be treated differently by their parents and one result is the turning to others for reassurance when anxious. The marketing application is especially relevant for high-involvement purchases for which there are opportunities for marketers to make additional contact with first borns in order to provide this reassurance. Relational marketers can easily identify first borns and so *ordinal birth position* might therefore become a surrogate measure of *personality* – a variable marketers have struggled to include in their market dissection attempts over many years (Evans *et al.* 1996:139; Snyder and DeBono 1985).

Data fusion

Exhibit 2.3 suggests that many of these data sources are being fused by relational marketers with a view to developing clearer understanding of their customers for closer relational interaction. A later section shows how data is fused and then mined, but it is worth summarising the above under the heading 'biographics'.

Biographics

Indeed, this fusion is the essence of biographics. Depending on whether the relational marketer starts with in-house customer transactional data or buys in profiling data such as geodemographics or lifestyle lists, there will be a progression from profile data to transactional data (or vice versa). Either way, transactional data tends to become the main data source for many databases, and, overlaid with this multitude of profile data, we have moved into the era of *biographics*. This is the fusion of profile and transaction data which provides a detailed description of customers and prospects relevant to their buying behaviour, analogous to the biography in literature.

The industry structure for biographic fusion is the data warehouse (Exhibit 2.7). This is the process of creating one large collection of data in a single location. Typically, this requires gathering and storing data from multiple sources which then becomes the single focal point for all types of data analysis. The data warehouse allows fast queries on potentially any data attribute it contains. 'The data warehouse … can be defined as a system that collects data from various applications throughout an organisation, integrates that data, stores it and then exploits it to deliver information throughout the organisation' (Read 1997). This definition by the director of marketing at the SAS Institute – one of the world's largest software companies – shows that it goes beyond the marketing function and is an integrator of a variety of business functions. A word of warning, though: Humby (1996) describes the interrogation of data from a variety of sources but also states that it is not worth including 'everything'. There is always the danger of 'paralysis by analysis'!

EXHIBIT 2.7 Data warehousing

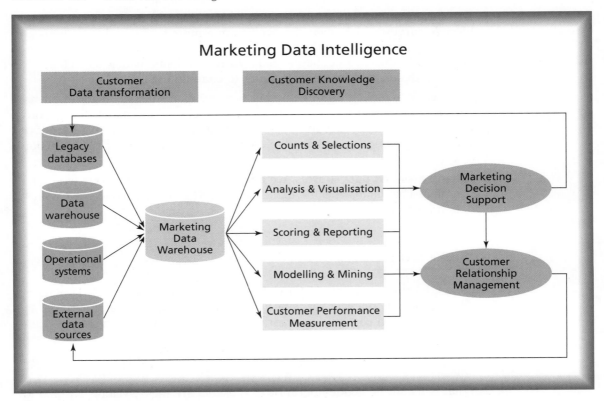

(Source: Chablo 1999)

This is the point at which it is appropriate to turn from the types and sources of data to how it can be mined, analysed and used.

Summary

- This chapter has explored a range of data sources for the interactive relational marketer. These include data on the organisation's own customers in the form of their transactional behaviour and other profile characteristics. We will see in the next chapter that this is very useful for identifying those customers who are worth most to the organisation.

- Then there is a range of additional profiling data from outside of the organisation. The availability of Census-derived geodemographic systems was a major catalyst in the UK. The 1981 Census was the first to be commercially available and perhaps can be described as a quantum leap from the profiling of (anonymised) samples of around 1 000 that were profiled on the basis of age, gender and social grade, to a database of all UK households that enables profiling of 60 or more variables.

- This began an industry of personalised data. The next development was the lifestyle survey which is far removed from a more traditional (anonymised) form of lifestyle research that we explore in Chapter 6 because the version described in the current chapter requires respondents' names as well as personal details and interests, in order to compile lists.

- Our coverage moved on to a number of other data sources, including that derived from various syndicated consortia, such as from panels that record direct mailings and from consortia that share marketing data. We introduced a number of ethical questions that could be asked concerning the collection of very personal data.

- Having explored data sources, we now turn to what can be done with all this data. The database is the tool and the next chapter is concerned with data mining and analysis.

Review questions

1 For a consumer market of your choice, consider the sources of information which might be relevant for data fusion (including the range of existing databases which could be relevantly linked). What could each source contribute to a relational marketing operation?

2 Discuss the contribution to direct and interactive marketing of transactional data.

3 What is meant by geodemographics? On what are these systems based and what are their uses to relational marketers?

4 What are the implications of the 'opt-out' that is now offered for the electoral roll?

5 What is meant by biographics? Explore the contribution of biographics to the relational marketers and indicate the implications of this for consumers.

Further reading

Evans, M.J. (1998) 'From 1086 and 1984: Direct Marketing into the Millennium', *Marketing Intelligence and Planning*, 16(1), pp. 56–67.

Sleight, P. (1997) *Targeting Customers: How to use Geodemographic and Lifestyle Data in Your Business*, 2nd edn, Henley: NTC Publications.

References

Acland, H. (2001) 'Ruling puts DM Industry Firmly on Back Foot', *Marketing Direct*, December.

Anon (1999) 'UK Perspectives Airs Photographic Census', *Precision Marketing*, 24 May.

BBC (2003) *Analysis*, Radio 4, March.

Borrof, R. (2001) 'Jigsaw Group Appointments PPS to Oversee Data Collection', *Precision Marketing*, 13 July, p. 1.

Brindle, D. (1999) 'Census Check on Partners', *Guardian*, 5 March, p. 12.

Briscoe, S. (2003) 'Doubts over Reliability of Population Census', *Financial Times*, 20 May.

Broderick, A. (1999) 'Information Processing Styles', IDM Educators Conference, May, London.

Chablo, E. (1999) 'The Importance of Marketing Data Intelligence in Delivering Successful CRM', White Paper, smart FOCUS.

Denny, N. (1999) 'Marketing Success is Judged by Cash Criteria', *Marketing*, 13 May.

Dixon, L. (2000) 'DoubleClick Sues over Data scandal', *Precision Marketing*, 7 February, p. 10.

Evans, M. (2001) 'Direct and Database Marketing', in P. Kitchen and R. Proctor *Marketing: The Informed Student Guide*, London: Thomson Learning.

Evans, M., Nairn, A. and Maltby, A. (2000) 'The Hidden Sex Life of the Male and Female Shot', *International Journal of Advertising*, 19(1).

Evans, M., O'Malley, L. and Patterson, M. (1996) 'Direct Mail and Consumer Response: An Empirical Study of Consumer Experiences of Direct Mail', *Journal of Database Marketing*, 3(3), pp. 250–62.

Evans, M., O'Malley, L., Patterson, M. and Mitchell, S. (1997) 'Consumer Reactions to Database-based Supermarket Loyalty Schemes', *Journal of Database Marketing*, 4(4), pp. 307–20.

Exon, M. (1998) 'The Moral Marketing Maze', *Precision Marketing*, 28 September, p. 12.

Foenander, J. (1992) 'The Use of Smart Card Technology for Target Marketing in the Retail Sector', *Journal of Targeting, Measurement and Analysis for Marketing*, 1(1), pp. 55–60.

Humby, C. (1996) 'Opening the Information Warehouse', *Marketing*, 18 September, pp. 34–7.

Kemeny, L. (1998a) 'Data "Tank" for Bank Practices', *Precision Marketing*, 16 November, p. 1.

Kemeny, L. (1998b) 'Financial Services Think [Tank] for Common Pool', *Precision Marketing* 14 December p. 5.

Larkins, V. (2003) '10 Million Tick Electoral Roll Opt-Out Box', *Marketing Business*, February, p. 6.

Marsh, H. (1998) 'What's In Store?', *Marketing* 15 October, p. 37–8.

McGoldrick, P.J. (1990) *Retail Marketing*, London: McGraw Hill.

Mitchell, A. (1996) *You and Yours*, Interview transcribed from BBC Radio 4, January.

Morris, C. (1998) as reported in Davila, G. (1998) 'UK Catalogue Firms Asked to Share Data', *Precision Marketing*, 19 October, p. 1.

Nairn, A., Evans, M. and Maltby, A. (1999) 'Gender Differences for Financial Services Direct Mail', *Journal of Financial Services Marketing*, 4(2), p. 139–62.

Nancarrow, C., Wright, L.T. and Alakoc, B. (1999) 'Top Gun Fighter Pilots Provide Clues to More Effective Database Marketing Segmentation: The Impact of Birth Order', *Journal of Marketing Management*, 15(6), pp. 449–62.

Patron, M. (1996) 'The Future of Marketing Databases', *Journal of Database Marketing*, 4(1), p. 8.

Peppers, D. (2003) 'Customer-Centricity is Key', *Research*, February, p. 21–2.

Read, G. (1997) 'The Future of Data Warehousing', *Business and Technology*, February, p. 64.

Richards, A. (1998) 'Can Unity Beat the Retailers?', *Marketing*, February, p. 18.

Rubach, E. (2003) 'Industry Hail Robertson Defeat', *Precision Marketing*, 23 May, p. 1.

Schultz, D.E., Tannenaum, S.I. and Lauterborn, R.F. (1993) *The New Marketing Paradigm*, Lincolnwood IL: NTC Books.

Shaw, R. (1991) 'How the Smart Card is Changing Retailing', *Long Range Planning*, 24(10), pp. 111–14.

Snyder, M. and DeBono, K.G. (1985) 'Appeals to Image and Claims about Quality: Understanding the Psychology of Advertising', *Journal of Personality and Social Psychology*, 49, pp. 586–97.

Stannard, H. (1999) reported in Anon (1999) 'UK Perspectives Airs Photographic Census, *Precision Marketing*, 24 May, p. 5.

Stone, M., Davies, D. and Bond, A. (1995) *Direct Hit: Direct Marketing With A Winning Edge*, London: Pitman, p. 70.

Tunney, D. (1999) 'Harnessing the Subconscious to Bolster Sales', *Marketing*, 13 May, p. 20.

Webster, E.C. (1999) 'Secrets of War: Spies in the Sky', History Channel, 3 July.

3 Data metrics

Learning objectives

Having completed this chapter, students should:

- Be able to analyse and evaluate the analysis and use of transactional and profile data.
- Be able to explore the nature and power of marketing databases in a relational marketing context.
- Understand how data is fused and mined.
- Understand contemporary relational marketing metrics such as RFM and LTV analysis.
- Understand practical examples of how some statistical techniques can be applied to database analysis.

Seagram

Seagram is a major supplier of alcoholic beverages in the UK. The database covers promotions and research into the consumption behaviour of consumers across a number of Seagram's key UK brands. The database will need to drive strategies for projected growth of the designated brands. It had to be capable of accurately reflecting values and consumption of individual consumers. The database contains 650 000 records, information is obtained from direct mail responses, sales promotions, Duty Free campaigns and distillery visitor centre visits as a result of SUK marketing activities. The questionnaires are a subset of one large questionnaire; therefore data imports into the SUK database are easily performed upon receipt of data from the respective house. Seagram have a number of business objectives, which require the income, generated through direct fundraising activity supported by the database:

- Acquisition of new customers
- Retention of existing customers
- Monitoring existing consumption rates
- Increase loyalty and usage
- Increase point of sale response rates
- Increase DM promotion response rates
- Improve cost efficiency and effectiveness
- Test marketing on consumers
- Conversion of competitor brand loyalty.

The use of Sequel Server permitted future enhancements; fast data retrieval and the functional requirements were satisfied by Visual Basic. A traditional approach was adopted where the business requirements were captured by holding a variety of workshops. Following sign-off, these requirements were converted into a systems specification. Scope were actively involved in the Testing and User acceptance of the system.

- Microsoft SQL Server 7.0 – Database
- QSS Namebase to analyse and standardise consumer names
- Capscan Matchcode PAF to enhance/standardise postal addresses
- The REaD Group's Gone Away Suppressions File to examine the occupants of specific addresses within the UK, for the purpose of cleaning direct mailing lists.
- The Mailing Preference Service file to specifically not mail people who have 'opted out' of direct marketing activity.
- The Bereavement Register to prevent marketing to the deceased, normally causing embarrassment to SUK and undue distress to relatives of the deceased.

The system has been responsible for increasing the number of new and repeat consumers and increasing the cost efficiency and effectiveness of the business.

(Source: Reproduced with the kind permission of Talking Numbers)

Introduction

The previous chapter explored some of the sources of contemporary data for direct and interactive relational marketing and this chapter now explores how such data can be fused and mined.

Technology has clearly been a factor in the growth of relational marketing, with the most significant developments being the increasing capabilities of computers and advances in relational databases, as we introduced in Chapter 1. The power, speed, memory and storage capacity of computers have been continually improving over the past ten years. Indeed, although the oft-cited phenomenon that computer power doubles every 18 months might not always be literally true, it is certainly the case that it is highly dynamic. It also leads to a related decline in the costs associated with the acquisition of technology.

The existence of a customer database enhances the speed and efficiency of accessing and analysing customer data. Equally, the database plays an important role in measuring response to relational marketing programmes, via the 'metrics' we explore in this chapter. Although, in practice, the database lies at the heart of operationalising much relational marketing in fmcg markets, it should not be *the* central focus or the *only* driver; this position should still be reserved for the right balance between organisational and customer goals, the latter being properly identified and anticipated via 'customer insight'. We explore aspects of customer insight in Chapters 5 and 14. Having said this, it is equally clear to us that 'data' is essential for *informing* relational marketing and it is to this area that we now turn.

Database basics

Information on a database is usually structured on the basis of files, records and fields. In order to understand how a database works, a simple analogy is a manual filing system. A manual system is made up of filing cabinets, within which there are individual suspension files. The database is the equivalent of the manual filing system, individual files are the filing cabinets, records are the suspension files (which might pertain to individual customers), and fields the different pieces of information held within those files. Files could hold information on all customers, products or transactions. These files are composed of a series of 'records'. Each record contains data about someone or something, for example a customer or potential customer. Each record is then further divided into 'fields' which store particular data items such as postcode, name, age, gender and so on.

The reason why 'field' data is held separately is because a marketer may want to extract those customers in a particular age category, or of a particular gender, for analysis or targeting purposes. Marketers therefore need to be able to identify those categories in a discrete way while taking care to avoid having too many data fields jumbled up together, as this would not allow us to be as selective as individual targeting requires. For example, although keyword searches extract the relevant records, without separating these records into fields the search time would be greater because all of the data in the homogenised record would have to be searched. Conversely, when records are divided into fields, this means that only those fields in which the relevant characteristics are stored would need to be searched. Also, if all of the individual field data were jumbled together and a lifestyle category of the 'Hooray Henry' was to be extracted for the targeting of trendily styled and fluorescent yellow mobile phones, we might extract everyone whose name is also Henry (first name or surname!).

Types of database

There are a number of different types of database available to organisations. These include:

- hierarchical
- network
- relational.

Hierarchical databases are the oldest form of marketing database. They store information in a structure similar to that of an organisational chart where there are analogous 'parent' and 'child' relationships. Consequently they are somewhat inflexible, because the routes of access are embedded in the data. As a result, hierarchical database systems are best suited for large, transaction-orientated databases in a mainframe environment. They can be designed to produce very high performance for specific queries, but this performance comes at the cost of fixing views of data. For example, while alternative views are possible, they are difficult to create once the primary structure has been created. Most bank databases have traditionally been hierarchical, and can process data on transactions (of which there are potentially millions) very quickly. However, it has proven difficult to utilise the database for marketing purposes. For example, it may be possible to access data by account number or name, but exceptionally difficult to generate a list of all 18-year-olds for direct marketing purposes.

Network databases are similar to the hierarchical model in that there are owner and member relationships. The system also uses pointers to identify records needed for analysis purposes. Such a system allows multiple access points to exist, and is therefore more flexible than a hierarchical database. However, it is also more expensive and complex to run. For example, routes to access data are embedded in its structure, and therefore the user will need to understand the data structure in order to manipulate the data effectively. This makes its use difficult for many routine marketing analysis purposes.

Relational databases are currently the dominant database architecture (or design) for systems developments. Relational databases store data in two-dimensional tables of rows and columns. A single row represents all attributes (data) for a given entity (such as a customer), while a column represents the same attribute for all records. Thus, routes of access are independent of the data, and files can easily be joined in new logical structures. The tables are linked together by a common key, such as a customer number. This link allows users to create dynamic views of data and to add new data with minimum difficulty. Relational databases have provided a huge boost for direct marketing applications.

An example will illustrate how relational databases are more useful than traditional hierarchical databases for direct marketing purposes. Hierarchical databases deal with only one file at a time. Think of a mail-order business operating in the music market. This business would need to be able to store a customer's order and to update stock records when the music CDs are transferred from stock to customer. A hierarchical database would only be able to deal with either the stock or the customer record at one time – they can't 'talk to each other'. On the other hand, the relational database allows both records to communicate with each other. The catalogue code for the customer's order for The Beatles 'Abbey Road' might be '28 1F' and the relational database allows the stock level of this CD to be checked and updated as the sale is made. The customer record is also updated so we now have a field containing purchased CDs against each customer from which a pattern of their music preferences can be analysed, together with whatever other data is being stored – quantities purchased, time of year when orders are usually placed, profile characteristics, method of payment and so on.

Exhibit 3.1 demonstrates the appearance of a database and shows that there can be customer 'records' with separate 'fields' for name, gender, address (with a different field for each component of the address) and so on. The exhibit also shows how entries might appear for data entry – for keying in data collected from some source or indeed for a telemarketing operator at time of collection. Also shown is the same data in tabular form, for many customers. Each row represents a 'record' (one for each customer) and the columns are the specific 'fields'. We would also need to have other 'tables' – for 'orders', 'stock levels' and 'stock reordering'. The exhibit also indicates how links can be made between such databases and demonstrates how linked data can be retrieved for personalised communications. Thus, it becomes clear that a relational database allows for a variety of links between different tables. These include:

- **One-to-one:** where each record in one table can be linked with one record in another table. This is typical of list management applications.
- **One-to-many:** where each record in one table can be linked with many records in another table.
- **Many-to-many:** where each record in one table can be linked with many records in another table and each record in that table can be linked with many records in the first table.

The Customer table stores customer details – name, address, geodemographic profile. The Order table stores all orders by date together with delivery and invoice dates, delivery address and delivery company. The Stock Level table stores each product in stock together with quantities and the Stock Reorder table stores order number and stock number together with quantity of the order. One-to-many links will be needed between each of these tables.

As stated in the Preface, we provide more material on the accompanying website and this includes a live Access database. You can explore the records and fields in this database using Microsoft Access. It contains details of 510 individuals and their cars.

Case study 3.1 shows some screenshots from this database to whet your appetite.

EXHIBIT 3.1   Database appearance of relational data

Orders			
Customer ID	**Surname**	**Initial**	**Code**
016	Evans	M	28 1F
017	Patterson	M	14 1B
018	O'Malley	L	10 2F

Stock		
Stock ID	**Name**	**Number in stock**
28 1F	Abbey Road	400
05 6C	Joshua Tree	330
20 9F	Sticky Fingers	635

RELATIONAL DATA

Name and address
details can be retrieved
from the Customer
table for an existing
customer

Invoice

BACK BEAT REVOLUTIONS

To: **Martin Evans**
       Penny Fields
       Gracelands
       CF10 3EU

Customer no: 01661
Order no: 0009567
Invoice date: 20 March 2004
Delivery date: 24 March 2004
Salesperson   Jennifer Pegg

Product descriptions can
be accessed from the
Products table using the
Product code.

Item	Product Code	Description	Quantity	Unit Price	Value	VAT
1	28 1F	Abbey Road	1	11.06	11.06	1.94
2	42 5B	Tapestry	1	11.06	11.06	1.94

Customer	**Order**	**Order item**	**Product**
Customer no.	Order no.	Item no.	Product code
Name	Customer no.	Order no.	Description
Street	Invoice date	Product code	Price
Town	Delivery date	Quantity	
Postcode	Delivery co.		
	Delivery street		

CASE **STUDY** 3.1

Access database: marketing academics, their cars, families, interests and financial profile

Record 26 of 510 is shown in Exhibits 3.2–3.7.

EXHIBIT 3.2 Customer Contact Form

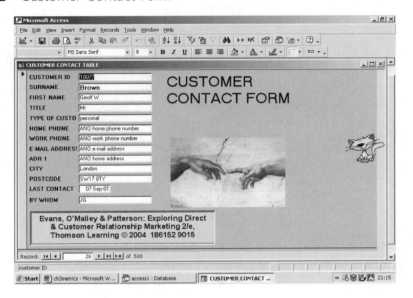

EXHIBIT 3.3 Family Data Form, giving details of children

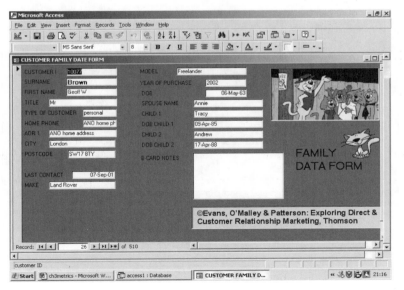

EXHIBIT 3.4   Code for interest in sport, financial profile and RFM (see later section on Recency, Frequency and Monetary Value (RFM))

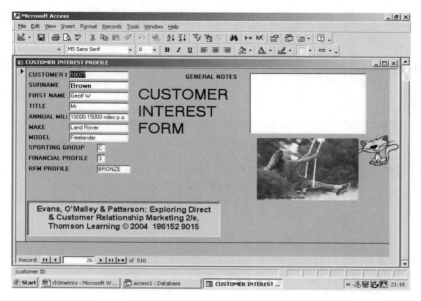

EXHIBIT 3.5   Car Form

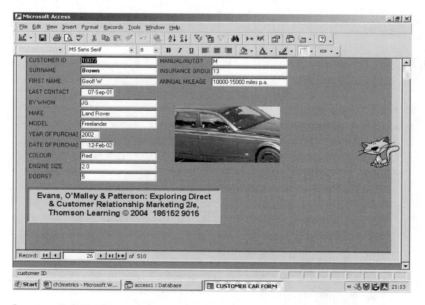

Note the linking Customer ID (10077) in each form.

EXHIBIT 3.6 Table showing customer details: name, address and other personal details

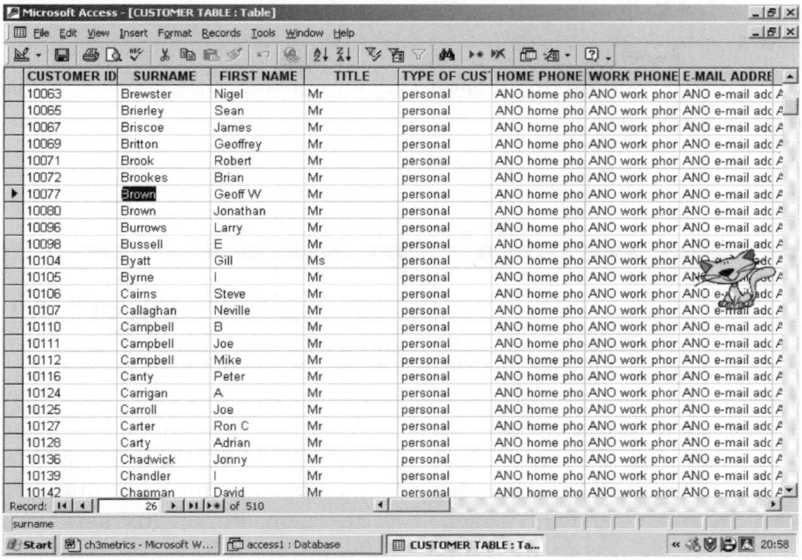

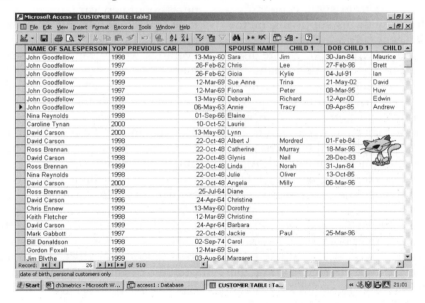

EXHIBIT 3.7 Table showing customer details: car type and salesperson concerned

You can experiment with this Web-based file and you will find that you can sort by a variety of variables and extract those names and addresses that fit specific sets of parameters in which you might be interested.

(Source: Reproduced by permission of Jennifer Pegg)

Database analysis

Consider the following case study, which demonstrates what even very basic data can reveal.

Relational potential, from very little data

A motor car dealer has read Chapters 1 and 2 of this book. As a result, he discovered that he has much more information about his customers than he previously realised. Before reading the book he was really rather reactive in his marketing – waiting for customers to book services/repairs for their vehicles and, apart from some cooperative local advertising with his supplying motor manufacturer, generally waiting for people to come into the showroom. Now he realises that he can be proactive and understand his customers and potential customers much more – and on an individual basis.

He was shown that every time a car was purchased he actually gathered significant amounts of information on the purchaser – name, address, telephone number etc. Also, when there was a credit agreement, information on the customer's financial and occupational circumstances was revealed. As a result, he began to send letters (and sometimes even telephone calls) asking about the new customer's evaluation of how well he/she was treated during the purchase process, thus potentially starting a relationship with that customer. He also used this process to gather a little bit more information about the customer – including lifestyle details which he realised could help with the targeting of relevant offers.

At regular intervals, he began to mail his customers to remind them about servicing.

After several 'services' he had information on the usual mileage of each customer, thereby making the reminders more timely. He also began to send out reminders regarding MOTs by simply checking the purchase date in the log book. At appropriate intervals he sent out mailings with news about new car launches and modifications, therefore offering up-selling opportunities for his dealership. Wine and cheese evenings were arranged for selected customers at appropriate launches.

Cross-selling was also possible because he could contact the customer with details of car alarm systems and other accessories. The customer's partner became an important target as well – the second family car might be a used vehicle and targeting for cross- and up-selling was approached in a similar way. He also became aware of the ages of the couple's children and was able to target them when they reached the age of 17.

He found that an analysis of address locations of customers, geodemographically profiled, was particularly helpful in defining his catchment area, and identifying where his customers lived. As a result, he mailed prospects in similar areas with regard to launches and other events.

Over time, the dealer found that with regular contact a relationship developed and he realised that if he was able to retain this customer and his family, over several years, the 'lifetime value' of their business would be quite significant and at the same time cheaper than new customer acquisition. This dealer also now has a 'list' which he is considering selling on to, for example, warranty or 'breakdown' companies, thus making money out the process itself!

But would you be happy about this?

Such data can also be used to 'score' customers. Most items of data are scorable. For example, we might know from previous campaigns that we have had a greater success rate when marketing to those with the 'Mr' title rather than Mrs or Ms, in which case we can give a quantitative weight to 'title'. Postcode is especially revealing because we can profile geodemographically from this and again compare with previous success/failure rates to score the geodemographic cluster and the postcode itself, at different levels. For example, do we have more success in Cardiff (CF) or Bristol (BS)?

This is an example of scoring from two of the most basic elements of data. By adding lifestyle and transactional data and scoring all those in our database on a weighted index which incorporates all of these variables, we can produce very useful league tables for targeting purposes.

Data mining

IN THEORY

Data mining is a 'process of extracting hidden or previously unknown, comprehensible and actionable information from large databases' (Antoniou 1997). From this there are two approaches that data mining can adopt. The first is verification-driven: 'extracting information to validate an hypothesis postulated by a user' (Antoniou 1997). This would be where a segmentation model, for example, has been decided upon and data analysed within this framework. For transactional data, such a model might look like a family tree, with the customer's life stage as the starting point with a cascading down, for each category, into vegetarianism, diabetic etc. so that the resulting number of segments at the bottom of the 'tree' could be quite large. The second approach refers to the digging around in databases in a relatively unstructured way with the aim of discovering links between customer behaviour and almost any variable that might potentially be useful. This second approach is discovery driven: 'identifying and extracting hidden, previously unknown information ... (to) scour the data for patterns which do not come naturally to the analysts' set of views or ideas' (Antoniou 1997). There is a parallel with market research versus environmental scanning, discussed in Chapters 5 and 14, because the former focuses on specific problems and the latter has a wider-ranging brief to identify anything in the marketing environment that might have a relevant impact upon the marketing operation.

Relational marketers have tried a variety of unusual or unexpected areas in which to mine. For example, some have examined consumers' individual biorhythms and star signs as predictors of their purchasing patterns (Mitchell and Haggett 1997) *and others have linked their transactional and profile data with meteorological databases to predict, perhaps months ahead, what demand there might be for ice cream or woolly sweaters!*

Another example of data mining is afforded by the linking with a GIS database to target down to newspaper round! This is usually around 150–200 households and by linking transactional data with lifestyle, geodemographics and panel data (see our coverage of panel data in Chapter 5) a very accurate picture of individual buying patterns emerges. The newspaper round – or milk round – can be used for door drops or direct mail as well as for local catchment area analysis. In addition to product delivery, there could be a delivery service for samples and vouchers and a delivery and collection service for questionnaires.

We now turn to a number of contemporary 'metrics' used in data mining.

RFM analysis

Our database 'data' also becomes 'information' when we identify the 'recency, frequency and monetary value' (RFM) of customer orders.

- **Recency:** Just knowing that a customer has purchased from the organisation in the past is important but not sufficient. Marketers are clearly more interested in a customer who has purchased in the last six months than in a customer who last bought from the organisation in 1984.
- **Frequency:** A one-off purchase may also make a customer less attractive (depending, of course, on the product-market in which we operate). So knowing how often they buy from the organisation is an important measure.
- **Monetary value:** The value of orders from the customer.

Small orders are usually less attractive than larger ones, so this is yet another measure of significance. Indeed, as has already been discussed, marketers are increasingly concentrating on their 'better' customers – those who have the highest monetary value (and frequency) of purchase – and are segmenting on the basis of 'volume' because in this way they are more cost effective, because they concentrate on those who bring greater returns. Vilfredo Pareto's theory of income distribution has been transferred and borrowed by relational marketers to support the proposition that 80% of sales come from just 20% of customers – in many markets the ratio can be even more polarised (95:5 is not uncommon). The Pareto principle is often quoted by relational marketers and is certainly relevant to this discussion of RFM analysis.

RFM analysis clearly, by the nature of the variables involved, means that transactional data must be tracked by the database – actual purchase history is needed. In addition to leading to the identification of volume segments and best prospects, the RFM information also contributes to the calculation of 'lifetime value' – another of the relational marketer's cornerstone measures.

Lifetime value analysis

'Lifetime' is perhaps a little of an overstatement – it doesn't mean the lifetime of the customer, but rather a designated period of time during which they are a customer of your organisation. Depending on the type of products or services on offer, lifetime might be as little as six months (as in purchases for baby products) or as long as ten years (as in the automotive market). Essentially, different sectors have worked out the probable lifetime value of the 'average' customer and calculate accordingly. Whatever period is relevant, however, the concept of what that customer is worth to the organisation in sales and profit terms over a period of time is a critical concept within relational marketing.

To take an extreme example, if a car company is only concerned with acquiring customers and does nothing to retain them, there is a fair chance that each customer who buys one of their cars this year will go on to buy another make next time – and the time after that and so on. The value of the sale might be £10,000 but subtracting acquisition costs, production and other costs could mean a net profit of just a few pounds.

With a more dedicated retention programme the company could expect that customer to buy one of their cars every third year for, perhaps, 12 years – not just at £10,000 but as they progress through their life stages they may be able to buy more expensive models. So, with lower costs of retaining a customer than acquiring him/her in the first instance, together with repeat buying and the prospect of up-selling over a period of time, the sales value could be as high as, say, £70,000 (£10k + £12k + £14k + £16k +£18).

Consider the smaller case of a home delivery curry business – Farooq's Tandoori. Assume 3 000 customers per year with overall sales amounting to £180,000. His costs of running the business were about 60% of sales so profit was £72,000.

The business, because it 'delivers', is able to record customers' names and addresses and the amount they spend. After the first couple of years of such recording Farooq was alarmed because he discovered that only 30% of his home delivery customers ever returned. Farooq decided to apply some of the material he had recently learnt by reading this book!

He analysed his database of customers. With 3 000 customers and revenue of £180,000 the first simple calculation was that the average spend per customer was £60 per year (on average this represents two orders per year, each order being for three meals averaging £10. Taking the 3 000 customers from year 1, only 30% returned and this we take as the 'retention rate'. Table 3.1 shows the initial calculations.

Table 3.2 demonstrates how Farooq extended this basic analysis into the second and third years and Table 3.3 shows how, from these calculations, he ultimately calculated the lifetime (after 3 years) value of his customers. Because only 30% of customers were retained, the decline in returning customers is shown under years 2 and 3 as 900 and 270 respectively.

With these smaller numbers of customers, but assuming the same average spend of £60, total revenue from the 'loyals' falls in year 2 and in year 3. The 'knock-on' effects for costs and profits are also shown in Table 3.3.

Because the value of profit is less in years 2 and 3 than in the current year 1, Farooq made an adjustment to the figures to take account of this – the calculation is the 'net present value'. This essentially converts tomorrow's money to today's

TABLE 3.1   Lifetime value calculation

	Year 1
Customers	3 000
Retention rate	30%
Average spend	£60
Revenue	£180,000
Costs as % of sales	60%
Costs	£108,000
Profits	£72,000

TABLE 3.2   Extended analysis

	Year 1	Year 2	Year 3
Customers	3 000	900	270
Retention rate	30%	30%	30%
Average spend	£60	£60	£60
Revenue	£180,000	£54,000	£16,200
Cost as % of sales	60%	60%	60%
Costs	£108,000	£32,400	£9,720
Profit	£72,000	£21,000	£6,480

TABLE 3.3 Lifetime value calculation

	Year 1	Year 2	Year 3
Number of customers	3 000	900	270
		(30% of 3 000)	(30% of 900)
Retention rate	30%	30%	30%
Average spend	£60	£60	£60
Revenue (Spend × No. of Customers)	£180,000	£54,000	£16,200
Costs as % of sales	60%	60%	60%
Costs (60% of revenue)	£108,000	£32,400	£9,720
Profit (Revenue − costs)	£72,000	£21,600	£6,480
Discount Rate	1.00	1.44	1.73
NPV (Profit / discount rate)	£72,000	£15,000	£3,746
Cumulative NPV	£72,000	£87,000	£90,746
Lifetime value per customer (NPV/3 000 customers)	£24.00	£29.00	£30.25

value. The starting point for this calculation is the interest rate – which Farooq knows has just moved to 10%. However, to be prudent, he bases his calculations on double this rate – all sorts of things might happen over the next three years: another home delivery service might start up, or the town bypass that has been discussed for years might eventually be built.

Having decided on a rate of interest of 20%, he now has to 'do the sums'. The formula for calculating the rate at which to 'discount' future money to today's level is:

$$D = (1+i)^n$$

Where i = the selected rate of interest (in this case 20%) and n = the number of years beyond the current first year that we are considering.

So, for Farooq:

For year 2, $D = (1+ .20)^2 = 1.44$
For year 3, $D = (1+ .20)^3 = 1.73$

What this means is that in order to discount future profit (in years 2 and 3) to today's value, we need to divide the actual profit figure by 1.44 in year 2 and 1.73 in year 3. The first year's profit is not discounted because today's money is at today's value! Table 3.3 shows the effect of the discount rate on profit. In years 2 and 3, the rates for discounting those years' profit to today's value produce 'net present values' of £15,000 and £3,746 respectively. Cumulatively, this means that profit figures amount to £87,000 by the end of year 2 and to £90,746 by the end of year 3.

Dividing these figures by the number of customers Farooq started with (3 000) produces the estimate of lifetime value per customer per year. As can be seen, the lifetime (over 3 years only, in this case) value of the loyal customer is £30.25.

The reason why the original 3 000 customers are used to divide into the cumulative NPV is because Farooq is concerned with the lifetime of each new customer – based on certain assumptions regarding retention rates and cost structures. The resulting lifetime value can be used in predictions about alternative marketing strategies and is therefore an immensely valuable planning calculation. To demonstrate some of this, assume Farooq decides to be a little more proactive in retaining customers – he has seen the increased value to be gained from the return of regular customers and now wants to implement a retention strategy.

Farooq develops a reward card scheme whereby his returning customers get a 10% discount and either a free onion bhajee or banana fritter for each main meal ordered. He sends all of his customers a questionnaire asking for their views on his home delivery service and the food. On the questionnaire he also asks for some additional personal details. He asks for their date of birth and names and dates of birth of others in the household. He now sends birthday cards to those on his database together with a birthday menu of 'special occasion' meals. Also enclosed with these mailings is an offer of a further discount, if they recommend Farooq's service to others who go on to purchase a meal. Every new customer, of course, is added to his database, because the home delivery system means name and address are essential prerequisites for delivery. The other side to the offer is half-price meals for the first order after a referral makes a purchase. Farooq thinks that this 'member get member' scheme will lead to about 5% of his existing customers 'recruiting' new customers – he bases this on the experience of some friends in the relational marketing industry. In addition to birthday cards, he also sends Christmas cards with a special 'winter curry' menu with the aim of increasing ordering at Christmas and New Year – and a calendar for the next year. He calculates that the additional costs are as shown in Table 3.4.

Farooq thinks that the entire scheme will have a positive effect on retention rates such that rather than the mere 30% of customers returning, he will now see 50% retained. The above programme, he estimates, will increase the number of orders per year from each customer – after all, he is offering discounts and other incentives for them to buy more frequently. The home delivery service is made more salient because of the regular mailings, tailoring to birthdays and promotional offers. Overall, Farooq estimates that the value of each customer's orders over the course of a year will now rise from £60 to £120 (each *order* will still be for an average of 3 meals @ £10, but now four times per year rather then just twice) – but this does not take account of the discounts and free items from which they will benefit. In addition, the MGM scheme will cost a further 50% of one order for the 5% of customers who make a referral.

Table 3.5 summarises the effects of the above retention programme on Farooq's sales, costs, profits and lifetime values. The referral rate from the MGM scheme has no effect in year 1 and then is based on an extra 5% of customers of those retained (after the effect of the 50% retention rate has impacted).

TABLE 3.4 Additional costs of marketing activities

Marketing activities	Cost
Discounts (10% of order value per customer per year) £120 × 10%	£12.00
Free Bombay Duck or Chapatti (50p per meal per year: 3 meals per order & 4 orders per year = 12 meals)	£6.00
Birthday cards (average 3 per household @ 50p)	£1.50
Christmas cards (1 per household @ 50p)	£0.50
Special menus (average 4 per household @ 20p with one for each of 3 birthdays plus Christmas)	£0.80
Mailing costs (4 @26p per year)	£1.04
Total (per household per year)	£21.84

TABLE 3.5 Lifetime value calculation

	Year 1	Year 2	Year 3
Referral rate	5%	5%	5%
Referred customers from MGM scheme	0	150 (5% of 3 000)	83 (5% of 1 650)
Retention rate	50%	50%	50%
Customers including retention	3 000	1 500 (50% of 3 000)	825 (50% of 1 650)
Total customers including referrals	3 000	1650 (1500 + 150)	908 (825 + 83)
Average spend	£120	£120	£120
Revenue	£360,000	£198,000	£108,960
Costs as % of sales	60%	60%	60%
Costs	£216,000	£118,800	£65,376
Additional costs (£21.84 per customer)	£65,520	£36,036	£19,831
Total costs	£281,520	£154,836	£85,207
Profit	£78,480	£43,164	£23,753
Discount rate	1.00	1.44	1.73
NPV	£90,480	£29,975	£13,730
Cumulative NPV	£90,480	£120,455	£134,185
Lifetime value per customer: (based on cohort of 3 000 customers: NPV/3 000)	£30.16	£40.15	£44.73

In addition, different lifetime values can be calculated for each segment we might be targeting differently (e.g. by postcode, age and so on). The point here will be to identify the effects of our different marketing strategies for each segment, in order to modify our approach. In this way, such calculations are not merely 'nice to know' but make a real contribution to the iterative nature of relational marketing planning and evaluation.

It must be pointed out, however, that several estimates – and even guesses – contributed to the above calculations, for example in terms of referral rates and increased spend. These could be inaccurate and the whole scheme could produce negative results. As the scheme moves along, revised figures can be built into the calculations, iteratively, to improve accuracy, but the risks should not be swept under the carpet. Relational marketing is full of 'try it and see' programmes – not all succeed by any means, but if you never try you never succeed! Lifetime (or 'long time') values can be calculated for each segment targeted; our calculations have aggregated any possible segments into one, to make it easier to follow the logic. Indeed, lifetime values can even be calculated for each individual customer and perhaps this should be the ultimate aim.

Based on their consulting experience, Dawkins and Reichheld (1990) claimed that a 5% increase in customer retention led directly to an increase in the net present value (NPV) of customers. This increase amounted to between 25% and 85% depending on the industry concerned. 'In a relationship, a seller seeks to minimise their costs and maximise their revenues. Customer retention affects both elements of the profitability equation, where Profit = Revenue − Expenses or Costs' (Ahmed and Buttle 2001).

A problem, however, with the LTV concept in practice is that marketers very often analyse their databases as they are *now*. Many segments, however, are extremely dynamic. Take an extreme case of the 'best' customers at a DIY store. There may only be about 5% of these who are also 'best' customers in the fourth quarter of a year compared with the first quarter. This can easily be explained by DIY projects at home that they may be involved with at the beginning of the year, but as soon as they are completed, their store patronage dies, yet they might be targeted as high LTV customers with a relationship marketing programme.

LTV and RFM analysis can lead to those customers who are not considered to be strong contributors to the company being *deselected*. They would not be sent relevant offers or, in the case of financial services, for example, they would be offered accounts that require higher initial deposits than they can afford. Indeed, the Halifax bank was discovered, via a flip chart left in a branch after a company training session, to refuse to allow certain groups of people to be customers at all (Mackintosh 2002). We explore societal implications of 'exclusion' in Chapter 13.

Allowable cost

For this calculation a 'mini' profit and loss account is created for the 'average' sale. Promotional costs are excluded (because we are attempting to estimate these) but other costs and the desired profit are included. Table 3.6 shows a simple example in which the selling price of a directly distributed computer is £1,000, its cost of production is £600, order handling is £40, 'p&p' is £20 and the desired profit is £250. Costs total £660 so the 'contribution' is £340. If the selling price is £1,000 and the sum of costs and profit for the average sale is £910 (£660 costs + £250 profit) then the allowable cost is £90 (£1,000−£910).

As an average figure this means that we can afford to spend £90 on each sale and that the resulting profit will be £250. This figure can now be used to calculate the response rate that would be needed from a mailed promotion. Table 3.7 shows that if the mailing costs are £26,000 and we allow £90 per order, then we need to get 289 sales (26 000÷90). If the mail shot is to 28 000 people a response rate of 1.03% will be required.

There is an additional use of these two calculations. From Table 3.6 it was shown that the 'contribution' was £340 and if we divide this into the cost of the promotion (£26,000) we can see that the break-even point is at 76 orders. That is, once there have been 76 orders, the costs of the mailing will be covered.

This analysis can be done for different selling prices and different promotional campaigns and shows again how relational marketing can be measurable and accountable. We have not delved into the intricacies of different costing structures because our intention is to show the allowable cost principle and how it can be used.

TABLE 3.6 Allowable costs

Selling price of computer			£1,000
Costs	Cost of product	£600	
	Order handling	£40	
	Postage & packing	£20	
Total cost		£660	(£660)
Contribution: (selling price−cost)			£340
Desired profit			(£250)
Allowable cost per order (selling price−costs−desired profit)			£90

TABLE 3.7 Response rates

Mailing cost	£26,000
Allowable cost per order	£90
Sales required (25,000/90)	289
Size of mailing	28 000
Response rate (required sales/size of mailing expressed as percentage)	1.03%
	(289÷28 000)×100

Cost per thousand

If we have been given quotations from different mailing companies – A costs £26,000 for a mailing of 28 000 and B costs £30,000 for a mailing of 32 500 – there is a standard measure to compare cost effectiveness though this does not take into account any difference in likely response rate from the two mailings (Table 3.8).

The message here is not to go for the cheaper mailing or, conversely, for the one that reaches more people, but rather to combine these factors in the 'cost per thousand' calculation.

Cost per order

Here, the cost per order is found by dividing total cost by total orders:

Cost Per Order	Total Cost ÷ Total Orders

Response per thousand

This is found by dividing total response by the total mailed:

Response per thousand	(Total Response ÷ Total Mailed) × 1 000

Note that 'cost per thousand' divided by 'orders per thousand' will also give 'cost per order'.

TVRs

When it comes to television audience research it is commonplace to calculate 'television ratings' (TVRs). This is a measure of how far a communications channel 'reaches' into the target market. For example, specific TV commercial time slots might 'reach' 100% of the target audience. It might also be thought that to make an 'impact', three exposures would be needed. This is known as 'opportunities to see' (OTS). In this case, the TVR would be $100 \times 3 = 300$ TVRs. But is it realistic to expect 100% of target market would be reached? Would they all be watching these specific commercials? Probably not, so different calculations can be made based on experience or further research.

TABLE 3.8 Cost per thousand

Cost per thousand	(Cost ÷ Size of mailing) × 1 000
Mailing A:	(£26,000 ÷ 28 000) × 1 000 = £928.57 per thousand mailed.
Mailing B:	(£30,000 ÷ 32 500) × 1 000 = £923.08 per thousand mailed.

Perhaps 50% of the target audience might more realistically be reached and it might be thought that there should be more exposures of the commercial to make an impact (often six have been found appropriate).

So now the TVR calculation would be $50 \times 6 = 300$ TVRs.

Clearly this adds cost because each exposure is costing air time (often £50,000 per 30-second commercial). So this has to be balanced against the realistic 'reach' of time slots and the estimated number of needed OTS.

Case study 3.3 provides a useful summary of many of the points made so far in this chapter.

CASE **STUDY** 3.3

Data clinic: customer retention modelling

Many companies use customer retention modelling along with a loyalty programme to retain or re-activate customers. If you can identify those customers most at risk of lapsing and then offer them a suitable incentive to stay with your company, you can significantly increase profits.

1. Prepare your data

Before undertaking any analysis or building a statistical model you will need to audit your data. The most powerful data on your customer database will usually be transactional information. With transactional data you can segment and analyse your customers according to RFM – Recency, Frequency and Monetary value of purchase, quickly providing valuable customer insight.

Always isolate missing, under-populated or incorrectly coded data fields. You may also want to clean or validate your customer name and address information. A powerful model will not work if your customers are goneaways, complainers or even deceased.

Many of the factors that determine customer retention are triggered by events such as moving house, getting married, having children or changing career. This data is often best gathered via third-party data selections such as Census information,

lifestyle data and geodemographics. External data sources are also useful when trying to analyse and predict the behaviour of recently acquired customers. If, say, a customer has been with your company for less than six months you may lack enough information to make an informed decision about their future purchasing patterns.

Whatever data you use in your model, ensure that you will continue to have access to that data in the future. A model cannot work if it is based on data that you no longer capture.

2. Building the model

First consider who you want to analyse and pick the right customers:

Will you build a retention model for each of your products, services or brands, or one that works across your entire portfolio?

The time frame for analysis is likely to vary according to product or market sector, but typically analysts look at the lapse rate of customers recruited at the beginning of a 12-month period. Will you be trying to predict propensity to lapse (often used by companies offering a subscription-based service such as book clubs or satellite/ digital television providers), or propensity to renew (often used by companies where the customer is invited to renew on an annual basis, e.g. insurance or loans).

It is important to identify at the outset which approach you will take and that this matches the marketing programme you wish to implement. The model here will target potential lapsers.

Customer retention models are usually built on representative samples of the total customer base, as statistical software is more capable of handling these smaller files.

Before building the model, a random validation sample is held back from the modelling file (usually between 30% and 50% of the file). The model is built on the remaining development sample and its robustness subsequently checked by applying it to the validation sample.

The two main propensity-modelling methods used in CRM and database marketing are regression and decision tree techniques (see jargon buster below).

Remember, the outcome is not guaranteed so always test before roll-out.

3. Interpreting the results

Generally you should look to gain the maximum predictive power from the least number of variables. Too many variables in a model can lead to 'noise' and 'over-fitting'. A simple non-statistical measure of your model's performance is the classification table. The model is applied to the validation sample to assess how many lapsers and non-lapsers were correctly predicted.

In the example above, 1 000 of the customers within the validation sample who were predicted to lapse actually had, and 1 250 who were predicted to be loyal had actually remained so. This means that out of 2 750 records in the validation sample, 2 250, or 82%, were correctly classified. Accuracy usually varies between 60% to 90%. Any model with accuracy over 70% is considered valid. A gains chart can offer savings by assessing how lapsers fall within the whole

database; by telling you if your model can identify 70 of all potential lapsers within only 30 of the total database, you can achieve significant potential mailing cost savings. Always employ intuition as a final sanity check – look at the variables that appear in your model and the composition of your predicted lapser segments. Do they resemble your image of a customer who might be about to stop buying your products or defect to one of your competitors?

4. Implementing the model

The customer retention model is best applied in conjunction with some measure of value, be it revenue, profit or customer lifetime value. The resulting risk/value matrix can be used to identify customers you need to incentivise.

You can assess how successful your retention incentive programme has been by holding back a sample from the high score group who do not receive the incentive: do you lose more of these people over the period of the campaign than those who received the incentive? You can also test the model itself by comparing the lapse or churn rate of those in the top 10% of the model compared to that of a control group. Keep monitoring the performance of your model. The profile of your customer base as a whole, and your lapsers in particular, will change over time. Seasonality or competitor activity may also affect the model's performance, so be prepared to learn from new data and experience. It is particularly valuable to gather information on why your customers are lapsing or defecting. By adding this data to your model you can develop a really powerful retention programme.

(Source: Lee Witherall, director of analysis and consulting at Claritas, *Direct Response*, 31 August 2002, reproduced from *Direct Response* magazine with the permission of the copyright owner Haymarket Business Publications Limited)

Statistical metrics

When many variables on the database are to be examined for possible meaning, we are concerned with multivariate analysis. This in turn can be categorised into structural and dependence analysis.

In structural analysis the interrelations between variables are explored in order to create a structure that is simpler than the original variables. Typical examples of structural analyses include factor analysis, cluster analysis, multidimensional scaling, and correspondence analysis. With factor analysis, a battery of one hundred lifestyle statements may be reduced to six or seven underlying factors. This is much easier and more relevant to report than the scores on all one hundred statements. Structural analysis is used by marketers for simplification of complex structures as in lifestyle research, attitude and image analysis in categorisation and positioning.

In dependence analysis the relationship between a dependent or criterion variable and a set of independent or predictor variables is studied (e.g. the variables that predict or explain the market share of a brand). Typical examples of dependence analyses include multiple regression, multiple discriminant analysis, analysis of variance and conjoint analysis.

Another important distinction is between the types of data that can be analysed: metric and non-metric data. Metric data are interval-level data (for example, where the 'rating' reflects a standard distance between categories, such as temperature or distance) and ratio (for example, where 'rating' is based on standard distances between categories but where there is also a true zero, such as with income). Metric data are often based on correlations and variances. Most multivariate analyses are possible if the data input consists of metric data. Non-metric data are ordinal (for example, a rating scale) and nominal-level (for example, the mere coding of variables such as gender or postcode) data, often based on similarity coefficients and preference ratings. Only non-metric techniques are allowed with non-metric data input. In Table 3.9, some of the types of multivariate analyses are classified according to these two distinctions.

We summarise these techniques here and provide some case examples of their application.

Further coverage is outside the scope of this book but there are plenty of good reference texts on statistical analysis, some of which are listed at the end of the chapter.

TABLE 3.9 Classification of types of multivariate analysis

	Structural analysis	Dependence analysis
Metric data	Factor analysis	Regression analysis
Non-metric data	Cluster analysis	CHAID
	Correspondence analysis	

Factor analysis

Factor analysis is a multivariate technique to structure a large array of variables into a smaller set of factors. These factors are underlying constructs that summarise the set of variables. Variables are often highly intercorrelated. These sets of intercorrelated variables are then summarised by one factor. Attitude questionnaires are often factor analysed to reduce the large set of questions to a meaningful small set of factors. This is an exploratory application of factor analysis, called principal components analysis.

Factor analysis is useful to direct marketers because it can 'reduce' large amounts of data by identifying more meaningful relationships. Factor analysis may also be applied to test for the number and type of underlying factors in a dataset. The researcher may have an idea about how many factors and what type of factors could be expected. This is called confirmatory factor analysis.

CASE **STUDY** 3.4

Attitudes to direct mail

In a study investigating consumer attitudes toward direct mail, a large dataset was analysed through factor analysis. Over 700 questionnaires, each containing in excess of 100 variables, were factor analysed and the results are summarised here. Varimax rotation was favoured since it allowed the factors to remain uncorrelated with each other, thus providing clear factors.

Two factors emerged from this analysis, firstly, a generally positive group, and secondly, a more negative group. Table 3.10 summarises the findings with respect to factor analysing the Likert-scale variables under the question 'Do you feel that buying products and services as a result of direct mail is ...?'. Of the two groups to emerge, one could be termed 'sceptical' and the

TABLE 3.10   Factor analysis – 1

'Do you feel that buying products and services as a result of direct mail is . . .'

Variable	Factor 1 'Scepticals'	Factor 2 'Comfortables'
Convenient	.3729	.7257
Foolish	.7834	.2808
Appealing	.3049	.7632
Difficult	.7260	−.0067
Quick	−.06981	.8065
Risky	.7645	.2314
	46% variance	18% variance

other would appear to be more 'comfortable with DM'.

Table 3.11 reflects the factor analysis concerning the Likert-scale variables under the general question 'Thinking about the personalised direct mail you receive, do you think it is...'. In this instance, one group appears to view direct mail as being 'useful entertainment' and the other views it as generally being a 'nuisance'.

Table 3.12 summarises the findings with respect to factor analysing the Likert-scale variables under the question 'How important to you personally is it for direct mail to ...'. Of the two groups to emerge here, one appears to want direct mail to be 'accurately targeted' and the other appears to want direct mail to be more 'privacy conscious'.

A fourth factor analysis explored the variables concerned with the perceived

TABLE 3.11 Factor analysis – 2

'Thinking about the personalised direct mail you receive, do you think it is ...'

Variable	Factor 1 'Useful entertainment'	Factor 2 'Nuisance'
Interesting	.8876	.1608
Informative	.8719	.1778
Intrusive	.2158	.7729
Entertaining	.7897	.0307
Damages the environment	−.0045	.8467
Relevant to you	.7960	.0642
	50% variance	20% variance

TABLE 3.12 Factor analysis – 3

'How important to you personally is it for direct mail to ...'

Variable	Factor 1 'Accurately targeted'	Factor 2 'Privacy conscious'
Be interesting	.8296	.0193
Be informative	.8529	−.0515
Have my personal details in order to understand my needs	.7284	.1634
Be entertaining	.7443	.0026
Not damage the environment	−.2155	.6443
Be relevant to you	.7643	−.2760
Not share my details with other organisations	.1261	.8155
Respect my privacy	.0263	.8477
Be accurate in terms of my personal details	.7332	−.2003
	41% variance	21% variance

importance of a variety of factors involved with purchasing products and services: 'When buying products and services, how important to you personally are the following . . .' (Table 3.13).

Here, three groupings emerge. The first clusters around the issues of trying new things; saving time; knowing what is available and getting products which are not in the high street shops. This 'busy innovator' contrasts with the next group which appears to be more concerned with following advice. The third group, the 'cautious control freaks', value being in control and avoiding risks. This analysis reinforces the importance – to different market segments – of convenience, risk, control and privacy issues.

TABLE **3.13**   Factor analysis – 4

'When buying products and services, how important to you personally are the following . . .'

Variable	Factor 1 'Busy innovator'	Factor 2 'Followers'	Factor 3 'Cautious control freaks'
Saving time	.6916	− .0221	.1385
Avoid risky decisions	.1337	.0116	.7890
Getting bargains	.5149	.3257	.3298
Getting products not in the shops	.7951	.1157	.0492
Being aware of what companies have	.7003	.1136	.2661
Being personally In control of the buying process	.1260	.0733	.7788
Trying new things	.7457	.2704	.0802
Following advice from friends	.1574	.9045	.0027
Following advice from family	.0896	.9019	.0837
Following advice from workmates	.1574	.7753	.055
	50% variance	20% variance	

Cluster analysis

Cluster analysis provides a set of procedures that seek to separate the data into groups. The goal in such applications is to arrive at clusters of objects, cases or persons that display small within-cluster variation relative to the between-cluster variation. The goal in using cluster analysis is to identify a smaller number of groups such that objects belonging to a given group are, in some sense, more similar to each other than to objects belonging to other groups. Thus, cluster analysis attempts to reduce the information on the whole set of n objects to information about, say, g subgroups where $g < n$.

One of the major problems in marketing consists of the orderly classification of the myriad of data that confront the researcher. Clustering techniques look for classification of attributes or subjects on the basis of their estimated resemblance. Cluster analysis is an exploratory method that seeks patterns within data by operating a matrix of independent variables. Usually, objects to be clustered are scored on several variables and are grouped on the basis of the similarity of their scores. The primary value of cluster analysis lies in the pre-classification of data, as suggested by 'natural' groupings of the data itself. The major disadvantage of these techniques is that the implicit assumptions of the researcher can seriously affect cluster results. Cluster analysis can be applied in direct marketing for clustering buyers, products and markets, as well as key competitors. It has been found to be a particularly useful aid to market segmentation (such as in analysing and reducing data for geodemographic or lifestyle clusters) or experimentation and product positioning. Several questions need to be answered with respect to a given cluster solution, including:

- How do the clusters differ?
- What is the optimal (i.e. correct) number of clusters?
- How good is the fit of the solution for a pre-specified level of clusters?

The first question concerns the distinctiveness of cluster profiles. The second question concerns the trade-off between parsimony, in the sense of fewer clusters, and some measure of increase in within-cluster homogeneity resulting from having more clusters in the solution. The third question concerns cluster recovery, which can be viewed in terms of the fit between the input data and the resulting solution – this should be high.

An alternative to cluster analysis has been proposed by Curry *et al.* (2003). The Kohonen Self Organising Map (SOM) can be used to categorise respondents into segments. It differs from cluster analysis in that it uses a two-dimensional grid within the data space and therefore the clusters represented by adjacent points on the grid are spatially linked to each other.

Correspondence analysis

Correspondence analysis is a robust, yet relatively simple method of enabling multivariate data to 'speak for itself' in the form of maps. These maps provide user-friendly, global snapshots of the patterns of, for example, consumers' perceptions in terms of the significant factors within a particular area, and the relationships between those factors. Participants are allowed to contribute at whatever level they feel comfortable and can avoid areas that they don't feel qualified to comment upon. As they are unaware of the fact that they are creating a map, they don't feel pressurised into giving the 'right' answers. Correspondence analysis is a particularly useful means of revealing patterns of association without the need for *a priori* speculations.

Correspondence analysis is a visual or graphical technique for representing multidimensional tables. It is in fact a picture of a table of figures. It can often be impossible to identify any relationships in a table and very difficult to account for what is happening. Correspondence analysis unravels the table and presents data in an easy-to-understand chart. This technique is particularly useful to identify market segments, track brand image, position a product against its competition and determine who non-respondents in a survey most closely resemble. Correspondence analysis provides a joint space (i.e. a configuration of both objects/stimuli and attributes of these stimuli), whereas multidimensional scaling of similarity data provides a single space with only objects/stimuli (Case Study 3.5).

CASE STUDY 3.5

Correspondence analysis

The authors conducted a research pro-gramme into consumer attitudes toward direct marketing, employing group discus-sions, and respondents were asked to complete a questionnaire detailing their perceptions of various forms of direct

EXHIBIT 3.8 Correspondence map

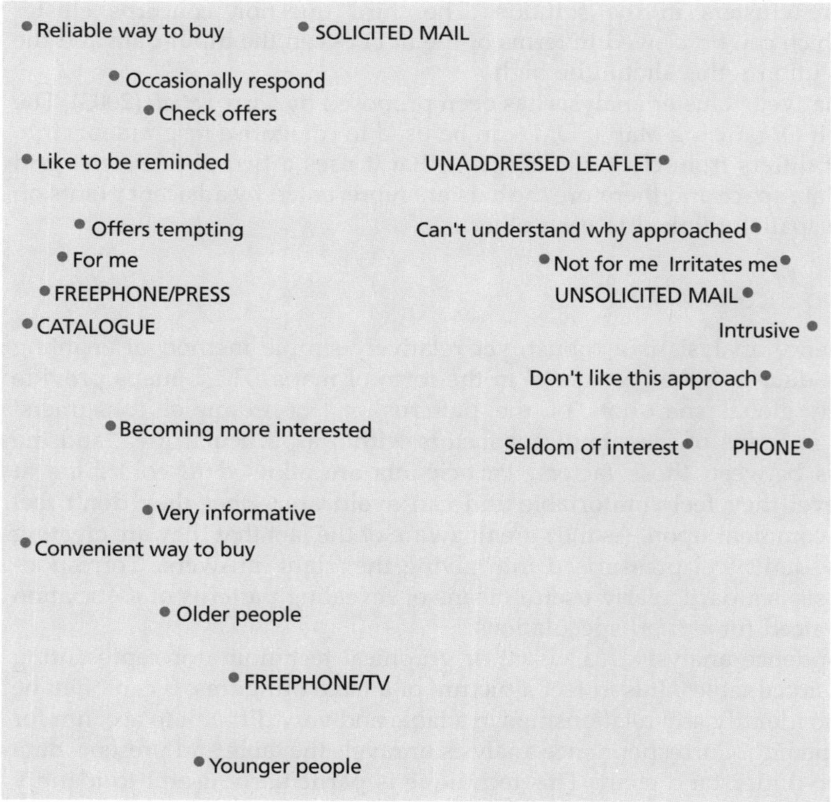

marketing prior to and after the group discussions. Using correspondence analysis, a series of maps were produced for the total sample and for various segments reflecting class, gender and age. The 'before' maps provide pictures of where 'they were coming from', while the 'after' maps showed how perceptions had changed, if at all, following exposure to the group discussions. Analysis of the maps revealed a surprisingly high degree of unanimity across the sample and the before and after comparison revealed that perceptions were resistant to change (Exhibit 3.8).

The analysis explained 92% of the data in the first two factors, making it unnecessary to represent the data any further. The horizontal axis (which explains 88% of the data) is very important in determining perceptions, and the map is graphically divided between favourable (left) and unfavourable (right) sides. In addition, the further from the centre of the map a factor

is, the more distinctive or discriminated it is. Table 3.14 shows the percentage influence of each form of direct marketing in shaping the whole map. Each of the direct marketing methods is clearly relatively distinctive (i.e. none of the methods is viewed as being typical of all direct marketing communications methods).

Catalogues (22%) and freephone/press (16%) clearly organised favourable perceptions on the left, while phones (34%), unsolicited mail (12%) and unaddressed leaflets (8%) had little influence. Table 3.15 displays the percentage influence of each attribute in shaping the whole map.

The top four influential attributes: Intrusive (12%), Don't like this approach (11%), Irritates me (10%) and Seldom of interest (10%) are all negative and are closely associated with Phone, Unsolicited mail and Unaddressed leaflets (Patterson *et al.* 1997). Attributes with positive associations clearly had less influence in organising the map.

TABLE 3.14 Percentage influence of forms of direct marketing

Phones	34%	Unaddressed leaflets	08%
Catalogues	22%	Freephone TV	05%
Freephone press	16%	Solicited mail	03%
Unsolicited mail	12%		

TABLE 3.15 Percentage influence of attributes

Intrusive	12%	Not for me	06%
Don't like this approach	11%	Occasionally respond	05%
Irritates me	10%	Check offers	03%
Seldom of interest	10%	Very informative	02%
Offers appealing	08%	For older people	02%
Convenient way to buy	08%	For younger people	02%
Reliable way to buy	06%	Becoming more interested	02%
Can't understand why approached	06%	Like to be reminded	01%
For me	06%		

Multiple regression analysis

Multiple regression is the best-known and most frequently used type of dependence analysis. Metric data are needed, both for the dependent and the independent variables. For the independent variables, dummies may be used: variables with only two values (e.g. the presence or absence of an attribute). With a set of independent or predictor variables a proportion of the variance in the dependent variable may be explained. The dependent variable may include sales, response rates and attitude. Independent variables may include previous use of a direct mail service, profile characteristics such as age, gender, income, geodemographic and lifestyle group, distance from the nearest 'physical' supplier of the product concerned, number of households in a catchment area, and other factors that may explain or predict the dependent variable.

Regression analysis may be used in an explanatory and predictive sense. Regression may be used to explain variations in a dependent variable (e.g. to explain which of a number of variables to 'attitude towards direct mail' contributes most significantly (Case Study 3.6)).

CASE **STUDY** 3.6

Regression analysis

Table 3.16 shows a summary of the results for the authors' survey mentioned earlier in connection with attitude research (Patterson *et al.* 1997). It can be seen that the more significant contributors (where the significance level is 0.05 or less) to attitude towards direct mail are (positive contributors): convenience; ease; product assortment (choice); relevance; previous exposure. The more negative contributors include risk, with inaccurate details and intrusion approaching significance. Both convenience and product assortment were discussed in the literature as being the most important

perceived advantages of direct mail. Perceived risk is also significant as a contributor, indicating that purchase through direct mail remains a risk for some consumers. Where p is < 0.05 and at a similar level for several factors, the higher the t value, the greater the 'contribution' towards the dependent variable. Overall model fit is assessed by the R^2 and F statistics; we observe that (a) the independent variables explain 50.8% of the variation in identification and (b) the postulated model is significant ($F = 46.04$, $p < 0.000$).

TABLE 3.16   Regression analysis

Dependent variable: How do you feel about buying products and services as a result of direct mail – is it: 'appealing – unappealing'? (five-point scale)

Independent variables	Question no.	Question	Regression coeff.	T value	Sig.
Convenience	Q5.1	Is buying as a result of direct mail: 'convenient – inconvenient'	0.30522	9.61	0.000
	Q5.4	'difficult – easy'	0.08669	2.80	0.005
	Q5.5	'quick – time consuming'	0.09780	3.13	0.002
Product assortment	Q35.4	How important is it for you to get products that aren't in the high street: 'very – not'	0.10358	3.46	0.001
Perceived risk	Q5.6	How do you feel about buying products and services as a result of direct mail – is it: 'risky – safe'	−0.11449	−3.31	0.001
Experience	Q7.1	For the direct mail you receive, is it: 'interesting – not interesting'	0.06513	1.37	0.171
	Q7.2	'informative – not informative'	0.05897	1.37	0.171
	Q7.4	'entertaining – not entertaining'	0.03187	0.88	0.381
	Q7.6	relevant – irrelevant	0.11518	2.91	0.004
Exposure	Q3	Do you buy as a result of organisations contacting you through the mail: 'often – never'	0.16055	2.97	0.003
Physical privacy	Q1	Do you consider the amount of direct mail you receive to be: 'too little – too much'	−0.05850	−1.40	0.161
	Q7.3	Is the direct mail you receive 'intrusive – not intrusive'	−0.04966	−1.67	0.096
Information privacy	Q22.6	Personal details are being kept by organisations for reasons unknown to me	−0.03157	−1.05	0.293
	Q22.4	I really don't mind about marketers having my personal details	0.04857	1.60	0.110
	Q22.5	There is a need for strong laws to control the sharing of personal information	−0.00570	−0.14	0.888
	Q22.13	Marketers should inform me before selling on my details	0.02837	0.66	0.509
	Q22.14	There are sufficient safeguards to my personal details	0.01831	0.50	0.620
	Q23.4	Direct marketing shouldn't share my details with other organisations	−0.06144	−1.82	0.070
Accuracy	Q22.7	For the direct mail I receive, the marketers have generally got my details correct	−0.06144	−1.82	0.070
Environmental concerns	Q7.5	For the direct mail you receive, does it 'damage the environment – does not damage the environment'	−0.02638	−0.92	0.359

R-Sq = 50.8%

AID and CHAID

Most types of cluster analysis start with single cases and form clusters by adding similar cases to an existing cluster. These types of cluster analysis are of a 'growth form'. Automatic interaction detection (AID) is a type of cluster analysis in which large samples are broken down into homogeneous subsets. AID and Chi AID (CHAID) are cluster techniques with a dependent variable. Based on scores on the dependent variable, clusters are formed that differ maximally between clusters on the dependent variable. The program develops clusters in which the objects or cases differ minimally. At the same time, the differences between the clusters should be large. Large samples are needed to apply AID or CHAID. The clustering stops if the clusters become too small or if the differences between the clusters become too small. The AID program can only split a group into two subgroups. With CHAID other splits are also possible, based on a Chi-square criterion.

An example of a dependent variable is the response rate to a direct mailing in a large sample. In the total sample this response rate may be 6.5%. With the AID program subgroups are distinguished with significantly lower or higher response rates. AID and CHAID are useful techniques for market segmentation and are becoming very popular amongst direct marketers.

EXHIBIT 3.9 CHAID tree

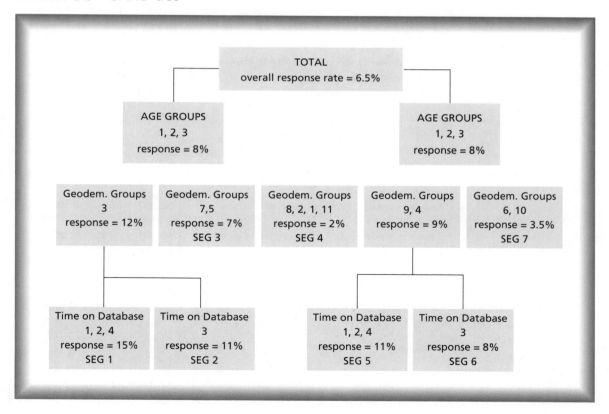

If, for example, a direct mail operation is building a predictive model on the basis of length of time customers have been on the database, geodemographic category and age, the direct mail company analyses response rates to a large test mailing (say, 20 000). CHAID will produce a tree-like analysis which identifies different segments based on the variables themselves but also on the effects of the variables interacting with each other (regression doesn't automatically do this). Where there is no significant difference between some of the variables, such as age categories, CHAID will combine these into a larger 'segment' (Exhibit 3.9).

For example, there may be six age groups (1 to 6) but CHAID might detect no significant difference between some of them and is able to group them into just two – say, under and over 50 (1,2,3 and 4,5,6). If there were 11 geodemographic groups involved in the overall response, CHAID might combine them as shown in the 'tree', thus reducing data to more meaningful groups on the basis of statistical significance. Length of time on the database might be classified according to four periods (less than 6 months, 6 months to a year, 1–2 years and more than 2 years) and again CHAID could reduce these to more significant groupings. The program will calculate response rates for each category/segment (shown in the exhibit) and numbers of responders (not shown). The resulting reduction of an enormous amount of data to just seven significant segments, based on different combinations of factors, is clearly of tremendous value to the direct marketer. Without this, there would have, potentially, been 264 ($6 \times 11 \times 4$) segments but without much significant value. CHAID is also able to do this on data for which regression might have produced an overall low level of explanation (low R^2) of the dependent variable (response) by the independent variables (age, geodemographics and length on the database).

The following case study incorporates an example of CHAID analysis and is a good example of the application of some of the other data mining approaches discussed in this chapter. The case demonstrates the use of a specific data mining tool. A number of these are available for analysing databases and one such product is VIPER, which is a software package from SmartFocus in Bristol; Alterian, also in Bristol, offer their 'Alterian Studio' suite. These tools allow very fast linking and analysis of different databases and employ some of the techniques that are incorporated into computer games to create such speed of analysis.

CASE STUDY 3.7

Cross-selling using data mining

A financial services company markets several financial service products and wants to identify new segments within its existing customer base for a cross-selling strategy. Through the application of data mining/CRM software the company can easily identify those customers who have already purchased various of the company's products. Although CRM involves more than a software package, in practice, many organisations either selling or buying a CRM 'solution' tend not to venture much beyond the more narrow IT approach. The chapters on relationship marketing and CRM explore this issue further, but for the sake of our segmentation illustration, the software deployed is described as a CRM solution. As Exhibit 3.10 shows, the software produces a Venn diagram showing the number of customers who have purchased account type A, type B and type C; 83 048 people have account A only and their names and addresses are quickly displayed (these are obviously 'scrambled' for this exercise). This is a potential segment for a cross-selling campaign concerning another of the company's products, say account type B.

The company could target these customers immediately, with a promotional offer for account B. But this would undervalue customer and transactional data as an asset. In addition, the company would also want the highest return on marketing investment. As we have already mentioned, it is increasingly important to satisfy that strategic criterion for segmentation which is concerned with financial returns.

If the company mailed all 83 048 at say, £1 per piece, the spend would be £83,048 uniformly across the target, missing the opportunity to 'gravitate' spend towards more profitable groups. So instead the company could use the data mining/CRM software to interrogate existing customers who have both A and B accounts. Data mining can identify what makes these customers different from others and what makes them more or less likely to take both products.

Taking the overlap area in the middle of the top of the Venn diagram, the data mining/CRM software could be used to overlay geodemographic profiles for these customers (Exhibit 3.11)

The results show that the existing A and B account-holding customers come mainly from areas classified as Blue-collar owners, High income families, Suburban semis, and Low-rise council. This information could be vital to the identification of target segments for the cross-sell campaign, to acquire new customers for a different product, but from the company's existing customer base for another product.

The approach can also be valuable for other campaigns, especially acquisition segmentation strategies, where customer and

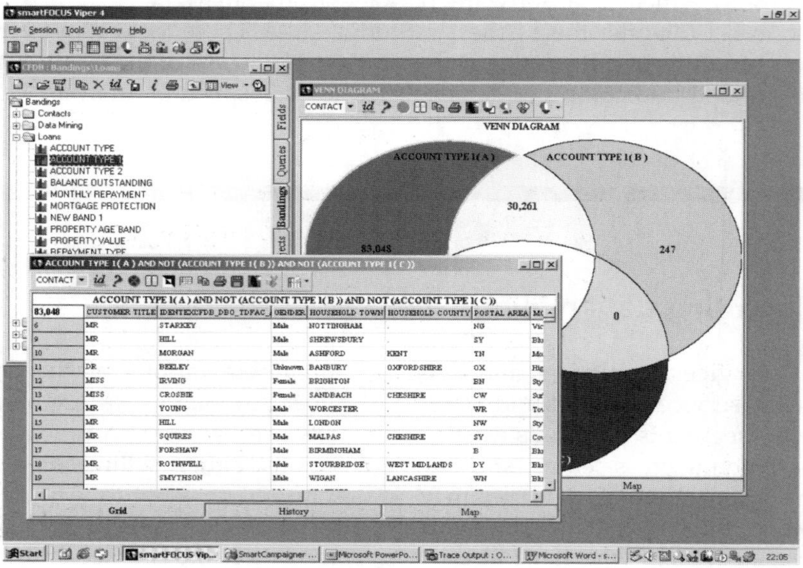

EXHIBIT 3.10 Number of customers who have purchased accounts A, B and C

transactional data on existing customers can be used to identify the characteristics of existing best customers in order to target others, not currently customers, but who possess similar characteristics. This is the identikit or cloning approach, an example of which is provided in the 'targeting' section.

Exhibit 3.12 takes the financial services example further. Transactional data can be fused with Experian's MOSAIC geodemographic system and MapInfo's geographical information system (GIS) to show 'hot spots' geographically of where these potentially best target segments might be found. As we have seen, MOSAIC uses postcodes and the data mining/CRM software has spatial analysis capabilities through a dynamic link to Mapinfo.

To further hone the characteristics of this 'best prospect' segment, the data mining/CRM software can be used to overlay other customer characteristics onto the map in order to redraw and filter this target segment further. Here, the first map has been filtered using Income over £35,000, Marital status = Married, and Age in the 40 to 60 band. These

are the characteristics that the same data mining/CRM software identified as being the ones possessed by the 'best' current customers of both account types A and B, according to their RFM profile. The data mining/CRM software extracts the names and addresses of customers with these same characteristics who currently have purchased only account type A as representing the best prospect segment for the cross-selling campaign for type B. This is done by merely selecting the 'hot spot zones' from the second map in Exhibit 3.12. Names and addresses are produced almost instantly, providing a contact list that satisfies the accessible criterion for segmentation. This target segment would presumably have a higher propensity to purchase both A and B products. Although the segment is composed of those who have currently only purchased A, it contains those who possess the characteristics of the best customers who have purchased both products.

There is more that can be done. The fullest benefit from existing customer data comes from looking at all of the attributes

EXHIBIT 3.11   MOSAIC profiles of customers who have purchased both A and B

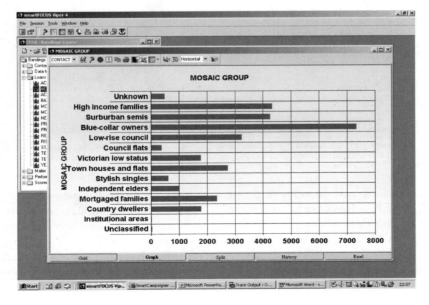

EXHIBIT 3.12　GIS data fusion

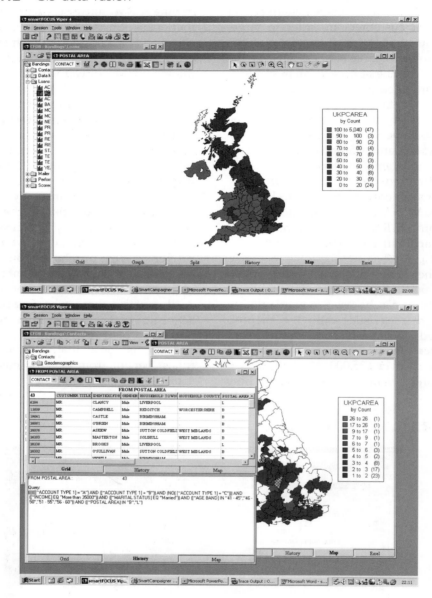

together. The easiest way to achieve this is via CHAID, which in this case is an integral component of the data mining/CRM software being used and of most similar packages.

As discussed earlier, this facilitates the breaking down of large datasets into homogeneous subsets. Based on scores on the dependent variable, clusters are formed that differ maximally between clusters on the dependent variable. The approach is very useful for market segmentation and is becoming very popular amongst data-driven marketers.

CHAID produces a tree-like analysis as shown earlier, which identifies different segments based on the variables themselves but also on the effects of the variables interacting with each other (regression doesn't automatically do this). Where there is no significant difference between some of the variables, CHAID will combine these into a larger 'segment'.

Here, various customer and transactional attributes have been investigated to see which best explain what characterises customers who have both A and B. A 'tree' structure represents different 'hot' and 'cold' 'branches' through the data. Each branch represents a different level of importance in explaining who the A and B customers are. Each attribute is assessed and the most important or 'significant' forms the first split. Taking the entire customer base in this instance, 26.44% of all customers have both A and B accounts (Exhibit 3.13).

By following the 'hottest branch' the company can understand which characteristics are possessed by those customers who have purchased both A and B account types. Exhibit 3.13 shows these to be: Married and Male. For this group of customers the percentage with both A and B accounts rises to 65.11% compared with 26.44% of the entire un-segmented base.

Further branches of the CHAID tree might cascade down to even more segments based on whichever variables prove to be significant. Space prevents showing further stages here, but assume the analysis produced 60 target segments. Each of these would have significant and different characteristics. Targeting could be done on a 'test' basis in which a sample from each might be targeted and those with better response rates could then be targeted with the full 'roll-out' campaign. Also, each could be targeted with different treatments, according to whatever gender, age, marital status or geodemographic characteristic might underpin the 'creative' (Exhibit 3.14).

(Source: This case has been provided courtesy of SmartFocus, Bristol)

EXHIBIT 3.13 Customers with both accounts A and B

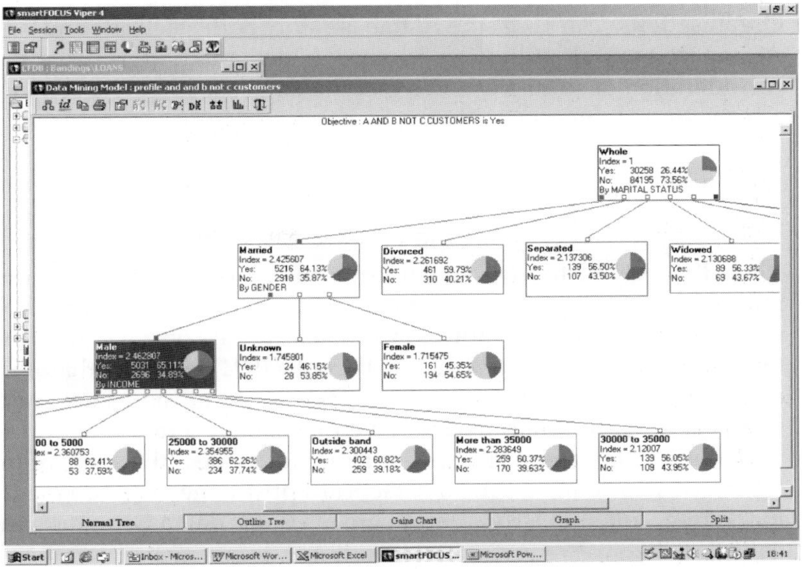

EXHIBIT 3.14 Targeted segments and differential treatment according to offer and creative, together with control groups

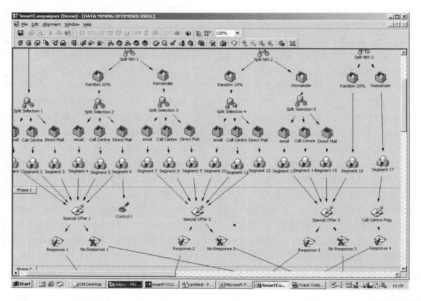

Strategic and tactical use of databases

Organisations can use the database for both tactical and strategic issues. Although tactical utilisation is very widespread, it is usually only through consideration of strategic issues that the database is truly a source of competitive advantage for the organisation.

Tactical utilisation of the database

If used merely tactically, the nature of the marketing database does not need to refer greatly to corporate strategy or organisational structure (Cook 1994). Under such circumstances it is more concerned with 'the next event' than with a longer-term view of customers (Bigg 1994). Cook (1994) suggests that it is actually more usual for organisations to employ the database at the tactical rather than at the strategic level, for the purposes given in Exhibit 3.15.

If the database is used only for tactical issues, this will ultimately relegate relational marketing itself to a tactical appendage of a broader, more strategic marketing function. Thus, strategic uses of database marketing need to be considered.

EXHIBIT 3.15   Tactical uses of the database

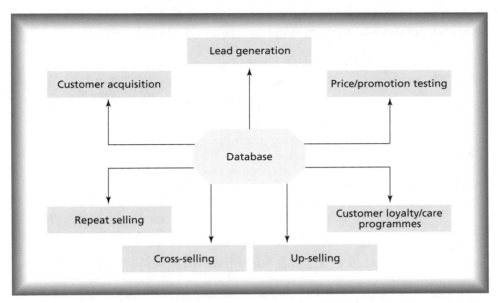

Strategic utilisation of databases

At a strategic level, decisions will need to be taken with respect to relational marketing planning and, in particular, segmentation and targeting, as outlined later in Chapter 6. In this sense the marketing database can focus on a whole range of different categories (e.g. new prospects, best prospects, loyals etc.) which are then utilised for acquisition or retention strategies. In this way, the creation and use of marketing databases will be quite selective.

Once created, the database has a variety of uses. It can clearly be used as a list from which to target customers via relational marketing activity. But, in addition, it can provide a wealth of information on the market and on customers and potential customers within it. In this context, the database provides data for both planning and analysis purposes: the database can be analysed for most attractive segments, for campaign planning and predicting campaign response. Strategically, the database can be used to change the basis of competition, strengthen customer relationships, overcome supplier problems, build barriers to entry and develop new products (Shaw and Stone 1988). Table 3.17 examines these further.

For example, Holiday Inn clearly believes in a positive strategic role for their marketing database which they see as allowing them 'to more accurately define strategies for the future and concurrently maximise short term marketing efforts' (Durr 1989). A new strategic use of the database which potentially could transcend all five categories is the sharing of data with other organisations in strategic alliances. We explore this in our coverage of knowledge management later. Shaw and Stone (1988) take this further by proposing a four-stage process of

TABLE 3.17 The role of database marketing as a competitive tool

Competitive opportunity	Marketing strategy	Role of information
Change competitive basis	Market development or penetration Increased effectiveness Better margins Alternative sales channels Reducing cost structure	Prospect/Customer information Targeted marketing Better control
Strengthen customer position	Tailored customer service Providing value to customers Product differentiation Create switching costs	Know customer needs 'Individual' promotions Response handling Identify potential needs Customers as 'users' of your systems
Strengthen buyer/supplier position	Superior market information Decreased cost of sales Providing access to supplier Pass stockholding on to supplier	Internal/External data capture Optimisation of sales channels Measure supplier performance Identify areas of inefficiency
Build barriers	Unique distribution channels Unique valued services Create entry costs	Knowledge of market allows improved service/value 'Lock in' customers, suppliers and intermediaries Immediate response to threats
Generate new products	Market-led product development Alliance opportunities New products/services	Market gap analysis Customer dialogue User innovation Information as product

(Source: Fletcher et al., 1990)

development of the marketing database (Shaw and Stone 1988). These phases are outlined below:

- In Phase One the database is merely a sales database originating from accounting systems and focusing more on product sales rather than customers.

- Phase Two occurs when a company has multiple databases for different sales territories or retailers and although they can be well used within the sector they cover, there can often be overlapping effort due to lack of communication and coordination – customers might receive direct mailings from the same company, but different and even conflicting ones from different parts of that company!

- In Phase Three there is evidence of a greater customer focus, with one database coordinating all communication with customers. Analysis is according to profiles, transactions and other relevant factors in order to determine how to target segments and individuals.

- In Phase Four there is evidence of true integration, with different organisational functions, not just the marketing one, linked with the marketing database.

If the organisation is not truly customer orientated then there will be only a tactical role for the marketing database, but if used strategically it has a central role to play – as outlined in the definition of database marketing offered earlier. Indeed, DeTienne and Thompson propose that the 'customer database is an opportunity for organisations to mechanise the process of learning about customers' and for this to be iterative because 'the database transcends the status of a record keeping device and becomes an implement of ever-increasing organisation knowledge' (DeTienne and Thompson 1996). This point is taken further in our coverage of knowledge management later.

Before ending this chapter, though, it is worth a brief discussion of who should deal with the database – in-house or outsourced.

In-house or outsourced?

Building and maintaining a customer, prospect or marketing database represents a significant investment for companies today. As such, it is important that the company carefully considers how the database will be used. Linton (1995) suggests that managers should address the following issues in order to assist them in selecting the appropriate database:

- How will the database support business objectives?
- What is expected from the system?
- What are the main requirements?
- What applications will it be used for?

Having answered these questions, managers should be in a better position to identify the type of database they need. It will also allow them to ensure that they have the appropriate computer power, speed, memory and processing capacity to run such a database.

A second issue which needs to be addressed is whether the database will be developed and maintained in-house, or whether an external supplier will be used. Keeping the database in-house certainly ensures that the organisation has more control, but it is often a more expensive option, particularly for smaller companies. Indeed, one of the current problems in the relational data-informed marketing industry is a skills gap (Mitchell 1996; Evans *et al.* 2002). There are all too few people with a strategic marketing vision coupled with the more technical database and analytical skills. As a result, it is often recommended that the database should be run by an outside company (Hughes 1996). We explore these issues in further detail in our coverage of knowledge management in Chapter 8.

The database needs to be capable of storing large amounts of data and of being analysed in sophisticated ways. It has to be constantly updated, de-duplicated, purged and merged (see the WH Smith Case Study below). Sometimes the software may also need to link directly into automated telephone contacts and so on. The software for these activities takes more than a couple of in-house seminars to learn and the company may not be able to afford to commit the time and resources internally to this. Outside database companies operate for multiple clients and therefore there are some economies of scale in the area in which they specialise. As a result, there may be certain advantages associated with outsourcing database management, including (Linton 1995):

- The database will not affect the capacity of the organisation's internal systems.
- There will be no need to recruit or train additional staff.
- The database will be managed by specialists.

However, as the partnership develops it sometimes evolves, because as with Tesco outsourcing its database operations to DunnHumby, there is now a formal link between the organisations.

CASE **STUDY** 3.8

WH Smith

In 1997, newsagent WH Smith introduced the first online loyalty card developed by a high street store. The customer data gathered by the use of the WH Smith Clubcard is used to analyse and profile customers and customer-buying patterns across its 600 stores.

In the first six months after its introduction, the Clubcard gained 2.5 million members. The scheme's membership now stands at over 5 million. The daily transac-

tion rate is over 100 000, with a peak at more than 250 000 transactions.

The primary objective behind the Clubcard was to use the data to understand WH Smith customers better, as well as constructing targeted specific offers and mailings to these customers. The company realised, however, that the success of this scheme was heavily dependent upon the accuracy of its customer data.

Although its initial customer data was proven to be of an already high standard (94% accurate), WH Smith needed optimum accuracy. In effect, it required a data cleansing service, and hired GB Information Management to conduct a bulk yearly-cleansing service. More recently, this has developed into a quarterly-managed service.

It involves the regular extraction and cleansing of WH Smith customer data in terms of Post Office address file accuracy, mortality file matching, and the like.

As a result of working with GB Information Management, WH Smith has subse-quently managed to progress this data accuracy to the exceptional level of 98%. Of course, improved data accuracy is only worth while if it enhances business processes and results.

Recent customer mailing offers to Club-card customers testify to the success of the project. The response to an offer on Delia Smith's *How to Cook* gained an 8% response rate, while a promotion for the *Science Fiction* TV video achieved a similar take-up.

(Source: Adapted by the authors from Direct Response 2001 Smart Award Case Study in Brown 2001)

Data realities

Although we have devoted significant space to discussing data sources and how this data is dealt with, we also have to present strong cautionary notes.

There is still unease over the quality of data being gathered, as is exemplified by the Jigsaw Consortium's concern over the accuracy and recency of some of the data it manages (Anon 2003).

Also, data fusion itself has been assessed as 'not containing much in the way of internal validity checks, creating the real possibility that decisions will be made using a fused database which does not represent reality' (Jephcott and Bock 1998). So, all of the above might lead to a kind of 'future shock' if the resulting targeting is based upon flawed analysis.

In research by Nairn and Bottomley (2003), a dataset was split, with one half being randomised to make the data meaningless. The same statistical procedures were conducted on the real and dummy data and both produced clusters that managers thought were meaningful for potential segmentation. Only when further and more sophisticated data analysis was carried out did the dummy data break down. The concern here is that data might need to be subjected to far more rigorous analysis than often is the norm and, in any case, managers are not often able to evaluate data sufficiently.

We have the classic 'garbage in, garbage out' but accentuated by so much more garbage and so few who can spot garbage when it's there!

To revisit our earlier discussion of CRM, we said that in practice this is too often equated with data-handling technology. The following case reinforces the point about relational marketing being overly centred on software technologies.

CRM

The phrase customer relationship management (CRM) is credited with many things, none of which are entirely positive. Massive expenditure on CRM solutions followed by minimal returns is the most commonly cited. Then there's the fact that every company under the sun, from software houses to consultants, seems to be offering CRM expertise. Yet the statistics make gloomy reading. Of the £5.7 billion estimated to have been spent last year on CRM in Europe, nearly £4 billion will not be used effectively. Chris Tatner, director of Proximity Consulting says: 'all too often in organisations the focus is internal. It's about putting in the software and pushing it out to customers, rather than asking what the customer wants. That's why a lot of CRM schemes fail.'

(Source: Acland 2002. Reproduced from *Marketing Direct* magazine with the permission and the copyright holders Haymarket Business Publications Limited)

In this chapter we have explored what the technology is and how it can be used, but we must reiterate that this is necessary but not sufficient for relational marketing. As Xu *et al.* (2002) suggest, 'the integration of CRM ... has more to do with culture and processes than software and data flow ... the failure of CRM implementations is a problem of completeness'. If the narrow perspective continues, we suggest the abandoning of the CRM concept in favour of CDM (customer data management). Our perspective is that data needs to be converted into knowledge and this knowledge shared across functions and partners, and clearly this takes us beyond a narrow 'software' perspective of data-informed marketing. These issues are explored in the next chapters, here within Part 2.

Summary

- Technological change is facilitating database development and, as we discussed in Chapter 1, there is demand for a more individualised marketing approach. The database provides a vehicle for understanding and analysing markets and customers and the merging of the data sources explored in Chapter 2 and leads to the development of *biographics*.

- Databases provide relational marketing with one of its main reasons for claiming to be more measurable and accountable than more traditional forms of marketing. The calculation – and strategic use – of lifetime values and allowable costs are examples.

- There are often questions concerning the accuracy of data held on marketing databases, so although this chapter has explored a range of methods of fusing and mining data and indeed cleaning it and keeping it up to date, in practice these are not always implemented. Abbott *et al.* (2001), for example, have researched this area and found that clean and accurate data are key to successful segmentation and targeting of markets.

- Segmentation and targeting strategies are the theme of Chapter 6, but we turn next to more metrics, involved with procedures needed to 'test' different targeting approaches. This is then followed by Chapter 5, which explores the value of traditional market research to add further insight to what can be gleaned from these tests.

- It is interesting, though, to remember a prediction from Shubik (1967): 'the computer and modern data processing provide the refinement – the means to treat individuals as individuals rather than parts of a large aggregate … the treatment of an individual as an individual will not be an unmixed blessing. Problems concerning the protection of privacy will be large.' This is not a misprint – it *was* 1967.

Review questions

1 What is meant by 'RFM' and the 'Pareto Principle'? What is their value to relational marketers and what are their implications for customers?

2 What is meant by 'lifetime value'? What is its value to relational marketers and what are its implications for customers?

3 For a consumer market of your choice, consider the sources of information that might be relevant for data fusion (including the range of existing databases as discussed in Chapter 2 and which could be relevantly linked). What 'metrics' can be applied to this data and what could such analysis contribute to a relational marketing operation?

4 Select two organisations with which you are familiar and analyse in which stages of database development they currently are – and discuss how they reached that stage and how they might progress further.

Further reading

Berry, M.J.A. and Linoff, G. (1997) *Data Mining Techniques: For Marketing, Sales and Customer Support*, New York: John Wiley.

David Shepard Associates (1995) *The New Direct Marketing*, Chicago: Irwin.

Hughes, A.M. (1996) *The Complete Database Marketer*, New York: McGraw Hill.

Kelly, S. (1994) *Data Warehousing: The Route to Mass Customisation*, Chichester: John Wiley.

References

Abbott, J., Stone, M. and Buttle, F. (2001) 'Integrating Customer Data into Customer Relationship Management Strategy: An Empirical Study', *Journal of Database Marketing* 8(4) pp. 289–300.

Acland, H. (2002) 'Focusing on CRM implementation', *Marketing Direct*, July/August, p. 13.

Ahmed, R. and Buttle, F. (2001) 'Customer Retention: A Potentially Potent Marketing Strategy', *Journal of Strategic Marketing*, 9, pp. 29–45.

Anon (2003) 'JIGSAW Chief Laments Data Quality', *Precision Marketing*, 14 February, p. 1.

Antoniou, T. (1997) 'Drilling or Mining? Handling and Analysis of Data Between Now and the Year 2000', *Marketing and Research Today*, May, pp. 115–20.

Bigg, A. (1994) 'Techno Tactics', *Campaign*, 8 July, pp. 37–8.

Brown, D.D. (2001) 'More Power to Your Database', *Direct Response* April, pp. 51–4.

Cook, S. (1994) 'Database Marketing: Strategy or Tactical Tool?', *Marketing Intelligence and Planning*, 12(6), pp. 4–7.

Curry, B., Davies, F., Evans, M., Moutinho, L. and Phillips, P. (2003) 'The Kohonen Self-Organising Map as an alternative to Cluster Analysis: An Application to Direct Marketing', *International Journal of Market Research*, 45(2), pp. 191–211.

Dawkins, P.M. and Reichheld, F.F. (1990), 'Customer retention as a competitive weapon', *Directors & Board*, Summer, pp. 42–7.

DeTienne, K.B. and Thompson, J.A. (1996) 'Database Marketing and Organisational Learning Theory: Toward a Research Agenda', *Journal of Consumer Marketing*, 13(5), pp. 12–34.

Durr, J.L. (1989) 'The Value of the Guest Register', *Direct Marketing*, September, pp. 48–55.

Evans, M., Nancarrow, C., Tapp, A. and Stone, M. (2002) 'Future Marketers: Future Curriculum: Future Shock?', *Journal of Marketing Management*, 18(5–6), July, pp. 579–596, ISSN 0267–257X.

Fletcher, K., Wheeler, C. and Wright, J. (1990) 'The Role and Status of UK Database Marketing', *Quarterly Review of Marketing*, Autumn, pp. 7–14.

Hughes, A.M. (1996) *The Complete Database Marketer*, Homewood, IL: Irwin.

Jephcott, J. and Bock, T. (1998) 'The Application and Validation of Data Fusion', *Journal of the Market Research Society*, 40(3), pp. 185–205

Linton, I. (1995) *Database Marketing: Know What Your Customer Wants*, London: Pitman, p. 22.

Mackintosh, J. (2002) 'Halifax Sorry for Snob to "Cash Heavy" Businesses', *Financial Times*, 27 February.

Mitchell, S. (1996) 'Training and Support Given to Users of Marketing Databases', *Journal of Database Marketing*, 3(4), pp. 326–430.

Mitchell, V.W. and Haggett, S. (1997) 'Sun-Sign Astrology in Market Segmentation: An Empirical Investigation', *Journal of Consumer Marketing*, 14(2), pp. 113–31.

Nairn, A. and Bottomley, P. (2003) 'Something Approaching Science? Cluster Analysis Procedures in the CRM Era', *International Journal of Market Research*, 45(2), pp. 421–61.

Patterson, M., O'Malley, L. and Evans, M.J. (1997) 'Database Marketing: Investigating Privacy Concerns', *Journal of Marketing Communications*, 3(3), pp. 151–74.

Patterson, M., Evans, M., O'Malley, L. (1999) 'UK Attitudes Toward Direct Mail', *Journal of Database Marketing*, 7(2), pp. 157–72.

Shaw, R. and Stone, M. (1988) 'Competitive Superiority through Database Marketing', *Long Range Planning*, 21(5), pp. 24–40.

Shubik, M. (1967) 'Information, Rationality and Free Choice in a Future Democratic Society', *Daedalus*, 96, pp. 771–8.

Witherell, L., (2002) 'Data Clinic', *Direct Response*, 31 August.

Xu, Y., Yen, D.C., Lin, B. and Chou, D.C. (2002) 'Adopting Customer Relationship Management Technology', *Industrial Management and Data Systems*, 102(8) pp. 442–52.

4 Testing in direct relational marketing

Learning objectives

Having completed this chapter, students should:

- Understand the various forms of experimentation available to a relational marketer.
- Be able to calculate appropriate sample sizes for conducting tests.
- Be able to devise and evaluate test programmes.

Bears, knickers or chocs?

A mail-order gift company has a list of 1 million customers. It is finalising its Christmas range and has space for just one additional product. The company has the opportunity to distribute one of the following: teddy bears, sexy knickers or boxes of chocolates. The managing director has a bent for knickers, so decides to include these in the Christmas range. The company had no idea of the response rate to the 'knicker' mailing but, after mailing, it turns out that 5% of the 1 million strong customer list respond to this mailing by purchasing. The gross margin of £4 per sale means that 50 000 orders lead to an overall margin of £200,000. How good does this sound? The point of testing is that each of the alternatives can be tried in order to determine which is likely to be the most effective.

In this case, if all alternatives were tested before final roll-out, the likely response rates of each would be estimated. For example, suppose the company tested each of the three products on different sub-samples of 5 000 customers from the customer database. Response rates to this test might be: 9% for the bear, 5% for the knickers and 2% for the chocolates. Following the

99

test, any roll-out would have to exclude the 15 000 customers in the test; they would not appreciate a confusing offer, so the final mailing list would be 1 000 000 less 15 000 = 8 985 000. With the same margins of £4 per sale, the margin for the 'winning' bear would be:

Bear: 9% of 985 000 × £4 = £354,600

Compare this with the knickers which would produce only £200,000.

Indeed, if the company had not tested and gone for the chocolates instead, the resulting margin would merely have been 1m x 2% × £4 = £80,000.

The value of testing is clear: it enables companies to select the alternative that is likely to be the most effective.

Introduction

Our coverage of data metrics leads us to another example of data-informed marketing, the use of 'testing'. Testing is but one form of marketing research but is the one within which there is the greatest degree of control over the variables being measured. The continuum shown in Table 4.1 incorporates testing under the 'experimentation' category. As one moves through the categories from left to right, the degree of control that is exercised over the variables being researched tends to increase. For example, under 'observation', the point is to monitor what happens, not to control that behaviour; under interview, the degree of structure in the questions will determine the level of control over the issues being researched. If more qualitative questioning is used, such as 'why do you think people buy brand X?', the open-endedness of this does not control the direction in which the respondent will answer. If, however, the question is closed, such as

TABLE 4.1 The research/testing continuum

Observation	Interview	Experimentation
Little control over what is being studied. Highly objective because actual behaviour is recorded as opposed to what the researcher thinks is important.	Degrees of control depending on the method used. In group discussions participants can veer off into areas of little interest, whereas more structured surveys restrict the range of answers to what the researcher feels to be the relevant issues.	High levels of control over variables (e.g. mailing list or content and style of mailing) but require complicated and expensive experiments to cover all the factors which might account for the relative success of one variant.

'Do you think people buy Brand X because it is a) of good quality, b) well advertised c) widely available in shops?, then the respondent's answer is controlled to the alternatives provided.

But with experimentation the aim is to control variables and to measure effects and results. It is with this last category that this chapter is concerned and in it we explore the widespread use of 'testing', as it tends to be called by direct marketers. The other categories of research are explored in Chapter 5.

The continuum represents an holistic approach to the research/testing area.

Experimental design and testing

It is under this heading that we discuss direct marketing 'testing'. We introduced the Jigsaw consortium in Chapter 2, this being a data alliance between Kimberly-Clark, Unilever and Cadbury Schweppes. In 1998 it mailed 150 000 personalised magazines in a national test mailing (Anon 1998). Three different versions of the magazine were sent to the various segments defined by lifestyle and life stage. The 'winning' version, based on response, would then constitute the full 'roll-out' mailing to 1 million households. This is an example of the scale of direct activities but also of the importance of getting testing 'right'.

Direct marketers tend to focus their testing on five major elements (Forshaw 1993): the target audience; the offer or 'proposition'; timing; format and creative treatment; and, in some cases, the product or service itself. Given that one of the cornerstones of direct marketing is that it can be *'measurable'*, there can be a reasonably good prospect of quantifying and predicting outcomes, which is what makes testing so useful.

The testing of target audiences centres largely on the use of lists and media. The marketer needs to ensure that he or she is communicating with the correct audience and thus the customer or prospect list assumes paramount importance, as do the media through which we try to reach this audience. In Chapter 2 we discussed the fact that lists can be created internally or can be obtained from external sources. Internal lists are likely to be well suited to the organisation's requirements, though the testing of different segments within those lists may still be needed. There are in the region of 3 000 external lists available and these are likely to require greater testing. No external list is going to be perfectly suited to the organisation and therefore testing will help to identify those sections of the list which are most appropriate. The number of lists to be tested and the degree to which each list is tested depends largely on the budget available and time constraints (Purdom 1996). Marketers also have a large number of media at their disposal and media choices can be tested for each individual campaign.

The offer or proposition relates to that element of the direct communications campaign that encourages the target audience to respond. Relational marketers, in particular, are fortunate in having a great deal of flexibility in this area and there are a number of characteristics of the offer which can be tested, including (Stone *et al*. 1995):

- price levels
- benefits
- exclusivity
- ways of using the product
- competitive comparison
- newsworthiness
- image
- drawback of non-use
- celebrity endorsement.

Middleton and Evans (1998) found that 'lists' and 'creative' were the most tested and then there were progressively fewer mentions for each of the following: lists, creative, offer, recency, frequency, pack format, incentives, number of items in mailer, layout, letter, seasonality.

For many direct marketers the timing of the offer is crucial to such an extent that high levels of non-response are usually attributed to poor timing. While issues such as seasonality are general aspects of timing that need to be accounted for, timing, more often than not, is specifically related to the product or service in question (Forshaw 1993).

The testing of different formats is also commonplace among direct marketers and it tends to centre on issues such as size, number of components, quality and types of envelope etc. (Forshaw 1993). In addition to making sure that the format is appropriate for the target audience, the marketer must also strive to maintain consistency between each of the elements in the communication; they must come together as a coherent whole. It is in this area that testing plays a major role.

Most organisations will already have decided upon the product or service and thus there will be no need for testing. However, in developing new products/ services or in tailoring them to suit the needs and requirements of specific market segments, some testing may be required.

Two general types of testing can be distinguished: first, when we want to compare the results from different lists or creative, and secondly, when we want to test a relational marketing approach on a small scale in order to predict how it will work in full. The former type is a comparative test and the latter is a predictive test.

Comparative tests

In such tests, direct marketers test response rates to:

- different lists: Experian versus Claritas lifestyle lists;
- timing of campaigns: whether business-business customers are more likely to spend their budgets at the beginning or end of a financial year;
- different creative treatment: whether different wording for men and women produces different response rates;
- response mechanisms: coupon versus telephone;

- production/print: whether a C5 envelope in green produces a better response than a C4 in orange, and so on.

It is also possible to test combinations of these, so we are not restricted to a single experimental variable. The structure of experimental design is discussed in a later section.

Predictive tests

A predictive test is where the direct marketer wants to estimate the future impact/response of a full roll-out based on a test sample. This might be a where a test sample from a mailing list is being used to predict the level of response if the full list is used.

A/B splits

This is when inserts in different newspapers or magazines can be tested or where different copy can be tested in the same newspaper. These are often referred to as 'A/B splits' because version A is inserted into one batch of the newspaper, version B into another batch, either in an interleaving way or stacked in groups of each version. The interleaving method is based on printing machines that print two copies simultaneously. For these, one half of the output is geared up for version A and the other half for version B. The result is each alternative copy of the publication containing 'A' or 'B'. Although this sounds very good, there can be problems of unequal numbers of 'A' and 'B' going out due to machine breakdowns, which would not always be notified to the client. This could destroy the reliability of the test because response rates would not be based on equal (or even known) sample sizes. There might also be restrictions on the style of insert – in terms of size, shape and material – if the publisher is not able to handle such differences. As well as testing copy in this way, if different publications are used, then medium can also be tested.

Test designs

In a simple test format, a test would be devised to assess something new against a 'control' pack (the 'banker' which had obtained the best results in the past). As this pack has a proven track record, the purpose of the test is to see whether the new variant can outperform the existing standard. If it can, and if it can do so reliably (probably not just on one small test), the new variant would become the 'banker' and it would be tested against a further new variant, and the cycle would continue.

A simple example demonstrates some of the considerations involved in designing experiments or *tests* and the following case study provides these.

CASE **STUDY** 4.1

Experimentation

Suppose a marketer believes that sales are low because of inefficient advertising, and wants to establish what will happen if some change is made in advertising. A new advertising campaign is developed and launched, and sales are monitored and compared with sales before the new campaign. In terms of experimentation this would be a simple before–after design, in the following manner:

Before measure   YES (initial sales = X1)
Experimental variable YES (new advertising)
After measure   YES (new level of sales
                        = X2)

The difference between the two levels of sales is taken to be the effect of the new campaign. So, if X1 is 5 000 units per month and X2 is 6 000 units per month, the organisation might conclude the new campaign to be effective. Clearly, this would not necessarily be valid. If, for example, competitors' distribution systems delayed delivery of competing products to the shops during the time of this new campaign, the customers may be purchasing the test product, not because of an effective advertising campaign, but because of the lack of availability of alternative brands.

It is clearly impossible to control competitors' marketing activity when conducting marketing experiments, and there are many other uncontrollable variables to take into account when designing and analysing experiments. For example, there might be a general trend of increasing sales and, perhaps, sales might have been even higher if the old campaign had continued!

There are dangers of simply comparing sales before and after the introduction of an experimental variable. The effect of time has to be considered, and it might be, as, for example, with poster advertising, that the time delay before achieving any influence might be substantial.

Another problem with the experiment above is that the wrong dependent variable (that is, the variable that is measured to judge the effect of the experimental variable) may be selected. Much depends on what the advertising campaign is trying to do, of course, and it may therefore be more valid to measure changes in attitudes or perceptions rather than sales.

When analysing the results of a test it is important to examine one issue at a time, rather than looking at the whole mass of data all at once. This means that even if the test had been devised as a complicated matrix, it could be analysed logically and systematically by isolating each individual test. A crucial issue is to try to keep other factors constant while examining the particular results of interest. If similar tests have been done in the past, then, in order to make results comparable, conditions should be kept constant. While appreciating that this would be the case in an ideal world, in real life it is often not possible to control for everything necessary and therefore there might be a trade-off between what is ideal and what is practical.

Controlling variables is important and this leads to the use of *control groups*, which measure the same dependent variables but in the absence of the experimental variable. This allows some degree of assessment of uncontrollable variables. For example, if for the experimental group (that is, those exposed to the experimental variable) the *before–after* calculation showed increased sales from 5000 to 6000 units per month, but for a *control* group sales rose from 4000 to 4800 per month, then the 20% increase for both groups might mean that there had been little effect of the experimental variable. This type of design is referred to as *before–after with control* as shown in Table 4.2 and the following case study provides an example of the use of control groups.

TABLE 4.2 Before–after with control test design

	Experimental group	Control group
Before measure (initial sales)	X1	Y1
Experimental variable (new direct mail 'creative')	Yes	No
After measure (new level of sales)	X2	Y2
Therefore, effect of experimental variable = (X2 − X1) − (Y2 − Y1)		

CASE **STUDY** 4.2

Blockbuster

Renting a film or game is no big deal for most people, which can make spending patterns volatile. Half the customers active in one quarter can be inactive the next. To counter this, Blockbuster established its Premier programme, targeting its best customers. Five mailings were distributed between April 2001 and March 2002. These were segmented to reflect customers' individual interests, such as DVD, VHS or games, and each included a bonus card to drive loyalty. Behaviour was monitored against that of a customer segment receiving no communications. The first mailing went to 740000 customers. Over a 60-week period, visits by these customers increased by 15.9%. This equates to two million incremental transactions worth £8.4m, from an investment of £826,000.

(Source: Adapted from material provided by DMA from the Blockbuster Entertainment Award Winning Case Study, DMA/Royal Mail Awards 2002)

In direct marketing it is often relevant to be able to test several variables at the same time. Under such circumstances a test matrix would be developed, like the one in Exhibit 4.1.

Each cell is an independent variable and referred to as a factor, and this form of experimental design is a *factorial design*.

In addition to measuring the effects on dependent variables, the direct marketer can also identify any effects of *interaction* between the variables (factors). This could be important because two variables might affect each other – they might be *interdependent* – but if they were tested separately this would not be identified. Direct marketers can employ a great variety of factorial designs, such as in Exhibit 4.2.

Marketing experiments can use data from consumer panels or retail audits, with the advantage of being able to demonstrate changes over time more effectively than *ad hoc* research. The test market is the largest marketing experiment because the whole relational marketing 'mix' is tested, rather than just one of several variables. Panel data are particularly useful in test markets, because not just sales, but customer profiles (and 'by name and address'), new and repeat buying levels, attitudes, retail preferences, and so on, are analysed over a period. As mentioned earlier, this data is now being used as an overlay to other sources of individual records in marketing databases.

EXHIBIT 4.1   Test matrix

Mailing lists	Versions of 'Creative'		
	version 1	version 2	version 3
list 1			
list 2			
list 3			

EXHIBIT 4.2 Types of factorial design

2 × 2 Factorial design

	Direct mail	No direct mail
Free newspaper inserts	1	2
No inserts	3	4

Test sample 1 receives direct mail shots and inserts in their free newspaper. Sample 2 receives only inserts, 3 gets only direct mail and 4 receives neither.

2 × 3 Factorial design

	Direct mail	No direct mail
Free newspaper *colour* inserts	1	2
Free newspaper *black & white* inserts	3	4
No inserts	5	6

Test sample 1 receives *colour* direct mailings and inserts in their free newspaper. Sample 2 receives only *colour* inserts, 3 gets *B&W* inserts AND direct mail, 4 receives only *B&W* inserts, 5 gets only direct mail and 6 receives none of these.

2 × 2 × 3 Factorial design

	Direct mail		No direct mail	
	Telesales	No telesales	Telesales	No telesales
Free newspaper inserts	1	2	3	4
No inserts	5	6	7	8

Test sample 1 receives direct mailings, inserts and a telesales call, sample 2 receives inserts, direct mail but no telesales, 3 gets inserts, telesales but no direct mail, 4 receives only inserts, 5 gets direct mail, telesales but no inserts, 6 receives direct mail only, 7 receives telesales only and 8 gets none of these.

Sample size

Clearly, in the practical world, the cost-effectiveness criterion is of paramount importance in determining how many people should be contacted in a test mailing, interviewed or observed. The fact is that while decision makers want results to be accurate, generally increased accuracy comes with increased sample size (for the same sample design). Indeed, there is normally a trade-off between possibly dramatic increases in research costs and increased research accuracy or other benefits. However, other resources such as time and human resources are also important. If a larger sample cannot be resourced, or if it would push the estimated completion date too far, then the smaller sample may be acceptable.

IN THEORY

Sample size

The size of the list or market segment concerned is not relevant to sample size determination.

Where levels of accuracy are important in determining sample size, the relationship can be summarised in the following way. For example, if we are designing a predictive test for a new mailing list we are not going to use the full list, until we have the results of a mailing of 'n' names from it. But what is the size of 'n'? The aim here is to reveal results in percentage terms, that is, the response rate percentage, and the formula for helping to determine sample size in such cases is:

$$\text{Sample size} = \frac{R \times (100 - R) \times Z^2}{E^2}$$

where R is the estimate of what the response rate percentage (the 'population' percentage) might be, E reflects the degree of accuracy desired in the estimated percentage and Z is a parameter which reflects the degree of confidence we desire in the result. For 95% confidence Z is 1.96 and for 99% confidence it is 2.58.

This model is based on the characteristics of the normal distribution (Exhibit 4.3). To briefly explain this, if many test samples are taken from a population (say, the mailing list), their results would vary but would be normally distributed. For such a distribution, about 34% of test samples would be one standard error away from the mean on either side and approximately 48% would be two standard errors away from the mean. Adding these divisions together, it can be seen that 95% of the items will be between +1.96 and −1.96 standard errors (or 'Zs') away from the mean. An element in this context would be what each sample estimates the response rate (population percentage) to be.

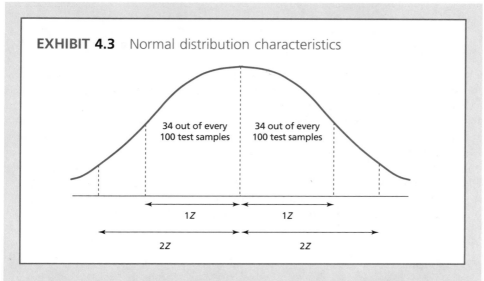

EXHIBIT 4.3 Normal distribution characteristics

34 out of every 100 test samples

34 out of every 100 test samples

$1Z$

$1Z$

$2Z$

$2Z$

In our example, we feel that, based on previous experience of similar lists, the response could be around 5% and we decide that we want to be 95% confident that our findings will be within a range of + and −0.6% of the projected response. In this case:

$$\text{Sample size} = \frac{R \times (100 - R) \times Z^2}{E^2}$$

where: R = our estimate of the response rate being about 5%;
Z = our 95% level of confidence identifies 1.96 'Zs' or standard errors from the mean;
E = our requirement for the result be in the range of ± 0.6% of the projected response.

In our example this produces:

$$\text{Sample size} = \frac{5 \times (100 - 5) \times 1.96^2}{0.6^2}$$

$$= \frac{475 \times 3.84}{0.36}$$

$$= 5\,069$$

That is, if, for the mailing list, the response rate will be 5%, a sample of 5 067 from our list (irrespective of the size of that list) would mean that we would be 95% confident that when we 'roll out' the campaign the response will be within the range 4.4% to 5.6% (± 0.6%).

Let us suppose that the test mailing produces 233 responses. This would be 4.6% of our sample of 5 069 and is within the range of 4.4% to 5.6% (± 0.6 around 5%) for which there is a 95% confidence level. It is likely, therefore,

→

that the full roll-out would produce a response rate within this range. In probability terms, our sample/test result does not challenge the proposition that the full roll-out response rate (population percentage) will be 5%.

If, however, our test mailing produced a response of 172 (that is, 3.4% of our sample from the list), it would fall outside the range for which we could be 95% confident of the full roll-out response being 5%. That is, although not *all* tests would produce the same response rate, the chances of a sample test producing a 3.4% response if the overall response rate is actually 5% would be so rare that we would question whether the 5% response rate is a realistic one to expect. In that case we could conclude that it would be likely (not definitely, because all of this is based on probabilities, not certainties) to be significantly less than 5%.

If we want to be 99% confident of our test results being within ±0.3 percentage points of the test response rate, then the size of the test sample would have to be:

$$\text{Sample size} = \frac{5 \times (100 - 5) \times 2.58^2}{0.3^2}$$

$$= \frac{475 \times 6.66}{0.09}$$

$$= 35\,150$$

This demonstrates how increases in accuracy can lead to extremely large increases in test sample size required and points again to the 'compromise', in practice, between the variables of accuracy, time and resources. The above analysis can be used in a slightly different way to estimate the range for the response rate during roll-out, from the test sample.

Then the range for the roll-out response rate (standard deviation) is given by:

$$E = Z \times \sqrt{\frac{R \times (100 - R)}{n}}$$

where n is the size of our test sample.

For example, if our test mailing of 5 000 on a list produced a response rate of 2% and we want to be 95% confident of the range of response (remember that the factor associated with a 95% confidence level is 1.96):

$$\text{Range } (E) = 1.96 \times \sqrt{\frac{2 \times 98}{5\,000}} = 0.39$$

We can therefore be 95% confident that the range of roll-out response is 1.61% to 2.39%.

Let us now put several of the above strands of theory and practice together in a fuller testing example.

CASE **STUDY** 4.3

Testing

'Datacon' is a credit card company and has decided to launch a new 'lifestyle' membership scheme in which members will be offered discounted domestic and foreign holidays and short breaks. A variety of activity holidays, long- and short-haul breaks and special interest holidays such as aeroplane spotting and fishing will be offered along with business conference venues.

You have been asked to produce a plan for testing mailing and e-mail lists in order to acquire new members.

You have been allocated a budget of £105,000 for the test and have been tasked with maximising return on investment. It has been agreed that profitability will be based on a £50 margin per new member.

The costs, per 1 000 names selected from the lists are:

Per 1 000 names	
List rental	£100
Data cleaning/deduping/mail merge	£30
Printing	£50
Letter/Offer	£50
Envelopes	£40
Mailshop (enclosing & collating)	£30
Post	£200
Costs per 1 000	£500

In addition, there are fixed costs for a test or roll-out of £5,000. A number of lists have been sourced from a list broker, together with their associated costs and characteristics. These are shown in Table 4.3.

TABLE 4.3 Lists

	List size
From Lists R Us:	
List 1: Plane Spotter List From subscribers to *Plane Spotting Monthly* and similar magazines	120 000
List 2: Fisherman's Friend List From membership of fishing clubs and subscribers to Fishing magazines	150 000
List 3: Holidays on the Edge List E-mail list from subscribers to e-mail online communities for such activities as Pot-Holing Weekly and Swimming with Sharks	180 000
List 4: Conference List From conference and exhibition attendees	80 000
List 5: International Travellers List From overseas travel insurance companies	50 000
List 6: Home Hols List From the registers of major UK hotel chains	15 000
List 7: Fly Far Away List From e-mail purchases of long-haul travel	50 000

The company could decide to select from all of these lists or it could decide to select from only some. As with the 'gift' example above, the rationale here is that testing provides more reliability in predicting the likely response from each list and without this, the company would not know if one list would produce a response of 1% or 50%. Let us assume that the company is a total novice in direct targeting and, on the basis of previous experience and of discussions with contacts around the same industry, it is thought that these sorts of lists tend to produce response rates of around 3%.

For the purposes of this case, assume that response equals conversion to sales.

It is now necessary to determine the sample size that would be needed for each list test.

From the earlier discussion of this, the following formula is used:

$$\text{Sample size} = \frac{R \times (100 - R) \times Z^2}{E^2}$$

In this case, the company wants to be 95% confident that the test results will be ±0.5%:

$$\text{Sample size} = \frac{3 \times (100 - 3) \times 1.96^2}{0.5^2} = 4\,472$$

That is, for each list from which a sample is drawn, a sample of 4 472 is needed. However, the list broker will only sell in multiples of a thousand, so it is probably fair to settle on sample sizes of 4 000.

If you think that all of these lists could target relevantly, it might be worth testing them all.

If so, the 'spreadsheet' shown in Table 4.4 emerges.

At this point it is still not known which lists produce the better response rates, so now is the moment of truth. The test is conducted and the resulting response rates are:

List	Response rate
1	1.3%
2	3.8%
3	2.7%
4	4.2%
5	2.2%
6	5.1%
7	0.5%

This is perhaps surprising: the 'Far Away' list, for example, might have been expected to have been a better performer for long-haul travel and it might not have been anticipated that the 'Home Hols' list would turn out to be the best performer. But this, of course, is the value of testing. The spreadsheet can now be extended as shown in Table 4.5.

TABLE 4.4 Spreadsheet – 1

List	Sample size	Variable costs (£500 per thousand)	Fixed costs
1	4 000	2,000	
2	4 000	2,000	
3	4 000	2,000	
4	4 000	2,000	
5	4 000	2,000	
6	4 000	2,000	
7	4 000	2,000	
Total variable cost		14,000	
Total fixed cost			5,000
Total test cost:		19,000	

Remember that there is a fixed cost for a test or roll-out of £5,000, so the final profit for the test is £20,400.

The decision now has to be made concerning which lists to use to maximise return on investment within the initial budget of £105,000. This budget includes the cost of the test, but in this case we have actually made a profit from the test itself of £20,400, meaning we have £125,400 for the rollout. However, there is a fixed cost of £5,000 for the roll-out, reducing the final budget to £120,400.

In order to calculate return on investment we can look again at the data so far. Table 4.6 summarises this and shows this is determined by dividing the 'return' (the profit or loss) by the 'investment' (the variable costs) for each list.

A further useful guideline can be calculated: the break-even point for response rates. It is known that the variable cost for testing each list is £2,000; therefore, to cover this, revenue needs to be £2,000, which, with a margin of £50, means that 40 need to be converted to sale.

Remember, we assumed that response rate actually *is* conversion to sale in this case. The response percentage needed, therefore, in order to achieve break-even percentage, is:

$$\frac{40}{2\,000} \times 100 = 2\%$$

TABLE 4.5 Spreadsheet – 2

List	Sample (excl Fxd cost for test (D-B)	Variable costs	Response	Margin (£50)	Profit/Loss	
1	4 000	2,000	52 (1.3%)	2,600 (52 × 50)	600	(2,600−2,000)
2	4 000	2,000	152 (3.8%)	7,600	5,600	
3	4 000	2,000	108 (2.7%)	5,400	3,400	
4	4 000	2,000	168 (4.2%)	8,400	6,400	
5	4 000	2,000	88 (2.2%)	4,400	2,400	
6	4 000	2,000	204 (5.1%)	10,200	8,200	
7	4 000	2,000	20 (0.5%)	1,000	−1,000	
				Overall:	£25,600	
				Less (fixed cost)	£5,000	
				=	£20,600	

TABLE 4.6 ROI

List	Variable costs	Profit	ROI%
1	2,000	600	30 (600 as a % of 2,000)
2	2,000	5,600	280
3	2,000	3,400	170
4	2,000	6,400	320
5	2,000	2,200	110
6	2,000	8,200	410
7	2,000	−1,000	−50

In other words, a list achieving less than 2% response is contributing to loss and a list achieving more than 2% response is contributing to profit. Lists 2, 3, 4, 5 and 6 would, on this basis, contribute to profit. And as can be seen from the return on investment table, Lists 6, 4, 2, 3, 5 are the better performers (in this order).

For the selected lists for the roll-out, we would not mail or e-mail the full quantity from each because some on these lists have already been contacted, so the roll-out number for each selected list would be the list size less 2 000.

We can now start allocating our budget of £120,400.

The best performers would suggest the following for the first stage of list selection in Table 4.7.

We could 'work down' this list until we have spent our £120,400. This would mean that our roll-out is maximising return on our investment and would be within the allocated budget.

In this case, we could select lists 6, 4 and 2 which would leave us with a small budget balance of £900.

TABLE 4.7 First stage of list selection

List	ROI %	Quantity – 2000 Number	Costs (500 per '000) £s
6	410	15,000 – 2,000 = 13,000	6,500
4	320	80,000 – 2,000 = 78,000	39,000
2	280	150,000 – 2,000 = 148,000	74,000
3	170	180,000 – 2,000 = 178,000	89,000
5	110	50,000 – 2,000 = 48,000	24,000

This case provides a useful examination of the testing procedures that can be transferred across a number of different contexts. The next section explores further metrics that can be applied in testing.

Significance testing

We use an example to provide another practical point of reference for this type of statistical analysis. Suppose that last time your direct mailing on a full list produced a response rate of 5%. You now carry out a test of a new mailing list, randomly selecting 10 000 consumer names, and this produces a response of 5.7%. Does the new list perform significantly better than the old one? To answer this basic question, a significance test can be used to provide information on the chances of 5% still being the true response rate. That is, we test the 'population percentage' (not the 'sample' percentage of 5.7%). If the test suggests that 5% is *not* likely to be the true response rate then the response rate for the new list is said to be significantly different from 5%.

If (say) 100 different mailing tests, of the same size, were undertaken to discover the response rates, then we could expect that from such a large number of separate tests, the average of these 100 tests would be pretty close to the true figure. Owing to sampling variations, we would not be surprised to find some of these test samples producing slightly better response rates and other test samples producing slightly worse response rates. The distribution of the response rate measurements for the 100 test mailings could be described as Exhibit 4.4 with the mean being 5, if the response rate from the full mailing list (i.e. the 'true population percentage') is 5. The distribution of sample results does not, however, give any indication of how much of a spread there is of individual test mailing response rates. For this, the standard error is required. One standard error away from the mean would contain approximately 34% of all the test results. (This figure is taken from normal distribution tables – when reading the figure in the table against one 'Z', 0.3413 is identified, which means that the probability of an item in the distribution taken at random being between the mean and one standard deviation away from the mean is 0.3413.)

The standard deviation is the measure of the spread of a normal distribution, and normal distribution tables provide the size of the area under the curve between the mean and various numbers of standard deviations away from the mean. When dealing with distributions of sample (in our case, test) results, the same tables and logic apply, but the measure of spread is referred to as the standard error.

For the example given at the beginning of this section, the mean of the sampling distribution is taken to be 5, and its standard error (SE) is calculated by:

$$SE = \sqrt{\frac{\Pi(100 - \Pi)}{n}} = \sqrt{\frac{5 \times 95}{10\,000}} = 0.22$$

EXHIBIT 4.4 Sampling distribution

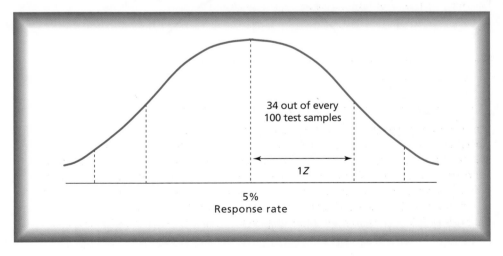

Π is the population percentage (response rate from the full mailing list, in our example) being tested, which is 5% in this case, and *n* is the size of sample taken, given in the example as 10 000. This has converted one standard error into 'response rate' percentages. Thus, if Z is 0.22 (in 'response rate' terms), it can be useful to label the horizontal axis of the sampling distribution as ± Z (from left to right), being 4.78 and 5.22 respectively. The results so far can be summarised as follows. If 5% is the true response rate from using the full mailing list, 34 out of every (similar sized) 100 tests would probably produce response rates somewhere between 5% and 5.22% and another 34/100 tests would produce response rates between 4.78% and 5%.

It is necessary to calculate how 'rare' our test result of 5.7% is, if the true response rate is 5%. To do this we need to relate it to the probabilities as described by the sampling distribution in Exhibit 4.5.

The approach is to position our 5.7% somewhere along the horizontal axis. That is, we must convert our 5.7% into standard errors and this is done by employing the following calculation.

$$Z = \frac{p - \Pi}{SE}$$

Here, *p* denotes the sample percentage as found by our test and Z is used to denote the number of standard errors that our sample percentage figure (5.7%) is away from the mean (5%) of the sampling distribution. The logic of this calculation is that it is not merely the actual difference between the two percentages (5.7 − 5) that matters – but this difference relative to the sampling distribution as described. In this case:

EXHIBIT 4.5 Sampling distribution

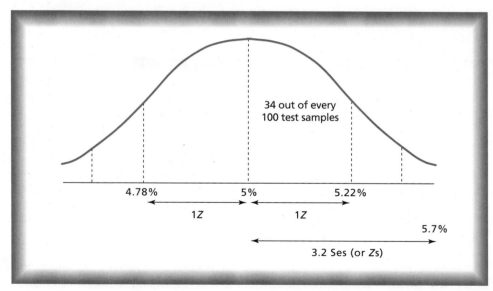

$$Z = \frac{5.7' - 5}{0.22} = 3.2$$

Therefore, 5.7% is 3.2 standard errors away from 5%, and from the normal distribution tables it can be determined that, if 5% is the true figure, the probability of a test estimating the response rate to be 5.7% or more would be about 0.0001 (i.e. when $Z = 3.2$, the area under the curve from the mean to this point = 0.4999%, and because the area to the right of the mean = 0.5, then the area to the right of $Z = 3.2$ is: $0.5 - 0.4999 = 0.0001$, or 0.01%). Thus, if the true response rate from using the full mailing lists is 5%, due to sampling variations of test mailings we could expect only *one* out of every *ten thousand* (!) similar sized test mailings to estimate it to be 5.7% or more – technically possible but somewhat rare, and we would probably conclude that the true response rate for our new list is likely to be significantly greater than 5%. Note that the conclusion is not that the true figure is 5.7% or any specific figure at all, just that it is significantly different from 5% – that is, it is statistically significant. At first sight the difference between a hypothesised response of 5% and a test response of 5.7% might not appear too great, but this example demonstrates the value of conducting statistical significance tests.

It is tempting to use the significance test as a 'decider', that is, to allow the test to make a decision, but it cannot validly do this. All the test provides is additional information on the chances of the figure tested being true, when a sample suggests something else. In the above example, the levels of chance associated with the test mailing result of 5.7% were so clear that we could make the decision without further processing. However, where such calculations produce a Z position of the test result of (say) something around $Z = 2$, what sort of conclusions should then be drawn?

To help sort out such grey areas, two levels of significance have been traditionally used. One uses the argument that if a sample result is so rare (if the true figure is the one being tested) that less than 5% of all sample results would produce a similar figure, then the result is significant, and the figure being tested would therefore be rejected. The other significance level is the 1% level and uses the same logic in the case of a sample result in the extreme 1% minority. Note that the logic here is the reciprocal of what we discussed under 95% and 99% confidence levels in the section on sample size determination.

Sometimes a sample result concerns just one end, or tail, of the sampling distribution (i.e. for one-tailed tests), and sometimes both ends of the distribution are relevant (two-tailed tests). Exhibit 4.6 shows these significance levels for both one- and two-tail tests, and their associated Z values which give the beginning of the rejection areas – that is, if the sample result Z is further away from the mean than this, the null hypothesis may be rejected. To demonstrate how this might operate, referring back to the example testing the 5% response rate, whichever significance levels were chosen, the sample result of 5.7% would fall in any of the 'rejection areas', thus providing further justification for our conclusion that the test result challenged the population figure of 5%. A relatively formal structure such as the following sometimes helps:

1 An hypothesis is set up (e.g. an assumption about the value of a population parameter). This is the null hypothesis and is the initial assumption, the

EXHIBIT 4.6   Significance levels

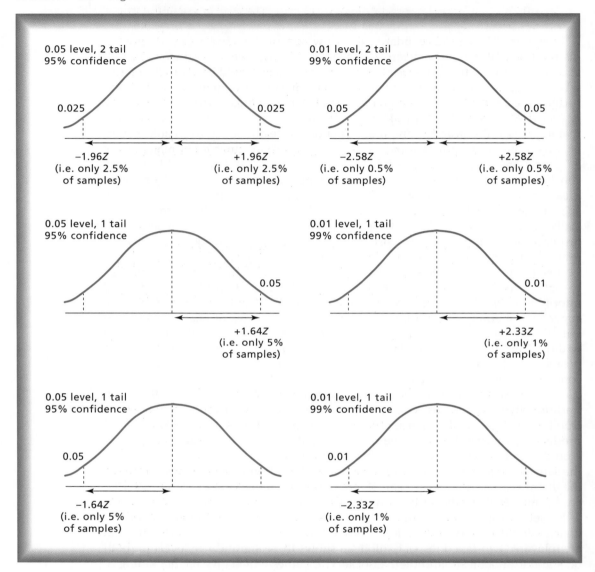

parameter that the significance test goes on to test. For the example this was 5% (i.e. NH: $\Pi = 5$).

2 An alternative hypothesis is defined. This is important since it specifies what happens if the null hypothesis is rejected. In the example, it could have been stated that AH $\Pi > 5$ (i.e. if the response rate is not likely to be 5% then it is likely to be something *more* than 5% – rather than less than 5%). This means that this particular example is concerned with only the right-hand side of the sampling distribution and is therefore termed a one-tailed test.

3 An appropriate significance level is chosen, either 5% or 1% usually. Assume a 5% level for the example and, referring to the above paragraph and to Exhibit 5.25, it can be seen that for a one-tailed test using the 1% level, the 'rejection' level begins at 2.33 standard errors away from the mean of the distribution. Thus if the sample result is calculated to be more than 2.33 'Zs' away from the population parameter being tested (which is tested by being the mean of the sampling distribution) then it could indicate that the chances are that the population figure being tested is wrong and, in this instance, is likely to be something *greater*.

4 The standard error of the sampling distribution (which has a mean equivalent to the population parameter being tested) is calculated according to:

$$SE = \sqrt{\frac{(100 - \Pi)}{n}}$$

Types of significance testing other than the one appropriate for this first example require different formulae and these are described in some of the sources listed at the end of this chapter.

5 The position of the sample result in the sampling distribution under test is found from the following calculation:

$$Z = \frac{p - \Pi}{SE}$$

This value is compared with the 'Z' value for the rejection of the null hypothesis as specified in stage 3 and if it is further away from the mean than this figure, the null hypothesis can be rejected in favour of the 'alternative' hypothesis.

In the example, we test 5% (response rate) being the mean of the sampling distribution in which our sample result is 5.7% (response rate). Because this is over 3 standard errors away from the mean, and well into the 'rejection area', which starts at 2.33 standard errors from the mean, we would indeed reject the null hypothesis and accept the alternative hypothesis, that because our test sample produced a response rate of 5.7% we could expect the use of the full list to deliver a response significantly greater than 5%.

It should be pointed out, however, that these tests are strictly only applicable to research based on some form of random sampling, because only these are in turn based on the laws of probability. Indeed, it is generally taken by purists that only simple random sampling allows such testing, but in practice most surveys use some other sampling method, and many depart from randomness and employ non-probability techniques like quota sampling. Koerner (1980) has discussed the compromises that can be made in order to conduct data tests. He suggests that once the standard error has been calculated according to the appropriate statistical test, it should be weighted by a design factor (e.g. this might be 1 for a simple random sample, and perhaps by 1.5 for a quota sample).

Comparing test and control sample results

When we want to compare response rates from two sub-samples, for example when a control group is used, against which the test sample response rate is to be compared, a variation on the statistical formula is needed.

For example, one sample from a mailing list tested the new version B of the copy and another sample from the same list used the established version A of the copy. In this case there would be two sample results, each of which is an estimate of the true response rate for each version of the copy. If a randomly selected test of 5 000 consumers from a list produced a 5% response rate to version A (the one mailed to them) and a sample of 6 000 from the same list produced a response rate of 6% to version B, then there is a significance test which helps determine whether there is likely to be a difference in response rate between the two versions of the mailing copy tested.

The starting point for this test is that the null hypothesis assumes *no* difference between the actual levels of response for the two versions. Thus the response rate (population percentage) for version A is the same as the response rate (population percentage) for version B.

Working through the five steps:

The null hypothesis is that $\Pi_1 = \Pi_2$.

If (1) is rejected the *alternative* hypothesis is that $\Pi_1 \ \Pi \neq \Pi_2$.

Here the concern is with a difference which could be either side of the mean, therefore it becomes a two-tailed test.

A significance level is selected, for example 0.05 which, for a two-tailed test, identifies the beginning of the rejection areas as 1.96 standard errors either side of the mean.

If there is *no* difference between the response rates for the two versions of copy and if a large number of (pairs of) tests were conducted then it is likely that, on average, the difference between these pairs of test results would be *nil*.

Thus where P1 and P2 refer to response rates (sample percentages) for version A and B respectively, this significance test tests the likelihood (rarity) of our pair of samples producing a difference of 1% (6%−5%) if there is no difference between the population percentages in reality.

$$SE = \sqrt{\frac{P1(100 - P1)}{n1} + \frac{P2(100 - P2)}{n2}}$$

(where $n1$ and $n2$ denote sample sizes for version A and B respectively)

$$\text{Thus } SE = \sqrt{\frac{5 \times 95}{5\,000} + \frac{6 \times 94}{6\,000}}$$

$$= .095 + .094 = 0.44$$

From this, if there is *no* actual difference between the two versions in terms of response rate, it could be expected that 34 out of every 100 pairs of test samples taken might estimate a difference of between nothing and 0.44%, as shown in Exhibit 4.7.

Our pair of test samples produces a difference of 1% (6% − 5%), so the 'Z' value of this has to be found from:

$$Z = \frac{(P1 - P2) - (\Pi_1 - \Pi_2)}{SE}$$

$$= \frac{1 - 0}{0.44} = 2.27$$

This shows that the 'Z' value is not merely the difference between P1 and P2 but the difference between *their* difference – with a difference of nil (i.e. the assumption that there is no difference between the two versions), and this is 'relative to' the spread of the distribution as described by its standard error.

Our pair of test samples produce a difference that is within the rejection area (the 'Z' value for a difference between response rates for the two versions (of 1%) is further away from the mean (i.e. a difference between the two versions of 0%) than the beginning of the rejection area (at 1.96) as defined in stage 3. A conclusion might be that this is such a rare event, if there really is a significant difference between the two versions of copy, that we can challenge the validity of our initial (null) hypothesis and accept the alternative hypothesis – in other words, it is likely that there *is* a significant difference between the two copy versions in terms of response rate.

EXHIBIT 4.7 Testing two sample percentages

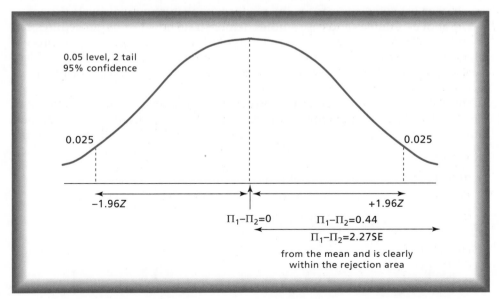

Calculating likely results for roll-out can now take place. If our test samples produced a difference of 1% (6% − 5%) and we want to operate at the 95% confidence level, the range for the difference between the two versions of copy will be :

$$\text{range } (E) = Z \times \sqrt{\frac{P1(100 - P1)}{n1} + \frac{P2(100 - P2)}{n2}}$$

$$= 1.96 \times \sqrt{\frac{5 \times 95}{5\,000} + \frac{6 \times 94}{6\,000}} = 0.86$$

This means that it is likely that on roll out, the *difference* in response rate between version A and version B will be from $1 - .86 = 0.14$ to $1 + .86 = 1.86$.

Analysis of variance (ANOVA) is another type of statistical analysis, related to the sorts of experimental test designs discussed earlier. In an experimental design, differences between conditions are studied. For instance, in some mailings from a list the creative is changed (group B), in another mailing from the list prices are lowered (group C) and in a third mailing batch from the list, nothing is changed (group A). If the three mailings are similar with regard to other factors, ANOVA may be used to test the significance of the response rate differences between the three mailings. In a more complex 2×2 design, four types of mailing may be distinguished, according to the four groups in Table 4.8. In group D, both the creative and the prices are changed. In an ANOVA analysis, the significance of the effects of creative and prices may be tested, as well as the effect of a combination of both effects (interaction effect). In order to study the interaction effect, the inclusion of group D is necessary.

There are other types of significance but space does not permit further coverage here. For example, where a factorial design of several 'cells' is used, the *chi-square* test of significance would be appropriate. The references at the end of the chapter list some sources for the reader who wants more of this!

The above examples and case studies demonstrate how testing procedures can be applied. We have presented this in terms of how the 'mechanics' of the process might operate. It is possible that in practice there would be additional and less mechanistic considerations, such as the more qualitative 'impact' assessment of each list.

The concentration on testing is, however, both a strength and a weakness of direct data-informed marketing. On the one hand, organisations can 'try out' different approaches under reasonably rigorous statistical conditions yet, on the

TABLE 4.8 A 2×2 experimental design

	Standard creative	New creative
Standard prices	Group A	Group B
Lower prices	Group C	Group D

other, such tests do not in themselves provide the 'why' of all of the outcomes. For example, Middleton and Evans (1998) found that marketing *agencies* are committed to the idea of testing as it is perceived to be fundamental to the operation of direct marketing. Their clients were also reported as being supportive of testing either because they believed in it themselves or because they took the agencies' advice and did what they suggested. A minority of agencies believed that their testing procedures negated the need for market research.

Indeed, we have already commented upon concerns over the shift towards mechanistic testing in data-driven relational marketing. For example, in a research project funded by the UK Chartered Institute of Marketing (CIM) into the effects of technology on marketing and marketers (CIM, 2001), marketers' commitment to understanding customers in the new era was explored and 'data' of the sort discussed above was often seen to be more important than qualitative understanding:

ff I've been going to these groups for 20 years . . . the number of occasions on which the director of marketing has turned up to these groups you can count on one hand . . . therefore when a marketing director gets to present to the board, does he really know as much as the sales director sitting next to him? Very likely not. **JJ** (Consultant, FMCG sector)

Mitchell (2001) recently quoted a director of one of the largest retailers in UK:

ff We've given up trying to understand our customers . . . helping us cut a lot of complexity from our business. The academic's instinct is to gather a large amount of information, formulate a theory, and apply it to a situation . . . (this) creates waste in the form of the wrong information at the wrong time, leading to the wrong decisions . . . or . . . fruitless attempts to predict or alter customer behaviour. **JJ**

The favoured approach by this company, 'sense and respond' (Haeckel, 2001), is to react quickly on the basis of customer contact via call centres, the Internet, interactive digital TV, and infomediaries. This is understandable in the current context of pressure to achieve short-term profit in order to provide shareholder value. However, it can lead to a subordination of the key components of the marketing concept itself, namely relational customer satisfaction and any underpinning customer understanding, other than what can be gleaned and inferred from, for example, tracking transactional data. It is clearly at odds with the concept of a relational paradigm, which by definition would encourage longer-term interactions.

Although Chapter 5 explores more traditional research applications within the relational context, it is worth linking the current chapter with that one, via the following case study. It shows the importance of data-driven decision making but also the contribution of more affective research to 'understanding' such relationships.

Testing vs. research

In a qualitative market research project (Evans *et al.*, 1997) into consumer attitudes towards direct marketing, some of the older women in particular declared that they received substantial quantities of direct mail on behalf of charities. They also said that this was not 'junk mail' because it was of interest to them – the matching of 'causes' with their own interests was very accurate. They were so moved by the direct mailing that they felt it important to donate – and they did just this. As far as the direct marketer is concerned, this 'response' reinforces the donors' status on the database and they will be targeted again – and probably by related charities who are likely to share lists.

But in the qualitative research, the women went on to say that they were barely able to afford to donate, but felt they 'had to' and were almost in tears over the issue. The reaction of the direct marketing industry was 'but it worked' – such reliance on mechanistic experimentation (testing) at the expense of more insightful research is submitted here as being an issue that the industry would do well to address. Although this targeting might 'work' in the short term, what problems might be being stored up for the future – not only when the 'targets' decide 'enough is enough' and refuse to donate any more and 'bin' all subsequent mailings – but if they merely spread ill will about the charities' direct marketing approach?

Summary

- It is clear that the large datasets that are now available to marketers mean that statistically rigorous tests of different approaches can be conducted and this chapter has explored some of the statistical and testing methodology involved.

- One issue, however, is that as marketing moves more and more towards direct and data-based approaches there is a real danger that more affective research will be displaced by experimentation. This in turn relies on behavioural response rather than attitudinal measures.

- Much database data, such as transactional and profiling data, provides valuable information on who is buying what, when, how and where, but it is market research that can get beneath the surface even further and discover reasons 'why' behaviour is as it is. The following chapter explores the contribution of more traditional market research.

Review questions

1 A retailer of music CDs has set up an online/e-commerce subsidiary (*BackBeat Sounds*) and is working on a promotional e-mailing campaign for a new *Kylie* CD. It wants to test two alternative lists of customers. List A is of customers who have previously purchased *Atomic Kitten* CDs but not *Madonna* CDs. List B is of customers who have previously purchased *Madonna* CDs but not *Atomic Kitten* CDs. They want to achieve reasonable levels of accuracy (95% degree of confidence). Current response rates for similar lists have recently been in the region of 6%. What sample size is needed for the result to be in a range of ± 0.2% of the actual response rate?

2 *BackBeat Sounds* decides to go for the sample identified in 1) and the test produces a response of 5%. Within what range can we be 95% confident of the actual response rate?

3 Explain the rationale behind the calculations required above.

4 How would you select a sample of 500 within a geographic area, using a) random sampling methods and b) quota sampling?

Further reading

Hughes, A. (2000) *Strategic Database Marketing*, 2nd edn, New York: McGraw-Hill.
Roberts, M.L. and Berger, P.D. (1999) *Direct Marketing Management*, 2nd edn, Englewood Cliffs, NJ: Prentice Hall.
Silver, M. (1992) *Business Statistics*, London: McGraw Hill.

References

Anon (1998) 'Consumer Consortium Sends Test Magazines', *Marketing Direct*, November, p. 1.
Chartered Institute of Marketing (2001) 'The Impact of E-Business on Marketing and Marketers', October, Cookham. Website for CIM Direct purchase: http:// www.connectedinmarketin.co.uk, tel. 44 (0) 1 628 427427
Evans, M., O'Malley, L., Patterson, M. and Mitchell, S. (1997) 'Consumer Reaction to Database-based Supermarket Loyalty Schemes', *Journal of Database Marketing*, 4(4), pp. 307–20.
Forshaw, T. (1993) 'Testing: The Direct Route to Continuous Improvement', *Direct Response*, July, pp. 28–9.
Haeckel, S. (2001) in Mitchell, A. (2001) 'Playing Cat and Mouse Games with Marketing', *Precision Marketing*, 16 March, p. 14.
Koerner, R. (1980) 'The Design Factor: An Under-Utilised Concept?', *European Research*, 8(6), pp. 266–72.
Middleton, S. and Evans, M. (1998) 'Testing and Research in Direct Mail: The Agency Perspective', *Journal of Database Marketing*, 6(2), pp. 127–44, ISSN1350–2328.
Mitchell, A. (2001) 'Playing Cat and Mouse Games with Marketing', *Precision Marketing*, 16 March, p. 14.
Purdom, N. (1996) 'Lists: The Best Way Forward', *Marketing Direct*, September, pp. 73–8.
Stone, M., Davies, D. and Bond, A. (1995) *Direct Hit: Direct Marketing With A Winning Edge*, London: Pitman, p. 240.

5 Marketing research for customer insight

Learning objectives

Having completed this chapter, students should:

- Understand marketing research techniques and applications within relational marketing.

- Comprehend the implications for relational marketing of both 'data-informed' and more 'affective' research.

- Beware of quantitative and qualitative market research approaches.

- Recognise some of the emerging ethical issues concerning information and research for relational marketing.

Signode

Signode is a company that supplies parts and repair services within the packaging industry in the USA. The company explored the trade-off between service levels and price in their mature markets. The database analysis was conducted using the company's customer profile and pricing model but was complemented via more affective research amongst the salesforce, which was, of course, in regular face-to-face contact with customers. The combined data was then cluster analysed and four segments emerged:

- **Programmed buyers**, who were smaller-volume customers who paid full price and did not need much service.
- **Relationship buyers**, who knew more about the products and services offered by the various competitors in this market and paid lower prices but needed more service than programmed buyers.

- **Transactional buyers**, who were around twice as large as relationship buyers and because the products were of great importance within their operations they needed above-average service levels. They were also very knowledgeable of pricing levels in this market and received (on average) 10% discounts from Signode. They tended to be less loyal to companies, instead favouring those that offered the best price at the time.

- **Bargain hunters**, who were very large-volume customers and benefited from the greatest price discounts and highest service levels. They switched supplier easily, often and quickly if dissatisfied.

It was recognised that the blending of data-based knowledge with more affective understanding led to the identification of very practical segmentation bases on which new account management policies improved profitability significantly.

(Source: Rangan *et al.* 1992)

Introduction

The previous chapters in Part 2 discussed the danger of relational marketing being 'data driven' rather than 'knowledge informed'. The specific issue is whether data can all too easily be used as a surrogate for real insight into customer behaviour. We have seen how data from a variety of sources can be fused and mined and we have explored how important 'testing' is to data-informed marketing. This chapter is also concerned with some of the techniques for researching markets but in ways that ensure anonymity of respondents and which can reveal more affective and psychological factors that in turn can add the insight that we suggest can sometimes be missed if relational marketing is driven too much by data.

Market research

In this context we discuss some aspects of relatively traditional market research approaches that are of particular value in relational marketing. There are, of course, many textbooks devoted to marketing research, so our coverage can only be both selective and relatively cursory. Indeed, we would anticipate that many readers will have been through a marketing research module of some description.

We view the variety of market research tools as constituting a continuum that reflects the degree of control that can be exerted over the subject of study and we introduced this in Table 4.1 in the preceding chapter.

'Marketing research involves the diagnosis of information and the selection of relevant inter-related variables about which valid and reliable information is gathered, recorded and analysed' (Zaltman and Burger 1975). This definition indicates that marketing research is both 'systematic' and 'formalised' and it introduces a sequence of research events, from diagnosing marketing information requirements through data collection to data analysis. This leads to the structuring of research programmes around a series of stages in the research process, as shown in Table 5.1. Such stages can be of great help, both in the planning of research programmes and in their control and evaluation.

As already stated, other texts are able to devote more space to these stages and indeed to coverage of methodologies and techniques, so our coverage is necessarily selective. We will, however, spend a little time on the first stage in the process suggested in Table 5.1.

It has been suggested that of all the stages in the research process, it is often this one that can be riddled with error and bias in practice. Although error and bias can occur at any stage of the process, if this first stage is not fully explored and agreed between decision maker and researcher, the entire programme can waste time and money.

Consider the difficulties created by poor definition and clarification of the marketing problem as evidenced by the following case study.

TABLE 5.1 The marketing research process

Stage 1	Defining and clarifying the marketing problem and determining what information this requires.
Stage 2	Determining cost-effective sources of information.
Stage 3	Determining techniques for collecting information
Stage 4	Data collection
Stage 5	Data processing
Stage 6	Communicating results

CASE STUDY 5.1

Poster or media research?

An advertising research programme was commissioned by a brewery to evaluate a poster advertising campaign for a new beer. Levels of awareness were evaluated and attitudes measured using a questionnaire and street interviewing and the results were gratefully received by the brand manager concerned. However, later feedback from the organisation revealed that the decision maker resided in general marketing management and while the research results were relevant and useful, they had their limitations. The problem materialised as poor communication: while the brand manager briefed the researchers in line with his perception of the problem, the marketing manager wanted to use the information to decide whether to launch a new lager using, predominately, a poster campaign. The point is that the initial research problem was broader than evaluation of one campaign.

Other instances of difficulties caused by faults in problem analysis and the briefing of researchers are provided by England (1980) and the dangers are generalised by Millward (1987):

> The utility of any research project is critically dependent upon the quality of the original brief ... too often research is neither communicated effectively to the decision takers nor relevant to their decisions ... make sure that the real decision makers attend key presentations ... the best briefing session is a two-way discussion which both crystallises and challenges current management thinking.

The problem definition stage should lead naturally to the listing of appropriate informational requirements (the 'data list') in the context of the decision areas concerned. To address these 'gaps' of information, secondary and/or primary data sources can be used and it is the determination of cost-effective sources of information that is the next stage in the process. The former involve information that already exists, such as customer lists, internal company records or previous reports, government statistics, newspaper and journal articles and commercial market research agency reports. Table 5.2 lists some examples of the wealth of information that exists and serves to demonstrate that it is always worth exploring the possibilities of using secondary sources as a *first* resort before commissioning what would usually be a more expensive and time-consuming programme of collecting new information using primary research methods.

Because of the heavy use of secondary sources, there is a need to adopt a critical perspective in using them. The researcher should evaluate such sources for impartiality in order to be reasonably sure that there is no bias in the information resulting from the source provider or compiler attempting to make a case for or against something. The researcher should ensure that sources are *valid*. That is, he or she should check that the information provides the researcher with what he or she wants to know. The researcher should also clarify the *reliability* of sources. In other words, the information should be representative of the group it purports to describe (e.g. a sample of twelve consumers is unlikely to reflect all consumers in a national population). Finally, the researcher should make sure that sources provide information with *internal homogeneity* (e.g. consistency within a set of figures).

TABLE 5.2 Secondary data sources

KOMPASS	Names & addresses of companies (possible competitors) by country & by product category.
Kelly's Guide	Addresses & description of main activities of industrial, commercial & professional UK organisations. Listings are alphabetical according to trade description & company name.
Key British Enterprises	Register of 25,000 top UK companies providing company name, address & basic data (e.g. sales, number of employees & Standard Industrial Code – SIC).
UK Trade Names	Trade names & parent company.
BRAD (British Rate and Data)	Costs of advertising in press, radio, poster, cinema, TV & all other mass media.
The Retail Directory	Details of Retail Trade Associations & lists retail companies according to type (co-op, multiple, department store etc.) & according to geography (e.g. lists the retail outlets within many towns).
MEAL (Media Expenditure Analysis)	Information on competitors' advertising spend on specific brands per month. Also gives ad agency concerned.
Business Monitor	Statistics for different products (e.g. number of manufacturers, industry sales & import levels).
Henley Centre and The Future Foundation	Projected future social attitudes, lifestyles, income and expenditure. Reactions to direct marketing.
Target Group Index (TGI)	34-volume annual profile of most product-markets in terms of who buys what. The research uses a geodemographically determined sample design and analysis is demographic, geodemographic and now includes hundreds of lifestyle questions (see Chapter 6).
Regional Trends	Plots population size & structure trends through the regions, together with regional income & expenditure.
Electoral Register	Useful to help define catchment areas of retail outlets & to calculate number of potential customers. Also used to draw samples for market research. Links can be made with postcodes to identify potential targets by name and address. Now there are two registers: one for citizens who have not opted out of commercial use of their name and address and the other for those who have.
National Readership Survey	Profile of readers of newspapers & magazines. Useful for direct response & other advertising media selection when matched with profile of target market.
Who Owns Whom	Firms & their parent organisation.
Trade Associations	Usually have information on numbers of competitors & size of market.
Family Expenditure Survey	Average weekly expenditure on many products & services according to different regions, size of household, age of head of household & household income levels. Useful for estimating market size & potential sales levels.
Market Intelligence (MINTEL)	Monthly profiles of different markets (both customers and competitors).
Local Chambers of Trade	Have statistics on companies in their trading area & information on trading conditions.
Retail Business	Monthly profiles of different retailing markets (both customers and competitors).
Internal database	It mustn't be forgotten that one's own database can provide a wealth of data for analysis purposes – for profiling and targeting customers and potential customers and for evaluating the effectiveness of alternative relational marketing campaigns via the tracking of split run tests.
Online databases	Including some market and company information. Others are more specialised and provide 'key word' search of many newspapers and journals for information and articles on the topic concerned. Internet sources continue to proliferate and offer databases, even mailing lists, as well as market and marketing information in a variety of forms.

So great is the amount and variety of secondary sources that quite large books are published which do nothing other than list possible sources of information related to various topics and areas of concern. The government's Statistical Service publishes an annual booklet entitled *Government Statistics: A Brief Guide to Sources* together with another guide, *Profit from Figures*, which illustrates some of the main uses of government statistics.

The sort of internal data from customer transactions which is stored and analysed via the organisation's database capability (and additionally profiled by external data), as discussed in Chapters 2 and 3, is also a major component of secondary data but at this point we merely refer the reader back to those chapters for coverage of these issues.

Many of these are free (either because they are to be found in most public libraries or because they are available from government departments). Even some of the expensive commercial reports can be found in some libraries.

Primary sources, on the other hand, involve collecting new information, first hand, for the particular research programme. A distinction worth making within primary data collection methods is between *ad hoc* and *continuous* research. When the *same* respondents are observed or interviewed repeatedly over a period, then this is referred to as continuous research as opposed to an *ad hoc* study, which would only collect data on one occasion from the same respondents. Repeated surveys, therefore, even if they use the same questionnaire and the same sample design, would only be continuous if exactly the same respondents were interviewed each time.

The *retail audit* is an example of continuous research. A sample of retail outlets allows sales patterns to be analysed and sold. The main benefit is to discover customer activity with respect to *competitor* stores and brands, on a regular, continuous basis. Sales of specific brands are recorded; often this used to be by means of physical stock checks by observers at regular intervals. The replacement of manual stock and shelf counts by laser scanning is now commonplace.

The other example of continuous research is the *consumer panel* (not to be confused with a group discussion). Here, respondents – often in the form of 'households' – agree to report on their buying behaviour or media habits over a period of time. The original method was for respondents to complete a type of diary every week and to post this to the research agency concerned. For example, in a panel for media studies, the radio stations listened to would be noted on a pre-printed chart for each day of the week, and a grocery panel would require the brands, pack sizes, prices paid and stores used to be recorded, for the product categories being studied. The Royal Mail operate a panel (the *Mailmonitor*) with the research agency RSGB, to study the receipt of different types of mail, from a variety of sources and in a variety of source categories, including of course, from direct marketers: 'the panel consists of a clustered, stratified sample of some 1 350 households made up of around 2 700 individuals recruited on a nationally representative basis according to gender, age, social class, size of household and TV region. In each of these households, everyone over the age of 16 completes a daily diary. The data is collected weekly but analysed on a 4 weekly basis' (Francis 1995). One of the advantages of a panel such as this is that it facilitates the running of *ad hoc* surveys with the panel respondents. There are significant economies of scale since the infrastructure is already in place with respect to sampling, mailing and data analysis. The research into 'gender effects in direct mail', discussed in the next chapter, employed the Mailmonitor panel to test the main hypotheses, which emerged from group discussion research.

Increasingly, however, many panels do not involve any form of interviewing. Some, for example, use a special audit bin, in which the packs of products are placed for a researcher to monitor, or, as is discussed below, mailshots are collected. Measuring TV viewing is now conducted by means of a set meter (e.g. for exposure to DRTV commercials) and in this form can be categorised as a form of observation research.

Households are commonly selected on the basis of random sampling (using electoral registers and/or geodemographic lists and multi-stage sampling of the type discussed shortly) rather than quota sampling. The major problem with panels is the high mortality rate of panel members. That is, the withdrawal rate due to boredom (and indeed because of members moving home and so on) is high – perhaps up to 40% after the first interview. Clearly, the aim is that replacements should be as representative as possible. However, the problem of recruiting replacements, together with the need to offer members some form of inducement or payment provides a constant danger of panel composition being unrepresentative. For example, once recruited, new members sometimes change their behaviour, so it might be appropriate to exclude the results from these households for some time until their behaviour reverts to normal.

The basic working of the panel system involves operators compiling reports (e.g. consumer profiles, matching behaviour with names and addresses and other aspects of their buying behaviour, such as stores used, brands preferred, times of purchase and so on) and selling these to their clients. These firms can thus monitor their competitors' marketing activity, as well as their own, with the additional advantage that a time series of information is built up, allowing the identification of trends over time. This is important because marketers would get a biased reading of their customers' loyalty if they relied exclusively on their own transactional data – repeat purchase rates for *our* store or brand might be encouragingly high – but panel data might reveal even greater repeat patronage of competitors' brands or stores. Because one of the characteristics of relational marketing is that marketing activity is less obvious to competitors (mailings and telephone contacts are less observable than are media advertising campaigns), the analysis of panel data can reveal competitor activity. Two panels that do just this are DART, by ThomsonIntermedia, and the MMS/Nielsen Panel (Exhibit 5.1). These ask panel members to send their direct mailing to the agency which will profile the sorts of recipients of mailings across product markets and brands and provide useful competitive data concerning the nature of the mailings themselves and their targeting profiles.

T-Groups

This is another version of the data fusion concept and some marketers are linking their databases with market research data.

EXHIBIT 5.1 MMS panel

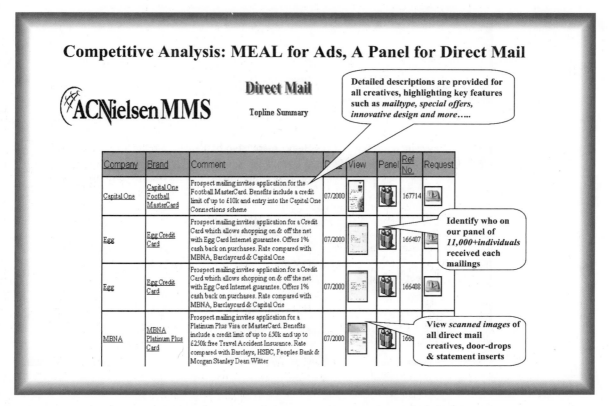

As Ward says: 'imagine a cube which represents everything you need to know about the UK's 23 million homes ... databases collect from a strip across the top of the cube, while market research samples from a thin strip to its depth. Where they cross is the T-Group ... if you can identify and understand that group you can fill in the rest of the cube' (Ward 1997).

Overall, then, relational marketers are linking panel data with other databases to provide additional richness to their data. *First T*, linked with DunnHumby, provides a service for clients. The company 'matches' transactional data with TGI and other data such as lifestyle survey data (Goldsmith 1999). The logic is to explore in some depth the nature of those specific named individuals who are both on the company's transactional database and on the TGI database. In this way, there is 'data matching' between the two databases. Profiles are then transferred across other customer groups, based on similar characteristics, and the resulting segments are made available to clients. Because the TGI is a 'traditional and anonymised' survey, only segment-level data is released, not by name and address, so the Market Research Society's Code of Conduct is not breached.

Exhibit 5.2 summarises how such data matching might 'drill down' to reveal not only the nature of customers' transactions with the company but also how these customers have responded to the hundreds of product and service

EXHIBIT 5.2   First T for a (hypothetical) grocery retailer

Our high-value customers 31%	Our medium-value customers 59%	Our low-value customers 10%
Ages: 18–35 Heavy viewers of ITV Heavy cinema going Grocery shopping at X	Ages: 36–54 Low ITV viewing Heavy readership of the *Financial Times* Grocery shopping at Y	Ages: over 55 Heavy viewers of satellite TV and radio listening Grocery shopping at Z
18–30 type holidays Ford and Vauxhall cars Heavy use of credit cards Enjoy eating out	Quiet foreign holidays BMW and Mercedes cars Pay off credit immediately, on credit cards Enjoy gardening	Frequent short breaks in UK VW and Renault cars Savings and pension-related spending Interests in photography and walking

questions and indeed to the 250+ lifestyle statements in the TGI survey. This also provides information on which other companies the individual buys from.

Not everything variable that is 'matched' for each individual will hold meaning for the client, but many will and these can aid in more effective and relational targeting.

It has also been found that during lifestyle and other surveys some respondents are economical with the truth with regard to buying patterns, but the panel, being a record of actual buying, can be used to weight some of these responses.

In this way, also, consumer panels can be linked with geodemographic or lifestyle databases. The 'T' means that 'horizontally' database data provides tremendous breadth of data over millions of consumers but the 'vertical', from market research (e.g. panels), provides greater depth of information over a period of time (because panels are 'continuous' data sources) (Miller, 1997). Exhibit 5.3 summarises the characteristics of the T-Group.

It was from such research that the claimed levels of purchasing in lifestyle surveys have sometimes been found to be extremely over- or under-represented in actual buying behaviour. One version of linking panel data with lifestyle database is the SMARTbase system developed by Taylor Nelson/Claritas, the former running a number of different consumer panels and the latter, lifestyle surveys (Walker 1996).

EXHIBIT 5.3 T-Groups

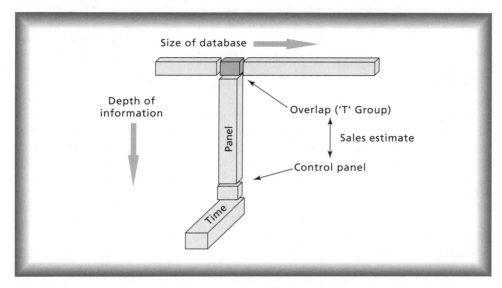

(Source: Cowling 1996)

Today, panels are generally conducted with even more sophisticated technology. The typical approach is for panel households to be equipped with TV *set meters* which identify which programmes and channels have been watched. These link the TV with a phone line and the research agency is able to download the data unobtrusively during the night. The problem of whether people are actually watching the television when it is switched on has also been addressed, though only partially. *People meters* (Exhibit 5.4) allow panel members to press a coded button whenever they enter and leave the room, one of which is

EXHIBIT 5.4 Meters and bar code readers

dedicated to each household member (even visitors can be coded). One of the authors was a panel member and although it is far from scientific to base conclusions on a sample of one – indeed oneself! – the reader will no doubt be thinking about the likelihood of every panel member *always* indicating when they enter and leave the room. This potential flaw in the methodology has also been cited by Ritson (2003).

This form of research is 'observation' because respondents' behaviour is monitored with no questions being asked. In another piece of observation research, this form of observation was itself observed! Ritson (2003) describes an ethnographic research project (see our later coverage of qualitative research) that involved observing household members during commercial breaks. This research revealed disquieting news for conventional mass media advertisers. Households in the project tended not to watch the advertisements very much even if they had been engrossed in the programmes around the commercial breaks. This is further reinforcement of the 'demand' for a new and more targeted relational approach as discussed in our coverage of technological targeting. As the number of people in the room increases, Ritson (2003) suggests there is less notice taken of TV advertisements even if the people meters imply otherwise. The research did, however, suggest that advertisements were watched more, later in the evening, especially leading up to midnight. So there could be encouragement for TV advertising to shift to these later time slots which can be cheaper and reach fewer people, but the ones they do reach are more receptive.

Another piece of equipment often provided to panel members is a hand-held *bar code reader* (Exhibit 5.4) and households in relevant panels are asked to scan all their groceries, key in prices of every item, scan a bar code on a card to indicate from which store it was purchased and whether there was a special offer involved. They may also be asked to scan bar codes which indicate the newspapers and magazines that were read that day and to which radio stations the household had listened. Again, the reader might wonder whether those willing and able to perform all these tasks daily are really representative of the population!

The panel in which one of the authors was a participant provides a good example of the uses of this technique. The ITV region of concern was HTV which is a 'split' region, there being HTV Wales and HTV West. The panel was set up in South Wales where many households tune in to one or the other transmitter. The panel was funded in association with retailers and split-run experiments were possible, with different versions of the same DRTV advertisement being broadcast via the different transmitters. The results could be tracked through analysis of viewing, response to the DRTV commercial and subsequent purchase via the scanned shopping baskets. The author may not have been an ideal panellist due to lack of dedication to the scanning tasks, but the household concerned was able to receive both HTV Wales and West and occasional 'channel hopping' did indeed reveal different versions of some commercials being transmitted at the same time!

This example provides another relevant dimension to our discussion in the previous chapter on experimentation (testing) because it demonstrates a practical way of broadcasting alternative DRTV commercials to different, but matched, audiences. Effectivess can be monitored via 'shopping baskets' as measured by the panel members' bar code scanning of their purchases. All in all, this review of the consumer panel has introduced all three forms of primary data collection method: observation, interview and experimentation.

We provide a discussion of observation techniques, because these are increasingly using technology for data collection, and several interviewing approaches that build on our earlier arguments about the need for greater insight.

Observation

As in human relationships, there are voyeurs in relational marketing. In a formalised research programme, observation may be used in an unstructured form to record aspects such as general purchasing behaviour, as opposed to the more structured observation of such factors as the gender of purchasers of a specific brand of toothpaste. Indeed, a fairly unstructured observational approach may serve as exploratory research in attempting to explore and clarify the focus that is needed in conclusive research. Marketers will record the behaviour of customers via loyalty cards – which products they buy, in what quantities, when and through what payment method. In more specific terms, such as a direct marketing test, response rates to different mailing creative will be monitored (observed).

It is usually more realistic to observe in actual or real conditions, such as recording the number of people who respond to a mailing. Sometimes this is not possible, for instance when evaluating new direct mail creative – reactions are required before roll-out and the marketer might use an eye camera with a sample of respondents to check which colour combinations for the direct response mechanism attract most attention. This research would be an example of the contrived category because respondents would not be viewing the mock advertisements in a real environment but more typically in a research room.

Perhaps the greatest potential problem of observation is that of modified behaviour – people who know they are being watched may not act as they otherwise would. For example, for the continuous studies to record respondents' television viewing habits and record the grocery products they purchase, it has been found that some respondents watch different programmes, or buy different products, during the first few weeks of such recording, until reverting to their more normal habits. Indeed, in Ritson's (2003) study to investigate what people do during the commercial breaks, the first week's data was ignored.

Various mechanical and electronic devices offer alternatives to a human observer watching an event. The marketer can use checkout EPOS scanning linked with loyalty cards to record customer purchase behaviour. This is observation research, because no questions are asked of the customer.

We have already considered the use of set meters to observe television viewing habits and other examples include the digital recording on the Internet of which websites are visited and by whom. Mechanical observation techniques may use devices like the psychogalvanometer, or lie detector, one version of which records changes in perspiration rates as a result of emotional reaction to stimuli such as test advertisements. Similarly, the tachistoscope allows an object, such an advertisement or a product package, to be illuminated for a fraction of a second to test it for initial impact, legibility, recognition, and so on. The marketer can use such techniques to pre-test alternative colour combinations or positions for their brand name, response mechanism, copy headline and so on. Another machine being used to great effect by the marketer is the eye camera – as mentioned earlier. Direct mail can be checked for how the reader's eye moves over the copy (RSCR 1997). This can also check for how different colour combinations might lead the eye to desired points on the mailshot or direct response press advertisement, or screen print of websites or pack designs and so on.

The advantage of observation is objectivity because what actually happens is recorded, compared with the subjectivity of questioning approaches, which, as will be shown shortly, by the very nature of question wording and interviewing can introduce some bias. However, as discussed above, such objectivity is lost if subjects are aware of the observation and modify their behaviour. In practice, the researcher may be unable even to approach the ideal of effective data collection through observation. The fact that the researcher does not have to gain respondent cooperation poses an ethical problem, but marketers generally feel that there are sufficient safeguards to consumer privacy in this regard.

Consider the case of the 'cookie'. This allows the tracking of how Internet 'surfers' move around the Internet and records their details. Many e-mailing lists are compiled in this way and are sold, often without the individual being aware of either the form of data collection or their use to which it is put by companies. It might lead to relevant and timely communication from organisations or it might be regarded as irrelevant 'spam'. Is this ethical or is it a legitimate way for relational marketers to get closer to their customers?

What cannot be condoned is clearly unethical espionage. But sometimes this is disguised by the euphemism 'competitor intelligence'. Equipment can be located in mobile vans that are parked outside competitors' buildings and record what is being displayed on VDU screens inside – plans for new products, marketing creative, databases and so on. Clearly we do not legitimise this as an example of observation in market research but it does raise an interesting point about where to draw the line between market intelligence and industrial espionage – and it is likely that this issue will become more pronounced as more sophisticated technology becomes available. The Market Research Society's Code of Conduct explicitly states that 'any form of espionage' shall not be associated with marketing research.

From the above, we can see that to consider that market research involves little more than questionnaires and clipboards is a misconception. Much useful information can be gleaned from a much wider range of research techniques. But the interview method is, of course, included in market research's repertoire and it is to this that we now turn.

Interview survey methods

There are, in fact, various types of interview used in research surveys, and typically a distinction is made between personal, telephone and postal interviews. Further distinctions can be made between structured and unstructured interviews, and the personal interview can be of a depth or group variety. Indeed, new technology provides another kind of interviewing, where the computer provides a vehicle for asking questions and collecting responses, in some cases using the interactive facilities of telephone-linked television sets (e.g. Sky Digital services). Other texts cover the pros and cons of different contact approaches so we will not dwell on these here. (See Moutinho and Evans 1996; Malhotra and Birks 2000.)

However, we will briefly explore a few issues here because they are relevant to an argument we are about to build up. Whatever form of contact traditional market research employs, it is based on anonymised responses. That is, respondents' replies are collected and analysed 'in confidence'; it is the nature of their replies that is important, usually cross-referenced with the profile characteristics of respondents but not their actual names and addresses.

The distinction here is between traditional and contemporary lifestyle research (Chapter 6), which raises the issue of 'data under the guise of research' (dugging).

It is a time of uncertainty with respect to the collection of consumer data, as Castle (2002) explains: 'there is an element of consumer boredom ... they've seen them (lifestyle surveys) before, done them before and don't feel they need to do another'. One solution appears to be to link the lifestyle survey with a specific brand in order to rejuvenate interest (May 2002). Examples include lifestyle survey operators linking with BA and Thomas Cook where there is obvious synergy.

However, we extend this theme here because the trend towards 'data-informed' organisation-customer interaction is, by definition, heavily focused on 'data'. This provides a wealth of detail of who buys what, when and how, but the quantitative approach is less able to explore the 'why' of customer behaviour. The plea for greater linkage is also made by Cooper and Goulds (2001), Leventhal (1998), Liddicoat (1998), Dwek (1998) and Mouncey (1998).

In this context we now turn to a brief exploration of how qualitative research can contribute to the more affective insight that can be needed to balance the data-informed approach.

Group discussions

A useful alternative that is better able to explore 'why' is the group discussion (or focus group) which is generally unstructured and qualitative. With this method several respondents (possibly between six and ten in number) are brought together and the interviewer guides the discussion through relevant topics, leaving most of the talking to members of the group. This method is widely used to pre-test advertisements. While the costs per respondent may be high with group discussion work as a result of the degree of skill required by the interviewer and the time that a group discussion takes, group discussions may still prove cost effective relative to large-scale sample surveys. The cost of one group discussion can exceed £2,000, which would include screening participants for relevant characteristics, devising the interview schedule, paying group participants, organising an appropriate venue, recording and transcribing events and analysing results. Since groups revolve around the sociology of group dynamics, it is not surprising that the interviewer must possess the skills necessary in dealing with issues such as the different roles respondents adopt, as described by de Almeida (1980) (Table 5.3).

There are a number of commonly cited criticisms of group discussions which must be acknowledged. The method is seen to lend itself to providing evidence to support preconceptions and relies heavily on the moderator's interpretation.

TABLE 5.3   The personas that group discussion participants can adopt

The competing moderator	The compiler
The rationaliser	The conscience
The choir	The rebel
The super ego	The pseudo-specialist

CASE STUDY 5.2

Using group discussions to investigate consumer reaction to supermarket loyalty schemes

The authors undertook this study in the mid-1990s. The choice of a qualitative methodology was predicated on a desire to explore consumers' reactions to loyalty schemes with minimal prompting from the researcher. Six discussion groups were conducted within an exploratory and relatively unstructured framework that was group orientated rather than moderator influenced. A highly structured discussion guide was not used since the purpose of the group was to 'experience the experience of respondents' (Calder 1977). The use of a flexible guide promoted the maintenance of a good rapport with respondents, facilitated interaction between group members, and provided the opportunity to improvise, 'to

pursue unexpected but potentially valuable lines of questioning' (Basch 1987). In terms of analysis, emphasis was placed on extensive verbatim quotes from group members, as the objective was to communicate respondents' perspectives in their own words (Calder 1977).

By way of introduction, the groups were given a brief scenario dealing with the introduction of a hypothetical supermarket 'loyalty scheme' as a way of initiating discussion. The subsequent agenda was determined largely by respondents who were encouraged to explore their experiences of the rewards, satisfactions, dissatisfactions and frustrations of loyalty schemes within a wider context of direct and database marketing. Respondents were recruited by professional recruiters on the basis that they had received some direct marketing communication in the last three months. The groups (eight respondents per group) were split as follows:

The scenario presented was: 'Your local supermarket launches a "loyalty scheme which will allow you to accumulate points based on how much you spend. These points will then be redeemable in terms of money off future purchases. In order for you to participate in this scheme you are required to fill out an application form regarding your personal details.'

To demonstrate the additional richness to emerge from 'groups', this particular project found that nearly all of the group participants or their partners were members of a retail loyalty scheme but many participants volunteered comments like:

- 'If you shop in that store anyway – it's a good idea.'
- 'It's a bit bloody cheeky I think really, they can obviously bring the prices down because they can operate the scheme, so just bring the bloody prices down.'
- 'People shop because of convenience.'

So alongside general participation, there are concerns about the low level of discount and that such schemes don't result in much switching behaviour. A more structured survey approach to these issues would probably lack this richness of comment.

Motivation research

We make no apology for including these more specialised approaches in a book on relational marketing because we believe that they provide something of an antidote to the concentration on testing. It is these more qualitative techniques that can provide the marketer with explanations as to *why* a certain approach works or doesn't work. We have already discussed group discussions and so now turn to projective techniques.

Projective techniques

If people are relieved of direct responsibility for their expressions, they will tend to answer more freely and truthfully. Projective tests are designed to achieve this end. These are called projective tests because respondents are required to project themselves into someone else's place or into some ambiguous situation. Consider the following examples of projective tests:

- **Third-person tests**: The respondent is encouraged to reply through some third party. The rationale is that there are both 'good' and 'real' reasons for behaviour. 'Good' reasons are socially acceptable (e.g. to buy environmentally friendly products). 'Real' reasons are sometimes not socially accepted. While 'good' reasons will probably be given in response to a direct questioning approach, such as 'Why did you buy this?', these answers may be only partially true. There may be a 'real' reason for behaviour that either the respondent is unwilling to admit or unable to recognise. An indirect question, for example 'What sort of people buy this?' or 'Why do people buy these?', might be sufficient to reveal 'real' reasons for behaviour.

- **Word association test**: This type of test, also known as free association, involves firing a series of words at respondents who must state immediately which other words come into their minds. Word association tests can be used to determine consumer attitudes towards products, stores, advertising themes, product features and brand names. The response 'junk mail' to 'direct mail from Evans Direct' but not to 'Patterson Direct' would suggest a lower level of accurate and relevant targeting by Evans Direct.

- **Psychodrama**: Here, the respondent is asked to play a role and, to do so, he or she is given a complete description of the circumstances. For instance, the role-playing of respondents to depict two alternative pain killers with other respondents playing the role of the pain. How 'the pain killer' tackles 'the pain' might lead to the copy strategy in direct response and other advertising campaigns (Cooper and Tower 1992).

- **Cartoon test**: The cartoon test is a variation of the TAT method and is commonly referred to as a 'balloon test'. Informants are presented with a rough sketch showing two people talking. One of them has just said something represented by words written into a 'speech balloon' as in a comic strip. The other person's balloon is empty and the informant is asked what he or she is replying (Exhibit 5.5).

- **Means-end chain analysis and laddering:** A useful technique is to repeatedly ask the respondent (words to the effect of) 'what does that mean to you?' For example, it is typical to start with product or service *attributes* such as those shown in Exhibit 5.6 and to encourage the respondent to work back through a series of '*consequences*' towards their own *motives and values*.

EXHIBIT 5.5   Cartoon test

EXHIBIT 5.6 Laddering

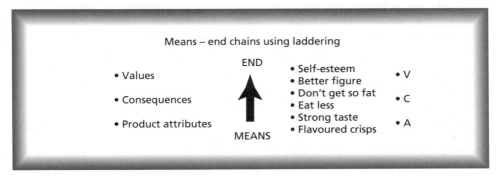

Means – end chains using laddering

- Values
- Consequences
- Product attributes

END ↑ **MEANS**

- Self-esteem • V
- Better figure
- Don't get so fat • C
- Eat less
- Strong taste • A
- Flavoured crisps

Issues and problems involved in motivation research

It should be noted that motivation research is not without its own special problems and issues. A major problem is the fact that all the above-mentioned techniques require the use of highly skilled interviewers and analysts trained in psychology. This, of course, is a problem which can be overcome, albeit at a cost. Potentially more serious issues and problems relate to the extent to which these techniques are scientific and ethical. With regard to scientific status, the controversy continues. Critics argue that the techniques are shaky to say the least, with little comparability between various research studies. On the other hand, confirmed advocates of motivation research suggest that the techniques are powerful marketing tools. With regard to ethical status, critics have long argued that the use of such techniques is tantamount to an invasion of the privacy of the consumer's mind and lays the customer open to manipulation. No doubt the debate will continue, although it must be said that in recent years the use of these techniques in consumer research has probably declined somewhat. The marketer would perhaps be best advised to keep an open mind, picking and choosing from the techniques available, as and where appropriate. Indeed it is increasingly being recognised that there is a need for great variety in the range of techniques from which to draw: a 'bricolage' (Barker *et al.* 2001)

We feel this point needs reinforcing because despite our earlier exploration of linkages between 'data and research' there is also evidence of relational marketers becoming narrower in their use of information and turning away from research in favour of being more data-driven (Mitchell 2001).

Attitude measures

So, with the plea for 'affective' understanding in mind, we review some techniques for measuring consumer attitudes. Marketers should clearly be interested in discovering consumer attitudes towards their and their competitors' offerings. Attitude measurements require special consideration because it is far too easy and superficial to ask a respondent questions like: 'What is your attitude towards Smith Direct?' only to receive a reply along the lines of 'I like it', or 'It's all right'. While such feelings may be important, it would be of greater use to uncover the reasons for such feelings and the type of actions in which they are likely to result. This perspective views an attitude as more than a global evaluation, and considers its structure to be composed of the:

- **cognitive component**, which includes what is known, the beliefs about the topic concerned, even if part of this is a misperception;
- **affective component**, which is the feelings and evaluations about these beliefs resulting from what is known about the topic;
- **conative component**, which includes the behavioural intentions resulting from the cognitive and affective components.

If intentions are based on specific elements of knowledge (beliefs) and evaluations, these beliefs and evaluations need to be discovered if the results are to be meaningfully used. Furthermore, such attributes are perceived by respondents with varying degrees of strength, so that the concept of degree in measuring attitudes is unavoidable. While some form of scale is required, the straightforward like/dislike continuum would be of only limited value. A more useful approach is to compile a series of scales, each measuring a different attribute of the same attitude. If a department store wishes to identify any scope for improvement on the one hand and perceived strengths to accentuate on the other, there are a variety of attitude scaling methods that can be employed and these are outlined below.

Semantic differential

The semantic differential incorporates a set of 5- or 7-point bipolar scales (Exhibit 5.7). The scales are characterised by opposites such as good/bad, active/passive, hot/cold, rough/smooth and strong/weak. One advantage of the semantic differential is that it provides a convenient way of comparing attitudes to different elements (e.g. direct mail, telemarketing, leaflets, inserts, direct response television), on the same scales and on the same pictorial representation.

Likert scales

Respondents may be presented with a series of statements about the topic concerned, and asked to indicate their degree of agreement with each, according to a 5-point scale ranging from 'strongly agree' to 'strongly disagree'. It is important, though difficult in practice, for the range of statements offered to cover the range of cognitive, affective and conative aspects that the topic involves. Exhibit 5.8 shows a version of the Likert scaling technique, where a mixture of positive and negative statements allows respondents' consistency to be checked.

EXHIBIT 5.7 Semantic differential

For the direct mail you receive, in general do you think it is:

Interesting	1	2	3	4	5	Uninteresting
Informative	1	2	3	4	5	Uninformative
Intrusive	1	2	3	4	5	Not Intrusive
Entertaining	1	2	3	4	5	Not Entertaining
Damaging to the environment	1	2	3	4	5	Not Damaging to the Environment
Relevant to you	1	2	3	4	5	Not Relevant to You

EXHIBIT 5.8 Likert scales

Please indicate your level of agreement or disagreement with the following statements:

	Strongly agree				Strongly disagree
I like having product or service information communicated to me by organisations	1	2	3	4	5
I like to decide for myself when and where to look for product or service information	1	2	3	4	5
The more that organisations know about me, the better they can meet my needs	1	2	3	4	5
I really don't mind about marketers having my personal details	1	2	3	4	5
There is a need for strong laws to control the sharing of personal information	1	2	3	4	5
For the direct mail I receive, marketers have generally got my details correct	1	2	3	4	5
I like to deal with organisations over the phone	1	2	3	4	5
I like to deal with organisations through the post	1	2	3	4	5

Both the semantic differential and the Likert scale can be used quantitatively by assigning values to each scaling position, and average scores for all respondents' replies can be calculated, either for each scale, or in an overall summation.

Fishbein provided another useful approach by suggesting that respondents might be able to score brands or products along each semantic differential scale (belief) but that they might not regard all bi-polars with equal importance or favourableness. So the idea is to elicit not only a rating along each belief scale, but also a favourableness rating of each scale. Multiplying the two for each scale and aggregating the scores provides a more meaningful analysis. The attitude is the summation of the weighted belief scores.

Attitude towards object model

An example of the use of the Attitude Towards Object Model comes from the authors' own experience (Patterson *et al.* 1999) through a research project into consumer attitudes towards direct marketing. Exhibit 5.9 summarises the identified contributors to 'attitude' and the relationship with 'intention'. Our coverage of statistical analysis techniques in Chapter 3 reviews the results we obtained from this model.

Internet survey research

A relatively recent phenomenon is the use of the Internet for conducting surveys. Indeed, both quantitative and qualitative research is being conducted through this medium. The obvious limitations concern self-selected samples, but it is clear that very widely dispersed populations can be researched.

As would be expected of a new and emerging technique there is a need to be cautious in implementing the approach (Scholl *et al.* 2002; Nancarrow *et al.* 2001; Jeavons 1999; Furrer and Sudharshan 2001).

For example, in research into the use of online communities, an online focus group was conducted (Evans *et al.* 2001). Gaiser (1997) suggested that online focus groups present opportunities for methodological innovation 'only limited by our own imagination'.

Certainly, online focus groups provide opportunities for synchronous and asynchronous interaction, with immediate availability in digital format of the discussion results for analysis. A typical approach is to place a welcome message on the Internet and explain what you are hoping to achieve.

A possible concern, however, is that 'the lack of non-verbal communication impedes ... understanding of the respondent's ideas, making the analysis and interpretation a difficult task' (Scholl *et al.* 2002). It is interesting that experienced qualitative researchers were able to convert online reactions quite well and draw valid conclusions.

EXHIBIT 5.9 Fishbein and Ajzen Multi-Attribute Model: used for investigating consumer attitudes towards direct mail

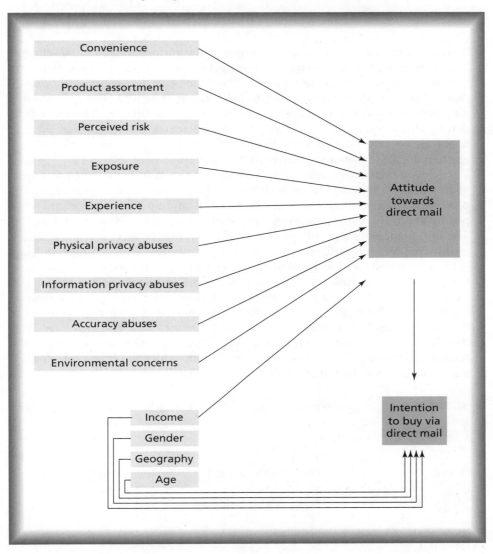

IN THEORY

It is appropriate to broaden our discussion of the various forms of marketing information, including research and testing, by drawing attention to different research philosophies. These represent 'the basic belief system or worldview that guides the investigator' (Guba and Lincoln 1994:105). There is some disagreement over the issues involved here, as this In Theory box demonstrates. It is useful to start with the polarised perception that often abounds, concerning two key 'schools of thought' that embrace differing epistemological positions: positivism and interpretivism (Silverman 1993). Data-driven relational marketing is heavily concerned with positivist testing of hypotheses, such as the ones discussed in the previous chapter (List A produces a higher response rate than List B and so on). The origins of positivism in the natural sciences can clearly be seen, therefore, in 'testing'. The importance of more interpretive research, however, has been suggested in this chapter as contributing greater insight into the 'why' of phenomena. This is founded on the basis that issues can only be studied from the perspective of research participants rather than monitoring what they do, from the perspective of the researcher. These different perspectives are often manifested in the type of data collected: often polarised between quantitative (positivistic) and qualitative (interpretive). Quantitative research can be described as a method which measures (e.g. tests) a phenomenon, whereas qualitative research is centrally concerned with understanding a phenomenon (Gordon and Langmaid 1988). See Table 5.4.

TABLE 5.4   The two social research paradigms as polar opposites

Philosophical and practical issues	Positivism	Interpretivism
Ontology	External to the individual	Individual is active participant in reality
Epistemology	Objective, single reality, realism	Subjective, multiple realities, idealism
Nature and development of knowledge	Nomothetic Deduction	Ideographic Induction
Type of data	Quantitative, standardised	Qualitative, non-standardised
Approach to data collection	Scientific rigor, systematic	Unscientific, first hand data collection
Inquiry aim	Explanation, prediction and control	Understanding, reconstruction
Goodness or quality criteria	Reliability and validity	Trustworthiness, authenticity
Values	Excluded, influence denied	Included, formative

(Source: Adapted from Guba and Lincoln 1994:112)

As we suggest, there is a range of views on research philosophy: Guba and Lincoln (1994:105), for example, disagree with association between methods and paradigm, and take the position that qualitative and quantitative approaches can be used with any research paradigm. The terms should be reserved for describing types of methods, rather than being employed synonymously with 'paradigms'. 'It takes what it takes' might summarise this position.

Whatever view is taken, it is important that research methodology satisfies certain criteria. First, 'validity', which is 'nothing less than the truth, known through language referring to a stable social reality' (Seale (1999:34). 'Reliability' refers to the stability of the data, that is the extent to which 'repeat measurements ... under broad terms, qualitative research tends towards high validity, in its various forms (Sykes 1990) and quantitative research towards high reliability. 'The main doubts about the reliability of qualitative research methods are that their inherent characteristics (their flexibility and the absence of rigid experimental control) are not conducive to replicability' (Sykes 1990:309). It is this sort of argument that is often reflected in relational marketers who are more orientated to testing methodologies.

'Constant conditions will give the same result' (Moser and Kalton 1971:353).

Objectivity is linked to the neutral and distanced position of the researcher or observer. These criteria are linked to the four questions traditionally used to establish the trustworthiness of research (Lincoln and Guba 1985:290), as summarised by Table 5.5.

TABLE 5.5 Questions in quality and related criteria under conventional and interpretivist paradigms

Question	Issue	Criterion under conventional inquiry	Criterion under interpretivist inquiry
1. How can the level of confidence to be placed in the truth of the findings (for respondents and in context) be established?	Truth value	Internal validity	Credibility
2. How can the extent to which the findings apply to other contexts or respondents be determined?	Applicability	External validity	Transferability
3. How can the repeatability of the findings, using a replicated study, be determined?	Consistency	Reliability	Dependability
4. How can the degree to which the findings are determined by the respondents and inquiry conditions, and not by researcher bias be discovered?	Neutrality	Objectivity	Confirmability

(Source: Adapted from Seale's (1999:45) presentation of the work of Lincoln and Guba (1985))

The future

However, it is worth raising an ethical issue here because data-based relational marketing has changed the nature of collecting details about individuals. Traditional marketing research was more concerned with respondents' buying behaviour, attitudes, characteristics and so on, but relational marketing wants names and addresses as well, in order to target relevant individuals. The Market Research Society's Code of Conduct used to outlaw the collection of personal details for selling purposes (*sugging*: Selling under the guise of research) and indeed most marketing research was based on more anonymised statistical analysis of data. But relational marketing needs to be able to identify individuals. Even if relational marketers do not use the personal details for immediate selling, they are keen to develop databases of personal information – *'dugging'* (data under the guise of research), as proposed by Santry. These issues are well explored by Fletcher and Peters (1996) and their research revealed practitioners to be reasonably comfortable with the situation. Researchers and sellers were keen to make clear to their informants the purpose to which personal details might be put. However Fletcher and Peters show that privacy issues are highly relevant here and have not been resolved. We delve more deeply into marketing privacy concerns in Chapter 13.

As it stands at present, however, the 1997 MRS Code overcomes the conflict with the phrase: 'members shall only use the term *confidential survey research* to describe projects which are based upon respondent anonymity and do not involve the divulgence of names or personal details of informants to others except for research purposes' (Market Research Society 1997).

The new code excludes, from its 'confidential research' principles, the collecting of personal data for sales or promotional approaches to the informant and for the compilation of databases which will be used for canvassing and fund-raising. In such circumstances the data collector should not claim to be involved in a confidential survey and should make this clear to the informant.

Summary

- This chapter has provided a framework for designing and implementing marketing research programmes. Both quantitative and qualitative research have been discussed and the authors contend that both have a strong role to play in relational marketing.

- Conventional marketing researchers would be surprised that this statement needs to be made at all, but with the growth of the database in marketing, there are suggestions that that is all that's needed. However, as we have shown, qualitative research can help marketers to discover how the 'direct' approach makes the customer feel (Phillips and Miller 1997).

- At the same time, however, what is clear is that the database has changed marketing research forever. It allows marketers to study actual buying patterns via analysis of transactional data and to evaluate the actual effects of different relational marketing campaigns in terms of response rates. Both camps will move towards each other and learn through a mutual synergy. As Dunn suggests, 'some purist market researchers are sticking their heads in the sand ... database marketing isn't going to go away' (Dunn and Summers 1995).

- Relational marketing has raised some issues, however, because marketing research has long prided itself on the ethic of not using research to sell products. The database is used to store data about specific individuals and the resulting lists of names and addresses used to target those individuals. This issue has been well addressed by Fletcher and Peters (1996). The Market Research Society itself has redrawn its Code of Conduct and this provides differently for what would be classed as traditional market research and what is clearly database-driven.

- The amalgam of data sources, data mining and research and testing paves the way for the identification of market segments to be targeted in appropriate and relevant ways. This is the theme of the next chapter, in which some additional insight from the behavioural sciences should enhance our understanding of such segments if we are to implement relational interaction with them.

Review questions

1 What is the role of motivation research in relational marketing?

2 What are T-Groups and what can they contribute to relational marketing?

3 How do consumer panels and retail audits operate and what are their uses?

4 Observation is objective, interviewing is subjective. Discuss.

5 How and why are group discussions employed in marketing research?

6 What is the concern over the use of 'testing' rather than 'research' by relational marketers?

7 To what extent do you think that the collection and analysis of personal details of consumers is an invasion of personal privacy?

8 What are the issues involved with collecting individualised data for database marketing, from a market researcher's perspective, a relational marketer's perspective and the consumers' perspective?

Further reading

Malhotra, N.K. and Birks, D.F. (2000) *Marketing Research: An Applied Approach*, European Edition, Harlow: Financial Times/Prentice Hall.

Miles, M.B. and Huberman, A.M. (1994) *Qualitative Data Analysis*, 2nd edn, London: Sage.

Moutinho, L. and Evans, M.J. (1992) *Applied Marketing Research*, Wokingham: Addison-Wesley.

Silverman, D. (1993) *Interpreting Qualitative Data: Methods for Analysing Talk, Text and Interaction*, London: Sage.

References

Barker, A., Nancarrow, C., and Spackman, N. (2001) 'Informed Eclecticism: A Research paradigm for the 21st Century, *International Journal of Marketing*, 43(1), pp. 3–28.

Basch, C.E. (1987) 'Focus Group Interview: An Underutilized Research Technique for Improving Theory and Practice in Health Education' *Health Education Quarterly*, 14(4), pp. 411–48.

Calder, J. (1977) 'Focus Groups and the Nature of Qualitative Marketing', *Journal of Marketing Research*, XIV, pp. 353–64.

Castle, D. (2002) as reported in May, M. (2002) 'Strength by Association', *Marketing Direct*, October, pp. 43–7.

Cooper, T. and Goulds, A. (2001) 'The Marriage of Market Research and Database Marketing', *Journal of Database Marketing*, 8(2), pp. 150–8.

Cooper, P. and Tower, R. (1992) 'Inside the Consumer Mind', *Journal of the Market Research Society*, 34(4), pp. 299–311.

Cowling, A.B. (1996) 'Big Issues for the Next Five Years: Data Fusion, Reach the Parts Others Don't', *IDM Symposium*, May.

De Almeida, P.M. (1980) 'A Review of group Discussion Methodology', *European Research*, 3(8), 114–20.

Dunn, E. and Summers, D. (1995) 'A Point in Question', *Financial Times*, 29 June.

Dwek, R. (1998) 'Data Double Act', *Marketing*, 30 April pp. 33–4.

England, L. (1980) 'Is Research a Waste of Time?', *Marketing*, 16 April, pp. 5–7.

Evans, M., Wedande, G., Ralston, L. and van t'Hul, S. (2001) 'Consumer Interaction in the Virtual Era: Some Solutions from Qualitative Research', *Qualitative Market Research: An International Journal*, 4(3) pp. 150–9, ISSN 1352–2752.

Fletcher, K. and Peters, L. (1996) 'Issues in Customer Information Management', *Journal of the Market Research Society*, 38(2), pp. 145–60.

Francis, N. (1995) *Panel Data Friend or Foe? How the Royal Mail Use the Panel*, Portsmouth: Royal Mail.

Furrer, O. and Sudharshan, D. (2001) 'Internet Market Research: Opportunities and Problems', *Qualitative Market Research: An International Journal*, 4(3) pp. 123–9, ISSN 1352–2752.

Gaiser, T. (1997), 'Conducting on-line focus groups', *Social Science Computer Review*, 15, pp. 135–44.

Goldsmith, J. (1999) 'Crossing the Great Divide', presented at the conference: The Marriage of Market Research and Database Marketing, 27 April, Whitehall Place, Henry Stewart Conferences.

Gordon, W. and Langmaid, R. (1988) *Qualitative Market Research: A Practitioner's and Buyers's Guide*, London: Gower.

Guba, E.G. and Lincoln, Y.S. (1994) 'Competing Paradigms in Qualitative Research', in N.K. Denzin and Y.S. Lincoln (eds) *Handbook of Qualitative Research*, Thousand Oaks, CA: Sage, pp. 105–17.

Jeavons, A. (1999) 'Ethology and the Web', *Marketing and Research Today*, May, pp. 69–76.

Leventhal, B. (1998) 'Databases and Market Research are Getting their Acts Together', *Research*, July, pp. 54–5.

Liddicoat, I. (1998) 'On the Road to Fusion', *Research*, July, pp. 56–7.

Lincoln, Y.S. and Guba, E.G. (1985) *Naturalistic Inquiry*, Beverley Hills, CA: Sage.

Malhotra, N.K and Birks, D.F. (2000) *Marketing Research: An Applied Approach*, European Edition, Harlow: Financial Times/Prentice Hall.

Market Research Society (1997) *Proposed Revised Code of Conduct*, London, p. 3.

May, M. (2002) 'Strength by Association', *Marketing Direct*, October, pp. 43–7.

Miller, R. (1997) 'The Human Face of Data', *Marketing Direct*, May, pp. 52–6.

Millward, M. (1987) 'How to get better value from your research budget', *AMSO Handbook and Guide to Buying Market Research in the UK*, pp. 6–10.

Mitchell, A. (2001) 'Playing Cat and Mouse Games with Marketing', *Precision Marketing*, 16 March, p. 14.

Moser, C.A. and Kalton, G. (1971) *Survey Methods in Social Investigation*, London: Heinemann.

Mouncey, P. (1998) '20 Years on, Is It Time for a Reunion?', *Research*, July pp. 50–3.

Moutinho, L. and Evans, M. (1996) *Applied Marketing Research*, Wokingham: Addison-Wesley.

Nancarrow, C., Pallister, J. and Brace, I. (2001) 'A New Research Medium, New Research Populations and Seven Deadly Sins for Internet Researchers', *Qualitative Market Research: An International Journal*, 4(3), pp. 136–49.

Patterson, M., Evans, M. and O'Malley, L. (1999) 'UK Attitudes Toward Direct Mail', *Journal of Database Marketing*, 7(2), pp. 157–72.

Phillips, D. and Miller, R. (1997) 'The Human Face of Data', *Marketing Direct*, May, pp. 52–6.

Rangan, V.K., Moriarty, R.T. and Swartz, G.S. (1992) 'Segmenting Customers in Mature Industrial Markets', *Journal of Marketing*, 56, October, pp. 72–82.

Ritson, M. (2003) 'Talking, Reading, Tasking . . .', *Financial Times*, 3 February.

RSCR (1997) 'Focal Points: Eye Flow Research Centre', *Academy of Marketing Annual Conference*, Manchester.

Santry, E. (1994) *Research*, June, p. 337.

Scholl, N. Mulders, S. and Drent, R. (2002) 'On-Line Qualitative Market Research: Interviewing the World at a Fingertip', *Qualitative Market Research, An International Journal*, 5(3), pp. 210–23.

Seale, C. (1999) *The Quality of Qualitative Research*, London: Sage.

Silverman, D. (1993) *Interpreting Qualitative Data: Methods for Analysing Talk, Text and Interaction*, London: Sage.

Sykes, W. (1990) 'Validity and Reliability in Qualitative Market Research: A Review of the Literature', *Journal of the Market Research Society*, 32(3), pp. 289–328.

Walker, J. (1996) 'SMART Move but will it deliver the goods?', *Precision Marketing*, 6 May, pp. 18–21.

Ward, G. (1997) reported in Miller, R. (1997) 'The Human Face of Data', *Marketing Direct*, May, pp. 52–6.

Zaltman, G. and Burger, P.C. (1975) *Marketing Research*, Illinois: The Dryden Press.

6 Technological targeting

Learning objectives

Having completed this chapter, students should:

- Understand the implications of the collection, analysis and use of personalised customer data, for segmentation and targeting of markets.

- Be able to show that the relational paradigm leads inevitably, in theory at least, to more personalised and (attempted) relational and one-to-one targeting.

- Appreciate relevant dimensions of segmenting and targeting, such as demographics, psychographics and geodemographics.

- Understand the fusion of personalised data from a variety of sources, which leads to biographical segmentation and targeting.

- Be able to demonstrate segmentation using transactional data.

Tesco case study

In the supermarket wars, the loyalty battleground is where the bullets fly thickest. And the grocer thought to have the most potent loyalty weapon is Tesco. Yet one of the great mysteries of the data world is just how customer insights mined from Tesco Clubcard's data mountain help make it the UK's biggest (and most profitable) grocery chain. In early 2001, six years after Clubcard's launch, Tesco bought a majority share in DunnHumby, its data analysis supplier. The word in data land was that something big was on the cards. So it proved. Until 2001, Tesco and DunnHumby had typically restricted analysis samples of customers to around 10%, in order to control the cost of data storage and transmission. The sea change came with lowering costs of technology, and Tesco's growing desire to delve deeper into the data for consumer insights. The challenge was to make sense of the 104 billion rows of data stored at any one time. Tesco Lifestyles was the result –

a segmentation and modeling system based on customer shopping behaviour. 'Lifestyles is ultimately about trying to understand factors that drive shopping behaviour, for example price, promotions or healthy eating, together with measurement of Tesco's share of a customer's wallet or purse,' says DunnHumby chief executive Edwina Dunn. 'We wanted to capture more spend from each customer, and nudge them into buying products from Tesco that they might buy elsewhere.' DunnHumby began by rooting through customers' shopping baskets, looking for products that are predictive of a need or a lifestyle – such as weight-watching goods. The data was then mined to identify other products that were highly correlated with these. The analysis revealed 25 shopping dimensions, or typologies – such as how 'green' a product was, how family-oriented or calorie-conscious. 'We were entering into areas where traditional statistics couldn't help, so we had to devise our own approaches for working with this data,' says Dunn. The segmentation was developed by studying customer shopping behaviour over time against the typologies. The next trick was to apply the segmentation commercially. The most obvious by-products of Lifestyles are the more recent Clubcard statements and vouchers, whose content has been shaped by the various Lifestyles segments. More than eight million Tesco customers now carry a Lifestyles code, used to target mailings. The challenge of these mailings, says Dunn, is to strike a balance between reinforcing shopping behaviour, by saying 'thanks very much', and encouraging changes in it. In July 350 000 young families received mailings geared to their tastes, offering ideas on summer activities and discounts on related products. The insight offered by Lifestyles is also having a more subtle influence on Tesco strategy. By modeling Lifestyles to geodemographic and electoral roll information, Tesco can predict the Lifestyle make-up of a store before it opens and allow local management to plan an appropriate range of products. A Tesco Metro in flat-land might, for instance, have a range to suit single-occupancy shoppers. How does Tesco Lifestyles differ from the classic lifestyle models such as ACORN and Mosaic? 'Lifestyles builds on the ideas behind those classifications,' says Dunn, who began her working life working on Census data in the 1980s. 'The difference is that Lifestyles is a much more sensitive indicator: it changes as shoppers' behaviour changes. For instance, you can spot where an area is beginning to hurt through unemployment. When you have such a massive tracker of consumption, where you let people define their own behaviour, you can be sensitive to change.' Tesco's 2 000 or so suppliers also benefit. As an offshoot of the initiative, reports are available measuring how a particular brand stacks up against a category, what type of shoppers buys that brand, and so on. Procter & Gamble, Mars and Walkers are already using Tesco Lifestyles to assess what it implies for their customer strategy. Direct mail is not Tesco's only route to Clubcard holders. More recently, customers have started receiving money-off coupons on their till receipts for products that match their Lifestyles profile. Tested in stores throughout Wales, the till coupon scheme has the advantage of being significantly cheaper than direct mail and may presage a cut-back in Tesco's

→

mail usage. Of course, the ultimate test of Lifestyles is what impact it has on the bottom line. To that end, Tesco says that a recent statement containing money-back reward vouchers and more than four million variations on coupons resulted in a sales uplift of over £30 million. The sales effectiveness of new stores has increased by 50% since adopting the Lifestyles approach.

(Source: Noelle McElhatton, Direct Response, August/September 2002, Data Clinic. Reproduced from *Direct Response* magazine with the permission of the copyright owner, Haymarket Business Publications Limited)

Introduction

This case study introduces a number of issues arising from the previous chapters' exploration of data sources and how such data can be fused and mined to identify relevant segments. The current chapter extends this into the subsequent targeting of these segments within relational interaction.

Some additional reasons for the desirability of more individualised targeting are also presented. However, a major issue for Part 2 is that 'data' can all too easily take over in the new relational era, as we have discussed in the preceding chapters. It is important to remember that what should drive marketing is not data *per se* but rather an understanding of customers and it is here that various bases for segmenting markets can go a long way to explaining different customers' buying behaviour.

The basic principle of market segmentation is that markets are not homogeneous and that it makes commercial sense to differentiate marketing offerings for different customer groups. The days when customers could buy a car 'in any colour as long as it was black' are long gone. Markets have fragmented and technology provides for greater variation in production. Marketing itself can more easily identify more and smaller market segments and indeed it can target selected segments more effectively. In this respect, developments in the collection, analysis and use of personalised customer data has been a major driver of many of the developments in relational marketing and these issues are discussed in this chapter.

Background to relational segmentation and targeting

Strategic aims to shift the marketing paradigm from a transaction-based one to being more relational, together with practical attempts to operationalise this, have real implications for segmentation and targeting. Developments over recent decades have meant that marketers are more able to analyse customer behaviour at an individual level and they increasingly aim to be able to cultivate long-term relationships with those customers who contribute most to the financial position of the organisation. We explored some of the mechanics of technology-driven, data-informed relational marketing in the previous chapters. In Chapter 1 we reviewed some 'demand' and 'supply' drivers. But here it is worth providing further background to the rise of this paradigm.

On the demand side we pointed to consumers' desire to be treated more as individuals, while marketers required more effective media to target consumers. Evidence of the trend towards individualism was uncovered during the 1970s and led, amongst other things, to the Reagan and Thatcher election campaigns from the late 1970s and into the 1980s based on 'self-reliance' (BBC, 2002). 'Standing on one's own feet' and 'freeing the individual from the state' were the sorts of mantras of those elections and were manifestations of research at the time that revealed individualism, as the creator of the VALS lifestyle research in the USA confirmed more recently (McNulty 2002).

The logical extension of this is that if more consumers want to express individuality (whether as true individuals or within the safety of tribes (Patterson 1998) or style groups (Evans and Blythe 1994) then it provides marketers with opportunities to treat them individually and offer more self-expressive products via more personalised targeting. For teenagers, especially, the search for individuality is manifested in a 'search for identity and belonging' (Davidson 2003), thus supporting the importance of tribes: 'the majority tend to be more transient and consumer led. Kids can buy a look, an identity and an attitude' (Davidson 2003). Technology has helped again, of course, because the old days of the Ford Model T (any colour as long as it's black) have gone because production processes facilitate smaller production runs of niche products cost-effectively. 'You can even purchase a potato peeler that reflects your "crazy" personality' (Davidson 2003).

On the supply side, we have explored technological developments, which have influenced the way in which market information can be collected, stored and utilised. We have also discussed the nature and role of databases in fusing and mining data from disparate sources, in order to provide greater intelligence of individual customers in order for more personalised targeting to take place. The latter is increasingly being facilitated by technology-driven new interactive media such as the Internet and mobile telephony. Whereas we devote specific chapters to 'interactive media', we do introduce several issues in this chapter within the context of 'targeting' segments.

Segmentation involves identifying homogenous buying behaviour within a segment (and heterogeneous buying between segments) such that each segment can be considered as a target for a distinct marketing mix.

IN THEORY

a) To help with the segmentation process, potential segments should satisfy a number of criteria (Frank *et al*. 1972). The four main and nine sub-criteria are (van Raaij and Verhallen 1994):

1 Typifying the segments
  - Identification: Differentiation of segment from other segments.
  - Measurability: Identification of segments in terms of differences in individual and household characteristics or other 'measurable' characteristics should be possible.

2 Homogeneity
  - Variation: Heterogeneity between segments in terms of behavioural response (Engel *et al*. 1972).
  - Stability: Although this criterion suggests that segments should be relatively stable over time and that switching of consumers from one segment to another should not be frequent, the use of data mining tools allows the identification of individuals' changed circumstances or behaviour such that they can now be switched from one target group to another.
  - Congruity: Homogeneity within segments in terms of behavioural responses.

3 Usefulness
  - Accessibility: Segments should be accessible in terms of communications media and distribution outlets. This means that it must be possible to reach the segment. Traditionally this meant the selection of those advertising media that match the segment's media profile in demographic terms, or selecting appropriate distribution channels, again through a matching of demographic profile with the equivalent profile of those most likely to frequent different types of retail outlets. Increasingly, however, especially since around the start of the 1980s more sophisticated market profiling and targeting dimensions have been deployed. The date is significant because it reflects the first use of the national Census for marketing purposes, as is explained later.
  - Substantiality: Segments should be of sufficient size to enable specific marketing actions. This does not mean that segments need to be especially large, but profitable enough to have distinct marketing mixes aimed at them. Again, new 'marketing metrics' have facilitated greater sophistication in calculating not only the most profitable segments but also even the most profitable individual customers.

4 Strategic criteria
- Potential: The segments should have enough potential for marketing objectives, e.g. profitability.
- Attractiveness: Segments should be structurally attractive to the producer, e.g., create a competitive advantage for the company (Porter 1979)

b) The generally accepted linear model of 'segmentation, targeting and positioning' (STP) is logical but perhaps misses a stage. The basic model leads to positioning in terms of how customers and potential customers perceive the organisation's offering and this might be regarded as being at more of the operational context of marketing communications.

In new research (Ellson 2003) it is suggested that the organisation's culture and the personality of its leader are precursors of a more strategic positioning of the company rather than individual brands, in terms of defending against competitors.

As a result, Ellson suggest that the model should be more inclusive:

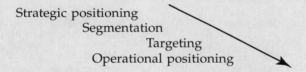

Strategic positioning
Segmentation
Targeting
Operational positioning

This possibly produces a certain 'chicken and egg' situation. On the one hand, positioning (according to Ellson) is concerned at the strategic level with adapting organisational personality to reflect the needs of the market, but on the other hand, at a more operational level, it more often deals with the manipulation of consumers' 'mind-sets' to suit the organisation. A possible problem with adapting the more macro-organisational personality (as opposed to individual brands) is the need to balance this with a reasonably constant maintenance of core values and purpose (Collins and Porras 1996).

Segmentation categories

Segmentation approaches can be categorised as being objective or subjective. An objective base may be measured unambiguously, e.g. age and gender, or may be taken from registrations of transactions, e.g. checkout scanning data. Subjective bases need to be measured with the respondents themselves and are often 'mental constructs' such as attitudes and intentions.

As suggested in the previous chapters, new metrics for segmenting markets are shifting the balance towards the former category in many segmentation programmes.

Further categorisation of segmentation bases can be made, as shown in Table 6.1. Here, three 'levels' are proposed. At the general level, segmentation is based on permanent or relatively long-lasting consumer characteristics such as gender, education level, occupation, family composition, and lifestyle. These characteristics are the same for different products, services and usage situations.

For domain-specific segmentation, there are different product classes and consumption domains, such as breakfast, washing clothes, or commuting. When these are taken into account, segmentation is domain-specific.

For specific-level segmentation, customers are segmented into, for example, heavy and light users of specific brands. Segmentation of present customers is also at the specific level.

Combining the three levels of segmentation and the distinction of objective and subjective variables are shown in Table 6.1. All segmenting bases can be categorised within this framework.

TABLE 6.1 Classification of segmentation variables

	Objective	Subjective
General level (consumption)	age education level geographic area	lifestyle general values personality
Domain-specific level (product class)	usage frequency substitution complementarity	perception attitude, preference interests, opinions domain-specific values
Specific level (brand)	brand loyalty (behaviour) usage frequency	brand loyalty (attitude) brand preference purchase intention

'Traditional' segmentation bases

The previous chapters of Part 2 explored a range of 'data-sourced' segmentation variables such as transactional data and geodemographics, so we will not examine these so fully here.

It is worth, however, revisiting some of the more 'traditional' segmentation bases. These provide an extra degree of underpinning explanation of how customers behave as they do and can, therefore, be extremely useful in adding more colour to what can sometimes be relatively monotone data.

Demographics

Age is still a valid base for many markets and holds important and sometimes not too obvious implications for relational marketers. This section focuses on two specific age segments, the baby boomers and first, young consumers. The latter have become important spenders, demanding their own products and searching for their own identity. A complicating factor is that this group has been found to be especially individualistic and sceptical of marketing activity. This doesn't make them difficult to reach, but it is proving harder to influence them. A decade ago they were labelled as 'Generation X'; Coupland (1991) and Ritchie (1995) have analysed their behaviour and attitudes and these have been further reported by Bashford (2000). It is possible that relational marketing can provide some of what Generation X might be looking for – greater interactivity and participation in marketing communications. We explore this further in the chapter on creativity. The current 16–24s have been termed Generation Y or the Millennial Generation (Adam Smith Institute 1998). Many in this category have been found to be materialists, brand orientated, risk takers, keen on business, hedonism, illegal drugs and have a disrespect for politics. The Future Foundation (2000) extended this research and found them to be more accepting of multinationals and with less interest in protesting. Further analysis of Generation Y has been conducted by Shepherdson (2000) and Gofton (2002). If this group were targeted, this profile could provide useful clues as to the sort of message and media to use to reach them.

It has been suggested that whereas 'adults' define themselves by their occupations, youths are 'defined by their consumption patterns. Brands and products are therefore of critical importance to teenagers' (Gillespie 2003) and this is clearly congruent with the multiple roles of self-expressive behaviour discussed earlier as an antecedent of relational marketing.

Indeed Davidson (2003) discusses teenagers of the early 2000s (labelled Generation Z) as being introspectively and self-expressively motivated: 'they are only interested in their personal lives, the parties they go to, the clothes they wear … the absence of community … the cult of celebrity provides an exciting surrogate community … celebrity (provides) a real identity in a sea of mock individuality'.

Of an even younger group, the largest increase in Internet usage is among the 7–10-year-olds (20% increase from 2002 to 2003, Datamonitor 2003). This is perhaps an omen for the future, when very significant proportions of the population will be accessing the Internet and, among other uses, interacting with companies.

The 'camouflage' (Army) case study of Chapter 9 is a useful example of targeting young markets, before they become able to become adopters, in order to develop a relationship that could continue to adoption. The following case study is another good example of looking into the psyche of the market targeted, in order to develop relational interaction.

Youth psyche

Bored youngsters through the decades have had a constant and familiar moan: 'There's nothing to do around here.' Craik Jones has taken that lament and made a campaign of it. ATOC (Association of Train Operating Companies) asked the agency to increase sales of the Young Person's Railcard (YPRC) and grow its database. Three-quarters of 16- to 25-year-olds use trains for leisure travel, but only a quarter have a railcard, which gives them a third off the fares for many journeys. The card costs £18 a year, but one reason for the relatively low uptake of it is confusion about eligibility. Craik Jones ignored the easy option of writing about exciting places to visit. Instead, it burrowed into youth psyche, and the embarrassment of being seen as a stick-in-the mud, with the message 'Don't be a local'. This was an integrated, multimedia campaign. Given the strategic thinking behind it, the level of creativity and the excellent results, it is hardly surprising that it won Golds in the travel/leisure and multiple media categories, and a Bronze in outdoor/ambient media. Although there were at least a couple of other strong contenders on the final shortlist, it was the judges' unanimous choice for this year's Grand Prix. They praised its engaging humour. 'The youth market is tough,' they added. 'This was

highly relevant to the target audience, and the combination of media used was really good.' The campaign opened with awareness-building press ads in magazines such as *Mixmag* and *Kerrang*. Online data gathering followed, driven by an inspirational competition to win a weekend away for a group of ten. Viral e-mails were used to get interested youngsters to persuade their friends to enter. While the theme of 'Don't be a local' was constant, it had a number of twists. Computer banners and drop-downs were used to target computer geeks. When they responded, they were teased for being so sad, before being switched to the competition microsite. In similar vein, a range of ambient media in local pubs, from beer mats to heat-sensitive urinal stickers, lured customers into 'saddo' games and then urged them to get out more. A third of all competition entrants clicked through to the main YPRC website for more information. Awareness of the card increased by 4% but the all-important awareness of eligibility rose by 14%. More than 17 500 names were added to ATOC's database, laying the groundwork for testing future electronic acquisition and retention activities.

(Source: DMA (2002) Grand Prix Award)

Now, consider the over-50s. It is foolish to lump these together in just one segment. The 'baby boomers', those born in the years following the Second World War, have very distinctive attributes and have become a very important target for marketers. They were involved in a massive social revolution which changed music, fashions, political thought and social attitudes forever. They were the generation to grow up in the 1960s when the term 'teenager' hadn't been used previously. They were not 'small adults' who, in previous generations, had worn similar clothes to their parents. The new generation wanted their own culture, their own fashions, music, and their own social attitudes which rejected the values of their parents. Coupled with this desire for ownership of their thoughts and lives, the baby boomer generation was the most affluent (generally) of any 'youth market' until their era, so they were able to engage in the consumer market and marketers responded with a fashion and music explosion of which we had previously never seen the like.

Such a consumerism-literate market should be extremely attractive. Indeed, in the USA a baby boomer turned 50 every 6.8 seconds in 2001. Not all the over-50s are baby boomers, of course. Those in their 60s and 70s and indeed the over-70s are from other generations with lifestyles and attitudes of their own. Overall, the over-50s have been termed the 'third age'. They represent about a third of the population (in the late 1990s) and are some 18 million strong in the UK. By 2020 they will represent about half the UK population and will rise from 20 million in 2000 to 27 million in 2025 (a 35% increase). In general terms, the ageing baby boomer generation is the most wealthy, in terms of inheritance from their parents. That previous generation was 'blessed' with low house prices when they bought and a lifestyle which was much less materialistic. As a result, their estates have often (but clearly not always) been cascading down to the new over-50 market. Indeed the over-50s in UK hold 80% of the country's wealth and 40% of spending (£145 billion p.a.) and is not only the only segment that is growing but has more disposable income than all the others combined (Cummins 1994).

Research amongst the over-50s has revealed several characteristics. The over-50s don't like to be portrayed as 'old' but at the same time would see through attempts to portray them as 'young', so caution is needed.

There are differences between those in their 50s, 60s and above. Those in their 60s generally prefer to use cash and are rather cautious consumers. Those over 70 are perhaps even further along this continuum. There has certainly been an explosion of magazine titles aimed at various over-50 groups, demonstrating that the market is not homogeneous and that the various groups can be reached. The profiling in this sector is not merely on the basis of age, however; social grade and geodemographics are also being used and there is a trend towards overlaying this with attitudinal research. An example of this comes from the analysis of the TGI in 1993 (Cummins 1994) which found, based on shopping attitudes and behaviour, that there are 'astute cosmopolitans', constituting about 19% of the 50–75s, and who are discerning consumers. There are also the 'temperate xenophobes' (20% of 50–75s) who are less likely to go abroad or eat 'foreign food'. The 'thrifty traditionalists' make up 20% and a further 19% are 'outgoing funlovers'. The largest group is the 'apathetic spenders' (21%) who use credit cards to extend their purchasing power beyond what they can really afford (Cummins 1994).

Consider this view from within the motor industry:

❝ The car dealers often despair of the marketing initiatives they see. The focus is on the young or the young family, even for the point of sale in showrooms ... older people often have 2 or 3 cars per family, yet manufacturers get hung up on items like cup holders. ❞ (Pulham 2003)

A major issue, then, is that marketers tend to target younger age segments yet the 50–60 segment buy two-thirds of all cars, more long-haul holidays than younger segments and even 25% of all toys (Sclater 2003). Datamonitor (2003) speculates that one reason for the relative neglect is that half the staff in advertising agencies are themselves under 30 and it has been suggested that it is not always seen to be 'cool' for these to design creative for older segments (Cooper 2003). It probably isn't a case, however, of allocating older staff to older accounts, as Cooper suggests: whatever age group media planners are shouldn't affect what they're planning. They should be experienced enough to target the demographics of their clients irrespective of their own interests. In relational terms, the over-50s can be more loyal:

ff the problem with young consumers is that they are 'flippy'. As soon as someone else targets them they jump ship. The mature consumer tends to be more loyal and they tend to do more business. **JJ** (Cooper 2003)

There is another issue for relational marketing here: 'as soon as you target the mature sector, people are worried that it's going to upset their youth market, but not if you use niche channels like direct mail and the Internet' (Cooper 2003). Saga is a major direct marketer, for instance.

So the points here are that relational marketers neglect or inappropriately target their older customers at their peril. Relationships can be longer lasting and more lucrative and there are ways of 'hiding' the targeting from younger segments if it is thought that this might alienate the younger segments.

Gender

Gender stereotyping has been used extensively over many decades, but it hasn't always escaped criticism. Reliance on 'mother' or 'mistress' or 'career woman' images of women in advertising sometimes attracts complaints on sexist or offensive grounds, as have some more recent demeaning images of men. Increases in the divorce rate and the 'singles' market (imposed through divorce or by decision) have added to the more general changes in sex roles, with women becoming more individualistic through their own careers rather than being housewives *per se*. Marketing to women, however, may still be in need of updating. There are new female roles such as the independent assertive woman, independent passive woman and independent sexual woman. Some of these clearly relate to what in popular culture has been termed 'girl power'. As female roles change, so inevitably do those of men. We have seen a variety of male stereotypes such as the 'caring sharing new man', the 'family' man, the 'yob lad', 'modelling' man, 'househusband' man, as well as gay images. Relational marketing cannot afford to assume all women to be homogeneous (and similarly for men). Indeed, as we continue to act out multiple roles, 'in the post millennial society individuals will be able to pick and choose different gender schemes or choose not to care about gender at all' (Kacen 2000).

Another implication of gender differences is information processing style between men and women. Information processing style has been generally reviewed by Kitchen and Spickett-Jones (2003) but the point here concerns possible gender differences. In a major research project it was found that men and women do react differently to certain features of written communication. Women respond well to bright colours, photographs and images and men respond well to bold headlines, bullet points and graphs (Evans *et al.* 1999, 2000). This study drew from findings in neurology based on MRI scans of male and female brains as they processed information (read things). Female brains generated more activity from more areas of the brain than did male brains, the proposition being that women were using more elements of messages (colour, imagery, words etc.) to form meaning and as a result left and right, front and back areas of their brains 'lit up' when reading material. As for men, their brains showed less activity (do you agree, girls!) and the supposition was that they were focusing more on fewer specific elements of the messages, mostly the words, to make sense of it (Exhibit 6.1). So, again an apparently straightforward demographic characteristic hides a multitude of implications for the marketer.

The exception within this study concerned cars. Women appeared more interested in the facts such as running costs, safety features and fuel consumption and men more concerned with image and appearance (Exhibit 6.2).

Earlier, the gay market was briefly mentioned. Indeed, it is worth commenting that marketing is increasingly interested in this segment. Gay men, for example, spend twice as much on clothing and four times as much on grooming as straights. They are often relatively more affluent, with few dependants. In terms of satisfying the accessible criterion, these segments are easier to reach nowadays because there are more gay magazines and TV programmes as well as being able

EXHIBIT 6.1   Male and female mail packs

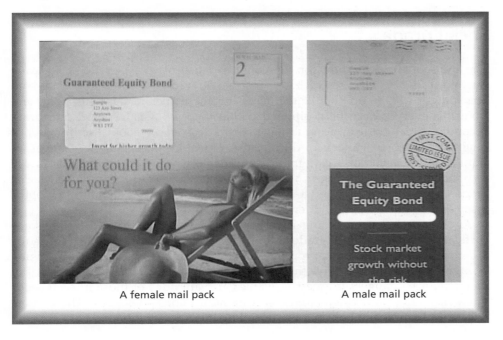

A female mail pack   A male mail pack

EXHIBIT 6.2   Boys and their toys

to reach them via the Internet and sponsorship of gay events (for example, by Smirnoff, Levi's and Virgin). Men in the gay market have also been found to be more responsive to new products and might be a good target in the early stages in the life of new products and services. This is explored further in a later section.

Social grade

The traditional justification for the continued use of social grade is basically twofold. It is simple to research. All that is required is for data to be analysed according to the occupation of the 'chief income earner in the household' and from this everyone can be positioned within the A, B, C1, C2, D, E categories. Secondly, social grade appears to have been a reasonably good discriminator of buying behaviour. However, during the 1980s in particular, a number of significant criticisms of social grade were made. It was also shown that of 400 respondents to earlier surveys who were reinterviewed to confirm their social grade, 41% had been allocated to the wrong group, and this is an indication of the instability of the system (O'Brien and Ford 1988).

Another problem concerning social grade is that although there might be some correlations between social grade and purchase, how can this be used ? Certainly it is relevant for selecting appropriate advertising media based on the matching of segment social grade with the social grade profiles for different media. But there could be dangers in inferring values and attitudes of those in each social grade in order to create marketing communications messages. These more affective dimensions might not be caused by one's occupation.

Recent attempts to improve social classification do not bode well, either. The Census of 2001 has produced eight (rather than the previous six) categories but excludes the over-75s (Zelin 2003). Indeed the new system has been found to be not as good in discriminating purchase activity as the 'ABC1' system and Rose *et al.* (1999) could not recommend it as a replacement for social grade. However, the previous system was based on households (occupation of chief income earner in the household) whereas the new system is at individual level, so the relational marketer might be tempted at least to experiment with this because of the stronger relational potential of data at individual level.

Family

The family life-cycle concept is particularly well exploited in relational marketing. Many financial services companies and supermarkets segment their markets, based on transactional and profile data, on the basis of Lifestage. This approach shows how the family unit's interests and buying behaviour change over time. A simple model is the progression from the single bachelor stage, to newly married, married with children, empty nester who is married with children who no longer live in the parental home, and finally to the solitary survivor stage. Buying needs, values and behaviour clearly differ for the various stages. A recent promotional campaign by Barclays Bank depicted the life stages through which their customers go, by picturing a young single man, then a couple with a family and an older couple whose children had left home, and suggesting that the Bank has financial service products to suit not just each stage 'now' but each individual as they progress through these stages of the life cycle. The Prudential even used a caterpillar to reflect how we metamorphose through life stages – promising equally evolutionary financial products to match each stage.

Life stage is clearly of increasing interest to relational marketers. The British Market Research Bureau (BMRB), for example, now offers a Lifestage segmentation product which identifies twelve life-stage groups which are further divided into ABC1s and C2DEs, producing a 24-way segmentation model (BMRB 2003).

The following case study shows how Lifestage was successfully used by Center Parcs.

CASE STUDY 6.2

Center Parcs and Lifestage targeting

The company had low occupancy at certain times of year coupled with over-demand at peak periods. A firm believer in direct mail, Center Parcs already had a programme to try to plug these gaps, with major campaigns to its customer database every January and September supported by smaller mailings throughout the year. But still the problem persisted. The aim was to fill up the periods of low occupancy while smoothing out the demand curve in the oversubscribed times of year. The first move was to join forces with data solutions provider Talking Numbers to build models identifying who was coming at what time of year. The major objectives were to focus targeting, to find the catchment areas for each village, and to establish who goes into which villas. With villas ranging from one to four beds, it would, says Nick Begy (Marketing Manager), be pointless targeting a family of four with offers for a one-bed villa. Previously, the holiday provider had identified when and where the gaps in occupancy were at short notice, then sent out postcards to its database to try to fill them. Begy identified a few errors in this approach. 'We weren't looking at lifestyle,' he says. 'We were looking at people who'd booked in September before but we really needed to be looking at who'd booked at short notice before, recognising the stock we had left and identifying who out of these people would be likely to go into them.' Basically, it's all about good old propensity modelling. Working with Talking Numbers, Begy and his team took everything Center Parcs had done before in terms of targeting and turned it on its head, starting propensity modelling at the end of November last year. This has signalled a number of significant changes. Sorting out the catchment areas has proved particularly useful, especially as April's fire at its Elveden site has left that village out of action for now. Rather than targeting all prospects in this area, Center Parcs can now decide which of Elveden's regulars should be targeted with information on which of the other two sites. This year Center Parcs has also brought in Claritas's PRiZM Household tool to refine its targeting further by profiling customers and prospects. The main component of this is Claritas's Lifestyle Database, combined with information such as census and subscription data. To provide a clear picture of customers, information on life stage and income is overlaid with lifestyle components like car ownership, readership, and cultural interests. This segments households into one of 52 distinct groups, such as 'most affluent empty nesters who like outdoor pursuits'. Data, such as party composition and number of bookings, has also proved useful in identifying these targets, as David Dipple, technical director at Talking Numbers, explains: 'We look at the number of adults in a party who book at a certain time of year and use this information to predict what will happen this year and target them appropriately.' Having worked all this out, Center Parcs is now tailoring messages to particular groups such as empty nesters which it recognises are more likely to take advantage of offers to visit out of season, and are also good bets for one-bed units. The September brochure mailing now goes to around 50 disparate segments with each one receiving a different offer and letter. Not only is modelling helping Center Parcs improve its targeting, but on a deeper level it enables the company to build up profiles of the visitors to each village. These very different profiles are also influencing the way people are now being targeted. For example, visitors to the Longleat Forest village have a very different profile to other guests. They tend to be from a slightly higher affluence band, with more public-school-educated children, which also means school holiday peaks tend to fall slightly differently than at the other villages. 'There are distinct groups of customers,' says Dipple. 'Elveden has people with big wads of cash, and they spend a lot there. Longleat is the old rich; there's a different atmosphere.' This insight has resulted in Dipple and Begy producing different profiles for each break at each village. These are then given to the villages, helping them to work out in advance if there's likely to be a lot of babies, male groups or teenagers at any one time. These are all factors that can lead to staffing issues. 'We can now say that if A happens, then B will follow. It allows us to be more predictive,' adds Begy. This new confidence in targeting has led Center Parcs to give cold lists a go again – something that hadn't been particularly effective in the past. PriZM Household is proving especially useful here. For this September's big brochure launch, it brought in large quantities of cold lists and overlaid them with the system, nailing prospects down to the exact postcodes Center Parcs wanted to target. The promotion for the brochure launch is the new spa at Sherwood Forest. This is something that wouldn't suit all customers so, using PriZM Household, low affluency groups and people with young children were excluded from this particular offer. It is still less than a year ago that Center Parcs and Talking Numbers started working together, yet in that time they have thrown up a wealth of data, including some unexpected findings. Apart from the differences in village profiles, the biggest learning so far, according to Dipple and Begy, is that promotions often stimulate more bookings even after the offer period is over. This was demonstrated after this year's January's campaign went out. Postcards were targeted at different lifestyle groups with empty nesters receiving cards focusing on adult activities like the spa, while the pre-school market was sent pictures of babies in the pool or crèche facilities. It reaped rewards during the promotional period but the surprise came when they looked at the number of bookings made after the promotional period had ended. 'Ten times as many people who were sent the promotion booked outside the promotional period as within it, so missing out on the discount,' says an astounded Dipple. 'We hadn't realised this before.' Even better, it's having a huge effect on profits. Although hesitant about actual figures, Begy admits that this particular campaign made 150 times the money spent on it in incremental terms. This year has been a steep learning curve. 'We're constantly refining what we do with every learning,' says Begy. So far the DM is working very well, and it's all down to modelling. 'By using models,' expounds Dipple, 'we can get the who, what and when right. So when we have one-bed apartments lying empty in September we know who to contact.' It doesn't stop there. In the pipeline are plans to marry up qualitative analysis with transactional and behavioural information to get an even clearer picture of behaviour and attitudes. But both Center Parcs and Talking Numbers are wary of jumping ahead of themselves too soon – tempting as it is with so much data now at their disposal. The important thing, says Dipple, is to remember what is useful. 'We're like kids in a candy store,' he says. 'But we have to make sure what we're doing is always working properly.'

(Source: May 2002. Reproduced from *Marketing Direct* magazine with the permission of the copyright owners Haymarket Business Publications Limited)

Lifestage is also a component in the 'Fruits' segmentation approach within the financial services sector (Berry and Leventhal 1996). Along with financial strength, demographic and the range of financial products held, this leads to the following classification:

- Plum: married man, living in the South, high income and savings. Heavy user of financial services.
- Pear: retired homeowner, earning moderate income with accumulated savings. Has stocks and shares, and favours safer forms of investment.

- Cherry: married, two children, 35–54, high earner. Heavy user of credit products.
- Apple: left school at 16, works part-time or self-employed. Pension plan but less likely to use credit cards.
- Orange: young, single, renting or first-time buyer. Good prospect for future products.
- Grape: lives in large house, average income, heavy debts, no savings.
- Date: female, widowed, over 55, low income, but likely to have savings and insurance.
- Lemon: female, living alone, below-average user of financial services.

Lifestage can clearly be a valuable tool in relational marketing because, if used relevantly, it could reflect 'adaptation' in relationships. For example, if a financial services company receives an inbound contact from a customer to change their address, it could merely update its database. However, there is an adage in the relational industry: ECHO (every contact has opportunities). If discreet questions were asked about the reason for the change it might be found that the customer is getting married. This could be a trigger point for the financial services company itself to move to another stage of interaction with the customer. This next stage of the family life cycle could mean relevance and timeliness for the company's 'marriage pack' to be sent with details of insurance, assurance and savings schemes for couples (Hughes and Evans 2001).

Related to the family life-cycle concept is the influence of children within the household and specifically 'pester power' which, as Carter (1994) found, is highly observable. Children react to peer group pressure and some marketers target their advertising at a slightly older age group so that the 'trickle down' theory operates – younger kids see the product being used by their elders and want to follow their lead. By the time it has trickled down to them, the older ones have been enticed to the next craze.

The concept of a 'brand' is probably just beginning to be understood by children when they reach 5 or 6. Parents are targeted with a 'sensible' message and kids with a more persuasive one. With children of about 7 or 8, parental influence is less constraining and the children themselves develop a repertoire of acceptable brands, TV advertising and observation of older children being the main influences. Parents might be motivated to buy their children those products that help their development but often they are persuaded to buy things which add to their children's street credibility – the 'right' brand.

When children are of primary school age it is often school friends who become more important product influencers than parents. Observation and word of mouth are then very important in developing children's preferences.

Many marketers have really taken this on board and have started to get into schools with various sponsorship and 'educational' ventures. Schools need help to ease financial hardship associated with their budgets but some teachers are uncomfortable with this way of targeting the children's market. This approach is highly relational, with sponsors and educational authorities working together.

Any viewing of TV at 'children's viewing times will confirm saturation by commercials aimed at children. Younger children may merely watch these as entertainment but as they grow, the brand and image become important and salient in children's minds as a result of associative learning processes and vicarious learning (seeing others using the product). Personalities and cartoon characters are also heavily used to target children.

As well as child-related consumption, we are also concerned here with the role of children in determining more adult purchases. That is, which car the parents will buy and where to go on holiday and so on. Parents have succumbed to a youth culture and look to their children for what is 'hip' to buy. In one survey (BBC 1997) it was found that 72% of parents admitted to £20 of their weekly spending being influenced by their children, 22% of parents thought that up to £50 of weekly spending was a result of pester power and 4% even thought that up to £100 of their weekly spending was based on this. This would amount to £5bn per year if averaged across the UK.

Adults are pictured as living through the brands they buy rather than 'mainstream institutions' (Castell 2002) but children also want to 'experience' life through brands: the days when slogans and commercial messages induced people to 'buy it', 'try it', 'drink it' are long gone. Brands are now placing consumers in the centre: Diesel days' 'successful living', Xbox advises 'life is short, play more', Coca-Cola tells us 'life tastes good' but to Nintendo 'life's a game' … the personal happiness to be gained from using precisely that brand' (Lindstrom 2003).

Clearly there are ethical issues here. The pursuit of brands rather than 'real' life is but one. Also, children have not fully matured, by definition, yet they are being heavily targeted, sometimes in subtle ways, by marketers who want them to develop brand preferences. Some retailers even have loyalty schemes for babies! The Royal Bank of Scotland obtained details of children from subscriptions to the Disney Book Club and sent them offers for a credit card. Children as young as 5 received the mailing offering a 9.9% APR (Anon, 1997).

The previously mentioned increase in the use of the Internet, by 7–10-year-olds especially, is probably at least partially a result of pester power where children convince their parents of the importance of the Internet for their school homework. Consider the issues raised in Case Study 6.3.

CASE **STUDY** 6.3

Kids' privacy

The Internet has become a key medium for brands wanting to target kids. But UK legislation has yet to include clear laws on gaining permission to gather personal information from children. There is nothing in the Data Protection Act that lays down the age at which a child can use a website without parental consent. The Electronic Communications (Data Privacy) Directive, which will become law in the UK by October 2003, establishes opt-in policy for e-mail and SMS marketing, but the DTI has yet to publish draft regulations on how this will work in practice. To bridge the gap, the UK Information Commissioner has issued guidance on compliance, suggesting that

→

brands gain 'explicit consent' from parents. If there is no adequate method of verifying parental consent online, it proposes postal clarification as the only option. So where does that leave brands that target kids now? In practice, it is extremely difficult to verify parental consent. Even when a child has provided his or her parent's e-mail address and consent has been sent from that address, how can anyone be certain that the parent was the sender? In such circumstances, the Information Commissioner suggests it would be advisable to revert to postal communication. This undermines many of the benefits of the Web, especially its immediacy. It is questionable whether children will ask their parents for consent, and whether parents will take time to confirm consent by post. The situation will not be practicable until there is widespread domestic use of electronic signatures. If the Commissioner chose to enforce that guidance, it would seriously hamper the development of e-commerce and online marketing. Marketing departments for companies seeking to develop relations with children online have a real dilemma, since the Commissioner advises that any proposed marketing activity to children be abandoned if verifiable consent has not been received. Explicit consent is not law, but a suggestion. We are working with clients such as Kellogg and Disney as if it is law, as that is the appropriate brand response. Almost every brand that deals with children will be aware of consent, but I'm sure a lot of them don't follow the guidelines. I think the burden of compliance is on the new media agencies to monitor, as clients come to us for consultancy – just as it is for television or radio advertising restrictions. The online restrictions may put some children off, as part of the fun of the Internet for kids is doing things out of their parents' reach. But there are plenty of things brands can do online with kids without having to gain consent. It will make fmcg brand

owners look at a larger number of ways to deliver loyalty retention with new concepts and ideas. We require consent from any child under the age of 16. If children are interested in joining our e-mail list, they can do it at our offline events or in print competitions, where we require name, e-mail address, date of birth, gender and parent's signature. Online applications must provide the e-mail address of a parent. We check legislation and try to go beyond that to show responsible care. There is no foolproof way of ensuring the e-mail address given is actually the parent's, but you can generally tell if it is genuine by the type of content a 12-year-old would include in the mail reply. We have a three-level opt-in process to make sure the child is keen to join our club. We may lose a few registrations as a result, but we know we are getting true fans. Clients are relatively unaware of specific codes of practice and legislation, whether we are talking mobile, Internet or classic advertising. There is the expectation that agencies will be aware and comply. It may be problematic for large companies to entrust such responsibilities to smaller new-media agencies. It is somewhat of a grey area until there is actually an issue where a company steps over the boundaries and is challenged. How this is handled by companies will depend on where the new-media spend falls. If it is part of the general ad budget, it will be more closely monitored, because brands tend to have long-term contractual relationships with suppliers. But if it falls into below-the-line spend, there will be fewer controls because activities such as promotions and design are handled on a project-by-project basis. There is a greater chance that client compliance with new legislation will fall through gaps.

(Source: Mark Sweney, *Revolution*, 7 August 2002. Reproduced from *Revolution* magazine with the permission of the copyright owners Haymarket Business Publications Limited)

Another topical base for segmentation concerns ethnicity. The following case study explores many of the issues involved in this respect, for the relational marketer.

CASE STUDY 6.4

Minority marketing

Treating any one group as a homogeneous mass is a risky marketing strategy but particularly if the target audience are ethnic minorities. They make up approximately 5.5% of the UK population, with about 30 different ethnic groups in London alone. And, according to a report by multi-discipline agency Interfocus, 'Marketing to Ethnic Minorities; Why Bother?', two of the largest groups, the Asian and the African-Caribbean communities, have disposable yearly incomes of about £7 billion and £5 billion respectively. Ethnic minorities are clearly a market worth targeting, but with such a broad mix of cultures and attitudes represented within this group, how can marketers successfully crack such a diverse audience? Louise Ellerton, strategic planner at Interfocus, believes companies tend to ignore the possibilities: 'Many brands are closing their eyes to the fact that they have a very lucrative market on their hands. They're not realising there are ways of tapping into that market above and beyond simply talking to them like everyone else.' One of the challenges facing marketers is the lack of lists available. The 1998 Data Protection Act has cracked down on the use of personal data, especially that considered sensitive, such as the ethnic or racial origin of a data subject. This means that for data supply firms, this is one area they can no longer cover, as Caroline Kimber, director of direct marketing at CACI, explains: 'You have to have explicit consent to use sensitive personal data. Therefore, we've had to say,

unfortunately, we can't do it, much as we'd like to. We have to adhere to the Act.' But there are still ways of collecting data, within various stiff constraints. 'You have to have two clear provisos,' says Roger Williams, UK marketing manager at Claritas. 'The first is that the person has given explicit consent to allow data to be collected and used, and secondly, the way the question is worded must imply clearly and precisely how the data will be used. You have to be very clear on who's going to use the data.' And when your product or brand appeals to the majority, as many do, it can seem pointless targeting individual groups. As Williams explains: 'Lots of products are universal, so the ethnic dimension doesn't come into it.' Marc Nohr, managing director for agency Lion, which has worked with a number of organisations targeting ethnic minorities, believes any company approaching its campaigns with this thinking is missing out. 'Mainstream marketing is colour-blind,' he says. 'It assumes ethnic differences aren't drivers, saying "we want everyone to buy our product, black, white or blue". Yet ethnicity is an important driver.' Nohr doesn't see targeting ethnic minorities as being quite as difficult as some would make out. 'The marketing community has the skills, it just has to use them. It's not as if we're not used to understanding segments.' He suggests moving away from the standard DM campaign trail. 'Why not use field marketing, face-to-face marketing, or try advertising in their press, or on their TV channels?' he asks. 'Some communities are geographically concentrated, so look at a map.' Another method is to use community leaders to reach an audience. If someone the community respects advocates a particular brand or product, those in the community are more likely to give it a try. Claire Davidson, Lion's strategic communications director, says: 'Spend time getting to know the community you're talking to, and get to know who the community leaders are – people who culturally influence the community – like the hairdresser or grocer.' To get it right requires effort. Nohr believes the provision of a complete service is the only way to do it. There's little point sending out an effective mailer if, when a non-English-speaking customer contacts you, whether by phone or letter, there are no facilities in place to translate for them. Another mistake is assuming everyone under the ethnic minority banner is the same, and approach-

ing them all in the same way. Paul Seligman, MD of agency 141, believes this mistake is a common one: 'Marketers assume all Bangladeshis, for example, have the same purchase patterns. We have to tread carefully. There's a tendency to make generalisations.' It would be easy to think that without any of the data usually available from lists, segmenting the ethnic community audience is near impossible. Ellerton believes otherwise, but acknowledges that it's easier once you actually have some data to work with. She says: 'We're seeing a lot of interest from companies that know they have an ethnic customer base, but don't know the proportion. It's a matter of data analysis to work out the numbers, research into the customer base and look at the clusters to see how relevant a marketing campaign would be.' One method of segmenting the ethnic market, according to the Interfocus report, is basing clusters upon levels of cultural

TABLE 6.2   Interfocus' ethnic segments

Cluster 1: least culturally integrated	More at ease with items closely related to their own culture Tend to live in close-knit family groups and ethnic dwelling areas Low-income and blue-collar workers Very limited knowledge of English language
Cluster 2: moderately integrated	Have working knowledge of English language Prefer to speak their native language Behavioural patterns are influenced by their subculture's values Combine some characteristics of groups one and three
Cluster 3: highly integrated	Fluent in both English and their native tongue At ease in a predominately Caucasian environment Live in areas not predominately ethnic oriented Behavioural patterns are largely driven by dominant culture
Cluster 4: totally integrated	Fluent only in English Have little knowledge of their ethnic culture Likely to be born in the UK View themselves as English and have patriotic feelings towards England

(Source: May (2001) 'Minority Marketing', *Marketing Direct*, October, pp. 15–16. Reproduced from *Marketing Direct* magazine with the permission of the copyright owner Haymarket Business Publications Limited)

integration (Table 6.2). Although fairly crude, it provides a starting point for marketers to build a picture that can be overlaid with other indicators of consumer behaviour. Targeting ethnic communities isn't impossible then, but the majority of multi-discipline agencies are simply not experiencing demand for this kind of work. Seligman doesn't believe the Data Protection Act is entirely responsible: 'It probably made it harder and discouraged people further from undertaking campaigns, but it's not as if there was a good of work before.' The reason, he says, is that much of the work goes to people the group in question is already familiar with, or to specialist agencies, such as the government's agency for publicity procurement, COI Communications. It recently worked

with the DTI to raise awareness of the national minimum wage among ethnic minorities. Lion, too, works with a number of agencies targeting ethnic minorities. For the RSPCA recently, it produced a campaign targeting Asian shopkeepers, encouraging responsible care of guard dogs. It included a leaflet produced in a range of languages. Clearly certain companies and brands are seeking out ethnic minorities as a target audience, and there are agencies ready and willing to do the work. It just needs every-one to open their eyes a little wider and see the possibilities that exist.

(Source: May (2001) 'Minority Marketing,' *Marketing Direct*, October, pp. 5–16. Reproduced from *Marketing Direct* magazine with the permission of the copyright owners Haymarket Business Publications Limited)

Psychographics

This name covers lifestyle, personality and self-image. We provide only cursory coverage of the last two, which can be discovered in most consumer behaviour books, but lifestyle is worth some discussion, especially because it is important to differentiate traditional from contemporary lifestyle segmentation. The latter was covered in Chapter 2, but the following is an analysis of how lifestyle segmentation was originally conceived. The discussion goes on to show, via a case study, how these approaches are being blended.

Lifestyle

Traditional lifestyle segmentation was based typically on the presentation to respondents of a series of statements (Likert scales). Table 6.3 reproduces a short selection of the (246) lifestyle statements used in the Target Group Index annual research programme (BMRB 1988)

Respondents are presented with these statements and asked to give their degree of agreement with each.

A UK lifestyle typology was named Taylor Nelson's Applied Futures (McNulty and McNulty 1987) and identified the following segments: the Belonger, the Survivor, the Experimentalist, the Conspicuous Consumer, the Social Resistor, the Self-Explorer and the Aimless. The Self-Explorer group was the fastest growing and further reinforces one of the propositions of this chapter, namely that some markets have become more orientated to self-expression and

TABLE 6.3   Examples of lifestyle statements

I buy clothes for comfort, not for style
Once I find a brand I like, I tend to stick to it
I always buy British whenever I can
I dress to please myself
My family rarely sits down to a meal together at home
I enjoy eating foreign food
I like to do a lot when I am on holiday

individualism. This traditional form of lifestyle (AIO) segmentation provides useful insight into what makes people 'tick'. It is based upon traditional market research: administering Likert-scaled statements concerned with activities, interests and opinions to a sample of consumers. The data is anonymised and the resulting profiles are very useful for determining the style and mood of promotional messages.

As discussed in the preceding chapter, contemporary lifestyle segmentation is very different, being based on respondents ticking boxes against products and services in which they claim to be interested and the data being attributed to name and address for the explicit purpose of building marketing databases.

A recent development has been to resurrect the Taylor-Nelson type of clusters but based on large-scale samples of consumers whose data is matched in a database with their name and address and which reveals both AIO data and product-specific data.

CASE STUDY 6.5

The Values Company

The Values Engine surveys 4 000 consumers every week through the agency IPSOS-RSL in order to explore AIO-type dimensions and the results are then applied to Claritas' database of lifestyle data in order to infer similar patterns and segments across the population (Exhibit 6.3).

The diagram shows how AIO data and product data are overlaid onto the inner–outer-directed value framework and Exhibit 6.4 takes the analysis further by showing how the segmentation model can be applied to traditional adopter categories which in turn can be used to inform marketing activities over the product life cycle (segmentation over time).

(Source: The Values Company)

EXHIBIT 6.3   Values and brands

(Source: values Engine™ 2003)

EXHIBIT 6.4   Values and the product life cycle

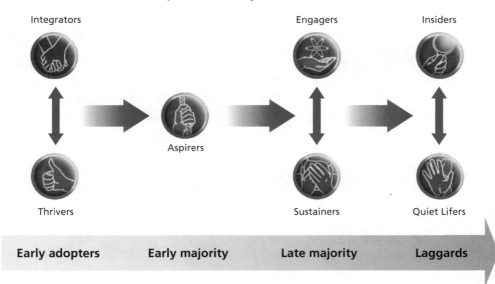

(Source: The Values Company)

Another dimension that is blended within Case Study 6.4 is the concept of innovativeness. This leads to potential segments based on customers' degree of interest in newness. This is a personality characteristic so also falls within the psychographics category. A proposition here is that over the life of a product, marketing activity might need to change because different segments of adopting customers are salient at different points in time. The characteristics of each adopter category and the importance of two-step flows of communication via opinion leaders can be found in more detail elsewhere (Evans and Fill 2000), but the case above is a useful introduction to this concept. Indeed, an interesting if slightly disquieting discovery in the car market was the acknowledgement by public relations managers of the potential value of targeting the more innovative customers who might be high in opinion leadership (Evans and Fill 2001) yet there was an almost total lack of implementation of this approach via the PR function. It was found that database departments often collected details of customers who purchased cars early in that model's life cycle and targeted the same individuals when the next new (relevant) product launch was launched. This data was generally not shared with PR people. Again we have an example of a lack of integration of databases and this serves to reinforce the need for such data to be properly shared across functions and partners. This point is explored further in our coverage of knowledge management in Chapter 8.

Other examples of separating 'innovative' customer details and targeting these individuals when other new products are launched is provided by Phillips and Sony who operate on this basis in the electronics sector.

Benefit segmentation

It has long been recognised in marketing that customers do not buy 'things', they buy benefits: we don't buy drills, we buy holes, cosmetics companies don't sell soap, we buy hope, and so on!

A useful illustration of segmentation is the toothpaste market in terms of the benefits shown in Table 6.4. What is shown is that even in such an apparently non-differentiated market, there are different consumer segments that buy in

TABLE 6.4 Toothpaste consumer benefit segments (Haley 1968)

	Sensory segment	Sociable segment	Worrier segment	Independent segment
Main benefit	flavour, appearance	bright teeth	decay prevention	price
Demographic factors	children, young people	teens, families	large	men
Lifestyle factors	hedonistic	active	conservative	concerned with value
Brands, label	Colgate, Stripe	Ultra Brite, Macleans	Crest	cheapest own-label, brands on sale

different ways for a variety of reasons and on this basis can be targeted with different marketing mixes. This is a fundamental rationale for market segmentation and fits neatly with relational approaches if there is to be an understanding of customers and any meaningful organisation–customer interaction.

There is renewed interest in benefit segmentation, as research into this form of segmentation in the financial services market by Minhas and Jacobs (1996) and Machauer and Morgner (2001) suggests.

Person–situation segmentation

This approach is strongly related to benefit segmentation because it is based on the interaction of consumer characteristics, product benefits and occasions of use (Dickson 1982; Dubow 1992). People with specific characteristics may want to use products with specific benefits in specific situations. Table 6.5 provides an example with respect to the suntan lotion market with four situations and four target groups. In principle, four times four products may be designed. Taking skin colour and skin factors into account, even more product formulas may be marketed.

TABLE 6.5 Person–situation segmentation (Dickson 1982)

Situations	Young children	Teenagers	Adult women	Adult men	Situation benefits
Beach/boat sunbathing	Combined insect repellent		Summer perfume		– windburn protection – product can stand heat – container floats
Home-poolside sunbathing			Combined moisturiser		– large pump dispenser – won't stain wood, etc.
Sunlamp bathing			Combined moisturiser and massage oil		– designed for type of lamp – artificial tanning
Snow skiing			Winter perfume		– protection from rays – anti-freeze formula
Person benefits	– special protection – non-poisonous	– fits in jean pocket – used by opinion leaders	– female perfume	– male perfume	

Relational segmentation

One framework that might provide a basis for segmenting along relational lines concerns 'loyalty'. This is more than regular purchasing, as Dick and Basu (1994) in their conceptualising of the loyalty phenomenon suggest. 'Relative attitudes' are also important. That is, loyalty depends not only on positive attitudes towards the store or brand, but on differentiated attitudes towards the alternatives. In other words, if a consumer is positive towards store A, and not very positive towards B and C, then the consumer might indeed develop loyalty towards A. On the other hand, if there are fairly similar positive attitudes towards A, B and C then there is unlikely to be real loyalty. In this case the consumer might patronise a particular store regularly but because of factors such as convenience and familiarity.

This analysis is useful because it is an explanation of why apparent loyalty (at least regular patronage) might not be true loyalty. Conversely, it contributes to our understanding of why some consumers exhibit aspects of real loyalty without holding particularly strong positive attitudes towards that store. In this latter case the argument would be that a positive but weak attitude towards A might be accentuated by even weaker positive attitudes towards B and C.

Dick and Basu (1994) describe a situation in which relative attitude is low (little to choose between the alternatives) but which is also characterised by high store patronage and they describe this as 'spurious loyalty'. Where, alternatively, there is low patronage but strongly differentiated and positive attitudes towards A, this is 'latent loyalty'. Otherwise expected high patronage in this case might be inhibited by co-shoppers' preferences, for example (Exhibit 6.5).

When it comes to real loyalty itself, it is clear by now that they see this as where there is both high patronage and a positive attitude towards the store,

EXHIBIT 6.5 Loyalty segments

		Repeat patronage	
		High	Low
Relative attitude	High	Loyalty	Latent loyalty
	Low	Spurious loyalty	No loyalty

(Source: Dick and Basu 1994)

which is not matched by similarly positive attitudes towards alternative stores. The potential market segments which marketers would want to progress are towards the upper left quadrant. There is fuller coverage of this model in Chapter 9.

A concern is encapsulated by Gofton's (2001) summary of QCI research which found that few organisations distinguish between the satisfaction levels of their most and least valuable segments:

> **❝** Only 16% (of the 51 blue chip companies interviewed) understand what the main drivers of loyalty are . . . 30% never look at this and only half carry out some research to identify loyalty. **❞**

Related to several of the above bases is Mitchell's (2003) proposition that consumers can be grouped into segments on the basis of the attitudes they hold towards privacy issues related to direct, interactive marketing.

As we have already mentioned, we are concerned that some of these more 'affective' bases for informing relational interaction can sometimes to neglected in favour of the more mechanistic 'what, how and when' of transactional data and the data-based segmentation summarised in the next section.

Data-driven segmentation

Based on transactional data overlaid with other data such as geodemographics and financials, the 'biographic' profiles discussed in the previous chapter can be determined from fusion and mining of data.

Tesco in the UK, for example, has analysed its loyalty card data and it has been reported (Marsh 2001) that mining the mountain of transactional data from its 10 million Clubcard users, it has identified 100 000 different segments, each targeted with a different set of money-off vouchers via a customer magazine. A similar example is provided by Tower Records. This company has segmented its customer database and e-mails offers to selected targets, and 'out of every 10 000 e-mails sent, no more than three people receive the same offer' (Marsh 2001).

Chapter 2 explored geodemographics but it is worth giving some examples of how this base can be used for market segmentation. Exhibit 6.6 demonstrates one such use of geodemographics. It is possible to profile a catchment area (for example) for the potential siting of a retail outlet. The MOSAIC (in this case) category overlays of the local map show where different segments live. If, for example, the retailer is mainly targeting the 'stylish single' segment, the map shows the area of greatest concentration of this segment. Indeed, names and addresses of those in this segment can be purchased in order to target these potential customers personally. This particular map shows a five-minute off-peak drive time from Cardiff Business School (CF10 3EU).

Another example of the use of geodemographics is provided in the following case study.

EXHIBIT 6.6 Five-minute off-peak drive time from CF10 3EU

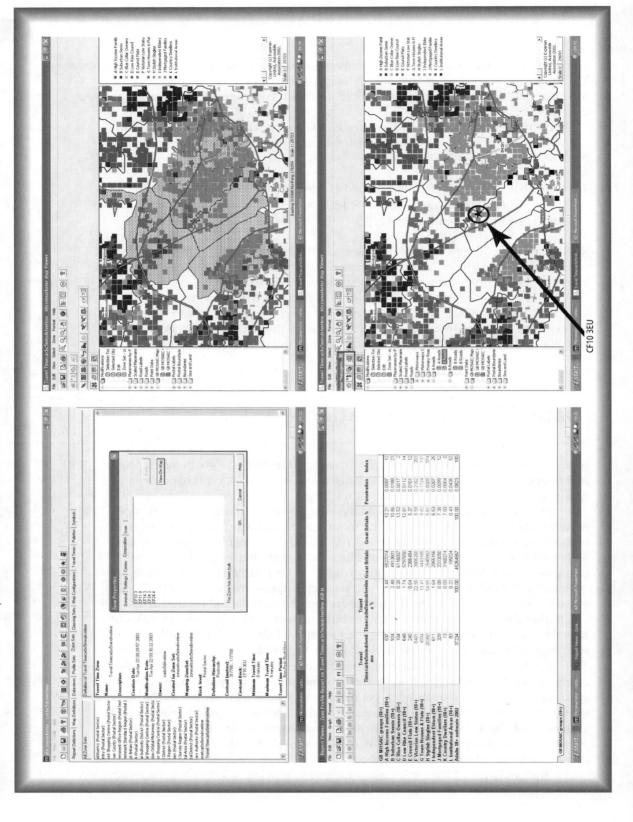

CASE **STUDY** 6.6

Rico Pasta Sauce

The client, Rico Pasta Sauce, provided their agency, JD Media, with the brief to raise awareness of their brand and to position it as the premium stir-in pasta sauce within the entire pasta sauce market. The raising awareness campaign was going to be composed of a mixed media regional campaign, consisting of leaflet drops to households (known as 'door dropping activity' or 'door-to-door'), posters (known as 'outdoor') and magazines, centred within the South East region.

With a lack of any customer data available from Rico Pasta Sauce, which could then be used to produce a MOSAIC Lifestyle Profile, TGI (Target Group Index) was used as the source for producing a MOSAIC Lifestyle Profile of Rico Pasta Sauce users. TGI market share is widely used in the media sector for advertising sales purposes. Used in area-based applications such as catchment analysis for new site locations, direct mailing, door-to-door distributions and geographical rankings, TGI profiles are particularly useful when a client has no customer data of its own for profiling, or to understand the whole market rather than simply profiling their own customers. Because MOSAIC has been appended to TGI respondent data, MOSAIC cross-tabulations of any of the questions on the TGI survey can be conducted. This allows MOSAIC types to be profiled by product usage and leisure interests, providing valuable extra information that can be used in the analysis and targeting of customers.

The index calculation is used as a means of identifying the target MOSAIC groups in which Rico Pasta Sauce consumers have the highest propensity to be found. The index compares the target percentage with the base percentage using the following calculation to show the extent to which the profiles differ: (Target % divided by Base %) × 100. This shows under- or over-representation of each group or type in the customer profile compared to the base profile. An index of 100 indicates that the MOSAIC group or type shown is represented at the same level in the customer profile as it is across the base profile (usually Great Britain in geographical analysis, or the total number of adults aged 15+ with the TGI profiles). Therefore, an index of 200 would show that the MOSAIC group or type has twice the representation. On the other hand, an index of 50 would show that it has half the representation when compared to the base. Generally speaking, a MOSAIC type with an index of below 80, or above 120, is statistically significant.

The MOSAIC Lifestyle Profile shows that Rico's target market consists of the following MOSAIC groups: High Income Families (index 188), Country Dwellers (index 155) and Suburban Semis (index 139). The Rico Pasta Sauce consumer base is therefore relatively affluent and upmarket. The penetration percentage of the target MOSAIC groups was then calculated in all newspaper circulation areas falling within the South East region. This percentage shows the geographical concentration of households of a particular MOSAIC group or type in relation to all households falling within a particular area, broken down by postal sector. If the target MOSAIC households in an area amount to 1 500 and all households amount to 3 000, then the penetration percentage would equal 50%. In other words, target MOSAIC households account for 50% (or half) of all households in the area: (1 500 / 3 000) × 100.

EXHIBIT 6.7 Penetration of MOSAIC groups in relation to all households for each postal sector

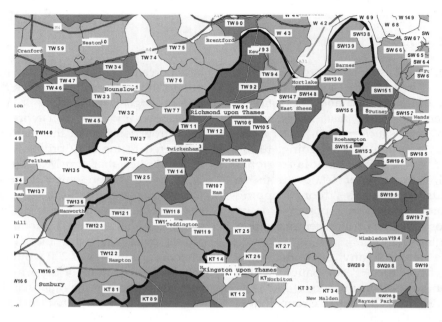

EXHIBIT 6.8 Areas where a poster campaign would have most impact

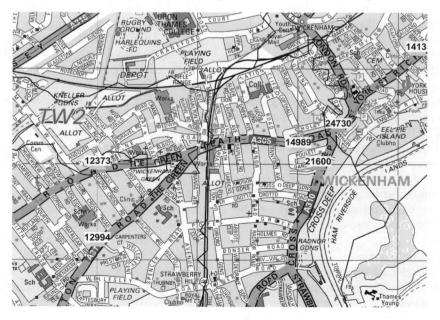

Newspaper circulation areas are defined by postal sector geography (TW12, KT33, etc.). Exhibit 6.7 illustrates the penetration of the three MOSAIC groups in relation to all households for each postal sector within the *Richmond and Twickenham Informer* circulation area. Areas shaded in red indicate a penetration of between 80 and 100%. JD Media then used this information to effectively target the placement of inserts for Rico Pasta Sauce: only those postal sectors falling within those newspaper circulation areas where the penetration of target MOSAIC households was over 80%, therefore limiting wastage and its consequences.

In terms of attempting to identify the most suitable areas in the South East for the outdoor advertising of Rico Pasta Sauce, annual average daily traffic flow counts (provided by the DETR[1]) were mapped and plotted by postcode census point and overlaid with the MOSAIC group postcode classification. Areas with a high traffic flow count in accordance with obvious clusters of Rico Pasta Sauce's target MOSAIC audience provided an indication of areas where a poster campaign would have most impact in terms of raising consumer and product awareness (Exhibit 6.8).

In order to identify those magazines and editorials offering the best potential for marketing Rico Pasta Sauces through advertising and inserting money redemption vouchers, a technique known as 'Media Matching' was undertaken. The aim of media matching is to identify which national and/or local media are most appropriate in which to advertise a product. This is done by matching the MOSAIC profile of that product with that of each medium. The resultant report matches all the media alternatives with how well the profile of those media match the profile of Rico Pasta Sauce users. An index calculation is subsequently created and, in simple terms, the higher the index, the stronger the profile of the media in the Mosaic groups that are also

EXHIBIT 6.9 Result of matching the MOSAIC profile with that of each medium

Magazine	Similarity
National Geographic	High
Sainsbury's Magazine	High
The M&S Magazine	High
BBC Gardeners World	High
Saga Magazine	High
Horse and Hound	High
The Times Educational Supplement	High
Radio Times	High
Safeway Magazine	High
Country Life	High
BBC Homes & Antiques	High
Golf Monthly	High
Reader's Digest	High
BBC Wildlife	High
Hello!	High
Garden Answers	High
AA Members Magazine	High
Private Eye	High
The Somerfield Magazine	High
What Car?	High
New Scientist	High
The Ford Magazine	High
The Garden	High
Viz	Low
Max Power	Low
More!	Low
Big!	Low
Match of the Day	Low
Top of the Pops Magazine	Low
TV & Satellite Week	Low
Shoot	Low
Best	Low
TV Quick	Low
Mizz	Low
TV Hits	Low
Chat	Low
Woman	Low
Woman's Own	Low
Bella	Low
That's Life	Low
Take a Break	Low
Cable Guide	Low
Inside Soap	Low
What's On TV	Low
Smash Hits	Low

strong in the Rico Pasta Sauce user MOSAIC p[rofile. For ease of interpretation, the index calculation has been banded, with indices of 120 and above being classed as 'high' and indices of 80 or below being classed as 'low'. On looking at Exhibit 6.9 above, it is evident that the relatively upmarket nature of the Rico Pasta Sauce user MOSAIC Profile corresponds with the (somewhat expected) affluence portrayed by the MOSAIC Profiles of quality editorials such as *Sainsbury's Magazine*, *The M & S Magazine* and *Safeway Magazine*. All three represent titles both falling within the right market and reaching the right audience. Unsurprisingly, on the other hand, low matches include *Viz.*, *TV Hits* and *Smash Hits*.

The overall campaign proved to be extremely successful: JD Media retained Rico as a client; there was a good response from the inserts placed in local newspapers and voucher redemption rates were above average. The vouchers also asked for some customer details, such as name, address, postcode and date of birth, in order that the customer database could be enhanced and further profiling of customers could be conducted. Rico is now looking to 'roll out' the campaign on a national basis.

(All names used within this case are purely fictitious.)

(Source: Ross Facer, Experian Micromarketing)

Another case study provides an interesting example of how data-informed segmentation can lead to quite wide-ranging marketing decisions. In this case, the store profiled catchment areas of its branches and very different catchment area profiles emerged. These led not only to what to stock but even the sort of music to play in each branch.

Jackson's

CASE **STUDY** 6.7

This convenience store (C-store) chain profiled the catchment areas of its branches and overlaid transactional data profiles with geodemographics. The different catchment areas were grouped into four main segments:

Cluster 1 – The Manor Born

The Manor Born typifies areas of high income/dual income families, living in large houses in the leafy suburbs of towns, with a typical age range of between 45 and 54 years old. These shoppers are professional or managerial, with an increased tendency to work from home, which may open up new opportunities for the C-store. Car ownership is high, as is disposable income and standard of education. Also with this group we find older couples who have retired to their own homes in very wealthy villages, or to luxury apartments by the sea.

In both variations of The Manor Born, we see a high spend generally on food, but this tends to be within a supermarket or at speciality stores, where fine wines and gourmet foods are purchased. The choice available to them is also fairly high due to either their location or their high mobility. This shopper tends to read *The Times, Daily Telegraph* or *Daily Mail*, along with regional newspapers in order to keep up to date with community issues. They are likely to be seen enjoying the theatre or an expensive restaurant.

These stores are in better areas of smaller country towns or outskirts of larger towns. The people around these stores reap the benefits of both town and country living. Most inhabitants will own their own homes and be in a professional occupation. There is typically a higher disposable income present around these stores. Most-read newspapers are *The Times, Daily Express, Daily Mail*, and *Daily Telegraph*. Shoppers like to shop regularly at small independent shops and speciality stores, as well as supermarkets such as Waitrose, Safeway and Sainsbury's. Shoppers are willing to experiment with new food, and like to purchase fine wines, cheese, pâté, game etc.

These stores experience the highest spend of all stores. Stores are not particularly profitable. Ranked second in terms of average square footage. Lowest total sales of all the clusters. But these provide the lowest Grocery sales in the Jackson's portfolio. Comparable sales of Frozen, Chilled, Produce and Off Licence sales with rest of portfolio. Sales in News slightly lower than other three clusters. Looking at this cluster, there are two sub-groups to target within the cluster:

- professional/managerial;
- older households.

Both treat the store very differently, yet both are looking for the added value possible in a rural setting.

The upmarket shopper

Shop at least once a week in a supermarket. Do not use C-stores to top up grocery shopping.

But do shop for: Milk (73%), Newspapers & Magazines (53%), Lottery (35%), Soft Drinks (28%), Tobacco (22%), Confectionery (26%).

The older shopper – older households

Try to shop at least once a week in a large grocers. Do use C-stores to top up grocery shopping. Looking for a community store to serve as many needs as possible. Key areas outside the core categories: Fruit & Vegetables, Tinned Food, Household Goods. This group is the highest purchaser within these categories.

Opportunities

- Alcohol: With money to spend, a range focusing on premium wines and spirits is beneficial.
- Enhance the community feel by providing services: Bakery, Post Office, ATM, Video Rental, Dry Cleaning, Confectionery (26%).
- Typical in-store music: Paul Simon.

Cluster 2 – Keep Up Appearances

Keep Up Appearances stores are those surrounded by affluent blue-collar, maturing families, on newer owner-occupied estates, or those better-off council areas located in rural settings. Again, a fairly high disposable income is enjoyed, as mortgages are close to being paid off and children are late teens, students, or in their first jobs. A very family-orientated shopper, it is likely that the female of the house still performs the main shop for the entire family, typically at a store such as Tesco. Indeed, many of these areas will have a large superstore located nearby. In the rural areas, however, the C-store may act as a full service provider, and should try to meet the needs of the surrounding area as fully as possible.

These stores are in areas historically built around industry. The people around these stores aspire to the trappings of middle-class lifestyles and typically live in owner-occupied housing, a percentage of which is ex-Council. These people will typically be in skilled manual occupations and have a higher than average wage for blue-collar workers. Most frequently read newspapers are the *Daily Mail* and *Daily Express*. Inhabitants around these stores are just as likely to use smaller local stores as larger supermarkets such as Tesco. These areas have the highest spend on groceries. Beer is preferred to wine and spirits. There is an above-average tendency for people to try new food, although traditional is preferred to foreign.

Top-up shopping does play a part in this cluster. Families use the store to supplement their busy lives: this cluster has the highest purchasing of Bread and Milk. Alcohol & Household goods are the two most common purchases outside the core categories. Surprisingly, Fruit & Vegetables, Chilled & Frozen are not important.

Opportunities

- Alcohol is the biggest winner here. There needs to be a step back from the cosmopolitan range of Cluster 1 but still offer a mid-price range. Price-led promotions will work particularly well.

- Again, services are important but it is now the link to leisure time that is the key: Video Rental, ATM, Meal supplements (Sauces etc.) to capture the time-poor/cash-rich element.

- Promotions: Price is the key element but some multi-buy activity may work. POS delivery is important as the store is mainly used for the core categories. Where the store is found in an extreme suburban location, there is a crossover with Cluster 1.

- Typical in-store music: Barry Manilow.

Cluster 3 – Royle Family

This group really forms the backbone of the Jackson's estate, accounting for 40 of the 88 outlets. Truly council orientated, this group ranges from better-off, optimistic council areas where council homes may have been bought out in the 1980s, through the spectrum of council estates, to those where apathy and even anger have taken hold of the residents as they struggle with many social difficulties. In some areas, a strong sense of pride prevails. Residents are proud of their working-class roots, and a strong sense of community abounds. Although housing is small, much is now owned outright, so disposable income is relatively high. These are no-nonsense areas, often politically left wing, but conservative in attitude.

Local retailers serve these areas well, as to go further afield would usually mean catching a bus into town. At the other end of the scale, we have those council estates where high unemployment, sickness and crime are unfortunate factors of everyday life. Low incomes, low opportunities and low expectations mean that residents are reliant on public services, income support, and the support of family and friends.

Income is the main driver in these households.
Price perception in-store is vital.
Mainly shop in Kwik-Save, Iceland & Co-ops. C-stores as a whole are seen as expensive.

Main drivers within the core categories are: Lottery & Tobacco. Are the second biggest purchaser of Bread, Milk & Fruit/Vegetables.

Opportunities

Outside the main categories this cluster has the highest purchase rate across the others: Alcohol (21%), Tinned Food (21%), Pet Food (17%), Household Goods (25%), Toiletries (21%). Lack of transport/ease of use contribute to this. Key to this is price.

Must be competitive but not necessarily the cheapest. Must be advertised. Re-education of pricing within the Jackson Store is important.

Promotion

Price is important. Bulk purchasing is attractive so multibuys can be used. Stores extremely important to this cluster: 'Buy as you need' mentality. Highest purchasers of Ready Meals and chilled foods. Depth of choice important due to the cosmopolitan population. Varied tastes and willing to try new products. Very high purchasing within the core categories. Leads in Soft Drinks & Confectionery.

Opportunities

Alcohol: biggest purchaser of alcohol. Try new products, so the latest brands are important.

Perceived depth of choice important. Ready Meals. The only cluster that could really sustain this category. Inviting delivery of product – upright chillers/freezers. Other 'grocery' categories only require a range to satisfy distress purchasing.

Leisure wise, the Royle Family areas enjoy watching ITV, reading tabloid newspapers such as *The Sun* and *The Star*, and spend a high proportion of their disposable income on bingo, gambling, the pools, and satellite TV. When the Royle Family goes shopping, it is either to mid-size, local retailers, or to fascia such as Iceland and Kwik Save. A lower than average spend should be expected. Royal Family shoppers are looking for cheap, discounted groceries, usually branded, so money-off coupons, competitions and 3 for 2 offers etc. should fare well.

These stores are in areas where public housing is common and access to stores is poor The labour force is mostly partly skilled labour, often employed in manufacturing Most frequently read newspapers are *The Star*, *News of the World*, *The Sun*, and *The*

Record. There is a high consumption of fats and sugars, and smoking and drinking are popular. Shoppers frequent midsize and local stores such as Co-op and Kwik Save; symbol stores are important. Traditional food is preferred to anything foreign. Tins and packets are preferred to frozen goods. These stores have above-average profitability compared to other clusters. Marginally below-average spend. Ranked fourth in terms of average square footage. Comparable total sales to other clusters. Above-average sales in News compared to rest of Jackson's portfolio. Comparable sales in Grocery, Tobacco and Off Licence to other clusters. Lower sales in Chilled, Frozen and Produce.

Typical in-store music: Abba

Cluster 4 – Young Ones

Young Ones describes those stores located in inner city or inner urban areas, surrounded by young residents falling into one of three categories: Firstly students, who form a big part of this segment, secondly, ethnic minorities living in inner city areas, or thirdly, young singles or co-habitees in their first job. Within these areas we can see evidence of high crime rates, high unemployment, low incomes, higher than average single-parent families, and general overcrowding. In some cases, an entire family may live in one small house. These areas are populated almost exclusively by people for whom English is not their first language. Similarly, within student areas, we find small houses, or large houses which have been converted into flats, low disposable income, low car ownership, a mix of social class, origin and cultural background. Small local housing association-run estates are also prevalent in these areas. Also within the Young Ones we find young professionals in their first jobs, choosing to live in cheap and convenient rented accommodation, close to work and all that a city has to offer in terms of nightlife and leisure.

Some of the Young Ones shoppers will be living close to or on the poverty line, being able to afford only the bare essentials on a day-to-day basis. However, this does include a high spend on cigarettes and alcohol. Others will be shopping on a daily basis due to their lifestyle, and buying a different meal solution to suit each day's activities. Purchases will be made just in time, and will typically be from local C-stores or discount retailers.

These stores are in inner city or town areas, often located near to a university or college. Accommodation typically comprises non-private housing (rented or council). The people around these stores are typically younger in age (18–24), and many are emerging professionals looking for their first job and house. Frequently read newspapers are *The Times*, *The Guardian*, *The Observer*, and the *Financial Times*. The emphasis when shopping for food is on price and convenience. Shoppers frequent local stores, freezer centres and speciality stores, and are willing to experiment with new food. Takeaways are popular. Ethnic minorities are particularly over-represented in these areas.

Store characteristics

The most profitable stores on average in Jackson's portfolio. Highest sales on average of all Jackson's stores. Highest no. customers on average of all clusters. Ranked third in terms of average square footage. Spend is comparable to other clusters.

Category sales

Sales are good in Grocery, Chilled, Frozen and Produce. Comparable sales to other clusters in Off Licence and Tobacco. Below-average sales in News.

Promotions: Price more important than multibuying. New products very important. Use store most often so only need to highlight the bigger events. Price sensitive but only if insulted, are willing to pay for the convenience element (24-hour opening). Leisure is the key again (Big Night In), therefore video rental an option.

Typical in store music: Oasis.

(Source: Jackson's Stores and Experian Micromarketing)

We hope this case demonstrates the power of data-informed relational marketing. From relatively unsophisticated data, the range of relational activities from stocking to in-store music policies is impressive. The relational approach is clear: note phrases like 'enhance the community feel'. Note, also, the links with much of our earlier coverage of segmentation bases, such as the recognition of those new innovative segments that are interested in trying new products.

Biographic and one-to-one segmentation

We have already explored the fusion of transactional and profile data in earlier chapters, so will merely restate the point about a significant trend in relational marketing towards biographic segmentation. The following case is useful in demonstrating how transactional data can be used to segment and target customers in differential ways.

MVC

Background

MVC is a chain of over 50 music stores, part of Kingfisher, with almost 2m 'members'. Ninety-seven per cent of transactions are made using cards and RSCR was asked to analyse the data and produce proposals for a precisely targeted, six-month mailing campaign designed to increase store traffic and generate incremental sales.

The process

The first step was to profile the customer base to find the most effective and practical segmentation model. The second stage was to use this model to devise a customer reactivation programme. A programme of offers and promotions to maximise sales from every pack was then mailed.

By combining Sales Band and Frequency of Purchase, a useful and simple segmenta-

tion model was identified based on 'Activity Levels' (Exhibit 6.10):

'Casual': 1 purchase, up to £50 sales
'Regular': 1–4 purchases and £50–£75 sales
'Loyal': 1–10 purchases and £75–£200 sales
'Extreme': 11+ purchases and sales >£200

Recency is a very useful decision support tool for planning reactivation activity.

Of the 1.3m customers, 867k were 'Active'; 17% had bought in the last 4 weeks, and over 50% in the last 8 weeks (analysis period included Christmas).

These were classified into Active, Warm, Lukewarm and Cold categories (Table 6.6) using calculations of average frequency by spend band.

An 'event-triggered' reactivation programme was implemented, based on clear ROI criteria. Customer transaction history by product range was examined, in particular identifying customers spending over

EXHIBIT 6.10 Segmentation by account data

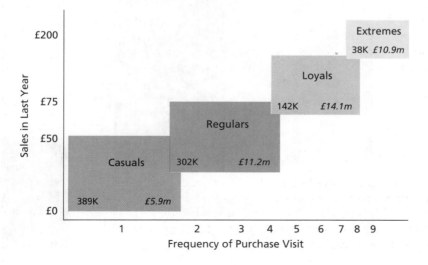

TABLE 6.6 Active to cold segments

Spend Band					Time Since Last Sale (Excluding Zeros)					
	<4 Weeks	5–8 Weeks	9–12 Weeks	13–17 Weeks	18–21 Weeks	22–25 Weeks	26–51 Weeks	52–78 Weeks	79–104 Weeks	105+ Weeks
£0.01–£25	39 675	94 509	36 405	25 387	16 197	16 976	89 656	99 037	29 428	45 615
£25–£50	23 907	60 855	21 952	13 719	8 499	8 264	40 402	36 621	10 327	16 969
£50–£75	15 374	35 830	12 372	7 399	4 606	4 084	20 142	14 625	4 393	6 292
£75–£100	11 001	23 619	8 123	4 714	2 890	2 480	11 292	7 291	2 271	2 857
£100–£200	25 151	45 458	14 323	8 239	4 883	3 918	16 993	8 668	2 814	3 220
£200–£300	11 762	16 540	4 569	2 594	1 476	1 145	4 230	1 809	576	622
£300–£400	6 415	7 047	1 851	1 053	597	415	1 593	601	196	243
£400–£500	3 757	3 445	886	483	262	188	743	249	83	106
£500+	8 345	5 127	1 238	653	386	258	987	314	118	137
Total	145 387	292 430	101 719	64 241	39 796	37 728	186 038	169 215	50 206	76 061

'Active'   241 638
'Warm'   65 013
'Lukewarm'   37 839
'Cold'   46 202
             390 692

50% in one range. Indeed, some small pockets of customers accounted for up to 40% of category sales.

This information was used to overlay a selectively inserted leaflet programme, using 'propensity to buy' to maximise relevance (Exhibit 6.11).

Over a six-month mailing period, the programme generated £750k in incremental sales against non-mailed control groups –

the equivalent of a virtual store! The promotions succeeded in tempting back lapsing customers, converting rental-only customers to buyers and developing multi-purchase behaviour among new members, and overall this segmentation model is now used throughout the chain for targeting marketing effort.

(Source: MVC/Experian Micromarketing)

EXHIBIT 6.11   Reactivation programme

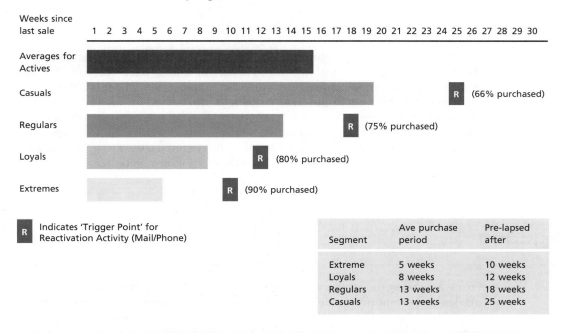

The general point being made here is that markets are being analysed in ever more sophisticated and detailed ways and this is leading to the identification and targeting of smaller but better defined (at least in theory) segments. But although this gives the impression that we have moved to 'segments of one', one-to-one marketing is not the norm and perhaps is more rhetoric than reality. There might be personalised targeting, in the sense that the individual is addressed by name, and there might be some data-driven offer that matches the data mining outcome for the segment to which the individual is allocated, but this is not the same as understanding customers on a true individual basis as we would in a human relationship context. Even the 'personalised' approach to relational marketing, however, might experience future flack. Digital printing technology allows personalisation to a higher degree. 'You can personalise page by page, it's easy to put a name anywhere throughout the copy' (Arnold 2002). A development of this in the USA was an apparently handwritten mailing targeted at members of a particular healthcare segment. So convincing was this that over 150 people complained on the basis that it looked like a friend writing to them telling them they needed to lose weight! (Rubach 2002). Technology will also facilitate more examples of personalised targeting of segments. It is now possible to target an individualised TV message, analogous to personalised mailing, to a unique address via fibre optic cable (Channel 4 1990).

As Shaw *et al*. (2000) note:

" Market segmentation should be driven by customer needs and wants . . . these techniques are well understood in the academic world but corporate practice seems to be in the dark ages. **"**

Indeed, a study amongst pharmaceutical companies found that when asked what the key challenges are for the introduction of CRM, only 6.5% of the issues mentioned related to improving customer satisfaction (Clegg 2001). So one wonders at happened to the likes of benefit segmentation, for example. Actual behavioural response does not necessarily equate with an understanding of consumers. If responders become the central focus (because they are cheaper to retain than new consumers are to acquire) then aren't we storing up trouble for the future in attending less to why the others are non-responders?

Targeting

From a marketing strategy point of view, selection of the appropriate target market is paramount to developing successful marketing programmes. Market targeting requires the evaluation and selection of one or more market segments to enter.

With regard to the question of each segment's structural attractiveness, the marketing manager's primary concern is, as has been discussed, accountability and profitability. It may be the case that a segment is both large and growing but that, because of the intensity of competition, the scope for profit is low. Several models for measuring segment attractiveness exist, including Porter's five-forces model. This model suggests that segment profitability is affected by five principal factors:

1 industry competitors and the threat of segment rivalry;
2 potential entrants to the market and the threat of mobility;
3 the threat of substitute products;
4 buyers and their relative power;

5 suppliers and their relative power.

Having measured the size, growth rate and structural attractiveness of each segment, the marketing manager needs to examine each one in turn against the background of the organisation's objectives and resources. In doing this, the marketing manager is looking for the degree of compatibility between the segment and the long-term goals of the organisation. It is often the case, for example, that a seemingly attractive segment can be dismissed either because it would not move the organisation significantly forward towards its goals, or because it would divert organisational energy. Even where there does appear to be a match, consideration needs to be given to whether the organisation has the necessary skills, competences, resources and commitment needed to operate effectively. Without these, segment entry is likely to be of little strategic value.

The company has also to decide on how many segments to cover and how to identify the best segments. There are four market-coverage alternatives:

1 undifferentiated marketing (marketing mix for the mass);
2 differentiated marketing (separate mixes for each segment);
3 concentrated marketing (separate mix but for only those segments selected);
4 custom marketing (separate mix for each customer).

On a more sophisticated level, organisations may pursue one of a number of targeting strategies in an effort to seek out prospects (Exhibit 6.12) (Blattberg *et al.* 2001):

EXHIBIT 6.12 Targeting strategies

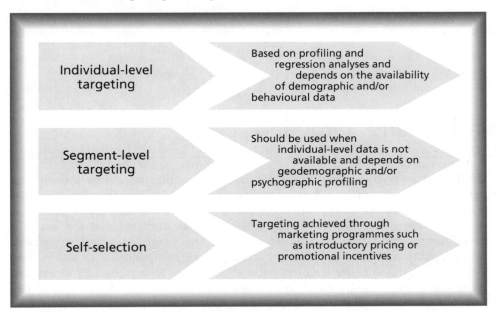

1 **Individual-level targeting**: The advantage of individual-level targeting is primarily that the offer can be personalised to the prospect. This will naturally require the use of information on individual prospects, and success is dependent upon how well the organisation understands those prospects. Conventional wisdom suggests that there are six factors that lead to success (McCorkell, 1997): product, targeting, offer, format, copy and timing. Ensuring success therefore requires not only having the right product and the right offer, but also relies upon the effectiveness of targeting, the format, the offer, and the timing of communication to individuals.

2 **Segment-Level targeting**: We have explored the use of geodemographic and psychographic profiling and segmenting in our earlier coverage in this chapter and the point here is that in the absence of true one-to-one relational interaction, most organisations are still targeting segments, albeit well-defined ones.

3 **Self-selection**: The use of a direct response mechanism through mass media has the advantage of reaching a potentially larger audience than a mailing, and more importantly, produces hot prospects. That is, prospects have self-selected themselves by showing interest in the offer. When using direct response in non-personal (broadcast) media it is important to make it easy for the prospect to respond, for example by using an 0800 number or Freepost facility. If an immediate response is required, the use of penetration pricing, or the suggestion of a 'one-time-only offer' or availability for a limited period may prompt warm prospects to become 'hot prospects'. Inclusions of a free gift, or opportunity to enter a free draw, have also proved useful in this regard. For some products or services, initiating a request for further information is likely to be a less risky option for a customer than a straight purchase, and therefore is likely to prompt a higher response rate. Whether the offer is one-stage (buy the product) or multi-stage (request information or receive a catalogue) will depend greatly on the offer, the company and the target prospects (McCorkell 1997).

Target selection and 'targeting'

Traditional marketers might target all customers within selected segments, but data-driven marketers can choose how many and which customers to target, as indicated in the coverage of segmentation metrics. Data-driven relational marketers are increasingly striving to select those segments that are likely to contribute more financially to the organisation. This in turn is driven by the need for marketing activity to be more accountable. Some companies, such as a leading electronics retailer in the UK, track the sales of newly launched products and those customers who purchase within the first few months of launch are then targeted for new complementary products.

Important metrics for analysing segments' likely financial worth were discussed in Chapter 3 and include RFM and LTVs.

At the beginning of this chapter we introduced the notion that a major 'supply'-side factor in driving relational interaction is the availability of new technology-driven media to facilitate more personalised targeting. Our coverage of 'media' in later chapters provides more details of this, but it is worth a brief discussion of the sort of developments concerned. The Internet is an obvious example of how more personalised targeting can be operationalised: via e-mail marketing and the integration of media such as advertising that drives potential customers to a website for relational interaction and possible purchase.

Telephonic technology now facilitates real-time targeting of potential customers via, for example, satellite location analysis so that a consumer walking past a store can be contacted at that moment via their mobile phone, with offers that might be based on their transaction or profile characteristics.

The film *Minority Report* demonstrated real-time recognition of customers as they entered a store or even just walked around a shopping mall. Recognition was via automatic retina identification and on this basis customer transactional and profile records were accessed and relevant promotions and offers delivered at the same time. This might have been futuristic at the time of the film's release (2002) but the technology is certainly available, indeed the company got into trouble over using an audio clip of the film (Tom Cruise's voice asking where his minority report was). This clip, together with heavy breathing, was sent as a phone message to individuals who had opted-in to receive information about films. However, 19 people complained to the Advertising Standards Association, claiming that it caused offence, fear and distress. The complaint was upheld but the company has said it will continue to use this approach (Rosser 2003). There was also annoyance over having to pay to access the voicemail message which they clearly didn't approve of in any case. How do you feel about this?

A London department store and a casino have already introduced biometric recognition (facial recognition software) so that their 'special' customers can be recognised as they enter and then quickly greeted personally by a manager (Steiner 2002).

It is important to remind ourselves of some of the points made in the previous chapter, as well as in the current one, concerning data quality and whether the resulting targeting is actually good targeting. There are still perceptions of 'junk mail' despite the wealth of data and sophisticated data handling technologies we have discussed. The Direct Mail Information Service conducts longitudinal attitudinal research into consumer perceptions of direct targeting as even in 2003 consumers thought they received twice as much direct mail as they actually do and from 2001 to 2002 there was a 24% increase in those registering for the Mailing Preference Service (MPS), which is a list against which the industry should clean their own targeting lists (Frankel 2003).

Having determined which segments to target – and indeed which customers and/or potential customers to target within these, the next stage is to consider how to position the product or service in the market.

Positioning

The third strand of what is referred to as STP (segmentation, targeting and positioning) involves deciding on the position within the market that the product or service is to occupy.[2] In doing this, the company is stating to customers what the product or service means and how it differs from current and potential competing products or services.

This involves mapping competitive offerings in the minds of customers and potential customers (Ries and Trout 1986) in order to influence their perception of reality. It isn't just via promotional messages, but by the entire mix.

Positioning is therefore the process of designing an image and value so that consumers within the target segment understand what the company or brand stands for in relation to its competitors. In doing this, the organisation is sending a message to consumers and trying to establish a competitive advantage that it hopes will appeal to customers in the target segment. In essence, therefore, the marketing mix can be seen as the tactical details of the organisation's positioning strategy. Where, for example, the organisation is pursuing a high-quality position, this needs to be reflected not just in the quality of the product or service, but in every element of the mix, including price, the pattern of distribution, the style of advertising and the after-sales service. Without this consistency, the believability of the positioning strategy reduces dramatically.

Multidimensional scaling and correspondence analysis can be used to build perceptual maps. These procedures involve algorithms that start with measures of similarity between pairs of products and try to find a geometric representation of the brands in the product category. These techniques position products that are perceived as similar close to one another and locate dissimilar products far apart. Dimensions of perceptual maps are not named by the multidimensional scaling programmes. Researchers have to interpret the dimensions themselves based on the geometric representation. Additional information may be gathered from consumers to name the dimensions. The attributes that are the most important in consumers' perceptions of a product category can be determined from survey research.

In this way, positioning is not actually something that is done to the product, rather it is something that marketers do to the minds of consumers. It relates to how consumers perceive the product in terms of image relative to competing offerings (Ries and Trout 1986).

Exhibit 6.13 shows an example of positioning for travel agencies. This suggests that the segments of customers labelled 'specialist', 'price buster' and so on require differing degrees of a) control over the travel/tour buying process and b) the degree of specialised or standardised 'package' the agency provides. Whether this approach would be adopted by travel agencies is debatable, but it could be a significant and worthwhile change in how different known customers are treated in store; perhaps even a good example of the one-to-one segmentation that this chapter has questioned.

EXHIBIT 6.13 Travel agencies: service needs

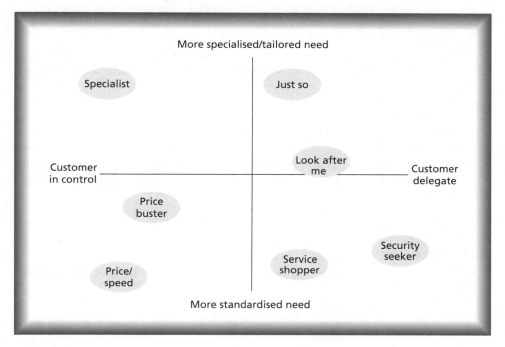

(Source: Forster 1997)

Summary

- Market segmentation is a real cornerstone of relational marketing but although there is now a much wider range of potential bases to inform segmentation, there are dangers of over-relying on those data-driven approaches that are not as affectively based. Our 'triangle' framework presented in the Preface includes the comment concerning 'more data but less understanding'.

- This chapter has explored some of the traditional approaches to segmenting and targeting markets and highlighted the value of these more affective ones, in terms of helping to identify salient needs and requirements.

- The previous chapters in Part 2 provided examples of how those segments that hold greater potential for the organisation can be identified via the data metrics employed in data mining. We also explored a variety of issues involved with researching this behaviour. There was the more mechanistic procedures involved with 'testing' different approaches in direct relational marketing and the previous chapter then explored how to add greater insight by turning to more traditional market research methods.

- With a blend of data-driven and more affective approaches, coupled with the more behavioural understanding that has been presented in the current chapter, appropriate segments can be identified and targeted. Further exploration of the vehicles for targeting takes place in our coverage of 'media' in Part 4. But we now move on, in Part 3, to explore the relational implications of the data and informational drivers that we have analysed in Part 2.

Review questions

1 If a market is segmented according to age, gender and social grade, what are the contributions of these variables to satisfying the various criteria for segmentation?

2 What are the implications of biographic segmentation for:
   (a) markets;
   (b) marketing?

3 Does increasingly personalised segmentation and targeting inevitably lead to:
   (a) one-to-one marketing;
   (b) relational marketing?

Further reading

Dibb, S. (2003) 'Market Segmentation', in S. Hart (ed.) *Marketing Challenges*, London Thomson.

Evans, M. (2003) 'Market Segmentation', in M. Baker *The Marketing Book*, 5th edn, Oxford: Butterworth Heinemann, pp. 246–83.

Tynan, A.C. and Drayton, J. (1987) 'Market Segmentation', *Journal of Marketing Management*, 2(3), pp. 301–35.

References

Adam Smith Institute (1998) *The Millennial Generation*, London.

Anon (1997) Taking Advantage of Children, *Sunday Times*, 28 September

Arnold, C. (2002) reported by Rubach, E. (2002) 'Up Close and Too Personal', *Precision Marketing*, 1 February, p. 12.

Bashford, S. (2000) 'Generation X Uncovered', *Marketing Direct*, October, pp. 17–19.

BBC (2002) *Century of the Self*, November.

BBC2 (1997) *Money Programme*, October.

Berry, J. and Leventhal, B. (1996) 'The Development of a Market Wide Segmentation System for the UK Consumer Financial Services Industry', *Journal of Targeting, Measurement and Analysis for Marketing*, 5(2), pp. 111–24.

Blattberg, R.C., Getz, G. and Thomas, J.S. (2001) *Customer Equity*, Boston, MA: Harvard Business School Publishing, Chapter 3 'Managing Customer Acquisition'.

BMRB (2003) British Market Research Bureau, London, website: www.bmrb-tgi.co.uk, accessed 16 April.

British Market Research Bureau (BMRB) (1988) *The Target Group Index*, London.

Carter, M. (1994) 'Kids Take Control of the Trolleys', *Marketing Week*, 4 November, pp. 21–2.

Castell, S. (2002) 'The Fantastic Elastic Self', *Research*, December, pp. 20–2.

Channel 4 (1990) *Direct Marketing*, Equinox Series.

Clegg, A. (2001) 'Strong Medicine', *Database Marketing*, March, pp. 14–20.

Collins J.C. and Porras, J. (1996) 'Building your Company's Vision', *Harvard Business Review*, Sept–Oct, pp. 65–77.

Cooper, P. (2003) in I. Sclater, 'Challenging Perceptions', *Marketing Business*, February, pp. 16–17.

Coupland, D. (1991) *Generation X: Tales for an Accelerated Culture*, London: Abacus.

Cummins, B. 'Time Pundits', *Marketing Week*, 8 April, pp. 29–31.

Datamonitor (2003) 'Report on the Grey Market', reported by Sclater, I. (2003) 'Challenging Perceptions', *Marketing Business*, February pp. 16–17.

Davidson, A. (2003) 'From Why to Z', *Research*, February, pp. 31–3.

Dick, A.S. and Basu, K. (1994) 'Customer Loyalty: Toward an Integrated Framework' *Journal of the Academy of Marketing Science*, 22(2), pp. 99–113.

Dickson, P.R. (1982) Person–Situation: Segmentation's Missing Link', *Journal of Marketing*, 46(4), pp. 56–64.

Dubow, J.S. (1992) 'Occasion Based Vs User-Based Benefit Segmentation', *Journal of Advertising Research*, March/April, pp. 11–22.

Ellson, T. (2003) 'Positioning and Culture as a determinant of Strategy', Unpublished PhD Thesis, Cardiff University.

Engel, J.F., Fiorillo, H.F. and Cayley, M.A. (1972) *Market Segmentation. Concepts and Applications*, New York: Holt, Rinehart & Winston.

Evans, M. and Blythe, J. (1994) 'Fashion: A Paradigm of Consumer Behaviour', *Journal of Consumer Studies and Home Economics*, 18(3), September, pp. 229–37.

Evans, M. and Fill, C. (2000) 'Extending the Communications Process: The Significance of Personal Influencers in the UK Motor Market', *International Journal of Advertising*, 19(2), pp. 43–65.

Evans, M., Nairn, A. and Maltby, A. (1999) 'Gender Differences for Financial Services Direct Mail', *Journal of Financial Services Marketing*, 4(2), pp. 139–62.

Evans, M., Nairn, A. and Maltby, A. (2000) 'The Hidden Sex Life of the Male and Female Shot', *International Journal of Advertising*, 19(1), February, pp. 43–65, ISSN 0265 0487.

Forster, S. (1997) 'Direct Marketing in the Travel and Tourism Sector', IDM lecture, UWE, Bristol, May.

Frank, R.E., Massy, W.F. and Wind, Y. (1972) *Market Segmentation*, Englewood Cliffs, NJ: Prentice-Hall.

Frankel, H. (2003) 'Awareness Drive Fails to Combat "Junk Mail" Image', *Precision Marketing*, February, p. 1.

Future Foundation (2000) *Responding to the Future*, London.

Gillespie, M. (2003) 'In Search of Lost Youth', *Research*, February, pp. 28–9.

Gofton, K. (2001) 'Firms Fail to Relate to Customers', *Marketing Direct*, January, p. 10.

Gofton, K. (2002) 'In the Heat of the Night Club', *Research*, February, pp. 20–2

Haley, R.I. (1968) 'Benefit Segmentation: A Decision Oriented Research Tool', *Journal of Marketing*, July, pp. 30–5.

Hughes, R. and Evans, M. (2001) 'Relationships are Two-Way: The Neglected Role of "Inbound" Contact in the Financial Services Sector', World Marketing Congress, June.

Kacen, J. (2000) 'Girl Power and Boy Nature: The Past, Present and Paradisal Future of Consumer Gender Identity', *Marketing Intelligence and Planning*, 18(6/7), pp. 345–55.

Kitchen, P. and Spickett-Jones, G. (2003) 'Information Processing: A Critical Literature Review and Future Research Directions', *International Journal of Market Research*, 45(1), pp. 73–98, http://212.135.234.170/bmrb/tgi.asp?p=725&r=4214.983, accessed 14 January 2003.

Lindstrom, M. (2003) 'Junior Consumer', *Marketing Business*, March, pp. 26–7.

Machauer, A. and Morgner, S. (2001) 'Segmentation of Bank Customers by Expected Benefits and Attitudes', *International Journal of Bank Marketing*, 19(1), pp. 6–17.

Marsh, H. (2001) 'Dig Deeper into the Database Goldmine', *Marketing*, 11 January, pp. 29–30.

May, M. (2001) 'Minority Marketing', *Marketing Direct*, October, pp. 15–16.

May, M. (2002) 'The Data Plunge', *Marketing Direct*, October, pp. 29–30.

McCorkell, G. (1997) *Direct and Database Marketing*, London: Kogan Page.

McElhatton, N. (2002) 'Data Clinic', *Direct Response*, August/September.

McNulty, C. (2002) interview on BBC *Century of the Self*, November.

McNulty, C. and McNulty, R. of Taylor Nelson (1987) 'Applied Futures, Social Value Groups'.

Minhas, R.S. and Jacobs, E.M. (1996) 'Benefit Segmentation by Factor Analysis: An Improved Method of Targeting Customers for Financial Services', *International Journal of Bank Marketing*, 14(3), pp. 11–14.

Mitchell, S. (2003) 'The New Age of Direct Marketing', *Journal of Database Marketing*, 10(3), pp. 219–30.

O'Brien, S., and Ford R. (1988) 'Can we at last say Goodbye to Social Class?', *Journal of the Market Research Society*, 30, pp. 289–332.

Patterson, M. (1998) 'Direct Marketing in Postmodernity: Neo-Tribes and Direct Communications', *Marketing Intelligence and Planning*, 16(1), pp. 68–74.

Porter, M.E. (1979) 'How Competitive Forces Shape Strategy', *Harvard Business Review*, 57(2), pp. 137–45.

Pulham, A. (2003) reported in Sclater, I. (2003) 'Challenging Perceptions', *Marketing Business*, February, pp. 16–17.

Ries, A. and Trout, J. (1986) *Positioning: The Battle for Your Mind*, New York: McGraw Hill.

Ritchie, K. (1995) *Marketing to Generation X*, New York: Lexington Books.

Rose, D., Elias, P. and McKnight, A. (1999) 'National Statistics Socio-Economic Classification: An Overview', Market Research Society Conference, Brighton.

Rosser, M. (2003) '20th Century to Persist with Voicemail Ads', *Precision Marketing*, 14 February, p. 1.

Rubach, E. (2002) 'Up Close and Too Personal', *Precision Marketing*, 1 February, p. 12.

Sclater, I. (2003) 'Challenging Perceptions', *Marketing Business*, February, pp. 16–17.

Shaw, R. McDonald, M. and White, C. (2000) 'Marketing's Black Hole', *Marketing Business*, Jan–Feb, pp. ii–vii

Shepherdson, N. (2000) 'Life's a Beach 101', *American Demographics*, May.

Steiner, R. (2002) 'Watch Out, Big Spenders, Big Brother is Watching You', *Sunday Times Business*, 11 August, p. 1.

Target Group Index (TGI) (2003) 'TGI Lifestage', http://212.135.234.170/bmrb/tgi.asp?p=149&r=7691.546, accessed 14 January 2003.

van Raaij, W.F. and Verhallen, T.M.M. (1994) 'Domain-specific Market Segmentation', *European Journal of Marketing*, 28(10), pp. 49–66.

Zelin, A. (2003) 'Good Housekeeping', *Research*, February, pp. 24–5.

Notes

1 The Department of the Environment, Transport and the Regions (formerly the Department of Transport). Traffic flow counts provide annual average daily flow counts and annual traffic estimates based on information gathered from a rotating census carried out by trained enumerators and from a core census using electronic equipment.

2 But see an alternative view as proposed in our In Theory box towards the beginning of this chapter.

PART 3
Relational Marketing

7 Relational interaction

8 Knowledge management

9 Acquisition, retention and loyalty strategies

Referring back to our 'triangle' in the Preface (Exhibit 1), we have explored some of the origins of direct relational marketing and some of the drivers that have contributed to its emergence and accentuated momentum. These included origins in direct distribution, direct promotion and database marketing. Drivers included a need to be more accountable and to satisfy fragmented and self-expressive markets and were fuelled by the dynamic technological environment which provided faster and more powerful computers and data mining software.

The contribution of transactional data to metrics such as RFM and LTV is clear and we have explored this in Part 2. But these particular metrics, although they can identify the 'best' segments in order to rank attractiveness and even deselect some, are relatively mechanistic and do not always provide too much insight.

When overlaid with geodemographics, a clearer picture of the world in which the customer lives emerges. We can envisage their neighbourhoods and profile characteristics. If overlaid with lifestyle data, we can see what products and services they are interested in, and we cannot glean this from their transactions with 'us' alone.

A range of additional profiling such as the sources discussed in Chapter 2 leads us to another level.

Through the wealth of data, linked with more affective insight from market research, we start to believe that we *know* our customers. The old days of 'a nation of shopkeepers', when the neighbourhood shopkeeper knew all his customers, their names, wants, purchasing patterns, family circumstances, power balances in their households, their pastimes and so on, might have largely gone. But the above data becomes a sort of surrogate and we perhaps start to think that we can use this to develop a relationship between individual customers and our own organisation.

This is the point of departure for Part 3. We delve more deeply into what constitutes relational marketing and explore the importance of broadening the relational notion beyond organisation–customer interaction to the wider network paradigm. We explore issues involved with converting data into knowledge and managing this across functions and partners.

The manifestation of all this is then analysed in the final chapter of Part 3, which provides coverage of how to acquire and keep customers via direct relational marketing programmes that aim to develop loyalty and mutual long-term benefit.

7 Relational interaction

Learning objectives

Having completed this chapter, students should:

- Have a conceptual understanding of the potential benefits for contemporary organisations of pursuing a relationship marketing strategy.

- Understand the different types of relationships that exist between organisations and their customers.

- Understand the nature and importance of the concepts used to differentiate successful and unsuccessful relationships.

- Appreciate the potential of direct marketing in initiating and managing customer relationships.

Harley Davidson relationship marketing

It was back in 1983 that Harley Davidson introduced their relationship marketing strategy, via the owners club (Harley Owners Group – HOG). The brand has long been an icon in the motorcycle world and this has been reinforced by the strong associations of its appearance in such films as *Easy Rider* and *Terminator II*. Harley's relationship strategy was kick-started by the informal meetings held by Harley fans. They nicknamed the bikes 'HOGS' in any case, so it wasn't a huge jump to set up the 'HOG' relationship club.

To add a more social slant to the image of bikers, Harley Davidson associated the company with the Muscular Dystrophy Foundation and held events to promote the charity. Now, Harley owners hold rallies and rides for quite a range of charities. The strength of emotion towards the brand is reflected in the feeling that it is driveway jewellery. Indeed, via the Owners Group this is supported by the range of bike merchandising, including accessories, jackets and caps. It all adds to a way of life that HOG members have bought into and there are few relationship strategies that are so 'affectively' based. There are tangible retention devices as well, though: customers can upgrade to a bigger model one year after purchase with trade-in at full value. Now, potential owners of second and even third bikes are targeted for relational treatment.

The channels of relational interaction are also extensive: 'multi-lingual customer care will be provided through a newly centralised call centre, allowing the delivery of dedicated bespoke service to HOG's 70 000 strong user base. Customers will be able to use telephone, fax, e-mail, or mail to find out about forthcoming rides, event tours and merchandise with a view to offering a web and SMS service in future' (Rubach 2003).

(Source: Rubach 2003. Reproduced with the permission of the copyright owner, Haymarket Business Publications Limited)

Introduction

HOG is a strong example of relationship marketing based on both emotion and financial incentive. A range of traditional and new media facilitate contact and this is not only between company and customers but is also customer–customer relational interaction.

In Chapter 1 we explored the B2B and service origins of the relational approach and these led to the proposition that relationship ideals could be applied in mass markets (Dwyer *et al*. 1987). While the problem of limited interpersonal interaction remained an issue, technology can be used to maintain records on each customer, personalise interaction, identify important customers, calculate their lifetime value and identify opportunities for up-selling and cross-selling (Dwyer *et al*. 1987), and all of this added practical momentum to the paradigm shift.

Moreover, arguments that it is cheaper to retain a customer than to acquire one, that existing customers are more likely to re-buy and that loyal customers generate more positive word of mouth (Donaldson and O'Toole 2002) proved compelling for fmcg marketers. Accordingly, firms developed strategies to retain customers either by locking them in, or, more in keeping with the relationship ideal, through the creation of meaningful customer value propositions (Rowe and Barnes 1998) that lead to mutually beneficial relationships and create mutual value. The idea that both parties can derive value from a relationship requires consideration of the motivations, expectations, costs and rewards accrued to both firms and customers in a relationship.

This chapter explores conceptual issues involved with relationship marketing and sets the scene for the wider perspective in Chapter 8, which explores relationships that go beyond the organisation–customer level. It also lays the theoretical foundation for the practical implementation of relationship marketing (in terms of acquisition, retention and loyalty programmes) as explored in Chapter 9.

Direct relational marketing

The relationship marketing ethos offers much to consumer goods marketers. The marketplace is increasingly dynamic and competitive, and 'with so much choice for customers, companies face the end of loyalty' (McKenna 1991). Moreover, in such an environment core product and service offerings are becoming more similar (Rowe and Barnes 1998) and customers are happy to switch suppliers at the slightest provocation (Sisodia and Wolfe 2000). Thus, the economics of customer retention (Reichheld and Sasser 1990) suggested that, unless loyalty can be re-created, marketing costs could soar while marketing successes could dwindle.

Marketers, then, see immense opportunities in taking relational principles and applying them in large consumer markets. Rather than competing on economies of scale as had been the norm, organisations could leverage these relationships and compete on economies of scope (Gordon 2000), and resources would be directed to the areas that provided most value for customers. By building upon the data-based techniques discussed in Part 2, RM could access information about each customer that was 'complete, specific and pertinent (Larson 1996) in order to understand *'real* customers on an *individual* basis' (Sisodia and Wolfe 2000, original emphasis) and communicate with them appropriately. This is particularly important for new product and service introduction whereby all new initiatives would be the 'outcome of a process of collaboration' (Gordon 2000) rather than guesswork based on statistical representations of customers (Sisodia and Wolfe 2000). In this sense, customers get more of what they value in terms of the product and associated services, and marketers incur fewer costs while increasing both relevance and value.

Customers, on the other hand, seem open to newer and more enlightened forms of marketing because of their 'long experience with never-ending promotions and a long history of over-promising and under-delivering' (Sisodia and Wolfe 2000). Perhaps they value continuing relations with known suppliers because of the opportunities provided for risk reduction, simplification of buying decisions and greater sharing of product relevant information, as well as the provision of social benefits and/or special status (see Peterson 1995; Sheth and Parvatiyar 1995; Gwinner *et al.* 1998; Gruen 2000).

Combining the two sets of motivations, the successful implementation of RM would also make marketing more efficient because (wasteful) expenditure on advertising and promotion could be reduced by encouraging customers to increase their involvement through self-service, self-ordering and co-production (Sheth and Parvatiyar 1995). Thus, RM leads to greater value creation through cooperative and collaborative relationships, with this value benefiting all parties (customers and organisations) engaged in the relationship (Tzokas and Saren (1997); Parvatiyar and Sheth 2000). So compelling was the promise of RM that it became widely embraced by mass marketers (Rowe and Barnes 1998).

Although RM was previously considered inappropriate in mass consumer markets owing to the anonymity of the marketplace and the lack of interpersonal interaction, these obstacles were surmountable by direct and database marketing. The database can be used to identify and track individual customer behaviour, while direct marketing facilitates personalised communication with individual customers. This, and new interactive communications media, overcomes both the problems of customer anonymity and those of two-way interaction.

While retention or loyalty is primarily beneficial for the marketer, a *relationship* results in an even better outcome for both customers and marketers. Thus, in this way, the goal of mass marketing came to be the engendering of customer relationships and the tools and techniques were borrowed primarily from the data-informed marketer's repertoire, as we have seen in Part 2.

In relational marketing that is both direct and interactive, interaction can be person to person, or it can be through the organisation's technology or via the traditional marketing-mix functions of facilitating the right product, in the right place, at the right time and at the right price. These mix elements and the nature of relational interaction with them are not mutually exclusive. Every interaction has an impact upon a customer's perception of an organisation, and thus in every interaction there is a possibility that the relationship will deepen, or that the relationship will become weaker. Clearly, organisations wish to deepen the relationship in order to gain a number of benefits.

Möller and Wilson (1995) suggest that the role of marketing within RM is to establish the process of relationship management. Thus, O'Malley *et al.* (1997) define RM as follows:

> ❝ Relationship marketing involves the identification, specification, initiation, maintenance and (where appropriate) dissolution of long-term relationships with key customers and other parties, through mutual exchange, fulfilment of promises and adherence to relationship norms in order to satisfy the objectives and enhance the experience of the parties concerned. ❞

This definition is influenced by contributions from diverse relational schools. It incorporates the purpose, process, focus, and key elements of RM:

1 The purpose is to satisfy the objectives and enhance the experience of the parties involved.
2 The focus is on key customers and other parties.
3 The process involves the identification, specification, initiation, maintenance and dissolution of relationships.
4 The key elements include mutual exchange, fulfilment of promise and adherence to relationship norms.

The synergy of these arguments and those throughout Parts 1 and 2 lead us to propose that direct relational marketing is:

The use of understandings of well-defined market segments or even individual customers, prospects and partners in order to develop and maintain mutually beneficial (and in the case of organisations, measurable) interactions for as long as the parties desire.

As a result of participating in a number of different relationships, certain benefits accrue to the organisation:

1 Supplier relationships improve value or reduce costs through more efficient ordering systems.
2 Relationships with distributors accommodate new product introductions.
3 The network of relationships in which the organisation is involved will enhance its competitive position. That is, all of these relationships in some way contribute to adding value, reducing costs, increasing innovation etc.
4 This combination of relationships ultimately helps the organisation to enhance its relationships with its own customers.

For customers, true relational interaction can be very satisfying:

• They feel an affinity with the organisation beyond mere repeat purchase and this can add to the 'experiential' nature of much current consumer behaviour.
• They can feel 'known' to the organisation, not just as an anonymous customer but akin to the personal interaction of restaurateur and regular customer.
• They often receive special treatment and extra pampering by the organisation.
• They are likely to receive timely and relevant communications of offers that would be of interest to them at that moment.

So, as introduced in Chapter 1 and extended through the metrics of Part 2, Relational Marketing is not concerned simply with a one-time sale but aims to build long-term relationships with customers as a way of realising their lifetime value. The connections are based on the mutuality of interaction between equal partners and characterised by trust, commitment, communication and sharing, which result in the mutual achievement of goals. This is probably somewhat idealistic but there are signs that the principles might be regarded as normative objectives.

Moreover, the ties that bind customers and their suppliers go beyond mutual economic value to incorporate social and structural bonds (Berry 1995). Developing relationships that go beyond purely economic bonds is to search for the ultimate differentiation strategy (Morgan 2000).

Marketers seek relationships with *special status* (Czepiel 1990). Such relationships are generally characterised by mutual trust, respect, loyalty, affection and communication (Sheaves and Barnes 1996). Because such relationships are socially complex and hence difficult to imitate, the ability to foster them is important for sustainable competitive advantage (Rowe and Barnes 1998).

Towards ideal relational components

In considering the nature of relationships we need to appreciate the idealised notion of a relationship as well as the more usual components or elements that are believed to be present when a relationship exists. Thus, this section will consider both of these elements.

The ideal relationship

The template that is most generally employed to discuss and describe relationships is that of marriage. In the early 1980s Theodore Levitt made a striking comparison between business relationships and contemporary marriage. According to Levitt (1983):

> The sale merely consummates the courtship. Then the marriage begins. How good the marriage is depends on how well the relationship is managed by the seller.

The marriage metaphor guided subsequent authors toward the marriage literature in order to better understand relationships. McCall's conceptualisation of marriage in turn adopted a social exchange perspective: (McCall 1966):

> Marriage [is a] restrictive trade agreement. The two individuals agree to exchange only with one another, at least until such time as the balance of trade becomes unfavourable in terms of broader market considerations.

In talking about commercial relationships (as marriages) we assume that the parties in the relationship are on an equal footing, and there are certain values that we implicitly rely upon. For example, we assume that relationships involve *partners* who should be *committed* and *loyal*. The *long-term* nature of the relationship is emphasised over the *one-night stand*, and there is an underpinning suggestion that such relationships should be *monogamous.*

Such conceptions of commercial relationships lie in stark contrast to other dominant metaphors in marketing. For example, utilising the marriage metaphor suggests that marketing should no longer be about *manipulating* customers or undertaking *strategic warfare*. Rather, it should be about *mutuality and fairness*. It is probably the case that this is somewhat idealistic and although rarely implemented at present, some might strive for this model. There might also be a concern that although the metaphor approach is useful in many cases, to compare one's relationship with one's marriage partner with how we interact with a supermarket, car dealer or bank is stretching pragmatism a little.

In their seminal paper Dwyer *et al.* (1987) recommend that organisations pay 'attention to the conditions that foster relational bonds leading to reliable repeat business'. Thus, the objective of relational marketing is for organisations to turn customers into clients, and prospects into partners (Ahmed and Buttle 2001).

Having briefly considered the implications of thinking about marketing in terms of relationships, it is worth while considering what we understand to be the core elements of successful relationships.

The following case study reflects one company's efforts to create personalised relationships that can lead to mutual benefit and go beyond the mere personalising of salutation in order to sell something based on previous transactions.

CASE **STUDY** 7.1

O$_2$

The mobile phone operator O$_2$ has a loyalty programme that involves a quarterly analysis of each customer's bill. It then provides unambiguous advice about the most economical tariff for each individual. The churn rate for customers in the loyalty programme is half that of other customers. Every 1% saving in churn rate contributes around £5m in profit. This demonstrates that relational power can go beyond mere pestering of customers for more sales to individualised understanding which can lead to benefits to both customer and organisation.

(Source: DMA Award 2002)

Key relational constructs

There are a number of concepts commonly employed to explain and describe successful relationships (Sheaves and Barnes 1996). These are useful in developing an understanding of the kind(s) of relationships contemporary organisations hope to create and maintain with their stakeholder groups.

Trust

Trust is considered to be the basis for exchange and the glue that holds a relationship together. Conversely, in the absence of trust, exchange becomes increasingly difficult. Scott (2002) highlights that it is useful to:

> ❝ Think of trust as a natural resource, like water. It oils the machinery of human interaction in everything from marriage and friendship to business and international relations. There are reserves of trust, in a perpetual state of replenishment or depletion. And in this parched and suddenly sweltering spring, it is not just water supplies that are looking ominously low. ❞

Because trust is central to all human interaction and not just business exchanges, it has been subjected to much debate and discussion in a whole range of disciplines. Indeed, given its centrality to social and economic life, an academic school dedicated to the study of trust has emerged (Gambetta 1988). However, trust is a complex issue and, despite the extensive attention it has received, it remains illusive.

Unless there is a minimum level of trust between parties, it is unlikely that a relationship will be initiated at all. Similarly, if trust breaks down the relationship is likely to be dissolved. Furthermore, it remains difficult to identify exactly why trust intensifies or decreases. In practice, trust may be a function of the reputation and perceived expertise of the organisation and its employees. Organisational reputation is communicated to customers through corporate and brand image, through advertising, through product and service quality and through the behaviour of its employees. In marketing we generally understand trust as 'a willingness to rely on an exchange partner in whom one has confidence' (Moorman *et al.* 1993). This exchange partner may be an individual, an organisation, or something more abstract such as a quality symbol (e.g. FSA) or brand. Put simply, we will engage in market exchanges when we trust (rely on or have confidence in) the word of an individual, organisation or brand. The fundamental building blocks of trust for organisations are (Bowen and Shoemaker 1998): achieving results, demonstrating concern and acting with integrity.

Thus, for consumers to trust an organisation they must have confidence in that organisation's ability and willingness to keep its explicit and implicit promises (Grönroos 1994). Trust is particularly important for services, which by their nature are highly intangible (for example, banks and insurance companies) because there is a need for a minimum level of customer trust before service delivery is initiated. (Liljander and Strandvick 1995). As a result, organisations must carefully consider the implications of the promises they make. Equally, visible elements of the organisation's activities (e.g. personalised communications) signal to customers the quality of other, less visible organisational activities. Thus, engendering trust also involves paying attention to the details that matter to customers.

The trust a customer places in a service provider is mainly based upon their own experience with that provider or their experience with similar organisations. Thus, your ability to trust a particular estate agent will be influenced not only by your knowledge and experience regarding that agent and their behaviour, but also by your previous experience with other estate agents.

Customers' insecurity is reduced as a result of trust, and the presence of trust in turn brings about harmony and stability in the relationship, which further strengthens trust.

Commitment

In addition to trust, commitment is also considered to be central to successful relationship marketing (Morgan and Hunt 1994). In marketing, commitment is typically associated with notions of *solidarity* and *cohesion*. Organisations that engender commitment in their employees exhibit lower levels of employee turnover (Allen and Meyer 1990). Moreover, committed employees are more motivated in their jobs, and more involved with their organisations (Sweeney and Swait 2002). In considering commercial relationships, commitment is commonly employed to denote successful versus unsuccessful relationships. Commitment operates in much the same way as trust. That is, an initial level of commitment is required to initiate the relationship, and, as the relationship deepens, so too does the existence and evidence of commitment. Moreover, without commitment, no relationship is believed to exist. Referring to consumer markets, De Wulf *et al.* (2001) define commitment as 'a consumer's desire to continue a relationship ... accompanied by this consumer's willingness to make efforts at maintaining it'.

Furthermore, commitment involves behavioural, attitudinal, affective and calculative components (Geyskens *et al.* 1996):

1 Behavioural commitment refers to the actual behaviour of parties in the relationship, the efforts they make and the choices they take. Parties find it relatively easy to assess the level of commitment displayed in their partners and tend to use perception of effort as a proxy measure (Harris and O'Malley 2000). Similarly, higher levels of investment in the relationship (in terms of time, money, resources or skill development) suggest greater commitment.

2 Attitudinal commitment refers to 'an implicit or explicit pledge of relational continuity' between relational partners (Oliver 1999).

3 Affective commitment relates to positive feelings towards the service provider. As a result of these feelings, the customer is not tempted to seek alternatives or to engage in any cost–benefit analytical schemes. Affectively committed customers voice strong intentions to remain in the relationship and are willing to invest in that relationship (Samuelson and Sandvik 1997).

4 Calculative commitment, in contrast, is partly instrumental. In this case, calculative commitment may be the outcome of a perceived lack of alternatives or estimation that the switching costs might outweigh likely benefits. Customers who remain in a relationship as a result of calculative commitment will only do so as long as their cost–benefit analysis provides no incentive to leave. However, such customers are only loyal while it is instrumentally rewarding for them to be loyal (Samuelson and Sandvik 1997).

Loyalty

Loyalty is clearly important in relationships and the rationale behind relationship development is often to engender loyalty amongst the customer base. Indeed, a small increase in loyalty can boost profits significantly (Reichheld and Sasser 1990). Traditionally, direct and relationship marketers have measured loyalty as a function of the recency, frequency, and monetary value (RFM) and lifetime value (LTV) of their customers. On one level this makes a lot of sense; loyal customers buy regularly, and continue to spend a high proportion of their money with the organisation. However, recent work in the area suggests that such a measure may be misleading because customers may only be loyal as a result of a lack of choice. Behavioural loyalty is therefore insufficient on its own, and increasingly loyalty is recognised as the degree to which a customer exhibits repeat purchase behaviour from a service provider, possesses a positive attitude towards that provider, and considers only using this provider when the need for this service arises (Gremler and Brown 1996).

IN THEORY

Dick and Basu loyalty theory

Dick and Basu (1994) proposed a framework (Table 7.1) that results in four categories of loyalty (no loyalty, spurious loyalty, latent loyalty and loyalty) determined by two dimensions (relative attitude and patronage behaviour):

1 *Relative attitude* focuses not only on attitude to the entity, but also incorporates comparison to other organisations or brands.
2 *Patronage behaviour* includes traditional retention measures such as RFM, share of wallet, purchase sequence etc.

TABLE 7.1 Four categories of loyalty

Category	No loyalty	Spurious loyalty	Latent loyalty	Loyalty
Relative attitude	Low relative attitude	Low relative attitude	High relative attitude	High relative attitude
Patronage behaviour	Low repeat patronage behaviour	High repeat patronage behaviour	Low repeat patronage behaviour	High repeat patronage behaviour
Manifestation	Does not patronise the company, and does not wish to.	Patronises the company, but does not have a high relative attitude. This may be as a result of other factors, including location, convenience, lack of alternatives.	In this case, the customer wishes to patronise the organisation, but perhaps is not able to do so – store location may be inconvenient, favourite brands not stocked etc.	The individual enjoys a high relative attitude, together with high repeat patronage behaviour.
Implications	Management may attempt to generate 'spurious loyalty'.	'Spurious loyalty' cannot be relied upon. The customer is clearly open to better offers.	Managerial efforts are best focused on removing the obstacles to patronage for the customer.	Loyalty must be continually reinforced, and the value offered must remain acceptable.

(Source: Adapted by the authors from Dick and Basu 1994)

Loyalty therefore involves a favourable attitude towards the brand or organisation and positive re-purchase intentions. This can be further understood by investigating the elements of loyalty (Oliver 1999):

1 cognitive loyalty, in which the brand is cognitively compared with alternatives (generally on functional grounds);

2 affective loyalty, in which the customer likes the brand or organisation as a result of previous satisfying experiences;

3 conative loyalty, which reflects an intention to re-purchase;

4 action loyalty, which relates to 'a deeply held commitment to rebuy or repatronise a preferred product/service consistently in the future ... despite situational influences and marketing efforts having the potential to cause switching behaviour' (Oliver 1999).

Mutual goals

Mutual goals are important because they explain the motivation for relationship development. However, the goals of relational partners do not have to be the same. Rather, both parties must simply have the possibility to achieve their goals through the relationship. For example, the organisation wishes to engender loyalty amongst its customers because it has been proven that it is more profitable to service existing customers than to constantly attract new ones (Reichheld and Sasser 1990). Similarly, customers may wish to reduce the time and effort (search costs) of shopping around and this is possible by remaining loyal to a good supplier. Customers may also accrue the extra benefits of shopping in a familiar environment and having the product or service customised to their requirements at no extra cost (Sheth and Parvatiyar 1995).

Social bonds

Social bonds refer to the degree of mutual personal friendship and liking by the parties involved in exchange. These are important because people enjoy doing business with people they like. Thus, social bonds are viewed as important in developing loyalty, particularly when competitive differences are not strong. The existence of social bonds has been used to explain the success of relationships in a wide variety of settings (e.g. between advertising agencies and their clients (Halinen 1997), between market research agencies and their clients (Crosby and Stephens 1987), and between barristers and solicitors) (Harris and O'Malley 2000). It has been suggested that 'favourable personal relationships are an important medium in exchanging information, resolving conflicts and producing personal rewards' (Halinen 1997). Some customers like to be recognised, they like to be kept informed through regular communication and they like to receive special treatment as a result of their being acknowledged as a valuable customer (Berry 1995). Thus, social bonds highlight the importance of the personal element in relationships and compel us to remember that, fundamentally, relationships develop between people.

Since the functional quality of the interaction has been elevated in importance, people skills are likely to become ever more crucial. In particular, the development and fostering of personal contacts become significant. This is because personal contacts facilitate the transfer of 'soft' information, enhance subjective judgments through frequent interaction in both formal and informal situations (Turnbull 1979) and make individuals more tolerant of service failure (Crosby *et al.* 1990). This personal dimension will 'result in a double bond ... between the two: a personal bond and a professional or economic bond' (Czepiel 1990). In addition, relationships can act as a form of crisis insurance (Turnbull 1979) so that in times of crisis rapid action will be requested or preferential treatment sought.

Structural bonds

Structural bonds refer to situations where partners are closely bound together as a result of underpinning systems or structures. For example, an inter-organisational relationship may involve a supplier of important machinery who also services that machinery and manages training for its customer's employees. In this case, although the machine could be purchased elsewhere, the additional services (training and servicing) create a structural bond. Such bonds 'create impediments to the termination of the relationship' (Wilson 1995). The following case study provides an example of a company creating structural bonds.

CASE **STUDY** 7.2

Structural bonds

HDoX, a producer of hydrogen peroxide, created structural bonds with Office Furnishing, one of its most important customers. HDoX invested in a telemetry and electronic data interchange (EDI) system that enabled it to monitor the level of inventory at its buyer's storage tank directly. The company automatically sends new supplies when the volume in the tank falls below a specific stock level.

(Source: Ahmed and Buttle 1999)

In consumer markets, the provision of financial services (loans etc.) may also create effective structural bonds for customers.

Shared technology can act as an extremely important structural bond in relationships. The now famous link between Intel and a number of computer manufacturers (Intel Inside) is one example of this.

We explore structural bonds further in Chapter 8, in our coverage of sharing knowledge across partners.

Adaptation

Adaptation refers to the need to be flexible in a relationship. Although the notion of adaptation is more widely used in inter-organisational relationships in terms of adapting systems, processes and even products and services to the customers' specific requirements, it can also be used to explain customised offerings to individual consumers. For example, overriding billing systems to deduct charges for late payments for credit-card customers who are highly valued by the organisation.

Satisfaction

Customers are not motivated to engage in relationships unless they are satisfied with the offer made by the supplier (Tzokas and Saren 1997). However, buyers evaluate satisfaction on other criteria also. For example, economic satisfaction refers to an 'evaluation of the economic outcomes that flow from the relationship' and social satisfaction to the 'psychological aspects of [the] relationship' (Geyskens and Steenkamp 2000). Thus, satisfaction is a multi-dimensional construct that must include the quality of the core product or service as well as the economic and social aspects of the relationship. Linked to this is the comparison level of alternatives, which simply acknowledges that satisfaction is always relative. That is, customers are happy to remain in any given relationship so long as they believe there are no better alternatives out there. To a large extent, this concept explains why individuals remain in relationships in which they express unhappiness. For example, a lot of banking research suggests that although consumers are not particularly satisfied with their current bank, they believe that the level of service in other banking establishments is the same, if not lower.

Cooperation

Cooperation is another variable that recognises the interdependent and interactive nature of relationships. Relational partners must be willing and able to work together to improve relational outcomes. Cooperation is essential for achieving mutual goals and is a necessary prerequisite for any adaptations to products, services, systems or processes to occur.

Non-retrievable investments

Non-retrievable investments are investments made in relationships that are of no value unless the relationship is maintained in the long term. Such investments are therefore an important indicator of commitment. In an inter-organisational relationship, investments in technology necessary to meet the requirements of one particular customer (but unlikely to be relevant to other customers) are one example of this. In the consumer marketplace, lending, particularly to students, is another interesting example. It has been proven that students incur significant costs and do not return profits for at least five years. As such, the investment in the relationship (e.g. offering a loan) cannot be recouped if the student subsequently switches their more profitable business (e.g. a mortgage) to another bank in the future.

Attraction

Attraction is a concept that has hitherto been largely ignored in explaining relational strength but is increasingly being recognised as important (Dwyer *et al.* 1987; Halinen 1997). Essentially, it is suggested that at least one party must find the other attractive in some sense for a relationship to be initiated. Attraction results when one party is perceived to offer economic, resource or social rewards to the other. Economic attractiveness is the extent to which higher value or lower costs are likely to result from relationship formation. Resource attractiveness may result from access to particular products, services, technologies, and customers that are necessary to further specific goals. Finally, social attractiveness refers to the possibilities of furthering social bonds and accessing social situations or individuals that are desired. Although one of these possible rewards may be the motivation for relationship development, the presence of all three is likely to signify a closer and more enduring relationship. Similarly, if attractiveness decreases (because more compelling alternatives arise) commitment to the relationship will decrease. Thus, attraction is a particularly compelling explanatory variable (Harris *et al.* 2003).

Having identified these important concepts, it becomes clear that relationships involve a complex and dynamic mix of elements that explain relationship strength and endurance. It is not necessary for all of the above variables to be strongly present in all relationships, or indeed at all times in the relationship. Rather, their relative importance will vary depending on the type of relationship and that stage of development that characterises any given relationship at any time. Thus, to further understand the nature of relationships we need to explore (a) the diversity of relational types and (b) models of relationship development. These are dealt with in the sections below.

Exploring relationship diversity

Although the stated aim of most contemporary organisations is to build relationships with their customers, this is an incredibly ambitious goal and is too broad to be meaningful in devising a relationship strategy. Although the use of the marriage metaphor implies the development of close and long-term relationships, not all commercial relationships can, or should, be of this nature. Moreover, an organisation's choice of strategy is not predicated on a simple dichotomy between transactional marketing on the one hand and RM on the other. Rather, it is more useful to consider a transactional–relational continuum (Grönroos 1994) on the left of which lie transactions (discrete exchanges, having a short duration and a sharp ending), and on the right lie relational exchanges (longer in duration and ongoing). Between these two extremes, we can find relationships with different degrees of intensity and characteristics.

Manufacturers seek long-term relationships with their distributors; retailers work hard to gain the commitment of their suppliers; service providers attempt to engender and maintain relationships with their customers; and many contemporary organisations now recognise the importance of building lasting relationships with their employees.

We explore these wider relationships within the context of sharing knowledge and understanding for mutual benefit, in the next chapter.

Thus, we begin to recognise that relationships with customers are only one of the many important relationships that an organisation might be involved in. Gummesson (1997) considers the ultimate customer to be only one of 30 possible relationships (30Rs) that impact upon how an organisation interacts with the world.

Although early evidence seemed to imply that firms should puruse relationships with all their customers and should ultimately strive for zero migration, that is, keeping customers at all costs, more recent research suggests that more relationship building is not always better, but rather, that building the right type of relationship is critical (Reinartz *et al.* 2002).

Different relational types

The initial impetus for RM in consumer markets was Dwyer *et al.*'s (1987) assertion that, like business-to-business situations, consumer marketers could also benefit from a relational orientation. However, one of the key distinctions between business-to-business, services, and consumer markets relates to relationship structure. On this basis, the background to a relationship will influence the type of relationship that ensues. Relationships occur against three different backgrounds: firm-to-firm (inter-organisational relationships); individual-to-individual (including many service marketing dyads); and individual-to-firm (as characterised by many relationships in consumer markets). (Iacobucci and Ostrom 1996). In turn, these backgrounds produce four distinct types of relationship:

1 Informal and social relationships are generally fair, harmonious and are characterised by low risk and uncertainty (e.g. spouses, neighbours, and consumer/small business). These are generally the kind of interpersonal relationships that inform our (idealistic) views of how commercial relationships ought to be.

2 Antagonistic and adversarial relationships have incompatible goals, unequal power, and are often hostile (e.g. divorced couples, prisoners and guards, business rivals, and boss/employee relationships).

3 Close and long-term relationships are intense and difficult to break (e.g. parent/child, business partners, patient/doctor, client/attorney, organisation/advertising agency). Such relationships are kept close by structural bonds (e.g. by birth in the case of parent/child; through contracts in the case of business partners and agency/client relationships; and

through history and expert knowledge in the case of doctor/patient). As a result of the longevity of such relationships, they often exhibit strong social bonds as well.

4 Casual and distant relationships typify those where history and the existence of trust are of little importance (e.g. interviewer/job applicant, waiter/restaurant patron, bank teller/bank customer, consumer/mail order sales person, large company/consumer, and consumer/credit card company). In the most casual and distant relationships, there is no history and no definite possibility of future interaction. The focus is predominantly on the transaction, although it is acknowledged that, over time, transactions may evolve into relationships (i.e. become closer and deeper). Even then, the best that can be hoped for is a transactional relationship (Stone *et al.* 1996) 'typically short-term and less intense in comparison to individual-level dyads' (Iacobucci and Ostrom 1996).

Understanding the different backgrounds, types, and possible targets of relationships is therefore important in relationship development. If this were not already complex enough, organisations also need to consider the level of relationship they wish to pursue. That is, it may be considered appropriate to initiate different levels of relationship with different customers. There are three basic levels of relationship (Berry 1995):

1 Level-one relationships are primarily based upon pricing incentives and other tangible rewards and are the weakest level at which a relationship exists. Tangible rewards include discounts, gifts, frequent flyer miles etc. to customers as a reward for their continued patronage (Peterson 1995). Many loyalty schemes represent an RM strategy in this sense (Sheth and Parvatiyar 1995). Loyalty programmes operate within a classical conditioning framework of reward and punishment. However, there is increasing recognition that loyalty schemes often achieve little more than spurious loyalty despite significantly raising costs (O'Malley 1998). More recently, it was found that the tangible rewards generated by such schemes do not boost customer retention, though their absence was found to disappoint customers (De Wulf *et al.* 2001).

2 Level-two relationships relate to the social aspects of RM as exemplified by regular communication with customers, recognising them, and referring to them by name during an interaction. Communication is central to relationship development and maintenance (Duncan and Moriarty 1998). For the majority of relational programmes involving massive numbers of customers, direct mail is a hugely important element of the relational strategy, though this is increasingly shifting to media such as the Internet and static and mobile telephony.

3 Level-three relationships offer structural solutions to customers' problems. Interestingly, such solutions are 'designed into the service-delivery system rather than depending upon relationship-building skills' (Berry 1995). This represents an organisation's underlying philosophy whereby the customer is placed at the centre of all activity (Palmer 1996).

Customer relationship management

CRM is variously understood as customer relationship marketing and/or customer relationship management. Although philosophically in line with relationship marketing, the focus of CRM is, in practice, on the technology; particularly that technology which attempts to manage all customer touch points and facilitate the integration of various database systems to provide a single picture of the customer (O'Malley and Mitussis 2002; Pine *et* al. 1995; Ryals and Knox 2001).

In practice, the most usual interpretation and operationalising of organisation–customer relationships is essentially this sort of data fusing and subsequent mining, which is used to identify and classify customer segments for differential targeting. It is unfortunate that many companies see a software package as all that is required. If the management of this resulting knowledge is not integrated and shared across relevant organisational functions, there is little chance of there being sustainable relational marketing. Knowledge management, as it is often termed, is a framework for moving data-informed marketing to a more strategic position. This is an approach that includes intra- and inter-company networks within what should be a broader CRM paradigm and this is the focus of the next chapter.

Summary

- In this chapter we have discussed a number of important concepts and issues that form the theoretical basis for direct relational marketing. The potential benefits of pursuing an RM strategy by contemporary organisations were discussed.

- Increased loyalty and retention of customers can be effected through the creation of relationships and the strengthening of relational bonds. This also enhances new product development and reduces the opportunity for competitors to encourage switching behaviour.

- Customers enjoy improved interaction experiences as a result of relationship participation. They receive better, perhaps even customised products and services, and they gain from confidence and social benefits as well.

- In attempting to understand commercial relationships in greater detail, attention was paid to identifying relationship success variables and describing their likely impact on those relationships. Here we identified and discussed the role of trust, commitment, mutuality, social bonds, structural bonds, satisfaction, adaptation and attraction.

- Although significant benefits may be derived from successful RM, we cautioned that close, long-term relationships are not always viable or desirable with all customers (or from the customer's perspective, with all organisations). To this end, the transactional–relational continuum highlights that a diverse range of relationships can exist, each with very individual characteristics.

- Furthermore, we explored different types of relationships and articulated the level at which relationships exist. This leads us to explore relationships that extend beyond the organisation–customer level and include alliances and data sharing across organisational functions and across organisations themselves.

Review questions

1 Why is trust so important in successful relationships? What are the fundamental building blocks of trust for commercial organisations?

2 What is spurious loyalty? How can it be avoided?

3 For a company of your choice, identify the relationships with which they are involved and why. In your answer, specify which relationships are interpersonal, which are inter-organisational and which involve some combination of both.

4 For the following relationships, which key relational constructs are likely to be most important for a consumer: local bakery, supermarket, mail order firm, expensive restaurant.

5 What challenges face organisations that wish to build relationships with their customers through technology rather than through face-to-face interactions?

Further reading

Bruhn, M. (2003) *Relationship Marketing: Management of Customer Relationships*, Harlow: FT Prentice Hall.

Donaldson, B. and O'Toole, T. (2002) *Strategic Market Relationships: From Strategy to Implementation*, John Wiley, Chichester

Egan, J. (2001) *Relationship Marketing: Exploring Relational Strategies in Marketing*, Harlow: Financial Times/Prentice Hall.

Foss, B. and Stine, M. (2002) *CRM in Financial Services*, London: Kogan Page.

Gummesson, E. (1999) *Total Relationship Marketing*, Oxford: Butterworth Heinemann.

Little, E. and Marandi, E. (2003) *Relationship Marketing Management*, London: Thomson Learning.

References

Ahmed, R. and Buttle, F. (1999) 'Retaining Business Customers through Adaptation and Bonding: a Case Study of HdoX', in D. McLoughlan and C. Horan (eds) *Proceedings of the 15th Annual IMP Conference*, Dublin: University College Dublin.

Ahmed, R. and Buttle, F. (2001) 'Customer Retention: A Potentially Potent Marketing Strategy', *Journal of Strategic Marketing*, 9, pp. 29–45.

Allen, N.J. and Meyer, J.P. (1990) 'The Measurement of and Antecedents of Affective, Continuance, and Normative Commitment to the Organisation', *Journal of Occupational Psychology*, 63, pp. 1–18.

Berry, L.L. (1995) 'Relationship Marketing of Services – Growing Interest, Emerging Perspectives', *Journal of the Academy of Marketing Science*, 23(4), pp. 236–45.

Bowen, J. and Shoemaker, S. (1998) 'The Antecedents and Consequences of Customer Loyalty', *Cornell Hotel and Restaurant Quarterly*, 39(1), pp. 12–25.

Crosby, L.A. and Stephens, N. (1987) 'Effect of Relationship Marketing on Satisfaction, Retention, and Prices in the Life Insurance Industry', *Journal of Marketing Research*, XXIV (November), pp. 404–11.

Crosby, L.A., Evans, K.R. and Cowles, D. (1990) 'Relationship Quality in Services Selling: An Interpersonal Influence Perspective', *Journal of Marketing*, 54 (July), pp. 68–81.

Czepiel, J.A. (1990) 'Service Encounters and Service Relationships: Implications for Research', *Journal of Business Research*, 20, pp. 13–21.

De Wulf, K, Odenkerken-Schroder, G. and Iacobucci, D. (2001) 'Investments in Consumer Relationships: A Cross-Country and Cross-Industry Exploration', *Journal of Marketing*, 65(October), pp. 33–50.

Dick, A.S. and Basu, K. (1994) 'Customer Loyalty: Toward an Integrated Framework', *Journal of the Academy of Marketing Science*, 22(2), pp. 99–113.

Donaldson, B. and O'Toole, T. (2002) *Strategic Market Relationships: from Strategy to Implementation*, Chichester: John Wiley.

Duncan, T. and Moriarty, S.E. (1998) 'The Role of Relationship Quality in the Stratification of Vendors as Perceived by Customers', *Journal of the Academy of Marketing Science*, 26(2), pp. 128–42.

Dwyer, F.R. Schurr, P.H. and Oh, S. (1987) 'Developing Buyer–Seller Relationships', *Journal of Marketing*, 51(April), pp. 11–27.

Gambetta, D. (1988) *Trust: Making and Breaking Cooperative Relations*, New York: Basil Blackwell.

Geyskens, I. and Steenkamp, J.-B. (2000) 'Economic and Social Satisfaction: Measurement and Relevance to Marketing Channel Relationships', *Journal of Retailing*, 76(1), p. 13.

Geyskens, I., Steenkamp, J.-B., Scheer, L. and Kumar, N. (1996) 'The Effects of Trust and Interdependence on Relationship Commitment: A Trans-Atlantic Study', *International Journal of Research in Marketing*, 13, pp. 303–17.

Gordon, I. (2000) 'Organising for Relationship Marketing', in J.N. Sheth and A. Parvatiyar, A. (eds) *Handbook of Relationship Marketing*, Thousand Oaks, CA: Sage, p. 512.

Gremler, D.D. and Brown, S.W. (1996) 'Service Loyalty: Its Nature, Importance and Implications', in B. Edvaardsson, S.W. Brown, R. Johnston, and E. Scheuing (eds) *Advancing Service Quality*, New York: ISQA Inc., p. 173.

Grönroos, C. (1994) 'From Marketing Mix to Relationship Marketing: Towards a Paradigm Shift in Marketing', *Management Decision*, 32(2), pp. 4–20.

Gruen, T.W. (2000) 'Membership Customers and Relationship Marketing', in J. Sheth and A. Parvatiyar (eds) *Handbook of Relationship Marketing*, Thousand Oaks, CA: Sage Publications Inc., pp. 355–80.

Gummesson, E. (1997) 'Relationship Marketing as a Paradigm Shift: Some Conclusions from the 30R Approach', *Management Decision*, 35(4), pp. 267–72.

Gwinner, K.P., Gremier, D.D. and Bitner, M.J. (1998) 'Relational Benefits in Services Industries: The Customer's Perspective', *Journal of the Academy of Marketing Science*, 26(2), pp. 101–14.

Halinen, A. (1997). *Relationship Marketing in Professional Services: A Study of Agency Client Dynamics in the Advertising Sector*, London: Routledge Advances in Management and Business Studies.

Harris, L.C. and O'Malley, L. (2000) 'Maintaining Relationships: Lessons from the Legal Market', *Service Industries Journal*, 20(4), pp. 62–84.

Harris, L.C., O'Malley, L. and Patterson, M. (2003) 'Professional Interaction: Exploring the Concept of Attraction', *Marketing Theory*, 3(1), pp. 9–36.

Iacobucci, D. and Ostrom, A. (1996) 'Commercial and Interpersonal Relationships; Using the Structure of Interpersonal Relationships to Understand Individual-to-Individual, Individual-to-Firm, and Firm-to-Firm Relationships in Commerce', *International Journal of Research in Marketing*, 13, pp. 53–72.

Larson, M. (1996) 'In Pursuit of a Lasting Relationship', *Journal of Business Strategy*, 17(6), p. 31.

Levitt, T. (1983) *The Marketing Imagination*, New York: The Free Press.

Liljander, V. and Strandvick, T. (1995) 'The Nature of Customer Relationships in Services', *Advances in Marketing and Management*, 4, pp. 141–67.

McCall, M. (1966) 'Courtship as Social Exchange: Some Historical Comparisons', in B. Farber (ed.) *Kinship and Family Organisation*, New York: John Wiley & Sons Inc, pp. 190–210.

McKenna, R. (1991) *Relationship Marketing: Successful Strategies For The Age of the Customer*, Reading, MA: Addison-Wesley.

Möller, K. and Wilson, D.T. (1995) 'Business Relationships – An Interaction Perspective', in K. Möller and D.T. Wilson (eds.) *Business Marketing: An Interaction and Network Perspective*, Norwell, MA: Kluwer Academic Publishers, pp. 23–2.

Moorman, C., Zaltman, G. and Deshpande, R. (1993) 'Relationships Between Providers and Users of Market Research; The Dynamics of Trust Within and Between Organisations', *Journal of Marketing Research*, 29 (August), pp. 314–29.

Morgan, R.M. (2000) 'Relationship Marketing and Marketing Strategy: The Evolution of Relationship Marketing Strategy Within the Organisation', in J.N. Sheth and A. Parvatiyar (eds) *Handbook of Relationship Marketing*, Thousand Oaks, CA: Sage, pp. 481–504.

Morgan, R.M. and Hunt, S.D. (1994) 'The Commitment–Trust Theory of Relationship Marketing', *Journal of Marketing*, 58(July), pp. 20–38.

O'Malley, L. (1998) 'Can Loyalty Schemes Really Build Loyalty?', *Marketing Intelligence and Planning*, 16(1), pp. 58–67.

O'Malley, L. and Mitussis, D. (2002) 'Relationships and Technology: Strategic Implications', *Journal of Strategic Marketing*, 10, pp. 225–38.

O'Malley, L., Patterson, M. and Evans, M.J. (1997) 'Intimacy or Intrusion: The Privacy Dilemma for Relationship Marketing in Consumer Markets', *Journal of Marketing Management*, 13(6), p. 542.

Oliver, R.L. (1999) 'Whence Consumer Loyalty', *Journal of Marketing*, 63, pp. 33–44.

Palmer, A.J. (1996) 'Relationship Marketing: A Universal Paradigm or Management Fad?', *The Learning Organisation*, 3(3), pp. 18–25.

Parvatiyar, A. and Sheth, J.N. (2000) 'The Domain and Conceptual Foundations of Relationship Marketing', in J.N. Sheth and A. Parvatiyar (eds), *Handbook of Relationship Marketing*, Thousand Oaks, CA: Sage Publications Inc., pp. 3–38.

Peterson, R.A. (1995) 'Relationship Marketing and the Consumer', *Journal of the Academy of Marketing Science*, 23(4), pp. 278–81.

Pine, J.B. II, Peppers, D. and Rogers, M. (1995) 'Do You Want to Keep Your Customers Forever?', *Harvard Business Review*, March–April, pp. 103–14.

Reichheld, F.F. and Sasser, E.W. Jr. (1990) 'Zero Defections: Quality Comes to Services', *Harvard Business Review*, 69 (September–October), pp. 105–11.

Reinartz, W., Drafft, M. and Hoyer, W.D. (2002) 'Measuring the Customer Relationship Management Construct and Linking It To Performance Outcomes', *10th International Colloquium in Relationship Marketing*, University Kaiserslautern, Germany, October, pp. 313–31.

Rowe, G.W. and Barnes, J.G. (1998) 'Relationship Marketing and Sustained Competitive Advantage', *Journal of Market Focused Management*, 2, pp. 281–297.

Rubach E (2003) 'Harley Gears up for Euro Loyalty Assault', *Precision Marketing*, January, p. 1.

Ryals, L. and Knox, S. (2001) 'Cross-Functional Issues in the Implementation of Relationship Marketing Through Customer Relationship Management', *European Management Journal*, 19(5), pp. 534–43.

Samuelsen, B. and Sandvik, K. (1997) 'The Concept of Customer Loyalty', in *26th Annual EMAC Conference: Progress, Prospects and Perspectives*, Warwick Business School, Coventry, England.

Scott, J. (2002) 'Once Bitten, Twice Shy: A World of Eroding Trust', *The New York Times*, 21 April, p. 5.

Sheaves, D.E. and Barnes, J.G. (1996) 'The Fundamentals of Relationships: An Exploration of the Concept to Guide Marketing Implementation', *Advances in Services Marketing and Management*, 5, pp. 215–45.

Sheth, J.N. and Parvatiyar, A. (1995) 'Relationship Marketing in Consumer Markets. Antecedents and Consequences', *Journal of the Academy of Marketing Science*, 23(4), pp. 255–72.

Sheth, J.N. and Parvatiyar, A. (eds) (2000), *Handbook of Relationship Marketing*, Thousand Oaks, CA: Sage Publications.

Sisodia, R.S. and Wolfe, D.B. (2000) 'Information Technology: Its Role in Building, Maintaining, and Enhancing Relationships', in J.N. Sheth and A. Parvatiyar (eds) *Handbook of Relationship Marketing*, Thousand Oaks, CA: Sage Publications, Inc., pp. 525–63.

Stone, M., Woodcock, N. and Wilson, M. (1996) 'Managing the Change from Marketing Planning to Customer Relationship Management', *Long Range Planning*, 29(5), pp. 675–83.

Sweeney, J.C. and Swait, J. (2002) 'The Power of Commitment: An Empirical Study in the Context of Consumer Services', *10th International Colloquium in Relationship Marketing*, University Kaiserslautern, Germany, October, pp. 703–15.

Turnbull, P.W. (1979) 'Role of Personal Contacts in Industrial Export Marketing', *Scandinavian Journal of Management*, 7, pp. 325–39.

Tzokas, N. and Saren, M. (1997) 'Building Relationship Platforms in Consumer Markets: A Value Chain Approach', *Journal of Strategic Marketing*, 5(2), pp. 105–20.

Wilson, D.T. (1995) 'An Integrated Model of Buyer-Seller Relationships,' *Journal of the Academy of Marketing Science*, 23(4), pp. 335–45.

8 Knowledge management

Learning objectives

Having completed this chapter, students should:

- Understand the process of how data can be converted into knowledge for competitive advantage.

- Be aware of the barriers involved with this, for example in terms of a major skills-gap amongst marketers.

- Have seen examples of knowledge management in practice via case studies of sharing data across functions and partners.

Jigsaw

Jigsaw boasts around a quarter of the top 100 grocery brands as 'clients' ... manages a database of ten million people and has an ongoing relationship with one million through a magazine. Liz Harlow was the first employee of the Jigsaw Consortium, the UK's most ambitious fmcg data warehousing project ever. The premise behind the launch of Jigsaw was straightforward but surprisingly ahead of its time in the fmcg sector. Four likeminded but non-competing companies, Kimberly-Clark, Unilever, Cadbury-Schweppes and Bass, came together in 1997 to discuss the value of sharing customer data. They were united in a common problem – how could relationship marketing deliver a return on investment with products of low value? They rightly recognised that in order to make CRM work for a brand of deodorant, chocolate bar, or sachet of soup, it would have to be on a collaborative basis. Although Bass subsequently sold its leisure business and pulled out of the Consortium as it no longer shared the key Jigsaw audience of mothers with children, the initiative has flourished. The primary vehicle for data capture and relationship building is a quarterly magazine *Voilà!* which is ABC audited and ranks as the second largest woman's lifestyle/fashion title behind Boots' *Health and Beauty* magazine. The magazine contains a detailed questionnaire and includes features around the themes of cooking, health and beauty and activities. The content is tailored to the individual and includes coupons and offers which again are linked to the information Jigsaw already knows about the recipient. 'I couldn't count the levels of segmentation that we do,' says Harlow 'It's as many different types as can physically be done on the production line.' She says that not only are recipients 'totally clear about the value exchange', but research has shown that they enjoy filling out the questionnaire. 'They are chiefly housewives looking after their families and rushing around supermarkets picking products off shelves either through habit or because of offers. It is interesting to them to sit down and reflect on what they do and where their money is going.' Harlow will not be drawn on the subject of response rates conceding with a small smile that results are 'pleasing' and around double that of the solus mailings they have conducted. However, an extranet site, Jigsaw wisdom, charts all mailing activity off the back of the database and includes detailed information about response rates. 'Members can go in, see what has been done before and learn from other companies' experiences. It is very much a shared learning culture,' says Harlow. So, how effectively are brands using the wealth of data available to them? A recent example is the rebranding of Jif to Cif to bring it into line with the rest of the world. Lever Fabergé used the Jigsaw database to identify people who had already bought Jif from across its repertoire of spray, mousse and liquid products. They were sent a mailing inviting them to 'C the difference' and including the offer of a free eye-test at Dollond & Aitchison to consumers who purchased a product from the range. But Lever Fabergé also used the database to reach new customers. By identifying characteristics that linked existing buyers, the company could match this against the rest of the database and target a second wave of 'unconverted' consumers. Different creatives were used and a total of two million people were targeted – all off the Jigsaw database. Kimberly-Clark also tapped into the Consortium for its £10 million relaunch of feminine hygiene brand Kotex. In last month's edition of *Voilà!*, 500,000 people (half of the entire circulation) received a 30p money-off coupon and a sample of the new product along with a competitor product. The coupon was personalised and coded so Kimberly-Clark was able to track coupon redemption to an individual level and conduct follow-up activity. According to Jigsaw communications manager Gareth Waterman, Kimberly-Clark identified seven groups of people it wanted to target with Kotex samples, adding that much deeper segmentation is possible. 'The breadth and depth is phenomenal. It's not "we want to reach female pet lovers" but "we want to reach female pet lovers who like skiing, shop in Tesco and eat a certain number of jars of Chicken Tonight in a year". This is seriously refined targeting,' he enthuses. Waterman joined Jigsaw in July last year after a six-month secondment to Kimberly-Clark as acting relationship marketing manager from direct marketing agency Simpson Mahoney Parrock. Part of his remit is to look into online data collection ideas, including a digital version of *Voilà!* on the Web, WAP-based initiatives and interactive TV.

Harlow recognises the potential of new media channels but is taking a cautious approach to the emerging interactive world. 'We are currently doing an extensive programme of testing and will be doing something online later this year. But we're very aware of our core competencies and are not going to rush off and collect e-mail addresses unless we know exactly how we're going to use them and link that to current activity.' For the moment she believes there is much more that could be done with the existing data the Consortium holds, from category management to media planning and new product development. 'It is a tremendously exciting project,' concludes Harlow. 'An investment was made by three very brave companies and that will give them a safe passage into the new world of CRM.'

(Source: Acland H (2001) 'One Giant Jigsaw', *Marketing Direct*, April. Reproduced from *Marketing Direct* magazine with the permission of the copyright owner, Haymarket Business Publications Limited)

Introduction

This case study illustrates the potential power of sharing knowledge across partners and, together with the conceptual issues discussed in Chapter 7, we see the broadening of the relationship marketing paradigm. We have already said that CRM should be considered from a much broader perspective than merely software-driven data management. This prior coverage lays the foundation for this chapter which is concerned with how to turn what are, all too often, failed CRM programmes into more successful integrating strategies. We explore the importance of extending data into knowledge and how this can be 'managed' within relational marketing. Davenport *et al.* (1998) define knowledge as 'information combined with experience, context, interpretation and reflection'. This moves us further forward from the more mechanistic processes that IT can provide in analysing and interpreting data. It also raises an issue of who possesses the relevant skills for deciding how data should be analysed with what strategic vision.

CRM problems

We have alluded to many of the issues here. There is the rhetoric rather than the reality of relational interaction. As Rigby *et al.* (2002) suggest, before implementing CRM software it is important to first do the 'basics' of 'traditional customer acquisition and retention strategies ... effective customer relationship management is based on good old-fashioned segmentation analysis' (see Chapter 6).

A second problem is again due to being too IT focused, but this time to use software before the organisation as a whole is customer-focused: 'believing that CRM affects only customer-facing processes ... is like trying to paint a house without sanding the walls first ... according to a survey, when asked what went wrong with their CRM projects, ... 87% pinned the failure ... on the lack of adequate change management' (Rigby *et al.* 2002).

Earlier sections have already explored the dangers of equating relationship marketing with IT solutions alone. Relationship marketing can be implemented in low-tech ways but, as companies grow, it is more difficult to know all customers' characteristics and interests, so data is clearly important. But as Rigby *et al.* suggest, 'start by vetting the lower-tech alternatives first – you may not need more'.

We have, again, explored the issues involved with different types of relationship. The key point is that all relationships between organisations and customers are (or should be, to avoid the 'rhetoric only' label) both mutual and relatively unique.

> " Relationships are two-way streets. You may wish to forge more relationships with affluent customers but do they want them with you? ... if your best customers knew you planned to invest $130m to increase loyalty how would they tell you to spend it? Would they want you to create a loyalty card or would they ask you to open more cash registers and keep more milk in stock ... unfortunately managers tend to ignore these considerations while using CRM." (Rigby *et al.* 2002) "

Technology by itself has not yet matured to being able to make informed and strategic interpretations of data. Artificial intelligence and neural networks are developing but it still requires marketing skills (discussed towards the end of this chapter) that bridge the 'technology–strategy' gap and the organisation-wide use of this to inform relational strategies. The relevance of this is demonstrated by Peppers and Roger's model of stages and uses of customer data (Table 8.1). They show the progression that needs to be implemented in relational marketing: insight leads to knowledge and knowledge leads to strategy.

As Plakoyiannaki and Tzokas (2002) declare, a key problem with CRM programmes is the relatively narrow focus, especially on software. They propose a more holistic approach which includes this, but which is more market-orientated and leads to much greater integration of wider issues, as summarised in Exhibit 8.1.

Exhibit 8.2 extends this analysis by summarising the potential of integrating organisational analytical and learning capabilities at various operational and strategic levels.

Knowledge management

The above model also extends the more tactical focus of using data to inform relational targeting and interaction to the more strategic issues of converting data

TABLE 8.1   Stages and uses of data

Data applications	Implications	Focus
Raw data	Prioritisation across business Fundamental piece of customer-based strategy Fuels analysis, forecasting and trends Needs to be viewed as an important company asset **Data leads to insight**	**Infrastructure** Prioritisation across business units & channels Consolidate for easy access and future real-time use Establish accuracy/trust through data rules and best practices Invest in awareness-building throughout the company around the value of data Establish joint accountability for maintenance by IT and business side of the company
Insight	Basis for building proactive tactics Helps plan and manage resources more effectively Moves from mass marketing approaches to database marketing Helps becomes aware of customers and their needs Insight should be consistently used by different parts of the organisation, therefore the distribution of insight to key customer-facing entities and those tracking key business metrics is critical **Insight leads to knowledge**	**Customer management** Assign a cross-functional team to perform analyses and create insight Establish key drivers of value and costs across channels – use as basis for analyses Create and execute an insight distribution plan Conduct channel integration planning pilots could be used Educate customer-facing employees on how to interpret 'insight'
Knowledge	Gives a company competitive advantage – it is between you and your customer Enables closer customer relationships, therefore the anticipation of customer needs Knowledge is created by few, used by many, therefore controlled **Knowledge leads to strategy**	**Customer growth retention** Establish two-way dialogue to fully utilise, maintain and improve on customer knowledge Establish customer needs and value clusters so customer needs can be met and recognised in a cost-effective way. Design channel integration based on customer preferences Allow customer knowledge to help prioritise employee focus
Strategy	Strategy allows for customer-based focus at all customer touch points **Strategy leads to profit**	**Business results** Measurement Refinement Continued coordination Tie strategy execution and success to employee compensation

(Source: Customer Insight table © 2002 Peppers and Roger Group)

EXHIBIT 8.1   Relational integration

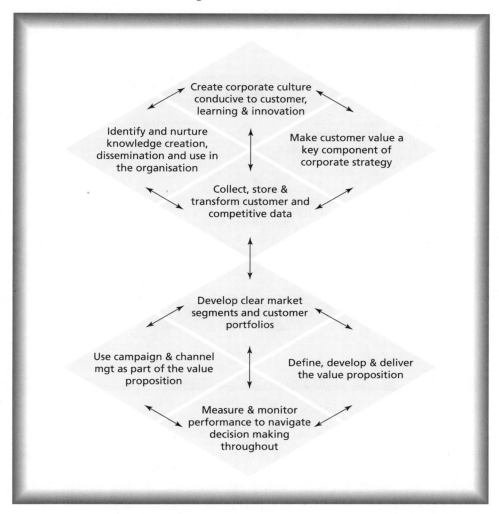

(Source: Plakoyiannaki and Tzokas 2002)

into knowledge within the context of a 'learning' corporate culture which in turn is concerned with 'customer value as a key component of corporate strategy'. This, together with the danger of 'data overload' arising from the many sources of data now drawn upon, means that there is a real need for appropriate knowledge management. As Chaffey (2002) suggests, it is important because organisational success is critically dependent on staff knowledge of the organisation's environment, including customers, suppliers, intermediaries and competitors. This is a reinforcement of marketing's 'outside in' philosophy and is needed to shape offerings to deliver customer service. Quintas *et al.* (1997) provide what is a rather generalised definition of KM: 'the process of continually managing knowledge of all kinds to meet existing and emerging needs, to

EXHIBIT 8.2   Importance of integration of capabilities

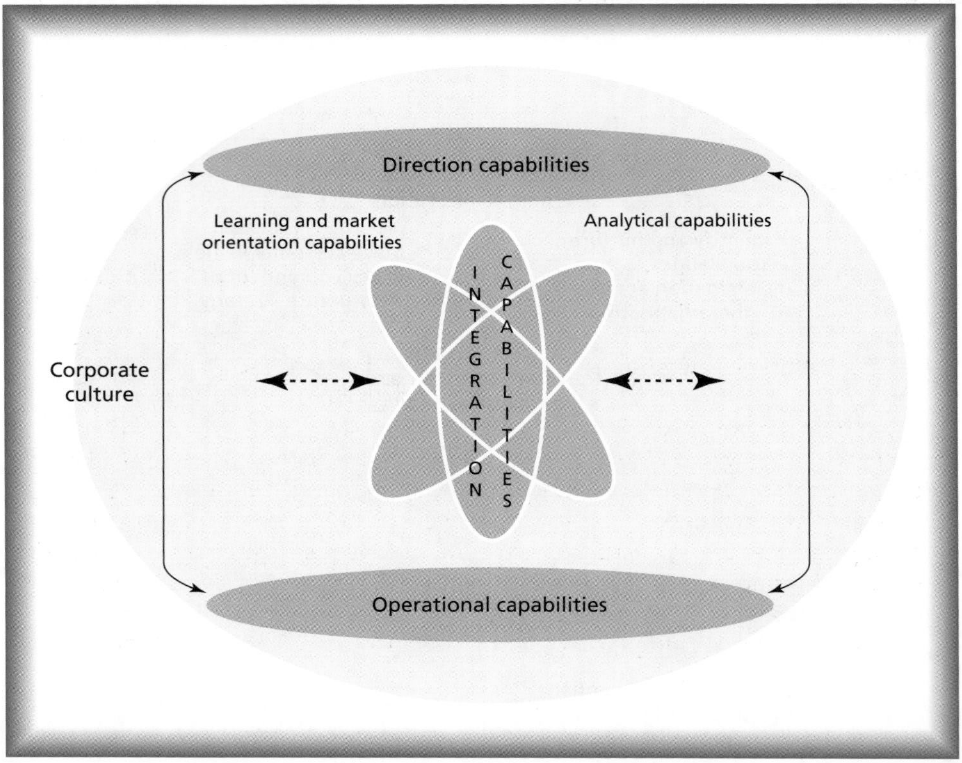

(Source: Plakoyiannaki and Tzokas 2002)

identify and exploit existing and acquired knowledge assets and to develop new opportunities'.

Knowledge management is concerned with the sharing of knowledge, increasingly across functions and departments within the organisation (intra-organisational KM). Sometimes such sharing is needed between partner or alliance organisations (inter-organisational KM). Indeed, as we have already mentioned, an increasing trend is towards strategic alliances, as illustrated by our earlier example of Jigsaw. A section will shortly explore some of the elements of this sort of strategic alliance within the context of knowledge sharing.

Indeed, if the management of this resulting knowledge is not integrated and shared across relevant organisational functions, there is little chance of there being sustainable relational marketing. Knowledge management is a framework for moving data-informed relational marketing to a more strategic position.

This is central to relationship marketing because as Corveillo *et al.* (1997) state, the manifestation of the relational paradigm is not only via database marketing and interactive marketing (based on relationship constructs and communications channels facilitated by new technology) but also via network marketing (up and down supply chains and across partners.

As Bennett and Gabriel (1999) concluded from their empirical research, 'the contributions of KM to both direct marketing and sales management were highly regarded'.

Relational variety

The variety of relational targets may be summarised under four broad categories (Exhibit 8.3) (Morgan and Hunt 1994): supplier partnerships, lateral partnerships, customer partnerships and internal partnerships. Within each of these categories we can further specify a number of particular relationships.

- **Customer partnerships:** These include relationships with intermediate customers (e.g. distributors, agents, dealers and retailers) as well as the organisation's ultimate customer. Organisations work closely with their intermediate customers to ensure that their products and services gain maximum positive exposure, to generate positive economic outcomes and to ensure that relevant and important customer and market information is communicated to them on a regular basis. Relationships with final customers are ultimately about securing customer retention, enhancing

EXHIBIT 8.3 Variety of relational targets

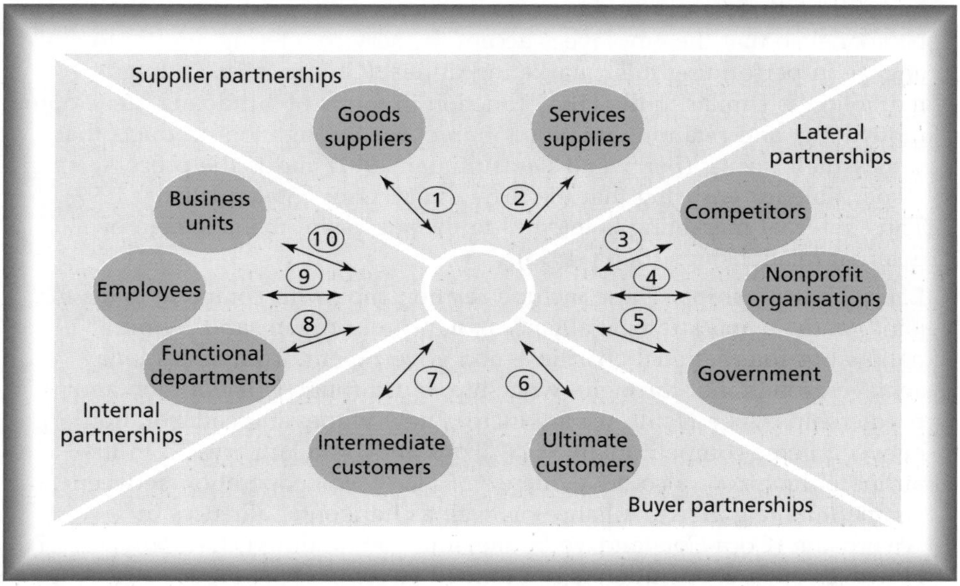

(Source: Morgan and Hart 1994)

profitability and improving the effectiveness and efficiency of marketing efforts through customer participation.

- **Supplier partnerships:** These represent important inter-organisational relationships, based primarily on providing the focal organisation access to important resources necessary to create offerings designed to satisfy its own customers. The impetus to build relationships with suppliers is likely to continue as we move toward a collaborative economy where 'supply-chain collaboration will intensify as pressure builds to cut costs, streamline the supply chain, and tie sales directly to production' (Mahoney 2001). As a result, rather than talking about the value chain as was traditionally the case, we need to think increasingly about collaborative nets which create specific competitive advantages as a result of the increased proximity of partners and members of other partner networks (Piller *et al.* 2002). For example, the Body Shop emphasises that it will only develop relationships with supplier organisations that deliberately attempt to minimise their impact on the natural environment. This is important to the Body Shop because it has a significant impact on their value proposition to ultimate customers.

- **Internal partnerships:** Although the relationship between an organisation and its various business units and departments is important here, the fundamental concern is the creation of sustainable relationships with employees. The focus on internal partnerships explicitly recognises that 'every employee in a firm has his/her own responsibility for creating superior customer value' (Hoekstra *et al.* 1999). Employees need to feel positive about their organisations and the roles they fulfil if the organisation is to be successful in its external marketing. This highlights the role of *internal marketing* (Grönroos 1994). Put simply, internal marketing reflects the recognition that 'a service must first be successfully marketed to the personnel so that the employees accept the service offering and thoroughly engage in performing their marketing duties' (Grönroos 1978). Internal marketing is similar to the HRM function in terms of 'attracting, developing, motivating, and retaining qualified employees through job-products that satisfy their needs' (Berry and Parasuraman 1991) and is the process responsible for ensuring that the firm is market orientated (Piercy 1997). Thus, internal marketing is integral to the successful management of external relationships (Berry 1995).

- **Lateral partnerships:** These include relationships with competitors (as in joint ventures and strategic alliances), non-profit organisations (local, national or international charities), and government. Companies today achieve growth, not through ownership, but through collaboration and partnerships. As a result, we are increasingly witnessing collaboration between fierce competitors like GM, Ford and DaimlerChrysler. In the airline industry we also see evidence of increased cooperation between competitors (e.g. STAR Alliance) as well as horizontal alliances in advertising (Coca-Cola and Vodafone) and co-branding (Marlboro–Ferrari). However, such cooperation is not limited to commercial organisations but also includes non-profit organisations such as charities and the arts.

Another way of analysing such knowledge alliances is to consider those that occur within the organisation (intra-organisational) and those that link organisations (inter-organisational).

Intra-organisational knowledge management

This concept is not new but is an important one. If CRM projects are to succeed it is not sufficient to buy-in (or outsource) a sophisticated data mining 'solution'. Data needs to be converted into knowledge and shared by all relevant parties in the organisation, as is epitomised by the Hewlett-Packard quote: 'if only HP knew what HP knows' (Sieloff 1999). The following short case study is a simple but powerful example of intra-organisational knowledge management.

CASE STUDY 8.1

Hewlett-Packard

Hewlett-Packard considered that it needed to improve its response to sales enquiries because the process of getting prospect details to salespeople took several weeks. The company developed a system it called QUILTS (Qualified Lead Tracking System). This involved an automated network in which such leads were transmitted to the telemarketing centre for qualification and ranking. The results were then electronically sent back to headquarters. The hotter prospects were telephoned directly to sales-people and the system reduced the turnaround time to 48 hours.

(Source: Lewington 1998)

This case is paralleled by the Spanish clothing retailer, Zara, which hired just-in-time staff from the motor industry who encouraged empowerment of shop assistants. When customers expressed liking for a 'top' but not with its current, rather military-style epaulettes, shopfloor staff were able to convey this to the Spanish suppliers and within days, a new 'epaulette-free version' was in stock. The store is also able to respond quickly to street-level reactions and stock is changed, on average, 17 times per year rather than the more usual four times for the sector as a whole (BBC 2003).

It makes obvious sense for appropriate customer data to be available to all who might be in contact with customers, whether they be in sales, invoicing, credit control, market research, customer service, complaints or wherever, but this does not always happen. Indeed, marketers need to be less insulated from other functions and even from the informational advantages and consequences of data shared with other organisations. For example, Depres and Chauvel (2000) distil literature from academics, consultants and practitioners on this issue and demonstrate (Exhibit 8.4) how (vertical axis) information can be transferred from the individual across groups (e.g. the marketing communications function) and to the organisation (other functions, even outside the marketing function). The horizontal axis in Exhibit 8.4 provides a 'process' that essentially reinforces the importance of 'sharing'.

By focusing on this, relational marketers will be able to devise effective strategies to meet the market needs and integrate with partners to deliver improved shareholder value. Exhibit 8.5 summarises another simple but clear methodology for managing knowledge (Rubenstein-Montana *et al.* 2001).

Organisations form such alliances for various purposes and this defines the type of strategic alliance. According to Burgers *et al.* (1993), strategic alliances are formed as a mechanism for reducing uncertainty for parties of the alliance and are not restricted to large organisations (Page and Marsland 1998).

A simple practical example will help here. In a research project into the use of multi-step flows of communication in the motor market, Evans and Fill (2000) found that motor company public relations managers make heavy use of motoring journalists as opinion formers (attempts are made to influence what these journalists say about new cars) but they are less able to make use of opinion leaders amongst car buyers. The problem is one of identifying these and then targeting them. However, the research revealed that in many of these companies there is also a database marketing communications department that records

EXHIBIT 8.4   Knowledge management

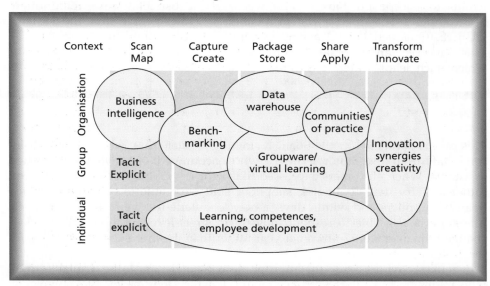

(Source: Depres and Chauvel 2000)

EXHIBIT 8.5 Knowledge management methodology

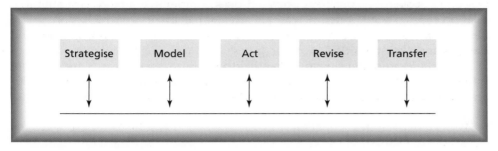

(Source: Rubenstein-Montana *et al.* 2001)

details of those who have purchased a new car early in its life cycle. These 'earlier adopters' include a high proportion of opinion leaders. But the worrying part of the research was that the PR managers usually claimed that this database was not shared with them and that marketing and PR are 'separate'!

Inter-organisational marketing

Since the late 1980s, the issue of inter-firm relationships has become more strategic because of the increasing emphasis on networks in securing sustainable competitive advantage. The focus on relationships remains relevant, however, because networks are formed by *webs of relationships* between organisational partners.

Unlike fmcg markets, organisational markets are not homogeneous; in fact they are heterogeneous with regard to both supply and demand (Anderson and Narus 1984). Furthermore, some buyers and suppliers are far more important than others, thus limiting the extent to which marketing programmes can be standardised. It is the so-called 'IMP' researchers who have explored these issues in some depth. They see marketing and purchasing of industrial goods as an interactive process between two parties but within a certain environment. Such an interaction cannot be considered in isolation, but must be analysed within the context of the relationship of which it forms a part and within the wider context of the environment in which it operates. This includes the up- and downstream interactions throughout the supply chain but also the inter-partner collaborations that abound in organisational marketing.

Although these are increasingly popular (and effective), it must also be remembered that conflict and competition are frequently experienced in such alliances.

The relational approach to inter-organisational research in the USA has a more recent history than its counterpart in Europe. This is attributed to a number of factors, including the large size of the domestic market (which made customer replacement relatively easy) and the predominance of adversarial business practice. As such: '... business operated on a competitive model, and although relationships existed, buying was an adversarial affair in which purchasing departments played sellers against each other to obtain concessions in price and other terms' (Wilson 1994).

The US literature developed in parallel to the European research and was not informed by the IMP work. As such, its two streams, channel research and buyer-seller research, merit discussion in their own right.

Channel research

In a similar approach to the IMP literature, Anderson and Narus (1984) analyse the commercial relationship between two participants (dyad) based upon their interactions. The integration of social exchange theory proved effective in enhancing the understanding of commercial relationships. It led to conceptual links being drawn between relational variables such as trust, communication, cooperation, conflict, relative dependence and satisfaction. Furthermore, both parties' desire to enter and maintain relationships was seen as a function of the expectations and satisfaction within a relationship versus the comparison level of the alternatives (Exhibit 8.6).

EXHIBIT 8.6   Model of manufacturer and distributor working partnerships

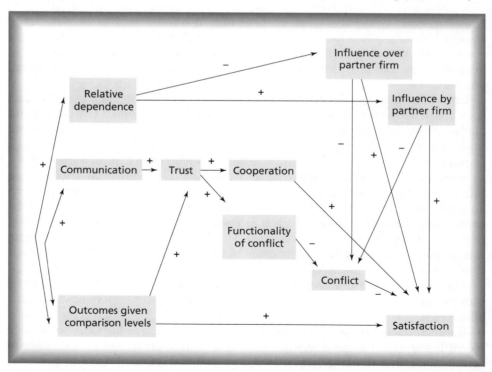

Buyer–seller research

Within the context of buyer–seller relationships, the work of Dwyer *et al.* (1987) is regularly cited as an important contribution to the literature in terms of explaining the development of inter-organisational relationships and their dynamics. It is heavily based upon Macneil's (1980) work on contractual relations, employs constructs from social exchange theory (Kelley and Thibaut 1978) and proposes a framework for developing buyer–supplier relationships. One of the principal contributions of this work is that it creates a conceptual distinction between discrete transactions and relational exchange. Discrete transactions refer to transactions that are predominantly governed by market forces and that are of specific content and duration. Relational exchange, on the other hand, refers to the interactive relationships that firms form. These are characterised by economic, social, legal, technical, informational and procedural bonds. The authors argue that relational exchanges include expectations that a relationship will endure over time, benefits and burdens will be shared, partners will experience mutual trust, and planning for future transactions will take place.

Networks

It was argued earlier that the focus on dyadic relationships is somewhat simplistic as it ignores the impact of webs of relationships on a single dyad. If there are strong ties in organisational markets then there is structure, connectedness and interdependence and the system can be described by the metaphor of a network (Easton and Araujo 1994).

After 1985 the focus of the IMP group expanded to include webs of relationships which link firms together in networks (Ford 1990). Within a network a single firm will occupy a number of different positions, which define its roles with respect to other firms in the network. As such, it is possible to distinguish between micro and macro positions within the network. 'Micro positions refer to positions with respect to a specific exchange partner and macro positions to positions with respect to the whole network or net' (Andersson and Söderlund 1988). Thus, the network paradigm recognised that a company is simultaneously involved in a number of relationships that 'both constrain its behaviour and provide it with opportunities to develop' (Cunningham and Tynan 1993).

Networks are 'complex, multifaceted organisation structures that result from multiple strategic alliances, usually combined with other forms of organisation including divisions, subsidiaries, and value-added re-sellers' (Webster 1992). More specifically, networks are purposeful arrangements (Jarillo 1988) between two or more firms, with each of the firms remaining independent along some dimensions. As such, networks are not examples of either vertical or horizontal integration. Networks are different from the traditional command and control hierarchy, in that they display 'a flat organisation form, involving interactions between network partners rather than multi-layered members' (Piercy and Cravens 1995). This has led to increasing recognition of the importance of the relational aspects of marketing.

The reshaping of organisations towards flatter, more responsive network forms and the rise of RM are related, not as cause and effect, but as part of the same phenomenon. Both are responses to environmental turbulence and pursue a common goal – the creation of competitive advantage in a changing world (Peck 1996).

The primary implication of the network paradigm is that the firm's marketing focus must change from 'internal parameter activities to exchange and positioning activities in the network' (Andersson and Söderlund 1988). This is usually a long-term activity, and thus must be acknowledged when devising marketing strategy. In terms of marketing strategy, the major issues relate to what Hàkansson (1982) calls handling and limitation problems. Handling problems refer to the development, maintenance and dissolution of individual relationships. In contrast, limitation problems embody strategic decisions with regard to the firm's overall portfolio of relationships. Because it is difficult to be simultaneously involved in relationships which demand different types of technology, organisation or knowledge, one limitation is the firm's own capabilities. Thus, it must restrict its involvement to certain types of relationships. In addition to handling and limitation problems, the firm must also formulate a relationship policy to decide whether all its relationships should be treated in a standardised way. Since some relationships are likely to be more critical than others, the firm must develop a policy in terms of how different relationships should be developed and managed.

Networks are described as being both stable and changing. A firm may attempt to change the nature of a single dyadic relationship (i.e. its micro position), or may wish to improve its macro position within the network. Thus, the behaviour of any given firm within the network has implications for the structure of the network. Bonds between exchange partners change over time through adaptations, new bonds are created, and existing bonds are broken. This increases complexity with regard to formulating relationship strategy (Ford *et al.* 1996). Furthermore, internal and external customers interact in networks of relationships. Because of this, 'the boundaries between the inside and the outside have dissolved and both can be seen as part of the same network' (Gummesson 1996).

The following case study provides a useful practical example of channel interaction that is also highly relational.

CASE STUDY 8.2

MCB publishing community

MCB University Press is a specialist publisher of management research and applied titles. Through the platform of its Internet site, MCB interacts with chain members and provides a framework of supporting information (resources) specifically for each chain member. The interconnectivity of the site allows specific resources to add value to the activities of the other chain members. Exhibit 8.7 illustrates how this is achieved, using a simplified illustration of the supply chain as an example.

Here, each element of the chain is provided with, and provides, value added

EXHIBIT 8.7   MCB relationship community

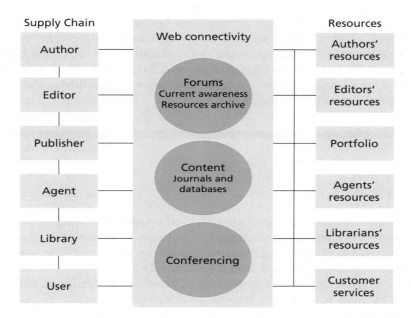

information through both their own resources and the resources of the other members. Web connectivity is further facilitated by forum networks and conferences which are underpinned by journal content.

MCB, as the owner and maintainer of this environment, is able to orchestrate the 'coming together' of chain members, provide them with added value, and extract its own value from the new relationships that have been created. One example of how this has been achieved is the development of Internet conferencing through a Virtual Conference Centre. The aim of this is 'to provide a journal sponsored forum to offer academics and professionals the opportunity to meet virtually and discuss the current issues in their subject area'.

The result is to provide a 'feedback loop' between authors, subscribers and the journal itself, together with an environment where interaction between key groups is facilitated. The proceedings of the completed conference are published in the supporting journal, allowing connectivity between authors and subscribers to impact on the published content.

(Source: Adapted from Hoey 1998)

KM across partners

As we have seen, there is an increasing trend for organisations to cooperate and share data and knowledge (Darrow and Belilove, 1978; Premukar and King, 1991). Strategic alliances are partnerships of two or more organisations or business units that work together and/or share resources to achieve strategically significant objectives that are mutually beneficial in improving their competitive positions. A strategic alliance is 'an agreement between firms to do business together in ways that go beyond normal company-to-company dealings, but fall short of a merger' (Wheelen and Hunger 2000). The following case is an example of a well-established and successful alliance that facilitates the management of knowledge across (competitive) partners.

CASE **STUDY** 8.3

SABRE

American Airlines developed a knowledge system that was originally for operations management purposes. A fuller and more strategic role for this was envisaged and it evolved into an electronic travel super-market shared by over 600 airlines, hotels and car hire companies across the world. Even the airlines' competitors saw the advantages of sharing this data and became partners. For a while, though, American Airlines implemented a system that meant that their own flights were displayed first. The other partners soon changed this, with threatened litigation!

(Source: Based on Hopper 1990)

Such cooperation is entirely consistent with the relational paradigm introduced in Part 1 and in Chapter 7. Indeed it is an integral component of many practical relational strategies. In fact, as Drucker has stated: increasingly command and control is being replaced by or intermixed with all kinds of relationships: alliances, joint ventures, minority participations, partnerships' (Drucker 1997).

There is an increasing trend towards multi-company alliances. As an example, a six-company strategic alliance was formed between Apple, Sony, Motorola, Philips, AT&T and Matsushita to form General Magic Corporation to develop Telescript communications software (McCreary et al. 1993). The opening vignette discussed the data-sharing alliance Jigsaw, but there are others. The following case shows the opportunities and potential problems encountered by the financial services alliance, Tank!, and several concerns are voiced by senior marketers. In particular, the focus on CRM software, as we have said, risks true relationship building and yet in principle the consortia approach is clearly seen to be a way forward in understanding product-markets.

Tank! questions the role of CRM

'Most people don't want a relationship with their bank.' This was the controversial opening statement made by Bob Tyrell, director of Sociovision, at this year's tank! Forum, the summit for direct marketers in financial services. His comments were particularly stark considering that the two-day conference in Nice last month focused specifically on CRM. Tank!, now in its fourth year, is a private club with hundreds of members from more than 80 firms in the UK and abroad. Drawn from senior decision makers, of whom 76% are at director level, all have one common goal: to consolidate best practice and raise standards of customer communications. Tyrell's words were a wake-up call to the delegates whose jobs are precisely about relationship building. CRM, as most of the audience understood it, he added, was dead: 'You have to get real and decide what your customers mean to you and why.' Every company, he asserted, must identify whether a one-to-one relationship with customers is really what they are striving for. If not, they must decide whether the relationship they seek should be purely value based. 'It's a choice between CRM – something that's important in the longer term – or CVM (customer value management), where the focus should be on the "now",' he said. 'You must put technology, churn and retention, and this year's profits above building a relationship with your customers.' But with technology often the reason why CRM projects fail in the first place, there were no surprises when the IDM's Julia Foster unveiled the results of Gartner's latest survey: 65% of CRM packages do not fulfil their promise. According to Caroline Marsh, sales director at Virgin One, technology should not be bought as an end in itself. Speaking to delegates, she said: 'Technology is an integral part of CRM, but it must be intelligently combined with people.' The critical issues up for debate, such as customer-centricity, had all been identified by delegates in the previous six months since the last forum. This sort of communication is at the heart of the summit, both in terms of networking opportunities and dissemination of industry knowledge and insight. But at this summit it was announced that the tank! Forum would no longer be about one-off, soon-forgotten events: it would now operate a 'continued learning process', according to Sean Larrangton-White, chairman of tank! and marketing communications manager at Royal Bank of Scotland. He revealed that he, along with fellow 'tank! drivers', will work to sustain dialogue. Tank! will communicate with delegates and designated people within their companies all year round by direct mail, e-mail, phone, fax, visits, and even one-day seminars. 'Tank! is unlike any other conference, anyway,' he explained. 'This will allow us to review the progress and learning gained in the lead-up to each future summit.' The ethos of tank! is based on the constant improvement of techniques and, as a result, the reputation of direct marketing in the financial sector. This is mainly achieved through the world's largest direct mail benchmarking system which it has in place, collated and monitored by ACNielsen MMS (see Chapters 2 and 5). Industry standard data is collected every six months from participating members in complete confidentiality and provides a chance to share and compare results with member companies. Using this direct mail library, tank!, in collaboration with the Royal Mail, created the People's Choice Awards.

Presented on the first night of the summit, it is the only consumer award to recognise direct mail excellence in financial services and identify those who are performing to the highest of standards. The mailings are split into categories and the winners were: credit cards: Egg; personal loans: Cooperative Bank; savings: Capital One Bank; general insurance: Prudential; and life insurance: M&S Financial Services. With 68 delegates, numbers were not as high as had been expected. 'But when you consider that 40% of UK conferences have been cancelled,

let alone international ones, it was a huge achievement,' said Larrangton-White. Delegates unanimously agreed that tank! is undoubtedly the only way forward for the industry. And the numbers of institutions taking part pays testament to its importance, proving that the financial sector is eager to improve its reputation.

(Source: Barnes 2001. Reproduced from *Marketing Direct* magazine with the permission of the copyright owner, Haymarket Business Publications Limited)

In Chapter 13, we explore other concerns arising from the consortia approach, such as the trend towards multinational data sharing consortia and the implications for consumer privacy of their personal details being moved around the world.

The sequence of knowledge management has been usefully analysed by Venkatraman and Henderson (2000) who provide the 'DIKAR' model in Exhibit 8.8. Data becomes information, which in turn becomes knowledge; knowledge results in informed actions and these produce business results.

This also provides alternative approaches to knowledge management. The more usual sequence is that data drives the process but we could start with results and deduce what knowledge will be needed to achieve them. This falls

EXHIBIT 8.8 DIKAR

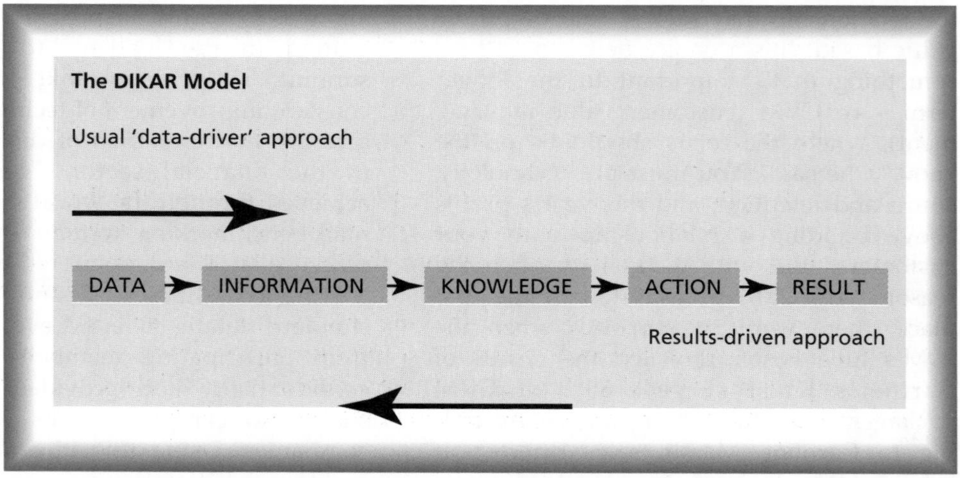

The DIKAR Model

Usual 'data-driver' approach

DATA → INFORMATION → KNOWLEDGE → ACTION → RESULT

Results-driven approach

(Source: Venkatraman and Henderson 2000)

into two categories: knowledge as body of information, which mostly can be processed by suitable database software and resides at the 'data' end of the flow; and knowledge as know-how, which requires more sophisticated 'people management' and is found at the action end.

CASE STUDY 8.5

United Biscuits

United Biscuits has two main operating categories: biscuits, of which McVitie's is the top brand, and snacks, which KP heads. Between them, they own some of the UK's most familiar products, including McCoy's, Go Ahead! and Oreo. Some have advertised online but, until recently, the company took a piecemeal approach, with each brand doing its own thing. A wise strategy, perhaps, as a packet of biscuits does not necessarily have much in common with a bag of crisps when it comes to target markets. But it also makes sense to look at brands together and let their online strategies feed off each other. That's precisely what United Biscuits decided to do some 12 months ago when it formed an 'e-business community', for which information systems director Mark Vickery has overall responsi-

bility. 'Often, companies don't coordinate their online activity or they go to the other extreme and set up whole dotcom businesses,' he says. 'We wanted something in-between to coordinate these activities, so we could learn from them. We try to set an agenda and priorities, and we're getting a more common direction and transfer of knowledge between brands.' Group brands manager Will Ursell says: 'When you look around the industry, there's very little best practice and if it does exist, it's generally not in the public domain. We need to base online activity on established marketing models. It's about seeing what has and hasn't worked on these brands and saying let's not make that mistake again.'

(Source: Adapted by the authors from Van Vark 2002)

Binney demonstrates the complexity of knowledge management via his 'KM spectrum' (Exhibit 8.9).

The interdisciplinary teams shown in Exhibit 8.9 can form the basis of 'communities of practice' which share and use knowledge via technology but must recognise the human dynamics within the teams as well (Adams and Freeman 2000). This is reinforced by Bhatt (2001) who states: 'KM is not a simple question of capturing, storing and transferring information, rather it requires interpretation and organisation of information from multiple perspectives. Only by changing organisational culture can an organisation gradually change the pattern of interaction between people, technologies and techniques.'

EXHIBIT 8.9 Binney's KM spectrum

Transactional – prepacked knowledge such as predetermined processes for help desks	Analytical – from CRM and data mining sources	Asset management – other 'explicit' and recorded knowledge and intellectual property	Processes evolving from TQM and reengineering – more internal process-based knowledge	Development – applying explicit knowledge within training programmes for empowering employees	Innovation & creation – inter-disciplinary teams to synergise knowledge from different perspectives

Relational value chains

A model developed by Porter (1980) describes the key activities that an organisation can perform or manage with the intention of adding value for the customer as products and services move from conception to delivery to the customer. An internal value chain is within the boundary of an organisation and an external value chain is where partners are performing activities.

Traditionally, value chain analysis distinguishes between primary activities that contribute directly to getting goods and services to the customer (such as inbound logistics, procurement, manufacturing, marketing and delivery of products) and support activities which provide inputs and infrastructure that allows primary activities to take place. These support activities include human resource, finance and information systems.

According to a survey conducted by Coopers and Lybrand, 54% of firms that formed alliances did so for joint marketing and promotional purposes (Coopers and Lybrand 1997). Companies are forming alliances to obtain technology, to gain access to specific markets, to reduce financial risk, to reduce political risk, to achieve or ensure competitive advantage (Wheelen and Hunger 2000). Coopers and Lybrand's study rates growth strategies and entering new markets among the top reasons for forming strategic alliances (Coopers and Lybrand 1997). New markets provide increased market uncertainty and greater operational uncertainty for an organisation, which can be reduced through strategic alliances. Technology was found to be the other major reason. Not all companies can provide the technology that they need to compete effectively in their markets on their own. Therefore, they are teaming up with other companies who do have the resources to provide the technology or who can pool their resources so that together they can provide the needed technology. In such cases, both sides receive benefit from the partnership.

As competition increases, the complexity of doing business increases as well. Major firms in the market start to refocus on their core competency, and outsource functions that are can be done in a better and cheaper way by others.

Tesco outsourced its data mining operation to DunnHumby but after a few years it was clear that a closer relationship was needed and now this has been formalised. The sharing of data between manufacturer and retailer is fairly commonplace. Category management involves the collaboration to grow the category rather than individual brands and the same principle applies to much data sharing. Tank! allows its financial services partners to evaluate response rates to different sorts of direct and interactive campaigns, for example.

A useful model can be used to show how to improve customer relational 'value' via the integration of different relational vectors (Exhibit 8.10).

These vectors are:

- customer data, which was a focus of much of Part 2;
- virtual integration (e.g. via EDI) with suppliers, which in turn enables the conversion of
- data into knowledge and power.

Indeed, from this, as each company has a number of supply chains for different products, the use of the term 'chain' seems limiting and supply chain network is a more accurate reflection of the links between an organisation and its partners; as should be clear by now, this is the position we take throughout this book. Indeed, Kalakota and Robinson (2001) describe the structure of a supply chain as a complex network of relationships that organisations maintain with trading

EXHIBIT 8.10   Relational vectors

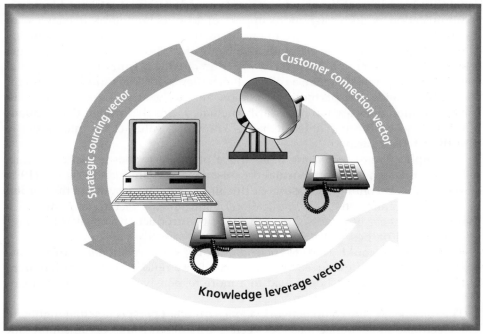

(Source: Venkatraman and Henderson 2000)

partners to source, manufacture and deliver products. The existence of such a network increases the need for electronic communications technology to manage and optimise this network. Communications technology is vital since managing relationships with customers, suppliers and intermediaries is based on the flow of information and the transactions between these parties.

According to Rayport and Sviokla (1996), the Internet enables value to be created by gathering, organising, selecting, synthesising and distributing information. They refer to this as a 'virtual value chain' that is mirroring the physical value chain. This description of the virtual value chain indicates the importance of information flow in the relational value chain models of today.

Deise *et al.* (2000) suggested a revised model that emphasises the importance of real-time environmental scanning (see Chapter 14) which has been made possible by the electronic communications links with distributors and customers.

Outsourcing

Since the 1980s there has been a tremendous increase in outsourcing of data-based knowledge management activities. As companies outsource more and more activities, management of the links between the company and its partners becomes more important (Chaffey 2002). Deise *et al.* (2000) describe network management as 'The process of effectively deciding what to outsource in a constraint-based, real-time environment based on fluctuation'. Electronic communication is becoming more important to outsourcing as it enables the transfer of information necessary to create, manage and monitor partnerships.

The danger, of course, is that with data being at the hub of relational strategies it is not always prudent to let it slip away to an outside organisation (Lacity *et al.* 1995). The compromise, again, as alluded to earlier, is for less formal outsourcing and more alliance and partnership relationships to emerge (Barnatt 1996). The communication links are not necessarily mediated directly through the company but may also be through intermediaries known as value chain integrators or directly between partners.

The implication of increasing outsourcing of core activities is that companies will move towards becoming virtual organisations. Benjamin and Wigand (1995) state that 'it is becoming increasingly difficult to delineate accurately the borders of today's organisations'. An implication of introducing electronic networks is that it becomes easier to outsource aspects of the production and distribution of goods to third parties.

This in turn could lead to boundaries between relational partner and organisation becoming blurred. The absence of any rigid boundary or hierarchy within the organisation should lead to a more responsive and flexible company with greater market orientation.

The relational value chain network offers a different perspective that highlights the electronic interconnections between partners and the organisation and directly between partners that enable real-time information exchange between partners. It shows the dynamic nature of this network and how it can be swiftly modified according to the market conditions. Different types of links in this network can be formed between different types of partners, from EDI links with key suppliers to e-mail links with less significant suppliers (Chaffey 2002). Adopting communications technology in this context is generally seen as a staged process. This has also been suggested by studies carried out by the DTI (2000). Companies start off using e-mail to communicate internally and with suppliers (step 1) before moving to offering product information and availability checking (step 2), online ordering (step 3), online payment (step 4), online progress tracking (step 5) and finally all stages are integrated (step 6) as suggested in this chapter.

Relationship constructs for relational partnerships

As our exploration of relational constructs would suggest, there need to be similar objectives, ability to share risks, and trust between partners and it is often the case that these are missing, leading to alliance failure or disbanding. Many organisations enter into an alliance without properly researching the steps necessary to ensure the basic principles of cooperation (Lewis 1992). Risk sharing is the primary bonding tool in a partnership. A sense of commitment must also be generated throughout the partnership and not just left to the odd individual in each organisation. If there is failure, it is usually because of more than one partner: shifting the blame does not solve the problem, but increases the tension between the partnering companies and often leads to alliance ruin (Lewis 1992).

Indeed, 'cultural clash' is probably one of the biggest problems that corporations in alliances face today. It is manifested in a variety of form, including semantic differences, personal egos and different business philosophies. After identifying these issues, measures can be developed to help avoid them. The most important of these is senior management's commitment to alliances. This is important not only to ensure that the alliances receive the necessary resources, but also to convince others throughout the organisation of the importance of the alliance so that the resulting knowledge can be fruitfully shared (Lorange et al., 1992). If not, alliances can be viewed as outside the organisational mainstream and therefore employees at all levels may tend to view them as not as important or as worthwhile as the organisation's core business.

Another factor, which influences the success of the alliance formation process, is the selection method. Partnership selection is perhaps the most important step in creating a successful alliance, as implied by the point above concerning organisational cultures. All concerned should recognise and facilitate 'speed, adaptation, and facilitated evolution ... a successful strategic alliance is laid during the internal formation process' (Lorange et al. 1992).

Also, as with any relationship, communication is an essential attribute for the alliance to be successful, otherwise doubt, misunderstanding and mistrust can result. In the same way that organisation–customer relationships have been compared with human relationships, so have organisation–organisation relationships. Kanter associates the process of alliance formation and maintenance directly to marriage, while the Business International Group uses a typology of alliance relationships matching different types of human couple relationships.

'An alliance is a lot like a marriage. There may be no formal contract. There is no buying and selling of equity. There are few, if any, rigidly binding provisions. It is a loose evolving kind of relationship. Sure, there are guidelines and expectations, but no one expects a precise, measured return on the initial commitment. Both partners bring to an alliance a faith that they will be stronger together than they would be separately. Both believe that each has unique skills and functional abilities the other likes. And both have to work diligently over time to make the union successful' (Ohmae 1989).

From this analysis, we suggest that knowledge management is really a 'people and process' issue not based on the application of technology *per se*. True, artificial intelligence and neural network technology are trying to capture human knowledge into technological systems but these are at a relatively primitive stage at present.

Tacit data

Much of the discussion so far has concerned relatively structured data (explicit data) such as customer transactional data and their profile details. Hopefully this will have been interpreted and converted via the visionary application of RFM, LTV and CHAID types of analysis into more strategic and tactical 'knowledge' (which segments to select for relational interaction and how such interaction should proceed etc.).

However, it is worth mentioning 'tacit' data (Kreiner 2002). This is less tangible and can be more 'affectively' based: expertise, gut feel, subjective insights, and intuitions – for example, how an individual customer reacts during telephone contact. This can be captured, and contemporary databases allow 'fields' to be included to accommodate such data. This is important because it can be shared across all those members of the organisation who might be in contact with the customer concerned. Perhaps experience suggests that our customer is a bit grumpy on Monday mornings.

Another example might concern customer complaints. The complaint itself can be recorded (explicit data) easily enough but the depth of emotion over the complaint (tacit data) can sometimes be lost.

There have been examples, however, of (surely innocent) errors occurring. For example, the sending of mailshots which include the 'tacit data field' within the salutation: 'Dear Mr Jones (pain in the arse)'. Such negligent abuse of data-based knowledge is not frequent but is clearly unacceptable.

By way of integrating explicit and tacit knowledge within a 'data to knowledge' framework, Nonaka *et al.* (2000) explore four constructs (Exhibit 8.11).

First, 'socialisation' shares new tacit information informally; secondly, 'externalisation' articulates tacit information into explicit knowledge; thirdly, 'connecting' disseminates this across relevant parties, often via the sorts of data mechanisms discussed in Part 2; and fourthly, 'embodying' in the organisational culture and shared context.

EXHIBIT 8.11   Modes of knowledge conversion

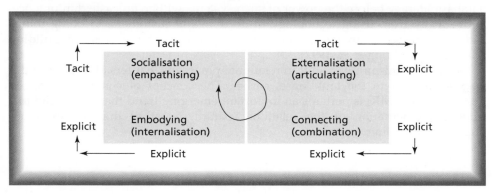

(Source: Nonaka *et al.* 2000)

Skills barriers to successful knowledge management

A major problem is that the new data-informed marketing is not always managed by marketers who possess the right skills to cope with the approach or even to talk the same language as those who can. In recent research conducted for the Chartered Institute of Marketing (Evans *et al.* 2002) this was identified as a major skills gap:

> ❝ Marketers should develop IT/new technology skills (maybe via 'junior mentors' – younger people who are 'IT savvy' and who can educate their senior colleagues). We cannot influence the development and usage of IT within companies unless we know something about it. ❞
>
> Senior manager, financial services multinational (Evans *et al.* 2002)

Indeed, Carson (1999) interviewed a group of leading US marketing practitioners and concluded that analytical skills and statistics topped the list of 'areas in which their education was lacking'. Businesses are demanding more accountability than ever before, making it essential for marketers to 'know how to do the numbers and prove their financial contribution to the bottom line'. Already we are seeing non-marketers taking over some of this ground and losing, for example, control of websites as reported by the CIM in their Marketing Trends Survey (CIM 2001).

We do not, of course, equate CRM success just with IT awareness. A major thrust of this chapter has been to show that CRM needs to go beyond software to wider knowledge-based interactions with customers, partners and suppliers. But at the same time it is clear that relational marketing is also heavily based on data-informed understanding as explored in Part 2, so the proposition in this section is especially pertinent.

The importance of holding a broader perspective and possessing multi-disciplinary skills has been highlighted by Long *et al.* (1992) who suggested that synergy is needed between marketing, operations, information technology and database literacy before the power of such systems will be unleashed in practice: 'move away from using technology to do things *to* customers, to doing things *with* customers by giving the customer a voice in the process of building relationships' (Long *et al.* 1992).

We explore this implied shift in relational power in Chapters 11 and 13, and it was introduced in the tank! case, earlier. The concept of customer-managed relationships (CMR) is perhaps an important emerging trend that could lead to a truer implementation of the relational paradigm rather than organisation-imposed interaction.

Summary

- The networked economy has important implications for relational marketing. We are in the era of the networked organisation and one in which relational contact is increasingly moving towards real-time and non-function-based interaction. The traditional organisation based on time and function 'silos' is moving to a more 'connected' model, in real time, and also from organisation-based focus on transactions to greater customer focus via relational interaction (Howard 2000). The interrelationships between various components and trends are shown in Exhibit 8.12.

EXHIBIT 8.12   The networked organisation

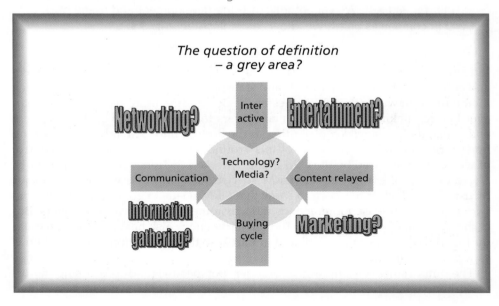

- The importance of marketing's role in managing knowledge, it is suggested, might be 'pushed closer to being an agent of the customer as opposed to the agent of the firm (Achrol and Kotler 1999). Their model reflects' 'layers' of networks: cross-functional teams, suppliers and other partners, linked via company databases. In this way, the analysis of the preceding chapters is synergised here.

- As Deshpache (1999) highlights, there is a need to take wider perspectives by using cross-cultural and cross-functional teams in order to focus on the 'customer centricity' needed for true relational marketing. Indeed, this reinforces Drucker's (1954) original perspective that 'marketing is the whole business seen from the customer's point of view'.

Review questions

1 Relational marketing goes beyond organisation–customer interaction. Discuss this statement.

2 To what extent do you think that the 'network' principle within relationship marketing theory is key to achieving true relational interaction?

3 Data-driven consortia are a notable extension of relationship marketing. How important are these? What are the factors that lead to their success? Are there any implications for customers?

4 What are the key skills gaps within relational marketing and how should these be bridged?

5 How might the failures in CRM implementation of the late 1990s and early 2000s be avoided in future?

Further reading

Journal of Knowledge Management, MCB Press.

Little, S., Quintas, P. and Ray, T. (eds) (2002) *Managing Knowledge: An Essential Reader*, London: Sage.

Marchand, D.A., Davenport, T.H. and Dickson, T. (eds) (2000) *Mastering Information Management*, Harlow: FT/Prentice Hall, Chapter 6, Knowledge Management.

Schlegelmilch, B.B. and Penz, E. (2002) 'Knowledge Management in Marketing', *The Marketing Review*, 3, pp. 5–19.

References

Achrol, R.S. and Kotler, P. (1999) 'Marketing in the Networked Economy', *Journal of Marketing*, 63, pp. 146–63.

Acland, H. (2001) 'One Giant Jigsaw', *Marketing Direct*, April.

Adams, E.C. and Freeman, C. (2000) 'Communities of Practice: Bridging Technology and Knowledge Assessment', *Journal of Knowledge Management*, 4(1), pp. 38–44.

Anderson, J.C. and Narus, J.A. (1984) 'A Model of the Distributor's Perspective of Distributor–Manufacturer Working Relationships', *Journal of Marketing*, 48(Fall), pp. 62–74.

Andersson, P. and Söderlund, M. (1988) 'The Network Approach to Marketing', *Irish Marketing Review*, 3, pp. 63–8.

Barnatt, C. (1996) *Management Strategy and Information Technology*, London: Thomson, p. 54.

Barnes, R. (2001) 'Tank! questions the role of CRM', *Marketing Direct*, December.

BBC (2003) 'Fast Fashion', in Store Wars Series, 19 February.

Benjamin, R. and Wigand, R. (1995) 'Electronic Markets and Virtual Value Chains', *MIT Sloan Management Review*, 36(2), pp. 62–73.

Bennett, R. and Gabriel, H. (1999) 'Organisational Factors and Knowledge Management within Large Marketing Departments: An Empirical Study', *Journal of Knowledge Management*, 3(3), pp. 212–25.

Berry, L.L. (1995) 'Relationship Marketing of Services – Growing Interest, Emerging Perspectives', *Journal of the Academy of Marketing Science*, 23(4), pp. 236–45.

Berry, L.L. and Parasuraman, A. (1991) *Marketing Services – Competition Through Quality*, New York: The Free Press.

Bhatt, G.D. (2001) 'Knowledge Management in Organisations: Examining the Interaction between Technologies, Techniques and People', *Journal of Knowledge Management*, 5(1), pp. 68–75.

Binney, D. (2001) 'The Knowledge Management Spectrum: Understanding the KM Landscape', *Journal of Knowledge Management*, 5 (1), pp. 33–42.

Burgers, W.P., Hill, C.W.L and Chan, K.W. (1993) 'A Theory of Global Strategic Alliances: The Case of the Global Auto Industry', *Strategic Management Journal*, 14(6), pp. 419–33.

Carson, C.D. (1999) 'What It Takes and Where to Get It', Working Paper, University of North Carolina.

Chaffey, D. (2002) *E-business and E-commerce Management: Strategy, Implementation and Applications*, Harlow: Pearson Education.

CIM (2001) 'Marketers Caught in Web of Intrigue – Control of Web Sites Wrestled Away From Marketers', Chartered Institute of Marketing, www.cim.co.uk.

Coopers and Lybrand (1997) 'Strategic Alliances Among America's Fastest-Growing Firms', *Barometer Survey*, New York.

Corviello, N.J., Brodie, R.J. and Munro, H.J. (1997) 'Understanding Contemporary Marketing: Development of a Classification Scheme', *Journal of Marketing*, 13, pp. 501–22.

Cunningham, C. and Tynan, A.C. (1993) 'Electronic Trading, Inter-organisational Systems and the Nature of Buyer-Seller Relationships: The Need for a Network Perspective', *International Journal of Information Management*, 13, p. 22.

Darrow, J.W. and Belilove, J.R. (1978) 'The Growth of Databank Sharing', *Harvard Business Review*, 56(6), pp. 180–5.

Davenport, T.H., De Long, D.W. and Beers, M.C. (1998) 'Successful Knowledge Management Projects', *Sloan Management Review*, 39(2), pp. 43–58.

Deise, M., Mowikow, C., King, P. and Wright, A. (2000) *Executive's Guide to E-Business, from Tactics to Strategy*, New York: Wiley.

Depres, C. and Chauvel, D. (2000) 'How to Map Knowledge Management', in D.A. Marchand, T.H. Davenport and T. Dickson (2000) *Mastering Information Management*, London: Financial Times/Prentice Hall.

Deshpache, R. (1999) 'Foreseeing Marketing', *Journal of Marketing*, 63, pp. 164–7.

Drucker, P.F. (1954) *The Practice of Management*, New York: Harper Row.

Drucker, P.F. (1997) 'Toward the New Organisation', in Hesselbein, F., Goldsmith, M. and Beckland, R. (1997) *The Organisation of the Future*, San Francisco: Jossey-Bass.

Dwyer, F.R., Schurr, P.H. and Oh, S. (1987) 'Developing Buyer-Seller Relationships', *Journal of Marketing*, 51(April), pp. 11–27.

Easton, G. and Araujo, L. (1994) 'Market Exchange, Social Structures and Time', *European Journal of Marketing*, 28(3), p. 81.

Evans, M. and Fill, C. (2000) 'Extending the Communications Process: The Significance of Personal Influencers in the UK Motor Market, *International Journal of Advertising*, 19(2), pp. 43–65.

Evans, M., Nancarrow, C., Tapp, A. and Stone, M. (2002) 'Future Marketers: Future Curriculum: Future Shock?', *Journal of Marketing Management*, 18(5–6), pp. 579–96.

Ford, D. (1990) *Understanding Business Markets: Interaction, Relationships, Networks*, London: Academic Press, Harcourt Brace and Co. Publisher.

Ford, D., Turnbull, P. and McDowell, R. (1996) 'Strategic Considerations in Networks', in J.A. Sheth and A. Parvatiyar (eds), *Emerging Perspectives on Relationship Marketing*, Emory University, Atlanta, Georgia, June.

Grönroos, C. (1978) 'A Service Oriented Approach to Marketing of Services', *European Journal of Marketing*, 12(8), pp. 588–601.

Grönroos, C. (1994) 'From Marketing Mix to Relationship Marketing: Towards a Paradigm Shift in Marketing', *Management Decision*, 32(2), pp. 4–20.

Gummesson, E. (1996) 'Relationship Marketing and the Imaginary Organisation: A Synthesis', *European Journal of Marketing*, 30(2), p. 40.

Hàkansson, H. (1982) *International Marketing and Purchasing of Industrial Goods*, Wiley: New York.

Hoekstra, J.C., Leeflang, P.S.H. and Wittink, D.R. (1999) 'The Customer Concept: The Basis for a New Marketing Paradigm', *Journal of Market Focused Management*, 4, p. 72.

Hoey, C. (1998) 'Maximising the Effectiveness of Web-based Marketing Communications', *Marketing Intelligence & Planning*, 16(1), pp. 31–7.

Hopper, M.D. (1990) 'Rattling the SABRE – New Ways to Compete on Information', *Harvard Business Review*, 68(3) pp. 118–25.

Howard, M. (2000) 'The Challenges of E-commerce: Creating Workable Models to Predict Consumer Needs in the Network Society, Future Foundations Report, London.

Jarillo, J.C. (1988) 'On Strategic Networks', *Strategic Management Journal*, 9, pp. 31–41.

Kalakota, R. and Robinson, M. (2001) *e-Business 2.0: Roadmap for Success*, 2nd edn, Boston, MA: Addison-Wesley.

Kelley, H.H. and Thibaut, J.W. (1978) *Interpersonal Relationships: A Theory of Interdependence*, New York: John Wiley & Sons.

Kreiner, K. (2002) 'Tacit Knowledge Management: The Role of Artifacts', *Journal of Knowledge Management*, 6(2), pp. 112–23.

Lacity, M.C., Willcocks, L.P. and Feeney, D.F. (1995) 'IT Outsourcing: Maximising Flexibility and Control, *Harvard Business Review*, May–June.

Lewington, J.A. (1998) 'Factors Affecting the Development of Sophisticated Database Marketing Systems', PhD Thesis, Open University Business School, Milton Keynes.

Lewis, J.D. (1992) 'The New Power of Strategic Alliances', *Strategy and Leadership*, 20(5) Sept/Oct, pp. 45–8.

Long, G., Angold, S. and Hogg, M. (1992) 'Who Am I?: A Preliminary Investigation into the Extent to which Data Collected via EPoS and EFTPoS Systems is Incorporated into Customer Databases Accessible through the Provisions of the Data Protection Legislation', in J. Whitelock *et al.* (eds) Proceedings of the Marketing Education Group Annual Conference, *Marketing in the New Europe and Beyond*, Salford, pp. 569–606.

Lorange, P., Roos, J.B. and Simci, C.P. (1992) 'Building Successful Strategic Alliances', *Long Range Planning*, 25(6), pp. 10–18.

Macneil, I.R. (1980) *The New Social Contract: An Inquiry into Modern Contractual Relations*, New Haven, CT: Yale University Press.

Mahoney, C. (2001) 'Global Supply Chains', *Executive Excellence*, 18(8), pp. 8–10.

McCreary, J.D., Boulton, W.R. and Sankar, C.S. (1993) 'Global Telecommunications Services: Strategies of Major Carriers', *Journal of Global Information Management*, 1(2), pp. 6–19.

Morgan, R.M. and Hunt, S.D. (1994) 'The Commitment–Trust Theory of Relationship Marketing', *Journal of Marketing*, 58(July), pp. 20–38.

Nonaka, I., Toyama, R. and Konno, N. (2000) 'SECI, Ba and Leadership: A Unified Model of Dynamic Knowledge Creation', *Long Range Planning*, 33(Feb), pp. 5–34.

Ohmae, K. (1989) 'The Global Logic of Strategic Alliances', *Harvard Business Review*, March–April, pp. 143–54.

Page, N. and Marsland, R. (1998) 'A World to the Wise', *Director*, September, 52(2), pp. 53–6.

Peck, H. (1996) 'Towards a Framework for Relationship Marketing – The Six Markets Model Revisited and Revised', in M. Baker (ed.) *A Vision of Marketing in 2025*, Marketing Education Group Conference, Strathclyde, July, 45.

Piercy, N. (1997) *Market-Led Strategic Change: Transforming the Process of Going to Market*, Oxford: Butterworth-Heinemann.

Piercy, N.F. and Cravens, D. (1995) 'The Network Paradigm and the Marketing Organisation', *European Journal of Marketing*, 29(3), pp. 18–19.

Piller, F., Schaller, C. and Reichwald, R. (2002) 'Indivualization Based Collaborative Customer Relationship Management: Motives, Structures and Modes of Collaboration for Mass Customisation and CRM', *10th International Colloquium in Relationship Marketing*, University Kaiserslautern, Germany, October, pp. 283–99.

Plakoyiannaki, E. and Tzokas, N. (2002) 'Customer Relationship Management: A Capabilities Portfolio Perspective', *Journal of Database Marketing*, 9(3), pp. 228–37.

Porter, M.E. (1980) *Competitive Strategy: Techniques for Analyzing Industries and Competitors*, New York: Free Press.

Premukar, G. and King, W.R. (1991) 'Assessing Strategic Information Systems Planning', *Long Range Planning*, 25(5), pp. 41–58.

Quintas, P., Lefrere, P. and Jones, G. (1997) 'Knowledge Management: A Strategic Agenda', *Long Range Planning*, 30(3).

Rayport, J.F. and Sviokla, J.J. (1996) 'Exploiting the Virtual Value Chain', *The McKinsey Quarterly*, 1, pp. 20–37.

Rigby, D.K., Reichheld, F.F. and Schefter, P. (2002) 'Avoid Four Perils of CRM', *Harvard Business Review*, February, pp. 101–9.

Rubenstein-Montana, B., Liebowitz, J., Buchwalter, J., McCaw, D., Newman, B. and Rebeck, K. (2001) 'SMARVision: A Knowledge Management Methodology', *Journal of Knowledge Management*, 5(4), pp. 300–10.

Sieloff, C. (1999) 'If Only HP Knew what HP Knows: the Roots of Knowledge Management at Hewlett-Packard', *Journal of Knowledge Management*, 3(1), pp. 47–53.

Van Vark, C. (2002) 'Take a Byte', *Revolution*, 25 September, pp. 22–5.

Venkatraman, N. and Henderson, J.C. (2000) 'Business Platforms for the 21st Century', in D.A. Marchand, T.H. Davenport and T. Dickson (eds) *Mastering Information Management*, Harlow: FT/Prentice Hall.

Webster, F.E. (1992) 'The Changing Role of Marketing in the Corporation', *Journal of Marketing*, 56(October), p. 9.

Wheelen, T.L. and Hunger, D. (2000) *Strategic Management and Business Policy: Entering 21st Century Global Society*, Upper Saddle River, NJ: Prentice Hall.

Wilson, D.T. (1994) 'Commentary by David T. Wilson', in G. Laurent *et al.* (eds.) *Research Traditions in Marketing*, Norwell, MA: Kluwer Academic Publishers, p. 343.

9 Acquisition, retention and loyalty strategies

Learning objectives

Having completed this chapter, students should:

- Recognise the importance of acquiring new customers.

- Understand how data-driven marketing can identify likely prospects for acquisition activities.

- Be aware of the dangers of focusing on acquisition at the expense of retaining existing customers.

- Be familiar with various approaches to encourage customer retention.

- Consider how loyalty and retention should be defined and how they should be measured.

- Be cognisant of criticisms of the contemporary focus on loyalty/retention.

- Appreciate the potential of direct marketing in managing acquisition, retention and loyalty.

Skoda: Simultaneous acquisition and retention campaign

Non-Skoda drivers see Skoda drivers as practical people who don't worry about image or street-cred. Skoda drivers, on the other hand, know they are driving a reliable car. With its new Octavia and Fabia models launched and targets to increase sales by £2.8 million, 2001 saw a very real brand challenge beyond the good work it had already started to address when it hired Chris Hawken as head of marketing at the start of 1999. Hawken's main criticism though was the lack of time devoted to non-Skoda owners. 'Research told us that there was 60 per cent brand rejection,' he says. By 2000, initial work was being conceived by Archibald Ingall Stretton (AIS). AIS and Hawken decided to run two mailers simultaneously – one to promote the Fabia, to be sent to 100 000 cold prospects, and the second for the Octavia, to be sent to 55 000 existing owners. This would invite them to upgrade to the latest models. Both were sent out between January and July 2001. 'The Octavia mailing would be preaching to the converted, so the brief was to communicate with much greater attention to detail. We wanted to invite people to go straight for a test drive without any call for data,' he says. 'The cold mailing, however, would require information back.' The cold list mailer was drawn from names on a variety of lifestyle and attitudinal lists with the creative approach linked as closely as possible to the current brand acceptance research. 'Above-the-line TV advertising had already done a good job of telling people that Skoda do actually make good cars,' says Hawken. 'It was just a case of dealing with people's fears that our cars still had the Skoda badge on it. As if by invitation, the Fabia mailing honed in on just this, by literally mailing out a genuine Skoda badge asking prospects to take it everywhere they went – even to bed with them. Also enclosed was a pre-paid reply card asking recipients to tell them what cars they were interested in, when they might be buying a new car, and inviting them to take the Fabia for a test drive. The Octavia mailing took a different approach. Sent in an A4 brown envelope, it was designed to look like a communiqué from the Skoda factory – complete even with fake Czech stamps on the outside. Inside it took the form of a spiro-bound policy document including extensive technical data. 'Skoda enthusiasts really love this,' says Hawken. 'This was more about saying you know the car, but did you know there have been 1 000 technical details changed to make it even better.' The Fabia mailing had a 75–25 split between older and younger customers respectively to test how the younger market performed. According to Hawken, the results of the mailings have been startling. In a competitive marketplace, the badge mailer drew a 3% response. Of these, 75% went on to take a test drive. This equates, he says, to a cost per enquiry of just £20 – about half the average in this sector. From the factory pack mailing, 5% of enquirers responded and 8% of existing owners requested a test drive. This resulted in a cost per test drive figure of £28.

Archibald says the similarity of response between Fabia cold prospects and Octavia enquirers is justification of the attention to detail the targeting process went through. 'This has been the first time we have mixed attitudinal and behavioural data together,' says Archibald. 'Within the overall response figures, we've found that the best prospects have come from specialist lists rather than lifestyle lists because specialist lists look more at attitude.'

(Source: Crush 2002. Reproduced from *Marketing Direct* Magazine with the permission of the copyright owners Haymarket Business Publications Limited)

Introduction

The above Skoda vignette is a good one to present at this stage. It links with some of our earlier exploration: of lists (Chapter 2) testing (Chapter 4) and attitudinal as well as behavioural data (Chapter 5). It also takes this into the realms of cold prospecting to acquire new customers and into strategies for retaining existing customers. Both of these areas form the main themes of this chapter.

Indeed, it could be argued, albeit narrowly and 'tongue in cheek', that these cover 'everything' in marketing. After all, what else is there once we've recruited customers and kept them? The fuller picture, of course, requires the exploration of data sources and data mining, the use of research and testing methodologies and the underpinning of relational constructs in order for the techniques of acquisition and retention to be wholly understood and applied. There is an obvious sequence here – organisations can't retain customers until they have acquired them – and this chapter explores this progression.

In terms of acquisition, the focus is on growing the customer base and then there are the important (and usually less expensive) retention strategies. There is much support for progressing beyond acquisition and criticism for neglecting retention: 'the front-end function of customer getting commands a substantial portion of budgets, top management attention, and talented marketing personnel. The back-end efforts of customer retaining generally are neglected' (Rosenberg and Czepiel 1984). The importance is increasingly being recognised and even though acquisition strategies can lead to business growth, further growth can be achieved by cross-selling and up-selling to existing customers and by reducing customer attrition rates (Ainslie and Pitt 1992).

Progression from acquisition to retention

A number of models of relationship development have been proposed in the literature (Table 9.1) and these clearly incorporate the progression from acquisition to retention.

We propose a six-stage model (Table 9.1 and Exhibit 9.1) with different phases of relationship development. The early stages reflect acquisition which then progresses into phases of retention.

Acquisition stages

'Companies must acquire assets before they can manage them. For this reason alone, customer acquisition merits our attention' (Blattberg *et al.* 2001). Acquisition is the life-blood of any business. Even those organisations with high

TABLE 9.1   Process models of relationship development

Ford (1980)	Dwyer et al. (1987)	Borys and Jemison (1989)	Wilson (1995)	Evans, O'Malley and Patterson, this volume
Pre-relationship stage	Awareness		Search and selection	Attraction
Early stage	Exploration	Defining purpose	Defining purpose	Interaction
Development stage	Expansion	Setting boundaries	Setting boundaries	Progression
Long-term stage	Commitment	Value creation	Value creation	Deterioration
Final stage	Dissolution	Hybrid stability	Hybrid stability	Cessation reclamation

EXHIBIT 9.1   Acquisition and retention

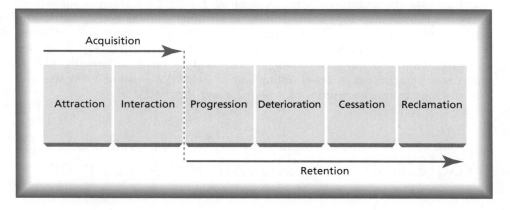

retention rates need to find new customers. More importantly, customer acquisition paves the way for successful customer retention because:

- The more efficient and effective an acquisition drive is, the greater the pool of customers whose retention values the organisation can capitalise upon.
- Every relationship begins with acquisition, and it is during this formative phase that the demands and expectations of the respective parties are shaped.

It has been argued that 'techniques for the acquisition of new prospects rest almost exclusively on subjective or experientially based judgement' (Lix *et al.*

1995). We are not convinced by this and the 'acquisition' case studies in this chapter hopefully demonstrate greater sophistication afforded by the new data-driven interactive marketing. One example is the case presented below which reflects the profiling of existing 'best' customers and the targeting of prospects who possess similar characteristics.

CASE STUDY 9.1

'Identikit' acquisition strategy

This case is based on a small mail-order wine business that is concerned about its customers and prides itself on providing more than just 'wine'. It also provides information about the types of wine and their vineyard of origin as added values. In this way the company is marketing orientated, it tries to adopt the marketing concept by being profitable through satisfying customer requirements and these are, in this case, for more than just 'cheap wine'. For many customers, the relational approach is a reality here because there is a degree of interaction at the personal level concerning the 'wider' interest in wines.

The company is able to analyse current customer profiles in a variety of ways. For example, its transactional data can be analysed for recency, frequency and monetary value (RFM) and long-time value (LTV). These are two important metrics in data-informed marketing, as we have already seen in Chapter 3, and many software packages include algorithms for these metrics. With the RFM metric, the company identifies the 'recency, frequency and monetary value' of customers and those with the highest rating according to this measure could be selected for targeting and those with poorer RFM scores might be ignored or even deselected. The wine company profiled the postcodes of its 'best' customers. Four

MOSAIC (see Chapter 2) groups emerged as representing these best customers:

- 'Clever Capitalists',
- 'Chattering Classes',
- 'Ageing Professionals', and
- 'Gentrified Villages'.

The company clearly knows where these 'best' customers live because it has their addresses, but the next stage was to identify where, geographically, others within these four MOSAIC groups live.

A map showing the 'hot spots' of where these groups are more likely to live was produced by Experian and the company was then able to narrow its geographical coverage of the UK to suit its own distribution operation. It wanted to focus rather more on the South East region and so it then approached Experian for a list of names and addresses of prospects (i.e. not existing customers, but people who are profiled as being in one of the four 'most likely' MOSAIC groups in that region). The company targeted these households in order to acquire more customers who would hopefully, via this 'identikit' approach, also become 'best' customers in terms of RFM and LTV.

In this case, even though the company is customer orientated, the selection and targeting via this 'identikit' method, which is based on the premise of 'more of the same', does not, *per se*, lead to targeting those who really are interested in this form of added value in the wine market. These geodemographic characteristics are just that – profile characteristics rather than anything affective that explains why they are interested in wine and its origins. For this, the company, in order to be more customer orientated, would need more affective understanding such as via qualitative research; an argument we have also explored earlier, in Chapters 4 and 5.

So, it is clear from this case study that an initial step in the acquisition process is to understand existing customers. Appreciating the characteristics and expectations of current customers will go a long way towards identifying the profile of likely relational targets. The next step is to generate an understanding of the prospects that the company intends to target. Cost-effective acquisition of new customers depends, in part, upon an organisation's ability to target prospects efficiently. A prospect is any individual, household or business who is not a current customer, but who is worth considering for acquisition. According to Hansotia (1997), these include:

- households, individuals and businesses with no prior relationship with the company;
- lapsed customers;
- customers of a parent or sister company;
- customers of strategic partners;
- inquirers.

We now turn to our 'acquisition–retention relational model' and provide analysis and examples of each stage.

Attraction

In many ways attraction is a pre-relationship phase. It represents the point at which one or other party finds another attractive in some way. It is the extent to which the potentially relational partners perceive past, current, future or potential partners as appealing in terms of their ability to provide superior economic benefits, access to important resources and social compatibility (Exhibit 9.2). Economic attractiveness is the extent to which greater profits or lower costs are likely to result from relationship formation. Resource attractiveness may result from access to particular products, services, technologies and customers that are necessary to further specific goals. Social attractiveness refers to the possibilities of furthering social bonds and accessing social situations or individuals that are desired. Although one of these possible rewards may be the motivation for relationship development, the presence of all three is likely to signify a closer and more enduring relationship.

It must also be remembered that attraction works both ways. Prospects will be attractive to organisations to varying degrees, but the organisation must also strive to make itself appear suitable to prospects as a possible relational partner. Prospects tend to be attractive to organisations primarily on the basis of economic

EXHIBIT 9.2   Facets of attraction

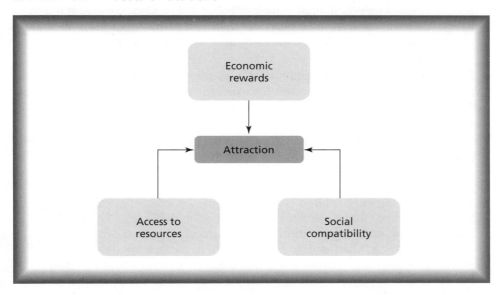

criteria. The principal argument that underpins the economic attractiveness of prospects relates to their potential lifetime (or long-time) value (LTV). We have discussed long-time value in some detail in our coverage of database metrics, but as a reminder, it is 'the total net contribution that a customer generates during his/her lifetime on a house-list (or customer database)' (Bitran and Mondschein 1997). The suggestion here is that marketers who wish to build long-term relationships with their customers must recognise that foregoing short-term profits may be necessary to generate substantial rewards in the future. 'The initial costs of acquisition are less of an issue since the organisation concerned recognises that it will make a return on this investment over the full duration of the relationship ... Once marketers understand how much a given customer might be worth to the organisation over time, they can tailor the offering to that customer according to the individual's needs/requirements, and yet still ensure an adequate lifetime ROI' (Sargeant 2001).

For their part, marketers also need to communicate their attractiveness to prospects. This attractiveness is likely to include resource and social components in addition to economic ones. Economic attractiveness is likely to centre on offering prospects value for money. However, the importance of economic criteria to purchasing is often overplayed and organisations need to consider how they might foster resource and/or social attractiveness also. Resource attractiveness is likely to centre on one or more of the following:

- **Time**: Growing work commitments and the pursuit of leisure interests have meant that contemporary consumers constantly find their time restricted. As such, time has become a valuable resource and organisations that can offer consumers time savings and convenience are likely to be viewed as very attractive indeed.

- **Information**: The decision-making approach to the understanding of consumption suggests that consumers deliberately collect information and weigh alternatives in making purchase decisions. Thus, organisations that provide information will facilitate such activities and may be deemed more attractive.

- **Experiences**: Many consumption decisions are not based on logical, rational problem solving but on the quest for experiences. Organisations may be able to enhance their attractiveness to consumers by focusing on experiential criteria. This places ever more importance on service elements of exchange.

- **Social responsibility**: Many consumers wish to act responsibly when they purchase products and services. As such, they wish to purchase products and services from organisations that behave in an ethical or responsible manner. Issues that may be considered here include purchasing products/services that are fairly traded with developing countries (e.g. Café Direct), buying cosmetics that have not been tested on animals (e.g. The Body Shop), dealing with organisations that in turn only partner with ethical organisations (e.g. Cooperative Bank). When organisations deliberately position themselves as socially responsible, information about this may feature in their communications with customers. Moreover, organisations that pursue corporate social responsibility find that this impacts upon their relational strategies. For example, the suppliers chosen by The Body Shop must also adhere to environment- and animal-friendly production methods if they are to enhance the company's positioning strategy. Thus, relationships influence strategy and strategy influences relationships.

Marketers may also appear attractive in social terms. That is, an interpersonal relationship may develop between an employee of the organisation and the customer that underpins the commercial relationship. As a result of this social exchange the customer might expect a greater degree of personal service and attention and this is consistent with understandings in social exchange theory (Kelley and Thibaut 1978) and within the marketing literature (Anderson and Narus 1984, 1990). Indeed, derived from social exchange theory, attraction explains why relationships are initiated and developed (see Kelley and Thibaut 1978).

The following short case demonstrates the importance of attraction in initiating relationships. This case demonstrates that even in the pre-customer phase, relationships can be developed with a view to cultivating a degree of commitment towards the organisation.

CASE STUDY 9.2

Camouflage

The British Army introduced a relationship programme at the pre-acquisition stage. The campaign was designed to keep potential recruits interested until they hit the age of eligibility. As one of the biggest employers of young people in the country, the Army needs to target its audience as early in life as possible. The solution was 'Camouflage' a youth loyalty scheme. Members of Camouflage, who must be UK residents aged between 12 and 16 years old, receive a magazine mailing three times a year. This is supplemented by e-mailings about events, exhibitions, competitions and a website featuring Army information and news. Images, copy and timing of delivery are carefully planned, with different packs sent to the various ages at key intake times.

Essential data such as date of birth, address and e-mail address are captured and augmented as membership continues. Launched in September 2000, the Army is delighted with the success of the scheme. Never before has it been able to track youth loyalty and conversions into recruits. Camouflage now has over 50,000 eligible members on its database, over a fifth of whom have converted.

(Source: DMA 'CRM' Award 2001)

So, some degree of attraction is a necessary precondition for the commencement of interaction, while ongoing attraction determines whether parties are motivated to maintain a relationship (Dwyer *et al*. 1987; Halinen 1997). Furthermore, the degree of attraction is likely not only to stimulate investment initiatives but also to influence the *level* of those investments (Halinen 1997). Given the important role of attraction, it is surprising that it remains largely unexplored within the RM literature. Perhaps it is because attraction is so essential to the formation and maintenance of relationships, so basic to the practice of marketing, that it has been taken for granted.

Communication is also a core element in a customer attraction strategy. Organisations need to signal their ability and willingness to serve the customer, and this can be communicated through advertising and/or direct marketing. However, organisations must be careful about the promises they make. Promises influence customer expectations regarding the interaction and their subsequent satisfaction with that interaction.

Interaction

Thus far we have proposed that the economic, resource and social content of marketing relationships determine perceptions of attractiveness. Furthermore, Morgan (2000) argues that these three elements of marketing relationships also represent antecedents of commitment and trust. Specifically, where superior economic benefits, access to important resources and social benefits can be delivered this generates enhanced levels of trust and commitment.

Person-to-person interaction forces buyers and sellers into intimate contact, thereby facilitating the development of relationships. As a result, there is increasing recognition that the (person-to-person) interaction between buyers and sellers, clients and providers is fundamental to the overall success of the marketing effort (Solomon *et al*. 1985).

Interaction is a fundamental behavioural aspect of relationships (Daskou and Hart 2002). Customers interact with organisations in a variety of ways: via telephone, mail, the Internet and, most powerful of all, face-to-face with service providers. These interactions can occur before, during and after service production and delivery. Both customers and service providers adopt roles, exhibiting the required and expected behaviour within this interaction (Solomon *et al.* 1985).

For customers, interaction with service providers has a strong impact on their expectations of service quality prior to delivery and to their perceptions of service quality after delivery. This interaction not only facilitates the immediate transaction but also plays a profound role in moving customer exchanges from transactions to relationships. Fundamentally, because there is high variability in the quality of service provision (i.e. heterogeneity), many customers are likely to seek continuity with the same provider when excellent service is experienced, particularly when that service is important, complex, and/or when the customer is highly involved (Berry 1995). The following case underlines the importance of interaction and personalisation to delivering customer satisfaction. Organisation–customer interaction is now multifaceted. Face-to-face interaction is complemented (or in some cases substituted) via technology-driven channels such as the Internet, telephony and kiosks, as is discussed later in our coverage of 'media'.

CASE **STUDY** 9.3

Amazon

Trailblazing e-tailer Amazon.co.uk's ambition is to be the world's most customer-centric company. The fact that 97% of its four million customer base profess themselves 'satisfied' or 'very satisfied' and that repeat purchase stands at 73% suggests it has gone some way towards achieving that aim. Personalisation is particularly important to Amazon.co.uk. Customers are able to edit the personalised recommendations they receive by rating their purchases to build a picture of what they like. A 'wish list' service allows customers to tell their friends and family what they would like for Christmas and birthdays, while the site's patented 1-Click ordering system means purchasers can buy products with one click of the mouse without having to fill in order forms. Amazon.co.uk's WAP service, Amazon.co.uk Anywhere, means customers can order products wherever they are. Updates are sent to consumers at every step of the ordering process. A record of all the addresses where orders have been sent in the past saves time and gives customers the option of sending to multiple addresses. Orders can be changed or cancelled at any time until the item is posted.

(Source: The Revolution Awards 2002. Reproduced from *Revolution* magazine with the permission of the copyright owner, Haymarket Business Publications Limited)

Attraction judgements are also made on a continuous basis and as such will determine the nature of the relationship as it progresses. This occurs because as interactions take place, changes occur in the relational knowledge of each partner. As Planalp (1987) outlines, people engage in interactions with a degree of knowledge about the behaviour appropriate to those interactions. Once they interact, this knowledge is updated and used in the next interaction. During the attraction phase of the relationship, perceptions of attractiveness and assessments of reward–cost outcomes are necessarily based upon supposition, as are assessments of commitment and trust (Ford 1980). However, as the relationship moves to the interaction phase, assumptions become more concrete as information is generated by the interaction. As such, relational knowledge can be used for both assimilation and accommodation (Planalp 1987). Assimilation refers to how relational knowledge is used to interpret interaction. As a result of interaction the parties involved will make some judgement as to how well that interaction went (Altman and Taylor 1973). Favourable outcomes, in terms of the economic, resource and social content of exchange relationships, may lead to increased attraction while unfavourable outcomes are likely to have the opposite effect. Accommodation (Planalp 1987), on the other hand, refers to how relational knowledge changes as a direct result of interaction. For example, Leuthesser and Kohli (1995) suggest that as individuals interact more frequently, they process greater amounts of information, and thereby reduce uncertainty and ambiguity. Thus, as the relationship progresses, and as assimilation and accommodation processes begin to work, a symbiosis develops between attraction and interaction, each having an effect upon the other.

Changes in relational knowledge may lead to subsequent changes in strategic intention. If, for example, because of interaction, a relational partner becomes less attractive, investment in the relationship may be reduced, the relationship may be dissolved and alternative relational partners pursued. Consequently, changes in attraction have strategic ramifications both for individual relationships and for positioning in networks (Johanson and Mattsson 1992), because they directly affect trust and commitment and, ultimately, influence the degree of cooperation between parties (Morgan and Hunt 1994).

Integration of interactive marketing contact is, as we have already stated, very important. For example, American Express credit card customers were showered with promotional brochures and telephone contacts from numerous different sales staff, each from different product groups and departments (Buss 1999). This was not only excessively costly and wasteful to the company but was also inconvenient for customers, and resulted in negative rather than positive associations with American Express.

Problems with focusing on acquisition

There are two main problems associated with an organisational focus on acquisition. First, many companies have failed to understand the costs associated with customer acquisition and, in many cases, acquisition costs may be so high as to undermine any profit associated with particular customers. This is particularly true of acquisition strategies on the Internet. Because of the extensive competition, it takes enormous marketing expenditure to set themselves apart from the crowd. As Hoffman and Novak (2000) highlight:

❝ Many e-tailers, in fact, are averaging more than $100 to acquire a new customer, and some are spending upwards of $500. If a merchant is selling high-ticket, high-margin items, or if it can be sure of a steady stream of repeat purchases, those costs may make economic sense. But for most, they're suicidal – their average customer acquisition cost is higher than the average lifetime value of their customers. **❞**

The short-sightedness of focusing all of the marketing effort on getting new customers is typified by the following statement from a marketing executive (Rosenberg and Czepiel 1984): 'The many ways companies relate to customers is akin to looking for a needle in a haystack, finding it, and then throwing it back to look for it again.'

Indeed, 'some companies seem hooked on steady doses of fresh customers to cover up regular losses of existing ones' (Rozenberg and Czepiel 1984). Recent business trends confirm that a continual focus on acquisition is expensive, and there is a new emphasis on retaining customers. This emphasis is born out of the realisation that customer defections impact negatively on profitability. Indeed, in many industries, customer defection can have a far more powerful impact than market share, unit cost, scale and a host of other factors generally associated with competitive advantage. It is not uncommon for a business to lose 15–20% of its customers each year. As such, many commentators have argued that reducing such defections can lead to phenomenal increases in profitability. We explored some of the metrics involved with this in our coverage of LTVs in Chapter 3 and the effect that retention strategies can have on customer value. By understanding the economics of retention and defection, organisations can justify investments in existing customers, can emphasise improvements in service quality over cost reduction, and can focus on new ways to grow the business.

Thus, it has been argued that marketing resources may be better spent on retention rather than acquisition (Fornell and Wernerfelt 1987). However, very few organisations have seriously attempted to measure the economic value of their customer retention strategies (Payne and Frow 1999). A study conducted in 2000 attempted to establish the importance of customer retention to UK organisations, based on a sample of 314 telephone interviews conducted at managerial/director level (Aspinall *et al.* 2001). Some of the findings are reported below and point to significant differences between theory and practice in relation to customer retention activities. For example:

- Over half the sample (54%) considered customer retention to be more important than acquisition. Only half of these had a definition of customer retention. More interestingly, 20% of those with a claimed definition stated that they did not know what customer retention was.

- Fifty-eight per cent stated that their organisation measured customer retention. Many of these measures were basic rather than sophisticated and included trends in sales; sales at individual level; percentage of customers buying; recency; and frequency.

- The major criterion against which retention was measured was a comparison with past performance (an introverted perspective). Only a few compared performance with competitors (external perspective).

Aspinall *et al.* (2001) conclude that despite the enormous attention given to customer retention in the academic and management literature, the actual practice of customer retention seems to be lacking. 'In particular, many companies that claim to consider customer retention as an important business objective do not define it well or measure it. On this basis, companies' claims to focus on customer retention need to be treated with a pinch of salt.'

The lessons learned from this study suggest that companies that are serious about retention should:

- define what retention means in their organisation;
- put in place operational measures that tell them whether they are achieving improvements in customer retention as a result of the strategies imposed.

All this suggests that while customer acquisition is certainly important, it can receive a disproportionate amount of attention, often to the detriment of satisfying existing customers. The competitive climate has changed, successful new products are few and far between, and in any case, me-toos are on the market much more quickly than in the past. Added to this, population growth has slowed down in many developed countries, making new customers more difficult to find. The focus on acquiring new customers is therefore questionable, as the leaky bucket analogy explains: lots of water is being poured into the bucket, which masks any leaks – the bucket remains full. If less water is available the leaky bucket eventually becomes empty as it cannot effectively retain its contents. So too with marketing. Before companies can identify what customers it gains and what customers it loses, it relies on a generic measure of market share (the amount of water in the bucket) for its effectiveness. New methods and approaches are required, and the tools and techniques in the direct marketers armoury offered some hope.

Thus, companies today must find the right balance between acquisition and retention strategies, and must develop different propositions for potential and existing customers. The subsequent stages progress potential relational interaction into the retention area (Exhibit 9.3).

Retention

Loyal customers, it is argued, cost less to serve than other customers, are prepared to pay more than other customers, and they are more likely to become company advocates promoting the company to others through word-of-mouth. In short, these customers are more profitable to serve. Because some marketers have assumed that growth can only be obtained from attracting new customers, they have often unwittingly minimised the importance of satisfying existing ones. As a result, current customers are treated as though they were prospects.

EXHIBIT 9.3   Acquisition to retention

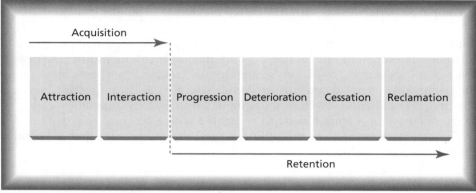

They often receive conflicting information, and their value to the company is continually undermined. Additionally, the company has little information about its customers, and this limits the ability to target customers with appropriate offers. Furthermore, such companies are often unaware which customers they have lost, and have no information as to why customers defect. This prevents the organisation from improving its strategies in the future.

Progression

The relationship between the customer and the organisation can now be seen as a collaboration providing benefits for both sides, but one that also demands input from both sides. At this stage the relationship can be considered to be continuous (Halinen and Tähtinen 2002; Tuominen and Kettunen 2002). That is, the relationship is progressing, both parties are happy, and the ending of the relationship is not anticipated.

Customers remain in relationships for two basic reasons (Bendapudi and Berry 1997): they either *want to* (dedication) or they *have to* (constraints). Wanting to stay can be based on customer satisfaction and trust, whereas having to stay is based on barriers to change (Tuominen and Kettunen 2002). Customers want to remain in a relationship when they receive ongoing benefits as a result of that relationship. Recent evidence suggests that tangible benefits are not that highly valued by consumers (Gwinner *et al.* 1998). Rather, core benefits include confidence benefits, social benefits and special treatment.

- Confidence benefits are critical outcomes of long-term relationships and relate to 'the sense of reduced anxiety, faith in the trustworthiness of the service provider, reduced perceptions of anxiety and risk, and knowing what to expect' (Gwinner *et al.* 1998). This notion is very close to, if not the same as, trust. As a result, confidence benefits are most highly valued by consumers.

- Social benefits include being recognised by service providers and, in certain cases, developing friendships with them.

- Special treatment includes the ability of relational customers to skip queues, receive special prices or promotional offers etc. It relates to 'a customer's perception of the extent to which a retailer treats and serves its regular customers better than its non-regular customers' (De Wulf *et al.* 2001). Interestingly, special treatment appears to be most valued when it is truly individualised and when it is fundamental (e.g. mechanic coming to collect the car when it won't start) as opposed to being peripheral (e.g. an invitation to a promotional evening for special customers) (Gwinner *et al.* 1998).

While wanting to stay in a relationship is a result of customer satisfaction as well as confidence, social and special treatment benefits, having to stay in a relationship is a result of an entirely different set of factors:

- Anticipated costs of switching include economic costs, psychological costs or social costs. Thus, the customer anticipates potential losses of time, money and effort already expended on the relationship and that would be required to initiate a new relationship. Equally, customers are exposed to the risk of making the right choice regarding the new supplier.

- There may be no obvious alternatives, thus forcing the customer to maintain the relationship.

Ford (1980) notes that 'relationships can fail to develop or regress depending upon the actions of either party or of competing buyers and sellers'. As such, relationship maintenance is not inevitable and the job of the marketer is to strengthen relationships continuously through individualised, interactive and integrated performance and communication (Shani and Chalasani 1992). Efforts to strengthen relationships with satisfied customers include inviting their participation in customer clubs and providing exclusive services for high value customers. The following, longer case study is a reflection of more continuous relational interactions that include many of the constructs here, such as special benefits.

CASE **STUDY** 9.4

Cause-related marketing

Cause-related marketing – where a brand links its product to a good cause, either as a one-off tactical promotion or a longer-term strategic campaign – is well established in the UK. But who exactly responds to these offers? Do they produce anything more than short-term gains for the products involved? And do they even risk diluting charitable giving by simply drawing funds away from other fundraising activities such as direct mail and above-the-line appeals?

To attempt to answer these issues, marketing services consultancy Dunn-Humby used its access to the Tesco Clubcard database to examine a number of cause-related marketing campaigns and →

assess their short- and medium-term impact on product sales. By being able to identify the type of customer purchasing the cause-related offer, it was also able to use the Target Group Index (TGI) to profile in greater detail the attitudes and opinions of the people responding.

In each case examined, sales increases did produce longer-term brand share gains for the parties involved – but there were also interesting insights into just who responded, showing clearly that these were people who were not normally regular givers to charity causes.

In terms of sales alone, Mr Kipling's Cherry Bakewell Red Nose appeal, one of three campaigns examined in detail, produced a massive uplift of 600% during the promotional period, but even after the promotion sales remained 40% higher – with 20% of the promotional buyers returning to the brand post-promotion.

Persil's involvement with Pants to Poverty saw not only gains for the lead product, but also uplift in sales for Persil brands not directly involved. This 'halo' effect was achieved at a time when other brands had increased their promotional activity to try to counter the Persil cause-related campaign.

Tesco's own Computers for Schools campaign, in which customers collect vouchers with their groceries, saw 190 000 customers spending significantly more over the six weeks of the promotion – an uplift in buying which translated into a sales rise running into tens of millions of pounds.

Finally, the TGI analysis indicated that the people who responded to the cause-related marketing schemes were not those likely to respond to conventional charity appeals through channels like direct mail, television or newspapers. So not only did sales rise, but also the money gained by the charities could not have been obtained from these 'donors' by other, more traditional, methods of fundraising. Given that some 43% of the population give less than £5.00 a year to charity, this suggests that cause-related marketing is drawing on a significant pool of untapped new donors without damaging the donations that come from regular givers. In short, they are a win–win promotion, bringing benefits for both the charity and the brand owner involved.

(Source: Case supplied by Nigel Lawrence, Dunn-Humby, 2003)

Deterioration

Relationships rarely move directly from a state of progression to dissolution. Rather there is a phase in between in which the relationship gradually deteriorates (Grönhaug *et al.* 1999). Deterioration is used to refer to situations where commitment and loyalty fade, although the relationship may continue to exist. 'A trigger of a fading process of a customer relationship is taken to be any element that affects the present status of the relationship in such a way as to initiate the process leading to the ending of the customer relationship' (Tuominen and Kettunen 2002).

In order to be able to manage customer relationships, marketers must recognise the triggers that initiate deterioration. Most significantly, if these elements can be identified, it may be possible to resolve problems and influence the relationship in a positive way. Fundamentally, there are two possible outcomes from deterioration: the relationship is *maintained* as a result of improvements in the relationship or the relationship is *ended*. The following case highlights the work that an organisation may conduct in trying to reverse the effects of deterioration.

CASE **STUDY** 9.5

Persil Grandmas

Lever Fabergé knew that one of Persil's most loyal segments, 'Modern Grandmas', was becoming alienated by recent brand advertising. A mailing was sent to 400 000 grandmas on its database asking for their laundry tips, which were collected in a booklet. A follow-up Christmas card con-

tinued the tips theme. Almost 8 000 tips were sent in – a response rate of 2%. Just under 24% redeemed a 50p Persil coupon.

(Source:Adapted from material provided by DMA from the Lever Fabergé Award Winning Case Study, DMA/ Royal Mail Awards 2001)

Cessation

Although relationships are viewed as long-term in nature, it is inevitable that at least some relationships will end. The end of a relationship may be the result of one or more incidents, it may be hardly recognisable (as with dormant bank accounts) or easily perceived, and either party may initiate it. This aspect of relationships has been largely ignored, though a number of studies are emerging in this area.

Because relationship endings are diverse, we can characterise different types of cessation (Halinen and Tähtinen 2002).

- **Termination**: refers to the deliberate ending of the relationship by one or more parties (or by an outside actor). As was explored in our coverage of databases, the new metrics such as RFM and LTVs allow companies to identify those customers who are not contributing as much revenue or profit as the company would like. This sometimes leads to a termination of relationship by the company by 'deselecting' or excluding these customers. They would not be sent relevant offers or, in the case of financial services, for example, they would be offered accounts that require higher initial deposits than they can afford. Indeed, the Halifax bank was discovered, via a flip chart left on open view in a branch office after a company training session, to refuse to allow certain groups of people, such as taxi drivers and others who deal mostly with cash, to be customers at all (Mackintosh 2002).

- **Dissolution**: refers to the natural ending of the relationship, without any deliberate decision to do so. For example, a mother with young children may trust Mothercare, be committed and loyal to Mothercare products and believe that she has a relationship with the organisation. However, as her children grow up, she has less and less need for Mothercare products and services and, as a result, the relationship naturally dissolves.

- **Switching**: refers to the ending of a relationship in which another service provider is substituted for the original provider. Switching may involve moving some or all of the business to the new provider, and may therefore involve either termination or dissolution of the original relationship. Not only does switching involve the ending of one relationship but it also involves the formation and strengthening of another (Halinen and Tähtinen 2002).

Customers may therefore choose to end a relationship for a variety of reasons, including the occurrence of unresolved critical incidents, the availability of preferred alternatives, or the absence of a motivation or need to maintain that relationship. Organisations may also choose to end a relationship with a customer, although this has received little attention in the literature. This lack of attention may be partly explained by the ideology of organisations being customer focused and customer centric (Helm 2002). However, loyal customers are not always the most profitable and, in some cases, the ending of relationships is both beneficial and desirable (Alajoutsijärvi *et al.* 2000). Some organisations attempt to measure the profitability and value of customers. In this case there is a trade-off between the supplier-perceived value of a relationship and the benefits and sacrifices incorporated into that relationship. The perceived value of an individual customer is usually termed customer profitability (Niraj *et al.* 2001). Such an approach combines the sales or revenues with the costs incurred by the customer. However, this results in a static view of customer value, as today's unworthy customers may be tomorrow's stars (Helm 2002).

There are also legal and ethical issues involved when considering the cessation of relationships by suppliers. For example, 'in some industries, business regulations such as obligations to contract in insurance markets, health care, postal services, public transport etc. render the discrimination of individual customers impossible' (Helm 2002). We explore some of these legal and ethical issues in Chapter 13. Moreover, when firms cherry-pick only the most profitable customers they may be undermining the moral basis of RM (Niraj *et al.* 2001). Furthermore, although cessation of some relationships may improve immediate profitability, negative word of mouth from terminated partners may cause other problems for the organisation (Halinen and Tähtinen 2002). For the moment then, it may be better to simply 'let the customer go (Knox and Maklan 1998). That is, the organisation should not actively cultivate the relationship and should only allow customers to choose from a standard menu of products, services and prices, thereby promoting dissolution rather than termination. There are signs that such problems are being addressed in UK where the government has set up a social exclusion department. Concerns include the closing of bank branches in favour of more direct methods and, as we state in Chapter 13, in the USA the Community Reinvestment Act is designed to prevent banks from closing in poor neighbourhoods. Such concerns remind us that 'marketing must serve not only business but also the goals of society ... and its contributions extend well beyond the formal boundaries of the firm' (Lazer 1969).

Reclamation

Companies, like telecoms, are increasingly realising the benefits of regaining profitable customers (e.g. BT). Customer reclamation 'encompasses the planning, realization, and control of all processes that the company puts in place to regain customers who either give notice to terminate the business relationship or whose relationship has already terminated' (Stauss and Friege 1999). It is not desirable to reinitiate all ended relationships, nor may it be cost-effective to do so. Thus, as a first step, marketers must analyse the reasons behind relationship cessation in order to assess the possibility of reclaiming the customer and to estimate the costs of doing so. Secondly, an assessment must be made of the customer value to consider whether reclaiming is desirable. Thus, organisations must segment their lost customers (Stauss and Friege 1999). Approaches to reclaiming customers might include initiating dialogues with these customers, and where desirable, making specific offers depending on the value of the customer and their reasons for ending the relationship. An award-winning example of reclamation is the case of Co-op milk deliveries (see Chapter 10).

The importance of the above analysis of retention can be drawn from Reichheld's (1996) perspective:

- Retained customers tend to be more profitable. They guarantee base profits because they are likely to have a minimum spend per period.
- Retained customers offer a reduction in costs as acquisition and operating expenses are amortised over a longer time period.
- Retained customers deliver growth in per-customer revenue, as, over a period of time, they earn more, have more varied needs and spend more.
- Retained customers pay price premiums because they are unwilling to wait for promotions or price reductions before deciding to purchase.
- Retained customers make new customer referrals free of charge. This saves on costly commissions and introductory fees.

McCorkell (1997) identifies a number of retention devices, primarily pioneered by direct marketers, but increasingly being used by many organisations. Most devices attempt to make repeat patronage the easy option for customers. These include:

- negative option;
- credit accounts;
- automatic payment;
- lease/rental;
- loyalty programmes.

Negative option marketing was pioneered by book and record clubs. Essentially, rather than requiring the customer to do something in order to remain loyal, negative option implies that doing nothing keeps the customer loyal. A simple example is a book club. The customer responds to press advertising (perhaps via a coupon) that offers four popular books at a significant discount. In order to purchase the books at this price, the customer is required to become a member of the book club. As a member, they are required to buy at least four books per year. Each quarter the customer is sent a catalogue from which to make their order. If the customer does not respond with an order within the required period of time they are automatically sent the 'editor's choice' and invoiced for this. Thus, the negative option implies that even when customers do not place an order, they still make a purchase. The customer will generally have the right to cancel (after a stated minimum period) but cancellation of membership will generally be required in writing. However, this requires some effort on the part of the consumer, who through inertia continues to remain a customer.

Catalogue retailers have traditionally offered to deliver the goods ordered within a specific period of time. They also offer a full refund if the goods are returned within, for example, three weeks. While many customers may wish to return the goods, this again requires effort on their part (repackaging, posting and its associated costs) – and as a result, due to customer inertia, they retain the goods and pay in full. Therefore negative option agreements operate on the principle that customer inertia can be used in their favour. The 'do nothing' option keeps the customer, while the 'do something' option is the opt-out. Although very successful from the direct marketer's point of view, negative option has attracted criticism in that it is not a very 'customer centred' approach to marketing. Also, customers who eventually 'do something' may be less inclined to enter similar agreements with other organisations. As a result, this method of retaining customers (although still quite prevalent) may be losing ground to more customer-orientated organisations. For example, a customer who wishes to return a product purchased from Next Directory simply has to telephone the company and arrange for the unwanted merchandise to be collected. Although this is an expensive service for Next Directory to operate, it considerably reduces the perceived risk for customers buying mail-order. The easy return service may be one of the reasons why Next Directory has achieved so much success.

Customers who have credit accounts tend to spend more and stay loyal to the organisation offering the account. Many accounts offer customers the option of paying the balance in full each month, or simply paying a percentage of the amount outstanding (usually 5% or £5, whichever is the smaller). Customers who pay the minimum amount each month are the best customers from the marketer's point of view. They remain loyal to the organisation while they are making repayments, they pay interest (often quite high) on the outstanding balance, and they continue to make purchases, thereby maintaining a balance. Although credit options still retain these benefits, they are becoming less effective, primarily because of the number of organisations with whom a single customer will have credit. For example, it is not unusual for a customer to have an M&S account, a Debenhams account, a House of Fraser account (and possibly a number of others). Although the customer may continue to buy at each of these outlets, the share of customer which each achieves does not vary significantly. Thus, credit accounts are primarily an advantage when competitors do not offer them. This is an increasingly rare occurrence. Today, customers expect to have a credit option for most purchases, so it becomes a requirement of doing business, rather than a differential advantage.

Credit accounts are most effective when the customer pays by direct debit. Although direct debit is more expensive to operate for the organisation, there is less likelihood of the customer paying their balance in full and closing the account. The minimum is paid each month via the direct debit, and therefore the 'do nothing' option is to maintain payments in this manner. Continuous authority mandates have a similar impact. For example, one of the authors pays for AA Relay annually by credit card. Each year notification arrives that the AA will debit the account by a specified amount. In this way, even if the cost of the service increases the AA does not have to get permission to take a higher amount. The option to cancel the agreement clearly exists, and the customer can look for alternative quotations. However, both of these require effort, and therefore without a strong reason to change, the customer remains a customer. Lease and rental agreements have a similar effect to credit accounts when retaining customers.

Loyalty programmes are another device used to retain customers. These are proving increasingly popular with organisations today, and therefore are deserving of greater attention, as is the nature of loyalty itself.

Loyalty, satisfaction and defecting

The sequential 'acquisition–retention' model (Exhibit 9.1) and the various acquisition and retention devices lead us to concept of loyalty. This is probably an over-used term in marketing today and in many cases it really only refers to the more behavioural dimension of repeat purchase rather than an affective or emotional attachment to a brand, store or organisation. Readers will be very aware of retail 'loyalty' schemes because these are employed by many retailers and it is possible that you personally have some form of loyalty card. This might encourage you to frequent that store more often but does it engender a feeling of greater emotional attachment with the store? For many consumers it is the convenient location of the store coupled with the extra 'discounts' (tailored via analysis of transactional data) that lead to repeat patronage and these, more tangible factors, are not the same as affective factors. So, what is 'loyalty'?

It would be logical to expect loyalty to depend, to at least some extent, on 'satisfaction'. As a result, measures of customer satisfaction have been widely used as proxy measures for loyalty. However, research from the Ogilvy Loyalty Centre suggests that 85% of automotive industry users report being satisfied but only 40% repurchase, while for packaged goods, 66% of people who identified a favourite brand admitted to having bought another brand most recently (McKenzie 1995). As a result, satisfaction measures have proved to be ineffective measures of loyalty (Reichheld 1988). But are marketers really wrong in assuming that satisfied customers will automatically be loyal?

As we might expect, the picture is more complicated. In extensive research in a number of different product-markets, Jones and Sasser (1995) (Exhibit 9.4) found that it is the degree of claimed satisfaction that is critical to levels of repeat purchase. The difference between repeat purchase behaviour for some who score '4' on 5-point satisfaction surveys and those who score '5' is six-fold. That is, high satisfaction (e.g. '4') is manifested in repeat purchasing far less than when it is extremely high (e.g. '5'). It is not enough, therefore, to satisfy customers, but to 'delight' them.

Jones tells a powerful story (1996) about this; see the following case study.

EXHIBIT 9.4 Need to 'delight'

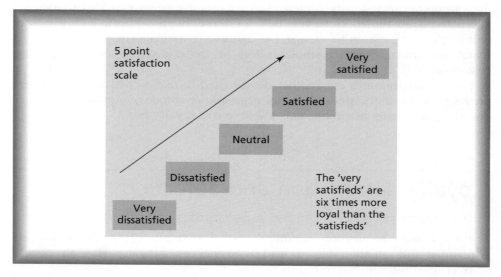

(Source: Jones 1995)

CASE STUDY 9.6

'Satisfaction' versus 'delight'

Professor Jones claims to have been satisfied with his BMW for ten years until the ashtray went missing after a service. He contacted the garage to be informed that they had found the ashtray and he could collect it later that day. He was not too impressed with this because he felt the garage should do the work to rectify their mistake; it wasn't him who had mislaid the ashtray! Coincidentally, a colleague had been interacting with the local Lexus dealer over a possible purchase and Jones wondered how

that Lexus dealer would have handled the ashtray issue, so he phoned them. They explained that he would not even need to visit their dealership because they would collect his car for servicing, leave him another for the day and return his later that day. They also said they were delivering a car in his neighbourhood and would stop off at the BMW garage, collect and deliver his ashtray to him. He was not targeted after this event by the Lexus sales force so it was not part of a 'marketing ploy' but rather the way they 'do business'. As it turned out, Jones eventually purchased a Lexus and by telling this story in a number of high profile presentations, he has even become an 'advocate' for Lexus after being very satisfied with BMW for over a decade (but clearly not 'delighted')!

(Source: Jones 1996)

This case raises the issue of 'customer defection analysis' which is concerned with developing an understanding of the sources of failure. If a customer defects, a lot can be gained by analysing the reasons why this occurred. At the very least the customer should be asked why they no longer wish to do business with the organisation. Information from individual customer defections can then be aggregated to identify if there are any trends in the reasons for defection. Perhaps the lessons for the BMW dealership in the above case study are clear.

Studies indicate a number of reasons for customer defection (DeSouza 1992; Keaveney 1995):

- Price – defecting in order to get a lower price.
- Product – defecting in order to purchase a superior product.
- Service – defecting for a better service.
- Defecting because of core service failure.
- Service-encounter failure or failed employee response to a service encounter.
- Inconvenience.
- Market – defecting to a different market; for example, a transport company which has moved out of road haulage and therefore no longer needs to buy trailers.
- Technological – a customer has converted from using one technology to another. Customers who initially abandoned high street banks in favour of banks that provided dedicated telephone or Internet banking would also fall into this category.
- Organisational – switching as a result of ethical or political pressures. For example, many customers who switched to the Co-operative Bank did so because they preferred to support the ethical position held by that bank.
- Involuntary factors.

Interestingly, many of these factors are actually controllable by the service provider (Keaveney 1995), and therefore a starting point is to initiate management programmes that reduce customer defection in the first place.

Because of the difficulties of using satisfaction measures as surrogates for loyalty, it is increasingly being subjected to behavioural measures which include purchase frequency, share of wallet, and purchase sequence. However, behavioural measures of loyalty have also been criticised as only capturing static outcomes. 'These definitions make no attempt to understand the factors underlying repeat purchase. High repeat purchase may reflect situational constraints, such as brands stocked by retailers, whereas low repeat purchases may simply indicate different usage situations, variety seeking, or lack of brand preference within a buying unit. The behavioural definitions, consequently, are insufficient to explain how and why brand loyalty is developed and/or modified' (Dick and Basu 1994).

IN THEORY

Loyalty

As a result of these deficiencies, Dick and Basu (1994) propose a framework that conceptualises loyalty as 'the relationship between the relative attitude toward an entity (brand/service/store/vendor) and patronage behaviour'. This definition combines both approaches to the understanding of loyalty, and results in four categories of loyalty (Exhibit 9.5), each of which has managerial implications. These four categories of loyalty provide a far richer conceptualisation of loyalty then previously existed. In order to understand the categories used, it is important to understand the dimensions on which these categories are based. We introduced this model in our coverage of market segmentation in Chapter 6 but it is worth exploring it in greater detail here.

- **Relative attitude:** Relative attitude focuses not only on attitude to the entity, but also incorporates comparison to other organisations or brands. For example, a customer may have a favourable attitude towards First Direct, but may prefer to deal with a high street bank.
- **Patronage behaviour:** Traditional retention measures, share of wallet, purchase sequence etc.

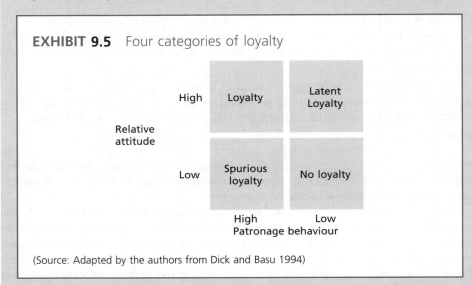

EXHIBIT 9.5   Four categories of loyalty

(Source: Adapted by the authors from Dick and Basu 1994)

These four categories are briefly explained below and summarised in Table 9.2.

- **No loyalty:** There is an absence of loyalty where the consumer's relative attitude is low, and there is no evidence of purchase behaviour. For example, research carried out by Shell in the early 1990s suggested that 85% of petrol buyers were not loyal to any brand or location (Dignam 1996). Motorists tended to stop for petrol whenever it was most convenient for them to do so. In this and similar cases, the best that management can do is attempt to generate spurious loyalty through such means as in-store promotions, loyalty clubs and special offers.

TABLE 9.2 Summary of Dick and Basu model

Category	No loyalty	Spurious loyalty	Latent loyalty	Loyalty
Relative attitude	Low relative attitude	Low relative attitude	High relative attitude	High relative attitude
Patronage behaviour	Low repeat patronage behaviour	High repeat patronage behaviour	Low repeat patronage behaviour	High repeat patronage behaviour
Manifestation	Does not patronise the company, and does not wish to.	Patronises the company, but does not have a high relative attitude. This may be as a result of other factors, including location, convenience, or lack of alternatives.	In this case, the customer wishes to patronise the organisation, but perhaps is not able to do so – store location may be inconvenient, favourite brands not stocked etc.	The individual enjoys a high relative attitude, together with high repeat patronage behaviour.
Implications	Management may attempt to generate 'spurious loyalty'.	'Spurious loyalty' cannot be relied upon. The customer is clearly open to better offers.	Managerial efforts are best focused on removing the obstacles to patronage for the customer.	Loyalty must be continually reinforced, and the value offered must remain acceptable.

- **Spurious loyalty:** Spurious loyalty is very similar to the concept of inertia. That is, although behavioural data indicate that there is high repeat patronage, in reality the customer does not believe that the alternatives are highly differentiated. In such cases, repeat purchase may be based upon the availability of deals, special offers, convenience or the influence of other people. As a result, the consumer may only temporarily display such loyalty, and is likely to be very open to competing offers. The management objective in this case is to convert spurious loyalty into loyalty. Enhancing the customer's relative attitude by communicating specific advantages can accomplish this. Alternatively, where competing offers are generally undifferentiated, managers can attempt to increase switching costs (effectively erecting a barrier to exit), that is, making it costly for a customer to switch between competing offers. One effective method of achieving this is through 'point accrual programmes' as used within many existing loyalty programmes. For example, petrol retailers have for a long time run point accrual programmes such as Tiger Tokens and Premier Points. These programmes aim to tie the customer into a particular supplier through the promise of future rewards. In this case, the points already accrued represent switching costs, because the customer loses the benefit of previous purchases if he or she switches suppliers.
- **Latent loyalty:** This suggests that a consumer has a high relative attitude towards the company or brand, but this is not evidenced by any purchase behaviour. This is probably as a result of situational influences, including inconvenient store locations, out-of-stock situations, or the influence of other people, as in the case of restaurant patronage. Using the previous example, a motorist might have a preference for Shell, but it may be more convenient to purchase from BP, or his or her company may have a credit account at a Texaco station. In this case, despite a higher relative attitude for Shell, the motorist would exhibit low patronage behaviour. In the case of latent loyalty, managerial efforts are best focused upon removing the obstacles to patronage, for example by extending the branch network, or developing credit accounts with local businesses who provide company cars.
- **Loyalty:** When true loyalty exists, the customer regularly buys, and does so because of strong preferences (high relative attitude). As such, this is clearly the most preferred of the four categories. Where loyalty exists, managerial efforts are best aimed at continually strengthening relative attitudes, particularly as the customer may be the focus of aggressive marketing by competing organisations. This may involve maintaining a price advantage, and/or offering additional services that are of value to the customer. In the case of petrol retailing, these might include car wash, valeting or even oil-change facilities.

Jones proposes another version of a loyalty grid, shown in Exhibit 9.6. Here, the relationship between behavioural repeat purchase (loyalty in this analysis) and affective satisfaction is summarised. As can be seen, there are those who are satisfied with a current organisation but will switch to others easily if they see similar or higher satisfaction (mercenaries). Hostages are those who feel trapped because of lack of alternatives so repeat purchase but are not particularly satisfied with that organisation. Air travel where there is only one carrier will be an example (Tyrell 1995). Defectors switch easily and readily because they are not satisfied whereas the loyalists remain because they are satisfied with the organisation concerned. Jones adds the 'terrorist' category which includes those who may or may not be repeat purchasers but as dissatisfieds they will spread ill will concerning the organisation or even play games such as swapping loyalty cards to be awkward or to see what happens to their 'targeted' offers.

EXHIBIT 9.6 Jones' loyalty model

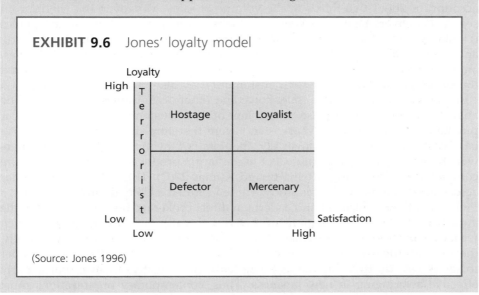

(Source: Jones 1996)

In both of the analyses in the above In Theory box, loyalty is seen to go beyond behavioural repeat purchase. In service companies, customers remain with the organisation when their expectations are met. Thus, strategies that focus upon closing the gap between customer expectations and experiences of service quality are appropriate to pursue. Social bonds can be created to cement business relationships where possible. As described earlier, social bonds refer to positive interpersonal relationships between employees in the buyer and seller organisations. While this is clearly most appropriate in business-to-business relationships, social bonds can also be fostered, albeit to a lesser extent, in service and consumer markets. Structural bonds can also be fostered between relationship partners, as we have also discussed, but overall it is clear that to focus on the 'behavioural' is only part of the relationship approach to loyalty.

Loyalty and profitability

Most firms accept at face value the proposition that if they retain more customers they will automatically increase profitability. However, the link between retention and profitability is not that clear-cut and simple, and, without a more thorough understanding, current expenditure on loyalty and retention may be unnecessary. To put the associated costs into perspective, the top 16 retailers in Europe collectively spent more than €1 billion (in 2000) on loyalty initiatives (Reinartz and Kumar 2002).

Research also demonstrates that all customers do not contribute equally to profitability. Rather, for most product categories, only one-third of buyers account for about two-thirds of the volume of sales. Moreover, this 'high-profit segment' delivers between six and ten times as much as the low-profit segment (Hallberg 1999). One US high-tech corporate service provider studied by Reinartz and Kumar (2002) decided to measure how profitable its retention strategy was, an initiative that cost them €2 million per annum. Their costing system measured the direct product costs for each customer. They also measured the associated costs on advertising, service, sales force and other organisational expenses. 'The answer took them by surprise. About half of those customers who made regular purchases for at least two years – and were therefore designated as "loyal" – barely generated a profit. Conversely, about half of the most profitable customers were blow-ins, buying a great deal of high-margin products in a short time before completely disappearing' (Reinartz and Kumar 2002). This finding was similar across other companies in this study. These included a US mail-order company, a French retail food business and a German direct brokerage house. As a result, the authors argue that the relationship between loyalty and profitability is much weaker – and subtler – than has been claimed over the past decade. Specifically, they found little evidence to suggest that loyal customers are necessarily cheaper to serve. Nor do they emerge as being less price-sensitive or even particularly effective at bringing in new business. Thus, contemporary organisations must recognise that loyalty is not a prize to be won at any cost. While some loyal customers may indeed be profitable, this does not automatically imply that all loyal customers will be profitable. Managers need to identify which loyal customers to focus on and which to ignore. While this sort of thinking flies in the face of the current loyalty mantra, it has resulted from the application of critical thinking on the part of researchers and managers. Moreover, the rapid increase in the amount of customer information and the technology by which that information can be interrogated means that such an understanding is within the reach of most organisations involved in CRM initiatives.

Reinartz and Kumar (2002) deal with the following related issues.

1 Loyal customers cost less to serve

Although it may be true that the costs associated with acquiring customers will be amortised over the life of the customers' relationship with the organisation, it is still necessary that customers are profitable over each of these transactions. Whether or not this is the case will naturally vary greatly among individual customers. However, it may indeed be true that loyal customers cost less to serve because of their increased familiarity with the company and its operations. In other words, because they require less hand-holding the company may find it cheaper to deal with them. For example, experienced customers of software products may be able to resolve problems online without needing to deal directly with a technical assistant.

Before addressing this issue in greater detail, it is important to point out that there is no *standard cost* associated with maintaining customer relationships. While this will certainly vary from industry to industry (sometimes by a factor of 100 or more), it is also likely to vary from company to company. These costs include not only the cost of facilitating a transaction, but also communication through mailings, telephone etc. Because different organisations communicate more or less via these methods and because the associated costs vary (quality of material, staff-related expenses), the costs of customer relationship management also vary considerably.

What emerges then is that the costs of retaining customers are largely company specific. The claim made by loyalty advocates is that loyal customers are almost always cheaper to serve. Although individual organisations can attempt to work this out for themselves, they rarely do so. Rather, they rely on published research and industry myths to justify the expenditure in this area. In contrast to much previously published material, this study found no evidence to support this contention in any of the four organisations investigated. Rather, the only correlation between customer longevity and costs that they found was that loyal customers were actually *more expensive* to serve.

The suggestion that loyal customers are more expensive rather than cheaper to serve goes very much against current understanding. However, in many ways, it makes a great deal of sense. Within the business-to-business environment, in particular, loyal customers almost always do business in high volumes and are very aware of their value to the supplying organisation. Indeed, the researchers point out than 'in its efforts to please the regulars, the corporate service provider had developed customised Web sites for each of its top 250 clients. At the click of a button, these customers could obtain personalised service from dedicated sales and service teams. The maintenance of these teams, not to mention the Web sites, cost the company $10 million annually' (Reinartz and Kumar 2002)

Equally surprising was that similar results were found across the other three companies in the study. The mail-order company, for example, had encouraged long-standing customers to switch their purchases from the telephone to the company's website. In spite of this, analysis of their database showed that the difference in cost of communication with new and existing customers was hardly differentiable. Indeed, customers who used the website expected lower prices for using this channel, thereby offsetting any savings to the company. Overall, then, the authors conclude that while in some industries long-standing or loyal customers may indeed be cheapest to serve, in other industries, *long-standing customers may actually be more expensive to service.*

2 From defection to retention

An organisation's ability to retain customers will be directly proportional to its understanding of why customers defect, and its ability to make appropriate changes in the future. Hirschman (1970) argues that failure to meet customer expectations is likely to result in one of three major responses from customers:

- **Exit**: When a customer is left dissatisfied the most common response is simply never to deal with that organisation again. At the very least the dissatisfied customer may seek out alternatives whenever possible. Dissatisfaction is not the only reason customers defect, however, as we discussed above in the In Theory box and Jones and Sasser's (1995) appropriately titled 'Why Satisfied Customers Defect' research. As suggested, it can be because another organisation's product or service seems more attractive, because the customers' needs have changed, or because they are simply seeking variety. Organisations cannot passively accept defections but should constantly monitor their customer base, determining opportunities to prevent exit.

- **Voice**: Many consumers give voice to their feelings about organisations. This voice may be positive (compliments) or negative (complaints) and may include feedback to the organisation itself or word of mouth to other consumers. Feedback, whether positive or negative, is very important to organisations. Complaints offer the organisation the opportunity to solve the problem. If such recovery activities are handled well, they may produce more satisfied customers. Unfortunately, customers are more likely to tell others about their experiences than to tell the organisation in question. Positive and negative word of mouth can have a tremendous impact on the behaviour of other consumers.

- **Loyalty**: Loyalty programmes are used both to acquire and to retain customers. In terms of retention, such programmes are seen to be a significant extension to traditional sales promotion discounting programmes, because these programmes not only provide customers with cheaper shopping, but also provide the sponsoring organisation with a great deal of information about individual customers. This information can be used to target relevant offers via direct marketing mechanisms, either at the point of sale or later in-home. Loyalty programmes are developed for a variety of reasons, including:
  - to generate information;
  - to reward loyal customers;
  - to manipulate consumer behaviour;
  - to increase switching costs.

Generate information

One of the advantages a loyalty programme can offer is that it provides information about the company's customers which, if used appropriately, results in highly specific targeting. The programme will provide information on the recency, frequency and monetary (RFM) value of purchases. This information can also be linked with customer data from a variety of other sources (geodemographic, lifestyle, credit history), in order to build up a fairly accurate picture of someone's life. The next phase of these developments is emerging, in the use of 'smart' cards on which can be stored vast amounts of cardholder information, from age and date of birth to previous purchases and medical records (Shaw 1991, Reed 1994). It has even been suggested that the Nectar loyalty scheme has been investigated by MI5 on the basis that it could provide a blueprint for a state ID scheme in the UK (Ambler 2002). More of this in Chapter 13.

The following case provides an example of another sophisticated 'smart card'-based loyalty scheme.

CASE STUDY 9.7

Smart Shell

Shell has developed one of the most technically sophisticated programmes in operation in the UK, and is believed to have invested almost £40 million on its Smart Promotion. The programme is based on the use of a Smart card, with each card having a computer chip capable of storing data on up to 500 transactions. This incorporates information about shopping patterns, spending habits, its holders and the outlets they use. The programme was launched in October 1994, and since then Shell is believed to have amassed a database of around 4 million customers. More recent reports suggest that one out of every six motorists now carry a Shell Smart Card. Points collected against purchases can be held on the card and redeemed against gifts, cinema tickets, Air Miles or donated to charity.

In 1995 Shell was using only 10% of the card's capacity, and was still building the database. This is what techies call a 'dumb smart card', an under-achieving Einstein. Even in the early stages data was transferred to a central computer via electronic readers at each outlet. This could then be analysed geographically, by outlet, type of product, frequency of purchase, and rewards redeemed. This information could then be used for direct marketing purposes. In 1997 Shell announced a landmark development with news of a consortium of retailers, including Dixons, Currys, Victoria Wine, Vision Express, John Menzies, the RAC and Hilton Hotels. If customers use the card for purchases in all of these outlets, the card promises to provide retailers with one of the most comprehensive pictures of customers' shopping habits and lifestyles. This is likely to result in even more effective targeting in the future.

Research in the later 1990s, however, found that relatively few of the companies were using 'their database as a strategic management tool. Corporate goals and objectives were often poorly understood, making the development of appropriate direct marketing strategy a somewhat 'hit and miss' affair ... there is little evidence of a strategic rather than promotional focus' (Shaw and Chudry 1999).

(Sources: Dignam 1996, Dye 1996, Hollinger and Talor 1997, Anon 1995a, 1995b, Shaw and Chudry 1999)

Reward loyal customers

Most programmes either offer a direct discount based on the amount of purchases, or allow customers to accumulate points that can be redeemed against a range of products. Both options aim to give a tangible reward to frequent shoppers. Other programmes offer more intangible rewards. For example, British Airways has segmented its customers according to the potential value of their business, and enrols them as members of a hierarchy of 'clubs'. Members of these clubs are offered a package of benefits and privileges related to their frequency of flying. Club membership is recognised at all points of contact with the customer, through booking to on-board service.

Another cautionary note here: companies often applaud themselves when they, in their words, 'lock-in' customers through such schemes. But some customers feel that being 'locked-in' is not the relationship that companies sometimes would like to think it is (Tyrell 1995).

Manipulate consumer behaviour

With a sophisticated system, the retailer and/or manufacturer can build a detailed matrix of demographic and behavioural data for each of its customers. On this basis, individualised communications can be generated, and incentives and coupons can be specifically tailored to individuals. These may be used to expose customers to products they have not tried, to encourage payment of premium prices, and to prevent switching to competing brands. Many loyalty programmes also aim to increase the amount spent by each customer. For example, the Tesco Clubcard is credited with encouraging members to spend as much as £3 more every time they visit the store than would normally have been the case (Dignam 1996).

Increase switching costs

Ultimately these programmes have the aim of increasing customer loyalty in order to retain a higher proportion of existing customers. They achieve this by developing higher relative attitudes through positively differentiating the offer from competitors, and/or enhancing value to the customer. Although financial tangible rewards may represent value for some customers, these are most easily copied by competitors, as evidenced by the proliferation of similar programmes in the marketplace. Thus the programmes that focus on using the information generated to truly understand their customers, and who then respond by continually enhancing value (often through intangible rewards), are likely to be most successful.

Other than the initial gathering of data, all of the other objectives are likely to take time to be realised. Loyalty programmes are also highly visible, so back-end failure can be particularly harmful. Entry costs are high, and pay-off is unlikely to occur until the second or third years. As such, loyalty programmes should be seen as a long-term investment, and not simply as the ultimate solution to customer retention – the direct marketing panacea of the 1990s. There are a number of limitations that must be acknowledged. Criticisms include (Hochman 1992; Dye 1996):

- They are little more than sophisticated sales promotions.
- They over-emphasise data collection.
- Loyalty is exhibited towards the programme, not towards the brand.

Sophisticated sales promotions

The comparison to sales promotion is as a result of the emphasis on discounts – although in this case the discount is on total spend over time, as opposed to offers on individual products for a short period. Loyalty programmes are seen as being more sophisticated than sales promotion because of their potential to target individuals, and their dependence upon the database.

The Loyalty Paradox Report described many loyalty programmes as 'mechanical hard sell promotions' (Henley Centre 1995). Although loyalty programmes have attracted a great deal of membership, many customers may simply be signing up because they patronise the organisation anyway. In this sense, programmes have been criticised for subsidising existing business. Furthermore, the emphasis on discounting may ultimately reduce profitability, and limit the ability to use price as a tactical weapon in the future (Dye 1996). Indeed, one commentator has suggested that using loyalty programmes as sophisticated sales promotions has been likened to the taking of drugs: 'constant discounting is the commercial equivalent of snorting cocaine – where an illusory short-term benefit leads to long-term disaster' (Bird 1991).

Despite the high numbers who have enrolled, customers are not entirely fooled by these programmes. For example, many consumers believe that the discounts offered are not large enough to warrant modifying their behaviour. Indeed, an NOP survey carried out in 1995 found that 43% of non-cardholders thought the savings too small to merit joining the programme (NOP 1995). Many supermarket programmes offer 1% discount on shopping over £10, and some participants in group discussions carried out by the authors were unhappy about the minimum expenditure required to be eligible for 'points' (Evans et al. 1997). This problem has been addressed by some retailers with lower purchase requirements for students and the elderly, although the 1% discount still applies. Furthermore, despite statements about the ability of programmes to generate targeted offers, many consumers feel that the offers they receive are based more on what the retailer wants to 'shift' rather than being determined by their needs. This equally applies to in-store offers, where, for example, Sainsbury's offer 'extra reward points' on certain products.

Sales promotions themselves have been criticised for encouraging promiscuity among customers, where customers shop for the best 'deal' rather than being loyal to any one brand. Loyalty programmes may also suffer from this problem, where one programme attempts to attract customers of a competing programme (Evans et al. 1997).

Data overload

The most important element in loyalty programmes is not data capture but the subsequent use of that data. Despite this, many programmes have emphasised the data-gathering benefits, so much so that many programme organisers find themselves suffering data overload. Rather than using the data to improve service, target offers or design new products, limitations of data processing systems have resulted in very basic uses of the information generated. For retail programmes, this is primarily manifested in untargeted money-off coupons. However, it is the ability to further utilise the information that will allow loyalty programmes to fulfil their initial promise.

Loyalty towards the programme, not the brand

'From a customer perspective, many loyalty programmes offer me-too benefits which may be nice to have (most people like to get something for nothing) but there are no guarantees of continued loyalty' (Uncles 1994). Too much emphasis on promoting the programme to consumers may result in a shift from loyalty to the company or brand toward loyalty towards the programme itself (McKenzie 1995). This suggests that rather than developing 'loyalty' to the company or brand (as defined earlier in the chapter), 'spurious loyalty' towards the programme itself is developed. An analogy can be drawn here to the fairly unquestioning loyalty of a dog (being loyal to the brand or company based on inherent brand properties) compared with the more cupboard love of cats (where loyalty is less pronounced and customers will switch brands if other 'offers' are seen to be more attractive) (Jones 1994). Failing to move beyond spurious (cat) loyalty could result in the destruction of any form of meaningful loyalty over time. One suggestion here is not to judge programmes simply by the scale of participation, but rather to focus upon measuring the impact on brand loyalty (Fitzgerald 1994).

Today, many organisations are being forced into running a loyalty programme, simply because their competitors are offering them. However, as we stated, loyalty programmes represent a considerable investment, and take at least two to three years to achieve any return on investment. That said, loyalty programmes are a very good way of developing a customer database, but this is only a first step in the process. Information must be carefully collected, and must then be used to provide added value for customers. Many existing programmes are data rich but information poor, and as a result are little more than sophisticated sales promotions. Given the earlier categories of loyalty, it seems that most of these programmes can achieve little more than spurious loyalty. That said, if organisations use the data they have, loyalty programmes can achieve their potential, and may engender real loyalty in the future.

When to consider a loyalty programme

The previous section discussed some of the benefits and limitations of loyalty programmes. This suggests that organisations should very carefully consider developing their own programme. It also seems that loyalty programmes are not necessarily appropriate for every single organisation. Hochman (1992) suggests that they are most effective for organisations that meet the following conditions:

- The organisation has a product that is purchased *frequently*, enabling the customer to work actively towards a level of reward.
- The product *margin* enables the organisation to support the programme.
- The product is a *parity item*, that is, where it is just as sensible and convenient for your customers to purchase a competitor's products.
- The product has a history of *brand switching*.
- The organisation is in a position to *commit all the resources* – £ plus marketing, systems and service staff support – required to sustain the programme.
- The company has a *service culture* in which concern about the customer is integral to the business.
- The company has an aggressive *commitment to excellence.*

Summary

- The future cash flow of a firm is generated by purchases from existing customers and purchases from new customers. 'Hence, if a firm makes sound investments in acquiring only the right customers and in developing existing customers, it should over time, continually enhance its value' (Hansotia 1997). This chapter has shown that both acquisition and retention are important for survival, and that marketers who focus only on the former are ignoring exciting opportunities and essential information.
- Although the customer battle in the early 2000s may be raging in the area of customer retention, acquisition remains the lifeblood of all organisations. As a result, organisations must develop differentiated strategies to deal with existing customers and new prospects.
- This chapter outlined the basics of the customer acquisition process. It then discussed the importance of retaining customers, and outlined the elements of successful retention strategies. Given the proliferation of customer loyalty programmes within the UK at the present time, the objectives, problems and future direction of such programmes were discussed.
- An important lesson from this chapter is that marketing alone cannot engender loyalty. As Frederick Reichheld said, 'marketing – acting alone – cannot create sustainable loyalty. Customers remain loyal, not because of promotions and marketing programmes, but because of the value they receive. Value is driven by a full array of features, such as product quality, service, sales support and availability' (Reichheld 1988). We explored this in Chapters 1 and 7.

Review questions

1 How might a mail-order wine company acquire new customers?

2 Why has customer retention become such an important managerial challenge?

3 What are the different categories of customer loyalty, and what are the characteristics of each?

4 'Some companies seem hooked on steady doses of fresh customers to cover up regular losses of existing ones' (Rosenberg and Czepiel 1984). Discuss the implications of this statement for business organisations in the 2000s.

5 What needs to be done by organisations in order to overcome criticisms that their loyalty programmes are nothing more than sophisticated sales promotions?

6 What impact has any of the retention devices used by organisations had on *your* behaviour?

Further reading

Coca-Cola/Boston Consulting Group Report (1996) *Knowing Your Customer: How Customer Information will Revolutionise Food Retailing*, London.

Dick, A.S. and Basu, K. (1994) 'Customer Loyalty: Toward an Integrated Framework', *Journal of the Academy of Marketing Science*, 22(2), pp. 99–113.

Pearson, S. (1996) *Building Brands Directly: Creating Business Value from Customer Relationships*, Basingstoke: Macmillan.

Pine, B.J., Peppers, D. and Rogers, M. (1995) 'Do You Want to Keep Your Customers Forever?', *Harvard Business Review*, March–April, pp. 103–14.

Reinartz, W. and Kumar, V. (2002) 'The Mismanagement of Customer Loyalty', *Harvard Business Review*, July, pp. 4–12.

References

Ainslie, A. and Pitt, L. (1992) 'Customer Retention Analysis: An Application of Descriptive and Inferential Statistics in Database Marketing', *Journal of Direct Marketing*, 6(3), Summer, pp. 31–43.

Alajoutsijärvi, K., Möller, K. and Tähtinen, T. (2000) 'Beautiful Exit: how to Leave Your Business Partner', *European Journal of Marketing*, 34, pp. 1270–89.

Altman, I. and Taylor, D.A. (1973) *Social Penetration: The Development of Interpersonal Relationships*, New York: Holt, Rinehart and Winston.

Ambler, T. (2002) 'Why Big Brother Believes Loyalty is Good for You', *Marketing*, 17 October, p. 10.

Anderson, J.C. and Narus, J.A. (1984) 'A Model of the Distributor's Perspective of DistributorManufacturer Working Relationships', *Journal of Marketing*, 48(Fall), pp. 62–74.

Anderson, J.C. and Narus, J.A. (1990) 'A Model of Distributor Firm and Manufacturer Firm Working Partnerships', *Journal of Marketing*, 54(January), pp. 42–5.

Anonymous (1995a) 'Bright Future for Smart Cards', *Marketing*, April 6, pp. III–VI.

Anonymous (1995b) 'Smart Cards on the table', *Marketing*, 9 February, p. 27.

Aspinall, E., Nancarrow, C. and Stone, M. (2001) 'The Meaning and Measurement of Customer Retention', *Journal of Targeting, Measurement and Analysis for Marketing*, 10(1), pp. 79–87.

Bendapudi, N. and Berry, L.L. (1997) 'Customers Motivation for Maintaining Relationships with Service Providers', *Journal of Retailing*, 73(Spring), pp. 15–37.

Berry, L.L. (1995) 'Relationship Marketing of Services – Growing Interest, Emerging Perspectives', *Journal of the Academy of Marketing Science*, 23(4), pp. 236–45.

Bird, D. (1991) 'Targeting Consumer Loyalty', *Marketing*, 27 June, p. 13.

Bitran, G. and Mondschein, S. (1997) 'Managing the Tug-of-War Between Supply and Demand in the Service Industries', *European Management Journal*, 15(5), pp. 523–36.

Blattberg, R.C., Getz, G. and Thomas, J.S. (2001) *Customer Equity*, Boston; MA: Harvard Business School Publishing, Chapter 3 'Managing Customer Acquisition'.

Borys, B. and Jemison, D.B. (1989) 'Hybrid Arrangements As Strategic: Theoretical Issues in Organisational Combinations', *Academy of Management Review*, 14(2), pp. 234–40.

Buss, B. (1999) 'The Organisational Form that Guarantees Successful Database Marketing', *The Journal of Database Marketing*, 6(4), pp. 330–8.

Crush, P. (2002) 'Skoda Revival', *Marketing Direct*, February, pp. 33–5.

Daskou, S. and Hart, S. (2002) 'The Essence of Business to Consumer Relationships: A Phenomenological Approach', *10th International Colloquium in Relationship Marketing*, University Kaiserslautern, Germany, October, pp. 499–515.

DeSouza, G. (1992) 'Designing a customer retention plan', *Journal of Business Strategy*, March/April, pp. 24–8.

De Wulf, K., Odekerken-Schroder, G. and Iacobucci, D. (2001) 'Investments in Consumer Relationships: A Cross-Country and Cross-Industry Exploration', *Journal of Marketing*, 65 (October), pp. 33–50.

Dick, A.S. and Basu, K. (1994) 'Customer Loyalty: Toward an Integrated Framework', *Journal of the Academy of Marketing Science*, 22(2), pp. 99–113.

Dignam, C. (1996) 'Being Smart Is Not the Only Redeeming Feature', *Marketing Direct*, September, pp. 51–6.

Dwyer, F.R., Schurr, P.H. and Oh, S. (1987) 'Developing BuyerSeller Relationships', *Journal of Marketing*, 51(April), pp. 11–27.

Dye, P. (1996) 'Don't Let Them Get Away', *Marketing Direct*, December, pp. 65–71.

Evans, M., Patterson, M., O'Malley, L. and Mitchell, S. (1997) 'Consumer Reactions to Database-based Supermarket Loyalty Programmes', *The Journal of Database Marketing*, 4(4), pp. 307–20.

Fitzgerald, J. (1994) 'The Database Argument', *Marketing Week* (Loyalty Supplement), 18 November, pp. 7–8.

Ford, D. (1980) 'The Development of Buyer–Seller Relationships in Industrial Markets', *European Journal of Marketing*, 14(5/6), pp. 339–54.

Fornell, C. and Wernerfelt, B. (1987) 'Defensive Marketing Strategy by Customer Complaint Management, A Theoretical Analysis', *Journal of Marketing Research*, 24, pp. 337–46.

Grönhaug, K., Hejnesand, I.J. and Koveland, A. (1999) 'Fading Relationships in Business Markets: An Exploratory Study', *Journal of Strategic Marketing*, 7, pp. 175–190.

Gwinner, K.P., Gremier, D.D. and Bitner, M.J. (1998) 'Relational Benefits in Services Industries: The Customer's Perspective', *Journal of the Academy of Marketing Science*, 26(2), pp. 101–14.

Halinen, A. (1997) *Relationship Marketing in Professional Services: A Study of Agency Client Dynamics in the Advertising Sector*, London: Routledge Advances in Management and Business Studies.

Halinen, A. and Tähtinen, J. (2002) 'A Process Theory of Relationship Ending', *International Journal of Service Industry Management*, 13(2), pp. 163–80.

Hallberg, G. (1999) *All Customers Are Not Created Equal*, New York: John Wiley & Sons.

Hansotia, B.J. (1997) 'Enhancing Firm Value through Prospect and Customer Lifecycle Management – Part 1', *The Journal of Database Marketing*, 4(4), pp. 350–60.

Helm, S. (2002) 'Customer Valuation-Based Dissolution of Relationships', *10th International Colloquium in Relationship Marketing*, University Kaiserslautern, Germany, October, pp. 169–87.

Henley Centre (1995) *Loyalty Paradox Report*, London.

Hirschman, A.O. (1970) *Exit, Voice and Loyalty: Responses to Decline in Firms, Organizations and States*, Cambridge, MA: Harvard University Press.

Hochman, K. (1992) 'Customer Loyalty Programs' in E.L. Nash, (ed.) *The Direct Marketing Handbook*, (2nd edn), New York: McGraw-Hill, pp. 781–99.

Hoffman, D.L. and Novak, T.P. (2000) 'How to Acquire Customers on the Web', *Harvard Business Review*, 78(3), pp. 179–86.

Hollinger, P. and Talor, P. (1997) 'Shell launches Smart card revolution: Retailers join discount scheme for shoppers', *The Financial Times*, March, 12.

Johanson, J. and Mattsson, L.-G. (1992) 'Network Positions and Strategic Action – An Analytical Framework', in B. Axelsson and G. Easton (eds) *Industrial Networks: A New View of Reality*, Routledge: London, pp. 205–17.

Jones, M. (1994) 'It's a Dog's Life Being at the Beck and Call of Marketers', *Marketing Business*, February, p. 48.

Jones, T.O. (1996) 'Why Loyal Customers Defect', *KeyNote Presentation*, IDM Symposium, 6 June, London.

Jones, T.O. and Sasser, W.E. (1995) 'Why Satisfied Customers Defect', *Harvard Business Review*, November–December, pp. 88–99.

Keaveney, S.M. (1995) 'Customer Switching Behaviour in Service Industries: an Exploratory Study', *Journal of Marketing*, 59, pp. 71–82.

Kelley, H.H. and Thibaut, J.W. (1978) *Interpersonal Relationships: A Theory of Interdependence*, New York: John Wiley & Sons: New York.

Knox, S. and Maklan, S. (1998) *Competing on Value*, London: Pitman Publishing, FT Management.

Lawrence, N. (2002) Case study supplied on behalf of DunnHumby, London.

Lazer, W. (1969) 'Marketing's Changing Social Relationships', *Journal of Marketing*, 33(January), pp. 3–9.

Leuthesser, L. and Kohli, A.K. (1995) 'Relational Behaviour in Business Markets: Implications for Relationship Management', *Journal of Business Research*, 34, pp. 221–33.

Lix, T.S., Berger, P.D. and Magilozzi, T.L. (1995) 'New Customer Acquisition: Prospecting Models and Use of Commercially Available External Data', *Journal of Direct Marketing*, 9(4), pp. 8–18.

Mackintosh, J. (2002) 'Halifax Sorry for Snub to "Cash Heavy" Businesses, *Financial Times*, 27 February.

McCorkell, G. (1997) *Direct and Database Marketing*, London: Kogan Page.

McKenzie, S. (1995) 'Distinguishing Marks', *Marketing Week*, 17 November, pp. 13–15.

Morgan, R.M. (2000) 'Relationship Marketing and Marketing Strategy: The Evolution of Relationship Marketing Strategy Within the Organisation', in J.N. Sheth and A. Parvatiyar (eds) *Handbook of Relationship Marketing*, Sage: Thousand Oaks, CA, pp. 481–504.

Morgan, R.M. and Hunt, S.D. (1994) 'The Commitment–Trust Theory of Relationship Marketing', *Journal of Marketing*, 58(July), pp. 20–38.

Niraj, R., Gupta, M. and Narasimhan, C. (2001) 'Customer Profitability in a Supply Chain', *Journal of Marketing*, 65, pp. 1–16.

NOP (1995) 'NOP Poll Proves Shoppers are Taking Part in Loyalty Programmes', *Loyalty*, November, p. 7.

Payne, A.F. and Frow, P.E. (1999) 'Developing a segmented service strategy: improving measurement in relationship marketing', *Journal of Marketing Management*, 15, pp. 797–818.

Planalp, S. (1987) 'Interplay Between Relational Knowledge and Events', in R. Burnett, P. McGhee and D. Clarke (eds) *Accounting for Relationships: Explanation, Representation and Knowledge*, Methuen: London, pp. 175–91.

Reed, D. (1994) 'System Shakedown', *Marketing Week* (Loyalty Supplement), 18 November, pp. 25–6.

Reichheld, F. (1996) *The Quest for Loyalty: Creating Value Through Partnership*, Boston, MA: Harvard University Press.

Reichheld, F.F. (1988) 'Loyalty and the Renaissance of Marketing', *Marketing Management*, 2(4), pp. 10–21, 15.

Reinartz, W. and Kumar, V. (2002) 'The Mismanagement of Customer Loyalty', *Harvard Business Review*, July, pp. 4–12.

Rosenberg, L.J. and Czepiel, J.A. (1984) 'A Marketing Approach for Customer Retention', *Journal of Consumer Marketing*, 1(Spring), pp. 45–51.

Sargeant, A. (2001) 'Customer Lifetime Value and Marketing Strategy: How to Forge the Link', *The Marketing Review*, 1, pp. 427–40.

Shani, D. and Chalasani, S. (1992) 'Exploiting Niches Using Relationship Marketing' *Journal of Business Strategy*, 6 (4), pp. 43–52.

Shaw, R. (1991) 'How the Smart Card is Changing Retailing', *Long Range Planning*, 24(1), pp. 111–14.

Shaw, T. and Chudry, F.A. (1999) 'Strategic Database Applications within Multi-Partner Programmes', *Journal of Database Marketing*, 7(2), pp. 107–19.

Shaw, T. and Chudry, F. (2002) Strategic Databases Applications within Multi-Partner Programmes, *Journal of Database Marketing*, 7(2), pp. 107–19.

Solomon, M.R., Surprenant, C., Czepiel, J.A. and Gutman, E.G. (1985) 'A Role Theory Perspective on Dyadic Interactions: The Service Encounter', *Journal of Marketing*, 49(1), pp. 99–111.

Stauss, B. and Friege, C. (1999) 'Regaining Service Customers: Costs and Benefits of Regain Management', *Journal of Service Research*, 1(4), pp. 347–61.

Tuominen, P. and Kettunen, U. (2002) 'To Fade or Not to Fade: Than's an Interesting Question in Customer Relationships, Too', *10th International Colloquium in Relationship Marketing*, University Kaiserslautern, Germany, October, pp. 719–34.

Tyrell, R. (1995) IDM Symposium Presentation, 6 June, London.

Uncles, M. (1994) 'Do You or Your Customers Need a Loyalty Programme?', *Journal of Targeting, Measurement and Analysis for Marketing*, 2(4), pp. 335–50.

Wilson, D.T. (1995) 'An Integrated Model of Buyer–Seller Relationships', *Journal of the Academy of Marketing Science*, 23(4), pp. 335–45.

PART 4
Relational Vehicles and Messages

10 Relational media

11 Virtual relationships

12 Relational messages

Part 3 provided an exploration of how marketing, which is increasingly data (and hopefully knowledge and insight) informed, can develop relational interaction with customers and potential customers. We analysed the nature of relational interaction itself and followed this with suggestions as to how 'CRM' should be viewed as a wider phenomenon than how it has often been perceived and operationalised, specifically by converting data into knowledge and insight across functions and partners. From this analysis, we presented various approaches to translating this paradigm into strategies for acquiring and retaining customers. Having reached this point it is appropriate to explore the range of relational vehicles for communicating with customers and potential customers and the messages that these can carry.

In Part 4, then, we explore the main forms of direct interactive media. As discussed in Chapter 1, there have been many concerns over the effectiveness of traditional media, and market fragmentation has resulted in diminishing audiences, media costs have soared and consumers are experiencing clutter. Factors such as these serve to make direct communication that much more competitive and effective. Furthermore, as we have discussed in Parts 2 and 3, organisation–customer contact is becoming more interactive and an aim is to take this to relational interaction. Part 4 covers developments in interactive media that can facilitate such interaction.

Moreover, as direct interactive marketing expenditure continues to increase rapidly (Barwise and Styler 2002), there is a reciprocal participation in dealing with organisations by direct methods on the part of consumers. Regarding the popularity of the telephone, for example, it is suggested that just over half the UK population are telephiles who are comfortable using the 'phone for telebusiness (Denny 1998). The use of the Internet is at a lower level at present but has been in a dramatic 'growth' stage, especially since the late 1990s.

Since its creation, the Internet has provided the infrastructure for greater direct marketer–direct consumer interaction. A movement that began with e-mail and mailing lists and a few news groups has – in some areas – already grown into a series of tremendously rich and influential virtual communities. We also, therefore, explore the relational opportunities for both marketer and customer of interacting via the Internet. The amalgam of new and old communications media means that we are in an era that can rightly be described as not only one of the 'direct marketer' but also of the 'direct customer'.

We conclude Part 4 with an analysis of the range of 'offers', messages and communications 'creative' from which relational marketers can draw and which are underpinned by contributions from concepts and theories from the behavioural sciences.

References

Barwise, P. and Styler, A. (2002) *Marketing Expenditure Trends*, London: London Business School/Havas and Kudos Research.

Denny, N. (1998) *The Telebusiness Report: The Definitive Report on Telebusinesses in the UK to the Year 2005*, London: Haymarket Business Publications.

10 Relational media

Learning objectives

Having completed this chapter, students should:

- Appreciate the range of media available to marketers who wish to communicate interactively with customers.

- Understand the characteristics and application of different media.

- Appreciate the importance of integration in interactive marketing communications.

Train railcards

More than three-quarters of 16- to 25-year-olds use the train for leisure journeys, but only a quarter have a Young Person's Railcard, entitling them to a third off many fares. In part this is because awareness isn't as high as it could be, and there is some confusion about who within what age bracket is eligible. (The answer: everyone.) Given those facts, it made sense to take one idea and present it in many different ways to reach a wide audience. That was the central thinking behind the train companies' integrated campaign to promote the card. Instead of pushing the wonders of travel, the campaign focused on the misery of not going anywhere with the message 'Don't be a local'. A prize draw with the prize of a weekend away for ten was set up. Press ads in young people's magazines like *Mixmag* and *Kerrang* were followed by e-mails to encourage online response. Viral e-mails were used to get members of the target audience to bring in their friends. Youngsters responding to the ambient media in pubs or to online pop-ups were urged to 'Get out more'. Sales rose by 24% after the press launch. Awareness of eligibility increased by 14%.

(Source: DMA Awards 2002)

Introduction

The opening vignette introduces this chapter well. It shows that we now have a tremendous range of vehicles that can facilitate interactive communications between organisations and customers (and between customers and customers) and it shows that many such vehicles can be combined within an integrated communications programme.

Consider the following list of media that can potentially facilitate relational interaction:

- addressed direct mail and mail order;
- customer magazines;
- telephony (static and mobile);
- Internet, e-mail and networked computers: static, laptop, palmtop;
- direct response (DRTV) and interactive TV (iTV);
- direct response print media;
- direct response radio;
- door to door;
- interactive kiosks;
- outdoor and ambient media;
- inserts.

There are several relatively new dimensions of the new use of media. It might sound tautological to say that interactive relational marketing requires the possibility of relational interaction. But how media are deployed will reflect the degree to which this is achieved. The interactive relational approach contrasts strongly with more traditional marketing communications: 'mass-marketing or segment based advertising is highly unfocused. It reaches millions of non-customers and the messages are untargeted, resulting in high advertising costs and questionable sales effects' (Blattenberg and Glazer 1994).

Another relatively new dimension of the new use of media is increased targeting and this, of course, is essential for relational interaction. We have already discussed the clutter of marketing communications. The average duration of each advertisement is falling, with the result that more companies are vying for the customer's attention but spending less time doing so. Consequently, in order for an individual company to stand out, it has to find a method of communicating with customers where the message does not have so much competition. Interactive relational marketing can overcome the difficulty with clutter and can also provide the sort of personalised communication that is a prerequisite for relational marketing.

Yet another trend is the convergence of media. In the past, there would be telephony, television and computers, for example. Now we have mobile phones that can access the Internet and receive television pictures. The TV itself can communicate interactively via the Internet. So 'convergence of media' is a clear development.

A final issue concerns whether outbound interactive media are addressed to named recipients or not. Media such as addressed mail, telesales and e-mails can clearly be addressed to specific people, whereas direct response radio and television advertisements are not. However, the distinction is now less important than previously because any resulting inbound contact is personalised by definition and can lead to continued personalised two-way interaction.

The point about whether 'outbound' is addressed or not depends to some extent on the level of knowledge of intended recipients in what would be acquisition campaigns. We would hope that any retention or loyalty or relationship campaign with existing customers would always be addressed, otherwise this would reveal a lack of recognition of recipients and therefore would not be relational.

We start by reviewing the nature and degree of expansion of direct interactive marketing and then explore some the media involved and their application within actual campaigns.

Growth of direct interactive media

To substantiate our earlier proposition that traditional less targeted, less accountable, more expensive media are, relatively speaking, under threat from the newer media that would claim the opposite characteristics, it has been shown that across major markets (the USA, Japan, Germany, the UK and France) there appears to be a significant and permanent shift towards interactive marketing and direct mail (Barwise and Styler 2002). In this study, 'interactive' marketing is taken as being 'internet advertising, marketing websites and extranets, email marketing and new media (iDTV, wireless)' (Barwise and Styler 2002). This category and direct mail were the only categories to gain share of marketing communications expenditure during the downturn in the world economy in the early 2000s. Indeed between 2001 and 2003 interactive marketing expenditure rose by over 19% and direct mail by over 7%, across these five countries. Within them there are even more dramatic increases: expenditure on interactive marketing, for example, increased between 2001 and 2003 by over 47% in the UK.

Also during that period, traditional media advertising might have still held the lion's share of marketing communications spend, but its share fell during consecutive years.

We will not labour these sorts of statistics much further, but it is worth reporting that across 15 European countries, direct marketing expenditure increased from just under €20,000 million in 1993 to over €43,000 million in 2000 (FEDMA 2003). In the UK over this period, expenditure rose by nearly 120% and in the Netherlands by nearly 160% (FEDMA 2003).

Germany, France and the UK have particularly strong direct mail industries. In the UK, in 2001, over 17% of marketing communications expenditure was allocated to this medium (compared with, say, less than 8% of Japanese spend) (Barwise and Styler 2002). Table 10.1 summarises some of the trends during the 1990s.

As can be seen, although direct mail continues to be the most important medium utilised by direct marketers, growth is now more obvious in other media. The growth in telemarketing may be due in part to the increasing use of inbound systems by companies to complement the extensive use of outbound contact.

Door-to-door distribution is enjoying rapid growth because of lower costs relative to mail. Also, the improved targeting accuracy offered by door-to-door distributors has encouraged companies. UK households receive twice as much unaddressed letterbox advertising as direct mail (Titford 1994). In 1992–93 the relative figures were an average of 10.4 unaddressed items and 4.1 direct mail pieces per month. By 2000, across 15 European countries, expenditure on unaddressed mail had risen to over €55,000 million from €21,000 million in 1993.

This trend is likely to continue – particularly for smaller service companies within clearly defined geographic areas. This type of direct marketing is designed to inform rather than to build relationships and, given this objective, can be relatively successful.

Direct response advertising has also experienced exceptional growth in recent years. Indeed, we suggest you watch an evening's commercial TV and compare the number of commercials that do and do not include a direct response mechanism such as a telephone number or website address. Even back in 1995, a DMIS survey found that 90% of all advertising in print media carried a direct

TABLE 10.1 Euro spend (€ million)

Country	Media	1993	2000
France	All direct	3 832	6 448
	Telephony	307	585
	Internet/online	–	144
	Addressed direct mail	3 578	4 300
Germany	All direct	5 670	8 896
	Telephony	1 534	3 017
	Internet/online	169	1 227
	Addressed direct mail	5 451	6 442
UK	All direct	1 163	3 372
	Telephony	769	3 980
	Internet/online	58 (1994)	260
	Addressed direct mail	2 436	4 664
Spain	All direct	1 581	2 638
	Telephony	77	386
	Internet/online	–	72 (1999)
	Addressed direct mail	807	796

response mechanism (DMIS 1995). In support of this more widespread utilisation, TGI found that nearly 35% of the UK population had made telephone calls as a result of advertisements seen on TV and in the papers over the previous 12 months (Young 1994). Direct response advertising is clearly set to grow, as more commercial airtime is available through satellite and cable. Despite what we have said about the relative 'mass' communications of traditional TV advertising, there is scope for reaching more tightly defined audiences. QVC and other shopping channels are available within many countries and have paved the way for further industry growth.

Addressed direct mail

The Federation of Direct Marketing Associations (FEDMA) defines direct mail as 'any piece of promotional material delivered to the consumer via a postal operator, including mail order catalogues' (FEDMA 2003). It has traditionally been the mainstay of UK direct marketing effort and in recent years has provided the impetus for growth within the industry. One positive side-effect of this growth in the volume of direct mail is that it has become a more accepted medium within marketing generally and consumers may also be more accepting of it. However, while direct mail continues to be a major weapon in the direct marketer's armoury, it no longer dominates, as the range of media available to direct marketing increases. Direct mail can be used for many purposes, which include (Taylor 1995):

- generating leads and enquiries;
- building customer loyalty;
- improving image;
- generating sales;
- building brand awareness;
- cross- and up-selling;
- building a database;
- supporting the trade.

The strategic use of direct mail means that organisations no longer use the medium simply to generate sales. Direct mail is also useful in terms of data collection and can be used to collect a wealth of information, particularly about existing customers. Furthermore, the medium plays a significant role in building and maintaining customer relationships because it is ideally suited to facilitating the meaningful dialogue so important to such relationships. At a strategic level, direct mail can be used to promote the image of the organisation and its brands.

Research conducted by Ogilvy and Mather Direct and The Qualitative Consultancy (TQC) in 1991 indicates that response to direct mail communications depends upon four factors: subject matter, brand relationships, personality types and creative execution (Exhibit 10.1). Perhaps the most powerful contributor to consumer response to direct mail is the subject matter of the direct mail piece itself. Having the right offer at the right time is paramount to success. This further emphasises the importance of ensuring that consumers receive direct marketing which is relevant to their lives. Having a brand relationship is also viewed as necessary for the successful implementation of direct mail programmes. Consumers seem to be far more willing to accept and respond to direct mail which comes as a result of the relationship between them and the organisation.

EXHIBIT 10.1   The determinants of consumer response to direct mail (TQC/Ogilvy and Mather Direct 1991)

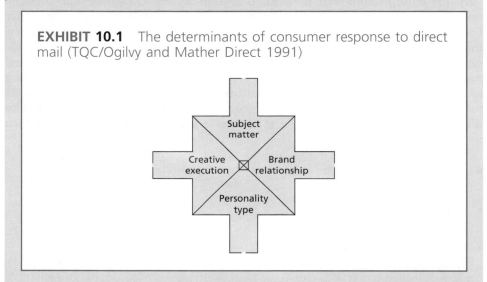

Personality type basically refers to whether the consumer has a positive or negative attitude towards direct mail in general and this also contributes to the level of response. The TQC/Ogilvy and Mather research further details personality types in this regard, as can be seen in Table 10.2. Finally, excellent creative execution will engage the recipient's attention and interest and may also encourage them to respond.

Direct mail offers the marketer a great deal of selectivity. As we have seen, targeting is crucial to interactive relational marketing. Because marketers can select mailing lists with specific relevance for them and because they can further select the prospects that offer the greatest potential

TABLE 10.2 Personality typologies in respect to direct mail (TQC/Ogilvy and Mather Direct 1991)

Type	Basic attitude	Motivation	Characteristics
Compies	Very positive	Entering competitions 'Something for nothing'	Not interested in subject matter Small/extreme group
Librarians	Positive	Value information Like storing things	Little compulsion to respond now Like financial services
Adults	Balanced	Look for things of value Ability to discriminate	Open most mail, feel in control Quick to filter out useful and not useful
Adolescents	Negative	Dislike pressure Attack & rejection of authority	Defensive and rebellious Feel threatened
Cynics	Negative	Scepticism Want to prove it's a con	Fear of being duped Want to show they can see through things
Conscientious objectors	Very negative	Anger Dislike intrusion	Fear of manipulation justified by rational arguments Concern for other defenceless people

from within those lists, direct mail offers the marketer more in the way of tightly defined targeting than many other media. Poor prospects can be removed from lists so that pinpoint targeting can be further improved. Direct mail is not a cheap medium to use. On a cost per thousand basis mail cannot compete with the likes of press or television, but that is just in terms of numbers reached. The extra targeting ability of mail means that cost per response and conversion can be much lower.

Direct mail is also a particularly flexible medium. It can be utilised for a wide range of applications and with an equally wide range of different formats. It enables the marketer to choose whichever format best suits his or her purposes. Depending on the demands of the campaign, the direct mail piece can be used to convey as much or as little information as is required. If the campaign requires that the consumer receives a large quantity of information (as can be the case in highly technological markets), then there really is no substitute for direct mail. The medium can also be used with equal efficiency in prospecting for new business, in customer retention drives and in communicating with other organisational stakeholders. Direct mail's creative potential means that organisations can send almost anything in the direct mail package: videos, scratch and sniff, samples, vouchers, competitions and teasers (see Exhibit 10.2). From a consumer perspective, direct mail's flexibility means that they don't have to read it straight away; they can take their time over the mailing; they can read it at their leisure; they can keep it for later – or, yes, it can be binned without even being opened!

Direct mail also offers the opportunity for personalisation of the message. However, personalisation involves more than just putting the name and address of the recipient on the envelope. Personalisation also means that the consumer receives an offer that is relevant to them. Many marketers have become engrossed in the minutiae of personalisation (Hill 1993). True personalisation (in our terms, true relational interaction) involves adapting the product or service, including the means by which it is communicated and the style of message used to convey the offer, to the needs of individuals in the target audience. In achieving this, marketers need to make more effective use of the consumer information we discussed in Chapter 2. This information can allow them to tailor the whole package (offer and communication) and not just the name and address on the envelope.

When recipients open and read a direct mail piece, there is no direct competition for their attention. This happens because with other media the message has to compete with other programme or editorial content, while direct mail does not have this problem. The main barrier is encouraging the recipient to open the envelope in the first place.

Direct mail facilitates the sort of testing operations we discussed in Chapter 4 and lends itself to measurability. Organisations can quickly and easily identify who is responding to their mailings, and can use this information to further refine their targeting efforts. One of the main advantages of direct mail as a marketing medium is its accountability. Response rates are easily judged and the exact success of a campaign can be rapidly evaluated. Methods of measuring success inevitably depend on the initial objectives of the campaign. They also depend on different levels of direct mail expenditure.

Direct mail has a wide variety of devices at its disposal which can be used to engage the involvement of the recipient while he or she is making a decision about whether or not to respond. This is important in light of the fact that it is becoming ever more difficult to gain the attention of consumers who are exposed to thousands of marketing messages every week. Gaining the attention of the recipient is made easier by the fact that it is difficult to ignore direct mail. While it is always possible to put direct mail straight into the bin, most people go as far as opening and reading the message before disposing of it.

The following case study demonstrates the use of direct mail in a cross-selling campaign. Generalised interests of men and women are reflected in this campaign and in the 2001 DMA Awards it won a Gold award in the Consumer Direct Mail category.

EXHIBIT 10.2 3D direct mail

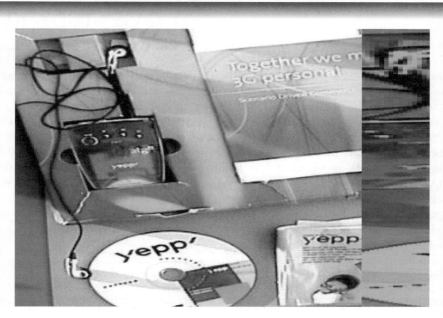

E-commerce provider ATG mailed an MPS player to 20 senior decision makers in key 3G licence-holding companies to target its services. The player contained a voice message explaining how ATG could achieve similar personalisation with future 3G customers.

Land Rover's Freelander 'Escape Mail Pack' included a map, video and miniature toothbrush (for the 'great escape' that can be a benefit of buying a Freelander).

Telewest mailed a locked safe and a website address to 2000 IT directors. The website gave the safe combination access number and the safe included shredded money to reflect a fraction of the sum that the company's secure data transfer system could save.

Vodafone

Vodafone wanted to encourage existing customers to use its mobile voicemail service. To achieve this the mobile operator's customers were sliced into three segments. Women under 35 were mailed a 'real' wedding invitation days after the event, while their male counterparts received a ticket to an England rugby match – four days out of date. Both sexes received a Tesco till receipt listing drinks bought for a party – days after it allegedly happened. The message conveyed in each mailing was that people can miss out on many slices of life if they don't use their mobile phone voicemail.

The mailing beat all the targets expected by Vodafone. To make a return on investment the mailing required a 0.7% response rate. The wedding invite recorded a 10.1% response, while the match ticket drew an 8.21% response. The packs are now a mainstay in cross-selling other Vodafone products, with around 75 000 mailed each month.

(Source: Adapted from material provided by DMA from the Vodaphone Award Winning Case Study, DMA/Royal Mail Awards 2001)

Royal Mail's Mailsort programme offers direct marketers a number of options in terms of direct mail delivery. The programme includes a number of different discounted tariffs related in the main to the speed of delivery required. Royal Mail also offer customer bar-coding (CBC) which utilises electronic bar-code readers to sort large volumes of mail. CBC is designed to reduce delivery times and improve the cost-effectiveness of the Mailsort programme. The bar code incorporates household-specific delivery point suffix (DPS) data which helps to make delivery that much quicker and more accurate (Couldwell 1997). However, in using CBC, marketers have to ensure that the lists they work from are extremely accurate (72% of addresses must include DPS data and 90% of the postcode information must be accurate). Set-up costs for the system can be quite high and organisations using it should view it as a long-term investment.

The deregulation of postal services in the UK from 2003 is seeing changes in the competitive nature of the market for delivery of direct mail but this is somewhat outside of the scope of this book and the reader is recommended to read the trade press for more up-to-date details; for example, an early article by Acland (2002) provides a useful summary of possible effects.

Direct mail is not without its problems. For many organisations the costs of direct mail still prove to be the biggest barrier to its implementation. Despite its attendant advantages, direct mail is not particularly cost-efficient for organisations who produce low-cost products and whose consumers are spread over a wide geographic area. These organisations are better served by traditional mass communications techniques, such as advertising, or by door-to-door marketing. Furthermore, direct mail has to some extent failed to live up to its promise of increased response rates following the introduction of complex modelling procedures, geodemographic and lifestyle profiling, and the detailed consumer information to which marketers now have access. One reason for the stagnation of response rates is the failure by many marketers to include response devices in their mailings. According to the DMA census in 1996, 30% of mailings do not incorporate a means for the consumer to respond. Furthermore, of those mailings that do include a response device, 40% require the consumer to pay for postage (Darby 1997). Increasing volumes of direct mail have also meant that the medium is developing a clutter similar to that experienced by traditional communications media. Such clutter serves only to alienate many consumers and the pressure is now on marketers to improve their targeting so that consumers only receive mailings which are of interest to them.

As with many other media, it is likely that this will be improved with the adoption of 'opt-in' permission marketing methods, which we will explore further in Chapter 13.

Mail-order catalogues

Also included within the direct mail category is mail order. This continues to play a major role within the UK direct mail sector. Indeed, as we saw in Chapter 1, it was one of the origins of the interactive relational approach we explore in this book. It accounts for nearly £5bn (Field 1997) annually and represents in the region of 15% (Anonymous 1997) of all UK direct mail. However, it has experienced a slight downturn in its fortunes in recent years, falling from a total of 369 million mailings in 1995 to 321 million in 1996. In an effort to fight the decline, many catalogue companies have extended their product lines to include financial services and in 1996, 6% (Anonymous 1997) of the sector's mailings were accounted for by such products as home insurance. This move has been made possible by the exploitation of customer databases and the extensive information which these organisations have held about their customers.

Mail order has had to change with the times. Not only does this involve the introduction of new product lines, but it also includes some fundamental changes in the way these organisations do business. The changing needs of society have perhaps had their greatest impact on the 'big book' catalogues such as Freemans, Littlewoods and Great Universal Stores. These big catalogues have traditionally depended on a network of agents for most of their business. These agents, cash-strapped housewives more often than not, earned commission by introducing others to the catalogue and ordering products on their behalf. However, today, these networks of agents are not as proficient as they have been in the past. The main reasons for this include the fact that there is an increasing lack of trust in society today, the population is generally more mobile than in the past, and agents have begun to play the system. In order to encourage agents to work for their catalogue, the likes of Great Universal Stores offer them incentives such as discounts on purchases and free gifts. Attracted by these incentives, many agents worked their way through the main catalogues collecting goodies as they went (Field 1997). Despite these problems, 'big book' catalogues are likely to represent a large proportion of the mail-order market for some time to come. The competitive advantage which these catalogues possess revolves around the easy credit terms which they have to offer and which customers cannot obtain elsewhere. Because the number of people in the UK existing on a below-average income is increasing, these credit terms are always likely to attract new custom.

One recent development of huge importance within the mail-order industry has been the growth of more specialised catalogues or 'specialogues' (Slater 1996). Specialogues compete on the basis of being more tightly targeted than their big book counterparts, focusing on particular segments of the consumer market. The specialogue market includes players such as Next Directory, Racing Green and Land's End but also incorporates even more tightly targeted offerings such as Divertimenti who offer upmarket kitchenware. Specialogues appeal to those consumers who are too busy to wade through huge catalogues and tend to focus on the more upmarket end of the consumer spectrum. They usually cater for the ABC_1 market, while the traditional mail order catalogues appeal to the C_2DEs (Field 1997). Specialogues don't necessarily work on the basis of easy credit terms but concentrate more on convenience. ABC_1 customers value convenience and quality, they are prepared to pay extra for these features, and this is what specialogues offer them. The high margins that specialogues earn mean that they don't have to worry too much about generating high volumes. Because specialogues are more highly targeted they tend to rely more on customer profiling (especially lifestyle profiling) than do the big book catalogues.

All, of course, are increasingly turning to CD-ROM and/or Internet-based catalogue support. When focusing on the specialised end of the market, companies need to be aware of their customers' interests in order to ensure that what they are offering is relevant. Another of the advantages of specialogues is the speed with which they can deliver. While big book catalogues have traditionally taken 28 days to deliver, specialogues such as Next Directory can have the products at your door the next day. If the big books are going to remain competitive, they too will have to improve the flexibility of their delivery systems.

Both mail-order catalogues and their Internet and CD-ROM equivalents need to find appropriate compromises in order to overcome issues of 'texture' of the products they promote. For example, mail-order catalogues sometimes include fabric swatches so that customers can feel the texture of the garments they are considering and Internet catalogues can include interactive 'virtual assistants' to show how different garments might appear on different models, or even on the customer, if he or she 'uploads' their own image.

A boost for mail order comes through collaboration, as we saw in Chapter 8, with data sharing consortia such as Abacus.

Customer magazines

Many organisations have added a new dimension to their customer loyalty programmes in the form of customer magazines. Originally used by the airline industry and financial services, customer magazines are now being utilised by retailers and fast-moving consumer goods companies such as Heinz. By building up detailed profiles of their customers these organisations are able to tailor the magazines to tightly defined customer segments. Indeed, some organisations are moving towards the development of individualised magazines – the only thing holding them back at the moment is printing technology. Maintaining loyalty is the major focus of these magazines and this advantage has led to brand manufacturers using them in the fight against own-label competitors. A secondary feature of these magazines is that they can be utilised for data collection purposes. Customer information can be gleaned from vouchers, coupons and competitions and used to identify prospects for other interactive marketing campaigns.

Customer magazines can be quite costly. It is rarely the case that production and distribution costs can be covered by advertising revenue. That said, in terms of the job they do, such magazines can be cost-effective and this effectiveness is easily quantifiable. Fostering customer loyalty comes at a price but does pay dividends in the long term.

Teleservices

Teleservices is probably a more apt name for what has traditionally been known as 'telemarketing' and is becoming increasingly prevalent in the UK. According to FEDMA (2003), teleservices use the telephone with the aim of generating sales, sales leads or maintaining a relationship with the consumer.

Many organisations have recognised the power of the telephone and it is now being used across a broad range of activities. These activities include (Roman 1988; Anonymous 1992b):

- new customer acquisition;
- reactivation of past customers;
- consolidation of and cross-selling to existing customers;
- upgrading current customers;
- screening and qualifying leads;
- servicing marginal accounts that don't justify a personal sales call;
- covering a wide geographical spread;
- retailer and dealer support and traffic building;
- market research and database building;
- customer care, loyalty building and helpline provision;
- direct response enquiry and order handling.

Many outbound telemarketing calls made in the UK continue to be to existing customers to stimulate interest in and cross-sell other products and services and to enhance loyalty. A large proportion of outbound calling remains in the business-to-business sector where recipients tend to be more comfortable with the medium. That said, there has been increasing incidence of the use of outbound telemarketing within consumer markets, though many remain sceptical of its utility. The legal requirement for organisations to clean their databases against the Telephone Preference Service lists of those who have registered as not wanting to receive unsolicited telephone calls means that outbound telephony is being encouraged to be somewhat more restrained.

The major growth within the sector has been in terms of inbound services and the rapid growth of the medium owes much to the increased use of direct response television (DRTV) advertising in the UK (Slater 1996). In addition to the effect of DRTV, the expansion of service industries and contemporary service culture, and the opening up of the telecommunications market and the introduction of freephone numbers and local-charge calls, have contributed to the rise of the telemarketing industry. Inbound telemarketing allows organisations to build and refine their databases, as we saw in Chapter 6. Such a process is invaluable to the success of an outbound telemarketing or other relational marketing programme which the organisation might initiate.

Once it is carefully planned and controlled, telemarketing, like direct mail, is highly selective in nature. Targeting is carried out in much the same way as with direct mail and telemarketing provides a quick and accurate means of collecting up-to-date and pertinent information about contacts. Future communications can thus be tailored to the needs of each contact: the information obtained can be used to build highly targeted consumer lists and follow-up strategies can be devised based on the media preferences of contacts. The profile (for example, geodemographic groups) of customers can be used to determine which 'script' is employed by the operatives.

Telephone-based contact does suffer from high costs, though these can be managed by maximising the effectiveness of the targeting process. The flexibility of it ensures that the medium can be used to contact consumers across a wide geographic area and calls can be timed to suit the contact and to provide maximum response levels.

The personal nature of telephone contact means that any queries can be resolved quickly and efficiently. The call handler may be able to develop a rapport with the contact and it may even be possible for a close relationship to be developed over time. This is less likely with what to many people is annoying: the impersonal automation that means the caller has to listen to minutes of a tune they don't necessarily like, before being asked to press a sequence of keys on their phone to access the appropriate department, via automatic call distribution (ACD). Often there will be the recorded message: 'your call is important to us but all our operators are busy, you are in a queue and your call will be answered in approximately 5 minutes'. The cynical caller may think that if the company really wanted to cultivate a relationship they would offer more personalised interaction or at least not be overly keen to cut costs by not employing enough operatives.

Customer loyalty can, however, be enhanced between sales by providing 24-hour access to the company and by using the telephone to check on customer needs and to make customers aware of new developments. Providing the customer with up-to-date information may also facilitate the achievement of programme objectives. Additionally, the two-way dialogue associated with telephone contact allows the call handler to quickly gauge the success of the marketing programme. It becomes possible to identify which techniques are working and which are enjoying less success.

Testing is also facilitated by telemarketing. The immediacy of telephone contact means that resources can be quickly deployed and elements of the marketing programme that are not working can be changed as the programme progresses. List accuracy can be also tested instantly and this helps to further improve targeting efforts and reduce wastage. Monitoring can take account of such factors as call rates, contacts reached, numbers unobtainable, positive and negative responses etc. Even the effectiveness of call handlers can be tested through the constant monitoring of their activities.

One of telephone contact's greatest advantages is the proficiency it offers in support of other media. It has been shown that the use of telemarketing as a support medium boosts success rates and provides incremental effectiveness (Roberts and Berger 1989).

The personal nature of telephone contact provides one of its major disadvantages as well as advantages. Outbound, in particular, has to be carried out with care and aforethought. It is most useful when a relationship exists between caller and contact. A telephone call from an organisation with which the contact already does business is likely to be viewed as a service and is welcomed. The very same call from an organisation that has had no previous contact is much more likely to be viewed as an intrusion (Nash 1986), and as we have stated, would be illegal if the recipient has registered with the TPS. Consider the following case study which reflects the growing use of SMS text messaging as the contact method.

CASE STUDY 10.2

Nickelodeon pushed new series through SMS

Nickelodeon sent out text messages to its 10 000-strong database of children alerting them to a new series of its most popular programme, *Sabrina, the Teenage Witch*. A new episode was to be screened every day over a four-week period in what became known as 'Sabrina September' last autumn. Apart from getting kids to tune in, the SMS messages had a secondary goal of encouraging viewers to enter a competition that would see the winners co-present the links between shows on the channel. For a chance of winning, hopefuls had to spot a 'magic letter' that would momentarily float across the screen during an episode. Over a complete week of shows, the letters added up to spell a word with a connection to *Sabrina, the Teenage Witch*. Once they'd guessed the word, kids could phone in with the answer and enter the competition. The initial message concerning the show and competition went out on the first Monday of the month, before the first episode was screened. In the first week, a second SMS was sent out on the Friday as a reminder. Messages were sent out on the Monday and Friday of all four weeks of the campaign, as the magic letter game was repeated each

→

week. 'This was the first time Nickelodeon UK had run an SMS campaign,' says Paul Lindley, deputy general manager of Nickelodeon UK. 'The feedback was that kids liked receiving messages from us, but craved a two-way dialogue.' The event, says Lindley, has paved the way for further SMS messaging of the database, this time one that comes with a reply mechanism, although Lindley stresses that all kids on the database have to get parental consent before they can be included. 'So long as the messaging is appropriate both in frequency and content, it's a good way to communicate with your audience,' he says. 'Kids are pretty savvy when it comes to messaging nowadays. 'If the messages aren't in their language or about what they're interested in, they won't work.' The Internet, video games and mobile phones have changed children's entertainment landscape dramatically, and, says Greg Childs, head of future TV at BBC youth arm CBBC: 'Right now there is the danger of *young* audiences turning away from TV.' A dwindling of children's TV audiences would create a headache for youth brands, as the box has always been an effective means of reaching children. But interactivity should be able to put everything straight on that score, ensuring TV retains its top billing in kids' entertainment. It should also boost brand communication, making it a two-way process so that children can communicate with the brands targeting them. As Dave Lawrence, planning director of brand consultancy Logistix, says: 'Young children are seeking a televisual experience that is more akin to what they get from the Internet or mobile phones.' Advertisers that are over-zealous in this area are in danger of getting a rap on the knuckles from watchdogs, and complaints have already been mounting over corporate SMS messaging; in a leaked report from a working group of the EU Commission's Directorate General for Health and Consumer Protection, the body voiced its concern over the way companies are target-

ing children through interactive communication. Nevertheless, programme creators continue to urge children to get involved with their favourite shows either via SMS or the red button on remote controls hooked up to digital televisions, which is good news for brands that want to market to kids. 'It makes it less of a passive message,' says Darrell Wade, kids' brand manager of fast-food company KFC, which has extended its sponsorship of Saturday-morning kids' show *SM:tv Live* to a section of its on-screen interactive offering. Developing a programme in this way does not take a great leap in imagination, according to Andrea Lippett, controller of iTV sales at Granada. 'Children have so little fear about new technology and they want to get involved with shows,' she adds. All children's broadcasters have an eye on building an iTV offering. Childs says all CBBC's new programmes are looked at for their interactivity potential while still on the drawing board. The BBC recently launched an interactive channel for under-fives, called CBeebies, and an interactive version of CBBC, which is aimed at six- to 12-year-olds. Both are available through digital satellite via Sky Active and digital terrestrial. Satellite digital viewers of CBeebies can choose storylines for shows featuring their favourite characters or play games. The experience for terrestrial digital viewers is less rich, with text-based interaction and fewer game-playing options. CBBC limits some of the more interesting interactive features to satellite digital viewers at present. Audiences of *The Saturday Show*, CBBC's interactive flagship, for example, can get a behind-the-scenes live broadcast of the show, request highlights of the previous week's show, or call up favourite cartoons. 'Children's programming is going to be at the forefront of the development of interactive TV,' says Childs. 'Kids don't find it difficult to interact with TV. In fact, they are demanding co-authorship of programmes. It begins at school, where they are encouraged to interact with information through CD-ROMs, for example. It follows that they'll demand some kind of interaction when they go home and watch television.' The BBC is also encouraging CBBC viewers to interact with broadcasting through SMS, under the banner 'Get Stuck In'. Viewers are asked to text daily magazine show *Xchange* with votes on issues and comments on its topical features. Meanwhile, kids' favourite *Newsround*, which now offers seven bulletins a day, is calling for editorial comments, and the between-programme presenters will soon receive votes, comments and competition entries via SMS. Childs has no fears of the BBC being swamped with text messages that could paralyse the telecommunication networks, as the current audience is relatively small. 'It's an audience whose size means texting numbers should be manageable,' he says. The channel's SMS offering has been put together by wireless youth marketing agency Aerodeon, whose managing director Andrew Jones says TV is only just catching on to text messaging's potential for developing a two-way channel of communication. 'Magazines are far ahead of TV, having built databases of readers who send and want to receive text messages,' he says. Jones believes that TV aimed at children, teenagers and young adults is catching up, though, and points to how hit TV show *Popstars* successfully integrated an SMS offering. More than 200,000 SMS messages containing gossip, behind-the-scenes insights and questions were sent to fans during the series. 'This age group is a fast-growing segment of the mobile phone audience,' he adds. 'They also love television more than they do the internet, which means combining TV with SMS is a great way to enable interaction.' Aerodeon has also worked with children's channel Nickelodeon, which targets seven- to 13-year-olds. Nickelodeon has embraced SMS and remote control interactivity, but it has yet to exploit interactive brand sponsorship possibilities. However, Paul Lindley, deputy

general manager of Nickelodeon UK, promises: 'We intend to take interactivity to another level this year.' Until now, the channel's incursions into interaction through texts and digital TV have focused on events such as the launch of series or school half-terms, which has helped it compile a database of viewers willing to receive SMS alerts. Last autumn, the channel sent out an SMS teaser message to the database telling kids to tune in to a new series of *Sabrina, the Teenage Witch*. It also sent out alerts prior to its 'Watch Your Own Week' programming event, which allowed kids to vote for the shows they wanted to watch during half-term. Neither alert came with a response mechanism for kids to reply to the message, but the channel plans to add this feature to future messages. Viewers could vote for the 'Watch Your Own Week' shows in a range of ways. The channel received 578 000 votes during the week – 293 000 via the remote control and the remainder through SMS, phone, e-mail or the website. 'Kids clearly like to interact with our channel and I see this offering great opportunities for brand communication,' says Lindley. Broadcasters are actively seeking sponsors in this area to take up some of the cost of interactivity. A brand can put up the cost of the outbound text messages and pay for, or subsidise, the cost of the return SMS or remote control vote. Simon Gunning, head of business development for interactive media at Telewest-owned Flextech, which oversees youth channel Trouble, is excited about the opportunities and envisages a raft of sponsorships in the near future. The channel is currently seeking sponsors to back SMS chat rooms, where viewers can share opinions on shows. If children's interactive television is in its infancy, interactive youth-focused iTV marketing has only just been born. But KFC's Wade is optimistic. 'Brands aimed at young audiences are definitely looking into these new communication areas,' he says. And Logistix's Lawrence adds: 'Any brand oriented to children that is actively advertising now will be looking into new fields such as interactive television.' Coca-Cola Enterprises' fruit drink brand Capri-Sun, which has a target audience of seven- to 11-year-olds, has its digital media agency i-level looking into the possibilities of iTV. 'It's something we're quite keen on getting involved in,' says Ben Simmonds, who plans and buys for Capri-Sun at i-level. The brand has already launched its own website, planetjuice.co.uk, where visitors are offered interactive games, which Simmonds believes will smooth a transition to interactive television. 'Children will have already been communicating with the brand through the Web, which should make it easier to build a dialogue through iTV,' he says, although he thinks iTV needs to improve its functionality first. 'The web is far superior in gaming at the moment. With iTV, the functionality isn't quite there.' Simmonds and Lawrence cannot agree on whether the remote control or mobile phone is the best way to interact with children. Lawrence is on the side of SMS. 'It's safer territory,' he explains. 'It's a great response route and there's a big buzz around it.' But Simmonds disagrees. 'I would have all communication go through the remote control handset,' he argues. 'It's simpler.' However, both agree that brands must be aware of the danger of falling foul of organisations such as the Independent Television Commission (ITC) due to an interactive communication strategy with children being deemed inappropriate. An EU working group recently compiled a report concluding that there were grounds for concern over the proliferation in commercial communication aimed at children leading to the compilation of personal data on youngsters. In response to this, the Direct Marketing Association has launched an information offensive called 'It's Your Choice'. Through leaflets and a website, www.its-your-choice.org.uk, the organisation informs consumers that they can legally demand a company stop sending them messages. The telecoms industry's involvement in SMS marketing is overseen by the Independent Committee for the Supervision of Standards of Telephone Information Services (ICSTIS). It fears that mobile phone owners, especially young children, are being duped into replying to text messages via premium-rate SMS services by unscrupulous businesses. The number of complaints to the ICSTIS over unsolicited messages, lack of pricing information and inappropriate subject matter has been increasing with the rising popularity in text messaging. ICSTIS, which can fine service operators or bar access to lines, wrote to all companies working in the SMS services sector calling on them to build consumer trust by stating the cost of responses if they are premium rate. 'There's great potential to exploit people, particularly children, through SMS,' says a spokesman for ICSTIS. 'It's harder to recognise whether a text message is at a premium rate compared with a telephone call, whose 090 code is normally enough of a clue.' Nickelodeon says it ensures that no reply text message can cost the sender more than 12p. The channel also asks parents to provide consent in writing (a form can be downloaded from its website) before adding kids to the database. Lindley says that apart from the fact that it's required in codes of conduct laid down by the ITC, there's a common-sense element to having parents on-side before communicating with their children. 'At the age group we're talking about, parents play a big part in their lives,' he says. Logistix's Lawrence believes that parents, especially mothers, are the gatekeepers through which brands have to pass to have an effective relationship with young children. The amount of caution needed in creating a dialogue with youngsters through SMS is similar to that required when creating branded sections on interactive television. The ITC demands transparency between what is programming and what is sponsorship. Whatever the target audience age, any branded section of a show's interactive offering must be 'two clicks' away from the broadcast stream. This means you can't suddenly go from watching a show to a section with an advertiser's message through one click of your remote control's red button, as the ITC believes it could create confusion over where the programme finishes and the advertising starts. The regulation is added to by restrictions during breaks between kids' shows, which ban commercials for alcohol, slimming products, medicines and adult films. With all these rules and the concern over communicating to kids in their language in a way that doesn't upset parents, it's no wonder brands are taking a cautious approach to marketing through iTV and mobile phones. But there is an inevitability about marketers coming to see interactive television as a great medium through which to target youthful audiences. 'Children are good at using handsets. There's the size of their hands and their experiences of gaming,' says Lawrence. 'Brands also want to create a two-way relationship with their audiences. It's a good match.' With a recent NOP survey revealing that 65% of 11- to 12-year-olds and 23% of nine- to 10-year-olds own mobile phones, and ever more households discovering digital TV, the audience is certainly there to be targeted.

What is your view of these developments? Are there dangers for children? Does this reflect good relational interaction?

(Source: Adapted by the authors from Jolley 2002)

Proper training and monitoring of personnel is vital because when used incorrectly it is all too easy for telesales to annoy. Nothing will irritate a consumer quite as much as a poorly timed, poorly conceived or poorly executed telephone call (Nash 1986). Outbound calls, however well targeted, can be inconvenient for the contact (Murphy 1997). With direct mail an unwanted solicitation can be easily discarded but with telemarketing we find it much more difficult to let the phone ring without answering it. Because outbound can be so intrusive, the initial part of a script must be geared to checking that the person is happy to talk at that moment (Murphy 1997). There is some evidence that some companies develop lists of customers who find it difficult to say 'no' over the telephone and pester them until they buy (Hughes 2002).

Consider the following case study. It reports a telephone-based campaign by a film company but attracted significant criticism and even complaints to the Advertising Standards Authority.

CASE **STUDY** 10.3

Twentieth Century Fox and *Minority Report*

In 2002, there were complaints to the Advertising Standards Authority by 19 citizens concerning a telephone message they received. The film company Twentieth Century Fox has a 'home entertainment' unit and for the launch of the DVD version of the film *Minority Report*, they used a sound clip from the film. Receivers of this telephone message were surprised to hear a man drawing breath and then saying 'Where's my Minority Report?' and then screaming: 'Do I even have one?' The voice was Tom Cruise, the star of the film. The message ended 'Don't miss out on your Minority Report. Buy it now on DVD and video.' The complaints were based on the phone message being offensive and that it could have caused distress and indeed that it did not make clear it was an advertisement. Some people who received the message had to pay to call their answer phone to retrieve the message if they had not been able to answer their phone when it was initially sent. Twentieth Century Fox Home Entertainment justified this by saying that it was only sent to those who had registered their details on the company's website (30 000 of them) and had actually asked for communications concerning films and DVDs. So the company considered it appropriate to communicate with those who had 'opted-in' for relational interaction. The company also thought that most people who had expressed this sort of interest would be familiar with Tom Cruise's voice. However, the ASA upheld the complaints on the basis that when consumers are out of the film context and going about their daily routine they would not necessarily be thinking of receiving a message from Tom Cruise and the nature of the message could indeed be seen to be somewhat menacing and could therefore cause offence.

(Source: Rosser 2002, 2003)

It is interesting to note that this campaign was actually based on a permission marketing (opt-in) strategy and perhaps even more interesting that despite the fact that complaints were upheld, the company has stated that it is likely to use a similar approach in future.

It is vital that telephone calls are carefully planned and controlled and used more often than not as part of a relationship-building programme. A blatant sales pitch should never be the first call that a consumer gets from a company.

The overheads associated with teleservicing and in particular the cost of maintaining a well-trained workforce can be very high. Automated call handling (ACH) can reduce costs but cannot always be used. The medium is also limited in terms of the amount of contacts that can be made. While traditional advertising and direct mail etc. reach large numbers of people in a short period of time, the number of telephone calls that can be made at any one time are restricted.

Although the role of technology within the teleservicing industry is increasing, the part played by people is arguably more important than ever (Darby 1996c). While technology has opened up the market for telemarketing expertise, this has effectively led to a burgeoning in the number and variety of tasks that personnel have to perform. No longer is the medium restricted to hard-sell outbound promotions. Contemporary teleservicing encompasses areas such as customer service, consumer complaint handling and technical support. This places pressure on the skills required within the industry. Having the right personnel is essential for the successful implementation of a modern teleservicing programme.

As we have already mentioned, there is convergence of media vehicles and this is especially the case between telephony and the Internet. Exhibit 10.3

EXHIBIT 10.3 Telephony and Internet integration

(Source: Aspect communications 1998 WebAgent, Demo CD, USA)

demonstrates how these two can be integrated. The customer on the left can talk over the telephone to an operative about possible investment opportunities and at the same time they can both view the same screen over an Internet connection and the operative can communicate ideas by drawing on the screen.

This brings us to the Internet as a relational vehicle, but because the next chapter explores this in greater detail, we will merely provide a brief overview at this point.

The Internet

❝ The Internet's secret: the Internet is more about people than technology. Any direct marketer needs to be clear about this. The Internet is a relationship medium uniquely suited to providing low-cost, near instant dialogue . . . Simply transposing traditional advertising and selling messages onto this new medium will not work. It is not the place for broadcasting image-building messages or sending out prospecting mail in the hunt for new business leads. But the medium is uniquely suited to developing higher levels of relationships, to establishing dynamic customer communities and allowing satisfied customers to become your champions 〞

(Cross 1994)

Originally used for scientific and military research in the USA, the Internet has evolved since the early 1970s into an elaborate communications system comprising electronic mail, thousands of specialised forums called 'newsgroups' and online 'bulletin boards' offering everything from Joan Rivers Jewellery to access to the Sunday Times Interactive Team Football. The Internet is an organic and democratic entity, owned and operated by no single authority and not covered on the whole by conventional legislation. Its rules of function or 'Netiquette' are unwritten or preserved only in a type of verbal precedence. Availing of this Marxist medium gone mad is relatively simple. An organisation using the Internet must understand and truly believe in relationship marketing, must appreciate niche marketing and not just treat the medium as the marketing equivalent of *soupe du jour*.

Relational marketers who use the Internet must remember that as a commercial environment it is highly democratic. Internet consumers can and do exercise more power than in any other marketing situation. They have ways of showing their disapproval of organisations that cross the boundaries of netiquette. These range from aggressive posting to blacklisting organisations that have defrauded customers, published misleading product information, been guilty of too much hype or simply advertised or sent direct communication where it was not wanted. This power has major repercussions for direct marketers, who can no longer use shotgun mailings.

Internet consultants emphasise the importance of delineating the objective for any proposed website (Darby 1996b). Marketers must employ cross-marketing techniques and use other communications media to drive traffic to their sites. In utilising the Internet to the fullest, organisations should take steps to capture details from those who visit the site. But just gathering information in a passive fashion isn't enough. A site must be supported with interactivity through the inclusion of offers, competitions and other means of data collection.

The Internet does have advantages over other interactive marketing media. It allows all but the smallest organisations to compete on what is more or less a level playing field, as start-up costs are relatively low. However, marketers need to approach the Internet with care. Also, hidden issues, such as the need for site development and support, can add to the cost.

The next chapter explores Internet-based relational communications in greater depth, including different models of use, such as consumer-to-consumer communities through which consumers exchange experiences of different companies or brands. Clearly companies will need to address this issue, otherwise the anarchic nature of word-of-mouse could get the better of them!

We now turn to direct response media. FEDMA (2003) describe these as mass media advertisements that carry a response mechanism for the consumer to contact the advertiser directly (for example, a coupon, telephone number or Web address).

Direct response and iTV

An area of significant growth within direct response media has been evident in the field of direct response television advertising (DRTV) and interactive TV (iTV). In excess of one in five television commercials now carry a response device (Reid 1995). Statistics such as this seem to imply that the insidious growth of direct response television advertising has the potential to swamp traditional TV advertising, while the majority remain blissfully unaware of its move into the mainstream. For many, DRTV has given direct marketing an air of respectability that had thus far eluded the industry. One could be forgiven for thinking that television advertising is something that would not sit well with direct marketers. After all, it appears to be extremely wasteful, it is ill targeted and costs are prohibitive (Fletcher 1996b). However, in the last decade of the twentieth century, consumers witnessed a veritable explosion in the communications network. There are now more television channels available through terrestrial, cable and satellite broadcasting than ever before. This revolution in television means that the various channels can now offer more tightly defined audiences. Direct response television advertising has also altered the direct marketer's perception of television campaigns. Traditional television advertising is subject to notoriously difficult measurement. DRTV, in contrast, provides instantly measurable results.

Contemporary direct response television ads take on a number of different formats. Perhaps the most famous and best loved is the infomercial, a long, tacky, low-budget affair designed to exhibit products in the manner of an in-store demonstration. These advertisements, largely broadcast in the dead of night, hope to inspire insomniacs to dust off their credit cards and take advantage of the offer of the century. While normal people enjoy the relative comfort of their beds, the insomniac is comforted by the knowledge that he or she is purchasing the *ultimate* gadget, *exclusively* available on a one-time offer only, complete with *inclusive* accessories at an *unbelievable* price of £9.99. Then there is the more sophisticated and respectable true direct response commercial which exists only to generate phone calls (Blackford 1997). Because of clever targeting the true direct response advert can side-step the expensive primetime slots so coveted by the traditional advertiser, and in so doing can avoid head-to-head competition for the viewer's limited attention. Placement around low-interest programmes are used as this makes it that bit easier to motivate the viewer to call. Within minutes of screening, the telephone lines begin to ring. Next, there is the traditional awareness ad with a last-minute inclusion of a response device tacked on at the end. In this case the inclusion of the phone number is simply a risk-free strategy designed to dispel the fears of clients. Finally, there is the most recent addition to the direct response advertising family, branding response television advertising (BRTV). Branding response television advertising, used increasingly by fast-moving consumer goods manufacturers, combines the creative brand-building properties of traditional television advertising with the measurability of response. BRTV is more about eliciting a two-way communication with consumers and does not necessarily intend to sell the consumer a product or service immediately (Darby 1996a). Today, there are numerous approaches which cultivate the brand and integrate response in the same advertisement. In so doing, the clever brand response advert can actually use the response as a branding device. Unlike DRTV, brand response aims to reach the largest audience possible. Because BRTV utilises peak viewing times it can cause problems in terms of call handling. However, it doesn't tend to generate the same level of immediate response as DRTV, the calls are shorter, and they can usually be handled by automated systems (Darby 1996a).

CASE STUDY 10.4

DRTV and iTV

At a time when the direct marketing industry is in a period of overall growth, increasing by 10% last year to reach an expenditure of £11.l4bn, you'd be forgiven for thinking it was good news all round. But according to the latest DMA Census (Marketing Direct July/August 2002), one quarter not doing so well is DRTV. The Census shows that while other DM media have been enjoying a steady increase in spend, DRTV expenditure has plummeted 26% in just one year. It fell from representing 16% of all DM expenditure in 2000, to representing 10.8%. 'It's been a bad couple of years and it is a symptom of the malaise in TV advertising in general. The budget's not what it used to be,' says Roland Mizon, marketing manager at DRTV production house Space City. But is the death knell sounding for DRTV? Pippa Easton, client services director at DM agency Clark McKay & Walpole, says she struggles to relate to the Census findings. 'A lot of our clients are going back into DRTV. There's a huge number of competing channels, so costs are low', she explains. Secondly, people are producing ads overseas where they can get high production values for low cost. This may explain why expenditure is down. Admittedly, Easton says, this mainly applies to the charity and financial services sectors but she refutes any claims that DRTV is on its last legs. Supporting this, CMW client the RSPB is actually returning to DRTV after a

five-year break. It tested it in the late 90s but stopped because it could not set up direct debits over the phone. 'Now many charities can fulfil paper-less direct debits, which has enabled them to go back into TV,' says Easton. This is all well and good, but the perception of many consumers and marketers alike is that DRTV is characterised by similar-looking charity and financial services ads. Dan Douglas, MD of DM agency DP&A, thinks that dumbing down is a big problem. 'Too many DRTV ads are formulaic,' he says. 'There's an amorphous template, particularly in financial services and charities, born of lack of ambition and a risk-averse culture.' Even the National Canine Defense League's marketing director, Adrian Burder, who spends £31 million on the medium and is a firm believer in the power of DRTV, is realistic about this view. 'In 1997 we had outrageous results,' he says. 'We still make money now, but there has been a fall. On satellite TV, there is one depressing charity after another. A certain amount of audience de-sensitisation is inevitable.'

'This is certainly one of the reasons why spend is down,' says Vincent Matthews, studio manager at DRTV production company Endorfin. 'People believe DRTV is only for charities, and if you're a marketing director, would you want to use a mechanism that people are tiring of?'

But is DRTV really restricted to charity and financial sectors? The answer is a resounding no. More companies are taking to DRTV, producing innovative and appealing ads. Tango led the way in the fmcg sector, getting into DRTV as early as 1994, working with agency HHCL. The two worked on a number of Tango's early DRTV projects still remembered today, including the Go Tan voodoo doll ads and more recently the megaphone ads showing a man being humiliated by orange-haired golfers. Viewers were asked to ring for their own voodoo dolls and megaphone. 'The voodoo ad ran for a couple of months and the phone line was open for a year,' says Richard Huntingdon, head of planning at HHCL. 'In that time we received around 400 000 calls and sent out 250 000 dolls.' In a departure from the DRTV norm, it also made money and increased brand awareness. This year has seen more fmcg brands take to DRTV, particularly cosmetics and toiletries. Pantène ran a sampling campaign between January and March this year. Aimed at driving the trial and brand awareness of Pantène Pro-V shampoo, it was a mystery unbranded campaign inviting women to ring a number and get a free sample. L'Oréal and Rimmel have also gone down similar routes. Interactive ads are also beginning to come to the fore. Mizon calls it 'a natural progression'. There are signs that advertisers are starting to look at interactivity to garner instant responses to ads. Douglas doesn't think the technology is there yet but agrees it has real potential. 'It's the place for DRTV to go at a meaningful level. Being able to click a button and make a purchase or donation has great value,' he says. The recent Depaul Trust ad using Publicis's VODKA technology took this a step further, allowing viewers to decide the narrative route of the ad themselves using iTV. However, only one platform provider, Kingston Communications, can provide this functionality so far. Matthews certainly has hope for the medium because of this potential, but also because of the players determined to take DRTV to new levels. Endorfin has recently done a DRTV ad for a watch brand, and is currently filming another ad on high-definition cameras of the type *Star Wars* was filmed with. 'We're trying to be more innovative,' he finishes. 'There is a lot of hope for DRTV, you just have to keep pushing at the boundaries.'

(Source: Adapted by the authors from May 2002)

Some direct marketers have criticised DRTV for failing to take advantage of customer response. They claim that many brand response advertisements don't take the opportunity to gather customer data when calls are made in response to the advertisement. Apple Tango, for example, no longer gathers details from callers. It has restricted itself to brand-building activities of which the response is merely a part (Darby 1996a). On the other hand, some companies are making the best use afforded by brand response advertising. Oxfam have integrated their branded advertising with a response element in order to achieve the twin objectives of soliciting donations and building the brand (Darby 1996a).

iTV

In a report commissioned by the DMA iTV has a bright future (DMA 2003). By 2002 nearly a third of advertisers had tried the medium and over three-quarters of these were pleased with the results and would consider running future campaigns. Indeed, during 2002, Sky TV saw an increase in the use of interactive commercials of 290%.

Rimmel cosmetics, for example, used an interactive advertisement through which prospects could complete an on-screen form which asked for their name, age and mobile phone number and which 'foundation' they currently used. Apparently, 63% of responders asked for further interaction (May 2003) and Rimmel cut cost per acquisition by 27%. The case study below provides a further illustration of this medium.

CASE **STUDY** 10.5

KFC adds interactive zone in *SM:tv* tie-up

Saturday-morning children's television show *SM:tv Live* extended its sponsorship by KFC to include an interactive offering launched towards the end of last month. The interactive element of the programme, aimed at children aged four to 11 as well as teens and adults, is accessed via the red button on the remote controls of digital TVs receiving either digital or terrestrial satellite. KFC linked up with the show to re-address an adult-focused bias in its marketing in previous years. It signed a year-long sponsorship of the show in November, which included a branded section on the interactive area. The fast-food chain felt that interaction between kids and the brand on iTV could be as popular as it had been via its website (www.kfc.co.uk). 'It appeared to be another great way of enabling us to communicate with a young audience,' says Darrell Wade, kids' brand manager at KFC. The interactive service offers competitions and dedicated sections on the show's presenters and guests. Viewers are encouraged to enter the area by prompts from the presenters during the show. KFC's branded section, which mirrors the look of other sections, although it features the chain's corporate red and black colours, offers games and information on menus and restaurants. In designing the interactive service, broadcaster Granada had to be aware of ITC guidelines governing the extent of product promotion allowed on interactive TV. 'The interactive offering has to be 65% editorial to 35% advertorial,' says Fiona Robertson, head of iTV at Granada Interactive.

(Source: Adapted by the authors from Jolley 2002)

Clearly, a prerequisite to the success of iTV is access to interactive television. The DMA (2003) report suggests that Sky had over 6 million subscribers to its digital interactive service (the interaction being via a telephone link to the TV programmes and commercials) and 40% of UK households have some form of digital TV service.

Direct response print media

Direct response advertising in newspapers and magazines presents the direct marketer with a cost-effective means of generating response from relatively large audiences. Both magazines and newspapers allow the direct marketer to provide substantial amounts of information, though in the case of magazines this can be further supported by high quality photography and artwork. In addition, the fragmentation of these media in recent years means that direct marketers can use them to reach more tightly defined audiences than was previously possible.

In looking in particular at magazines, Roberts and Berger (1989) suggest that the single most important criterion for selecting magazines to use in direct response advertising is the receptivity of the magazine's readership to such advertising. 'The direct marketer, then, must look not only for magazines that contain substantial amounts of direct response advertising, but also for those that continually feature direct response advertising for similar products.' Furthermore, according to Nash (1982), other considerations in using this medium will include:

- **Economics:** Because of the low cost per contact associated with magazines they may be suitable as a vehicle for direct response advertising if the margin is low or if the objective is to get information to a large number of prospects.

- **Credibility:** If the organisation and/or the product or service on offer is not very well known they might benefit from the halo effect of the magazine's own credibility. In other words, the authority and credibility of the magazine may rub off on any advertisement placed in it.

- **Lack of satisfactory lists:** If no suitable lists exist for a particular type of offer (as may be the case with innovative products), then direct response advertising in magazines may be a suitable approach as it reaches a large number of prospects. The organisation can then generate its own list as a result of the response generated by this element of the campaign.

Newspapers, too, offer a valuable means of direct response advertising to direct marketers and they also provide a number of distinct benefits (Roberts and Berger 1989):

- **Frequency:** Many newspapers are published on a daily basis and while they may only have a short shelf life, repetition serves to enforce the message of the advertiser.

- **Immediacy:** The deadline for submission of advertisements is usually pretty close to the day of publication. This allows the direct marketer to avail of up-to-the-minute information.

- **Reach:** Newspapers reach a high proportion of households in their primary geographical area. As explained earlier, access to such large markets comes with attendant advantages.

- **Local shopping reference:** Local newspapers are used by readers as the primary reference to local shopping opportunities and so represent an ideal media vehicle for local organisations.
- **Fast response:** Because of the frequency with which they are published, newspapers offer the direct marketer an excellent opportunity for close monitoring and testing of their activities.

The following case study was an award-winning one at the DMA Awards in 2001. Along with product samples and coupons being sent to kitten owners, an important direct response print media campaign was implemented.

CASE **STUDY** 10.6

Kittens

Kitten owners are most likely to be female, so Pedigree Masterfoods aimed a direct response press campaign at women offering a free Whiskas Kitten Care Pack. Along with a product sampling and mail campaign, this recruited 35% of the UK kitten-owning population. Exhibit 10.4 shows the direct response mechanism of phone and web address.

(Source: Adapted from material provided by DMA from the Pedigree Masterfoods Aware Winning Case Study, DMA/Royal Mail Awards 2001)

EXHIBIT 10.4   Direct response mechanisms

Direct response radio advertising

Direct response advertising on radio offers the direct marketer many of the opportunities afforded by its counterpart on television. According to Brook and Cary (1978), radio has a lot to commend it from an interactive marketing point of view:

- **It is ubiquitous:** The high incidence of radio ownership in the UK means that the medium is available around the clock to almost every consumer.

- **It is selective:** Fragmentation of the industry and the stylising of programme format have meant that independent radio stations in the UK reach relatively homogenous groups of highly defined target audiences.

- **It is economical:** Radio provides marketers with cost-effective reach, while production costs for radio advertising remain some of the lowest of any medium.

- **It offers rapid access:** Production times for radio advertising are relatively short compared to those for other media such as television. This means that the direct marketer can develop and air a direct response radio advertisement in a short period of time.

- **It is involving:** While many remain sceptical of the power of radio advertising, studies have shown that the personal nature of radio as a medium engages the audience. Listening to the radio, even when conducted as a secondary activity, has the ability to get the message across.

    Many people have discovered that compared, say, with television, radio can be very engrossing and personal. There is the old adage, 'the pictures are better on the radio', because the mind is able to be more active rather than merely react to how TV portrays images.

- **It is flexible:** The short lead times for production and airing of radio advertisements make it an ideal medium for testing purposes. Furthermore, should close monitoring of the campaign indicate that changes are required, these can be carried out quickly and with little cost.

CASE STUDY 10.7

AA Buyacar

The AA's radio segment of its integrated campaign promoted 'Buyacar', its online service selling nearly new and second-hand cars. 'This was amusing and brave of the AA,' said the judges. 'The ads got their point over very quickly, and the humour was excellent.' Across a range of media, the campaign compared buying a car from the AA, renowned for its skilled mechanics, with the risk of buying from strangers.

Radio was the core element. Although the ads sounded as if they were recordings of actual telephone calls, the agency in fact used highly trained improvisation artistes. The aim, of course, was to drive customers to the Buyacar web site. The site attracted over 200 000 visitors in its first four months – double the target figure. This compares with only 300 000 in two years for the comparable service from JamJar.com, the agency submitted (though the judges pointed out that the AA enjoyed the huge advantage of being an established brand). All responders and visitors to the site were added to a customer development communications programme to convert and cross-sell other AA services.

SFX	Phone being answered.
Man selling car:	Hello?
Man buying car:	Hello there, I'm calling about the car that you have advertised in today's paper.
Man selling car:	Oh excellent, excellent.
Man buying car:	Can you tell me what colour it is?
Man selling car:	Yes, it's metallic blue.
Man buying car:	And how thick is the paint on the car?
Man selling car:	(Laughs) Well, it's normal paint thickness . . .
Man buying car:	(Interrupts) It's just I need to know that it's between 80 and 120 microns, because that's the standard paint depth.
Man selling car:	(Interrupts) You what!?
Voice-over:	When you buy a used car online at AA Buyacar, the bodywork is thoroughly checked – right down to the thickness of the paint.
Man selling car:	Look, it's a standard paint job. Honestly, you can't expect me to know how many microns thick my paint is, I'm not a scientist . . .
Man buying car:	But you would be able to measure it for me while I wait? . . .
Man selling car:	(Interrupts) Of course not, I don't have that kind of equipment.
Man buying car:	You do have a micrometer, don't you?
Man selling car:	No! I have a car!
Voice-over:	AA Buyacar, You'll find us at the AA.com.

(Source: Adapted from material provided by DMA from the Automobile Association Award Winning Case Study, DMA/Royal Mail Awards 2002)

Door-to-door

Proponents of door-to-door direct marketing claim that its cost-effectiveness and new-found targetability bring it out of the basement of direct marketing media to take its rightful place alongside the likes of direct mail. Inexpensive and more accessible geodemographic targeting systems have vastly improved the accuracy with which door-to-door can be accomplished while still leaving it cheaper than its direct media counterparts.

Based on our earlier exploration of geodemographics, it is clearly possible to target at neighbourhood level, as is suggested in Exhibit 10.5.

EXHIBIT 10.5 Neighbourhood targeting for door-to-door communications

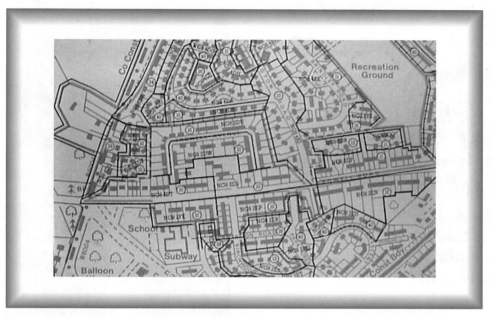

(Source: Experian Micromarketer)

Each 'circled number' might denote a different geodemographic group, thus paving the way for targeting that might even be via milk or newspaper round.

Talking of milk rounds, the following case study is an award-winning one, based on Co-operative Associated Dairies' door-to-door campaign.

CASE **STUDY** 10.8

Co-op milk

Associated Co-op Creameries had a problem: doorstep milk delivery is a shrinking market and a concept forgotten by many consumers. ACC needed to remind potential customers about the convenience of having Co-op milk delivered to their home. The solution was to be found in ACC's back yard, literally, and led to one of 2001's most evocative pieces of direct marketing. The ACC uses its own milkmen to leave empty bottles with notes for prospect households on their rounds.

The apparently handwritten note, signed by a Co-op milkman, wished them 'good morning' and a free pint of milk when they take up the service (Exhibit 10.6). The Co-op's milk bottle delighted the judges on many fronts. It had creative simplicity in using an instantly recognisable medium. 'The Co-op has plenty of spare bottles, so why not use them?' one judge asked. It also avoided the temptation to overload the message, keeping the note to a single page

→

EXHIBIT 10.6 Door-to-door campaign

> **Good Morning!**
>
> Wouldn't it be good to wake up every day with fresh Co-op milk on your doorstep? There's no delivery charge & I always deliver before 8·00am. So go on, place your order & wake up to a fresh start!
>
> Your Co·op Milkman
>
> P.S. If you order today, your first pint is free!

written in large, legible handwriting. As one judge joked, you could envisage yourself reading it at 6.30 in the morning. Prospects filled in the note and returned the bottle to the milkmen in droves: there was a 26% increase on rounds that employed the door-drop and a cost per response of less than 49p per new customer. The milk bottle has, not surprisingly, become a key weapon in ACC's acquisition armoury.

But perhaps the ACC milk bottle's biggest selling point for the judges was the door-drop campaign's effectiveness *vis-à-vis* other media. TV advertising of delivered milk, for instance, had clearly failed to stem the market's decline. As one judge summed up: 'It's a brilliant argument for why direct marketing is a better medium than any other. The milk bottle as a door-drop succeeds where conventional advertising has failed.'

(Source: Adapted from material provided by DMA from the Associated Co-op Creameries Award Winning Case Study, DMA/Royal Mail Awards 2001)

The response levels for door-to-door may not be as high as those for direct mail but its cost-effectiveness ensures its survival as a major direct marketing force. Although retailers continue to be the greatest users of door-to-door, many fast-moving consumer goods companies and financial services organisations are now using the medium to good effect.

Door-to-door marketing encompasses a number of options, including leaflets, samples, coupons (and milk bottles), though it seems that sampling offers the greatest advantages for direct marketers. Sampling allows the consumer to try the product for free, something that consumers are always going to like, and it takes the risk out of trying new products. 'Uniquely among marketing methods, sampling breaks down the adversarial psychological barrier between buyer and seller' (Denny 1995). Studies show that in the region of 95% of samples are tried by consumers and thus go some way towards influencing subsequent purchase (Sappal 1996). When launching new products, sampling probably works best if it's run in conjunction with a television advertising campaign and when the sample is coupled with a coupon or voucher. The television advertising helps to create awareness of the new product, the sample induces trial and the coupon encourages the consumer to buy the product for themselves if they like it. However, given the nature of sampling, it is better suited as a medium to products and services with wide appeal.

In recent years the remit of sampling has been widened by some organisations to include some element of market research (Derrick 1997). Data collection can be accomplished through the inclusion of data capture vehicles in prize draws etc. It is the requirement by client organisations for more up-to-date information that has encouraged samplers to get involved in market research. New technology such as hand-held computers allow door-to-door marketers to collect detailed information as they work. The client organisation can then access that information and use it to make decisions as the campaign is still running.

Kiosks

Interactive information kiosks are one of the most recent introductions to the marketer's armoury. Using touch screen technology, kiosks allow consumers to search for and retrieve the information that they want, rather than having it forced upon them by over-eager sales assistants. Kiosks have the ability to accomplish the following activities (Lord 1997):

- extending brand presence beyond existing retail sites and reaching many more potential customers;
- creating an unintimidating environment in which customers can make purchasing decisions;
- freeing up staff from answering basic enquiries;
- taking pressure off staff to make complex and under-informed recommendations;

- providing a greater range of information than a human being can offer;
- providing customers with a hard copy of the information they are after;
- allowing customers to work within a budget and compare prices easily;
- increasing awareness of complementary products and increasing average customer spend.

Kiosks also satisfy the need for specialist advice, a service which all too many sales assistants fail to provide. Furthermore, the interactive kiosk can reduce queues at checkouts as customers can find out in advance whether the product they wish to buy is in stock. Marketers need to be careful with the use of kiosks, however. This involves understanding that kiosks need to provide added value to existing retail operations. It remains unclear whether the kiosk is simply a primer, readying consumers for the onslaught of interactive technology, or whether the medium is here to stay. Whatever its future, the interactive kiosk is already providing direct marketers with yet another means of communicating personalised marketing messages (Exhibit 10.7).

The following case study, although not current, because Daewoo now has its own dealerships, does nevertheless demonstrate the sort of direct interaction that kiosks can facilitate.

EXHIBIT 10.7   Kiosks

That'll be the Daewoo

Perhaps the best-known and most successful interactive kiosk operation in the UK (was) run by Daewoo Cars. A subsidiary of the Korean industrial giant Daewoo, the company entered the UK market in early 1995. Right from the very beginning the interactive kiosk was central to its marketing strategy. Working in conjunction with Halfords and to a small extent with Sainsbury's, the company has now placed in the region of 140 kiosks around the country. The kiosks were all part of what the company views as an emphasis on customer service. They envisage themselves as being closer in orientation to high street retailers than car dealerships. They wanted to take the pressure out of buying cars and kiosks provided them with the means to carry it off. But kiosks were not the only direct marketing element of the Daewoo campaign. The launch of the cars in the UK was supported by an £11 million direct response television advertising campaign. The original direct response television advert offered UK 200 drivers year-long test drives of the new cars. Response to the offer was phenomenal and the company was able to build a list of 200 000 individuals. These individuals were then mailed a follow-up questionnaire which generated 60% response. Daewoo has been able to use the information from these activities to build up its own comprehensive database. The strategy has clearly worked. Daewoo has witnessed unprecedented success in the short time it has been operating in the UK. It has taken 1% (18 000 units) of the UK car market in its first year of operation.

(Sources: Lord 1997; Fletcher 1996a)

The UK-based Rover Group now allows prospective customers to 'configure' their own model via kiosks which have been introduced within Rover's dealers across UK and Europe.

There is a trade body that encompasses this medium: Point of Purchase Advertising International UK (POPAI). In 2001 the Acting Director General of POPAI stated: 'they offer advertising space, targeted content and response mechanisms' (Kingdom 2001).

As well as allowing prospects to order products and even 'design' them (at least state which 'options' they prefer), kiosks are, of course, deployed as data gatherers.

Some kiosks allow consumers to input their characteristics and for products to be tailored accordingly, for example Levi's provides such interactive kiosks for the 'direct' ordering of personalised jeans based on the customer's measurements. There are also an increasing number of telephone 'boxes' that act as kiosks to access the Internet.

In the next chapter, on virtual relationships, we provide a further example of kiosks. In Case 11.7 we show how the government is planning to put much of the

G2C and G2B services online, to be accessed, among other methods, via kiosks in most neighbourhoods.

Inserts

These are leaflets or other materials inserted loose in a publication. As we saw in Chapter 4, there are a variety of publications that will accept inserts, ranging from national and local newspapers to magazines.

Your own experience may suggest that such publications can sometimes be shaken over a waste bin without even looking at the inserts first. However, it does not take much of a response rate for inserts to prove cost-effective, again as we saw in Chapter 4, in the simulation (and also in the case study below). If the medium that carries the insert is carefully selected, then the old adage, 'the medium is the message', might come into play and inserts relevant to the theme and/or atmosphere of the publication can increase response rates.

CASE STUDY 10.10

Inserts

Launching the Superb, its first executive car for 70 years, was a brave move on Skoda's part, given the lingering associations with the brand's less than reliable past. A Millward Brown survey showed that 34% of potential purchasers rejected the brand. Skoda's desired new market of fleet managers might prove sceptical, not least because of the price tag of £25,000 for a Skoda. They were likely to purchase on brand first. The first step in the campaign was to conduct market research to ascertain barriers to purchase.

The findings revealed that the opportunity lay with those people who had a clear attitude to purchasing a fleet car – pragmatic and independent people who were looking for quality and value for money, rather than brand. These findings led to a media strategy of targeting key car and national press titles displaying pragmatic and independent attitudes.

Skoda wanted to promote the emotional and rational values of a Skoda to the new fleet market. The creative strategy was to have an insert showing that the Superb comes with a range of features such as air conditioning and a chilled glove box associated with more expensive cars. The 0.23% response rate was twice the forecast.

Skoda Fabia is regularly voted What Car? Car of the Year. Still, some people prefer to buy a less well-made and more expensive car. An insert aimed to save people the embarrassment of buying a supermini that was not the best in its class. Women were a target, so women's lifestyle magazines were used as well as the usual car titles. A response rate of 0.6% was achieved at a cost of £10 per head.

With the launch of the new Polo, VW wanted to appeal to a younger audience. The idea was that, because the car is so strong, owners felt they could take on the world. Two weeks after the launch of the above-the-line advertising, to exploit consumer awareness, came the insert disguised as an application form for a job as lion tamer. Response rates ranged from 0.02% to 0.66%.

(Source: Adapted from material provided by DMA from the Skoda and VW Award Winning Case Studies, DMA/Royal Mail Awards 2002)

Remember our coverage of 'testing' in Chapter 4? We provided a worked simulation that included the possible use of inserts. Our suggested response rates there might have seemed astonishingly low, but as can be seen from the above cases, there can be highly effective insert campaigns even when response rates are of this order.

Outdoor and ambient media

Traditional outdoor media such as posters are now incorporating more direct response mechanisms than ever, such as telephone numbers and website addresses. The medium is also much more technologically enabled than in the past. Billboards that have moving slants can show changing messages and the use of lights can enliven visual impact. Light-emitting diodes, for example, for a TV station, can move to the current time on electronic posters that promote that day's viewing, to show 'what's on' now. Exhibit 10.9 even shows how posters can be made interactive.

As for ambient media, this is partly a reaction to the clutter of traditional media and partly in search of more and more innovative and eye-catching communications methods. It also attempts to get beneath the emotional barriers that recipients of traditional promotion might raise because it places messages where we have not been conditioned to expect them.

Examples include messages on petrol pump handles, advertisements on the floor of stores (Safeway, for example, has used these) and the 'liveries' of buses and taxis. You can probably complete the list yourselves as more novel locations appear constantly.

The following case study is a good example of the creative use of ambient media. It was an award winner in the 2001 DMA competition.

Ambient bananas

To promote its sexual health line, the Family Planning Association recruited market stall-holders to place stickers on phallic-shaped fruit and vegetables (Exhibit 10.8). Customers were then offered a free condom.

EXHIBIT 10.8   Ambient media

Extending outdoor media via calls to action

One of new media's selling points has always been its ability to provide exact information about how many consumers see and act on ads. But being highly measurable is a double-edged sword. When the results are poor, as they often can be with banner click-throughs, it shows the medium in a bad light. Some argue that traditional media would be shown to perform just as indifferently if it could be measured to the same degree. Recording every hit of a TV ad or poster is impossible, no matter how sophisticated tracking techniques may be, they point out. However, that starts to change when advertisements invite a call to action, since their effectiveness can then be judged by the size of the response. Digital media have an increasing role to play in this, coming with offline formats to provide a greater level of accountability through direct response mechanisms. That's especially the case with posters and other ambient ads on taxis, in washrooms and on coffee cups and carrier bags. Not everyone wants the hassle and expense of holding a conversation from the street. But if they could text a message or access a WAP site and get specific information the response might be higher. The theory has been tested successfully by Rtn2Sndr, a wireless marketing agency based in Dublin, which handles campaigns for brands such as Nescafé and Fanta. Partnering with Viacom Outdoor, which handles transport media sales including London Underground and the UK's buses, it recently ran a poster campaign offering free cinema tickets to commuters who could identify the number by which James Bond is known. This won 2 000 responses within 14 days, five times greater than the level to be expected from a free-phone number. 'Accountability is something poster advertisers are not used to, so they love it when they get an effectiveness report at the end of every campaign,' says director Donald Douglas. 'The traditional new media metrics of impressions and click-throughs can be made to apply to them as much as to the Web.' One advantage of SMS is that it can extend the longevity of outdoor campaigns, Douglas adds. Consumers who receive a text message back will in many cases store it and use it to access a website as long as five weeks after the posters have come down. But as anyone who has tried to dial into a WAP site knows, tapping in a long string of letters and digits on a handset is a frustrating process. That barrier is being addressed by Bango.net, a service which provides a numeric equivalent to Web addresses in partnership with BT and operators of WAP portals. For as little as £19 each, a company can register numbers that link directly to complicated Web addresses, greatly reducing the time it takes to create a link. 'Mobile users find it difficult to enter long strings of characters, and some don't even know how to enter a forwards slash,' says Anil Malhotra, chief alliances officer at Bango.net. 'Dialling a number is second nature.'

(Source: McLuhan 2002. Reproduced from Revolution magazine with the permission of the copyright owner, Haymarket Business Publications Limited)

Exhibit 10.9 shows the use of outdoor communications that can also be interactive. The Adshell poster asked for the 'pressing' of a button under the model's bust and this then revealed information about the range of underwear (Beer 2002).

Apart from demonstrating the interactive possibilities of some traditional media, is this sexist?

Integration of relational media

A danger, especially in these times of media proliferation, is for a client company to brief different communications agencies. The campaign might involve sales promotion, direct mail, telesales and use of e-mail. Often, even though some agencies are now claiming to be 'one-stop shops', the client will need turn to

EXHIBIT 10.9   An interactive poster

different specialists (even if they are under the same roof). This paves the way for inconsistent briefing (or understanding of that briefing). Indeed, the client may need to use different sections of its own organisation to brief these fragmented specialists, so there is even further scope for lack of integration of message and media.

Peltier *et al*. (2003) propose a useful conceptual framework for linking database management (our coverage within Part 2) with interactive media, in order to achieve integrated communications (Exhibit 10.10).

The following case study demonstrates how a variety of media can be used in an integrated way to support each other and individually achieve slightly different ends. There is interactivity and much of the campaign was data informed.

EXHIBIT 10.10 Data-informed interactive IMC (Peltier et al. 2003)

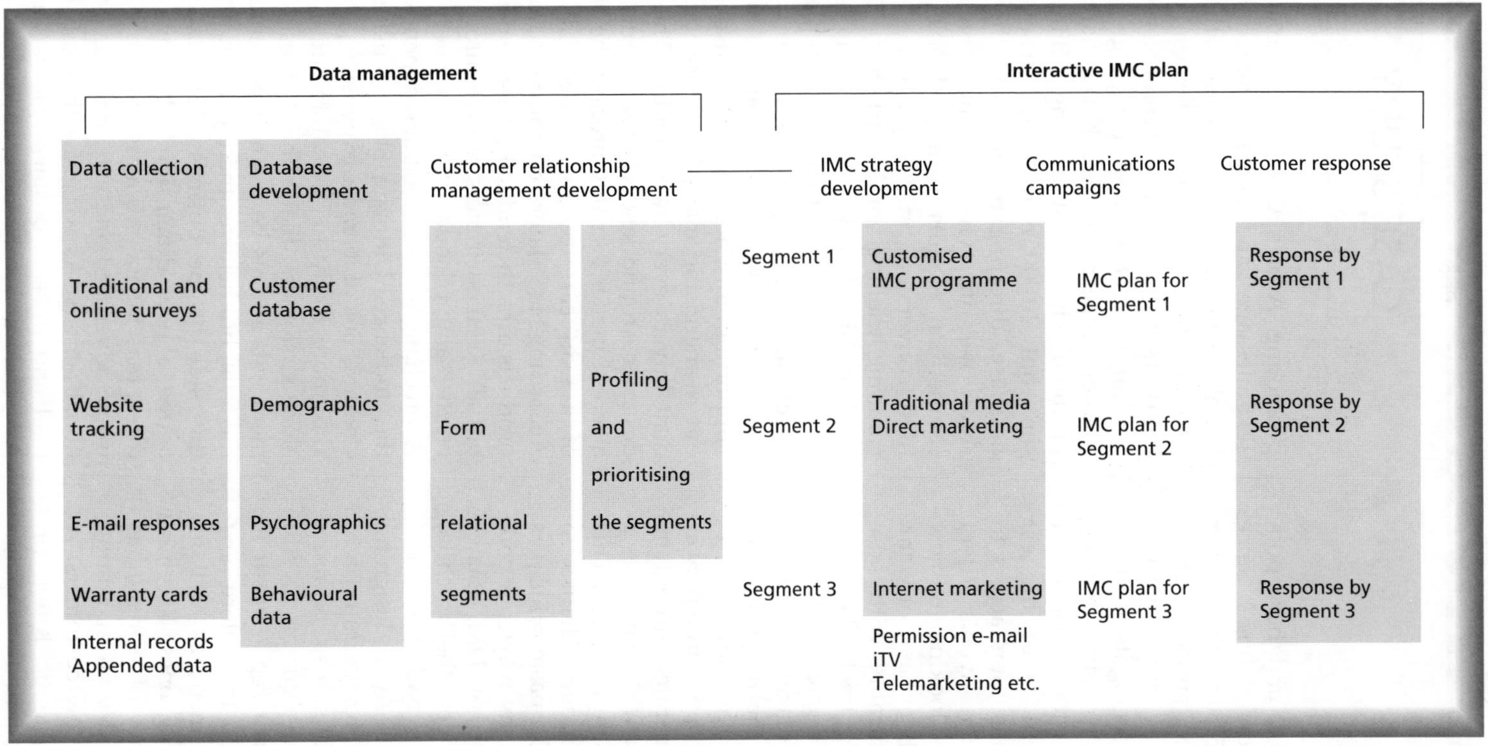

Data management

Data collection	Database development	Customer relationship management development	IMC strategy development
Traditional and online surveys	Customer database	Form relational segments	Segment 1
Website tracking	Demographics	Profiling and prioritising the segments	Segment 2
E-mail responses	Psychographics		Segment 3
Warranty cards	Behavioural data		
Internal records Appended data			

Interactive IMC plan

IMC strategy development	Communications campaigns	Customer response
Customised IMC programme	IMC plan for Segment 1	Response by Segment 1
Traditional media Direct marketing	IMC plan for Segment 2	Response by Segment 2
Internet marketing	IMC plan for Segment 3	Response by Segment 3
Permission e-mail iTV Telemarketing etc.		

More kittens

Remember the Avon lady and her eponymous greeting of 'Avon calling'? Since arriving in the UK in 1959, the direct seller of beauty products has continued to grow. Avon now has 160 000 UK representatives, with five million women seeing its brochure every week. A few things have changed over the years and now customers can order by mail, Web or e-mail. 'Our biggest challenge is in giving consumers access to Avon,' says Andrea Slater, Avon's VP of marketing. 'We're always looking for new customers but not all of them have, or want, access to a rep.' Communicating with those who prefer to shop without the help of a rep is where DM comes in. People ordering by mail, phone or Web just receive a brochure with every order, hence the importance of DM to keep up interest. This side of Avon wasn't set up until 1997, coming into play as a result of the demand generated through its advertising activity, all of which includes a phone number and Web address. This wasn't too difficult a move. Thanks to Avon's selling method, the basic principles were already there. 'In many ways our core business uses techniques of DM,' Slater explains. 'The consumer gets the brochure and the buying decision is made from this.' This experience also led to Avon designing its direct mail in-house. Five years on and the DM side of the business remains relatively small scale – most customers still prefer to buy through their rep – but it is providing a way for Avon to explore new channels to attract customers, as well as communicate with existing ones. Recently Avon, working with agency Bluestreak, has turned to e-mail, SMS and viral marketing as a way of bringing in new customers. A tie-in with pop group Atomic Kitten (in 2002) produced an integrated campaign

promoting Avon's Color Trend make-up. Text messages and e-mails went out to a largely teen audience, directing them to Atomic Kitten and Avon's websites. Following on from this success, Avon recently ran a viral marketing trial campaign called Mission Impeccable, which ran nationally promoting its nail wear range. Bluestreak sent out 20 000 e-mails to an external database, directing recipients to the main Avon website with the incentive of a competition. Results were good. 'We had a high conversion rate,' says Slater. 'We'll continue trialling viral marketing.' Direct mail is also used to reactivate lapsed customers. If the customer fails to place an order nine weeks after receiving a brochure, Avon sends them a reactivation mailer. Supporting this activity, Avon also sends out re-energising mailers to these independent buyers every two months. These are designed around key brochure events, with a recent mailer focusing around the launch of a skin care product called Ultimate. According to Slater, customers ordering products directly tend to be bigger spenders, but all Avon customers receive information on the same products. So, with every offer, Avon changes the proposition depending on the audience. Ultimate Skin Transforming Cream is one of its more expensive products and more likely to appeal to these go-it-alone customers. Slater thinks these customers will always be a small percentage of the total, but believes there is room to grow this side of the business. 'The Internet's added a new dimension,' she says. 'The direct mail business is a result of how much we've advertised and extended our promotional activity. As we grow this, our direct mail and Internet business grows with it.' All roads at Avon seem to lead to direct marketing. 'DM leverages so much of what we're doing so we get a very good ROI,' says Slater. And, with Christmas coming up, more DM activity is planned, so expect to hear 'Avon calling' somewhere near you soon.

(Source: Adapted from Anonymous 2002)

Summary

- In view of the tremendous success experienced so far by the industry, one would clearly expect growth to continue. The trend is already moving away from direct marketing as a stand-alone tactical element of the promotions mix. 'Indeed the vision of these media (telephone, mail, door-to-door) as being the "core" media of direct marketing, able to operate on their own and deliver results, is one of the past, rather than the present and the future' (Henley Centre 1995).

- The move towards direct response has dual benefits: it will facilitate more accurate targeting as a result of requests *from* consumers, thereby reducing 'junk' mailings, and it will allow marketers to move from prospecting to relationship building, an approach will require a totally integrated marketing and communications mix.

- Integrated marketing communications and direct response mechanisms imply that marketers will continue to bear the costs of traditional above-the-line approaches (although perhaps at reduced rates due to the choice of off-peak slots). But at the same time we see more personalised media such as the Internet, telephony and mail continuing strong growth.

- Companies will continue to demand further improvements in targeting capabilities, a demand which should continue to be met by technological advances, as we saw in Chapter 6. However, consumers are already exhibiting concerns over how parts of the industry operate. In particular, they are concerned with intrusions of their privacy, sale of their data, and some segments of the population (ABs, over-35s and the grey market) are already experiencing 'clutter' via the volumes of direct targeting they experience (Evans *et al.* 1995). These issues will clearly need to be addressed in the future and we explore some of these in Chapter 13.

Review questions

1 How would you use kiosks in a direct marketing strategy for any other marketing campaign?

2 What are the relative contributions to interactive relational marketing of direct mailings?

3 To what extent do you believe that the Internet will be a major force in direct marketing through this millennium?

4 What are the relative contributions to interactive relational marketing of telemarketing?

5 What are the relative contributions to relational marketing of direct response and interactive media advertising?

6 Do you approve of the use of SMS messaging as described in the 'Minority Report' case study? Why, and what are the issues that this raises?

Further reading

Fairlee, R. (1993) *Databased Marketing and Direct Mail*, Guildford: Kogan Page.
Kobs, J. (1992) *Profitable Direct Marketing*, Chicago: NTC Business Books.
Nash, E.L. (1986) *Direct Marketing*, New York: McGraw Hill.
Stone, B. (1996) *Successful Direct Marketing Methods*, 5th edn, Lincolnwood, IL: NTC Business Books.

References

Acland, H. (2002) 'A Slice of the Action', *Marketing Direct*, pp. 37–41.
Anonymous (1992a) 'The Miserable Life of The Careful Consumer', *Marketing*, 17 September, p. 20.
Anonymous (1992b) 'Telemarketing and What It Can Do For You', *Marketing*, 13 February, p. 20.
Anonymous (1997) 'A Catalogue of Failure?', *Marketing Direct*, June, pp. 20–1.
Anonymous (2002) 'Avon Tries New Channels', *Marketing Direct*, October, p. 21.
Aspect Communications (1998) WebAgent Demonstrations CD-ROM, San Jose, CA.
Barwise, P. and Styler, A. (2002) *Marketing Expenditure Trends*, London: London Business School/Havas and Kudos Research.
Beer, R. (2002) 'MCBD Creates Interactive Poster in First Campaign for Pretty Polly', *Campaign*, 1 November, p. 8.
Blackford, A. (1997) 'Never Mind The Quality', *Marketing Direct*, April, pp. 46–51.
Blattenberg, R.C. and Glazer, R. (1994) 'Marketing In The Information Revolution', in R.C. Blattenberg, R. Glazer and J.D.C. Little (eds.) *The Marketing Information Revolution*, Boston: Harvard Business School Press.
Brook, A.C. and Cary, N.D. (1978) *The Radio and Television Commercial*, Chicago: Crain Books, p. 11.
Brown, C. (2001) 'Easy Group Steals March on In-Store', *Precision Marketing*, 10 August, p. 12.
Couldwell, C. (1997) 'Dawn of the Machine Age at the Royal Mail', *Marketing Direct*, March, pp. 60–70.
Cross, R. (1994) 'Internet: The Missing Marketing Medium Found', *Direct Marketing*, 20(9), pp. 37–46.
Darby, I. (1996a) 'Calling For Attention', *Marketing Direct*, September, pp. 58–64.
Darby, I. (1996b) 'Spinning A Web Site', *Marketing Direct*, September, p. 31.
Darby, I. (1996c) 'The Right Staff', *Marketing Direct*, November, pp. 55–60.
Darby, I. (1997) 'Marketers Suffer Lack of Response', *Marketing Direct*, July/August, p. 10.

Denny, N. (1995) 'Sampling Takes The Top Slot For Launches', *Marketing*, 4 May, p. 8.

Derrick, S. (1997) 'Reaching A Captive Audience', *Marketing Direct*, June, pp. 37–40.

DMA (2003) *iTV – Coming of Age*, London: Direct Marketing Association.

DMIS (1995) *DMIS Factbook*, London: Direct Mail Information Service.

Evans, M.J., Patterson, M. and O'Malley, L. (1995) 'The Growth of Direct Marketing and Consumer Attitudinal Response' *2nd annual Conference on Advances in Targeting, Measurement and Analysis for Marketing*, London, 7–8 June, pp. 5–16.

FEDMA (2003) *Survey on Direct Marketing Activities in Europe*, Brussels: Federation of European Direct Marketing Associations.

Field, L. (1997) 'Hail The New Order', *Marketing Direct*, July/August, pp. 60–6.

Fletcher, K. (1996a) 'Dawning of a New Daewoo', *Marketing Direct*, May, pp. 36–9.

Fletcher, K. (1996b) 'Vera Goes A-Wooing', *Marketing Direct*, December, p. 32.

Henley Centre (1995) *The DMA Census of the UK Direct Marketing Industry*, London.

Hill, M. (1993) 'Delivering the Personal Touch', *Direct Response*, November, pp. 43–5.

Hughes, I. (2002) reported in *Precision Marketing*, 28 June.

Jolley, R. (2002) 'Get Them While They're Young', *Revolution*, 13 March, pp. 26–9.

Kingdom, M. (2001) as reported in Brown, C. (2001) 'Easy Group Steals March on In-Store', *Precision Marketing*, 10 August, p. 12.

Lord, R. (1997) 'Death of the Car Salesman', *Revolution*, July, pp. 38–40.

May, M. (2002) 'DRTV's New Direction', *Marketing Direct*, October, pp. 35–7.

May, M. (2003) 'Interactive Ads Winning Support', *Marketing Direct*, May, p. 11.

McLuhan, R. (2002) 'Call to Action', *Revolution*, 23 January, pp. 26–7.

Murphy, C. (1997) 'Coming In From The Cold', *Marketing Direct*, June, pp. 51–2.

Mutton, E. (2001) as reported in Brown, C. (2001) 'Easy Group Steals March on In-Store', *Precision Marketing*, 10 August, p. 12.

Nash, E.L. (1982) *Direct Marketing: Strategy, Planning, Execution*, New York: McGraw Hill.

Nash, E.L. (1986) *Direct Marketing: Strategy, Planning, Execution*, 2nd edn, New York: McGraw Hill.

Peltier, J.W., Schibrowsky, J.A. and Shultz, D.E. (2003) 'Interactive Integrated Marketing Communication: Combining the Power of IMC, the New Media and Database Marketing', *International Journal of Advertising*, 22, pp. 93–115.

Reid, A. (1995) 'Can DRTV Really be the Advertising of the Future?', *Campaign*, 14 July, p. 11.

Roberts, M.L. and Berger, P.D. (1989) *Direct Marketing Management*, Englewood Cliffs, NJ: Prentice Hall.

Roman, E. (1988) *Integrated Direct Marketing*, New York: McGraw Hill.

Rosser, M. (2002) 'ASA to Probe 20th Century Fox Campaign', *Precision Marketing*, 6 December, p. 1.

Rosser, M. (2003), 20th Century Fox to Persist with Voicemail Ads', *Precision Marketing*, 14 February, p. 1.

Sappal, P. (1996) 'Sampling The Market', *Direct Response*, November, pp. 63–4.

Shine, T. (1994) 'The Use of Targeting by Consumer Packaged Goods/Fast Moving Consumer Goods Companies', *Journal of Targeting, Measurement and Analysis for Marketing*, (2), pp. 105–14.

Slater, J. (1996) 'A Tightly Targeted Business', *Marketing Direct*, May, pp. 42–54.

Taylor, T. (1995) 'Direct Mail', *Campaign*, 19 August, p. 27.

Titford, P. (1994) 'Self-Regulation in Direct Marketing', *The Journal of Database Marketing*, 2(2), June, pp. 141–50.

TQC/Ogilvy and Mather Direct 1991, cited in Henley Centre (1991) *Positive Response*, p. 80.

Young, M. (1994) 'Direct Response Television', *Journal of Targeting, Measurement and Analysis for Marketing*, 2(2), pp. 125–38.

11 Virtual relationships

Learning objectives

Having completed this chapter, students should:

- Be aware of the Internet as a vehicle for developing relationships between organization customers.

- Undersatnd customer interactions with organisations via the Internet in terms of emerging models of e-commerce.

- Appreciate the potential for enhanced relationships of the commercial exploitation of online communities.

Levi's

'Lostchange.com' was part of a multimedia 'advertainment' adventure aimed at introducing the Silvertab jeans range to the 15- to 24-year-old 'urban nomad' audience. It also aimed to continue the brand's ongoing positioning as 'equipment for urban living'.

The campaign, which ran from July to November (2001), used online film, interactive games, e-commerce, rich-media ads, e-mail marketing, TV, print, direct mail and point-of-sale materials to achieve its goals.

Hollywood screenwriter Ernest Lupinacci, editor Barry Alexander Brown and photographer Albert Watson created an interactive, online film, *Lost Change*, which was released in weekly episodes between one and three minutes in length. It depicted a bag of money that was planted in a street and recipients who were filmed by a mysterious group of people known as The Agency. It was accessible from Lostchange.com, MTV2, AtomFilms and Real.com.

As well as hosting the film, the Lostchange.com website offered tie-in content such as games to hone users' agent skills, information on the gear needed to be a good agent and profiles on the main characters in the film.

(Source: DMA Awards 2002)

Introduction

The opening vignette won the prize for the best integrated campaign and the judges of the competition were impressed by the results of the campaign in terms of visitors attracted to the website as well as the integration of the wide range of complementary media employed. The e-mail campaign was based on Levi's internal database as well as partner databases (such as Atomfilms) and resulted in very high 'open rates'. The interactive nature of the case plus the possibility of online purchase is a good illustration of the integrated use of the Internet and how this medium can facilitate relational marketing, and this is the theme of this chapter.

The chapter is not concerned with e-commerce and online marketing *per se* because there are plenty of texts that deal with this (see further reading). Instead, the focus here is more on how online interaction can enhance relationship development and maintenance.

It is clear, though, that with the advent of e-commerce, communication technologies such as the Internet and e-mail marketing have become an essential way of integrating the different value-chain activities that we introduced in Chapter 8. These are also effective in reducing production times and costs (Chaffey *et al.* 2003). We have already discussed the role of new technology in fuelling the trend towards interactive and relational marketing. Also, in earlier chapters, we have explored 'data' in the form of internal transactional data and external 'overlays' and profiling data such as geodemographics and lifestyle data. However, as we have seen in Chapter 10, there is a range of new media arising from technological developments and the Internet is clearly a major example here. It can facilitate different forms of organisation–customer interaction.

This chapter's theme is the role of the Internet in relational interaction. We start with a brief outline of some of the mechanics of the Internet and provide indications of how the medium has developed and grown. We then explore its role and nature in relational marketing.

We discuss new models of interaction that reflect significant shifts of control from organisation to consumer and suggest that it is important not merely to provide static information via the Internet, but to provide more interactive transactional sites, which are linked to back-office systems containing customer data which can be accessed in real time.

Internet basics

Hamill and Gregory (1997) define the Internet as 'a global network of inter-linked computers operating on a standard protocol which allows data to be transferred between otherwise incompatible machines'. This protocol, termed 'Transmission Control Protocol/Internet Protocol' (TCP/IP), originated from a network set up by the US Department of Defense in the 1970s (Ellsworth and Ellsworth 1996). By the introduction of high-speed networks and other enabling technologies such as 'integrated browser packages', the Internet has developed from a network dedicated to defence and research to a 'network of networks', whose participants include governments, universities, companies and individuals, to name but a few. Clearly, this provides great potential for the sort of knowledge management and data alliances discussed in Chapter 8.

One 'phenomenon' which has been allowed to develop on the back of this interconnectivity is the 'World Wide Web' (WWW) or 'Web' for short. The World Wide Web, described by Winder (1996) as 'a hypertext-based information exploration tool', allows information to be produced using HyperText Mark-up Language (HTML) and comes in the form of 'Web pages' or sites. Like the Internet, the Web revolves around another protocol known as HyperText Transfer Protocol (HTTP). This allows a 'web browser' (or graphical user interface (GUI), for example Netscape Navigator and Microsoft's Internet Explorer) to communicate with Web servers on remote computers (Ellsworth and Ellsworth 1996). Hypertext was popularised and developed by Tim Berners-Lee at the European Particle Physics Laboratory (sometimes referred to as CERN) in the early 1990s (December and Randall 1995). Such has been the pace of development in recent years that the Web now allows users to interact with websites through text, sound, pictures and video.

XML for data interchange

XML enables people and companies to exchange information more clearly and completely than previous formats. It capitalises on two key trends in the electronic world: the growing use of websites for information distribution and the increasing use of electronic ordering and invoicing. XML can make websites more usable by making them more easily searchable, while simultaneously easing the difficult transaction of business-to-business communication by providing intelligible standards for data interchange. XML enables developers to create documents that both humans and machines can read. It provides a well-structured way of formatting and storing data using mark-up tags that look like labels in English (or any other language). The computer uses these mark-up tags to identify and direct it to the data it needs for processing. XML also provides the flexibility for data interchange between systems as it can be used to represent the contents of a relational database or even an object-oriented database. In addition to this, its structure of storing data enables programmers to interpret and manipulate data easily. The strong structure of XML makes it easier to create information that can be used by multiple processing applications and even extremely different processing applications.

EDI and XML

Electronic data interchange (EDI) systems have been used over the past 50 years to establish an infrastructure for exchanging information electronically. EDI systems have used data in structures that are fixed length or delimited fields neatly ordered into a file or table for processing. Although the method of transmission of data has changed drastically over the years – from mailing data tapes to directly connecting over data networks – the form of information sent in EDI hasn't changed at all. The technical architecture of EDI is too limited to absorb new ideas and methods of business interactions and, with the speed at which businesses are changing and evolving, EDI is unable to address new business needs. This is primarily because of its narrow focus of using one global exchange and routing protocol and its inflexibility in accommodating new types of data. EDI systems could only handle data in an agreed fixed format and any new changes to the format would involve major system changes. Also, the format used in EDI was highly customised and could not be used as a generic format for data exchange with multiple organisations, thus restricting its use only between companies who have strong partnerships.

XML offers businesses more flexibility than their current systems can offer, along with opportunities to create simple standards that can be extended to cover additional data structures as necessary.

Growth of e-marketing

Much has been written in the press concerning the development and importance of the Internet. On the other hand, Morgan (1996) stated that 'accurate figures regarding the use of the Internet and World Wide Web (WWW or "The Web") are impossible to obtain'. The technology may have advanced since that time, but the diversity of the domains involved still makes it difficult to provide meaningful figures. However, a common theme from all sources is that the Internet and World Wide Web are growing at a phenomenal rate. This new medium potentially offers a variety of opportunities for companies to communicate individualistically and to build long-term relationships with consumers.

However, some useful figures are provided by Barwise and Styler (2002) who report the shift from media advertising to the more direct and interactive forms of marketing communications. They show that across a range of countries (the USA, UK, Japan, France, Germany), chief marketing officers saw reductions of 2% in expenditure on media advertising from 2001 to 2002 and expected only a 1.6% increase from 2002 to 2003. In contrast, they saw direct mail expenditure increasing by 3.8% from 2001 to 2002 and expect a further increase of 7.4% from 2002 to 2003. But when it came to the 'interactive marketing' category (Internet, e-mail) these senior marketers saw a year-on-year spending increase of 6.6% between 2001 and 2002 and expected a further growth by over 19% from 2002 to 2003. Indeed, November 2002 was the first month when consumer purchasing via the Internet alone topped £1bn., showing continued expansion in both organisations' and customers' use of this interactive medium. The early years of the 21st century also saw, for the first time, some high-profile online companies beginning to make profits via their online activity (e.g. Amazon.com).

In parallel with marketers' engagement with the Internet (DMA 1998), consumers are also participating in dealing with organisations by direct methods on the part of consumers and the era can rightly be described as not only one of the 'direct marketer' but also one of the 'direct consumer' (Evans *et al.* 2001).

There is substantial evidence to suggest that e-banking, for example, is being significantly embraced by financial institutions and their customers. Research estimates that globally by 2003 more than 32 million households were banking online, which is well above the 6.8 million in 1998 (Simpson 2002). The Internet is eclipsing other electronic channels of delivery because of its convenience – but also because of its cost. It could be estimated that a financial transaction conducted within a branch of a bank might be in the order of 68p, but via the telephone it might be nearer 37p and online it might only be around 7p. The implications for cost control and indeed for disintermediation in other sectors are clear.

Since its creation, the Internet has provided the infrastructure for greater marketer–consumer interaction. A movement that began with e-mail and mailing lists and a few newsgroups has already grown into a series of virtual communities. With the growth of the World Wide Web interface, the potential has been unleashed for the widespread creation of online virtual communities on a commercial basis. As Loader (1998) has observed:

“ the global communication networks which make up cyberspace are claimed to be altering almost every facet of our lifestyles, including patterns of work and leisure, entertainment, consumption, education, political activity, family experience and community structures. **”**

E-relationships

As we have seen, relationship marketing is concerned with all the activities directed towards attracting, developing and retaining customer relationships. The Internet provides ample opportunity for organisations to learn about their customers over time by tracking their purchases and even, via cookies and 'SpyWare', their paths around the Web itself and therefore to reveal related interests. This latter point raises ethical and privacy issues which we take further later in Chapter 13.

Many of the main elements of relationship marketing come from research in industrial marketing which indicate that relationships are complex, long-term in nature, and mutually beneficial. It is no surprise, therefore, that the first area of marketing to take up the Internet on a significant scale (within its own sector) has been B2B. If relationship marketing is to be successfully applied within consumer markets, then such 'relationships' should incorporate these integral elements. Accordingly, the Internet provides a potentially useful vehicle for implementing such relationship marketing more widely – as we shall now explore and the following case is a useful example of how relationships can be developed online.

CASE STUDY 11.1

E-relations

Hypnosis Media takes artist promotion straight to fans

Hypnosis Media has designed numerous acclaimed music websites, including nme.com and Worldpop, as well as artist-specific sites for Pink Floyd, Craig David and Blur, among others. But it is also behind some innovative online marketing and viral tools that have helped promote new material. For Robbie Williams, Hypnosis developed the 'Robster' desktop application, designed to promote the *Swing When You're Winning* album. The downloadable application (from www.robbiewilliams.co.uk) sits on the fan's desktop, pumping updated news straight to the user. The application also provides a live chat facility – again on the user's desktop – and a Windows Media Skin, all branded in line with the artwork for the album. 'The exciting thing about this application is that it takes the music, the chat, and other value-added stuff to the user,' says Hypnosis head of account management Scott Muir. 'It is also highly visible branding.' Hypnosis has also produced numerous e-cards. A good example of the genre is one that Warners commissioned to promote Madonna – it is still active (www.madonnaghv2.co.uk). Once the card has been sent, Warners can update the content, thus expanding the shelf life of the card. The Madonna card has other features, including a special stamp collection viral incentive. Other techniques used by Hypnosis include skins – branded designs for Windows Media Players created for clients including animated band Gorillaz – and viral games. Three games have been developed for Travis, including the 'Sing Fling' game (available on www.travisonline.com), which generated 100 000 game plays and was even mentioned on Radio 1. Last year, Hypnosis created an online game for ex-Spice Girl Geri Halliwell based on her *Scream If You Wanna Go Faster* video. The game allowed players worldwide to play against each other online by racing a 'Geri' avatar.

(Source: Muir 2002, Reproduced from *Revolution* magazine with the permission of the copyright owners Haymarket Business Publications Limited)

We have constantly asserted the importance of interactivity in practical relational marketing and Sutherland (1996) has identified two kinds of interactive communication:

1 where the reader interacts with the message (e.g. CD-ROMs), and
2 where the reader interacts with the messenger (e.g. direct mail, telephone).

The Internet encompasses both kinds of interactive communication but 'probably the most valuable benefit which the net offers is that of the second kind of interactivity, that of establishing and maintaining a mutually profitable individual relationship over time'. Swinfen-Green (1996) states that interactive marketing has three advantages:

1 By asking an audience to respond to a message, people are more likely to retain information more accurately and for longer. We explore this in more detail in the next chapter on 'relational messages'.

2 Recipients can filter the information which is relevant to them at their own pace at any given time – if information is missed or not fully understood, a person can return or request more information.

3 Recipients can be allowed to customise the information they receive.

Online communications like that of the Internet and World Wide Web have several advantages over off-line systems:

- Information can be updated constantly.
- Over time, information released can be controlled – for example, out-of-date information can be isolated or deleted.
- They can offer an online user the option of entering into two-way communication or 'dialogue'.

Hoffman and Novak (1996) have studied the nature of the Internet and Web as communication media. They make a useful distinction when they state that *e-mail* is an example of a *'one-to-one'* communication medium, where as the *Web* is described as a *'many-to-many'* medium. Considering the nature of such media, their potential, either alone or when combined, can facilitate direct and in particular relationship marketing. 'One-to-one marketing', according to Greene (1996), is facilitated by the Internet when one considers that the Internet:

1 fosters two-way communication – the only medium other than personal selling that can truly provide immediate give and take;

2 provides advertising 'on demand';

3 shifts the point of purchase to the individual – changing the way companies market, sell and deliver products;

4 cuts advertising 'waste'.

Jones (1996) states that 'marketers can use e-mail in two ways beneficial to building the dialogue of relationship marketing':

1 'to use it to deliver a target message to a focused group of consumers within a particular market';

2 'to develop the fabled one-to-one relationship by maintaining a regular dialogue'.

The former is usually facilitated by companies who have influence over a usergroup's e-mail or integrated browser software and is often done in conjunction with the Web. Electronic mail, as described in both of the cases above, is a 'one–one' communication device. The ease with which it can be used, in particular with the WWW, should not be underestimated. Sending (whether direct of via a website) or replying to an e-mail can be made to be as easy as clicking or pressing on one button – 'the reply button'. When one considers the effort and processes involved in using other interactive marketing media, the convenience of using e-mail in 'two-way' communication would apparently be far more attractive to consumers – especially when one considers that the whole dialogue can be initiated and maintained while the consumer is in the comfort of his or her own home. This allows the consumer to be more proactive and this in turn shifts a degree of control in their favour. This is an issue to which we return in Chapter 13 when we suggest that this can help to overcome some of the concerns over personalised marketing.

E-reciprocity

The reciprocal nature of relational interaction is facilitated by the Internet, which allows 'individuals and organisations to communicate directly with one another regardless of distance and time' (Berthon *et al.* 1996a). Swinfen-Green (1996) also states that dialogue 'is very important to marketers who are able to solicit feedback about products and services, create customer loyalty through the development of "club like" sites, initiate transactions including sales, capture information . . . about potential customers, and carry out market research'.

Berthon *et al.* (1996b) also on the subject of interactivity, differentiate between website visits and hits. A *'visit'* implies an element of interaction between the 'surfer' and the Web page, whereas, in the case of a *'hit'*, the 'surfer' generally does nothing with the information on the site. From an organisation's perspective, the concept of interactivity of website 'visitors' will be valuable if not critical to building relationships online and these can be taken back into the real world. Poon and Jevons (1997) suggest evidence that there is 'considerably greater (by a factor of two to three, depending on the quality of site) likelihood of purchase at a retail level as a result of Web communications'. So, in terms of relationship building, this could provide evidence that the Internet has a real role to play in assimilating relationships which translate from online to real life.

Relationship knowledge and measurement

One of the fundamental building blocks to any relationship is that of one party's knowledge of another. According to Glazer (1991), '"Knowledge is power" is a well established social principle, and a major determinant of marketing power has always been the levels of information possessed by agents.' Further, they say that 'in the short run and in any given situation, depending on the context (and in particular who knew more originally), the balance of power might shift in the direction of buyers or sellers'. We have already alluded to the potential importance of such a shift of control and this statement reinforces the point.

From the consumer's perspective such relationship knowledge might be, in the first instance, limited to what an organisation allows to be communicated to the consumer via both the Internet and World Wide Web and other communications media. But due to the nature of the Internet and Web, the 'power of information gathering' might eventually be in favour of the consumer.

The Web, in itself, is a powerful research tool which otherwise might not normally be available to a consumer. Such a tool, if used, could provide additional information on an organisation (maybe published by a national or international third party) that could influence the development of a relationship.

This potential for consumer knowledge and therefore control could, at first sight, actually hamper an organisation's use of this medium, but we argue that it is exactly this that can lead to a more level playing field, upon which there is greater potential for mutuality in relational interaction.

Hamill and Gregory (1997) discuss the impact on prices: 'the net will lead to increasing standardisation of prices across borders, or at least, to the narrowing of price differentials as consumers become more aware of prices in different countries'. This potential threat to organisations wanting to build relationships through online communications and transactions might be solved by the use of local language, but hindered by the enhancement of language ability – including the growing use of computerised translators – by consumers in different countries.

From an organisation's perspective, 'relationship knowledge' can be developed quite naturally via the use of the Internet and World Wide Web. There are a number of ways in which an organisation can assimilate this knowledge of consumers:

- **Use of website statistics in log files**: 'visitors to websites can be tracked without their knowledge and software, especially for this purpose, can produce statistics on what content was viewed, for how long and by whom.
- **Monitoring 'cookie files'**: These are files within a browser where, through the use of tags, a site recognises whether a user has visited a website before and subsequently has a record of how they behaved last time.
- **Online forms**: These are 'data entry spaces' on websites, linked to a database, which allow users to input information. Forms can be designed to be optional or compulsory before allowing users to navigate further into the website. Possible uses of forms can be to gather demographic data, registration information (e.g. e-mail addresses) or more comprehensive information through online questionnaires.

The above methods of monitoring can provide valuable information which an organisation can use to develop profiles, tailor its communications and develop 'one–one' relationships accordingly.

The following case study provides useful information on Web measurement techniques.

CASE **STUDY** 11.2

Web measures

The value given to a website by its community is hard to measure, but music site Worldpop (www.worldpop.com) aims to do just that. It has a database of details on about 200 000 of its 250 000 unique users. This information can be broken down by the category of music they prefer. Users are mostly aged from 12 to 35, but the site's core market is 16- to 24-year-olds. Community is the cornerstone of the website's offer, and its message boards average 2 000 new postings a day on subjects such as the best song on the new Red Hot Chili Peppers album. Increasingly, Worldpop seeks to harness the power of its community to help clients with their marketing and measurement. Message board monitor Nurse Pop (real name Monica Stephen) is charged with recruiting Worldpop panels consisting of community members. These help create a buzz around new music community members to join 'eteams'. This turns music-lovers into marketing activists, who are encouraged to tell the world about the new songs of their favourite artists (or indeed other products) to help create a buzz and increase sales. In return, eteam members are rewarded with access to the latest pop gossip, exclusive merchandise and prizes. Eteams were used to boost interest in pop band Liberty X and to help promote the launch of series six of *Buffy the Vampire Slayer* on video. 'Moderation of our message boards is in-house, as we felt external moderators weren't doing it properly,' says Donia Salah, head of interactive marketing at Worldpop. 'We carry out qualitative studies on our audience. This helps clients measure, prior to release, which products go down well with which kind of audience.'

(Source: Salah 2002. Reproduced from *Revolution* magazine with the permission of the copyright owner, Haymarket Business Publications Limited)

The blend of quantitative and qualitative measurement in this case is in accord with our perspective of research, as explored in Chapters 4 and 5.

E-relational networks

Our earlier discussion of alliances and consortia is taken further here. Organisations are building electronic links with their partners and suppliers. Their goal is to take advantage of the efficiencies that flow from e-collaboration, whether for buying and selling, jointly designing products, co-marketing, improving customer services or information sharing. The collaborative technologies that are available these days can allow organisations to cut administrative costs and pass these benefits on to their customers in the form of lower prices (not that they always will!). What some organisations are looking for is integration with partner, suppliers and customers, in the mould of the networked relational marketing paradigm we have discussed in previous chapters.

Consider the following case study. This is a good example of an alliance (albeit a short one in this case) that was mutually beneficial for both partners.

KitKat/MSN

This relates to a link between Nestlé Rowntree and MSN (Microsoft Messenger) in 2001. Nestlé Rowntree wanted to emotionally (re)engage its market in its familiar associations with 'having a break' (the main theme of its media advertisements over many years). The approach was to contact consumers more often, when they had a break or felt in need of one. Nestlé Rowntree commissioned market research by agency m digital which suggested that 'breaks' had become more individualised. This certainly is in accord with our earlier exploration of individualism. The research also identified Microsoft's MSN Messenger as being associated with breaks. So the idea was to synergise the two. The resulting alliance between Nestlé and MSN included on-pack

(KitKat) presence (MSN logos on 50 million KitKats) and KitKat branding on MSN's home and Messenger pages. Indeed, for a while, MSN Messenger was renamed 'The KitKat Messenger'.

To add to the synergy, the KitKat Café (www.kitkat.co.uk) was linked and this meant that various features such as games and a downloadable 'breakmate' could be accessed. The breakmate worked like an alarm clock on the PC to inform the user when it was time for yet another break. The alliance ran for six months in 2001 and the KitKat site saw a 1 620% increase in traffic.

(Source: New Media Age 2002, http://www.newmediazero.com/awards02/catwin16_detail.html, Effectivess Awards, 27 June, London)

... for a ha'porth of tar

The Internet clearly has great potential for building and maintaining relationships and it can cut (some) costs for the marketer because of disintermediation and because of the relative cheapness of sending e-mails as opposed to mail or telephone contact. Sutherland (1996) highlights this: '(compared with) one-to-one' addressable media (mail and telephone), the Internet is cheap and e-mail in particular is 'as good as free'. Should online relationships develop to an extent where transactions are taking place, costs generally should be cheaper than retail transactions, but are likely to vary by product or service – so such cost-savings are not guaranteed.

However, we feel it essential to reinforce the point made by many other observers and researchers, that 'fulfilment' is needed: it is one thing having a glossy 'front end' website that attracts plenty of traffic, but when visitors purchase physical products, these will have to be stored, picked and delivered. Walker (2001), for example, comments: 'fulfilment costs are high in relation to sales ... reports of stock shortages and mislaid deliveries do little to engender commitment'. This is not cheap and is a major problem associated with 'e' marketers who have not fully thought through the implications of online trading. The following case study reinforces this point.

Fulfilment

Mailing and fulfilment house Reality offers its clients a range of delivery options. These include evening and weekend delivery but as a fall-back, should no one be in to receive the package, it uses secure codes. Pre-arranged with the customer, these codes tell the carrier where the customer wants the delivery taken in their absence, for example to a neighbour. Reality is also experimenting with Spar convenience stores as drop-off points for deliveries. Customers can specify that they would like their order to be delivered to their local Spar shop where they can pick it up at their convenience.

The BearBox is an intelligent home delivery box which anyone can deliver to with the owner's permission. It is wirelessly linked to the BearBox management centre which schedules deliveries and issues a unique PIN code for each delivery which expires on use. Once delivery has been made, the consumer is notified via e-mail or SMS. Boxes are made of a composite with inner steel cage and attached to the consumer's wall with an expandable steel bolt. It is currently being used by Boden, Tesco and Madaboutwine, among others.

(Source: May (2001) 'The Last Mile', *Marketing Direct*, November, p. 398–42. Reproduced from *Marketing Direct* magazine with the permission of the copyright owner, Haymarket Business Publication Limited)

The above cases discuss one barrier, namely what can be unreliable fulfilment, but it is also worth briefly exploring other barriers.

Trust and security

Trust and confidence are also attributes of a successful relationship. 'The need to guarantee from being cheated in Internet sales is important, particularly for more significant sales transactions' (Poon and Jevons 1997). They go on to say that Internet security still hampers 'the smooth transition from communication to sales'. From the perspective of relational marketing, trust and confidence are obviously important.

Online communication with organisations can, from a consumer's perspective, be potentially very misleading. For example, while not in the interest of building relationships, e-mails can be sent anonymously and the content and address of websites may not necessarily be what they seem. The following case explores some security concerns and provides some possible solutions.

In empirical research, Kunoe (2001) found lack of trust to be a major barrier to buying online.

Security

User authentication online is growing in importance as paid-for content rises in popularity. Site users want to be sure their account details are safe, while sites need to prevent hackers from compromising security and getting for free what others have to pay for. The standard access security model on the Web is a combination of user name and password. But there is unease in some quarters concerning the robustness of this method of authentication. 'About 99% of sites that provide user name and password-controlled access are flawed in a number of areas,' claims Neil Garner, technical consultant at Consult Hyperion, which provides strategic consultancy to clients including BT Cellnet and Natwest. 'When capturing the user name and password, the link between server and user may not be secure. Once the user has logged in, cookies or Web addresses stored on their machine may contain unique references to their account. And worst of all, if you forget your password, your user name and password may be sent to you via an e-mail that is not secure.' Many big organisations and high-risk consumer sites, such as those owned by banks, enforce 'gobbledegook' passwords that are changed regularly to minimise the security risk. But aside from triggering calls to technical support and system administrators relating to forgotten passwords, many account users jot down passwords on notes and business cards, and then misplace them or leave them lying around in insecure locations. 'I always remember being handed a business card by a security services sales executive that had the user name and password access details to his corporate intranet written on the back of the card,' reveals Garner. For several years,

smartcard technology has been touted as a more secure way to authenticate users than the user name and password approach. While it can be effective in a corporate environment, there is a problem for consumers – distribution. Although newer PC operating systems have been developed to include smartcard support, few come with a card reader as standard, and there is little sign of a change in the situation. An alternative is electronic 'tokens' that can be plugged into a computer's USB port – the plug in the back of the PC which can bolt on a variety of devices such as mice, printers and digital cameras – but again, this approach is more likely to catch on with corporate networks than with consumer users. This is one area where interactive television has an edge over the PC-based net, in that the set-top boxes required for the service need a smartcard to be inserted in order to function. Moreover, the user's box and address details are known to the operator, adding a level of security missing from the Web. One Web initiative that has attracted attention, though, is the Microsoft Passport scheme that was launched in 1999. Those who sign up to Passport – there are now 210 million Passport accounts, many of which are owned by Hotmail users – give their information to Microsoft, which stores it on a secure server. Account holders provide Microsoft with a minimum of two information fields – typically an e-mail address and a password – but can fill in up to 11 more fields to add depth to the authentication data. Individual sites then sign up to use Passport to make their authentication process more straightforward. Passport is positioned as a way of allowing people to move easily among participating sites without having to maintain separate passwords for each site and log in each time they return to those sites. Digital certificates authenticate a true Passport site – but concerns have been raised that it might be possible for hackers to run fake sites that would enable them to access a user's credit card information. Microsoft says that situation won't happen, but is also quick to point out that Passport is not a high-security option. 'Passport is a simple sign-in and authentication tool; it does not go to a deeper level,' says Microsoft. Net policy and regulatory affairs manager John Noakes. Garner is rather more scathing. 'Microsoft Passport: how crazy is this? So you use a single user name and password over the network that will unlock all your user names and passwords for individual sites,' he fumes. 'Crack the Passport user name and password and you have all a person's details. I suspect sensible people will only use Passport for storing throw-away credentials for unimportant services. If a service is important enough, it will have its own additional security features: digital certificates, client software, additional random questions, SMS and e-mail one-time-use passcode or smartcard.' SMS and other mobile phone technology is already being used to authenticate transactions both online and in high street stores. This works on the principle that the SIM (subscriber identity module) card within a mobile handset offers a smartcard-like tamper-resistant environment for the storage of signing keys. It also has the advantage of being a mass-market device used by millions of people around the world. In a multichannel environment, users can initiate a transaction on their PC and use their phone to sign in and authenticate themselves. Several operators worldwide are looking to deploy such services to subscribers. Last year, software developer Smart-Trust partnered with Vodafone to trial the use of mobile-based digital signatures. A

pilot was run with the Department for Trade and Industry, which saw staff use their handsets to sign expense and travel forms. 'Because almost everyone has mobile phones, you get rid of the whole distribution problem – getting the hardware out there is the hard part,' says SmartTrust head of product marketing Fredrik Broman. While SIM cards do not have a large amount of data capacity, Royal Bank of Scotland's head of strategy, e-commerce team, Andy Hunter, thinks this might be overcome by the addition of a second SIM in the handset or battery pack. 'Ideally, there would need to be a more powerful digital signature on the SIM,' he adds. 'But that would require a more powerful chip and that would add to the cost.' Payment service provider World-Pay has also developed an authentication service involving mobile phones. In association with Vodafone, it is trialling an 'm-wallet'. When shopping online, users can click on an m-wallet icon on sites that are signed up to the system, then key in a PIN number using their mobile phone handsets to activate the electronic wallet. 'There's no actual keying in of the credit card number – it can only be activated by the users, who would have their personal ID number and mobile phone in their hand,' explains WorldPay European managing director Phil Battison. Biometrics – using physical attributes such as fingerprints to ensure security – has also been much talked about as a means of authentication. As long ago as 1998, Net Nanny Software International unveiled a software product called BioPass-word that claimed to measure an individual's keystroke rhythm to create an electronic profile. But a consistent technological standard has yet to emerge. Today a number of companies are marketing keyboards with fingerprint sensors. But distribution is again a fundamental drawback. Such systems may work for access to corporate networks, but until there is mass consumer penetration, they will offer little for most websites. 'There is a lot more ground to be covered in the biometrics area and I wouldn't go for it yet,' says Ofir Arkin, managing security architect at @Stake, an Internet security specialist, whose clients have included the US Department of Justice, the US Air Force and NASA.

(Source: Adapted by the authors from Gray 2002)

Where a consumer's relationship with a company has moved from being passively communicative to actively supporting transactions online, security is a major issue.

For example, eBay is a major Internet company and its users have been targeted with bogus e-mails asking for details of their bank accounts. The 'scam' involved official-looking messages to inactive customers asking them for bank account numbers and even credit card details and PIN numbers if they wanted to remain as customers. In an earlier but similar scam, some of the fraudsters were enticed to the USA by an FBI undercover operation and it was found that 56 000 credit card numbers had been 'stolen' (Collinson 2003).

So it is obvious that the trust and confidence built up in a relationship may be reduced if the interaction between company and customer is seen not to be 'trustworthy'. A related problem between the sender and receiver, or transactor and transactee, concerns possible third parties which could intercept or tamper with information. This may potentially be a worry from a consumer's perspective, especially where transactions are involved, even though in conventional retail transactions, potentially the same risks occur. However, while this threat exists, there are ways to defeat it. For example, December and Randall (1995) highlight the use of 'public key encryption', where 'the sender uses the recipient's public key to produce an encrypted text; the recipient turns this text back into plain text using the private (secret) key'. The development of online transactions may necessitate the use of 'trusted third parties' which assist in the security of information routed over the Internet, for example credit card details.

Privacy

Privacy could be described as 'the right not to be disturbed, the right to be anonymous, the right not to be monitored and the right not to have one's identifying information exploited' (Gattiker *et al.* 1996). We explore privacy in greater detail in Chapter 13 but unfortunately, as Morris (1996) suggests: 'Many business organisations display – at risk of endangering customer trust and encouraging consumer backlash – an extraordinarily cavalier business attitude regarding human privacy in traditional direct response advertising as well as Internet based promotion'. He goes on to identify areas of privacy abuse on the Internet and World Wide Web which include the following.

An increase in the ease at which people can be monitored – with the use of cookies, as described earlier, nearly all of a user's movements can be monitored and logged when visiting a website. Such site logs or records may not then be private in themselves (Ellsworth and Ellsworth 1996). The act of being monitored is not just confined to the Web. There are organisations which log the e-mail addresses of users participating in 'themed' discussion groups and then offer the lists for commercial use.

One way organisations can reduce the backlash of privacy issues is to adopt a permission marketing (Godin 1999 and Chapter 13) strategy by building into their websites forms where visitors can 'voluntarily' give information. Such volunteering of information could provide valuable foundations in which dialogue could lead to relationships as long as volunteered information is not abused.

A factor that is probably underestimated is the time it takes to access a website and navigate through it to purchase. Kunoe (2001) terms this as 'patience' and found it highly significant as a barrier to e-commerce.

Of particular interest and importance to us here, in a relational context, is another of Kunoe's findings, namely that 'the relationship between the user and the vendor on the web can be compared to the absence of a one-to-one relation or what one experiences in a mass marketing context ... the hybrid of intimacy that many eCommerce vendors ... has little to do with one-to-one communication, dialogue marketing or relevant interactive marketing' (Kunoe 2001). Indeed, he concluded that major relational constructs were not sufficiently operationalised for relationship marketing to be a reality.

This is indeed an indictment but provides useful lessons for relational marketing to become a reality.

Other limitations of the Internet for relationship building are as follows.

Number and type of consumers online – quite simply, if an organisation's current or target consumers do not have online connections, relationship marketing strategies using the Internet and World Wide Web will not be feasible. As the number of online connections approaches the number of telephones and TVs, through either computers or Web set-top boxes (which facilitate Internet access through TVs), its attractiveness as a medium will increase. Overall, the rate of increased penetration is fast and, as we mentioned when discussing pester power in Chapter 6, the rapid increase in Internet use by children suggests that the future will see the majority of the population 'online'.

Telecommunication infrastructure – clearly, for effective relationships to flourish over the Internet, the telecom infrastructure should not be in any way limiting to communications. If not right, frustration concerning, for example, 'download times' or weak or non-existent connections could distinctly damage relationships. From an international or global perspective, this is important as telecom infrastructures in different countries are in various stages of development (Morgan 1996) and could be deemed less attractive for online marketing strategies. Again, this limitation will disappear over the next few years, as the telecoms organisations are forced (by both government regulation and customer pressure) to improve their terms of service.

Account switching – every private online user has an account with an 'Internet service provider' (ISP). There are usually two types of account: *dial-up* – where a customer is charged a flat rate fee for a monthly connection, and *online* – where a customer is charged an hourly rate. The pace of the development of the Internet is partly attributable to introductory offers from larger ISPs such as Freeserve and AOL. This has meant that consumers can utilise one 'offer' after another of free connections for a limited period. From a relationship perspective, this switching is detrimental. Therefore, consumer relationships are likely to flourish over the Internet when – as the telecoms providers offer better terms – consumers are more likely to stay with one Internet service provider. One of the foundations in relationships is 'commitment', and clearly this is damaged by such switching. More specifically, it results – from an organisational perspective – in problems of 'traceability' and 'administration'. More often than not, even though the technology exists to forward e-mail messages to other accounts or access e-mail accounts from around the world using 'telnet', a consumer could switch ISP and, if there are no other contact details for that consumer, they may then be untraceable. In terms of administration, unlike a consumer's address and telephone number, where changes are relatively infrequent, the rapid switching of ISPs can produce significantly increased administration costs concerned with maintaining databases etc. This could increase the cost of consumer relationships and offset the benefit of reduced costs of communications using this medium. Once more, this churning is likely to reduce once the tariffs stabilise and become more standardised across different providers.

Use of aliases – there is a common acceptance that personal details such as names, addresses and telephone number should be up to date, true and not misleading. In formal arrangements, the law often requires accuracy as a pre-requisite. However, third parties such as ISPs are now becoming involved indirectly in communications, whether this be as part of an ongoing relationship or otherwise. Accordingly, the existence of these third parties might prove an important factor in developing relationships online. These ISPs are utilised by the online users to enable their access to the Internet and establish a unique name for the purposes of e-mail communications.

It is the process of e-mail registration that may limit future relationships – without any real restrictions (unless abusive terms are used), users can register virtually any name or term to be used online. The use of conventional first name and surname, initials, first names and surnames, aliases or funny names are all possible – the permutations of possibilities are virtually unlimited. One thing that stops the use of a particular name or term with an ISP is if it has already been registered with that particular ISP. If it has, a person can try another ISP which uses a different domain name to register their preferred name or term. This can be very misleading and potentially damaging to building relationships online as the person with whom you think you are communicating could really be someone totally different.

More than one e-mail address – in addition, over time, consumers are more likely to have more than one e-mail address for communications: perhaps one at work and one at home. This may not prove to be overly limiting in building relationships, as consumers would normally volunteer which e-mail address they would prefer in communications. But combined with some of the limitations above, the existence of more than one address will add to the complexity for an organisation in maintaining relationships over the Internet.

The international 'strength' of the Internet can also be its 'weakness'. *Global e-relationships* – it is obvious that the Internet and World Wide Web can make a significant impact on the internationalisation or globalisation. Berthon *et al.* (1996a) state that a presence on the medium is 'international by definition' and 'compared to other media, the Web provides a more or less level playing field for all players, regardless of size'.

However, use across borders can be seriously hampered by heterogeneous markets. Some examples will demonstrate. Virgin Atlantic Airways maintained a website and placed details of its trans-Atlantic airfares. The website described a return airfare of under $500. A prospective passenger wishing to buy one of these tickets was, however, told that this special price was no longer available and the alternative was a ticket costing over $500. Under US law the airline was obliged to keep the information up to date and as it had inadvertently failed to do so it ended up paying the US Department of Transport $14,000.

Clearly, UK companies which do business with customers in other countries need to be aware of the laws applicable there when promoting their goods and services via the Internet. Perhaps the most problematic area will be in the financial services industry, as this sector is closely regulated in most countries. Case 11.6 does not focus on financial services but on another, more dubious sector.

CASE **STUDY** 11.6

Tattilo

The Italian company Tattilo Editrice SpA made erotic pictures available over the Internet. The milder pictures were made available to all visitors to the website, whether or not they had a subscription. More explicit pictures were available to those who wished to subscribe to a special service. Tattilo is an Italian company, based in Italy, and both services were made available from computer equipment located in Italy. The domain name (that is, the Internet address) of the website was playmen.it. Playboy Enterprises Inc. – the publisher of *Playboy* magazine – had failed to obtain protection for its Playboy trade mark in Italy in a previous case brought against Tattilo. However, Playboy brought proceedings against Tattilo in the New York courts, claiming that Tattilo had infringed Playboy's US registration of the Playboy trade mark by – amongst other things – its use of the playmen.it address because the service was available to US citizens. The court agreed and ordered Tattilo either to refuse subscriptions from US customers or to shut down its Internet site, even though that site was in Italy. Tattilo was also ordered to pay to Playboy the gross profits it had earned from subscriptions to the service by US customers and all gross profits earned from the sale of goods and services advertised on the Playmen site. Interestingly, the court stated that 'Cyberspace is not a safe haven.'

(Source: O'Malley *et al.* 1999)

This case clearly demonstrates the global *opportunities* of the Internet but also the *constraints*.

E-relationship effectiveness

Despite the growth of Internet marketing and the rapid technological developments which underpin its operation, the way in which it is used for relational marketing can be criticised. There are lessons to be learnt from the mistakes and concerns raised in various research findings. Some of these are presented in Exhibit 11.1. This summarises the results of research conducted by Shelley Taylor and associates in 2000 and shows a rather disappointing picture of websites.

Other research tends to echo the disquiet. Exhibit 11.2, for example, reports on a mystery shopping project into B2B websites.

Having explored some of the issues and concerns relating to relationship marketing via the Internet, we now extend this analysis into suggesting how relational marketing might become more relational.

Consumer control and new e-commerce models

It is clear that the 'electronic marketplace expands the range of information sources available to buyers' (Varadarajan and Yadav 2002) and this can have the

EXHIBIT 11.1   Poor e-relationships

Online Retailers assessed

- 50% don't make contact information avzailable throughout the site
- 88% don't have a link from their home page to shipping information
- 56% don't have any form of post-sale support
- 84% don't have access to return policies on the checkout path
- 39% don't offer live order tracking
- 36% don't include return instructions with the purchased item
- 70% don't provide information about Product availability near the product description

(Source: Shelley Taylor & Associates (2000) *100 retail Websites 70 in US and 30 in UK*)

EXHIBIT 11.2 B2B mystery shopping

B2B – 'Search stage: Mystery shopping via Internet

- Fairly quick response, but limited in content & few encouraged further contact
- 9% online forms reflected data protection
- Two-thirds responded via E-MAIL:
  - most within a day
  - but in an average of 30 words
  - less than one-fifth gave product info
  - less than one-fifth invited another contact
- Postal response by some:
  - most sent brochures
  - most acknowledged the website Q
  - but one telecoms co. said 'in response to phone call'!
  - none asked for clarification of what was wanted
- Phone response by some:
  - within 5 days
  - half acknowledged Internet contact
- Fax response by 1:
  - same company sent 2 on different days

Overall, only one-third asked what was wanted

(Source: Frost *et al.* 1999)

effect of increasing buyer power within organisation–customer interaction (Evans *et al.* 2001). C2C online communities can add to this by providing more information (from non-organisational sources) and in turn greater buyer power via what can be very influential 'word of mouse' (Evans *et al.* 2000). These are the issues we explore in this section.

Consumer control

A key factor concerning consumer interaction with relational marketing is 'control' (Evans *et al.* 2001). Consumers are perhaps increasingly valuing and seeking greater control over the consumer–organisation interaction. In qualitative research, the following consumer quotes demonstrate the issue:

❝ . . . I would prefer it if I didn't see anything in the post unless I had specifically requested it. ❞ (Female, 25–34)

> ❝ ... Personally, if I've got something that I want to do financially, I would look into it and go to my own people. I would search them out myself rather than look at something that came through on the carpet because generally you just pick it up and throw it away. ❞ (Female, 25–44)

> ❝ ... It's just its annoying to be sent things that you are not interested in. Even more annoying when they phone you up ... if you wanted something you would go and find out about it. ❞ (Female, 45–54)

(Evans *et al.* 2001).

Control has also been cited in other research as a dimension valued by consumers (Gober 2000). Indeed, there is evidence that perceived control could be used to encourage more to use the Internet:

> ❝ I have looked at internet sites ... only when I wanted to ... only because I was in the market. ❞ (Male 25–34)

> ❝ Holiday to New Zealand ... e-mailed ... car hire companies and whatever and they've been e-mailing me back with different rates and lots of information ... its great, because I've initiated it, I want to know the information. ❞ (Male 25–40)

(Evans *et al.* 2001)

Marketers could provide the means for consumer-controlled interaction via, for example, less unsolicited outbound contact and more opportunities for consumers to contact marketers in their own time and own way, such as via the Internet. Indeed, we would suggest greater use of 'inbound' customer contact in developing direct and relationship marketing campaigns, as was discussed under 'lifestage' in Chapter 6.

Emerging models

Table 11.1 suggests how the locus of control can shift towards the consumer. Traditional models of e-commerce are shown as the conventional business-to-business and business-to-consumer. However, as consumers band together, in loose but cooperative buying groups, they begin to wrest greater levels of control over the buying process, and at the same time engage with relational marketers even more. So, clearly, companies should not see this trend as a threat.

Case 11.7 summarises some of the many government initiatives aimed at creating government-to-consumer (G2C) and government-to-business (G2B) interaction. There are, of course, ongoing discussions about the government-to-government (G2G) version, in terms of the extent to which personal data held by one government department can be shared across departments.

TABLE 11.1 Emerging e-commerce models

	Business	Consumer	Government
Business	B2B EDI networks GM/Ford	B2C Amazon Dell	B2G VAT returns Payroll (P45/6)
Consumer	B2C Buying cooperatives	C2C Online communities eBay, Corporatewatch.org	C2G Tax returns
Government	G2B SME Service UK Online 4	G2C Office of Fair Trading Biz UK Online	G2G Criminal justice Social service KM of intelligence

CASE **STUDY** 11.7

G2 everything

Labour has identified 520 services which it plans to take online by 2005. The initiative was announced on 30 March 2000. According to figures released in autumn 2001 by the division of e-envoy Andrew Pinder, 256 of these services are now e-enabled (51%), 356 will be e-enabled by 2002 (14%) and 513 (99%) will be online by 2005. Some of the services already online include applying for a passport, booking a driving theory test, buying a TV licence and self-assessment for tax. Some services will never go online due to their sensitive nature, such as those dealing with asylum seekers or EU legislation.

Will there be a Britain not only with UK Online Centres in every major city but also with interactive kiosks in every village in the land.

(Source: Goddard 2002. Reproduced from *Revolution* magazine with the permission of the copyright owner, Haymarket Business Publications Limited)

Of particular note in Table 11.1 is the emergence of the 'community' model, and this is what we turn to next.

E-community relationships

The consumer-to-consumer 'community' model is relatively new but is a potentially useful approach for both organisations and consumers because the locus of control shifts towards the consumer and could facilitate a greater degree of (mutual) relationship building than other models. The importance of organisational involvement (or at least monitoring) of some virtual communities is clear from this example. If consumers are sharing (negative) experiences of the company and its brands, then this can be powerful 'word of *mouse*' that should not be ignored.

IN THEORY

Online communities

Social interaction now has a 'virtual' version as the concept of virtual (online) communities becomes a reality. Anderson (1999) has suggested that as social arrangements change, the nature of and the ground conditions upon which communities operate change profoundly as well. Recognising this fundamental notion is crucial for our understanding of the social environments of the present and the future. Furthermore, Anderson has observed that: 'Communities in the past – even the recent past tended to be closed systems. That is, they had relatively clear and impermeable boundaries, relatively stable memberships, relatively few linkages to other communities.' However, as no living system is ever entirely closed or entirely open, he further suggested that: 'even the most closed must exchange material and information with other systems; even the most open must maintain some boundaries, some continuing integrity of form'.

Moreover, the rapid developments of information and communications technologies are having a formidable impact and are facilitating the formation of new kinds of online communities. 'Cyberspace has become a new kind of social terrain, crowded with "virtual communities", in which people come together for sexual flirtation, business, idle gossip, spiritual exploration, psychological support, political action, intellectual discourse on all kinds of subjects – the whole range of human interests and needs' (Anderson 1999). Fundamentally, new technologies permit people to make direct connections with others by the elimination of the middleman, a process known as disintermediation. Further, the like-minded come together irrespective of time and space issues to form groups and a variety of networks, a process known as aggregation. Howard Rheingold (1993) has observed that 'the future of the Net is connected to the future of community, democracy, education, science, and intellectual life – some of the human institutions people hold most dear, whether or not they know or care about the future of computer technology'.

Wellman *et al.* (1996) observed that when people and machines became linked via computer networks and through the resulting interactions, social networks were formed which they described as computer supported social networks (CSSNs). They suggested that 'members of a virtual community want to link globally with kindred souls for companionship, information and social support from their homes and workstations. White-collar workers want computer supported co-operative work (CSCW), unencumbered by spatial distance ... and some workers want to telework from their homes ...' (Wellman *et al.* 1996).

In Sociology the term community could be defined and should be understood as meaning '(1) a group of people (2) who share social interaction (3) and some common ties between themselves and other members of the group (4) and who share an area for at least some of the time' (Hamman 1997).

Oldenburg (1991) has suggested a 'third place', after home and work; this includes places such as bars, hair salons and coffee bars and he called it the 'Great Good Place' where members of a community meet, leaving behind possible divisions such as class or rank in the spirit of inclusion rather than exclusion. 'The character of a third place is determined most of all by its regular clientele and is marked by a playful mood, which contrasts with people's more serious involvement in other spheres. Though a radically different kind of setting for a home, the third place is remarkably similar to a good home in the psychological comfort and support that it extends. They are the heart of a community's social vitality, the grassroots of democracy, but sadly, they constitute a diminishing aspect of the American social landscape' (Oldenburg 1991). These core settings of informal public life are necessary for community building. They become places where community members interact with each other and recognise the ties that bind them together. Therefore, in order for communities to develop, the existence of third places are vital. Oldenburg suggested that in the cities of the Western world such third places are in decline, with populations living in suburbs far from within walking distance to shops, local businesses and community centres which bring people together. Hamman (1997) observed that 'because of the lack of third places within easy reach of the majority of the population, many people, especially those with a high level of education and expendable income, have flocked to third places accessible through computer mediated communications technologies'.

The assumed separation between the definitions of physical and virtual communities is advanced as an unproductive dichotomy. Drawing upon the disciplines of human geography, sociology and cybersociology, the commonality between the 'traditional' and virtual definitions of community are particularly striking. The traditional concepts of community would indicate that spatial proximity does not necessarily create a community. The work of human geographers Bell and Newby (1978) and Schmalenbach (1961), who define community as something more than the sense of belonging to an active social network ('communion') and involves custom, shared modes of thought or expression, would be an apt description for many of the online virtual communities.

This analysis clearly moves 'community' close to the relational paradigm and therefore holds potential for relational marketing.

Cyberspace is a social space. Whether e-mailing a friend, exploring a MOO,[1] surfing the Web, or posting to a list service or newsgroup, users interact with one another. This communication – often random and sporadic, often prolonged and regular fosters a sense of community and can help to generate what Rheingold (1993) calls virtual communities.

Virtual communities of consumption

Research by Robert Kozinets (1999) points towards Internet user experience as a key determinant – at least so far – of participation within a virtual community. People use networked computers for social relating and, whether termed 'virtual communities' (Rheingold 1993) 'brand communities' (Muniz 1997) 'communities of interest' (Armstrong and Hagel 1996) or 'Internet cultures' (Jones 1995), research reveals that online groups are often market oriented in their interests. Kozinets (1998) refers to 'virtual communities of consumption'. These are a specific subgroup of virtual communities that explicitly centre upon consumption-related interests. They can be defined as 'affiliative groups whose online interactions are based upon shared enthusiasm for, and knowledge of, a specific consumption activity or related group of activities' (Kozinets 1999). For example, the members of an e-mail mailing list sent out to collectors of Barbie dolls would constitute a virtual community of consumption, as would the regular posters to a bulletin board devoted to connoisseurship of fine wine.

Kozinets's research outlines four distinct virtual community 'types'. The first of the four types are the *tourists* who lack strong social ties to the group, and maintain only a superficial or passing interest in the consumption activity. Next are the *minglers* who maintain strong social ties, but who are only perfunctorily interested in the central consumption activity. *Devotees* are opposite to this: they maintain a strong interest in and enthusiasm for the consumption activity, but have few social attachments to the group. Finally, *insiders* are those who have strong personal ties to the consumption activity.

Commercial aspects of virtual communities

In a research project funded by the European Social Fund and the Direct Marketing Association (Evans *et al.* 2000), nearly half (41%) of virtual community sites that people participate in are owned by individual companies, 10% by a group of companies and 30% by an Internet service provider. However, nearly a quarter of respondents did not know who 'owns' the virtual community sites that they use.

There appear to be commercial benefits for organisations that provide virtual communities on their sites. A substantial proportion (25%) of Internet users claim to have a more positive opinion about the owner of the sites they use. Over half stated that their opinion has not changed but a negligible number stated that they now have a more negative opinion. It therefore appears that companies who provide virtual communities on their site are likely to be perceived more positively by at least a quarter of users. Indeed, when asked directly, more than half of all respondents say they think it is a good idea for companies to provide virtual communities on their websites. A third of people would also like to use a virtual community to communicate with the company itself. Providing such facilities on a website may also strengthen the relationship that consumers have with organisations as 13% of Internet users say they feel closer to some brands/companies since participating in their virtual communities (Evans *et al.* 2000).

There are also more direct benefits for companies who provide virtual community facilities. A third of respondents claim to have purchased something on a virtual community site and 50% use these sites to find out more information about products and services. The 18–29-year-olds are even more likely to purchase online, with 39% of them having done so on a virtual community site. Virtual community sites may also lead to subsequent off-line purchases, as 15% of respondents have done so as a result of seeing something on the site (Evans *et al.* 2000).

Companies will need to be cautious regarding the level of commercialisation of the site. Over half of virtual community participants do not like it if a site is too commercialised and an even larger proportion (72%) consider Web adverts to be distraction; 18–29-year-olds are less bothered by Web advertising (Evans *et al.* 2000).

There are, however, several benefits of online communities that businesses can exploit:

- For the majority of virtual community participants, interacting within a virtual community is an effective way of connecting to a diverse group of people.
- Individuals can choose their level of interaction, gather and give information and advice and express their opinions – all while maintaining an important, perceived, level of control over the interaction.
- It helps them find information.
- They enjoy the interaction with other people and feel that they 'get something out of participating'.
- It's an opportunity to discuss topics that they are interested in.
- The majority of enthusiasts like to receive advice from other people. A smaller proportion like to give advice. This may be a good indicator for companies to use bulletin boards for posting product/service advice.

The relational potential of such communities is clear and because the locus of control is nearer the consumer, there is great scope for the online relational community because consumers can take more of the initiative and be proactive in their interaction with other consumers and with companies.

Case study 8.2 is a good illustration of a community approach to relational interaction between the various players in the publishing industry. From this case, it is recognised that the structure and content, together with the basic routines for forum management, must be in place and strictly adhered to if the forums are to become consistently useful and credible. The need for this is highlighted by Baym (1995) who states that 'community is generated through the interplay between pre-existing structures and the participants' strategic appropriation and exploitation of the resources and rules those structures offer in ongoing interaction'.

Communities create the prime opportunity to enhance marketing communications through the hypermedia environment. As Armstrong and Hagel (1996) observe, 'virtual communities not only gather potential purchasers together, but they also arm them with far more information than they have typically been able to access conveniently and cost effectively in the past'. By adding value through the provision of content (and facilitating information flows between members), companies can both draw customers in and expose them to the elements of the marketing communications mix.

United Biscuits has even introduced an internal online community for the sharing of experiences and knowledge across its various brands. The full case study for this can be found on the accompanying website and an extract is in Case 8.5, but we reproduce another extract here.

CASE STUDY 11.8

United Biscuits

The e-business community comprises staff from different areas of United Biscuits, separated into four main groups: commercial, operational, technology and business support. The point is not to homogenise online strategies across all brands, but to see what works and how it could be applied elsewhere.

(Source: Adapted by the authors from Van Vark 2002)

As well as demonstrating the relational use of an online community within a company, it also reinforces our earlier points (Chapter 8) about sharing knowledge for best practice.

Although not exactly an online community, the 'infomediary' is worth a brief mention. Companies 'enrol' with an infomediary consortium and provide product, price and availability details (Chen and Padmananabhan 2002). These are then available online for anyone to compare. Thus, customers' pre-purchase search procedures are helped and, for many people, this will be quicker and more convenient. It is generally recognised that the predominant use of the Internet in terms of the various pre- and post-purchase stages of consumer behaviour lies in the 'search' stages. A major effect will be on price levels because companies will see competitors' prices and customers will vote with their pockets.

Overall, we suggest that despite the tremendous growth of online marketing and the fact that some years after the 'dot com' failure era, we are seeing major 'onliners' moving into profit, there is still some way to go for these to achieve relational status with their customers.

Summary

- The exponential growth and global acceptance of the Internet as a source of information and a business communication tool has presented marketers with a unique and powerful marketing communications platform. Indeed, the Internet and World Wide Web would seem to be a promising medium for building relationships online. This might be due to the degree of interactivity and dialogue which is facilitated through such online communications.

- Organisations are also likely to benefit from decreased costs in building relationships online. Conversely, the convenience of communication and (potentially) product or service-based transactions may provide benefits to the consumer.

- While both parties in a relationship are likely to benefit in some way through using the medium, a number of issues and limitations which currently exist may limit the success of building relationships online.

- Privacy and trust in combination with security issues are likely to be the main concerns of consumers in relationships, though from an organisational viewpoint, the existence of Internet service providers and telecommunication companies, and the use of more than one e-mail address with possible aliases, may make the building and maintenance of relationships online more difficult then one might first have thought.

- While both parties may, through an online relationship, increase their knowledge of the other, the power of the consumer may be increased compared to conventional retail relationships as the Internet and Web provide a knowledge base and forums which would not normally be available to the average consumer.

- In the context of globalisation, the Internet and Web brings the consumer closer to a company, but language, culture, attitudinal differences – and the existing technology in place – may limit their use in relationship building across borders.

- New e-commerce business models have emerged, for example from B2C to C2C. The dramatic change in terms of how consumers interact with each other and potentially engage with marketers is epitomised by a change in the level of perceived control, with a shift towards consumer-controlled interaction.

- In addition, though, through the MCB and United Biscuits cases, we have illustrated the potential for corporate websites to communicate all aspects of the marketing mix and to allow a seamless link between the customer and the product and/or with other relevant partners.

Review questions

1 Consider your dealings with organisations via the Internet, either as a business customer or consumer. How are the relationship marketing constructs addressed by both you and organisations? How could they be more fully addressed?

2 The electronic communications technology available to both marketers and their customers means that the latter represent a fast-moving target – in terms of their rapidly changing demands. How have the recent technological developments affected the basic relationships between marketers and their customers?

3 What policies does your own organisation (company or university) have in place to guard the privacy of its customers? What strategies, if any, is it pursuing to build trust with its customers in general, and those coming through e-commerce in particular? Does it recognise the concept of permission marketing?

4 Do you belong to any such commercially sponsored virtual communities? If so, how has their existence changed your view of the sponsoring organisations? Has it resulted in you making extra purchases from it?

Further reading

Bandyo-Padhyay, N. (2002) *e-Commerce: Context, Concepts and Consequences*, Maidenhead: McGraw Hill.

Brown, S. (2000) Customer Relationship Management: A Strategic Imperative in the World of e-Business, Toronto: John Wiley.

Chaffey, D., Mayer, R., Johnston, K. and Ellis-Chadwick, F. (2003) *Internet Marketing: Strategy, Implementation and Practice*, London: FT Prentice Hall.

Coupey, E. (2001) *Marketing and the Internet: Conceptual Foundations*, Englewood Cliffs, NJ: Prentice Hall.

Eisemann, T.R. (2002) *Internet Business Models: Text and Cases*, New York: McGraw Hill.

Journal of the Academy of Marketing Science, Special Issue on Internet Marketing, Fall 2002, 30(4).

Mohammed, R.A., Fisher, R.J., Jaworski, B.J. and Cahill, A.M. (2002) *Internet Marketing: Building Advantage in a Networked Economy*, New York: McGraw Hill.

O'Connor, J., Galvin, E. and Evans, M. (2003) *e-Marketing: Theory and Practice in the 21st Century*, London: FT Prentice Hall.

Tassabehji, R. (2003) *Applying e-Commerce in Business*, London: Sage.

References

Anderson, W.T. (1999) 'Communities in a World of Open Systems', *Futures*, 31, pp. 457–63.

Armstrong, A. and Hagel, J. (1996) 'The Real Value of On-line Communities', *Harvard Business Review*, May–June, pp. 134–41.

Barwise, P. and Styler, A. (2002) *Marketing Expenditure Trends*, London: London Business School/Havas.

Baym, N.K. (1995) *Cybersociety: Computer Mediation and Community,* Thousand Oaks, CA: Sage Publications.

Bell, C. and Newby, H. (1978) 'Community, Communication, Class and Community Action: the Social Sources of the New Urban Politics', in D.T. Herbert, and R.J. Johnston (eds) *Social Areas in Cities: Processes, Patterns and Problems,* Chichester: John Wiley, pp. 283–302.

Berthon, P., Pitt, L., and Watson, R. (1996a) 'Marketing Communication on the World Wide Web', *Business Horizons,* Sept–Oct.

Berthon, P. and Pitt, L.F. and Watson, R.T. (1996b) 'The World Wide Web as an Advertising Medium: Towards Understanding of Conversion Efficiency', *Journal of Advertising Research,* January/February, pp. 43–54.

Chaffey, D., Mayer, R., Johnston, K. and Ellis-Chadwick, F. (2003) *Internet Marketing: Strategy, Implementation and Practice,* London: FT Prentice Hall.

Chen, Y., Iyer, G. and Padmananabhan, I. (2002) 'Referral Infomediaries', *Marketing Science,* 21(4), pp. 412–34.

Collinson, P. (2003) 'Email Fraud Targets 2m UK On-Line Customers', *The Guardian,* 31 May, p. 2.

December, J. and Randall, N. (1995) *The World Wide Web – Unleashed 1996,* Indianapolis: Sams.net Publishing, pp. 43–59.

DMA (1998) *Direct Marketing Association Census,* London.

Ellsworth, J.H. and Ellsworth, M.V. (1996) *Marketing on the Internet – Multi-media Strategies for the World Wide Web.* New York: Wiley & Sons, Inc.

Evans, M., Howard, M., Wedande, G., Van T'Hul, S., and Ralston, L. (2000) *Consumer Interaction in the Virtual Era,* ESF/DMA funded project.

Evans, M., Patterson, M. and O'Malley, L. (2001) 'Bridging the Direct Marketing-Direct Consumer Gap: Some Solutions from Qualitative Research', *Qualitative Market Research: An International Journal,* 4(1), pp. 17–24.

Evans, M., Wedande, G., Ralston, L. and Van T'Hul, S. (2001) 'Consumer Interaction in the Virtual Era: Some Solutions from Qualitative Research', *Qualitative Market Research: An International Journal,* 4(3), pp. 150–9.

Frost, F., Matthews, B. and Evans, M. (1999) 'Responses to General Enquiries Via The Internet: Targeting the Organisational Decision Maker', *Journal of Targeting, Measurement and Analysis for Marketing,* 7(4), pp. 374–86.

Gattiker, U.E., Janz, L., Kelley, H. and Schollmeyer, M. (1996) 'The Internet and Privacy: Do you know who's watching', *Business Quarterly,* pp. 79–82.

Glazer, R. (1991) 'Marketing in an Information Intensive Environment: Strategic Implications of Knowledge as an Asset', *Journal of Marketing,* 55, October, pp. 1–19.

Gober, M. (2000) 'The 12 Things Customers Really Want', *Customer Management,* January/February, p. 32–4.

Goddard, L. (2002) 'A Public Affair', *Revolution,* 20 February, pp. 26–9.

Godin, S. (1999) *Permission Marketing: Turning Strangers into Friends and Friends into Customers,* New York: Simon & Schuster.

Gray, R. (2002) 'Are Your Users Who They Say They Are?', *Revolution,* 17 April, pp. 26–8.

Greene, T. (1996) 'Netting Maximum Results for Marketing by Surfing the Internet', *Direct Marketing,* July, pp. 42–3.

Hamill, J. and Gregory, K. (1997) 'Internet marketing in the Internationalisation of UK SMEs', *Journal of Marketing Management,* 13, pp. 9–28.

Hamman, R. (1997) 'Introduction to Virtual Communities Research and Cybersociology Magazine Issue Two [Online] http: //members.aol.com/Cybersoc/is2intro.html

Hoffman, D. and Novak, T.P. (1996) 'Marketing in Hypermedia – Computer Mediated Environments: Conceptual Foundations', *Journal of Marketing,* 60 (July), pp. 50–68.

Jones, N. (1996) 'Internet Marketing – Talking Pages', *Marketing Week*, July, pp. 37–40.

Jones, S. (1995) 'Understanding Community in the Information Age', in S.G. Jones (ed.) *Computer-mediated Communication and Community*, Thousand Oaks, CA: Sage, pp. 10–35.

Kozinets, R. (1998) 'On Netnography. Initial Reflections on Consumer Research Investigations of Cyberculture', in *Advances in Consumer Research*, vol. 25, Joseph Alba and Wesley Hutchinson (eds), Provo, UT: Association for Consumer Research, pp. 366–71.

Kozinets, R. (1999) 'E-Tribalized Marketing? The Strategic Implications of Virtual Communities of Consumption', *European Management Journal*, 17(3), pp. 252–64.

Kunoe, G. (2001) 'Barriers to eCommerce', FEDMA Research Day, 14 September, Madrid.

Loader, B. (1998) 'Cyberspace Divide: Equality, Agency and Policy in the Information Society', in B. Loader (ed.) *Cyberspace Divide: Equality, Agency and Policy in the Information Society*, London: Routledge, pp. 3–16.

May, M. (2001) 'The Last Mile', *Marketing Direct*, November, pp. 398–42.

Morgan, R.F. (1996) 'An INTERNET Marketing framework for the World Wide Web (WWW)', *Journal of Marketing Management*, 12, pp. 757–75.

Morris, L. (1996) 'Privacy – It's everyone's business now!', *Direct Marketing*, April, pp. 40–3.

Muir, S. (2002) 'Hypnosis Media Takes Artist Promotion to Fans', *Revolution*, 7 August, p. 25.

Muniz, A.M. (1997) 'Brand Community and the Negotiation of Brand Meaning', in *Advances in Consumer Research*, vol. 24, M. Brucks and D.J. MacInnis (eds), Provo, UT: Association for Consumer Research, pp. 308–9.

New Media Age (2002) http://www.newmediazero.com/awards02/catwin16_detail.html, Effectiveness Awards, 27th June, London

Oldenburg, R. (1991) *The Great Good Place: Cafes, Coffee Shops, Community Centers, Beauty Parlors, General Stores, Bars, Hangouts and How They Get You Through the Day*, New York: Paragon House.

O'Malley, L., Patterson, M. and Evans, M. (1999) *Exploring Direct Marketing*, London: Thomson Learning.

Poon, S. and Jevons, C. (1997) 'Internet-enabled International Marketing: A Small Business Network Perspective', *Journal of Marketing Management*, 13, pp. 29–41.

Rheingold, H. (1993) *The Virtual Community: Homesteading on the Electronic Frontier*. Reading, MA: AddisonWesley Publishing Co.

Salah, D. (2002) 'Worldpop Offers Qualitative Study of its Message Boards', *Revolution*, 21 August, p. 29.

Schmalenbach, H. (1961) 'The Sociological Category of Communion', in T. Parsons *et al.* (eds) *Theories of Society 1*, pp. 331–47.

Simpson, J. (2002) 'The Impact of the Internet in banking: Observations and Evidence from Developed and Emerging Markets', *Telematics and Informatics*, 19, pp. 315–30.

Sutherland, R. (1996) 'The Web, the Net and the Direct Marketer', *Admap*, November, pp. 72–4.

Swinfen-Green, J. (1996) 'Why Interactive Marketing is Here to Stay', *Admap*, January, pp. 28–31.

Van Vark, C. (2002) 'Take a Byte', *Revolution*, 25 September, pp. 22–5.

Varadarajan, P.R. and Yadav, M.S. (2002) 'Marketing Strategy and the Internet: An Organising Framework', *Journal of the Academy of Marketing Science*, 30(4).

Walker, C. (2001) 'Why Web is Weakest Link for Grocery Chains', *Precision Marketing*, 20 April, p. 11.

Wellman, B., Sallaf, J., Dimitrova, D., Garton, L., Gulia, M. and Haythornwaite, C. (1996) 'Computer Networks as Social Networks: Collaborative Work, Telework and Virtual Community', *Annual Review of Sociology*, 22 February, pp. 213–38.

Winder, D. (1996) *All You Need to Know about the Internet – Your Indispensable Guide to Getting On-line*, Bath: Future Publishing, p. 20.

Note

1 Moo (Multi-User Dimension Object Orientated) is a computer program that allows multiple users to connect via the Internet to a shared database of rooms and other objects, and interact with each other and the database in synchronous time.

12 Relational messages

Learning objectives

Having completed this chapter, students should:

- Appreciate how the role of understanding consumer motivation can contribute to creating messages within relational marketing.

- Be aware of various theories of motivation and to show how motives can be considered to be driving forces derived from different levels of depth within the human psyche.

- Understand how concepts from psychology can contribute to understanding how consumers respond to relational marketing activity.

- Recognise that there are alternative bases on which to create marketing messages, such as emotions, logic and semiotics.

Land Rover and Freelander

a) Research has identified that the most powerful means to building loyalty to the Land Rover marque is to involve customers in off-road experiences. While most drivers never get to drive off-road, having the capability creates a desire to do so.

A selection of off-road Land Rover holidays called 'Adventures' (Exhibit 12.1) was the hook for a communication aimed at emotionally involving customers and enhancing brand perceptions.

Mailings, inserts and a website informed customers about holidays ranging from the UK to Botswana. The brochure, translated into four languages, has been mailed to 14 000 customers around the world and has achieved a 9.4% response rate.

b) Land Rover's Freelander needed to grow the market by appealing to people who have never considered a 4 × 4. The solution was a mail pack dubbed the Escape Kit. It generated 300% increases in response rates over the

EXHIBIT 12.1 Land Rover adventures

(Source: Land Rover, DMA Awards 2001)

previous campaign. Almost 3 500 leads were added to the database, of which 1 900 were passed on to dealers for extended test dealers. The Escape pack includes a map pin and miniature toothbrush – useful while escaping, though the pack emphasises that true liberation only comes with the Freelander (Exhibit 12.2).

EXHIBIT 12.2 Escape kit

(Source: DMA Awards 2002)

Introduction

The above case study is a good illustration of several issues explored in this chapter. It reflects motivational drivers to express oneself and achieve some self-actualisation (we discuss these drivers in our coverage of Maslow's hierarchy of needs) and the effectiveness of involving customers in participative marketing messages. The more mutual participation, the more likely is a relational outcome, and we discuss this in our coverage of Gestalt psychology later in this chapter.

The theme of this chapter, then, is the exploration of the sorts of messages that can be deployed. These reflect the way of conveying an offer, a call to action or other communication that the organisation considers appropriate to encouraging relational interaction between itself and the recipient. This is often referred to as the marketing communications 'creative' and should be based on an understanding of the target audience. We have already provided some underpinning in this respect, in Chapter 6, on 'targeting' but we extend this perspective by drawing more heavily in the current chapter on, especially, psychological processes and concepts. Because the human mind can only process and retain relatively small numbers of discrete points in communications messages at any one time, there is a creative skill in simplifying a complex world so that the message is accessible and does not overwhelm the recipient with too many points that would lead to too much 'noise' in the communications process.

Creativity

Creativity cannot occur in isolation. Rather it occurs against a backdrop of hard work and planning. As such, Wallas (1995) outlines a process whereby marketers can lay the groundwork for message creativity which incorporates the following four steps:

1 **Preparation**: Conducting various types of research in order to provide background information about the marketing problem and to give meaning to subsequent stages. This not only involves more traditional research methods but also includes reading about the product and the market in which it operates, listening to what customers have to say about the product or service in the field, using the product or service and learning about the client's business first hand by visiting the organisation (Moriarty 1986).

2 **Incubation**: Getting away from the problem at hand and using the information that has been gathered to help generate ideas. In order to develop potentially fruitful ideas the creative team will need to consciously avoid focusing too much on the problem and remain open to inspiration.

3 **Illumination**: This relates to the generation of ideas which might be later put to use creatively. This stage will make use of procedures such as brainstorming.

4 **Verification**: Refining the ideas generated and identifying whether or not they are workable and if they will provide a solution to the problem. The interactive relational marketer will often rely on testing during this phase, using samples of the target audience to evaluate different concepts and themes which have emerged from the illumination stage.

Creativity must also bear some relation to any marketing objectives which have been outlined. Of increasing importance in this area is the need to ensure that any communication takes account of the brand image the organisation is trying to foster. Brand image refers to consumers' subjective perceptions of how a brand performs across a range of criteria, both functional and non-functional, which they consider to be important for evaluation purposes. These subjective perceptions are organised by the consumer into a succinct picture of the brand which will play a part in that consumer's consumption behaviour (Engel *et al.* 1986). The brand image is compiled by the consumer through direct experience of the brand, through exposure to marketing communications, through packaging, and even through observation of what kind of people use the brand and the occasions and situations in which the brand is used (Gordon 1991). From the organisation's perspective, brand image aids in the establishment of the brand's position (Park *et al.* 1986), can protect against competitive attack (Oxenfeldt and Swann 1964), and thus leads to enhanced market performance (Shocker and Srinivasan 1979). A brand image has in itself a number of inherent characteristics which include, among others, brand personality and user image; we discussed the matching of brand and self-images in Chapter 6. In many ways the organisation lives or dies by the brand image it manages to foster and thus there is a distinct need in the creative process to be aware of these issues and to ensure that communications are consistent with them.

One of the points of discussion within marketing generally is whether interactive relational marketing is the poor relation in terms of 'creativity'. It has often been claimed by traditional above-the-line agencies that having to include direct response mechanisms in advertising stifles the creative effort and that as soon as an 0800 telephone number is plastered across a TV commercial, any creative value is immediately destroyed. However, times are changing and contemporary interactive relational marketing is fighting to be seen as creative in its own right. The marketing communications industry in general has realised this fact and interactive relational marketers are being recognised for their creativity with British Design and Art Direction Awards (Denny 1996).

Furthermore, the old above/below-the-line distinction is being displaced by the concepts of 'left' and 'right' of the line and by 'integrated marketing communications' (IMC). The distinction between above and below the line was based on whether the agency received commission from media owners for their buying of time or space. If they did, it was declared to be above the line, if not (e.g. traditional direct marketing and sales promotion), it was below the line. Now, this distinction has become blurred not only because many campaigns are paid for by fee rather than by commission but also because interactive relational marketing employs media through the use of direct response advertising. It is now more accepted to speak of left and right of the line which represents acquisition and retention strategies. It is also important to produce messages that, across different platforms, communicate consistently. The development of 'one-stop shop' agencies and the power of data in the trend towards not only integrated but interactive integrated communications (Peltier *et al.* 2003) further underpin the need for well-devised interactive relational messages.

The importance of understanding the audience

We have already touched upon the fact that good creativity springs from a thorough understanding and appreciation of the target audience. Of particular importance here is an awareness of the things that motivate consumers and the benefits they seek from different products and services.

Motivation theory

Motivation is a basic concept in human behaviour and thus also in consumer behaviour. Motivation can be described as the driving force within individuals that moves them to take a particular action. This driving force is produced by a state of tension, which exists as a result of an unfulfilled need that moves us away from psychological equilibrium or homeostasis (Exhibit 12.3).

Individuals will strive both consciously and subconsciously to reduce this tension by fulfilling their needs. Every individual has the same need structure but different specific needs will be to the fore in different individuals at various points in time. Thus, our proposition is that marketing does not create needs, rather it encourages us to *want* brand X by associating its acquisition with the satisfaction of a latent need. On this basis, interactive relational marketing creative can benefit from an understanding of the key aspects of motivation theory because specific message appeals can be based on such analysis. Perhaps the most widely acknowledged theory of motivation is that of Maslow, which is represented as a hierarchy of needs (Exhibit 12.4). Maslow's proposition is that needs at one level must be at least partially satisfied before those at the next level become important in determining our actions.

Maslow's hierarchy

We assume that most readers will be familiar with Maslow's hierarchy and thus we will not dwell on its details. However, the significance of the hierarchy to marketing is great. It clearly demonstrates that a need refers to more than mere physiological essentials. Other forces driving our behaviour can come from a concern for our safety, social integration, personal recognition, learning,

EXHIBIT 12.3   Homeostasis

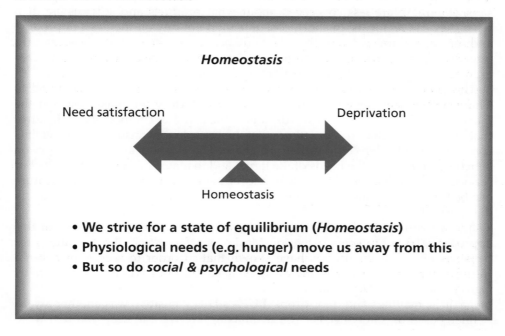

EXHIBIT 12.4   Maslow's hierarchy of needs

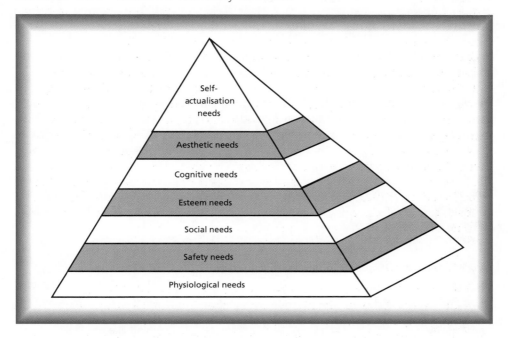

appreciation of our surroundings or from the perceived importance of spiritual satisfaction. We are less concerned about what products and services *are* than what they can *do* for us. In short, consumers do not buy on the basis of product and service features *per se*. Rather, they buy because of the benefits these features offer us. Recognition of this can be translated into message appeals and other aspects of interactive relational marketing creativity.

This point can be illustrated in many ways. A quotation often attributed to Charles Revlon of Revlon Cosmetics is: 'In the factory we make soap, in the market we sell hope.' In other words, it isn't the physical composition or features that are being purchased, but rather what they can do for consumers; the benefits consumers might derive from their purchase. The classic way of focusing in on benefits is to identify the needs of the target and to match one or more product or service features that are in some way relevant with each need. Then each feature can be converted, using a 'which means' approach, into a benefit that can satisfy that need (Table 12.1).

Interactive relational marketing creative often reflects the application of this approach. Playing to some extent on Maslow's safety level, direct mailings for pensions aimed at the 18–35s have shown that in order to secure an assured future, a second pension is increasingly desirable. Indeed, the campaign by Ogilvy and Mather Direct has won a variety of creative awards for its inserts in magazines, mailings and door-drops. BUPA's DRTV creative was another award winner, based on safety needs: 'You're amazing, we want to keep you that way.'

TABLE 12.1 Needs–Features–Benefits

Needs	Features	Benefits
Identify needs	Select relevant features	Convert features into benefits that satisfy needs
Newly married couple who have just moved into a newly built house.	This drill-bit set includes a quarter-inch masonry and a quarter-inch wood/metal bit.	This drill-bit set can help you turn your house into a home by allowing you to personalise it by hanging shelves, pictures etc.
Shy and retiring 18-year-old who has just started university and wants to make some new friends.	Brightly coloured designer-label jacket.	This jacket will help you fit in and become part of the in-crowd.
A young woman who wants to experience life to the fullest and wishes to make a statement about her individuality.	A navel-piercing service.	Piercing your navel makes a statement. It says something about who you are and you've never before experienced anything like the feeling it gives you.

This and direct campaigns for life assurance, especially covering family members, also relates to concerns for loved ones (i.e. social needs) and additionally to more personal esteem needs (our self-esteem can be enhanced by feeling we are looking after those for whom we have some responsibility). Social needs are also portrayed by BT's 'Friends and Family' and 'It's Good to Talk' DRTV campaigns.

Freudian motives

A very different perspective is provided by the application of Sigmund Freud's psychoanalytic theory which distinguishes three basic structures of the mind: id, ego and superego (Freud 1964) (Table 12.2).

TABLE 12.2 Id, ego and superego

Superego	Conscious level
Ego	Subconscious level
Id	Unconscious level

IN THEORY

Freudian motives

Id

The *id* is the unconscious, instinctive source of our impulses, a source of psychic energy. It is a beast looking for immediate hedonic gratification (pleasure), self-interest, and a short-term perspective. Freud argued that the libido, sexuality, is the driving force of the id but the more general interpretation is that the Id is the reservoir of 'base' instincts and there could sexual or violence-related or even traumatic experiences from the past which linger in the unconscious and exert influence on conscious and subconscious processes.

Many people believe that consumers may be influenced at the unconscious level by 'subliminal' advertising. Subliminal advertising is supposed to exert influence on behaviour while consumers are not aware of the influence attempt of this type of advertising. Examples of subliminal advertising are short flashes such as 'Eat popcorn' or 'Drink Coca-Cola' inserted in a film in New Jersey. These flashes are too short to be consciously observed (Packard 1957). Subliminal images may also be inserted in pictures, in a scrambled or hidden way, e.g. the word SEX to be read in the ice cubes in a glass of whisky (Key 1973). The suggestion is

→

that these hidden flashes or pictures are being unconsciously observed, processed and, without any cognitive defence or screening by the superego, transmitted to the mind of consumers. These subliminal messages exert a strong effect on behaviour without people knowing that they are being influenced. Recent research, however, does not support this view and there is conflicting evidence for its effectiveness. But if subliminal advertising does work, it would bring many ethical questions to the fore about whether this type of advertising should be allowed or not. A possible 'direct' application would be the encoding (glyphs) of personalised data into questionnaires when a guarantee of confidentiality is used in order to increase the likelihood of open and full responses.

Superego

The *superego* represents the internalised representation of the morals and values of those important to us in society and operates at the conscious level. Thus it consciously controls our behaviour by seeking to make it fit with these internalised norms. It is our social conscience and can conflict with the id.

Ego

The *ego*, on the other hand, responds to the real world and acts in a mediating role between the id and reality. It does not operate at the conscious level but neither is it submerged into the unconscious; instead, it is a subconscious mediator between the other two elements. Thus it controls our instinctive drives and tries to find a realistic means by which we can satisfy our impulses, or socially acceptable (to satisfy the superego) outlets that will adequately address the id drives (Exhibit 12.5).

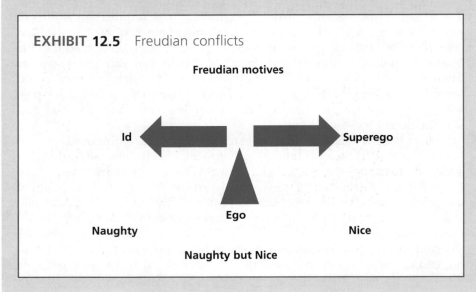

EXHIBIT 12.5 Freudian conflicts

Freudian motives

Id — Superego

Ego

Naughty   Nice

Naughty but Nice

It might be suggested that appeals to the id can be made in subconscious ways. Pack designs that could spark off a subconscious set of associations might be based on phallic and other symbolism in the designs, shapes, textures and materials.

CASE STUDY 12.1

Phallic vegetables and participative naked men

In Chapter 10 we explored relational media and described the use of 'ambient' media including the rather innovative use of phallic-shaped vegetables. Stickers were placed on these vegetables by cooperating stall holders in markets and free condoms were offered. This was on behalf of the Family Planning Association and the campaign also included placing cards in clubs, bars and cinemas. These cards showed a picture of a naked man with a hole punched out in his groin (Exhibit 12.6). Ninety per cent of these cards were picked up. As well as reflecting the use of phallic symbolism in a direct response campaign, it also demonstrates participation in campaigns. As we see later, if the receiver of the message can be 'involved' with the message, it is often more effective in communicating. In this instance, the nature of the participation is probably all too obvious.

EXHIBIT 12.6 Phallic participation

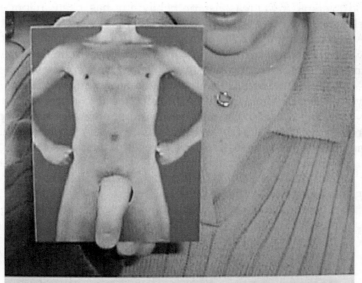

WHO CAN RESIST - THE CARD WAS DESIGNED TO ENGAGE AND ENTERTAIN DURING NATIONAL CONDOM WEEK.

(Source: DMA Awards 2002: Bronze Award for the Outdoor/Ambient Media Category)

Other messages might attempt to tap the subconscious id drives with what superficially would appear to be rather obscure references. Take, for instance, an advertisement in which a woman is about to eat a toffee apple. She wears a bracelet on her wrist in the form of a snake and the copy reads 'Adam just cured my fear of snakes'. The advertisement is actually for gold jewellery, but there is plenty of Freudian symbolism here (Adam and Eve, 'forbidden fruit' and the phallic symbolism of snakes!). This might go completely over or under the heads of the target market, at least at the conscious level, but if it reaches the id then it might well be doing what was intended. The problem with the subconscious, of course, is that it is very difficult to identify and research, even if it exists. Different psychoanalysts might well interpret research findings in different ways and so the whole approach attracts critical attention.

A classic piece of market research years ago investigated the reasons for poor sales of the newly introduced instant coffee. The widely quoted study of instant coffee usage illustrates that there can be 'good' and 'real' reasons for behaviour (Haire 1950). The indirect questioning approach employed in this project was to ask women what sort of housewife would have compiled the shopping lists shown in Table 12.3. Half the sample had the list which differed only by having instant coffee included. The instant coffee shopping list was seen to have been drawn up by a lazier, less well-organised woman who was described as not being a good housewife. Direct questioning, on the other hand, revealed good reasons for preferring real coffee, which revolved around the product not tasting as good as drip-grind coffee. Respondents were considered to be unwilling or unable to reveal their true (real) reasons for not buying instant coffee and the principle of 'good' versus 'real' reasons for behaviour has been a long-held premise in marketing.

A major element of this 'deeper' approach to motivation concerns the balance between the id and the superego. If a main tenet of the theory is the conflict and ultimate compromise between these components, consider the effects of alcohol. In a classic television anti-drink advertising campaign, the same sense was played twice, through the perceptions of the two main characters. First, a man was drinking more and more and, through *his* eyes, was becoming more and more sophisticated, suave and attractive to the women around him. Then the same episode was played through *her* eyes: a drunk was getting more and more

TABLE 12.3   Haire's shopping list

Shopping list 1	Shopping list 2
1½ lb hamburger	1½ lb hamburger
2 loaves Wonderbread	2 loaves Wonderbread
Bunch of carrots	Bunch of carrots
1 can Rumfords baking powder	1 can Rumfords baking powder
1 lb Nescafé instant coffee	1 lb Maxwell House drip-grind coffee
2 cans Del Monte peaches	2 cans Del Monte peaches
5 lb potatoes	5 lb potatoes

(Source: Haire 1950)

obnoxious. What this nicely demonstrates is the effect that alcohol can have on reducing the constraints of the superego. Indeed, in a series of advertisements for Pernod, the copy, in a variety of different settings, read 'Pernod: Free the spirit'. Apart from being the obvious play on words, it could also be equated with the notion of freeing the id.

Consider the id a little further. When on holiday in a foreign country we are often unaware of the local norms and some people will deliberately ignore them to such an extent that there is little perception of social constraints at all. In such situations the id can be free and this might explain the misbehaviour of the lager louts in Spanish resorts. The proposition, then, is that there can be *good* and *real* reasons for behaviour. Interactive relational marketers can use messages which reflect this to varying degrees. At one extreme would be the Club 18–30 approach where the real reason (i.e. sex on holiday) is barely disguised ('Beaver Espania', 'One Swallow Doesn't Make a Summer' etc.). We suggest that this sort of 'id' appeal would generally not be acceptable in mass media communications that reach the mass of the population with little targeting. But the direct approach perhaps allows for this, providing these risqué messages are targeted at the 'like-minded' in a discrete way, for example though direct mail. In this way, the more 'private' message that direct communications provide could give added momentum for Freudian messages.

At another extreme a more subtle set of imagery for a direct mailing can be used, for example for a sports car in which the *good* reasons appear to revolve around speed being a safety feature. This might be converted into the benefit of being able to accelerate safely during an overtaking manoeuvre. However, the underlying *real* reason might be that the sports car helps attract the opposite sex or is even a substitute mistress! This is not as far fetched as it might sound and was, actually the theme of advertising for the MGB GT car in the early 1980s. The copy headline for that advertisement read: 'Psychologists say a saloon car is a wife and a sports car a mistress'. In Chapter 6 we referred to research that suggested that it is in the car market that men tended to prefer the graphic imagery in mail packs (Evans *et al*. 2000) and perhaps some of this imagery can operate at the subconscious level. So again, we propose increased opportunities for Freudian messages arising from the direct and interactive media.

Another example would be direct mailings for 'men's health' books; the name reflects the good reason (perhaps more acceptable to the superego) but the message inside the mailing is about 'unleashing animal magnetism' and the books are mostly concerned with improving one's sex life (an appeal to the id).

In one sense this Freudian approach might suggest a role for symbolism as being a way of satisfying the id, but not in a direct way nor complete id satisfaction. One motivator is the sex drive and this could be open to this sort of 'substitution effect'. For example, Polhemus and Randall (1994) suggest that the relatively instant sexual gratification of earlier eras has been replaced to some extent by fantasy; for example, by the dressing up (down) of some club scenes.

Using the hierarchy of effects

There is a long-held belief in marketing that audiences respond to messages in a very ordered, sequential way: cognitively first (thinking), affectively second (feeling), and conatively third (doing). Based on this response sequence, numerous authors have developed what have become known as hierarchy of effects models (Table 12.4). These hierarchies of effects have received much criticism, mainly because this is not necessarily a sequence that consumers follow in all situations. As we discuss later, low involvement products might not elicit such an ordered or elaborate sequence of pre-purchase stages, whereas a product with which the customer is deeply involved may well do. However, such models do provide a framework with which to guide discussion of consumer responses to marketing actions and messages. In looking at how hierarchies of effects might provide insights for creative effort we will utilise the model proposed by DeLozier (1976). This is not the most recent but it does allow us to incorporate a good number of underpinning concepts from psychology. Indeed, even if the validity of sequential models has sometimes been questioned, it is useful to be able to apply behavioural science theories in a reasonably integrated way.

Exposure

Exposure involves ensuring that the communication is placed in such a way as to make it accessible to the target audience. Thus there are implications here for list selection, media selection and indeed for distribution channel selection. The major focus at this stage is on reaching the target audience. We explored aspects of this in Chapter 3 when we discussed media selection metrics.

TABLE 12.4 Hierarchy of effects models

St. Elmo Lewis Circa 1900	Colley 1961	Lavidge & Steiner 1961	McGuire 1969	Engel et al. 1986	DeLozier 1976
		Unawareness	Presentation	Exposure	Exposure
Attention	Awareness	Awareness	Attention	Attention	Attention
	Comprehension	Knowledge	Comprehension	Comprehension	Perception
					Retention
Interest		Liking			
Desire		Preference	Yielding	Yielding	Conviction
	Conviction	Conviction	Retention	Retention	
Action	Action	Purchase	Behaviour	Action	Action
					Post purchase

A number of years ago, Lea & Perrins sauce ran a campaign which incorporated door-drops of free samples, a small bottle of sauce banded onto magazine covers and sales of the bottle through Tesco for a loss-leading price of 19p (Lovell 1997). In all cases, targets were invited to send for a recipe book in exchange for providing data about themselves (nine questions-worth). The exercise was designed to gather data for targeting purposes. By matching the data collected with NDL lifestyle profiles it was found that Lea & Perrins customers were absolutely 'average', nothing peculiar to them seemed to emerge. However, one of the specific questions enquired about television viewing habits. 43% of the Lea Perrins users said they watched morning programmes on ITV. Had the company relied solely on their demographic and lifestyle profiling they would not have selected this particular medium (i.e. off-peak television advertising) and thus they saved valuable resources and satisfied presentation criteria very effectively.

Data-informed marketing clearly should aid the achievement of this 'exposure' stage. The metrics explored in Chapter 3 should, in theory, make it more likely for customers to be targeted appropriately, but as we have seen, the quality of data and how this is mined and used can sometimes leave much to be desired.

Attention

Even if the marketing message is in the right place, there is no guarantee that the market will see it. Consumers sometime discard mailings as 'junk mail' (even if it might be relevant to them if they opened it) and 'channel hop' when watching television if advertisements don't capture their attention. This is especially true of acquisition drives as relevance is not necessarily immediately apparent to the audience.

Although not an entirely reliable estimate, there are several suggestions that every UK consumer is exposed to at least 2000 promotional messages a day but that probably notice less than 5%. Americans are exposed to 18 million unsolicited telephone calls daily and receive 3000 coupons per year (Hallberg 1995). Davidson (1997) suggests that the average consumer in Spain and Italy is exposed to over 20000 commercials per year. He also submits that £1m worth of advertising probably only buys 0.1% share of consumer exposure. Godin (1999) suggests that in USA there are over 3000 marketing messages per day and that, on average, each US citizen had $1,000 spent on them via direct targeting in 1998. So there is a clear implication that once the communication is presented effectively, the next task is to ensure that it gets noticed. Four aspects of attention may be distinguished:

1 **Gaining attention:** This is especially important but difficult in the clutter of commercial messages.
2 **Holding attention:** Once gained, the attention needs to be held in order for the actual message to be conveyed.
3 **Leading attention:** Attention must be guided towards the message and not to peripheral elements in the communication.

4 **Distracting attention:** This is usually ineffective, unless the arguments of the message are weak. Distraction might prevent consumers from discovering the weakness of the arguments. However, as a means of convincing the audience, the use of distraction raises certain ethical questions.

Thus, during this phase interactive relational marketers are concerned with attracting and maintaining attention and there are particular techniques that can be employed to accomplish this. Among these is the use of colour. On a general level, colour tends to arrest the attention more than monochrome and indeed different colours have different attention values. The warm colours (orange and red) advance towards us in our perception, having the effect of making whatever it is appear larger, whereas the cooler colours (blue) recede in our perception, making the message appear smaller. On this basis, red is often cited as having the highest attention value. Having said this, there can be problems associated with the use of red. The Royal Mail's automated sorting machines cannot read addresses printed in black on a red background and this presents enormous difficulties every Valentine's Day when the use of red envelopes is commonplace.

Movement is another technique utilised to gain attention. Thus direct response advertising on television or in the cinema is often considered more efficient at generating attention than static press or direct mail messages. However, it is possible to simulate movement in a still picture and this is often done effectively with blurred backgrounds suggesting a moving foreground (e.g. a speeding sports car). Video cassettes which also allow the use of movement are becoming more popular for communicating direct messages, as are interactive communications via the Internet. A variation on movement is the use of sound, and modern technology enables the interactive relational marketer to send 'speaking brochures' containing a 'chip' allowing personalisation of each message.

The position of the message is also important in gaining attention. The back outside cover of a magazine, for example, means that the direct response advertising message can be noticed even without opening the magazine at all. Some interactive relational marketers might include the main component of the message on the envelope of a mailing to increase the chances of it being noticed. Others, however, believe that by doing this, recipients might be more likely to discard the piece before opening because it would be clear it was a piece of direct mail. Variations on this theme include letting an enticing part of the message (e.g. the incentive) show through the window of the envelope. Some believe that the right-hand page attracts more attention than the left, because as we leaf through the pages from the beginning, it is the right page that is uncovered first. Those, however, who start with the sports page on the rear of a newspaper may well disagree and argue that the left-hand page is the one that is usually noticed first. If a double-page spread is employed then there are no competing messages and so attention could be more likely because of this. A compromise is to cover a double-page spread with just half of each page. The 'golden section' technique or 'law of thirds', known by architects and artists, can also be employed. This suggests that if a rectangle is divided into thirds, both vertically and horizontally, then the eye goes to the points of intersection (Exhibit 12.7). Placing important parts of the copy or graphics at these points might therefore make them more prominent. Additionally, in the context of direct mail, if some of the message is moved to the postscript or 'PS', it is often the case that this will be the part of the letter that is especially noticed and remembered.

In Chapter 5 we explored marketing research and, from this, it is worth remembering the 'eye camera' which in the current context is useful for tracing the path that the eye takes over a 'space' such as a mailing or advertisement.

The size of the message has also been the focus of marketing discussion. This is not, however, a straightforward matter. Doubling the size of a message is unlikely to double attention. A suggestion is that attention increases as the square root of the message size (Rudolph 1947).

Yet another approach to gaining attention uses what might be described as known conditioned responses. We attend, almost automatically, to the sound of a telephone ringing and this approach is used to good effect in direct response radio advertising. Other examples include the introduction to a radio advertisement with a statement such as 'Here is a news flash'. A major direct marketer, Avon Cosmetics, uses a ringing door bell and the 'Avon calling' slogan in its promotional approach.

If a message is in some way different then because of its distinctiveness it may stand out and thus attract more attention. In practice, many marketers place the distinctiveness of their communications at the top of their priorities. The direct mail industry has a strong track record of employing unusual and attention-grabbing mailings. All sorts of items have been sent in mailings and this makes the medium extremely capable of delivering innovative creative ideas. Certainly, communications do need to stand out from the crowd but because many

EXHIBIT 12.7 The golden section

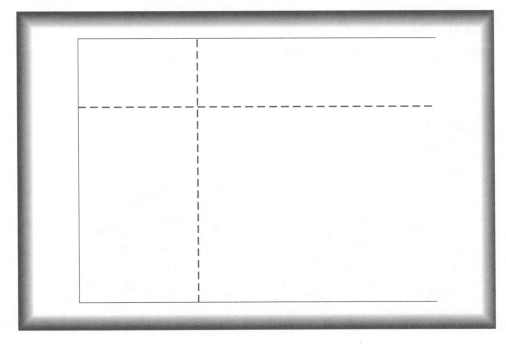

consumers may be risk averse, communications must also create a sense of familiarity. Thus, the marketer needs to be careful when using novel messages. For example, in an outrageous mailing in the USA, Barnes describes: 'a pigeon in a cage was first trialled ... the idea was that recipients would attach their response to the leg of the pigeon which would return "home". Surprised at the low response rate, post-campaign research revealed that instead of the birds being released, they were killed and eaten' (Barnes 2001).

Another problem, of course, is that novelty only lasts a short time so the employment of this approach must be especially dynamic in order to maintain its distinctiveness. The marketer will need constantly to test different approaches because each will not be effective for very long. See Chapter 4, which provided a review of testing techniques. It is clear, though, that interactive relational marketers are very proactive in this area and they do try different approaches (e.g. the use of envelopes of different shapes, sizes, colours and textures) (Exhibit 12.8). Indeed, when it comes to direct mail, the colour of the envelope is important: 'to seduce the recipient into opening the envelope ... financial companies (should not) use red as it's a danger colour ... (so) use a lot of blue' (Wright 2000).

An Oxfam mailing included a tape measure which could be used to measure whether one's child's arm was small enough that they could be classified as suffering from malnutrition. Posters for Disneyland Paris by Ogilvy Mather Direct are based on capturing images from 8mm cinefilm before production and end up as 3-D holograms which are expensive but attention grabbing (Stokes 1997).

One poster advertisement for Levi jeans actually had a pair of 501s glued to the poster itself. The result was that many people clearly noticed the message because many of them tried to get the jeans, but of course they were positioned

EXHIBIT 12.8   A novel envelope

too high on the poster for this to be an easy matter. Another version of this also involved a poster. A Ford car was glued to the poster, which was advertising Araldite, not Ford! A later version of this series actually saw two cars glued to each other on the poster.

Not only is it important to attract the attention of consumers, but the interactive relational marketer must also hold the attention and convey the message. Attention-getting devices are numerous, but if attention is attracted by methods inconsistent with the message or the situation, this attention is readily lost. Attention may be held by encouraging the audience to participate. Messages that work in this way might be ambiguous or incomplete and for this reason the audience is encouraged to attend to the message more than would otherwise be the case, in order to complete the message and to make sense of it (the Zeigarnik Effect, after B. Zeigarnik, 1927).

Perception

Once noticed, the message/offering should be perceived and understood in the intended way. In getting the audience to perceive a message in a particular way, interactive relational marketers can utilise a number of techniques. One application concerns visual illusions and, although space does not permit more coverage here, the reader will be familiar with line drawings that deceive the eye. An example for the interactive relational marketer could include the design of welcome packs which appear taller or broader than they really are, by employing thin vertical stripes or broad horizontal bands respectively (Exhibit 12.9). 'Figure–ground' relationships can also be employed to change the perception of graphic images, depending on which is identified as the background to the image.

EXHIBIT 12.9 Visual illusions

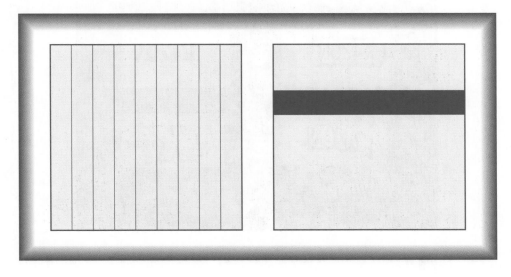

Consider the variations of a possible brand logo in Exhibit 12.10. These were used to demonstrate the importance of *how* messages are presented (Bernstein 1975). These four versions of a hypothetical brand are developed and respondents are asked what sort of product category they belonged to. Version 1 produced no uniform reply and nothing very spontaneous was forthcoming. It was seen by different people as being a range of very different categories. Version 2, however, started to produce more rapid replies and ones that were a bit more focused: on a brand stamped on a car tyre or tea chest, presumably because of the stencilled style. Version 3 was stronger again. Most people readily thought of a comic or a powerful cleaner. Version 4 also produced fairly spontaneous and similar responses: a travel company of some kind, such as a ferry operator, airline and so on. The point of this experiment was to convey the important message for marketers that the way in which something is presented can affect perception of it. That is, perception is not isolated to the substantive element of a message. Clearly there are important implications here for logo and pack design.

Because interactive relational marketing targets individuals, messages can be tailored to be congruent with the 'frame of reference' of each target. Even when targeting segments, the message can be tailored (e.g. mailings can be written specifically and differently for men and women or for different ethnic groups etc.). In the case of gender-specific mailings, it has been found, through exploring the issue in focus groups, that there are gender-specific styles which lead to different perceptions (Evans *et al.* 2000; Pidgeon 1997). Essentially what we are

EXHIBIT 12.10   Logo perception

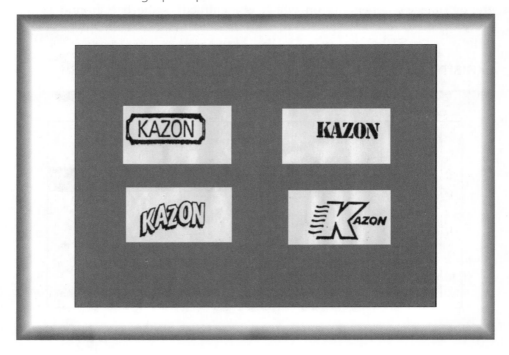

saying is that perception is selective. That is, different individuals might perceive the same message differently, or selectively. The task for the interactive relational marketer, who will be targeting customers as *individuals*, is to discover, through market research and database analysis, what the relevant 'fields of experience' of the intended audience are. Exhibit 12.11 shows that effective communication occurs where common frames of reference are used. If the sender of the message understands the experience and general frame of reference of the receiver and puts the message in terms that mean the same to both sender and receiver, there is a greater chance of effective communication. The receiver should then perceive and understand the message in the intended way.

For example, consider the graphics in Exhibit 12.12. A crooked sign in long-hand writing advertising fresh eggs, found along a country lane and outside a rustic country cottage, might be congruent with the receiver's frame of reference for 'happy hens' and free range eggs. The same sign in a city centre probably wouldn't be. Conversely, if the sign said 'flying lessons', the receiver might be less tempted to ask for further details in the rustic cottage than in the city centre!

Earlier, we discussed the use of colour in attracting attention. Colour is also an important consideration during the comprehension stage because different colours can transmit different meanings. Most colours have both positive and negative meanings and, of course, different colours are more or less fashionable at different points in time. Furthermore, different colours can mean different things in different countries, thus making any generalisations almost impossible to make. However, in Western cultures, red is often seen as being a fiery, passionate colour; white as being pure and virginal; black as being mysterious,

EXHIBIT 12.11 Schramm model of communication

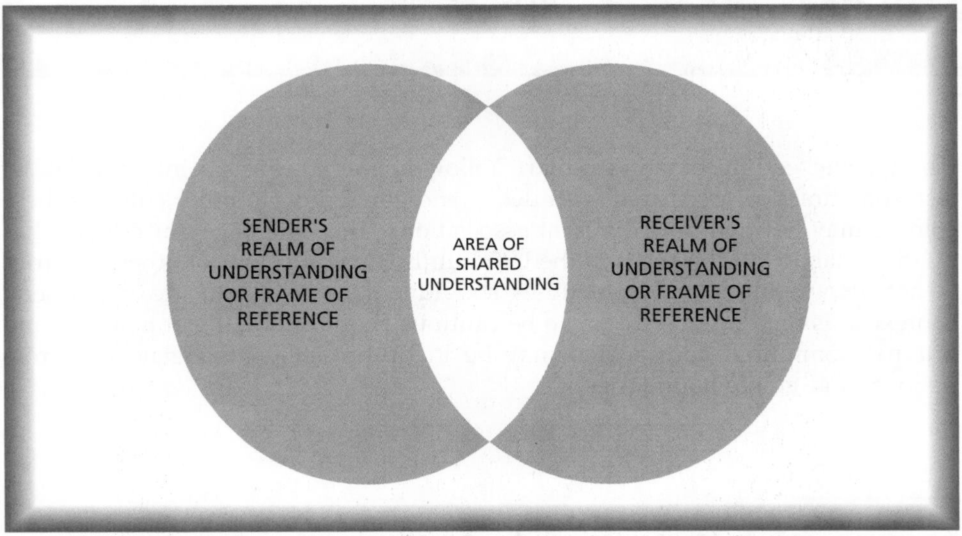

SENDER'S REALM OF UNDERSTANDING OR FRAME OF REFERENCE

AREA OF SHARED UNDERSTANDING

RECEIVER'S REALM OF UNDERSTANDING OR FRAME OF REFERENCE

(Source: Schramm and Roberts 1971)

EXHIBIT 12.12 Frames of reference

perhaps wicked but sometimes smart. Yellow might be seen as being cheerful but also sometimes as associated with deceit and cowardice. In other cultures these colours may have entirely different associations. The funeral colour of black has no major taboo attached to it in the UK, but the funeral colour of other countries is not always black and sometimes should not be used outside the funeral context. It is therefore necessary to be cautious about international mailings and Internet communications which may be inappropriately homogeneous across national and ethnic boundaries.

Retention

Assuming the message is interpreted appropriately, retention is concerned with ensuring it is remembered in the intended way. Marketing communication may be considered to be concerned with teaching consumers about various marketing offerings. If this is the case, marketing itself can benefit from a knowledge of how consumers learn about things. Two approaches to teaching customers to learn and remember are outlined here. Firstly, associationist learning theory, which is summarised in Exhibit 12.13 and secondly, Gestalt theory.

Associationist learning is based on the early work of the Russian physiologist Ivan Pavlov (1928) and on the work of Skinner (1938). Pavlov considered learning to be essentially concerned with stimulus–response relationships. His experiments included observation of dogs' responses to various stimuli. For example, when presented with food, dogs often salivate. There was nothing exceptional about this; it is a natural and even automatic response to that stimulus. Pavlov went on to present various other stimuli at the same time as presenting the food. Again the dogs salivated. When, however, this process of paired stimuli presentation was repeated very often, he then presented the other stimulus (the sound of a tuning fork, light bulb being flashed, etc.) by itself and the dogs salivated to that other stimulus even though no food was present. What he argued was that an unnatural response to the light or sound had been conditioned into the animals. This type of learning became known as classical conditioning.

Skinner's work resulted in the acknowledgement of operant conditioning. This recognises that learning can be encouraged through the use of positive and negative reinforcers. By pairing rewards or punishments with certain behaviours, Skinner showed that these behaviours could be reinforced.

Interactive relational marketing might not operate precisely at the level of Pavlov's or Skinner's experiments but the principles are used every day. If the

EXHIBIT 12.13 Associationist learning

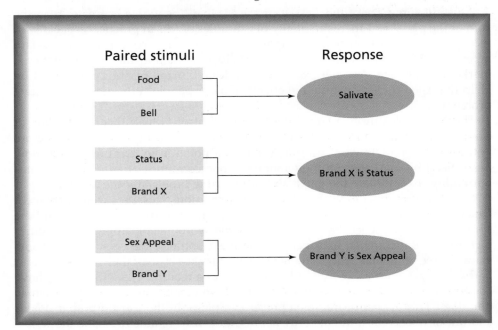

creative team understands what the intended market segment is interested in (e.g. status appeals or sex appeals), it can present the relevant appeal and thus the market is likely to respond favourably. Presenting a brand together with a benefit as paired stimuli in a repetitive fashion may mean that the market will learn to associate the brand with that particular benefit. The associations attached to a large number of well-advertised brands can be explained by this process. Marketing does not create needs, but rather encourages a want for a specific product because it associates its acquisition with the satisfaction of a need. This is the basis of the associationist learning approach.

Gestalt learning

Another school of thought which considers how we learn is the Gestalt school. Gestalt theory is based on the work of Köhler (1927) and his ape Sultan who displayed insight by being able to put the components of a problem together to form a (greater) whole, or solution. These experiments were conducted around the same time as Pavlov's but Köhler thought there was more to human learning than mere stimulus–response relationships. Köhler presented apes with a variety of puzzles. One such puzzle involved an ape in an almost bare cage, with a bunch of bananas hanging from the roof. However, because of the geometry the bananas were not directly accessible. There was also a table in the corner of the cage. The aim of the apes was to get the bananas but they were left to solve the problem of achieving this on their own. Nothing much happened for some time until one ape, Sultan, eventually moved the table underneath the bananas, stood on it and managed to reach the fruit. Köhler described this as an extra element of mental processing that was needed to solve the problem and the learning process therefore includes a degree of insight.

A useful summary of the Gestalt process is that 'the whole is greater than the sum of the parts' and there are plenty of examples of this in practice, especially in recent times. The direct mail example mentioned earlier concerning the Oxfam tape-measure is an example of real participation in the interactive relational marketing message. Another example includes a blurred plastic pack mailed by Help the Aged to demonstrate the effects of older people suffering from cataract problems.

The law of closure is a constituent component of Gestalt theory. The law of closure states that we tend perceptually to close up, or complete, objects that are not, in fact, complete. For example, the use of notation in text messaging (now being used by marketers in their mobile phone communications) demonstrates our ability to 'complete the gaps' and at the same time enjoy the 'game'.

In advertisements for Newcastle Brown, ambiguous messages were displayed. One pictured a can of the beer with the ring pull having just been opened and the spray forming a speech balloon in which the word 'woof' appeared. Another pictured an irate, arched-back cat confronting a bottle of the beer. Clearly, some extra degree of mental processing is needed to make sense of these messages and perhaps any 'Geordies' of Tyneside who might be reading this will already have added the one missing piece of information: Newcastle Brown being known as 'the dog'. This also appeared as a poster campaign in the Cardiff area in Wales and out of over 3 000 students only about a dozen were able to 'make the whole mean more than the sum of the parts'. The pieces of the jigsaw must be available to receivers and in this instance in Cardiff this was not the case.

A wonderful illustration of the law of closure and the encouragement of receiver participation is demonstrated by a series of Becks beer advertisements in the style magazines of the early to mid-1990s. These advertisements were superficially very surreal and ambiguous, with strange and 'off the wall' mixed-up images. The reader, however, was shown how to make sense of the message by folding the page along dotted lines. When folded the message was simplified and the words 'just buy Becks' were produced. It is a superb example of participation (even physical participation)! We explored the characteristics of Generations X, Y and Z in Chapter 6 and a common one is the desire to participate in marketing messages, rather than receive them in a passive way. Remember, these groups are knowledgeable and cynical of much 'upfront' marketing and are willing to 'play games' with messages.

What successful trend-spotters have found is that contemporary teenagers and twenty-somethings react best to playfulness, honesty and irony. Furthermore, DRTV advertising in particular may appeal to them because it gives them control over the solicitation of any further information, and kitsch, low-budget 'infomercials', designed to exhibit products in the manner of an in-store demonstration, are just the type of thing that appeals to this playful, ironic and anarchic postmodern television audience.

Law of continuity

The 'continuity' element can be manifested in a staged presentation over time, encouraging participation in the story. A classic example of this, of course, is the 'soap opera' style of episodic advertising employed by Nescafé with their Gold Blend brand. The Marlborough case below also reflects the continuity principle because the receiver of the message has to participate in a sequential way.

CASE **STUDY** 12.2

Marlborough

A competition asked for a telephone number to be called. This asks various questions and gathers some personal data for the database. If the quiz questions are correctly answered, a mail pack is sent (Exhibit 12.14); as can be seen, this includes a letter, a map and a video. Each contain 'clues' as to where the 'hidden treasure' can be found: the recipient plays the role of a treasure hunter. The competition is won if the treasure is found. This demonstrates the continuity principle because the recipient participates in a sequence of connected stages in the message.

(Source: Marlboro Customer Services (1998) Consumer Promotion, Hemel Hempstead)

EXHIBIT 12.14   Mail pack

The marketing implication of this is that by encouraging participation, because the problem is not solved at the immediate superficial level, marketers are tapping into this process of insight. Indeed, because of this, the approach is often considered to be more effective in helping with the learning of a marketing message.

There is evidence to suggest that 'online' marketers are turning away from banner advertisements in favour of more participative messages. Borroff (2001) reports a KPE (agency) study that predicts the growth of online interactive games that will be available via interactive TV and mobile phone as well as conventional Internet access. These are known as 'Advergames': 'promotion of a brand within the format of a computer game ... by becoming an intrinsic part of a game's content, the brand gains an exposure and credibility that it wouldn't otherwise achieve' (Borroff 2001). This approach allows for capture of the player's details and profile and, by sending as e-mail attachments, can easily be sent on to friends to form a viral campaign. For example, the Robbie Williams track 'Love be your energy' was supported by an Advergame which could be downloaded from the Robbie Williams website and e-mailed to other fans. There is clear potential here for interactive participation to enhance brand–customer relationships.

In the same way that we discussed selective perception earlier, there can be an equivalent at this stage as well: selective retention. The techniques and theory on which to base interactive relational marketing creative approaches, however, provide potential means for ensuring a reasonable degree of uniformity of response even though there is equally the potential for individualistic responses – and in any case the interactive relational marketer should be increasingly individualising not only the fact of targeting but the nature of targeting.

Conviction

If the sequence has 'worked' so far, then we have communicated the message via appropriate vehicles to reach the target market, have gained attention and ensured that the message has been interpreted and remembered in the intended way. We are now concerned with developing favourable attitudes towards the marketing offering. Coverage of attitude measurement in Chapter 5, on marketing research, explored this in greater detail, but it is worth a brief recap. The components of the structure of attitude are shown in Exhibit 12.15.

Focusing on such a structure helps in the definition of communications objectives, message creation and campaign evaluation. Objectives can be defined by discovering the nature of perception with regard to the interactive relational marketing offering, whether attitudes are favourable or unfavourable, what the antecedents of these attitudes are, and whether the target audience exhibit any intention to buy. Thus, messages can be tailored depending on what is discovered during this analysis. Campaigns may also be evaluated by measuring these same dimensions over the course of the campaign in order to identify if progress is being made.

EXHIBIT 12.15   Attitude components

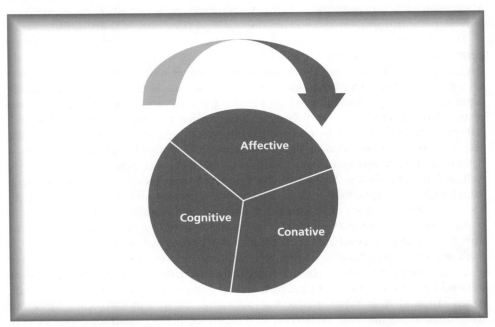

Action

The previous stages of response move potential customers through pre-purchase events so that there is a better chance of conversion. However, in order for action to take place, interactive relational marketing messages must include a 'proposition', a 'solution' and a 'mechanism' for facilitating response. Unfortunately, many such mechanisms are designed poorly and make it difficult for the target audience to respond (e.g. coupons which are too small to fill out completely or DRTV advertisements which do not provide ample time for the telephone number to be recorded).

Interactive relational marketers will be especially interested in the nature of this stage; measuring response rates and the time of response according to individual profiles and so on. It has been found that if direct mailings are written using 'you' (the consumer), rather than 'us' (the company), response rates are significantly higher. Similarly, adding words like 'now' or 'instantly' at the end of sentences such as 'If you buy this/donate to that' will also usually increase response rates.

It is worth mentioning impulse buying here. It might be assumed that no 'pre-purchase' stages would be relevant with this, but Bayley and Nancarrow (1998) found that there are different forms of impulse buying and we can assume that pre-purchase stages are relevant for some of these. For the 'accelerator impulse' category, for example, the purchase has already been decided but the sudden purchase is because the buyer decides to stock up, now rather than later. The 'compensatory impulse' occurs when the buyer either feels 'down' and low in self-esteem and uses sudden purchases as a prop, or if the purchaser rewards him or herself for achieving something or after completing a tedious or difficult chore and uses a surprise purchase as a reward. In an old chocolate advertisement, for example, Cadbury depicted people achieving something and then awarding themselves a medal: a CDM (Cadbury's Dairy Milk).

The 'breakthrough impulse' is intriguing. It includes some high value products such as cars and even houses! It appears that the purchaser suddenly decides that whatever underlying emotional conflict with which they have been wrestling can be resolved by a step change in their lives: 'a few years ago Winnie went out to buy a spare set of car keys and signed up for a new car' was how one respondent described an impulse purchase in this category. Another revealed: 'after a row with his wife he jumped into the car to drive around and cool down. He drove past a house for sale and something made him stop. He put an offer on it there and then and went back to tell his wife the good news.'

The final category is probably what we tend to think of as impulse buying: 'blind impulse'. Here, this 'may be a transient, dysfunctional captivation with an idea or aesthetic aspect of the product' (Bayley and Nancarrow 1998).

The interactive marketer could base messages on the first three versions of impulse buying by tailoring it to fit the underpinning rationale.

Response or purchase does not represent the end of the process. Interactive relational marketing is concerned with satisfied customers, good relationships with customers, loyal and repeat purchasing and/or the spreading of goodwill. After purchase has taken place, the provision of information via marketing communications, through packaging and labelling, is important for consumers to structure their product experience. Consumers who buy a bottle of Moldavian wine, like to learn about the country of origin of this wine the type of grapes and other information. Indeed, the wine may taste better knowing all of this. The same is true for Scottish single-malt whiskies. Background information helps to structure the experiences with the product and to appreciate it more. Direct mailings via loyalty and retention schemes can help create the relevant relationships through which the consumer can achieve this structure.

Post-purchase

Post-purchase activities can be better understood with reference to cognitive dissonance theory. Cognitive dissonance is a kind of psychological tension resulting from perceived inconsistencies in cognitions (Festinger 1957). For example, let us assume that you have just purchased a new car after a fairly extensive pre-purchase search and evaluation of alternatives. Your final choice is probably a bit of a compromise because no car is completely tailored to the requirements of each individual customer. Having said this, you are likely to view your choice as highly satisfactory. However, there may have been other cars available that you believed had some superior design features. These slightly contradictory cognitions can produce dissonance and you may ask yourself if you have made the correct choice. The level of dissonance is a function of the importance of the cognitions to the individual. So, if the point about other design features is very minor, the level of dissonance might be negligible. If, however, you drive your new car home and the next-door neighbour, whom you see as being especially knowledgeable about cars, says 'Why on earth did you buy that, that model has a terrible repair record?', your level of dissonance could be very substantial indeed.

Cognitive dissonance is a motivator in that the individual tries to reduce it. In the above example, a high level of dissonance over the car might lead the buyer to seek supporting evidence for his decision, to reassure himself that he has done the right thing. Indeed, much interactive relational advertising is aimed at people who have already made a purchase, in order to help them overcome dissonance, reassure them of their purchase decision and therefore ease the way for a repeat purchase or at least to spread positive messages to others. It is also worth emphasising that dissonance is not the same as dissatisfaction. Dissatisfaction produces dissonance, yes, but a generally satisfying purchase may also produce cognitive dissonance if some of the cognitions over it are slightly inconsistent with each other. Take the example reported by Jones (1996) which we discussed in Chapter 9, concerning the missing ash tray from his BMW. The Lexus dealer collected it and delivered it to his home and even though he had been a loyal BMW owner for ten years, the seemingly minor incident over the ash tray raised dissonance in him. The Lexus dealer's actions suggested to him that there would be less dissonance if he was a Lexus customer, so that's what he became.

Although we are discussing dissonance in the post-purchase phase, because it applies particularly well here, it can occur in the pre-purchase phase as well. We can usually perceive positive and negative cognitions whenever we are faced with alternatives, so the mental processing of these pros and cons can obviously lead to levels of confusion and doubt over the best choice. Therefore the onus is on the interactive relational marketer to provide the target with information which will help the individual overcome such dissonance. It might appear obvious to suggest that we emphasise consonant cognitions (positive aspects of the product). However, there are occasions when a slightly negative set of points can be made as well. The use of two-sided arguments has been suggested as being effective for more educated audiences. Direct charity marketers often draw attention to the 'downside' of, for example, parting with one's hard-earned money but for a very good 'cause'. The interactive relational marketer might also emphasise how many satisfied customers there are. For example, in the mid-1990s a satellite broadcaster, in direct response advertising, used the copy headline 'half a million people can't be wrong'. Interactive relational marketers can also extend this by targeting specific individuals as endorsers or opinion leaders. The targeting of opinion formers (e.g. journalists) is also a highly sophisticated business, as we saw in Chapter 6, with the aim of securing positive and relevant 'editorial' coverage by those who are likely to be perceived as being independent, credible experts. This can 'reassure' customers they have bought the right product.

Related to this is offering reassurance through after-sales service and warranties. This is again very prominent in the car market and reflects the pragmatic view that cars are complicated pieces of machinery and that no car is (yet) tailor-made for each individual customer, so there are bound to be both consonant and dissonant cognitions. However, by emphasising that if anything does go wrong then it will be taken care of, dissonance can be reduced. Mitsubishi, for example, have used the copy headline 'They would cost us a fortune if they were not so reliable'.

Exhibit 12.16 shows how marketing messages of a bygone era depicted, somewhat unethically, healthy people to reassure that smoking cigarettes will not do you harm. Indeed, the copy reads '. . . will not affect your throat'!

Involvement

As we stated earlier in this chapter, the sequential 'hierarchy of effects approach is not universally applicable and indeed has its critics. We will shortly review other approaches to message creation, but before we leave the sequential model it is worth saying that levels of involvement that customers have with the product category or the specific purchase issue can go some way to determining the value of these models (Exhibit 12.17). Consumers can have *enduring* involvement which continues out of sustained interest in the product category and *situation* involvement which is more short lived because the interest is related to an event (e.g. a wedding dress).

Low involvement has been associated with passive learning (Krugman 1965) which was suggested as a way of explaining how TV advertisements produced high recall but not much attitudinal change. It was postulated that the viewer is passively receiving the message and does not attend much to the advertisement. More recent research by Ritson (2002) tends to confirm this. Krugman's point was that TV is 'animate' while the viewer isn't. However, with the advent of interactive TV the viewer can be encouraged to be more involved with messages

EXHIBIT 12.16 Unethical reassurance

and, as we have seen, the more involved, the greater the interaction and possibility for relationship development.

Print media is inanimate so the reader has to be animate in order to make sense of messages, so involvement, although selective, can be positive. Where there is little interaction, however, based on Krugman, passively received TV messages would be more effective for low involvement products and the more interactive print media more appropriate for high involvement situations.

Exhibit 12.18 extends this by presenting a simple grid model used by Foote, Cone and Belding, a major advertising agency, to analyse consumer/product relationships. The grid also shows the typical locations of several different products. The FCB grid is based on two concepts: consumers' involvement and their salient knowledge, meanings and beliefs about the product.

Some products are considered primarily in terms of rational factors, such as the functional benefits of using the product. These are termed 'think' products in the grid model. Included in this category are such products as investments and car batteries, all products purchased primarily for their functional consequences.

In contrast, 'feel' products are considered by consumers primarily in terms of nonverbal images (visual or other types of images) and emotional factors, such as

EXHIBIT 12.17   Involvement and sequential models

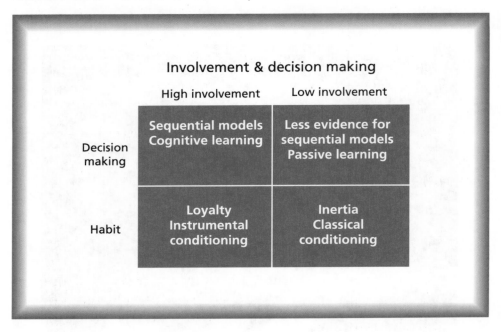

EXHIBIT 12.18   FCB grid

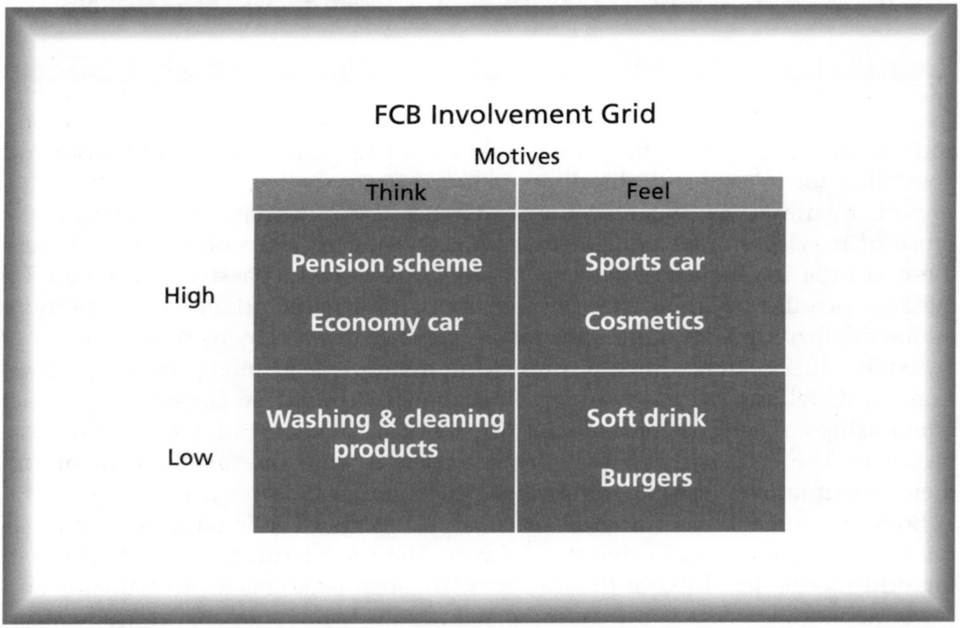

FCB Involvement Grid

Motives

	Think	Feel
High	Pension scheme Economy car	Sports car Cosmetics
Low	Washing & cleaning products	Soft drink Burgers

psycho-social benefits and values. For instance, products purchased primarily for their sensory qualities: ice cream and cosmetics, as well as products for which emotional consequences are dominant, such as flowers or jewellery, are feel products in the FCB grid. An example of the practical application of this concept can be seen on the use of scent strips for perfume products which allow consumers to experience 'feel' products. Marketing research shows that consumers are more likely to buy products that they have sampled. Scent strips can be included in direct mailings and can be a very effective marketing communication device.

The appropriate message strategy depends on the product's position in the grid. Sometimes, a product can be 'moved' within the grid, from a 'think' to a 'feel' product.

The following section extends this analysis by exploring the extent to which messages can be based more on 'emotion' than 'logic' or vice versa.

Moral principles, emotions and logic

In trying to persuade the target audience we must first decide whether we are to appeal to their moral principles, their emotions or to logic (Aristotle's *Ethos*, *Pathos* and *Logos*).

Ethos

In focusing on ethos the message will essentially refer to the source; the organisation sending the message. To this end, source credibility becomes a major consideration. 'Credibility is the extent to which the recipient sees the source as having relevant knowledge, skill, or experience and trusts the source to give unbiased, objective information' (Belch and Belch 1990). Obviously, organisations that are seen to have expertise and knowledge are likely to be looked upon more favourably than those that aren't. One means of achieving source credibility on this basis is to use accepted experts in the field to endorse the product or service. Trustworthiness may, however, be rather more difficult to achieve. 'The variable most universally accepted as a basis for any human interaction or exchange is trust' (Gundlach and Murphy 1993). Trust has been the subject of debate and discussion within a whole range of disciplines. Indeed, because of its centrality to social and economic life, an academic school has developed, whose primary objective is to understand and elucidate this single concept. Based on the work of Anderson and Narus (1990), we define trust as the consumers' belief that a firm will perform actions that will result in positive outcomes for them, and will not take unexpected actions that will result in negative outcomes. The more trustworthy an organisation is seen to be, the more likely that consumers will have positive attitudes towards the ideas they put forward (Giffin 1967; Hovland *et al.* 1953). This may be especially true when consumers are negatively disposed towards these ideas in the first place

(Sternthal *et al.* 1978). However, trust is not something that an organisation can truly convey through their communication alone. Trustworthiness depends first and foremost on the actions of an organisation as it conducts business.

Pathos

Messages that appeal to pathos 'involve creating an appropriate feeling in the receiver by appealing to feelings, values or emotions, by associating strong affective cues with the product or brand' (Percy and Rossiter 1980). Humans are emotional creatures and the emotions we express can also form the basis of interactive relational marketing creative appeals. Plutchik (1980) identifies eight basic emotions (Exhibit 12.19) which occur in four pairs opposite each other in the circle. Emotions that are adjacent to one another combine to create a composite emotion (e.g. joy and anticipation combine to form optimism). The following are examples of how some of these approaches might be used in interactive relational marketing communications.

- **Fear**: The intention here is to imply that something nasty or unfortunate might happen if the target does not take some action. Appeals such as 'Don't miss out on the opportunity of a lifetime' are often used.

The following case study reflects the use of a fear appeal in direct relational marketing.

EXHIBIT 12.19   Plutchik's emotion wheel

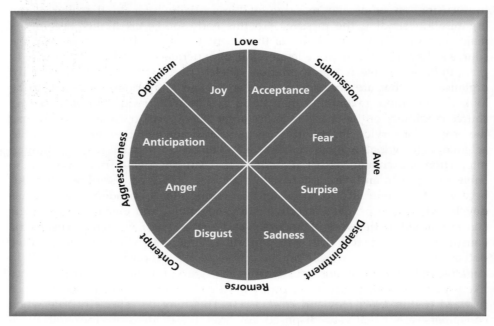

Fear appeal

Saatchi & Saatchi devised a campaign for the Multiple Sclerosis Society to coincide with the London Marathon. The ads appeared in the national press and on cross-track posters in the London Underground. The aim was to contrast the debilitating effects of the disease with the able-bodied runners, using a switch device to show the unpredictable way in which MS can switch off parts of the body (Exhibit 12.20). Part of the problem for the agency was the recognition that people donate to charities for which they feel empathy, yet relatively few have direct experience of MS. Hitting the right tone was essential to generate that empathy.

(Source: Adapted from material provided by DMA from the Multiple Sclerosis Society Award Winning Case Study, DMA/Royal Mail Awards 2002)

EXHIBIT 12.20   MS 'switches off' parts of the body: this one's the bladder

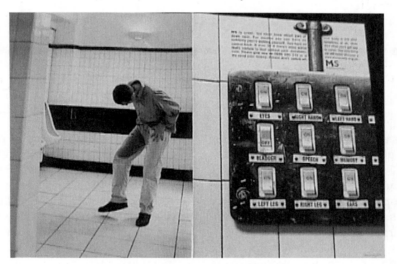

This case study demonstrates the sensitive yet powerful use of a fear appeal in a context that needs emotional involvement in order for the message to fully hit home.

- **Love**: Reflected in mailings for products and services associated with marriage or anniversary gifts, where the purchase of these items is an expression of the target's love.

- **Disgust**: Here the appeal is designed to shock the target so that they are mobilised into action. RSPCA pieces often use images of tortured or neglected animals in order to achieve this.
- **Anticipation**: The idea here is to engage the target and get them to seek more information. 'You could be the lucky recipient of £25,000. Just open this envelope for more details.'

The use of entertainment may also be useful in pathos appeals. Entertainment can break through the clutter of contemporary marketing communications and captivate the target audience. It tends to be used to best effect with products and services that are not highly differentiated, are frequently purchased, elicit low involvement and are relatively inexpensive (Burnett, 1993). Entertainment often involves the use of humour, hyperbole or borrowed interest. Devising a message which is considered humorous by everyone in the target audience is extremely difficult, and humour tends to wear out quickly. There is also a tendency for humour to overwhelm the other aspects of the message and in particular to draw attention away from the product. The following case reflects the use of both humour and the Gestalt principle of 'participation', discussed earlier in this chapter.

CASE **STUDY** 12.4

Humour

Humour was a key weapon in a test mailing by Smile.co.uk, one of the first wave of online banks in the UK launched in 1999. The mailing had a serious mission, however: to drive people online to find out more about Smile's products, and also to experiment with targeting people while at work.

Given that the target customer for Smile is much younger than the average bank customer, a traditional financial mailing was never an option. Humour and targeting would be critical to its success. Key influencers likely to publicise Smile by word of mouth were identified and mailed at work with a 'Pants' pack.

The inclusion of a pair of pink pants was guaranteed to cause a stir in the office. The appropriateness of the 'Pants' concept, being both a current vogue phrase in the youth lexicon and a play on the notion that you can wear what you like when banking from home, was not lost on the judges. 'A clever idea, well crafted' was their verdict. In a market where a 0.5 per cent response is considered average, the mailing achieved a response of more than 7%.

(Source: DMA Gold Award for Consumer Direct Mail (Low Volume), 2001 Awards)

Hyperbole or exaggeration may also be entertaining in its own right, though its primary purpose is to present some fact about the product in a form that is larger than life and therefore attractive. Inevitably, some products and services don't lend themselves too well to the use of entertainment. It is often the case, therefore, that the message will borrow interest by incorporating a focal point which has high inherent interest but which is not directly related to the product or service being sold.

Logos

'Logos appeals require the receiver to deduce the desired conclusion from a message based upon certain general principles presented or implied within the message that the receiver accepts as true; or they may require the receiver to induce the required conclusion as a result of believable evidence in the arguments presented' (Percy and Rossiter 1980). In other words, this is essentially a rational appeal that uses logic to develop a reason why, benefit, or position. Because the audience must follow through the logic, this strategy requires a moderate level of both interest and information-processing skills on the part of the audience. Such messages frequently make use of factual statements about the product or service which are used to introduce new products and to describe technical products. Alternatively, the interactive relational marketer may focus upon product or service comparison, outlining the benefits of their offering in relation to those of competitors. Demonstration of the product in use may also prove beneficial, although this naturally requires the utilisation of television, cinema or videos.

Symbolism

In addition to consideration of ethos, pathos and logos appeals, the interactive relational marketer will need to be mindful of the images and symbols incorporated in their communications. The study of signs such as these is referred to as semiotics. Semiotics comes originally from the work of Ferdinand de Saussure whose work was concentrated on linguistics but which is appropriate for the study of all signs. In looking at signs Saussure highlighted that every sign consisted of a signifier and signified and a typical Saussurian model is depicted in Exhibit 12.21.

The signifier is the form that the sign takes while the signified is the concept it represents. So, for example:

Sign: The written word 'house'
Signifier: The letters 'h-o-u-s-e'
Signified: The category 'house'

It must be remembered that there is no necessary connection between the signifier and the signified. While in English the letters 'h-o-u-s-e' represent the

EXHIBIT 12.21   Saussure's signifier and signified

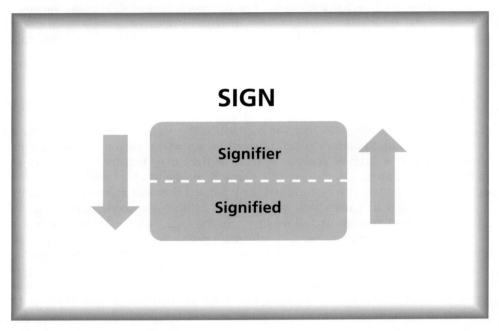

category we know as 'house' in French there is a totally different signifier (i.e. 'm-a-i-s-o-n').

Other major developments in the study of signs have been offered by Charles Sanders Peirce who, in contrast to Saussure's dyad, proposed a triad depicted in Exhibit 12.22. Peirce's model is different in that he highlights that the meaning of a sign comes from the sense that is made of it by an interpreter. Therefore:

Sign vehicle: The form of the sign.
Sense: The sense made of the sign by an interpreter.
Referent: What the sign stands for.

Of particular interest to marketers in the use of signs are the notions of metaphor and metonymy. The purpose of using metaphors is to imply a resemblance between something which is essentially unfamiliar to the target audience (usually the product or service) and something which is more familiar to them in order to convey a particular message. For example, in its advertising Solpadeine is portrayed using the metaphor of arrows shattering a pane of glass. This is done to signify the ability of this drug both to target pain and to overcome it. Interestingly, painkillers usually use one of two metaphors: strength in overcoming pain or soothing and relaxing properties. Thus, the use of metaphors, whether they be images or phrases, lends credence and strength to the message concerned. However, metaphors do rely upon the audience to make the connection and thus they must be used with care. Metonyms may also be visual or verbal and their purpose is to use an individual example to signify a related

EXHIBIT 12.22 Peirce's sign triad

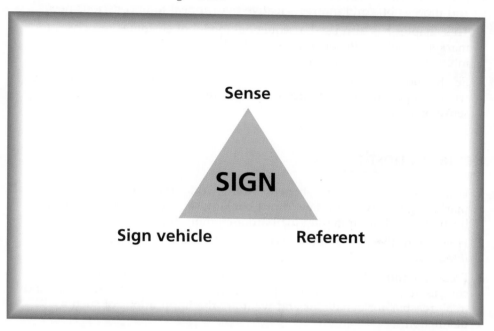

general category (e.g. the use of pictures of a starving child to represent the poverty and deprivation of the Third World). Thus the associations brought about by the use of metonyms can also lend power to our message.

'The necessity of differentiating products motivates sign competition. The competition to build images that stand out in media markets is based on a process of routinely unhinging signifiers from signifieds so that new signifier–signified relationships can be fashioned' (Goldman and Papson 1996). To all intents and purposes, signifiers, through constant use and appropriation, have become free-floating to the extent that marketers can now attach almost any signifier to their brands when communicating. For example, an image of a crawling baby might be used to signify a new generation of product, exploration, starting out on a new project and a whole host of other ideas and notions.

Summary

- The main emphasis of the marketing concept is on customer orientation, satisfying and anticipating the customers' needs and wants. Thus, understanding customers' needs, feelings, drives and emotions can provide the interactive relational marketer with valuable clues to how the creative strategy should be structured.

- People are not always aware of the real needs determining their behaviour and more subtle and indirect creative may appeal to unconscious needs.
- This chapter has also used a sequential model of customer responses to marketing actions to suggest the application of behavioural concepts to interactive relational marketing messages.
- Furthermore, we have outlined different strategies depending on whether we are appealing to the target audience's moral principles, emotions or sense of logic.

Review questions

1 Using the 'needs–features–benefits' framework, devise interactive relational marketing creative for a new direct banking service, a charity for battered husbands and an upmarket mail-order clothing catalogue.

2 How might theories of motivation be applied to the development of interactive relational marketing messages?

3 Freud identified the id, superego and ego. What are these, and can they contribute anything to relational marketing? What is meant by 'good' and 'real' reasons for behaviour and what are the implications of such a distinction?

4 Of what value to interactive relational marketing messages are 'sequential models' of customer response to marketing activity?

5 Discuss 'gestalt' psychology and its role in 'participative' interactive relational marketing messages.

6 How might interactive relational marketers use human emotion to develop their message appeals?

Further reading

Evans, M.J., Moutinho, L. and Van Raaij, W.F. (1996) *Applied Consumer Behaviour*, Harlow: Addison Wesley.

Percy, L. and Rossiter, J.R. (1980) *Advertising Strategy: A Communication Theory Approach*, New York: Praeger.

Thomas, B. (1996) *Royal Mail Guide to Direct Mail for Small Businesses*, Oxford: Butterworth-Heinemann.

References

Anderson, J.C. and Narus, J.A. (1990) 'A Model of Distributor Firm and Manufacturer Firm Working Partnerships', *Journal of Marketing*, 54(January), pp. 42–58.

Barnes, R. (2001) 'High Impact Mail', *Marketing Direct*, November, pp. 51–3.

Bayley, G. and Nancarrow, C. (1998) 'Impulse Purchasing: A Qualitative Exploration of the Phenomenon', *Qualitative Market Research: An International Journal*, 1(2), pp. 99–114.

Belch, G.E. and Belch, M.A. (1990) *Introduction to Advertising and Promotion: An Integrated Marketing Communications Perspective*, 3rd edn, Chicago: Irwin.

Bernstein, D. (1975) *Creative Advertising*, Harlow: Longman.

Borroff, R. (2001) 'Are Games the Future of On-Line Ads?', *Precision Marketing*, 31 August, p. 2.

Burnett, J. (1993) *Promotion Management*, Boston: Houghton Mifflin.

Colley, R.H. (1961) *Defining Advertising Goals for Measured Advertising Results*, New York: Association of National Advertisers.

Davidson, H. (1997) *Even More Offensive Marketing*, London: Penguin.

DeLozier, W. (1976) *The Marketing Communications Process*, New York: McGraw Hill.

Denny, N. (1996) 'Can We Win Creative Respect?', *Marketing Direct*, November, p. 12.

Engel, J.F., Blackwell, R.D. and Miniard, P.W. (1986) *Consumer Behaviour*, 5th edn, Chicago: The Dryden Press.

Evans, M., Nairn, A. and Maltby, A. (2000) 'The Hidden Sex Life of the Male and Female Shot', *International Journal of Advertising*, 19(1), pp. 43–65.

Festinger, L. (1957) *A Theory of Cognitive Dissonance*, Evanston, IL: Row Peterson.

Freud, S. (1964) 'New Introductory Lectures', in *Standard Edition of the Complete Psychological Works of Sigmund Freud*, 21, London: Hogarth (Original work published in 1933).

Giffin, K. (1967) 'The Contribution of Studies of Source Credibility to a Theory of Interpersonal Trust in The Communication Process', *Psychological Bulletin*, 68(August), pp. 104–20.

Godin, S. (1999) *Permission Marketing*, New York: Simon and Schuster.

Goldman, R. and Papson, S. (1996) *Sign Wars: The Cluttered Landscape of Advertising*, New York: The Guildford Press.

Gordon, W. (1991) 'Accessing the Brand Through Research', in D. Cowley (ed.) *Understanding Brands*, London: Kogan Page, pp. 33–56.

Gundlach, G.T. and Murphy, P.E. (1993) 'Ethical and Legal Foundations of Relational Marketing Exchanges' *Journal of Marketing*, 57(October), pp. 35–46.

Haire, M. (1950) 'Projective Techniques in Marketing Research', *Journal of Marketing*, 14, pp. 649–56.

Hallberg, G. (1995) *All Consumers are Not Created Equal*, Chichester: John Wiley.

Hovland, C.I., Janis, I.L. and Kelley, H.H. (1953) *Communication and Persuasion*, New Haven, CT: Yale.

Jones, T.O. (1996) 'Why Loyal Customers Defect', *KeyNote Presentation*, IDM Symposium, 6 June, London.

Key, W.B. (1973) *Subliminal Seduction*. Englewood Cliffs, NJ: Signet.

Köhler, W. (1927) *The Mentality of Apes*, New York: Harcourt Brace.

Krugman, H.E. (1965) 'The Impact of Television Advertising: Learning without Involvement', *Public Opinion Quarterly*, 29, pp. 349–56.

Lavidge, R.J. and Steiner, G.A. (1961) 'A Model for Predictive Measurements of Advertising Effectiveness', *Journal of Marketing*, 25, pp. 59–62.

Lovell, C. (1997) IDM Guest Lecture, University of the West of England, 30 January, Bristol.

Maslow, A.H. (1970) *Motivation and Personality*, 2nd edn, New York: Harper & Row.

McGuire, W.J. (1969) cited in Barry, T.E. and Howard, D.J. (1990) 'A Review and Critique of the Hierarchy of Effects in Advertising', *International Journal of Advertising*, 9, pp. 121–35.

Moriarty, S.E. (1986) *Creative Advertising: Theory and Practice*, Englewood Cliffs, NJ: Prentice Hall.

Oxenfeldt, A.R. and Swann, C. (1964) *Management of the Advertising Function*, Belmont, CA: Wadsworth Publishing Co.

Packard, V. (1957) *The Hidden Persuaders*, New York: McKay.

Park, C.W., Jaworski, B.J. and MacInnis, D.J. (1986) 'Strategic Brand Concept-Image Management', *Journal of Marketing*, 50(October), pp. 135–45.

Pavlov, I.P. (1928) *Lectures on Conditioned Reflexes: The Higher Nervous Activity of Animals*, 1, London: Lawrence and Wishart, translated by H. Gantt.

Peltier, J.W., Schibrowsky, J.A. and Schultz, D.E. (2003) 'Interactive Integrated Marketing Communications: Combining the Power of IMC, the New Media and Database Marketing', *International Journal of Advertising*, 22, pp. 93–115.

Percy, L. and Rossiter, J.R. (1980) *Advertising Strategy: A Communication Theory Approach*, New York: Praeger.

Pidgeon, S. (1997) 'The Success and Future of Gender-Specific Fund-raising Propositions', *Journal of Not for Profit Marketing*, Spring.

Plutchik, R. (1980) *Emotion: A Psychoevolutionary Analysis*, New York: Harper and Row.

Polhemus, T. and Randall, H. (1994) *Rituals of Love*, London: Picador.

Ritson, M. (2002) 'Why big audiences don't always mean big gains for advertisers', *Marketing*, 3 October, p. 16.

Rudolph, H.J. (1947) *Attention and Interest Factors in Advertising*, New York: Funke Wagnalls.

Schramm, W. and Roberts, D. (eds) (1971) *The Process and Effects of Mass Communication*, Urbana, IL: University of Illinois Press.

Shocker, A.D. and Srinivasan, V. (1979) 'Multiattribute Approaches for Product Concept Evaluation and Generation: A Critical Review', *Journal of Marketing Research*, 16(May), pp. 159–80.

Skinner, B.F. (1938) *The Behaviour of Organisms*, New York: Appleton-Century-Crofts.

St. Elmo Lewis, E. (circa 1900) cited in Barry, T.E. and Howard, D.J. (1990) 'A Review and Critique of the Hierarchy of Effects in Advertising', *International Journal of Advertising*, 9, pp. 121–35.

Sternthal, B., Dholakia, R.R. and Leavitt, C. (1978) 'The Persuasive Effect of Source Credibility: Tests of Cognitive Response', *Journal of Consumer Research*, 4(March), pp. 252–60.

Stokes, D. cited in Darby, I. (1997) 'Printing Gets all Creative', *Marketing Direct*, January, pp. 52–6.

Wallas, G. cited by Belch, G.E. and Belch, M.A. (1995) *Introduction to Advertising and Promotion: An Integrated Marketing Communications Perspective*, 3rd edn, Chicago: Irwin.

Wright, A. (2000) reported in Bird, J. (2000) 'A Question of Colour', *Marketing Direct*, July/August, pp. 49–50.

Zeigarnik, B. (1927) 'Uber das Behalten von erledigten und unerledigten Handlungen', *Psychologische Forschunnge*, 9, pp. 1–85.

PART 5
Direct and Relational Planning within a Societal Context

Parts 1 to 4 of this book have explored the development of relational marketing from a number of different origins and driven by a variety of factors. The role of personalised data has been shown to be of major importance in operationalising relational marketing and new interactive media have facilitated relational communications.

We now move into slightly more holistic areas. First, we explore wider social implications of direct relational marketing and then suggest how, synergistically, the earlier coverage plus this wider perspective can be incorporated within direct and relational marketing planning.

In terms of the former, we explore customer reactions to direct relational marketing, together with issues of privacy. These inevitably need to be considered because there is an obvious trade-off between individuals providing (knowing or unknowingly) personal details and marketers' being able to interact with customers and prospects as individuals. In addition to how the individual reacts to this, there are also wider implications for society and indeed the *societal marketing concept* comes into play here.

The approaches explored throughout this book are subject to a degree of regulation, both voluntary and legislative, and we explore relevant aspects of this regulation.

Our coverage of direct and relational marketing planning is an analysis of the series of iterative stages which comprise the process. We emphasise the importance of marketing's 'outside in' perspective by highlighting the variety of 'environments' within which marketing operates, along with techniques and processes for monitoring these and projecting their likely impact upon how the organisation operates.

The importance within direct and relational marketing of 'measurability' is again shown to be a cornerstone. This must be built into the planning process in terms of both objective-setting and results measurement. We also provide examples of integrated direct and relational marketing strategies.

13 Customer reactions and the regulation of data-driven marketing

Learning objectives

Having completed this chapter, students should:

- Be aware of the range of reactions that consumers can have to data-informed personalised and relational marketing.
- Recognise the impact of relational marketing in a wider 'societal' context.
- Comprehend the nature of privacy and its constructs and antecedents.
- Be familiar with the general principles of data protection legislation.
- Be able to seek specialised advice from the various voluntary regulatory bodies.

The consumer view

About 90% of my morning mail is separated out into 'junk' to be briefly scanned and then put out with the rubbish within one hour of its arrival (I'm not kidding). Otherwise the piles build up over the week to uncontrollable levels.

All unsolicited mail, often including cheap pens or other such inducements, like a ten pence and a two pence coin to support a charity's bid for attention, goes straight into the bin. This is not because I am a hardened, uncaring individual. This is because I refuse to be coerced by such marketing psychology. Allow me to mention a recent débâcle I had with Bose, the hi-fl products manufacturer. It all started when I was sufficiently impressed by an advert in the national press to call its telephone number. The ad promised swift responses. I gave the requisite details and awaited information about a 30-day trial period. It never arrived.

Some considerable time later a Bose package arrived addressed, not to me, but to the previous occupant of the household. He had left the property in November 1999. Clearly the information on Bose's database had never been updated, despite my intervening telephone call handing them my details on a plate. It was obvious that my details and interest in its own advertising campaign had not been passed on. I wrote back pointing out that its systems were clearly not 'joined up'. I also made it clear that the company had not only failed in its relationship management by telephone, but that it had lost a sale. I never heard anything again. It seems there is no clear-thinking individual within the organisation; if that is so, then Bose should take along, hard look at itself. My own experience of marketing is that it is full of acronyms and people who have been brainwashed into thinking that hard-hitting mail campaigns are enough 'in themselves'. I support permission-based marketing, but only so long as it is correctly carried out and keeps the promises that the consumer expects it to have made with them.

The 'correctly carried out' and 'promises being kept' parts are common sense, aren't they? You don't need a marketing psychologist to tell you that.

(Eileen de Bruin, housewife *Marketing Direct* (2002) 'How to Make Opt-In Work', Guide to Data and Permission Marketing Supplement, October, pp. 6–7. Reproduced from *Marketing Direct* magazine with the permission of the copyright owner, Haymarket Business Publications Limited)

Introduction

This opening vignette reflects the increasing knowledge about data-driven relational marketing that today's consumers possess. It also shows the cynicism that can be generated if so-called relational marketing is mere rhetoric.

This chapter explores many of the issues that arise from this. First, we revisit the nature of data that is – and might be – collected and this builds upon our coverage of Chapter 2. Next, we report research into how consumers react to attempts at interactive relational marketing. Not all consumers, by any means, have major privacy concerns over the use of their personal details but some do, and we delve into this issue. We then debate whether marketing should be mainly concerned with 'current campaigns' or the wider social impact that often, inevitably, will be a consequence of the data-informed paradigm. Reactions to some of these issues have been manifested in data protection legislation so we review some of the key components of this form of regulation.

Data sources revisited

In Chapter 2 (Exhibit 2.2) we reviewed a range of data sources. These included transactional data and a variety of additional profiling data such as geodemographics and lifestyle. However, we also referred to 'surveillance' sources such as global positioning satellites for identifying the location of mobile phones and aerial photography for the compilation of a topographical database. We now add further data sources that might become commonplace (see the additions in Exhibit 13.1).

We have added a 'genetics' layer. Clearly, for financial services companies, it would be useful to be able to assess insurance risks on the basis that gene patterns can indicate individuals' future potential susceptibility to illness or disease (Borna and Avila 1999). In the UK some patient data is available in the NHSnet database that can be accessed by healthcare professionals (Introna and Plouloudi 1999).

The possible acquisition of genetic data is a concern for some (Specter 1999). The accessing of individual medical records might be considered to be an invasion of privacy if what is thought to be confidential between doctor and patient is shared across financial services companies. In a survey of 3 000 UK households, three-quarters were against genetic tests for insurance underwriting, 85% against insurance companies rejecting applicants on this basis and 78% against insurance companies charging higher premiums on the basis of genetic tests. Indeed, 68% of the sample thought that this use of genetic data should be

EXHIBIT 13.1 Further data sources

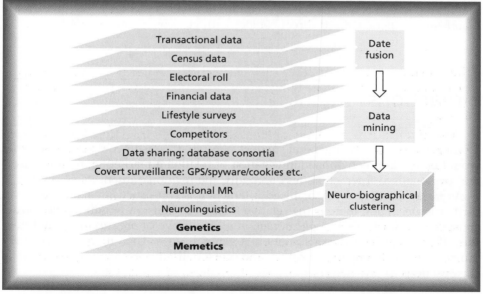

prohibited by law (Borna and Avila 1999). Introna and Plouloudi (1999) report that medics have expressed concern over this trend. The logical extension of the scenario is that those who don't need insuring will be insured and the rest will be excluded.

Our final addition refers to the science of *memetics* which has recently attracted significant attention (Dawkins 1989; Blackmore 1999; Marsden 1998, 1999; Williams 2002). Whereas a 'gene' passes forms of behaviour down (vertically) through the generations, a meme acts as a sort 'horizontal' communicator of how to behave – from person to person, similar to vicarious learning (Assael 1998). The difference, however, is that memes work more like a viral contagion. A good example of the principle is how it is often difficult not to start yawning if others are yawning (Marsden 1998). Could memes go some way to explaining the spread of extreme xenophobia, Nazism or ethnic cleansing? It might be an unconscious communication and one, that might be most enduring if instilled at an early age. Will it become possible to 'create' a meme that marketers can use to communicate through societies, with consumer becoming infected with the mind virus that is not recognised consciously, but which results in them suddenly joining the next fad or fashion? Some say this is nearly possible and research is being conducted to 'design and engineer highly infectious memes that could be used in marketing campaigns' (Marsden 1998).

Stating what is, admittedly, the extreme position, could this mean that we are on the eve of the kind of 'hidden persuasion' that brought the industry under the ethical spotlight of the late 1950s (Packard 1957)? It is interesting to revisit Packard at this point; he wrote: 'Eventually – say by A.D. 2000 – perhaps all this depth manipulation of the psychological variety will seem amusingly old-fashioned. By then perhaps the biophysicists will take over "biocontrol", which is depth persuasion carried to its ultimate' (Packard 1957:195). We explore wider social responsibility issues in greater depth later in this chapter.

We turn now to review some evidence of how consumers react to 'the new marketing' which is heavily based on data-informed strategies which in turn are manifested in personalised direct contact with customers and prospects.

Consumer reactions

There are, perhaps, two general matters here: first, consumer reactions to what would be the more obvious manifestation of relational marketing, namely direct and personalised interaction, and secondly, the relational intent itself.

As far as direct and personalised interaction is concerned, this subsumes yet further issues. First, there is the relative 'macro' dimension within an individual consumer's life of this sort of interaction with a range of organisations and how this affects their lives as consumers in a general sense. Then there are relatively 'micro' issues arising from direct and personalised interaction with specific organisations.

Reactions to direct and personalised interaction at a macro level for the consumer

From the more general consumer perspective, direct and personalised interaction is seen to offer a number of substantial benefits over traditional marketing. For example, the consumer can interact with organisations more conveniently (Darian 1987; Lavin 1993) by direct means such as mail, the Internet or telephony. They can conduct regular business in these ways rather than having to go to physical stores or bank branches, for example.

Because they can explore a range of different suppliers of products and services from the relative comfort of home (or office), they can access a more extensive product assortment (Rosenberg and Hirschman 1980; Gehrt and Carter 1992; Gillett 1976). Even a long trip around a large shopping centre might not unearth such an extensive range as that from an Internet 'surf' across the world. As a result, direct interactive marketing can be seen as appealing to the time-hungry, convenience-orientated, individualistic shopper of the 1990s and 2000s. We refer you back to our exploration in Chapters 1 and 6 in particular for more on this.

However, not everyone subscribes to the notion that the direct personalised approach offers substantial benefits over traditional methods of shopping or communication between organisations and customers. The issue of privacy is increasingly conceptualised as both influencing and exacerbating consumer concerns (Cespedes and Smith 1993; Milne *et al.* 1996; Maynard and Taylor 1996; Patterson *et al.* 1996). This has been of relevance in the UK given industry attempts to argue its ability to self-regulate in lieu of (restrictive) European legislation (Evans *et al.* 1995). Other inhibitors include poor targeting which produces irrelevant communications, often described by consumers in terms such as 'junk' communications. Indeed, this is where we can move into a brief exploration of how consumers perceive their interaction with organisations.

Reactions to direct and personalised interaction at a micro level for the consumer

From research into this area, Evans *et al.* (2001) found that the situation is complex. At the same time as expressing various concerns, consumers also participate in this type of interaction with organisations. They are, for example, simultaneously street-wise yet cynical, as the various 'paradox gaps' in Exhibit 13.2 summarise.

This shows marketers that although direct personalised marketing is clearly a convenience to the time-constrained contemporary consumer, it can also be its own worst enemy because the consumer can be bombarded by a mountain of mail with little time to sort it all or too many intrusive outbound telephone or e-mail contacts.

The volume of personalised marketing that consumers receive is likely to impact upon their attitudes towards it. We explore privacy issues in more detail later, but it is worth introducing some aspects of this here. Physical/interaction privacy is concerned with the physical intrusion of marketing communications

EXHIBIT 13.2   Consumer reactions to direct personalised interactive marketing

Knowledge paradox

Knowledgeable	gap	Partial knowledge
Heard of Experian		Big Brother concerns

*'Taking out a loan that goes on
what is called Experian...
the company that notes everything
you do in your life.'*

Female ABC1 45–54

Comfort paradox

Comfortable with DM	gap	Cynical
Heavy use of phone and mail		See DM as 'rip off'

(Use of phone): *'Yes...once a month...things like catalogues...
I do car insurance over the phone.'*

Male 25–34

*'The only reason they would want any more
information is to try and market to us,
which we don't want anyway.'*

Male 25–40

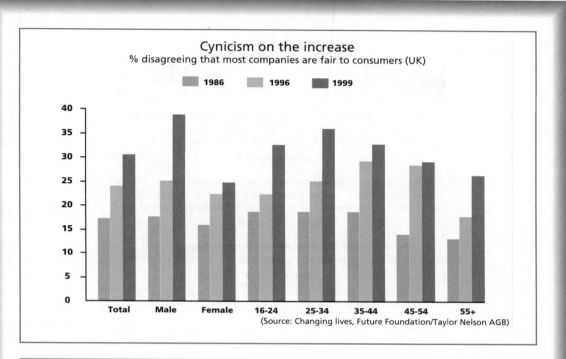

Cynicism on the increase
% disagreeing that most companies are fair to consumers (UK)

1986   1996   1999

Total   Male   Female   16-24   25-34   35-44   45-54   55+

(Source: Changing lives, Future Foundation/Taylor Nelson AGB)

Targeting paradox: relevance

Use of personal data — gap — Continued poor targeting

*'BT are really good at this, they'll send you a little
magazine or whatever saying do this, it will save
you this amount of money.'*

Male 25–40

*'Most isn't wanted, its not relevant and just clutters
up the table...you have to sort through it to get to the "real mail".'*

Male 45–54

Privacy paradox

| Provide personal data | gap | Privacy concerns |

*'I've nothing terrible to hide! It doesn't really bother me,
I'm just mildly interested to know how they
get hold of your name sometimes.'*
Female 45–54

*'I think it's quite unnerving really what people might know.
How much detail they do actually have on you regarding
income and credit limits. I don't know what details are stored.'*
Female 25–34

*'I don't mind companies knowing more about me
but that bit about meeting your needs is a load of bullshit.'*
Male 45–54

Control paradox

| Orgs want relationships with consumers | gap | Consumers don't |

*'Holiday to New Zealand...e-mailed...car hire companies
and whatever they've been emailing me back with different
rates and lots of information...it's great, because I've initiated it,
I want to know the information.'*
Male 25–40

*'I would prefer it if I didn't see anything in the
post unless I had specifically requested it.'*
Female 25–34

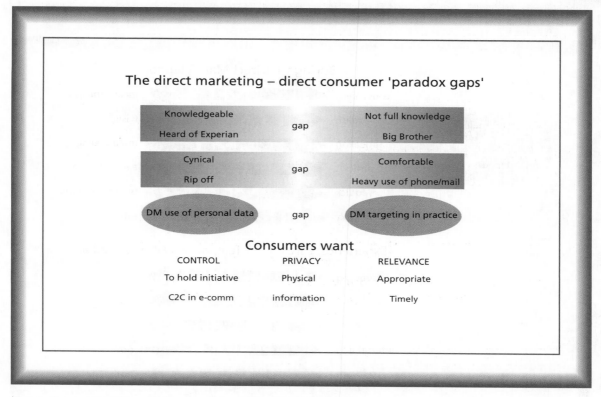

The direct marketing – direct consumer 'paradox gaps'

Knowledgeable	gap	Not full knowledge
Heard of Experian		Big Brother

Cynical	gap	Comfortable
Rip off		Heavy use of phone/mail

DM use of personal data	gap	DM targeting in practice

Consumers want

CONTROL	PRIVACY	RELEVANCE
To hold initiative	Physical	Appropriate
C2C in e-comm	information	Timely

(Source: Evans *et al.* 2001 and Future Foundation/Taylor Nelson AGB 2000)

into the lives of consumers, and the increasing volume of personalised marketing solicitations (see Chapter 10 for some statistics on this) has contributed to a degree of consumer dissatisfaction with marketers in the UK (Patterson *et al.* 1996).

Exhibit 13.3 summarises the results of a survey investigating UK consumers' attitudes toward direct mail and outbound telemarketing (Evans *et al.* 1998). It shows how outbound telephone contact is especially seen to be intrusive.

Consumer reactions to relational intent

The 'privacy paradox' issue summarised in Exhibit 13.2 suggested that some consumers are somewhat cynical about 'relational' interaction. Other research also points to this and this, is not merely as a result of coverage in the popular press of potential concerns. It is likely, as has been shown in the USA, that public concerns had evolved and were evident in the UK even before media coverage became widespread (Phelps *et al.* 1994). There might be a desire on the part of organisations to develop relationships with customers, but customers do not always want to reciprocate.

Marketers, for example, do not like the term 'junk mail'. It applies to mail which is perceived by the recipient as being uninteresting, irrelevant, untimely or

EXHIBIT 13.3   Direct marketing 'consequences'

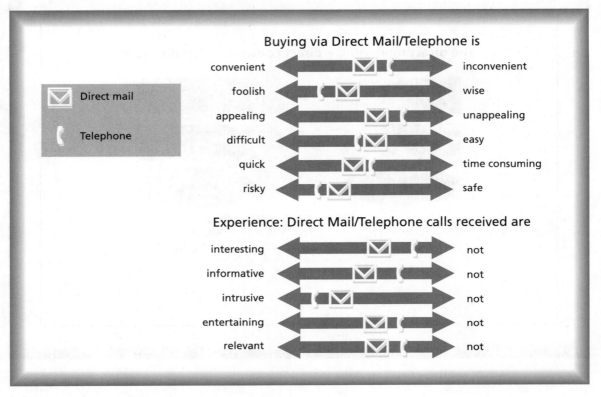

(Source: Evans *et al.* 1998)

inaccurate. The concept is equally transferred to e-mail, fax or telephone contact that is seen in the same way. The converse of this can apply and would therefore be nearer the 'relational' end of a 'continuum' that ranges from 'junk' and irrelevance to true relational interaction: 'if a person is interested in a subject and receives an unsolicited telephone call or piece of mail about it, he is not likely to view its receipt as an invasion of privacy ... it is relevant' (Sherman, 1991:40).

We believe that a key success factor in moving towards relational interaction is the balance of 'control' between customer and organisation. We have already discussed CRM (Chapters 7 and 8) and even the name suggests that the balance of control is in the organisation's favour (the management of customer relationships). As we have seen, the main manifestation of CRM in practice is data-driven marketing via data mining software. We have criticised this and suggested a wider role that incorporates insightful understanding of the customer-organisation interaction across functions and partners. However, for the current narrower CRM we would suggest that a more appropriate name would be CDM (Customer 'data' management).

As far as the consumer is concerned, there are different dimensions of 'control':

1 Control over one's personal information. Information privacy refers to the ability of individuals to determine the nature and extent of information about them being communicated to others (Westin 1967). The dilemma is the one above, of balancing consumers' rights to control access to their personal information and companies' rights to information access for business purposes (Simitis 1987).

2 Control over accuracy of data held and used. Consumer concerns are also likely to be exacerbated when the use of inaccurate data results in negative consequences for them (Cespedes and Smith 1993). As marketers obtain and utilise greater volumes of consumer information there is an increasing likelihood that errors will arise. Furthermore, consumers consider that the existence of inaccurate data reflects a lack of commitment on the part of the offending organisation (O'Malley *et al.* 1997). Commitment is a relational construct, so again this reflects a cynicism on the part of consumers over organisations' relational intent.

3 Control over the physical intrusion of personalised marketing – the amount of mail, e-mail or telephone calls received, as we have just said, is important in order to overcome perceptions of 'non-relational', 'junk' interaction.

As Goldwag (2001) suggests, 'Internet consumers know the value of their own personal data ... they expect something in return ... if they are going to give you permission to communicate with them ... it does not have to be a tangible incentive ... could be control over the e-mail in their in-box'. Mitchell (2001) thinks that tangible payment could be the answer: 'treat your customer's data as you would his home ... don't enter without permission ... once inside, respect his wishes and if you want to use his property/information for your own purposes to make money from it ... then pay him rent'. Indeed, this position extends the 'metaphor' approach to relationship marketing that we explored in Chapter 7, from personal human relationships to how these can be more contextualised within the comfort, security and privacy of customers' homes.

Perceived control, then, is a key concept to overcoming many of the more negative aspects of direct relational marketing: for example, consumers are concerned about the process of sharing data: 76% of 724 respondents to a survey (Evans *et al.* 1997) wanted direct marketers not to share their details with other organisations. Furthermore, 79% wanted marketers to inform them before sharing their personal details. Both of these measures relate to degrees of perceived consumer control.

This leads us back to the privacy issue which we outlined earlier but now explore in more detail.

Privacy issues

Following from our earlier discussion and analysis of consumer reactions to personalised marketing, privacy issues include:

- information privacy (control over one's personal information);

- physical/interaction privacy (control over the physical intrusion of personalised marketing);
- accuracy (control over accuracy of data).

Information privacy

Our exploration of consumer reactions to personalised marketing led us to propose 'control' as being a major factor and this is supported from a more conceptual perspective. Information privacy refers to the extent to which individuals can *control* who holds their data, and what is done with it (Westin 1967). Basically, it incorporates three issues:

- who controls consumer information;
- how information is collected and used;
- data security.

Information privacy has been the subject of debate for some time. On the one hand, there is the argument that consumers should have a right to determine what happens to their personal information. This is closely related to the notion of control. For example, in the USA many consumers already believe that they have lost all control over how information about them is used, with some even suggesting that if they could, they would add privacy to their constitutional rights to life, liberty and the pursuit of happiness (Schroeder 1992).

Indeed, there has been a plethora of books written on this issue in the USA in recent years. Examples include:

- *Privacy for Sale: How computerisation has made everyone's private life an open secret*, by Jeffrey Rothfeder (1992)
- *Privacy for sale: How big brother and others are selling your private secrets for profit*, by Michael Chesbro (1999)
- *The Unwanted Gaze: The destruction of privacy in America*, by Jeffrey Rosen (2001)
- *The Naked Consumer: How our private lives become public commodities*, by Erik Larson (1994)
- *Identity, Privacy and Personal Freedom: Big Brother v New Resistance*, by Sheldon Charrett (1999).

The extent to which the situation in the UK is similar to that in the USA is debatable, but it is certainly the case that consumers have traditionally guarded their privacy and find it undesirable that anyone else should possess personal information about them. Whereas many countries have had personal identity papers, some for many decades, the UK continues to debate the introduction of an 'ID' scheme with ferocity. Indeed, at the time of writing, there was another 'round' of discussion on the basis (at least superficially) of trying to reduce illegal immigrants (Travis 2003). The previously mentioned Nectar loyalty scheme has even been linked with the development of a national ID scheme (Ambler 2002).

Amber suggests 'unfounded rumours indicate that MI5 has infiltrated Nectar whose card is being used as a UK pilot ... Big Brother has discovered marketing'.

On the other hand, many organisations argue that they should have the right to access consumer information for business purposes. Indeed, many marketers believe that because they have committed valuable resources to the development of databases, the information held on them is their property to do with as they see fit (Cespedes and Smith 1993). They also argue that they have no interest in highly personalised information, but it is clear that they have a growing appetite for individual-level transactional and lifestyle data and this is, as we have discussed throughout this book, of major significance in developing and operationalising relational marketing.

Despite this, as we saw in earlier chapters, few marketers are using the full capacity of the data they already have. Indeed, they may not yet have any great or immediate use for some of the information they hold, but they are reluctant to have it removed from their databases in case it may prove to be of benefit in the future. While this is understandable from an organisational point of view, it suggests a worrying trend for consumers.

There is also the issue of how organisations acquire data. In the past, much data acquisition has been covert, with consumers unaware that data is being collected for marketing purposes. The growth of personalised relational marketing has created the need for data on a massive scale, and there seems to be some controversy over the extent to which consumers are happy to provide their personal data. For example, studies in the USA have claimed that consumers are generally quite happy to supply information in order to facilitate a specific exchange. However, many consumers believe that the data is necessary to facilitate the transaction, and give limited consideration to uses outside the specific transaction concerned (Cespedes and Smith 1993; Gandy 1993). In other words, they may not expect their information to be shared with other organisations: 'For the large majority of consumers (80%) in the UK, concerns and fears about information provision are currently balanced by a pragmatic understanding of the need to play ball with companies. However, we believe that this balance is relatively fragile and should not be taken for granted' (Henley Centre 1995).

In reality, consumers will have different thresholds of information privacy which will be determined largely by the kind of the information being collected (Exhibit 13.4) the organisation responsible, how data is collected, and the subsequent uses to which that information will be put.

Further complicating the issue of information privacy are increasing concerns regarding data security. As technology improves, and as greater numbers of individuals gain access to desktop computing facilities, the ability to control data security becomes more difficult. Consumers gauge for themselves whether or not they view a particular company as trustworthy, but it is impossible to determine the trustworthiness of individuals within that company, or, as we have suggested, 'other companies in the group' that may not even be known to the consumer. Many firms have been proactive in setting up data security measures, but it is impossible to ensure 100% protection. The consequences of a breach in security in many organisations would be serious. Indeed, the consequences could be disastrous for consumers if there was unauthorised access to an insurance

EXHIBIT 13.4   Consumer willingness to divulge personal details to direct marketers

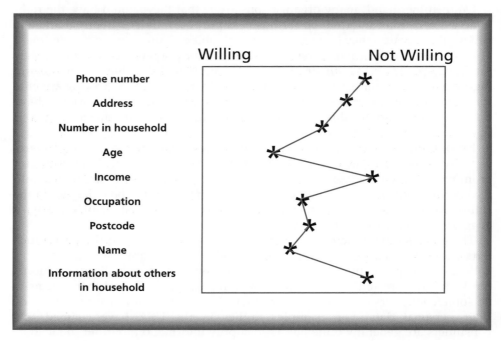

(Source: Evans *et al.* 1998)

company's database, particularly, for example, when we consider the degree of details stored about individuals' home security measures.

Thus, it seems that as marketers' appetite for information grows, consumers may become more protective of their data. As a result, Westin envisages a rise in what he calls 'consensual databases', where consumers consent to information surrender in return for some type of reward such as coupons, samples or money (Westin 1992). At the end of the day, if information held on databases is treated confidentially, and used in the development of a relationship between the marketer and the consumer, then consumer fears may be allayed to some degree (Fletcher and Peters 1996). However, as Mitchell states, 'permission isn't enough … is ticking a box once, permission to spam me for the rest of my life … there's only one way out: to put consumers in the driving seat, empowering them to specify what sort of messages they are looking for by time, place and category' (Mitchell 2002). It is to this proposal that we also subscribe. Godin (1999) is also keen on the permission marketing route: 'every marketing campaign gets better when an element of permission is added'. In his analysis, permission marketing is:

- anticipated: people look forward to hearing from the organisation;
- personal: the messages are of direct interest to the individual;

- relevant: the marketing concerns something in which the prospect is interested (Godin 1999).

He envisages that this encourages mutual interaction over time and therefore, in our terms, relational interaction.

It is worth revisiting the attitudes towards this issue that are held by some in the industry. The Information Commissioner's (IC) office ran a hard-hitting advertising campaign to warn consumers of the dangers of parting with their personal details. There was an outcry from many direct marketers; 'these ads have angered many industry figures and have been labelled excessive, shocking, inaccurate and, crucially, damaging to direct marketers' (Mutel 2001). Some went even further: 'just what in God's name does the IC think it's doing … the current radio commercial extolling the public to be wary of giving either written or verbal details does nothing but instil fear into the public's mind' (Ramsden 2001).

Exhibit 13.5 is another advertisement from the IC but this one was aimed not at consumers but at marketers who deal with personal data. It, too, attracted criticism from marketers.

We wonder why marketers are not able to see privacy issues as an opportunity rather than a constraint – what do you think?

EXHIBIT 13.5 IC Advertisement to *Data Marketers*, Campaign running 14–31 August 2000

Physical/interaction privacy

Physical/interaction privacy relates to the physical intrusion of marketing communications (e.g. direct mail, telesales, e-mails) into the daily lives of consumers.

When there is a 'positive and mutual relationship' it would be expected that direct and personalised communications would be welcomed but much personalised communication is a manifestation of acquisition strategies, because new business is the lifeblood of any company, and consequently marketers are constantly trying to recruit new customers.

The 'hottest' prospects are, somewhat obviously, targeted most heavily, such as those with the highest spending power. Ungoed-Thomas and Nuki (1998) reported their uncovering of a 'Midas' list of those between 25 and 45 earning more than £50,000 p.a. and who own lots of electronic products, engage in relatively expensive leisure activities and 'are being sent 250 mailshots a year, five times the national average'. If these people enjoy receiving information about even more things they can spend their money on, then there probably isn't a problem; however, many will feel this is just too much: 'every day it come through the door ... it's relentless ... I don't read it on principle because Britain is turning into a huge buying experience and I hate it' (Rule 1998).

However, returning to a key theme of 'control', consumers have little or no control over the prospecting efforts of companies (Waldrop 1994). In terms of traditional marketing communications, consumers have the ability to screen out unwanted communications by means of zapping, zipping and nipping, they possess control over the solicitation of further information (Kitchen 1986), and the advent of personal video recorders (PVRs) allows consumers to screen out the commercials automatically. Direct communications are likely to cause far greater difficulties in this regard, although the 'Preference Services' run by the UK Direct Marketing Association (DMA) have made a good start. These are:

- Mailing Preference Service (MPS)
- Telephone Preference Service (TPS)
- FAX Preference Service (FPS)
- Email Preference Service (EPS).

The regulations under these can be confusing, though. For example, although there is a legal requirement for companies to clean their databases against the telephone preference service (TPS) list of those who have asked not to be contacted by telephone by companies with which they do not have a relationship, the equivalent preference service for direct mail (MPS) is not legally binding. However, 'even use of the TPS, now mandatory, is not universal' (Reed 2001). Opt-outs are available, but when consumers opt out 'what they really mean ... is that there are certain things they want and certain things they don't want' (Waldrop 1994). The situation as it stands does not allow for consumer selectivity, because organisations, *not* consumers, determine who shares the data. It might be argued that lifestyle surveys go some way to determining this. These, as we have seen in Chapter 2, ask consumers for details of those products and services in which they have an interest and the industry might claim that the more knowledgeable consumer of today will understand that by providing this information, they are, in effect, opting in to allowing personalised contact over the ones they mention. Indeed, the Postal Preference Service (Chapter 2) is even clearer in its rubric which implies 'opt in'. It is perhaps unfortunate that the name of this list compiler is so similar to the opt-out preference services and might cause some confusion, for some, over its status.

Accuracy

Relational marketers clearly do not intend to use personal data inaccurately, but 'with the amount of data in use by direct marketers it is not surprising that mistakes happen' (Fletcher 1995). We have already discussed the problem of some 'fields' in databases inadvertently ending up as the solicitation in direct mailings (e.g. 'Dear Mr Jones (pain in the arse)). Even when the recipient's name and address are incorrect, this can lead to distrust and annoyance on the consumer's part.

Concern with respect to the accuracy of data held may be heightened in certain circumstances. If, for example, the data relates to the credit history of the consumer then the possibility for negative consequences is high. Inaccuracies in financial data may result in the consumer being turned down for a loan or mortgage. Indeed, the practice of County Court Judgments (CCJs) with addresses (via postcodes) has resulted in new residents experiencing difficulties with getting credit, not because of their own actions, but because of those of the previous household resident. Failure to update data held on a regular basis may lead a marketer to be unaware of changes in circumstances. Fortunately, this rarely has any significant effects. However, should a consumer have died, and yet continue to receive direct communications, then other family members may be very upset: 'it is said that dead men tell no tales, but their widows do. Either by writing to the company chairman or the local press, the unfortunate recipients of direct mail to a deceased spouse make their feelings clear. And the message is always the same: stop mailing people who have passed on' (Reed 2001).

Some consumers believe that the large amounts of unsolicited and irrelevant direct communications they receive come as a result of inaccurate data. However, consumers themselves may be unwittingly contributing to the problem. In an attempt to minimise abuses in both information and physical/interaction privacy, consumers may knowingly provide false information (Gandy 1993). Indeed, many UK consumers readily admit to such behaviour. For example, consumers may say that they earn more than they really do – simply to get more upmarket direct mail; others may lie about the number of people in their household for security reasons (especially when they live alone); finally, there are those who simply attempt to make it difficult for any organisation to process their data by writing illegibly, or giving false names or postcodes. While this may indeed solve the immediate problem of abuses in other areas, in the longer term it is likely to cause problems with direct transactions, or even contribute to abuses in physical privacy issues as the subsequent relevance of offers diminishes.

Maintaining data accuracy should be of paramount importance to industry participants. Accurate data facilitates the building of consumer relationships

(Smith 1994). The point is that, if organisations are going to utilise personal details on consumers for marketing or other purposes, the onus is upon them to ensure that the information they hold is correct, and consumers themselves feel that this should be the case.

IN THEORY

Privacy model

We conceptualise three levels of privacy antecedents, which interact, influence and are influenced by other antecedents and privacy concerns themselves (Exhibit 13.6). These are:

- the cultural environment;
- the ideological environment;
- the interaction-specific environment.

The cultural environment

Using Milne *et al.*'s (1996) conceptualisation, this includes country-level marketing technology and infrastructure, adherence to individual rights (norms), consumers' experience of direct marketing and individual demographic background.

EXHIBIT 13.6   Privacy and its antecedent variables

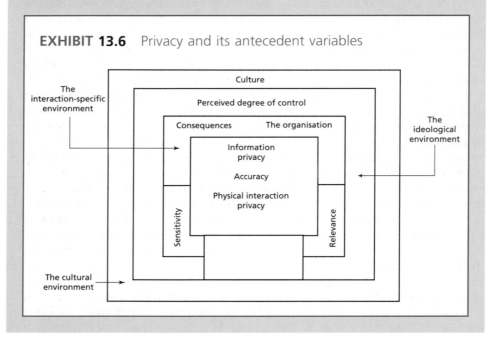

Infrastructure is important because the state of the direct marketing infrastructure within a country will, by consequence, dictate the level of direct marketing activity in that country. Despite the statistics presented in Chapter 10 on levels of direct marketing expenditure, it may be true to say that the UK industry is not as highly developed as its US counterpart. Consequently, consumer experiences in the UK are more limited. This may in turn explain the fact that although UK consumers have traditionally been protective of their individual privacy, concerns in relation to direct and personalised marketing have been relatively slow to evolve here (Patterson *et al*. 1996; Petrison and Wang 1995). Such concerns, however, are more strongly felt in Germany, for example.

The ideological environment

The ideological environment comprises consumer perceptions with regard to the level of control they have, and should have in the exchange process. Also of importance here is the level of knowledge which consumers possess in relation to database and direct marketing practices in general, existing legislation, and the process of seeking redress when privacy intrusions occur (Patterson, *et al*. 1997).

Relational marketing, by definition, is supposed to involve a mutually profitable exchange. While organisations may have traditionally enjoyed greater power in the exchange process than consumers, there is a growing danger that the consumer's position will be further eroded. Thus, in addressing the issue of social responsibility in personalised marketing, the notion of control becomes central, as we have already discussed. Lenk (1982) supports this view, believing that the concentration on privacy masks the real problem: that possession of personal details on consumers affords the organisation greater power at the expense of the individual.

In considering how personalised marketing may be used to foster relationship marketing, the notion of control is of even greater importance. Using a database to get close to customers has been described as 'customer intimacy' (Treacy and Wiersema 1993). However, such 'intimacy' has also been heavily criticised for amounting to little more than a means of gathering enough information on customers so that the organisation can market at them (Barnes 1994). This does not really foster relationship building as it centres on the interests of the organisation to the exclusion of those of consumers. Furthermore, the consumer may not be committed to the relationship, and may even be unaware that one is being developed. Increasing organisational power may diminish the role that the consumer has to play, allows the organisation to engage in manipulative behaviour, and as such does not represent a move towards relationship marketing (O'Malley *et al*. 1997).

Consumer knowledge of direct and database marketing practices in general is also an important mediating variable. This knowledge may come as a result of exposure to or experience of these practices. Concern is likely to be exaggerated when the consumer is largely ignorant of the demands placed on marketers for detailed consumer information, is unaware of legislation designed to protect the consumer body, or is not conversant with the means by which consumers can protect themselves. On the other hand, concerns are likely to be allayed when the consumer is cognisant of why personalised marketing uses the methods it does.

The interaction-specific environment

Perceived invasions of privacy are a function of the company involved, the knowledge that consumers possess about this particular instance of data collection and the specific uses to which the information will be put. It will also include the extent to which the consumer believes the offer/request to be relevant, the degree of sensitivity they associate with the particular information being collected and any negative consequences likely to result from information collection (Patterson *et al*. 1997).

If the consumer has a history of dealing with a particular organisation, and believes that organisation to be trustworthy, the likelihood of that offer/request being considered intrusive diminishes. Therefore, marketers must be seen as trustworthy in order to successfully communicate with and obtain information from consumers. However, because many marketers acquire consumer data through covert means, the result is a reduction of trust towards firms in general and, as we have seen, there is, in general, a decline in trust of companies in the UK.

When consumer knowledge of a specific instance of data collection or data use is reduced, control will also be reduced as the consumer will not be in position to prevent his or her data from being collected, to decide what information is shared with or sold to others, or to agree with the utilisation of that information. Thus, lack of interaction-specific knowledge is likely to aggravate privacy concerns. Consumers may also question efforts by companies to collect information if that information does not appear to be relevant to the transaction at hand: 'If a person is interested in a subject and receives an unsolicited telephone call or piece of mail about it, he is not likely to view its receipt as an invasion of privacy... It is relevant' (Sherman 1991). However, this relevance can only be achieved through improvements in targeting, improvements that require the use of personal data on individuals by companies. Placing restrictions on the uses to which companies put information may only serve to increase the amount of 'junk' consumers receive, and consumers themselves recognise this as a 'Catch 22'.

The degree of sensitivity that the consumer attaches to a piece of information will also determine the level of concern involved, as we saw earlier in this chapter. Most consumers will be quite happy to surrender personal details such as name and address, although they could be troubled by the fact that profiling may 'produce sensitive information from that which was not sensitive in its original form' (Gandy 1993). Ideally, marketers should only be using such information as is directly relevant for their marketing purposes, and 'information that by any reasonable standard would be considered personal, confidential or private should not be used in an inappropriate way' (Sherman 1991).

Because of the influence of the interaction-specific environment on perceptions of privacy, regulation in the area is potentially problematic. Ideally, the solution lies in companies conducting their business with the concern due to customers, and ensuring that those customers have some say in what happens to their data. Self-regulation guidelines are discussed later in this chapter.

Wider social responsibility

Even 'strategic marketers', who can (and should) plan beyond today's campaign, are being pressed to be more accountable in their activities and at the same time are increasingly time pressurised themselves, in today's corporate culture. Marketers are not always able to explore implications of current campaigns and strategies that extend beyond these. In terms of data protection legislation, for example, three-quarters of the sample of 200 companies was not prepared for the new data protection legislation of 1999 (GB Information Management 1999). The lack of awareness is a concern because it suggests that companies are more concerned with today's campaigns and, perhaps, feel that the new legislation is not particularly important. This last point was demonstrated at the FEDMA Council Day in 1998. During a presentation by the legal director, an off-the-cuff and unscripted remark was made to the effect that the new legislation being introduced throughout the EU was 'a solution looking for a problem'. There was spontaneous applause from the audience which was composed almost entirely of senior DM practitioners from several member states. Is this a reflection of the attitude the industry might really possess? It is further reinforced by the title of a paper in a practitioner-based DM journal, 'Beating the Data Protection Registrar' (Dineen 1999). So the proposals are sometimes seen to be a hindrance to how DM campaigns are run. Privacy issues should really be considered as opportunities, because if seriously addressed, they could pave the way for a move closer to the relational ideal.

We explore this wider societal impact under a number of headings:

- Data for other purposes: state data for marketing databases
- Data for other purposes: research data for marketing databases
- Data for other purposes: marketing data for state databases
- Data for other purposes: company databases to other companies
- Data for profit – and social exclusion
- Data for other purposes: criminal use.

Data for other purposes: state data for marketing databases

We have already discussed (in Chapter 2) the use of the Census. Whereas this was originally, and indeed for many decades, used for social planning (transport, housing and so on), from 1981 it has also been used commercially. The 2001 Census was the first to be announced to citizens as being for business planning as well as social planning (see Exhibit 13.7 for an introduction to the Census form itself).

New, industry-influenced questions, such as those attempting to identify gay markets, might be a privacy worry for some, but a main proposition here is whether 'social'/'state' data that ends up in marketing databases is a wider societal concern.

Perhaps it is *not*, at a simple and innocent level, but the creeping commitment of what individuals are required to divulge to the state, and then the incremental nature of what marketers can access from the state, is a legitimate concern.

Exhibit 13.8 shows some rather cynical headlines from the UK trade magazine *Precision Marketing* between November 2001 and February 2002.

Following these initial manifestations of the industry's obvious concern over the Electoral Roll (ER) issue, when a case to ban the use of the ER for credit referencing collapsed due to the complainant (Robertson) failing to secure legal aid, the reaction was similar: 'Industry hails Robertson defeat' (Rubach 2003) was the headline on the trade paper *Precision Marketing*. There *is* a degree of socially responsibility within this because without the ER there would be difficulties for the credit referencing industry if a major and reasonably accurate database listing names and addresses were not available to check identities. Indeed, there is already a significant worry about identity theft and without the ER this might escalate.

EXHIBIT 13.7   2001 Census form

count me in
Census2001

The future is in your hands

The Census is vital for Government and businesses to plan ahead. The information is used to plan everything from the health services we will need in the future, to where roads and new businesses should be built. Every question on the form is there for a reason.

EXHIBIT 13.8 Cynical relational marketers?

'Uproar across industry as decision favours privacy' (*Precision Marketing*, 2001)

'DMA poised to fight electoral roll ruling' (*Precision Marketing*, December 2001)

'Industry bodies slam new SMS Preference Service' (*Precision Marketing*, January 2001)

'Net industry in uproar as EU plans to abolish cookies' (*Precision Marketing*, November 2001)

The point we make, however, is the degree of gloating. Even the editor of *Precision Marketing* comments that the 'defeat of the direct marketing industry's old nemesis, Brian Robertson, that pesky retired accountant from Pontefract, has unsurprisingly been described as a victory for commonsense' (McKelvey 2003). He also tends to confirm the focus on the more immediate at the expense of possible wider societal impact: 'the truth is that in these tough economic times, data protection is not at the top of the boardroom agenda' (McKelvey 2003). We believe that in order for relational marketing to live up to the rhetoric, it needs not only to obey the letter of the law but also even to exceed its spirit.

Data for other purposes: research data for marketing databases

A popular adage within the data-driven marketing industry is that 'every contact (with the customer) has an opportunity (to gather more data)' (ECHO). Even in business-to-business contexts ECHO is relevant: a list of marketers might have been compiled from attendees at conferences and seminars and could include name, job title, company and even the name, drink preferences and dietary requirements of the '*secretary*'! Sometimes data is collected without there being clear commercial reasons but because it is thought it might be useful at some later stage of more sophisticated data mining. So again there is the issue of data collection for dubious purposes.

In not all instances are providers of further data aware that it will be used to update personalised records. This is analogous to the debate raging between traditional (anonymised) marketing research data and (personalised) data for selling and fundraising. This is another example of the collection of data for a different purpose from that which might have been perceived as the real purpose, and the issues of dugging, sugging and frugging are explored by Fletcher and Peters (1996).

Data for other purposes: marketing data for state databases

A further area for potential 'social responsibility' concern is the purchase of marketing data by government departments. CACI, for example, have an entire department dealing exclusively with government contracts for its ACORN geodemographic and related products. Geodemographic systems use an increasing range of financial data sources to overlay census, housing and demographic data, and the resulting 'financial' ACORN and MOSAIC products can easily be seen to be of potential value to the Inland Revenue (for example) to check financial details and trends against tax returns from those they want to investigate further (Key 2000).

A related development has been the interest shown by the government in loyalty-scheme data. The idea was to track consumers' food consumption patterns with a view to assessing the impact of genetically modified foods (Hansard 1999; Parker 1999). Is this the point beyond which the use of personal data, supposedly for marketing, becomes unacceptable – or is it entirely justified to use such data to investigate a serious health issue of public concern?

Another example: Experian has developed a database for vehicle insurance purposes which is being used by the police to reduce uninsured driving (Experian 1999). The 'end' might be laudable, but what is your perspective on the 'means' of achieving this?

Could it be that the state has been content to provide the marketing industry with space to collect, fuse and mine data from a variety of sources and then for various departments to buy or take what they can use for reducing fraud and for other instances of social (individualised) monitoring?

Data for other purposes: company databases to other companies

This includes the 'data consortia' phenomenon discussed in Chapter 8. It is interesting to note that the London 999 police service was under bid from a commercial consortium. The commercial opportunities revolve around non-emergency calls – such as washing machine problems or people locking themselves out of their homes. Scoot already operates in this way in Kent, Staffordshire, Greater Manchester and South Yorkshire (Anon 1999).

Another example of personalised data held by one organisation being transferred to another is that of a former student of one of the authors who was targeted by a funeral undertaker to purchase a coffin for her father. It seems that the hospital had given the names of patients in intensive care to this undertaker. The problem here was that the student was approached while the father was alive, making a difficult situation far more stressful. In any case, abuse results in negative perceptions, which may prove very difficult to alter in the future.

The Nectar scheme introduced in the autumn of 2002 recruited around 10 million members in just six months. But new partners are added regularly. By

May 2003 these included BP, Sainsbury's, Barclaycard, McDonald's, Ford, Vodafone and Blockbuster. But are all consumer-members happy to have their data shared amongst all of these – and other partners that will, presumably, have joined the consortium at the time of your reading this? Do you actually know all of the partners in the consortium? The 'small print' of this scheme states that 'information regarding the specific goods or services you buy from a particular participating company will not be passed to us or any other participating company except where required to do so to operate the Nectar programme' (Nectar 2002).

The sharing of data is an issue of lobbying in terms of the new legislation. Mail Marketing, for example, is to share some of its lists with Infocore, a US list company (Wood 1998). Amazon has also been accused of transferring data on UK consumers to the USA (Walker 2000). However, the latest Data Protection Act (1998) prevents companies from exporting personal information to countries that do not have adequate data protection – and this includes the USA. As the Data Protection Registrar has said, 'businesses exporting data must be satisfied that they comply with the law – otherwise I will simply prevent the activity' (France 1998).

There is a 'treaty' between the EU and USA which identifies certain US companies which are seen as implementing adequate data protection (the 'Safe Haven Treaty'). However, even the US President, George W. Bush, has weighed in to the debate and threatened to withdraw from this because it could hamper US multinational companies which are not part of the treaty (Walker 2001). Indeed, it is thought that only a handful of US companies have sufficient data protection to be covered by the treaty.

DoubleClick is a company that specialises in Internet advertising and was sued in California because it was claimed that it obtained and sold personal data unlawfully. The company acquired Abacus, a data-sharing consortium and this 'enabled it to combine anonymous internet usage data with personal consumer information ... can amass a range of detailed information on consumers visiting certain sites, including their names, addresses, age, shopping patterns and financial information' (Dixon 2000). In the UK, 216 catalogue companies are signed up to 'Abacus': 'its databases have been combined into one, holding information data on around 215 million catalogue transactions from 26 million individual consumers. This data is further enhanced by Claritas' Lifestyle Universe, which overlays income, lifestyle and life-stage data at an individual level for every UK household. Updated weekly, it gives users access to every mail order buyer in the UK' (May 2002).

These examples are all evidence of company databases of personalised details going to other companies. The 'opt out' clause allowing respondents to say they do not want their details passed on to other companies is perhaps being diluted because the usual wording refers to 'others in the group'. As the consortium approach escalates, 'the group' leaves consumers with less control over where their personal details go.

Another example of data being accessed for other purposes was afforded by a recent case in which pharmaceutical companies selling prescription data were informed by the High Court that this breached patient confidentiality and was unlawful (Savage 1999).

It has recently been revealed that another research base, *genetics*, is being used, especially by the financial services sector. Here, genetics are added to the layering of data for fusing and mining (Specter 1999) and perhaps even more serious ethical issues are likely to need addressing here.

Data for profit – and social exclusion

An outcome of data mining is the identification of specific customers' contribution to profit, as mentioned earlier. Tesco, for instance, has introduced segmentation based on this, via data mining that leads to 'gold', 'silver' and 'bronze' levels of purchasing (and hence loyalty card variants). However, might the less privileged become disaffected when they realise that others are being presented with the 'better' offers? It has been suggested, even from within the industry, that alienated customers might even see this as something 'Orwellian in nature' (Wright 1999). There are signs that this has been recognised by government – it has set up a social exclusion department and is concerned about banks closing branches in favour of data-driven approaches because of potential exclusion effects within some sections of the community. In the USA the Community Reinvestment Act is supposed to prevent banks from closing in poor neighbourhoods, so perhaps there are signs of the tide turning with respect to these sorts of wider social responsibility issues, even if Lavidge's vision appears rather rose-tinted by today's standards. On one day alone in the UK, [in April 2000] Barclay's Bank closed 170 of its branches.

By its very nature, targeting means that some members of society will be excluded from direct marketing offers. Cespedes and Smith (1993) argue that as 'people from different races, religions, and ethnic groups tend to live in distinct areas' and as geography is one of the major variables used in targeting, some sections of society will effectively be discriminated against. Although, in Britain, there does not appear to be the same degree of ghettoisation as in the USA, it may yet occur that as companies increasingly target neighbourhoods with high spending power, lower income groups will find their choices increasingly limited.

Also, as personalised marketing changes with the information age, and as more highly developed technologies and media are utilised, those within society without the resources to keep pace will suffer as they will be virtually unable to purchase goods through this medium.

Yet another aspect of exclusion, according to Cespedes and Smith, involves the ability of smaller companies and non-profit organisations to compete with larger organisations. Initially, it was these smaller organisations that first took advantage of the fact that direct marketing enabled them to use niche marketing as a means of combating companies with large mass media budgets. Stricter controls, legislation, and consumer backlashes may only have the effect of making the situation untenable for these smaller companies. The cost of acquiring and using personal information would inevitably rise, effectively driving smaller operators out of business. All this would serve to do is place consumers once more in the hands of the larger corporations and consequently reduce consumers' freedom of choice.

Perhaps it is entirely consistent with a permission marketing approach to decide also that it is not worth exploring relationships with all customers. We have discussed the 80:20 'rule' that suggests a large proportion of sales/profits are generated by a relatively small number of customers. In this way, it could be argued that some customers who are not contributing much should not be encouraged to remain as customers. Godin (1999) states: 'fire 70% of your customers and watch your profits go up'. But does this really reflect the 'mutuality' of relational marketing?

Data for other purposes: criminal use

One of the authors initiated a research programme with a UK police force to investigate the criminal use of marketing databases. Could databases of recently purchased desirable products be accessed to locate addresses to target for burglary? There has been some evidence of this, albeit anecdotal, but sufficient for the police to be concerned to discover if there are any patterns in this regard, and so we conducted the research over an 18-month period. The results were confidential between the researcher and the police force concerned, but clearly, if there are such links, we have yet another category of social responsibilities beyond the level of a specific personalised campaign and again reflecting marketing's wider social role.

The societal relationship marketing concept

So, how does the above discussion match marketing's theorised and practical 'societal role'? It was more than 30 years ago that the concept of wider responsibilities of marketing was posed. Lazer (1969) suggested that:

> ❝ Marketing must serve not only business but also the goals of society . . . its responsibilities extend well beyond making profits . . . and its contributions extend well beyond the formal boundaries of the firm. ❞

The late 1960s and early 1970s provided much debate about the role of business generally and of marketing in particular. Lavidge (1970), for instance, added to the criticisms of marketing's failure to help to deal with social rather than economic problems and, amongst other dimensions, cites poverty as an area for marketing consideration. He proposed that marketers should: 'help mitigate and ultimately eliminate the effects of poverty'.

However, one result of personalised data and its analysis is that the profit value of individual customers can be determined. For example, there is the use of long-time value (LTVs) and recency, frequency, monetary value (RFM) analysis. Those customers not considered to be strong contributors to the company in these respects are being deselected. They are not being sent relevant offers or, in the case of financial services, for example, they are being offered accounts that require higher initial deposits than these individuals might be able to afford.

On the one hand, there are arguments for a wider social role of marketing and, on the other, there are clearly increasing pressures for the marketer to focus (perhaps over-focus) on profits and shareholders.

The wider responsibility phenomenon has been conceptualised in various ways in the wider business ethics literature. For example, Carroll's (1978) classification of moral pressures (individual, organisational, association (profession related), societal and international (cultural differences)) is a useful model here (Exhibit 13.9). It demonstrates that the company (organisational level) will have its own codes and ethos, influenced by external forces such as the codes of conduct of professional bodies. There are also societal pressures which need to be addressed and the individual with his or her own moral codes is often torn in many different directions by these pressures.

Managers have been found to deal in different ways with these conflicts. Martin (1985) proposed five types:

- the *crook*, who knows that certain things are wrong and acts unethically;
- the *legalist*, who works to the letter of the law but doesn't worry about wider ethics or morality;

EXHIBIT 13.9   Carroll's model of moral pressures

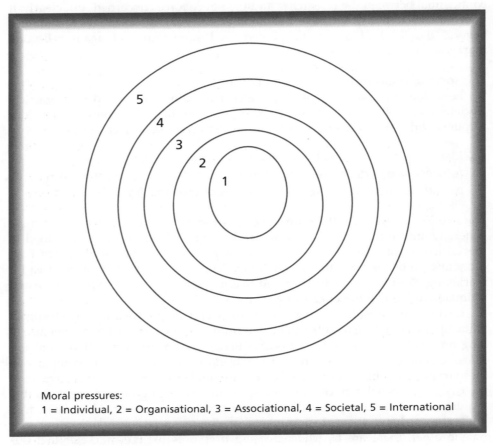

Moral pressures:
1 = Individual, 2 = Organisational, 3 = Associational, 4 = Societal, 5 = International

(Source: Adapted from Carroll 1978)

- the *moralist*, who is highly principled and tries to follow this through into his or her business actions;

- the *seeker*, who is not certain of ethical consequences but wants to do the right thing;

- the *rationaliser*, who might recognise ethical issues but will justify bypassing them on grounds of being the most efficient for the company.

Other models of business and marketing ethics are available and it is worth mentioning one more at this stage. Enderle (1995) presents a grid, with person-level, organisational-level and systems-level (macro effects) being matched with 'talking about ethics', 'acting ethically' and 'thinking about ethics'. The focus of this paper resides in the macro area and 'thinking' about the wider social implications of data-driven marketing.

It is important to recognise that companies need to compete effectively in order to be profitable enough to stay in business. They do not operate in an altruistic environment and therefore they may decide that it is imperative to 'go direct' if this is what their competitors are doing. The reasons are obvious – it can reduce costs by cutting out the face-to-face contact with customers traditionally enjoyed in branches, while at the same time it can take them closer to their customers because they collect so much data about them that their requirements are better understood. In addition, marketing is having to demonstrate greater accountability; in a study of UK company boards, the variables that marketers traditionally focused upon, such as awareness, market share and customer satisfaction, are being usurped owing to the perceived need to be financially accountable (Ambler 1999). Profits, sales and gross margins were the top three criteria for the boardrooms surveyed. Data-driven marketing, of course, provides for greater accountability and marketers will be encouraged to use those approaches that can be more easily translated into financial data.

Even some 'ethics thinkers' are modifying their perception of what is acceptable. Sternberg (1995), for example, proposes a 'teleological' model in which the maximising of wealth of the owners of the company is fine as long as the means to this end are conducted in a generally decent manner.

Recognition – and counter-action?

Awareness campaigns of, for example, the Preference Services and the opt-out can show consumers how they can reduce the amount of targeting if they so wish. Other media might allow for a shift in the balance of control from marketer to consumer – such as the Internet, or other direct response media (Evans *et al*. 2001), which allows the consumer to 'go looking' for his/her interests. Personal details may become the subject of a different sort of marketing transaction – one in which the consumer is the marketer. By perceiving 'property rights' (Davies 1997) to apply to personal details, the consumer may become a vendor of their own details to selected organisations for specified purposes. This shift in the ownership of information might see the rise of intermediaries, or infomediaries (Hagel and Rayport 1997), which would act as brokers on behalf of consumers. It might mean something more radical – such as making contracts with consumers whereby they are paid – or rewarded in another way – for revealing certain personal details to named organisations for specific purposes. This approach has been proposed by Westin (1992), who described it as the creation of 'consensual databases'. Godin also considers that the permission route should be regarded as an investment that can pay back via longer-term relationships (Godin 1999).

In a societal context, as Camenisch (1991) points out: '(Marketing) occurs in society, with society's permission and support, and purportedly, in part for society's benefit.' On this basis, it may be true to say that marketing managers should have to take into account the moral expectations of society. Star (1989) agrees; 'the social effects of the marketing process must, like all social phenomena, be looked at in some sort of trade-off matrix'. His analysis is derived from research into consumer reactions to marketing, which revealed different segments, ranging from those who 'have had their needs identified, had a marketing programme designed specifically around their characteristics and have been exposed to the marketing programme' to those who 'are exposed to the marketing programme even though they have no interest in it ... the marketing programme is likely to be distracting or even irritating' (Star 1989).

In truth, it makes good business sense to explore these sorts of social impact of marketing activity and not to over-focus on response rates or conversions to sale because, if organisations continue to disregard the moral expectations of society, they are putting themselves on a collision course with consumer dissatisfaction and alienation and an increase in the already cynical view of marketers who claim 'relationships' when the reality is mere rhetoric.

Despite this, it appears that most managers have given little thought to the social impact of data-driven personalised marketing (Cespedes and Smith 1993). Those who have given it any degree of thought have dismissed it. They seem to think that if they continue to believe that concerns do not exist, then they will not exist. Furthermore, they argue that discussions of social responsibility are all fine and well in academia but they have no place in the competitive world of business. Even much academic literature (but not all, see Crane and Desmond 2002) seems to have satisfied itself largely with the practical problems faced by industry participants, at the expense of the consumer and social implications in general (Whalen *et al.* 1991).

We end this exploration of personalised marketing's wider social responsibility by reviewing one final issue, the environmental impact of direct mail. The past three decades have seen a progressive increase in worldwide environmental consciousness. Recession tends to divert interest away from environmental issues, but underlying concerns appear to be strengthening with the recognition that business has been responsible for many of the problems associated with the environment. Consumers appear to be very cognisant of the environmental impact of direct mail and leafleting in particular. While industry participants satisfy themselves with low incidences of response, consumers recognise this as a waste. Denny draws an analogy between direct mail and the battle of the Somme in that vast quantities of direct communications are used to win a small number of sales sufficient to make the exercise profitable (Denny 1995). Adding to the problem is the fact that many direct mail pieces incorporate glossy paper which cannot be recycled. Yet as Bloom *et al.* (1994) point out, environmental groups are slow to react, as they are heavy users of direct mail themselves. Many UK consumers do have very real concerns about the environmental impact of direct mail.

The use of recycled paper, for example, may not be substantially friendlier to the environment because of the chemical processing involved. However, consumers are unaware of this. Their opinion is based upon not only the type of paper used in direct marketing, but also the vast quantities that move swiftly from the letterbox to the bin. Clearly, this does little to improve consumer perceptions.

Friends of the Earth (Cubitt 2003) has also criticised the results of the increase in direct mailings in terms of recycling the 'junk'. The government called for 70% of UK mailings to be recycled by the end of summer 2003, but only 11% had been achieved by May 2003. This compared with 64% of Austria's mailings. At least, in 2003, the UK's DMA was discussing, with an environmental agency, ways of developing better recycling.

A partial solution to this problem may lie in the ability of marketers to utilise information in such a way as to produce smaller, more tightly defined and relevant communications which reduce the wastefulness of their operations.

Looking to the future, relational marketers are going to have to do a better job of facing their responsibilities if the industry is to achieve its potential. With this in mind, there are a number of ways that they can tackle these difficult issues, including self-regulation, consumer education and legislation.

Self-regulation

Privacy and social responsibility issues, for companies, customers and legislators, may be alleviated by increased attempts by the industry to police itself. Self-regulation 'goes beyond the minimum requirements of legislation and has to be adhered to in spirit as well as to the letter.' (Titford 1994). A number of authorities and codes of practice have been introduced by the industry over the past decade (Titford 1994). Indeed, in terms of the policy of self-regulation the UK industry is considered one of the most successful. The introduction of the Preference Services are a clear recognition of consumers' rights and concerns. Unfortunately, unless more proactive measures are instigated, more and more people may register their wish not to be contacted. This will serve only to reduce the size and potential of the market available.

The British Code of Advertising Practice (Advertising Standards Authority) endorses several more specialised codes, such as that of the Direct Marketing Association. The Direct Marketing Association requires its member organisations to adhere to the spirit, not merely the letter, of its Code of Conduct. The Code is detailed and addresses many of the concerns we have raised in this book. We highly recommend a visit to the website to download this Code (www.dma.org.uk). The DMA also provides more specialised codes for e-commerce, SMS and e-mail campaigns and for direct marketing to children.

The Advertising Standards Authority's 'British Code of Advertising, Sales promotion and Direct Marketing' (CAP) Code is also excellent and we recommend visits to www.asa.org.uk. There is also the Mail Order Protection Scheme (MOPS) which provides financial recompense to consumers after off-the-page selling companies fail.

The industry response in terms of establishing new authorities and detailing codes of practice is clearly important. However, self-regulation will only succeed if marketers, at individual and company level, are committed to making it work. In order to promote the spirit of self-regulation, alleviate consumer concerns over privacy, reduce the threat of further restrictive legislation and generally further the interests of the industry, organisations involved in personalised marketing should become more open, honest and accessible. In order to adhere to the spirit of self-regulation, companies should find the following guidelines of some use (Evans *et al.* 1995):

- If running a campaign using an external agency, only use companies recognised by the DMA. The handbook of registered agencies is freely available and should be consulted by advertisers seeking to use third-party services to produce their direct marketing campaigns.

- If internal direct mail or telemarketing campaigns are being undertaken, ensure that the preference services' lists are consulted regularly. Do not, under any circumstances, cold call or mail consumers who have registered their wish not to receive unsolicited marketing communications.

- Never use the telephone book for indiscriminate cold calling. If you receive such calls yourself, report the offending company to the DMA.

- Regularly clean and update your own internal databases. Be particularly careful with mailing lists which you have purchased, and cross-reference them with the Postcodes Address File (PAF) and the Deceased Register to ensure that they are correctly targeted and addressed.

- Do not sell or swap lists without first ensuring that the proposed campaigns meet the BCAP requirements of being legal, decent, honest and truthful. If in doubt, consult the DMA.

- Do not attempt to sell to consumers via either mail or telephone under the guise of market research. Such practices serve to undermine both the market research and database industries in the long run and in any case contravene the Market Research Society's Code of Conduct (Fletcher and Peters 1996).

- Do not attempt to deceive consumers into thinking that a request for personal information is 'traditional/anonymised' market research when you are actually compiling a database comprising data attributed to name and address (dugging). The MRS has amended its code and allows personalised data to be collected for list-building purposes as long as the respondent is aware that the research is for this purpose.

- Monitor and evaluate campaigns, not just in terms of response per 1 000, but also in terms of consumer attitudes.

- Do not collect more data than you really need. Apart from being a principle within the Data Protection Act (1998), there is no point in collecting data that the organisation cannot (yet) analyse or use (Godin 1999). If *you* don't know why you collect some data, your customers will be even less understanding, and that is unlikely to enhance relationships.

The success of self-regulation will also be dependent upon consumers using the facilities provided to them (e.g. MPS, TPS, EPS and FPS) and registering complaints on offending companies. To this end, consumers and direct marketers will need to be better educated as to what is acceptable and what is not acceptable in the future.

Unfortunately, some companies refuse to abide by decisions made by regulatory bodies. We refer you to Chapter 10 and our discussion of Twentieth Century Fox's decision to continue to use film-based shock messages to promote its films even though the ASA upheld complaints about its 'Minority Report' mobile phone campaign.

Consumer education

On an industry level, it is important that consumers are made aware of their rights. Given that consumer knowledge of direct marketing practices is a factor in how they perceive the industry, direct marketers need to allow the consumer greater access to information. Consumers should be made aware of what constitutes acceptable and unacceptable behaviour in terms of data collection and utilisation by organisations. Additionally, they need to know how to protect their information, how to query information held on a company's database, and how to remove their information if they so desire. As the saying goes, a little knowledge is a dangerous thing. Without comprehensive knowledge on how direct marketers operate, why they need information and how they use it, consumers are likely to jump to their own conclusions and to be susceptible to scare-mongering by the media.

We refer you back, however, to the responses given by some in the industry to the issue of their wider social responsibility (for example, the trade press 'headlines').

Legislation

Relational marketers have a problem. There is no Direct Marketing Act, where all of the relevant law can be found in one convenient place. Instead, there is a proliferation of statutes, regulations, directives and precedents which have to be analysed. The following is a list of current (at the time of writing) legislation and EU Directives:

- Data Protection Act 1998
- Telecommunications (Data Protection and Privacy) Regulations 1999
- Regulation of Investigatory Powers Act 2000
- Freedom of Information Act 2000
- Communications Directive COM/2000/385
- ECommerce Directive (00/31/EC)
- Distance Selling Directive (97/7/EC).

To make matters worse, the position is always changing as new legislation comes from Parliament and Brussels, and the courts continue to interpret and reinterpret the legislation.

The Data Protection Act

It is interesting to note that privacy legislation in this country was enacted more as a consequence of pressure from the business community than from consumers (Petrison and Wang 1995). It was the business community that forced statutory recognition of privacy rights because British companies were becoming increasingly worried about the possibility of losing trade with organisations from countries where privacy legislation had been enacted and was thus restrictive.

The main legislation in this field is the Data Protection Act 1998. The purpose of this Act is to protect the rights of individuals when other people, such as direct marketers, collect information about them and store or process it on computers.

Under the Act, any direct marketing organisation that stores information about individuals on a computer must register with the Information Commissioner. It is a criminal offence to store or use personal information without being registered. Indeed, it is unlawful to use data for a purpose other than the registered purpose, for example when data from people entering a competition is used for mailings or list selling. The organisation must register various information, including:

- the sort of personal information held;
- the sources from which it is obtained;
- the purposes for which it is used;
- to whom it might be disclosed.

Having registered with the Information Commissioner, the organisation must comply with the eight data protection principles (Exhibit 13.10).

It is not automatically a criminal offence to break these principles, but it can give rise to liability to pay compensation to the individual concerned. Furthermore, if anyone reports the breach to the Information Commissioner he can issue an enforcement notice, and it is a criminal offence not to comply with one of these notices. If an organisation ignores an enforcement notice, the Information Commissioner will remove the organisation from the register and the organisation will then be unable to continue storing or using personal information at all.

Although there are some exceptions, in general individuals are entitled to be supplied with a copy of all information relating to them. If that information is inaccurate, they can obtain a court order that it be corrected or deleted.

Unless the user of the information can prove that he or she took all reasonable care to ensure that the information was accurate, individuals may be entitled to compensation for any injury, loss or distress suffered by them as a consequence of the information being inaccurate. For example, if information is collected about someone's health or lifestyle, but it is entered on to the computer incorrectly with the result that they are denied insurance cover, that individual may have a claim.

Similarly, unless the user of the information can prove that he or she took all reasonable care to prevent the loss of information relating to an individual, that individual may be able to claim compensation for any loss or damage he or she

EXHIBIT 13.10   Data protection principles

Data Protection (1998 Act)

Principles:
1– Personal data fairly & lawfully processed
   Consent to be given (or at least not withheld)
   for collection AND uses which can be 'for marketing purposes' – **but is this too vague?
   Act doesn't define lawful!**

2– Used for specific purposes & not further processed **(e.g. the Electoral Roll case, in Chapter 2)**

3– Adequate, relevant & not excessive for purpose
   But lots collect data that might be useful in the future
   (e.g. age as required field in on-line forms)

4– Accurate & up to date
   Complaints over incorrect names/addresses etc.
   Data decays quickly – **people move, die, change life stage etc.**

5– Don't keep for longer than necessary
   Decided on a case by case basis – **could do with greater clarity here**

6– Data subjects have rights to see data held on them

7– Organisation to take measures to avoid unlawful processing
   (can't just hope employees won't use database for crime etc.)

8– Don't transfer outside EU unless adequate data protection **(USA – only 69 in 2001 in Safe Haven!)**

Interpretation is case by case – is this too woolly?

Also, lots of issues can be avoided if you can show 'disproportionate effort' to do or find out

TPS is legally binding

MPS isn't but it is illegal to mail if they've written in to opt out

Illegal to fax at home but not work

Increasingly moving to opt-in

EU Communication Directive Oct 2003 – covering SMS, Internet etc.
(Cookies: OK if used to track effectiveness rather than individuals' web paths)

---

suffers as a result of that information being lost. For example, individuals may reply to a mailshot to register with a company that provides financial services so that they will be informed of suitable investment opportunities that arise. If their details are accidentally deleted, and as a consequence they are not notified of a particular investment opportunity, they may be able to claim the profit they would have made out of that investment.

EXHIBIT 13.11 The First Data Protection Commissioner Annual Report, 2000

In the 11 months to the end of February (2000) we received 4,570 complaints –
pro-rata more than we have previously received in any full year. Adjusted pro rata
this represents a 36% increase on the previous year.

Total complaints received 1988 to 2000

1988/89	1 122	1994/95	2 814*
1989/90	2 698	1995/96	2 950*
1990/91	2 419	1996/97	3 897*
1991/92	1 747	1997/98	4 173*
1992/93	4 590	1998/99	3 653*
1993/94	2 889	1999/2000	4 570†

*Figures since 1994/95 refer to the financial year 1 April to 31 March. The previous
period ran from 1 June to 31 May.
†This figure is for complaints received for the 11 months to 29 February 2000.

Complaints were received about

Other	51%
Direct marketing	18%
Consumer credit	31%

Outcome of investigated cases

direct remedy for complaint	45%	not upheld	14%
not followed up	17%	no action necessary	8%
indirect remedy for complaint	13%	not covered by the Act	3%

125 cases were submitted to the Legal Department for consideration of prosecution.
145 cases proceeded to court and 130 of them resulted a finding of guilty.

Convictions

	99/00
Unregistered data users	28
Cases of unlawfully procuring information	91
Cases of selling unlawfully procured information	0
Cases of data users 'using' data for unregistered purposes	7
Employee for using data for an unregistered purpose	0
Data user for disclosing data	0
Employee for disclosing data	0
Directors conniving offences by company	4

Similarly, unless the user of the information can prove that he or she took all reasonable care to prevent any unauthorised disclosure of information relating to an individual, that individual may be able to claim compensation for any unauthorised disclosure of that information.

Perhaps the most troublesome of these for the marketer is the principle that personal information must be obtained and processed fairly and held for no longer than is necessary for the purpose. Many marketers are collecting information that they think might be of use 'later', for example when a new data mining system is in place. But this is not good enough under the law. Data needs to be used lawfully, not kept for a rainy day.

There is no doubt that data protection is an increasingly important area which relational marketers must heed, and the 2000 Report of the Information Commissioner shows that marketing is indeed an area of concern for the IC.

Exhibit 13.11 summarises the Information Commissioner's 2000 report on complaints and outcomes.

Case Study 13.1 summarises some recent cases brought before the Information Commissioner (formerly the Data Protection Registrar).

CASE **STUDY** 13.1

IC cases, 2000

Misuse of data

The complainant, a student, received a letter from India from someone asking to become her pen pal. In his letter he said he'd come across her details when developing new software for a company in the UK to which she had applied for a loan. He had noted from the course she was studying that they had similar interests. The complainant was concerned that detailed information she had provided to the loan company in connection with her loan had been used in this way.

The complaint was pursued with the company, raising concerns firstly that live data had apparently been transferred to India for software testing purposes and, secondly, that the personal data had been used in this manner by an employee of the company.

It appeared that the loan application forms were passed by the loan company to contractors who sent the information to India, where it was keyed into a database and returned to the loan company by electronic transfer. The employee was not, therefore, a software test engineer but a data input operator. However, it was confirmed that all the employees at the site in India had signed confidentiality agreements and that as a result of the incident the individual concerned had left the contractor's employment.

Solicitors for the loan company contacted the contractors, emphasising the gravity of the incident. The contractor responded giving details of various steps that had been taken to prevent a recurrence. These included the placing of notices throughout the keying-in facility, and weekly meetings, reminding employees of the importance of confidentiality and data protection and the implementation of a targeted 'Employee Data Security Awareness' programme. Also, other employees were informed of the consequences of such a breach and it was cited as an example to future staff. In addition, employees were reminded of the effect of such an incident on the contractor's relationship with the loans company and the distress caused to those whose data had been misused.

It was clear from the steps taken by the loan company and the contractor that the incident was taken extremely seriously and that any recurrence of the events that led to the complaint was extremely unlikely.

Unsolicited mailings

A husband and wife received unsolicited marketing literature from a bank. Despite writing to the bank on at least six occasions to request that no further mailings be sent, the bank failed to comply with the request and continued to send literature. A complaint was made to the Data Protection Registrar which resulted in the bank amending its database to ensure that no further mailings were sent to this address.

Disclosure

A bank disclosed the details of a motor finance agreement to a car dealer without the complainant's consent. The car dealer in turn disclosed this information to the boyfriend of the complainant who had simply taken the car in for a service and had been asked by the complainant to make an enquiry about which cars might be available on a trade-in basis.

The complaint was raised with the bank, and the investigation revealed that the bank had disclosed details of the outstanding finance on the agreement to the dealer. The basis for the disclosure was that the customer's consent had been demonstrated by the dealer in providing the bank with the customer's name and agreement number. However, the customer had not provided the dealer with this information. The bank had not appreciated that some dealers would take steps to obtain such information from other sources, and as a result agreed to amend its procedure to raise this issue with its own staff and to ensure that dealers from whom it obtained business are made aware of their obligations under the Data Protection Act.

(Source: Information Commissioner Report, Case Studies 2000)

The Internet

The Internet – and the Worldwide Web in particular – has been heralded by many as the perfect tool and delivery mechanism for direct marketers. Already, users of Internet e-mail are regularly deluged by unsolicited e-mails advertising a full spectrum of products and services from suppliers all around the world. Of course, there are direct marketers using the Internet in a much more sophisticated manner. There are a number of legal issues which must be taken into account.

Law on the internet

Marketers who use the Internet for promotional purposes must ignore the siren voices which still persist in proclaiming that the Internet is unregulated. The truth is quite the reverse, and there has probably never been a more regulated medium.

The main problem is the very thing that makes it so attractive to marketers: its global reach. Everything the marketer puts on an Internet site is accessible from anywhere in the world unless access controls are put in place, and of course this would defeat the objective of mass distribution. E-mail can be sent more selectively, but has other problems.

New legislation, at the time of writing, concerns e-mail marketing. The EU's Directive on Electronic Communications and Data Privacy includes a 'soft opt-in'. This means that where there has been no previous contact with the consumer that consumer, must give prior consent in order to receive unsolicited e-mails. But where a sales context has already acquired e-mail addresses, they can be used.

Because Internet sites can be accessed from anywhere, the courts in many countries (including the UK and the USA) are treating things done on the Internet as within their jurisdiction no matter where the computer hardware is sited. Worse still, they are applying their own laws, not the laws of the country where the computer hardware is sited. One example is the issue of misleading price indications. Virgin Atlantic Airways maintained a website which included details of its trans-Atlantic airfares. The website described a return airfare of under $500, but when a prospective passenger asked for one of these tickets he was told that this special price was no longer available and the alternative was a ticket costing a little over $500. Under US law the airline was obliged to keep the information up to date, and as it had inadvertently failed to do so it ended up paying the US Department of Transport $14,000.

The result of this is that marketers must consider the legality of what they wish to do under the laws of every country, not just their own. And just in case some marketers believe this doesn't matter because foreign courts cannot get at them, it is worth noting that in many cases the judgments of foreign courts can be enforced very easily through our own courts (remember the Tattilo case study in Chapter 11).

It is interesting to check the level of compliance with the 1998 Data Protection Act. In a study of UK-based websites, UMIST and the IC (Macaulay and Bourne 2002) found a rather mixed picture. The larger companies and those in regulated industries exhibited high levels of compliance but smaller companies and those in unregulated sectors did not. Specific issues included the following:

- Small companies thought they were protected by their ISP, when this is not the case.
- Low levels of internal data security in some small companies.
- Many organisations will collect and use data even if they did not ask for it (for example, information entered into e-mails or discussion groups/communities). They can use data for which they have asked permission.
- Only 60% of children's sites had a privacy policy. 'One (children's) site has online discussion groups where the material (some of it containing sexual content unsuitable for children) is visible to all visitors, although registration is required to take part. A couple of sites which appear to be offshoots of a phone company collect information on children (and adults) in return for free ring tones for their mobile phone. At least one of them also requires the use of a premium-rate telephone call. However, the fact that they are an offshoot of a phone company is not made clear' (Macaulay and Bourne 2002).

Again, we reiterate: why not go beyond compliance if a mutually beneficial relationship is the real, not just rhetorical, intention?

Summary

- We have explored consumer reactions to direct and personalised marketing and several issues emerged. There are concerns over privacy and this is an area we analysed in some depth. We also proposed a model of privacy. A major contributor, we believe, to more successful relational marketing is to shift control over the process to consumers.

- There are wider social implications, as well, for marketers and we explored many of these, ranging from the use of personalised marketing data by the state to potential criminal use of this personal data. While marketing ethics must not be overlooked, the judgement of whether a decision proves to be unethical or ethical lies more or less with the individual concerned. In making ethical decisions, individuals must first be aware of the moral dimension of a particular situation. As such, there may be much to be gained by discussing social responsibility as this should go some way towards identifying the moral dimensions of particular situations.

- We have reviewed a number of possible solutions to these concerns, including voluntary and legislative regulation and increased education of consumers about the nature of the relational marketing industry.

- Permission marketing also appears to be worth exploring because it can redress the control balance between organisation and customer and this can be a major factor in achieving mutuality in relational marketing.

- We argue for relational marketers not only to recognise the letter of the law but even to exceed its spirit, otherwise claims of 'relationship' can all too often be seen cynically as mere rhetoric.

Review questions

1 What do you think would be the consequences for the direct marketing industry if 'opt-in' became the norm?

2 What concerns do UK consumers exhibit in relation to personalised direct and relational marketing? Outline the main foundations for each concern. What is your personal position regarding these issues?

3 What other issues should a socially responsible organisation consider?

4 Marketing 'occurs in society, with society's permission and support, and purportedly, in part for society's benefit' Camenisch (1991:246). To what extent do you think marketers should have to take account of the moral expectations of society?

5 What are the Data Protection Principles as given in the Data Protection Act (1998) and how do they affect direct marketing?

6 How is marketing via the Internet regulated?

7 Do you think there is a need for more legal controls of direct marketing? Why?

Further reading

Advertising Standards Authority: www.asa.org.uk and www.cap.org.uk

Crane, A, and Desmond, J. (2002) 'Societal Marketing and Morality', *European Journal of Marketing*, 36(5/6), pp. 548–69.

Data Protection Act (1998) The Stationery Office, London

Direct Marketing Association's Code of Conduct: www.dma.org.uk

Perri 6 (1998) *The Future of Privacy*, Vols 1 and 2, London: Demos.

References

Anon (1999) 'Consortia Begin Bids for London 999 Calls', *Precision Marketing*, 5 July, p. 44.

Ambler, T. (1999) 'Marketing Metrics study', London Business School as reported in Denny, N. (1999) 'Marketing Success is Judged by Cash Criteria', *Marketing*, 13 May, p. 3.

Ambler, T. (2002) 'Why Big Brother Believes Loyalty Is Good for You', *Marketing*, 17 October, p. 10.

Assael, H. (1998) *Consumer Behavior and Marketing Action*, PWS-Kent, p. 120.

Barnes, J.G. (1994) 'Close to the Customer: But is it Really a Relationship?' *Journal of Marketing Management*, 10, pp. 561–70.

Blackmore, S. (1999) *The Meme Machine*, Oxford: Oxford University Press.

Bloom, P.N., Adler, R. and Milne, G.R. (1994) 'Identifying the Legal and Ethical Risks and Costs of Using New Information Technologies to Support Marketing Programmes', in R.C. Blattberg, R. Glazer and J.D.C. Little (eds) *The Marketing Information Revolution*, Boston, MA: Harvard Business School Press, pp. 289–305.

Borna, S. and Avila, S. (1999) 'Genetic Information: Consumers' Right to Privacy Versus Insurance Companies' Right to Know: A Public Opinion Survey', *Journal of Business Ethics*, 19, pp. 355–62.

Camenisch, P.F. (1991) 'Marketing Ethics: Some Dimensions of the Challenge', *Journal of Business Ethics*, 10, p. 246.

Carroll, A.B. (1978) 'Linking Business Ethics to Behaviour in Organisations', *Advanced Management Journal*, 7, pp. 110–12.

Cespedes, F.V. and Smith, H.J. (1993) 'Database Marketing: New Rules for Policy and Practice', *Sloan Management Review*, Summer, pp. 7–22.

Charrett, S. (1999) *Identity, Privacy and Personal Freedom: Big Brother v New Resistance*, Boulder, CO: Paladin Press.

Chesbro, M. (1999) *Privacy for Sale: How Big Brother and Others Are Selling Your Private Secrets for Profit*, Boulder, CO: Paladin Press.

Crane, A. and Desmond, J. (2002) 'Societal Marketing and Morality', *European Journal of Marketing*, 36(5/6), pp. 548–69.

Cubitt, E. (2003)'FoE Blasts "pathetic" Recycling Initiatives', *Precision Marketing*, 23 May, p. 1.

Darian, J.C. (1987) 'In-Home Shopping: Are There Consumer Segments?', *Journal of Retailing*, 63(2), Summer, pp. 163–86.

Davies, J.F. (1997) 'Property Rights to Consumer Information: A Proposed Policy Framework for Direct Marketing', *Journal of Direct Marketing*, Summer, 11(3), pp. 32–41.

Dawkins, R. (1989) *The Selfish Gene*, Oxford: Oxford University Press.

Denny, N. (1995) 'The Quest for the Best Messenger', *Marketing Direct*, November, pp. 21–8.

Dineen, A. (1999) 'Beating the Data Protection Registrar', *Direct Marketing Strategies*, 1(1), pp. 13–16.

Dixon, L. (2000) 'DoubleClick Sued over Data Scandal', *Precision Marketing*, 7 February p. 10

Enderle, G. (1995) 'A Comparison of Business ethics in North America and Europe', Working Paper, University of Notre Dame, Indiana.

Evans, M., O'Malley, L. and Patterson, M. (1995) 'Direct Marketing: Rise and Rise or Rise and Fall?', *Marketing Intelligence and Planning*, 13(6), pp. 16–23.

Evans, M., O'Malley, L. and Patterson, M. (1997) 'Direct Marketing Attitudes: A UK Perspective', American Marketing Association Conference, Dublin.

Evans, M., O'Malley, L. and Patterson, M. (1998) 'Relationship Marketing and Privacy Issues: Building Bonds or Barriers with L. O'Malley and M. Patterson', *Journal of Database Marketing*, 6(1), pp. 34–47.

Evans, M., O'Malley, L. and Patterson, M. (2001) 'Bridging the Direct Marketing–Direct Consumer Gap: Some Solutions from Qualitative Research', *Qualitative Market Research: An International Journal*, 4(1), pp. 17–24.

Experian (1999) 'New Database Helps Police Reduce Uninsured Driving', *Vision*, Summer, p. 4.

FEDMA (Federation of European Direct Marketing Associations) Council Day, November 1998, Brussels.

Fletcher, K. (1995) 'Dear Mr Bastard . . .', *Marketing Direct*, July/August, p. 58.

Fletcher, K. and Peters, L. (1996) 'Issues in Customer Information Management', *Journal of the Market Research Society*, 38(2), pp. 145–60.

France, E. (1998) as reported by Davies, S. (1998) 'New Data privacy Storm Threatens Global Trade War', *Financial Mail on Sunday*, 29 March, p. 3.

Future Foundation/Taylor Nelson AGB (2000) *Changing Lives*, London.

Gandy, O.H. (1993) *The Panoptic Sort: A Political Economy of Personal Information*, Boulder, CO: Westview Press.

GB Information Management (1999) reported in Anon (1999) 'Most Firms Ignorant of New Data Rules', Marketing, 20 May, p. 10.

Gehrt, K.C. and Carter, K. (1992) 'An Exploratory Assessment of Catalog Shopping Orientations', *Journal of Direct Marketing*, 6(Winter), pp. 29–39.

Gillett, P. (1976) 'In-Home Shoppers – An Overview', *Journal of Marketing*, 40(October), pp. 81–8.

Godin, S. (1999) *Permission Marketing*, New York: Simon and Schuster.

Goldwag, W. (2001) 'Net Users Need Rewarding for Personal Data', *Precision Marketing*, 20 April, p. 14

Hagel, J. and Rayport, J.F. (1997) 'The Coming Battle for Customer Information', *Harvard Business Review*, Jan–Feb, 75(1), p. 53.

Hansard (1999) 'House of Commons Debates', 3 February, pt. 22.

Henley Centre (1995) *Dataculture*, London: Henley Centre, p. 3.

Information Commissioner (2000) The First Data Protection Commissioner Annual Report, Wilmslow.

Introna, L. and Plouloudi, A. (1999) 'Privacy in the Information Age: Stakeholders, Interests and Values', *Journal of Business Ethics*, 22, pp. 27–38.

Key, A. (2000) 'The Taxman: Snooper or Helper?', *Marketing Direct*, January, p. 7.

Kitchen, P. (1986) 'Zipping, Zapping and Nipping', *International Journal of Advertising*, 5, pp. 343–52.

Larson, E. (1994) *The Naked Consumer: How our Private Lives become Public Commodities*, New York: Penguin.

Lavidge, R.J. (1970) 'The Growing Responsibilities of Marketing', *Journal of Marketing*, 34(January), pp. 25–8.

Lavin, M. (1993) 'Wives' Employment, Time Pressure, and Mail/Phone Order Shopping', *Journal of Direct Marketing*, 7(1), pp. 42–9.

Lazer, W. (1969) 'Marketing's Changing Social Relationships', *Journal of Marketing*, 33 (January), pp. 3–9.

Lenk, K. (1982) 'Information Technology and Society', in G. Friedrichs and A. Schaff (eds) *Microelectronics and Society: For Better or Worse*, Oxford: Pergamon Press, pp. 273–310.

Macaulay, L.A. and Bourne, I. (2002) 'Study of Compliance with the Data Protection Act 1998 by UK Based Websites', Manchester: Information Commissioner/UMIST.

Marsden, P.S. (1998) 'Memetics: A new Paradigm for Understanding Customer Behaviour and Influence', *Marketing Intelligence and Planning*, 16(6), pp. 363–8.

Marsden, P.S. (1999) 'Help Advertising Evolve: Clone Consumer Thought-Patterns', *Admap*, March, pp. 37–9.

Martin, T.R. (1985) 'Ethics in Marketing: Problems and Prospects', in G.R. Laczniak and P.E. Murphy (eds) *Marketing Ethics: Guidelines for Managers*, Lexington, MA: Lexington Books, pp. 1–7.

May, M. (2002) 'DIY Data', *Marketing Direct*, July/August, pp. 43–4.

Maynard, M.L. and Taylor, C.R. (1996) 'A Comparative Analysis of Japanese and U.S. Attitudes toward Direct Marketing', *Journal of Direct Marketing*, 10(1), pp. 34–44.

McKelvey, C. (2003) 'Beware of Next Robertson Jam', *Precision Marketing*, 23 May, p. 15

Milne, G.R., Beckman, J. and Taubman, M.L. (1996) 'Consumer Attitudes toward Privacy and Direct Marketing in Argentina', *Journal of Direct Marketing*, 10(1), pp. 22–33.

Mitchell, A. (2001) 'New Consumer Expectations, New way of Life', *Precision Marketing*, 12 April, p. 14.

Mitchell, A. (2002) 'Permission to Target is not a Licence to Spam', *Precision Marketing*, 12 July, p. 14.

Mutel, G. (2001) 'Too Much Information – a Damaging Prospect', *Precision Marketing*, 31 August, p. 11.

Nectar (2002) Nectar loyalty programme Application Form.

O'Malley, L., Patterson, M. and Evans, M.J. (1997) 'Intimacy or Intrusion? The Privacy Dilemma For Relationship Marketing in Consumer Markets', *Journal of Marketing Management*, 13, pp. 541–59.

Packard, V. (1957) *The Hidden Persuaders*, London: Penguin, p. 195.

Parker, G. (1999) 'Tories Accused of GM Foods Scaramongering', *Financial Times*, 4 February, p. 8.

Patterson, M., O'Malley, L. and Evans, M.J. (1996) 'The Growth of Direct Marketing and Consumer Attitudinal Response to the Privacy Issue', *Journal of Targeting, Measurement and Analysis for Marketing*, 4(3), pp. 201–13.

Patterson, M., O'Malley, L. and Evans, M.J. (1997) 'Database Marketing: Investigating Privacy Concerns', *Journal of Marketing Communications*, 3(3), pp. 151–74.

Petrison, L.A. and Wang, P. (1995) 'Exploring the Dimensions of Consumer Privacy: An Analysis of Coverage in British and American Media', *Journal of Direct Marketing*, 9(4), pp. 19–37.

Phelps, J.E., Gozenbach, W.J. and Johnson, E.A. (1994) 'Press Coverage and Public Perception of Direct Marketing and Consumer Privacy', *Journal of Direct Marketing*, 8(2), pp. 9–22.

Ramsden, I. (2001) reported in Mutel, G. (2001) 'Too Much Information – a Damaging Prospect, *Precision Marketing*, 31 August, p. 11

Reed, D. (2001) 'New Life for Suppression', *Precision Marketing*, 6 July.

Rosen, J. (2001) *The Unwanted Gaze: The Destruction of Privacy in America*, New York: Vintage Books.

Rosenberg, L. and Hirschman, E. (1980) 'Retailing Without Stores', *Harvard Business Review*, July/August, pp. 103–12.

Rothfeder, J. (1992) *Privacy for Sale: How Computerisation has Made Everyone's Private Life an Open Secret*, New York: Simon and Schuster.

Rubach, E. (2003) 'Industry Hail Robertson Defeat', *Precision Marketing*, 23 May, p. 1.

Rule, J. (1998) reported in Ungoed-Thomas, J. and Nuki, P. (1998) 'Mailshot Firms Blitz "Midas" Consumers', *The Sunday Times*, 17 May.

Savage, M. (1999) 'Legal Rule Hits Health Data', *Research*, July, p. 6.

Schroeder, D. (1992) 'Life, Liberty and the Pursuit of Privacy', *American Demographics*, June, p. 20.

Sherman, R.L. (1991) 'Rethinking Privacy Issues', *Direct Marketing*, April, pp. 40–4.

Simitis, S. (1987) 'Reviewing Privacy in an Information Society', University of Pennsylvania Law Review, 135, pp. 707–46.

Smith, R. (1994) 'Setting and Maintaining Data Quality: An Overview', *Journal of Database Marketing*, 1(3), pp. 247–53.

Specter, M. (1999) 'Cracking the Norse Code', *Sunday Times Magazine*, 21 March, pp. 45–52.

Star, S.H. (1989) 'Marketing and Its Discontents', *Harvard Business Review*, Nov–Dec, 67(6), pp. 148–55.

Sternberg, E. (1995) *Just Business: Business Ethics in Action*, London: Warner.

Titford, P. (1994) 'Self-regulation in Direct Marketing', *Journal of Database Marketing*, 2(2), p. 341.

Travis, A. (2003) 'ID Cards to Cut Asylum Abuses', *The Guardian*, 23 May, p. 1.

Treacy, M. and Wiersema, F. (1993) 'Customer Intimacy and Other Value Disciplines', *Harvard Business Review*, 71(1), pp. 84–93.

Ungoed-Thomas, J. and Nuki, P. (1998) 'Mailshot Firms Blitz "Midas" Consumers, *The Sunday Times*, 17 May.

Waldrop, J. (1994) 'The Business of Privacy', *American Demographics*, October, pp. 46–54.

Walker, C. (2000) 'Amazon accused of data law "flout"', *Precision Marketing*, 25 September, p. 1.

Walker, C. (2001) 'US Threat to Axe Data Treaty Puts Multinationals on Alert', *Precision Marketing*, 6 April, p. 1.

Westin, A. (1967) *Privacy and Freedom*, New York: Atheneum.

Westin, A. (1992) 'Consumer Privacy Protection: Ten Predictions', *Mobius*, February, pp. 5–11.

Whalen, J., Pitts, R.E. and Wong, J.K. (1991) 'Exploring the Structure of Ethical Attributions as a Component of the Consumer Decision Model: The Vicarious versus Personal Perspective', *Journal of Business Ethics*, 10, pp. 285–93.

Williams, R. (2002) 'Memetics: A New Paradigm for Understanding Customer Behaviour', *Marketing Intelligence and Planning*, 20(3), pp. 162–7.

Wood, J. (1998) 'Mail Marketing Group to Share Leads with US Firm', *Precision Marketing*, 15 June, p. 6.

Wright, B. (1999) as reported in Beenstock, S. (1999) 'Supermarkets Entice the 'Ultra' Customer', *Marketing*, 15 April, p. 15.

14 Planning and executing direct relational marketing

Learning objectives

Having completed this chapter, students should:

- Recognise the stages in the planning process.

- Be able to conduct situation analyses and environmental scans.

- Understand the importance of measurability in defining objectives.

- Be able to synthesise earlier coverage of data sources, metrics, targeting and interactive media within an overall relational plan.

- Be aware of the importance of being able to cost plans within budgetary constraints.

- Be wary of problems of implementing plans, however well designed they might be.

Dell Computers

The tool for managing customers is Premier Dell.com, an ordering and fulfilment extranet service, customised for each buyer. Customisation is the name of Dell's game. The tale of how wunderkind Michael Dell revolutionised the industry with his made-to-order model is now part of business folklore. There is little dispute, even among rivals, that Dell has set the standard in the efficiencies of its direct model, where consumers and corporate customers buy made-to-order systems over the phone or via the Internet. Building to order is a double whammy for Dell. Because its PCs are assembled only when a customer actually parts with his cash, Dell has waved goodbye to the inventory millstone that dogs its rivals. And the rather useful by-product of such a highly optimised process is that Dell, a mass producer, has the power to treat each customer individually – the epitome of relationship marketing. Premier Pages takes this a stage further for business customers, be they SMEs or large corporations. Premier Dell.com is a support service and a system to track the progress of orders, no matter what stage they are at in the manufacturing and delivery process. It caters for the selling part of the relationship cycle first, short-circuiting the process through a personalised store where customers configure their desired PC online – down to whether they want their own corporate software images installed at the factory. Sales-wise the site has been judged a huge success, with closure rates on the telephone combined with the Web twice that of selling via the telephone alone. 'By the time the customer calls, he has been to the website and configured his system already,' says Slater. 'Instead of a 15-minute conversation explaining the options, they're having a five-minute call just about things they're concerned about.' Small wonder Michael Dell has declared that he wants 70% of all Dell's transactions carried out via the Web in three years' time. The relationship management phase kicks in with the site's order tracking capability. As each PC is dispatched, its bar code is swiped to update the factory system and the customer's Premier Page simultaneously.

The Premier sites receive about 90 000 technical enquiries a week and Dell's answer to keeping support costs down is to encourage self-help through information gleaned via the online support site. In the 20% of cases when this does not work, an engineer is dispatched. Dell knows from the outset the size of each of its business customers, asking the customer how big his company is as soon as he logs onto the website. It is now also introducing tiered levels of support into which customers can buy, taking into account a company's size. Silver and Bronze levels are soon to be joined by Gold and Premier, tailored for large businesses requiring high availability of on-site support. Despite such segmentation, Premier Dell.com is more a relationship tool than a direct sales one. Perhaps the most overt evidence of selling via Premier Pages is the occasional personalised message on a customer's home page, alerting them to the availability of new technology.

'We know when a page was last accessed by the customer,' Slater says. 'We can tell when they've not been there for a while, so maybe the relationship isn't going the way we want it. Our sales people can then make a call. That's a legitimate use of the Premier data, in the same way as when the phone doesn't ring. Nothing revolutionary.' There are many ways to measure the success of Premier Pages – there are more than 60 000 Premier Dell.com sites in 14 languages worldwide and 30% of B2B customers visit Premier Pages every week. But in a business where margins are being squeezed, Dell consistently outperforms the market. It recently unseated its chief adversary Compaq from a seven-year reign as the world's largest PC maker.

(Source: Adapted by the authors from McElhatton 2001)

Introduction

The Dell case shows how relational marketing can be implemented with, even in B2C markets, a high degree of personalised relational interaction. The computer market may be particularly subject to changes in the technological environment but all businesses are susceptible to the dynamic and uncertain nature of the environments in which they operate. The purpose of planning is to reduce uncertainty, to assist in the identification of strategies that maximise strengths and opportunities and minimise weaknesses and threats, to identify a coherent action plan, and to evaluate the effectiveness of the committed resources. On this basis, 'planning is essential when we consider the increasingly hostile and complex environment in which firms operate' (McDonald 1992). Thus marketing strategies must occur within well-thought-out frameworks, and with the required resource allocation in place if they are to be successful. Relational marketers argue that conventional strategic planning models can be adapted to plan for relational marketing:

> The only differences are that the microchip has empowered us to consider customers at a micro, not just a macro, level and, even more importantly, to study the dynamics of customer relationships. (McCorkell 1997)

Essentially, the argument is that given the detailed level of knowledge about individual customers and their relationship to the organisation that relational marketers possess, precise objectives can be developed which are then subject to rigorous measurement criteria. In this sense, the value of planning to relational marketers is perhaps greater than its value to strategic planners. As we explored throughout this book, relational marketers can accurately measure the success of their planning, and thus can identify their contribution to the profitability of the business. This in turn increases the legitimacy of relational marketing within the organisation.

In putting together relational marketing plans, it is important that managers ensure that they are easy to understand, that they are detailed and precise, that they are sufficiently flexible to allow for sudden changes in circumstance, that they are realistic given current resources and capabilities, that they cover all relevant market factors and that they clearly delineate the responsibilities of various members within the organisation (Holder 1993).

In this chapter we explore the relational marketing planning process and its constituent elements.

The relational marketing planning process

We envisage the relational marketing planning process as consisting of 12 steps, which we call the Relational Marketing Planning Wheel (Exhibit 14.1), the 'wheel' concept being of importance because it is intended to reflect the iterative nature of the process. Each stage should not be set in stone because it should be responsive to the dynamics of the marketing environment within which the organisation operates and indeed to responses to previous stages in the process: 'the process is highly iterative – requiring constant doubling back to earlier parts of the situation assessment as new insights about customers, competitors and competencies are introduced, issues are clarified, and new strategic directions are contemplated' (Day 1984).

Mission and scope

Mission and scope relate to the attitudes and expectations within the organisation with regard to the business that the organisation is in, how the organisation rates against competition, and how it fits in to its environment. Piercy (1997) divides mission analysis into two separate components: customer missions and key value missions. Customer missions focus on the customer needs which the organisation aims to satisfy and the competitive domain in which the organisation is going to operate. Key value missions, on the other hand, centre on what aspects of the

EXHIBIT 14.1   The relational marketing planning wheel

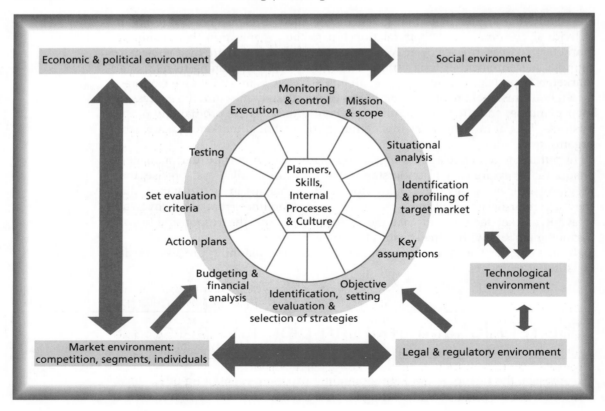

business the organisation deems important. Delineating the mission and scope of the organisation is an important step in defining the market in which the organisation operates. This in turn should go some way towards deciding who its customers are and how best it should go about satisfying customer needs.

Business objectives

Business objectives should be included at this stage in the plan. This is to ensure that relational marketing planners know what the priorities of the business are. At the business level, it is common to find objectives relating to profitability (ROI, £ profits); cash flow; utilisation of resources; market share; growth (revenue, units); contribution to customers (price, quality, reliability, service); and risk exposure (reliance on specific products, markets or technologies) (Day 1984). While at any time the business may have objectives in all of these areas, it is common practice that only the most important three or four are stated. This indicates management priorities, and facilitates the development of coherent plans. From the relational marketer's point of view, a thorough understanding of the business objectives will guide the formulation of relational marketing objectives and strategies, and ensure that they play their part in achieving organisational objectives.

Situational analysis

The situational analysis is the bedrock upon which the planning process is built. Broadly, it involves an assessment of the company's present position within its market(s). Thorough knowledge of the current situation is critical to the success of any plan, primarily because it helps the organisation to identify exactly what position it currently holds and what positions it might like to hold in the future. The situational analysis involves a detailed analysis of four individual elements: an analysis of the external marketing environment, an analysis of the company itself in terms of internal resources and capabilities, an analysis of trends in the particular market(s) in which the company operates and of product performance within that market, and an analysis of customers. These elements can then be combined into a summary statement of the company's internal strengths and weaknesses, and a review of its opportunities and threats. Given this information, it then becomes possible for the company to identify its critical success factors.

Environmental analysis

'A knowledge of the business environment must precede the acquisition of any degree of control over it' (Brownlie,1987). The problem is, however, that the business environment is in a constant state of flux. Moreover, the vast majority of changes in the business environment are not dramatic and happen over time, thus they are difficult to spot. As a result, firms have had to develop structured processes in order to monitor the marketing environment.

In addition, because marketing essentially holds an 'outside in' perspective (rather than the company itself deciding what the market wants), it is important to analyse potential customers, competitors and the wider environment within which it operates, in order to match company objectives and capabilities not only with current but also with future market requirements.

Understanding the marketing environment is therefore crucial and procedures must be put into practice on a continuous, not merely 'once a year' basis. Such understanding will obviously be based on information and how this is then converted into insight. We have already explored the nature and role of 'data' (Chapters 2 and 3), testing and research (Chapters 4 and 5) and knowledge management (Chapter 8) in relational marketing but now we need to examine the nature of, and processes for, the exploration of the organisation's wider environment. This, however, is not separate from these other sources of information and as a result the model in Exhibit 14.2 is useful in reflecting the ideal progression of 'data' to 'knowledge' and the various dimensions it can possess.

The importance of environmental scanning, especially for relational marketing, is because technological change is especially dynamic, as we mentioned in Chapter 3. Indeed, the pace of change means we can sometimes 'overestimate the immediacy but underestimate the profundity of underlying economic shifts. The digital revolution is not exception ... a wait and see strategy is usually wrong. It

EXHIBIT 14.2 Marketing information systems

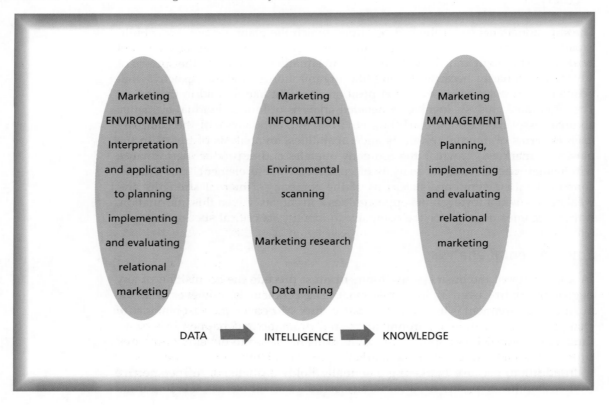

is better to fail five times over through trying too early than it is to fail once by being too late' (Evans 2000).

The implication here is that change needs to be monitored and as far as possible predicted in order for organisations to be 'there' when change actually affects their operations. Recognising change only when it has had an impact is usually going to be too late. On this basis strategic planning will take place on the continuous iterative basis, we have already suggested, rather than within any old-fashioned annual planning cycle.

Depending on the specific influence, marketing activities might be *directly* affected (new technology providing alternative methods of conducting the same activities, or legislation governing these) or, alternatively, *market behaviour* might change – due to changes in the social structure or social attitudes, or perhaps due to changed lifestyles resulting from technological and/or economic change. This would then hold *indirect* implications for marketing response. If marketing is to react in true relational manner then it is clear that it needs to be ready to do so when an event or trend is manifested in market behaviour and desires.

A further point is the interaction of influences – the combined impact of economic and technological change, for example, might give extra momentum to (say) the home-centred society in certain segments since in-home entertainment expands with technological development; home working becomes a reality for more people via Internet PCs linked to their employer; and enforced leisure time expands if there is high unemployment or with retirement (and, as we have seen, there is a significantly expanding baby boomer segment of retirees).

The competitive environment can be included because a greater under-standing of the competitive nature of the market environment is probably becoming more important – as Unger (1981) has suggested: 'knowing what the consumer wants is often not too helpful if a dozen other companies also know . . . a company must be competitor oriented. It must look for weak points in the positions of its competitors and then launch marketing attacks against these . . .'.

Again, as we have seen in Chapter 3, there are databased competitor intelligence sources and these should be used to plot likely competitor strategies.

Technology does bring with it some ethical issues concerning competitor intelligence. For example, technology mainly intended for political surveillance, such as so-called spy centres in, for example, Yorkshire, might have been involved in commercial business competitor intelligence. Some of these centres are RAF bases but are significantly controlled from the USA. There have been concerns over the unethical and even illegal use of this sort of technology on behalf of such companies as Enron in order to gain competitive intelligence for competitive advantage (BBC 2003).

As we have already discussed under data fusion in Chapter 3 and in our coverage of knowledge management in Chapter 8, the above would be perceived to be unethical by many; the intent is to plug into networks of intelligence sources and fuse data in synergistic ways. The importance of monitoring, projecting and even influencing change in this wider context has been reinforced by Moutinho *et al.* (2002): 'Marketing is poised for revolutionary changes in its organisational contexts as well as in its relationships with customers. Driven by a dynamic and knowledge-rich environment, the hierarchical organisations of the twentieth century are disaggregating into a variety of network forms including internal networks, vertical networks, intermarket networks and opportunity networks. The role of marketing in each network is changing in profound ways. Marketing increasingly will be responsible for creating and managing new marketing knowledge, education, real-time market information systems, intra-firm integration, conflict resolution, technology forecasting risk and investment analysis, transfer pricing of tangibles and intangibles and the coordination of the network's economic and social activities.'

Many of the issues raised here are explored in this book. We have already shown how the relational paradigm extends beyond organisation–customer interaction into intra- and inter-organisation relational interaction. The issues involved concerning networks and sharing of knowledge are covered within our discussion of knowledge management.

Although marketers might buy in to the relational paradigm, we believe that the dynamic nature of this environment requires constant vigilance and we therefore agree with Deshpande (1999) who calls for cross-disciplinary, cross-function and cross-cultural examination and sharing of knowledge. Moutinho *et al.* (2002) also suggest a 'scenario planning' approach for exploring marketing's future.

IN THEORY

Environmental scanning

Environmental scanning has been described concisely by Jain (1981) as 'an early warning system for the environmental forces which may impact a company's products and markets in the future'.

In this way, scanning enables an organisation to *act* rather than to *react* to opportunities and/or threats. The focus is not on 'the immediate' but rather has a longer-term perspective which is necessary for being in a position to plan ahead. Indeed, the whole effectiveness of organisations is to some extent dependent on their abilities to understand – and use this understanding – of environmental uncertainty. One key point is that environmental influence is not static but continuously changing, hence the need for continuous monitoring of various influences, both internal and external. A danger of not thinking in this way might be a kind of 'Future Shock'.

Some writers and researchers point to organisational problems in the practical implementation of scanning procedures – as well as more general aspects of marketing decision-making. Aguilar (1967), for instance, demonstrated that those who most need scanning information (top management) are not those who most deal with the collecting and analysing of such data and that this is a problem because there is quite a distortion and loss of information before it reaches the decision makers. A related consideration is whether scanning should be conducted centrally or decentrally. Jain (1981) and Johnson and Scholes (1984) point to the importance of being able to scan the environment more globally and therefore more synergistically – something that would be difficult if different environments were scanned by different departments for their own relatively narrow perspectives and uses.

Aguilar identified another problem related to all of this, that those collecting the information are not the decision makers and therefore there is the problem of whether the right kind and sufficiency of information is collected. These aspects (of the same problem), he suggested, also resulted in a lack of integration of the very diverse types of data.

Useful frameworks have been suggested under alternative terminology (market sensing) by Piercy (1997) and summarised by Piercy and Evans (1999), as appears in Exhibits 14.3, 14.4 and 14.5.

As can be seen, these provide practical grids for identifying and prioritising trends and events. Here again it is suggested that decision makers should be involved in the process rather than merely briefing others and then receiving results. As for sharing the findings and implications, databases can be used so that different departments and personnel in the organisation (and indeed in partner organisations) can access the same knowledge electronically. In other words, we have synergy of database technology (which is all too often merely used for processing data for more immediate campaign purposes) and data from the wider perspective of longer-term trends.

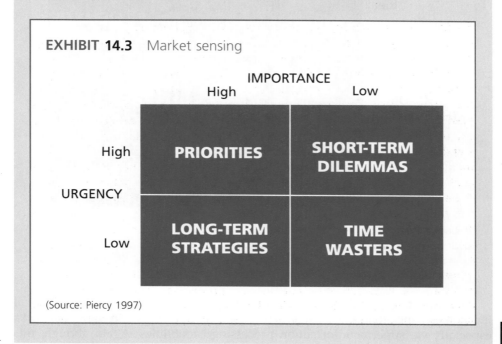

EXHIBIT 14.3 Market sensing

IMPORTANCE

	High	Low
High	**PRIORITIES**	**SHORT-TERM DILEMMAS**
Low	**LONG-TERM STRATEGIES**	**TIME WASTERS**

URGENCY

(Source: Piercy 1997)

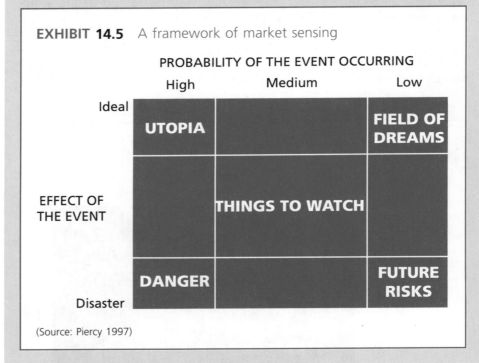

EXHIBIT 14.4 A framework for market sensing

| Environment | Timeframe |
| Dimension | Market |

Events	Specific Impacts	Probability
		Effect
1.		
Code:		
2.		
Code:		
3.		
Code:		
4.		
Code:		
5.		
Code:		
6.		
Code		

(Source: Piercy 1997)

EXHIBIT 14.5 A framework of market sensing

PROBABILITY OF THE EVENT OCCURRING

High   Medium   Low

Ideal

UTOPIA   FIELD OF DREAMS

EFFECT OF THE EVENT   THINGS TO WATCH

DANGER   FUTURE RISKS

Disaster

(Source: Piercy 1997)

To support this analysis, Achrol and Kotler (1999) discuss how 'relational mechanics' and the 'knowledge-driven society' synergise in new networks especially via superior information processing capabilities. Again, though, this requires the market-sensing procedures of Piercy (1997) and Day (1994) and, as

Day suggests, it is entirely congruent with the relational paradigm which he describes as 'market relating'.

These processes have become known as environmental scanning, the purpose of which, according to Jain (1990), is to enable the firm to deal with environmental change. Many environmental scanning models have been proposed, though they all more or less share similar characteristics (Exhibit 14.6).

The environmental factors that make up the wider marketing environment are essentially beyond the control of the organisation. Thus it is the organisation that must adapt to, or account for, changes in the environment.

Obviously, some of these environments have particular relevance for relational marketers, given the nature of relational marketing. Changes in technology have been increasingly evident in recent years and have had a dramatic effect upon the industry, especially in terms of factors such as the evolution of the database, analytical systems and the emergence of desktop publishing. Equally, given the targeted nature of relational marketing, changes in demographics or sociocultural factors are likely to have a profound effect on how a relational marketer conducts business, as do new relational vehicles that facilitate interactive relationships. The legislation that governs relational and database marketing is currently evolving and relational marketers clearly need to keep up to date with any relevant changes.

EXHIBIT 14.6   The environmental scanning process (Jain 1990)

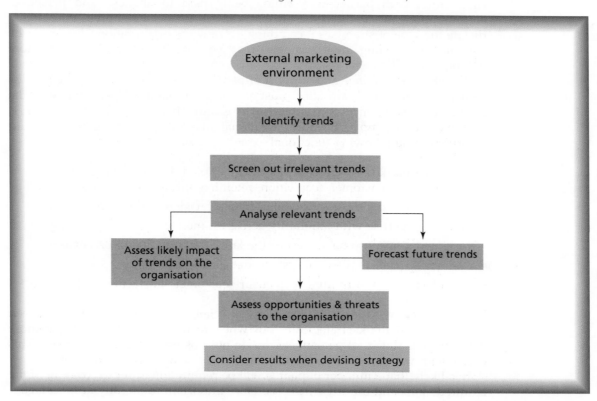

Indeed, as we have suggested, it is probably more appropriate (if 'relationship marketing' is not to be mere rhetoric) for organisations to go beyond the letter of the law and to reflect its spirit.

Changes in the economic environment may also have implications for marketers, and relational marketers in particular. For example, the resources available may be dependent upon economic conditions, target markets may become more or less appealing in times of economic crisis and the product or service offerings may need to be adapted to offer unique value to customers. Different market segments will be differentially affected by changes in the economic environment (which in turn is often a manifestation of political environments). For example, an increase in interest rates will reduce the disposable income of those with mortgages, credit card and other debt but for 'empty nesters' who have paid off their mortgages and do not have much debt for example, an interest rate increase will attract them to investing in savings products. Further examples of how different 'environments' affect marketing can be found elsewhere (for example, Evans 1988).

Internal analysis

In addition to forces from the external environment, internal or company-specific factors will also have a bearing on the planning process (Piercy 1990). The main focus during this phase of analysis will be on the organisation's resources and capabilities, with particular attention being paid to financial and personnel considerations. It stands to reason that a firm's financial resources will largely dictate the type of strategies it can pursue. For some organisations, however, the cost of not pursuing these strategies may be greater and thus they are more willing to take financial risks.

The skills, experience and support of personnel are paramount to the success of any strategy. The organisation must be confident that it has personnel with the appropriate experience and expertise to ensure that the planning process is effective. For example, the ideal relational marketing planning team should incorporate the following functional expertise (Holder 1993):

- relational marketing strategic planning, coupled with the analytical knowledge of customer acquisition, retention and lifetime value.;
- media knowledge across all media, from television to door-drops;
- creative expertise with familiarity across all media;
- production talent to be abreast of the latest techniques and processes;
- systems specialists who understand database marketing;
- manufacturing and fulfilment to ensure customer satisfaction and service.

We have already explored the problems associated with the 'skills gap' between those who can think strategically but who are not IT savvy and those more technical and statistical personnel who do not possess strategic awareness. This exploration was in our coverage of knowledge management in Chapter 8.

It is likely that a number of people will be required in order to cover all of the required skills and expertise. It is therefore important to identify at this stage if people with these skills are already involved in the planning process. Equally important, the team should consider what elements of the campaign can be carried out in-house, and what elements will be contracted out to an agency. This is important, as agency briefs need to be developed very early in the campaign in order to ensure that sufficient time is available for design, artwork, mailing, fulfilment etc. As we discussed in Chapter 10, there can be dangers of 'disintegrated' marketing communications if different media briefings are given by different client departments to different agencies or agency departments.

An organisation needs to be confident that its personnel have the capabilities to implement any strategies that are outlined. Furthermore, in a truly customer-centred organisation, it is imperative that the firm has the full backing of its employees so that everyone within the organisation is working towards the same goal. The field of internal marketing has been developed whereby employees are treated as internal customers in an effort to smooth the path towards successful implementation of external strategies (Berry 1981; Piercy and Morgan 1993). This is particularly important if relational marketing is to be used as part of a relationship-building programme.

Internal analysis should also help to clarify the organisation's competitive advantage and core competencies. Any strategy that an organisation pursues should enable it to identify its competitive advantage(s) and to focus on these to the benefit of the organisation (Jain 1990). According to Jüttner and Wehrli (1994), the majority of explanations of the origins of competitive advantage focus on what they refer to as 'resources' and 'competencies'.

For the relational marketer, the following resources are important (Roberts and Berger 1989):

- an extensive and accurate mailing list;
- a detailed database providing relevant and up-to-date information on customers and prospects;
- analytical techniques and models capable of extracting from the database the critical information on which to make managerial decisions.

Finally, internal analysis should take account of the structures and systems within the firm in terms of organisation, training and development, and intra- and interdepartmental communication, as we discussed in Chapter 8 on knowledge management. Key questions will centre on the ways in which decisions are made, the degree of autonomy at functional levels, and the process of internal communication and communication between partners and suppliers.

Market analysis and product performance

Market analysis refers to the process of monitoring changes in the markets in which the organisation operates. Factors for consideration will include the size of the market, whether the market is growing or shrinking, and any trends or developments that may be occurring within it.

Market analysis will also include a focus on the organisation's competitors. Given the intensely competitive nature of contemporary markets, this competitive focus is becoming increasingly important. Not only must the firm consider which organisations are competitors at the present time, but it must also try to gauge whether new competitors are likely to emerge in the near future. This is becoming ever more difficult, particularly with the move towards scrambled merchandising by many high-street retailers. For example, the major supermarkets have, in recent years, moved into the competitive domains of clothing, petrol, DIY, and even financial services. The move by Marks & Spencer, Tesco and Sainsbury's into financial services several years ago indicates the power of the customer database and the role of customer relationships. While future competitive actions are probably the most important to consider, they can be gauged to some extent by reference to past actions and performance. Continuous environmental scanning will also be of significant benefit here.

Next, the organisation will have to assess the performance of its product mix within these markets. The firm will need to identify the level of success that these products enjoy, the degree of funding and support they require, and the role each of them plays in customer acquisition and retention.

Customer analysis

A business can increase value in two ways: customer acquisition and customer development. In planning relational marketing strategy, the role of relational marketing in both these areas must be addressed. As such, customer analysis is critical to understanding a company's current situation. This is because ultimately it is customers and not products that generate profit (McCorkell 1997); it is through the behaviour of customers that the business will grow or decline. Traditionally, assets of the business included property, capital equipment and new product patents. Ironically, customers were not included in such an assessment. However, today, the existing customer base is viewed as one of the organisation's most critical assets. This is primarily because research suggests that existing customers are at least five times more profitable than new customers. We have dealt more extensively with customer analysis within Part 2 of the book and refer you to the chapters there.

It is, however, worth reiterating that relational marketers argue that the customer database is an invaluable source of information relating to customers, but that we are concerned about the perspective of some who believe that we can virtually ignore traditional market research techniques. We covered this in Chapter 5 but another view is summarised thus: 'conventional market research methods are sometimes too slow and almost always too imprecise to provide the right quality of planning information' (McCorkell 1997). While we agree that the customer database is invaluable, we have argued strongly against eliminating conventional research methods.

SWOT

This is a useful framework (Table 14.1) that is well covered in most books on strategy. It calls for an examination and evaluation of the internal strengths and weaknesses but also the external opportunities and threats. In running executive

TABLE 14.1 SWOT analysis

Attributes	So what?
Strengths	
Customer lifetime value is high.	This means that customer retention is particularly important to us, and so far we're pretty good at it.
Trend analysis suggests that the company has a good record of customer retention.	
Weaknesses	
The customer database is not very sophisticated.	We cannot capture a great deal of information about our customers. This affects our ability to target customers effectively, and leads to a great deal of waste.
The organisation does not have the resources to deal with high volumes of in-bound telephone calls.	Promoting telephone direct response may not be a viable option at this time.
Opportunities	
Research indicates that customers are more likely to purchase products via the mail or telephone if the organisation has an established returns policy.	We might make purchasing more attractive for customers if we used our existing distribution system to collect returns. Although this will involve additional costs, it also represents additional value.
The majority of our customers use the credit facilities we offer. There might be an opportunity to diversify into financial services.	We could use the information we already hold on our credit customers to offer them financial services products. We can also use this data to profile credit customers, and extend our target base.
Threats	
Environmental scanning suggests that financial services are being offered by a wide variety of organisations.	It's becoming increasingly difficult to identify competitors. The number of new entrants suggests that the firm will lose market share unless action is taken.
All of our competitors now run loyalty schemes.	We don't. Our competitors know more about their customers, and offer their customers more value.

programmes, the authors have experience that suggests the former is generally conducted more thoroughly but that managers are less able to explore external trends, so again we reinforce the importance of the environmental scanning procedures outlined above.

This summary should also note where the company already performs well, and where there is room for improvement. The SWOT analysis should make it relatively easy for the organisation to identify what the critical success factors in its market are likely to be. For example, from the above SWOT analysis, the critical success factors would include:

- Customer retention is one of the company's critical strengths.
- The inability to profile customers effectively is a critical weakness.
- Increasing the value offered to existing customers (through broadening the product line) represents a critical opportunity.
- Competing loyalty schemes may attract our customers if we don't respond very quickly.

Critical success factors represent areas that are crucial for success in a particular market. However, many organisations make the mistake of believing that these factors will not change (Day 1984). The company might now know its strengths and weaknesses and be aware of potential opportunities and threats, but before this information becomes really useful, the company must really understand who its customers are, and what it is they want.

Identification and profiling of target market

Gaining knowledge of customers is extremely important for marketers in general, but even more so for relational marketers. Comprehensive customer knowledge allows the relational marketer to choose which approaches to use in future acquisition and retention drives and, as a consequence, to make value judgements with regard to acquisition and retention costs.

Customer profiling is the process whereby the customer base is categorised into distinct groups according to customer characteristics. These characteristics may then be used in the search for future prospects and to tailor future communications and offerings to existing customers.

We again refer the reader to earlier chapters for fuller coverage of target market identification and profiling (Chapters 2, 3, 4, 5, 6 and 9, in particular).

We also make a plea for socially responsive targeting. We have explored 'junk' targeting and issues of data protection control and feel that for marketing to be truly relational, it needs to 'go beyond' the letter of the law in these respects.

Key assumptions

It is important to challenge key assumptions *before* developing strategies in order to avoid a situation where a lot of time and effort have gone into formulating a plan which is unacceptable to the organisation for a number of reasons. For example, it may be that the proposed strategy requires additional personnel or technology which will not be made available (Piercy 1997). In relational marketing terms, key assumptions that must be challenged include the following:

1 Is there an assumption that an external agency will be used for creative, fulfilment, media buying, or data capture? To what extent is this assumption valid? Will the required finance be available? Is it common practice to use external agencies or is the majority of work normally done in-house?

2 Does the campaign depend upon the purchase of new mailing lists? Is more research required in order to refine strategies? Will the media choice be acceptable to the organisation? If so, is it safe to assume that the organisation will support such requests?

3 Is there a need to access other datasets within the organisation in order to profile or generate a mailing list? Can you presume automatic access to such data?

4 Is the assumption that the campaign will be fully stand-alone, with no need to ensure the compatibility of either the offer or the message with other strategies? How valid is this assumption? Given the growing trend towards integrated marketing communications (IMC), who is the person or people with whom you should confer?

5 Will there be an incentive offered to increase response to the campaign? If this is based on the use of specific products or brands, is it safe to presume that this will be acceptable?

6 Does the campaign seek to secure direct sales? If this involves supplementing or bypassing retail channels, will this contravene existing policy?

7 If any of the financial analysis is based on the sale or sharing of mailing lists with other departments or organisations, is it a valid assumption that this will be supported within the organisation?

The assumptions that are made will differ greatly from company to company, and indeed, from strategy to strategy, and therefore the above list is illustrative rather than definitive. If you are happy at this stage that the appropriate resources will be available, and that in principle your strategy is compatible with the business mission, then you are in a position to formulate a detailed plan. It is now appropriate to identify the specific objectives for the relational marketing campaign.

Objective-setting

Setting objectives is another critical element of the relational marketing plan. Indeed, if objectives are inappropriate, unrealistic or inconsistent, then everything that follows is of little value. The first question to ask is: what is an objective? Day (1984) states that objectives are 'desired or needed results to be achieved by a specific time period'. This suggests that objectives are simply statements of the results that a business should achieve. However, it is important to note that objectives are hierarchical in many ways. We outlined earlier that the business mission and overall objectives should be stated in the Mission and Scope stage of the plan. This is because relational marketing objectives should go some way towards achieving the overall business objectives. Objectives can be developed in a number of ways which will be discussed shortly. However, before looking at the process of objective-setting, it is first important to identify what makes a good objective, and what are the elements which all objectives should incorporate. We suggest that objectives should

Communicate
Aspirational but
Realistic goals, with each objective having a
Precise focus (market share, product sales, increased retention), which is capable of
Evaluation (quantifiable measures), within a specific
Time period. This has led us to suggest the mnemonic CARPET, described below:

- **Communicate**: The purpose of a written objective is to communicate with other members of the organisation. This suggests that the language used should not be open to interpretation – it should communicate a clear message. Because objectives are written they are less open to subjective interpretation than objectives that are verbally stated.

- **Aspirational**: Objectives need to challenge and focus effort, particularly because businesses generally wish to grow, increase profitability etc. Essentially, business objectives focus upon improving on previous achievements. As a result, objectives should include some aspirational element. In this way, objectives act as motivators, and allow the organisation to strive to do better than in previous years, and/or in previous programmes.

- **Realistic**: Although there is some element of aspiration included within an objective, it is also important that objectives are achievable with the appropriate strategies, within budget, environmental and competitive constraints. Otherwise, objectives are just pipe dreams. If managers do not believe that objectives can be achieved, there is no motivational element involved.

- **Precise focus**: Objectives should focus on a specific element (e.g. share of customer, percentage of sales, product penetration). Where the company has objectives in more than one of these areas, several objectives are required. This results in clear, specific objectives which will subsequently provide more guidance for strategic and tactical choices.

- **Evaluation**: Objectives must be written to include clear evaluation criteria. If not, they become no more than a wish list, and it is impossible to determine if objectives have been met, or if strategies have been successful. These evaluation criteria refer to the precise focus of the objective. These could relate to volume, value, margin, market share, or profitability. In order to facilitate objective evaluation, the use of loose terms such as 'maximise', 'minimise', 'penetrate' and 'increase' should be avoided unless they are qualified by specific targets. Thus, the objective may be to increase market share by 10%, to increase customer retention by 20%, to reduce customer defections by 50% etc.

- **Time**: For an objective to be useful in terms of measuring performance, there must be a time limit involved in order for managers to determine if targets have been met or missed. If objectives do not have a specified time limit, it becomes unclear when evaluation is appropriate. Thus all objectives should specify the time period involved – this may be within one year, within one month of running an advertisement, or within two weeks of sending out a direct mailshot.

To reiterate, objectives are intended to communicate required results to managers and others. Objectives should focus upon single precise issues (market share etc.), should be capable of evaluation and should identify a specific time period. Given the focus upon customers in relational marketing, it is common practice for separate objectives to be set down for each target group – loyal users, competitive users and promiscuous consumers (McCorkell 1997). Indeed, in some markets, objectives may be established for individual customers, particularly where those customers account for a large proportion of sales.

Objectives can relate to a number of different results. For example, the objective may be to build awareness, or to inform or educate. Although relational marketing can assist in achieving such objectives, on its own, relational marketing tends to focus upon generating direct sales, generating sales leads, and/or creating a database of key prospects:

- **Generating direct sales**: Appropriate if the product can be sold through direct channels, and/or if the organisation wishes to bypass or supplement a retail network.
- **Generating sales leads**: Appropriate if a salesforce is required, a new market sector is entered or new prospects are needed. In this case, further work is required to make a sale. For example, double glazing and financial services generally require a sales visit – however, the job of the salesperson is more effective if they can spend time dealing with clients rather than trying to generate sales leads.
- **Creation of a database of key prospects**: The objective here is not only to generate a database containing key information but also to make this information accessible in order that it can be used to support and drive marketing initiatives (Linton 1995).
- **Build awareness/Educate/Inform**: Although traditionally the domain of mass communications, relational marketing can also play a role in achieving these objectives. For example, although direct marketing of pharmaceutical products is prohibited in India, direct marketing is used to build awareness. Mailings discuss patients' symptoms in general, in the hope that recipients will be encouraged to ask their doctor for further details (Anonymous 1997).

The objective-setting process

The process of setting objectives is particularly important. This is because a business will have several objectives, and indeed relational marketing may itself have several objectives. If the process is not taken seriously, objectives may not be consistent. That is, one objective may invalidate another. For example, objectives to increase customer retention may directly impact upon an objective to reduce costs (especially where cost reductions occur in customer service or product development). Because strategies are developed to meet objectives, there is a need to think carefully through the objectives to ensure that strategies are not counter-productive. Equally, objectives need to be acceptable to management. This is more likely where they have been actively involved in the objective-setting process, and where they believe that objectives are realistically achievable within the given budget and environmental conditions. Thus, 'one of the roles of the objective-setting process is to provide a structured basis for developing objectives that can be embraced by managers' (Day 1984). There are three broad approaches to setting relational marketing objectives: derive from business objectives; develop from database; and combine, negotiate, formulate.

Derive from business objectives

Within most businesses, senior managers are responsible for setting business objectives over time periods of one, three and perhaps five years. These objectives are generally set having taken stakeholders' expectations, environmental conditions and internal resources into consideration. Stakeholders include investors, unions, employees and perhaps even government. Senior managers are expected to weigh the often conflicting expectations of these groups, and to identify what is achievable within given business resources. On this basis, business objectives are set, which subsequently form the basis for marketing, financial, production and other functional objectives. These objectives then become the basis for lower-level objectives. For example, within this approach, relational marketing objectives are derived from distribution and communication objectives, which are derived from marketing objectives, which are derived from business objectives. The strength of this process is that lower-level objectives aim to achieve higher-level objectives, and, as a result, strategies should be compatible and higher-level objectives should be achieved. The major criticism of this process is that middle management are not involved in the objective-setting process, and that objectives are handed down with no thought to the extent to which they are achievable.

Develop from database

This approach to planning has also been called outside-in planning (Shultz *et al.* 1993; McCorkell 1997). Within this approach, objectives are based upon information derived from the database. Essentially, relational marketers 'work out what it will cost, using their back data and forecasting models as a guide, to achieve any given volume of sales and cut off their plan at the optimum level' (McCorkell 1997). This approach leads to the formulation of relational marketing objectives which are clearly achievable. Indeed, some argue that this approach is far superior to top-down approaches, in that it is 'based on the reality of what previous customer behaviour suggests is achievable, not the pipe dreams of stakeholders' (McCorkell 1997). Thus, this approach to setting objectives results in more realistic objectives. However, its main limitation is that such objectives do not include an aspirational element, and thus are limited in their ability to motivate managers to exceed previous performance. Secondly, objectives may be set unrealistically low – within this scenario objectives may be continually met – but the extent to which they contribute to business objectives is increasingly questionable.

Combine, negotiate, formulate

Both of the above approaches to setting objectives are commonly used in business today. It has been shown that each has particular strengths, and that each has particular weaknesses. By combining both approaches it is possible to maximise the strengths of each, and to minimise weaknesses. That is, the aspirational element is provided by top-down approaches derived from business objectives, while the realistic element is provided by reference to information held on the database. Of perhaps greater importance, however, is that negotiation involves managers in the objective-setting process. In this way, they begin to take ownership of objectives, and they are motivated by aspirational but realistic objectives. Where this process takes place, business objectives may even be changed to reflect the reality of what is achievable within the available resources. As a result, stakeholder expectations are more likely to be achieved.

In an ideal world, the preliminary objectives set by senior management will be achievable, and, as a result, all lower-level objectives will also be achievable. However, in practice the world is far from ideal, and business objectives often incorporate politically desirable objectives, or reflect stakeholder wish lists. Thus, there is a clear gap between business objectives and what previous information suggests is achievable. Negotiations are generally about compromise – compromise over what is required and what is achievable within budget and other constraints. This is likely to result in changing objectives, for example by reducing the level of aspiration, changing strategies, and/or increasing resources available in order to improve the expected performance of a strategy. Because it is more firmly based in reality, the negotiated strategy is probably best for most organisations. Within this process, unrealistic objectives are not imposed top-down, although there is some aspirational element involved. Equally, objectives are not just the same or incrementally higher than previous campaigns. Most importantly, management are aware that these objectives are clearly achievable. The combination of aspirational and achievable objectives is a powerful motivator for management. Furthermore, because managers have been actively involved in the objective-setting process, they have 'bought-into' the plan at an early stage. Thus, in summary, a negotiated process of objective-setting results in a number of valuable benefits:

- Objectives are both aspirational and realistically achievable.
- Management have ownership of objectives, and thus motivation is likely to be higher.
- The level of focus and discussion should also ensure that objectives are precise, capable of evaluation, and specify appropriate time periods.

Identification, evaluation and selection of strategies

Strategy is 'the major link between the goals and objectives the organisation wants to achieve and the various functional area policies and operating plans it uses to guide its day-to-day activities' (Hofer and Schendel 1978). Marketing strategies therefore outline the path or approach to be taken by an organisation in allocating resources towards achieving its objectives (McDonald 1992).

Day (1986) indicates that a strategy's applicability may be evaluated according to the following criteria:

- **Suitability:** Is there a sustainable advantage? Any strategy should enable a company to identify its strengths and competitive advantage(s) and to focus on these to the benefit of the organisation.
- **Validity:** Validity refers to the consistency a strategy has with assumptions held about the external product/market environment (Jain 1990) and on whether those assumptions are realistic.
- **Feasibility:** Does the company have the skills, resources and commitment? In selecting strategies, an organisation will have to make a decision regarding their willingness to commit to a particular way of doing things (Ghemawat 1986), which will inevitably involve the matching of resource requirements to strategic proposals.
- **Internal consistency:** Internal consistency, what Yee (1990) refers to as 'strategic alignment', relates to the degree of fit between proposed strategies and current operations.
- **Vulnerability:** What are the risks and contingencies? The degree of risk associated with any strategy is a reflection of the resources allocated to it.
- **Workability:** Can the company retain its flexibility? Ideally, the workability of any strategy should be subjected to quantitative analysis (Jain 1990). In the absence of such measures, recourse to managerial consensus is advisable. Littler and Leverick (1994) suggest that in markets where new technology is the driving force, detailed and structured marketing planning becomes difficult. As a consequence, it is likely that under such conditions decisions will be made quickly, managerial judgement and guesswork will be the order of the day, and decisions will be bold and sweeping.
- **Appropriate time horizon:** 'A viable strategy will have a time frame for its realisation' (Jain 1990).

The process of strategy evaluation can be quite difficult at first but becomes easier with experience. Using the criteria set out above, management should be able to test and refine the strategic options that lie before them. Some options can easily be eliminated as they clearly fail to meet the criteria. However, it is rare for one clear option to emerge. Instead, management are likely to be forced to choose between a range of options on the basis of the balance between the risks and opportunities they offer. Constant refinement and re-evaluation of the options against the evaluation criteria should eventually highlight the strategies to be pursued. This process of strategic evaluation is outlined in Exhibit 14.7.

EXHIBIT 14.7   The strategy evaluation process (Day 1984)

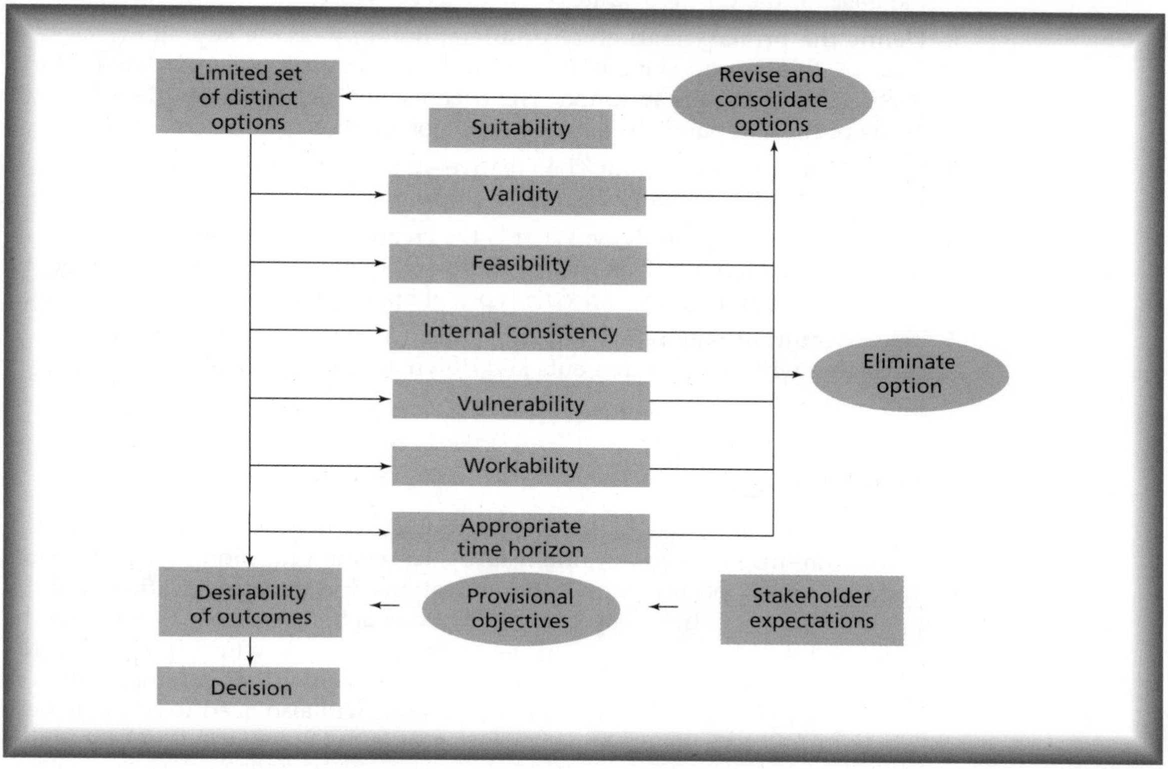

In relational marketing strategy terms, there are three main areas for consideration: media strategy, creative strategy and contact strategy.

Media strategy

We have already explored aspects of media strategy in terms of the range of media that can be selected (Chapter 10) and media selection metrics (Chapter 5) and refer the reader to these chapters for a reminder of the issues involved. Furthermore, scheduling and budgeting need to be flexible in order to allow for the sort of testing explored in Chapter 4.

Creative strategy

Again we refer you to earlier coverage for more detailed treatment. Chapter 12 explored relational messages and provided examples of how these are manifestations of relational marketing 'creative' as it is often termed. It is, however, worth adding Roberts and Berger's (1989) five steps:

1 **Develop the key selling concept:** The key selling concept relates to the core benefit on offer to consumers. Because consumers buy on the basis of

product or service benefits rather than attributes, using the core benefit as the basis of the creative strategy makes good sense.

2 **Define the primary marketing problem:** Building on the key selling concept, this second stage moves from the customer's point of view to the perspective of the organisation. The organisation needs to identify what, in terms of the campaign at hand, is its major marketing problem.

3 **Specify the desired action:** The creative strategy will differ depending on which particular action is desired of consumers.

4 **Create the message strategy:** What is the creative platform on which the message will be built? This will be expressed in general terms at this stage, to be broken down later into specific types of appeal, wording of the appeal etc.

5 **Take account of mandatory requirements:** Creative strategy must be consistent with the requirements laid down at organisational or divisional level.

Contact strategy

The information required to develop a contact strategy should come initially from a communications audit (Linton 1995). The communications audit compares customers' views of previous communications by the organisation and by competitors and identifies key communications actions needed to generate the desired result. Management will need to decide at which points in the relationship between the organisation and the consumer that communication is going to take place (Bird 1993). General decisions will also need to be made here with regard to when the customer or prospect is to be contacted and by which means.

The following case study demonstrates how contact can be scheduled according to relational trigger points.

CASE STUDY 14.1

Car dealership contact strategy

After purchase of a Land Rover Freelander, customers are contacted as follows:

Month 1   Welcome letter
If no accessories purchased, send accessories letter

Month 2   Free 3 000-mile service letter
After they book, send confirmation card
Follow up phone call after work has been completed

Month 11   12 000-mile service letter
After they book, send confirmation card
Follow-up phone call after work has been completed

Month 23   24 000-mile service letter
After they book, send confirmation card
Follow-up phone call after work has been completed

Month 35 MOT reminder
           36 000-mile service letter
           After they book, send
           confirmation card
           Follow-up phone call after work
           has been completed

Month 45 48 000-mile service letter
           After they book, send
           confirmation card
           Follow-up phone call after work
           has been completed
           Introduce allegiance programme

The allegiance programme offers discounted repairs and parts.

Also, if the customer appears to have lapsed his or her contact with the dealership, send allegiance letter, accessories letter and/or winter/summer check letters.

(Source: Adapted from material provided by DMA from the Land Rover/Freelander Award Winning Case Study, DMA/Royal Mail Awards 2001)

Budgeting and financial analysis

Setting budgets is one of the most detailed parts of the planning process. Essentially, the budget reflects the allocation of resources to strategies, and ultimately becomes a benchmark by which performance is measured. As such, developing budgets is also one of the most important parts of the planning process. The purpose of budgeting is to:

- communicate and motivate;
- allocate resources and accountability;
- control and coordinate activities;
- report results and provide feedback on performance (Stone *et al.* 1995).

Setting marketing budgets

Within marketing there are many different ways in which companies go about allocating resources to strategies. Indeed, many of these methods can also be used in budgeting for relational marketing. These are briefly outlined below:

- **Percentage of sales:** Budgets can be allocated either as a percentage of last year's sales or as a percentage of expected future sales. This method has received strong criticism in that sales form the basis of expenditure, rather than relational marketing expenditure resulting in sales. As such, budgets are either too low or too high, and tend to have little bearing on the stated objectives of a particular campaign.
- **Competitive parity:** This budgeting method has little to offer relational marketers, primarily because direct marketing is a below-the-line activity and thus it is difficult to determine how much competitors are actually spending. In any case, competitors spend to achieve their objectives, which may be very different from those stated in the relational marketing plan.

- **Objective and task approach:** Essentially, rather than starting with a fixed budget, relational marketers look at the objectives which have been agreed, and identify what tasks are required in order to achieve these stated objectives.

The first two methods (together with a number of others) work on the basis of allocating a fixed budget for a specified period of time. 'The very idea of a fixed sum to be spent each financial year or season is not sensible for relational marketers. The issue is: how much can I afford to spend to acquire a prospect, or to produce a sale for a customer?'(Bird 1993) Furthermore, the criticisms outlined above suggest that these methods are not particularly useful for relational marketers. As a result, the objective and task approach is much more applicable for developing relational marketing budgets. Additionally, because of the capacity to calculate the costs of relational marketing fairly accurately, this approach can be further refined (and improved) using the concept of allowable costs, as we explored in Chapter 3 (Kruegar 1996; McCorkell 1997). Thus, we call this refined approach 'objective and task within allowable costs'.

Objective and task within allowable costs

There are a number of stages involved in budget allocation using this method. These include:

1 Determine projected lifetime value of customers and prospects (see Chapter 3 for a detailed discussion of LTVs).
2 Financial analysis of previous relational marketing campaigns. Unless this represents a company's first relational marketing campaign, there will be information available on the success or otherwise of previous campaigns. It is important that this information be analysed thoroughly in order to enhance the effectiveness of the current process of budgeting, and indeed the overall planning process. The main performance measures used by relational marketers are (Stone et al. 1995):

   - **Customer acquisition costs**: Essentially a review of the average cost of acquiring customers as indicated by previous data. This will be an important input into determining the allowable costs of acquisition.
   - **Break-even volumes:** This indicates the minimum level of sales required in order to break even on campaigns to particular target segments.
   - **Attrition rate:** This is a measure of the rate at which customers are lost by the business. Further analysis is required to establish the reasons why customers defect.
   - **Lifetime values:** This may be further broken down to reflect the different lifetime value potential of different customer segments.
   - **Profit potential:** Based on previous data, calculate the expected profits of the campaign.
   - **Resource allocation:** Data on how all of the marketing resources have been deployed, and how effective resource allocation has been with different customer groups.

3 Determine allowable costs. (See Chapter 3 for a discussion of allowable costs.)

4 Review objectives and tasks, and allocate costs. Stages 5 and 6 of the planning process require that realistic objectives are set, and that the strategies chosen are capable of achieving the desired results. Because the availability of the budget is crucial to achieving success, setting objectives, choosing strategies and allocating budgets are highly interactive stages of the process (Table 14.2). Essentially, budgets are structured plans for the financial aspects of the campaign. Therefore costs need to be allocated to the various tasks which combine to form strategies. This requires a thorough assessment of the costs involved, because these will vary significantly depending on strategies chosen.

5 Ensure that the budget is feasible given the available financial resources. One of the potential problems with the objective and task approach is that the required budget may be far higher than expectations, and indeed far higher than the business can afford at this particular point in time. Thus, this last stage is essential to ensure that the resources will be available to implement the chosen strategies. If the required resources will not be available, then this is the stage to rethink the objectives, strategies or other elements of the plan.

TABLE 14.2 Costs related to direct relational marketing implementation

Media costs	Press, TV, radio, billboard etc.
Agency costs	Design, copy, artwork, consultancy etc.
Mailing	Envelope, brochure, postage etc.
Cost of handling response	Freepost, Freephone, maintaining and staffing a call centre, data capture etc.
Cost of meeting the response	Supplying and distributing the material that is required.
Cost of servicing the response	Sales or telemarketing costs in dealing with the potential volume of new business.
Testing	Separate budgets are required for testing format, publications, mailing lists etc. Test budgets generally show a loss because of fixed costs which cannot be allocated over a large volume.

Action plans

Action plans provide the means by which the organisation's ideas are turned into reality by being given a structure and a format through which they can be implemented. This involves not only the communication of ideas on a general level, but also the specific detail of any changes to be made and the programmes to be pursued. Piercy (1997) outlines a process by which action planning should occur (Exhibit 14.8).

Essentially, management's task is to identify the most critical areas for consideration, decide how any solutions should be accomplished and communicate these plans to the relevant people within the organisation. The general objectives and strategies outlined earlier must now be developed into precise objectives 'supported by more detailed strategy and action statements, with timings and responsibilities clearly indicated' (Christopher and McDonald 1995).

Set evaluation criteria

Measurability is the key attribute of response-generating activities, as we have shown throughout this book, and the type of measurement to be used must be planned in advance.

Effective measurement involves five key stages (Brannon 1993):

1 Every objective must be quantified and timed. If it is response you seek, of what kind, from whom, how many, at what rate and over what period of time?
2 Define what analyses will be used in evaluating the campaign and thus define the information needed for effective evaluation.

EXHIBIT 14.8   The action planning process

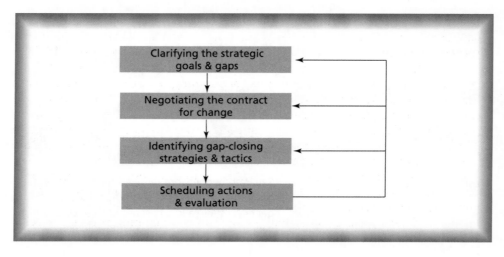

3 Identify how every response will be captured. Ensure that there are systems in place which allow every response to be logged, and identify the source of response. Such a system must also be capable of collecting all of the data deemed to be necessary for evaluation.

4 Identify how progress on each response will be tracked through to the final action dictated in your objective.

5 Identify how the results will be analysed.

Set target response levels

The simplest and most immediate measure of an interactive campaign is the response levels it achieves (Linton 1995). The organisation should aim for a realistic figure that is within the organisational budget, and that has taken into account the industry average and any other variables that might impact upon performance. We saw in case studies in Chapter 10 that inserts might produce what appear to be very low response rates, sometime less than 1, but that response to mailings can get into double figures.

Testing

Testing is a form of experimentation, as we saw in Chapter 4, and we refer the reader to the extensive coverage of testing in that chapter. The important point here, though, is that it helps to reduce costs by isolating the most cost-effective approaches and stimulates the creative process by identifying new goals. Above all, testing is customer centred because it recognises how consumers respond to relational marketing approaches they receive. It does not, to repeat an earlier discussion, explain why they respond as they do, so we again argue for a blend of testing and research (see Chapters 4 and 5).

Execution

'Most marketing plans are killed by inaction, rather than by deliberate rejection' (Nash 1986). This suggests that when the time comes to execute the plan it is important that everybody knows what they have to do, everybody is fully committed to making the plan work, and, above all, everybody actually *does* what they are required to do. The process of planning can be seductive, in that it is generally easier to plan, and to keep on planning, than it is to actually do something. Procrastination occurs because those involved are attempting to develop the *perfect plan*. However, it is important to remember that the objective of the planning process is *not* to develop the perfect plan, but rather to execute strategies capable of achieving agreed-upon objectives. As Drucker (1974) states: 'The best plan is only a plan, that is, good intentions, unless it degenerates into work. The distinction that makes a plan capable of producing results is the commitment of key people to work on specific tasks.'

Thus, in a sense, execution signals the end of the planning process. Specific action plans have been developed, budgets and resources allocated, evaluation criteria laid down and testing completed. The relational marketer is now ready to execute the plan, that is, to take the required action. Taking action involves:

1 reviewing implementation problems;
2 organising for implementation;
3 promoting customer response;
4 fulfilling orders;
5 managing customer service.

Reviewing implementation problems

Piercy (1997) argues that managers need to anticipate implementation problems as early as possible, and prior to implementation should ensure that:

- strategies are coherent and complete;
- strategies are capable of being implemented by the company at this time – e.g. structures are in place, and key resources are available; for relational marketers, these include database facilities, distribution channels, and fulfilment operations (Stone *et al.* 1995);
- the required support exists within the organisation.

Organising for implementation involves:

- mobilising the required resources;
- allocating responsibility for tasks to individuals;
- coordinating the activities of in-house and agency personnel;
- initiating an effective communication process;
- establishing the reporting process.

The relational marketing manager is now confident that the strategy is capable of being implemented, that the resources and budgets are in place, that personnel are aware of their roles and responsibilities, and that communication and reporting procedures are in place. He or she is now ready to implement the action plans developed earlier in the planning process.

Promoting customer response

The next step for the relational marketer is to initiate the activities intended to promote the customer response. These activities should be detailed in the action plans developed earlier in the planning process. Essentially, these should state *what* needs to be done in order to implement the chosen strategies. Such plans will include a schedule of activities indicating *when* tasks need to be initiated or completed. Because action plans translate strategies into structured frameworks, each action plan for each organisation will indicate different tasks and different dates. As such, there is no such thing as a generic action plan. However, action plans are likely to detail the following activities:

- creative activities (see Chapter 12);
- production (see below);
- purchase or rent of mailing lists (see Chapters 2 and 4);
- generation of customer target list (see Chapters 2, 3 and 9);
- purchase of media space (see Chapters 5 and 10);
- placing of advertising, conducting mailing, beginning teleservicing (see Chapters 5, 9, 10, 11).

We only explore aspects of the production process here because earlier chapters have covered the other activities, as indicated. Exhibit 14.9 summarises the flow of the production process for a direct mailing (Roberts and Berger 1989).

Graphics (artwork and photography) and copy (the words and phrases to be used) will be identified as part of the creative message process (see Chapter 12). These must now be subject to layout where the position and size of each element are determined exactly. This will then be ready for what used to be referred to as typesetting; although the term is still used, the old method of moving metal characters to the correct position in a template has been replaced by desktop publishing and other specialised software. Several detailed issues will be resolved here as well, such as preparation for colour printing; four-colour printing produces every colour, shade and tone because that is what the combination of red, blue, yellow and black can produce. Because each colour needs to be applied as a separate overlay, it might be acceptable to compromise over the number of colours used, as long as precise colour, tone and shade are not critical.

The gap between the creative and production teams is certainly narrowing as the importance of working together on these issues becomes critical (Darby 1997).

EXHIBIT 14.9 The production flow

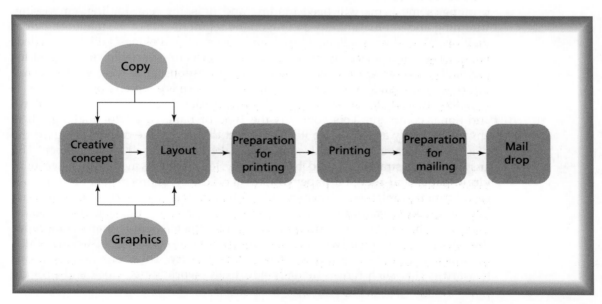

Clients are asking for ever more unusual mailings, as discussed in the context of developing 'novelty' creative treatment (see case studies in Chapters 10 and 12). This can be manifested in odd shapes, sizes and materials and although the creative team might come up with such ideas, it is the production staff who identify whether it can be achieved. Indeed, they will increasingly suggest methods based on their knowledge of ever-changing printing and production technology. In this synergistic sense, it is useful for them to work hand in hand. Improvements in digital printing technology mean that it is now possible for campaigns to be personalised (Reed 1998). Although improvements in database technology have promised the possibility of one-to-one marketing, print and production techniques have traditionally lagged behind. However, with the advent of digital printing one-to-one marketing is now firmly on the agenda and many loyalty schemes will now be mailing several million different personalised offer letters that would not have been feasible in the past. 'In traditional litho-printing, you have to typeset your page, scan it, impose it, expose the plates, make your plates, make the process ready, run "up to colour" (probably wasting a couple of hundred sheets) and then print. How much easier to have a digital file which is sent to print in much the same way as we send our day-to-day work to desktop printers' (Bloom 1997). Digital printing makes it possible to individualise every single print, thereby making its application in relational marketing extremely powerful. It is even possible to produce an individualised catalogue mailing for a responder to a DRTV advertisement within 24 hours. Digital printing therefore brings with it personalised and just-in-time mailings. Having said this, early experience of digital printing suggests that it can be expensive and of lower quality than litho-printing. However, as with most new technologies, it is likely that both these factors will improve as their use increases.

The next stage is for sample printings to be checked and then sent to print but we do not delve into the intricacies of the printing processes in this book. After printing, some items will need binding and finishing (e.g. folding, embossing, trimming and laminating, depending on the requirements of the mailing). Before mailing, also, items will be folded and inserted, envelopes will be labelled, personalised and sorted by postcode or other targeting variable and bagged for the mail deliverer. Once mailed, we await the response, but we must be geared up to receive it and to respond appropriately; these are matters of fulfilment.

Before turning to the issue of fulfilment in detail, a specific issue is worth additional comment. This concerns the type of paper used for mailings. It is environmentally as well as politically correct to do what we can to safeguard the planet's physical environment, so does it make sense to use recycled paper? The answer is not straightforward because recycled paper is more expensive than virgin paper and recycled paper can be significantly poorer in quality unless it goes through a relatively expensive bleaching process. Sometimes this can be an advantage: some charity mailings might even be more appropriate if printed on paper which is not so overtly opulent. Another factor here is that virgin paper does not come from hardwood forests but from faster-growing softwoods which are often managed especially for the paper industry. Thus, one argument put forward is that such forests actually add to the world's tree stock and provide useful habitats that otherwise would not exist.

In the late 1990s the direct marketing industry appeared to turn away from recycled paper, perhaps because the 'green' lobby is less vociferous over direct mail's threat to the environment then it was in the late 1980s and early 1990s (Teather 1996). Another view is that recycling means fewer managed forests dedicated to paper production and because these contribute significantly to *increasing* the number of trees, many are happy to use virgin paper from what can be argued is a *more* environmentally friendly source. 'The pulp and paper industry is one of the major planters of new forest. If we keep recycling more and more material there will be less intensive forest management' (White 1996). Another criticism of recycling comes from the head of print production at Rapier Stead and Bowden, Bonnie White, who says: 'a lot of recycled paper is of no use to the environment. The chemicals they use to de-ink are like caustic soda. That's more damaging than chopping down trees from managed forests' (White 1996) At any rate, recycled paper is not 100% recycled, but contains at least 75% recycled pulp, so even recycling requires a substantial input from virgin paper. The future is likely to see advances in how recycled paper is produced, resulting in quality improvements and cost reductions (Teather 1996).

A fairly typical number of different items to be included in a single mailing is half a dozen, but some mail packs can include more than 30. Any hiccup in the process which means that the odd item isn't ready at the time of mailing would disrupt the entire project. Each item also might need to be tracked, so codes need to be clear for the response handler. Additionally, the number of items obviously affects weight and therefore mailing costs. If costs turn out to be higher than estimated, the entire project can be dramatically affected: a ½p per mail pack can lead to an additional cost of £2,500 for a mailing of 500 000, which would be a relatively small campaign.

Fulfilment

Fulfilment is mainly concerned with receiving orders or enquiries via the mail, telephone, Internet or interactive TV. But handling complaints is also part of this aspect of customer service and carelines are becoming more prevalent and relevant (Hemsley 1997). Furthermore, as we discussed in Chapter 2 on sources of data, fulfilment offers an opportunity to capture data on potential customers. Fulfilment is a process in its own right. Systems must be set up to deal with receipt of customer mail/calls, then to capture their details, produce personalised response output, enclose and mail information or products (which in turn involves order picking, packing and dispatch), analyse the statistics on enquiry nature, level, and timing profiles, bank monies for orders and update stock control systems. Exhibit 14.10 summarises some of the stages and components of this system (Roberts and Berger 1989).

Fulfilment involves all of the activities required to fulfil a customer order after it has been received (Roberts and Berger 1989). It includes:

- handling responses;
- data capture;
- order processing;
- order shipment.

EXHIBIT 14.10 The fulfilment process

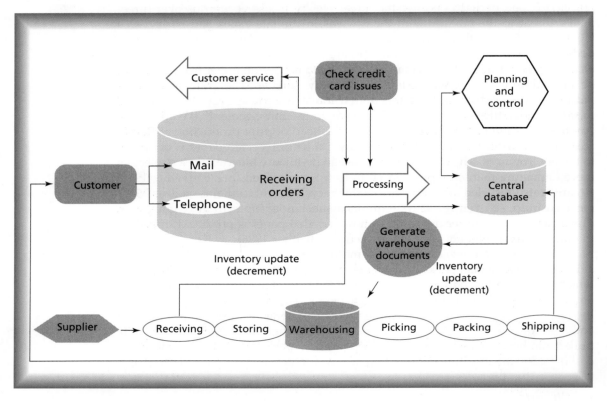

Handling responses

For many customers, their first contact with the organisation occurs when they respond to a mailing, a telephone call or a direct response advertisement. Because the organisation will not get a second chance to make a first impression, customer responses must be handled professionally. Additionally, there are a number of opportunities to collect data which will be invaluable in evaluating direct marketing, enhancing the customer database, and identifying opportunities for future strategies. Response handling includes:

- managing initial contact (via mail or telephone);
- collecting and recording relevant data (source of enquiry, order, method of payment, and additional profile information if required);
- responding to queries (customer service is not something that happens *after* the order is placed, but is something that should occur throughout the process).

Response services also need to be determined. There are a variety of alternative approaches, including the Business reply envelope or card and the Freepost system, both of which provide the responder with the means to reply free of postage charges. The PO Box system provides the marketer with a confidential delivery address but the responder has to pay for the postage.

Data capture

Data capture for use in the next stage, outbound contact, is a crucial component of the fulfilment process. Dedicated software (for example the Post Office Address tables) can check addresses for accuracy and this is important if we are to target individuals accurately. Otherwise we might be accused, justifiably, of sending 'junk mail'. The information provided by customers must be recorded in such a way that it is available for order processing, enhances the customer database, and can be used to monitor and evaluate strategy implementation. Most organisations have developed appropriate procedures and forms designed to capture and record this data on the database. Because the relational marketer has the capacity to communicate with individual customers in an individual way, capturing and recording the data become particularly important. For example, the database can be used to:

- make differentiated offers to prospects who respond to the advertising campaign;
- provide information for planning telemarketing or sales follow-up;
- target mailings precisely;
- provide telesales staff with customer information so that they can handle customer calls more effectively and productively;
- ensure that the salesforce has access to comprehensive customer information (Linton 1995).

Order processing/order shipment

In order to respond to the customer request, the order must be processed. Where this involves the sale of merchandise, two forms are generally raised: one goes to the warehouse to initiate fulfilment, and one to finance to request payment. When the warehouse receives the orders it will sort, pick, pack and ship the required merchandise to customers. Many organisations will guarantee shipment within a 30-day period, and thus processing and shipment must be able to respond quickly.

As we have seen, especially in Chapter 11 concerning online relationship marketing, a major barrier for many successful operations is poor delivery.

Customer service

Customer service must permeate the entire fulfilment process. In the initial stages personnel must be capable of dealing with customer queries and establishing customer expectations. Where guarantees are made, these must be adhered to. Where a goods return policy exists, this must be available to all customers. Where problems occur, sorting these out must become an organisational priority. Above all, the organisation must be able to respond to customers quickly and professionally whatever the problem may be.

Complaint handling is integral to this and it has also been found that customers who experience some level of dissatisfaction or concern and complain about this are more likely to be retained as customers than those who do not complain (Jones 1996). Dr O'Pattervans, in the case below, might have been more likely to use the rail service again if he had complained and had a satisfactory response. It might even be suggested (only slightly facetiously) that it might pay marketers to create situations over which customers would complain! Related to this, it has been found that those customers who are 'very satisfied' are up to six times more likely to be retained than those who are just 'satisfied' (Jones 1996), so the importance of 'delivering' the relational marketing service is very important.

Fulfilment is therefore not the end of the relational process; rather, it is a potential beginning. As more attention is paid to the quality of service as well as to products, it is important for the relational marketer to ensure that responses to DRTV, mailings, and telephone contacts are appropriate for the customer. In the past, there were two industries, one catering for the handling of responses from sales promotions such as coupons and competitions and the other for relational marketing. These are now becoming increasingly integrated.

Consider the following case study, which demonstrates the potential for relationship dissolution.

CASE STUDY 14.2

Dr O'Pattervans

A railway company offers direct booking of tickets and seat reservations via the telephone in addition to telephone-based timetable enquiries.

Dr O'Pattervans is invited to a meeting in London in two days' time and contacts the telephone enquiry line. He is informed of train times and ticket prices and is told that if he books before 2pm on the day before departure the ticket will be less than half the full fare. However, this will be conditional on seat availability because these particular tickets are allocated according to quotas. He is also given the number for the ticket booking service, which he then calls. Unfortunately, he is not successful in getting through; the line is either engaged or a recorded message tells him that 'all operators are busy, please try again later' and at that point the line is cut. Even when the line is engaged the 'ring back' facility is not available on that number. He tries again and

again, over a four-hour period, but to no avail. The alternative method of buying the ticket is not open to him because he cannot leave his desk that day to drive ten miles to the nearest booking office.

Dr O'Pattervans needs to know if there are seats available at the cheaper fare but can't phone his nearest station because the entire rail enquiry service has been routed through one telephone number. He tries this again but is told that they are not able to divert calls to individual booking offices and neither can they check availability of seats. A 'Catch 22'!

The following day, with only an hour to the 2pm deadline, he has still had no success getting through to the direct booking number so he decides to leave his work (despite the fact that things are extremely busy) and drive to the nearest booking office. On arrival he is informed that the cheaper fare is not applicable on the train he has to take to be on time for the London meeting. This contradicts the information the timetable enquiry service provided. Dr O'Pattervans ends up paying the full fare which he could have done on the day of travel. Indeed if he had, it would have saved several wasted hours trying to get through to the booking number and a round trip of another hour to buy the ticket in person. To complain would involve collecting and completing a complaints form, which would take more time and, on the basis of one previous experience of complaining (over a delayed train which meant he missed a job interview), he decided it wasn't worth it because all he had received that time was a brief letter of apology and a voucher for £2.

This tale of woe demonstrates that any direct service must be capable of delivering accurately, effectively and efficiently. In this instance, the customer would probably have been better off and certainly less stressed and annoyed if the direct service didn't even exist.

Other fulfilment issues are concerned with planning for levels and timing of response. For example:

- Once a DRTV advertisement is broadcast, how many calls might we expect within half an hour of the broadcast? In reality the burst of inbound calls is almost instant and, if anyone cannot get through, we might have lost them and their business forever.
- How long should we plan the time lag to be for responses to a poster campaign?
- What level of mailing response might we expect and has there been liaison with the Royal Mail about this?
- How many catalogues should we print?
- What stock holdings should be considered for product orders? Remember the fiasco when Hoover could not meet demand for their sales promotion offer of free flights to America with the purchase of a vacuum cleaner! (Peattie and Peattie 2003).

There are other points that need to be addressed, such as the coupon itself; has it been designed to allow enough space for a consumer to complete their full address and other details? – many are not! Also, the media code needs to be included in order to track the response effectiveness of different media used. Order forms need to be designed to help both the customer and the fulfilment house. Product codes need to be easy to include and record. Payment terms (e.g. credit facilities) need to be in line with the Consumer Credit Act, 1974 and there should be appropriate provision for credit and debit card 'numbers' (16 'boxes' are needed). If insurance for order delivery is relevant, provision must be suitable and pre-planned. Forms should also be designed to facilitate data capture, and data to be captured must be pre-determined and planned for. The type of analysis to be conducted on outcomes should also be planned for in advance, such as the production of response levels by media, cost per enquiry/order, geographic and geodemographic profiles of order/enquirers, stock control, financial reporting such as banking and credit card reports.

As with our discussion of database and knowledge management, there is a similar issue here, with respect to outsourcing a fulfilment specialist or keeping the operation in-house. Conducting the fulfilment operation in-house can be disruptive because usually there are peaks and troughs of fulfilment activity and if managed internally there might be few economies of scale. If, on the other hand, response handling is required on a more even and regular basis, an in-house operation might be less disruptive. Also, if the business operates almost exclusively on a 'direct' basis, such as Reader's Digest, then gearing entire internal business systems around direct contact – inward and outward – makes more sense.

It is more likely, then, that the outsourcing of fulfilment is more appropriate for many organisations. Fulfilment and response-handling houses work for others, so there are some economies of scale and concentration of expertise and equipment. This expertise and equipment can be significant and as technology changes the specialists are more likely to be at the cutting edge than would be the case with smaller internal operations. Also, there are often links between response handling and mailing operations. Response frequently involves some form of mailing, so again, those specialists who have the capacity for rapidly responding to clients' requirements for irregularly timed response activity are often worth using. They will also be more likely to have access to state-of-the-art printing and production equipment than the smaller internal operation is likely to be able to afford. The previous section on production gives some indication of what we mean by specialised equipment; folding machines, enclosing machines, printers, labellers, wrapping and strapping machines, weighing and counting machines, for mailing operations, and for telephone-based contact there can be fully automated digitised systems running to 2 000 lines or more! In addition, the points mentioned on order picking and packing, stock control, banking of monies and data capture are all worth considering for outsourcing.

Overall, the execution process is both sequential and cyclical. It is sequential in that response-generating activities precede customer contact, and the processes of data capture, order processing, shipment etc. must follow in a linear fashion. However, the execution process is also cyclical. This is because relational marketers can design activities so that customer response can be managed effectively. For example, mailings can be staggered to ensure that the organisation is not overwhelmed with responses in a particular time period. As a result, methods of generating customer response may be undertaken periodically throughout the campaign, and each time a response is initiated a sequential fulfilment process occurs. The timing of response-generating activities should be identified in the action plan prior to implementation. However, it is not always possible or even desirable to implement action plans exactly as laid out in the plan. For example, responses may be far higher or lower than expected, media or production costs may be subject to change, or the strategies themselves may need to be adapted. As Day (1984) points out, 'strategies are constructed in ambiguous environments in which many significant events cannot be forecast and planned for in their entirety. Some events will not even be contemplated when the strategy is chosen.' There is therefore a need to review if the chosen strategies are still feasible, if specific targets are being met, if the campaign is within budget, and if objectives are likely to be achieved. This suggests that execution needs to be continually monitored, in order to provide the necessary management information. Where problems or opportunities arise, management are then in a position to respond, and to maintain control of the process. Monitoring and control activities must therefore take place throughout the execution process. These activities are discussed below.

Monitoring and control

❝ In a world where it is increasingly difficult to control anything, direct marketing makes a considerable appeal because when properly conducted it is very controllable compared to less disciplined marketing activities. ❞
(Day 1984)

Monitoring and control of a relational marketing programme is particularly important because it allows managers to identify the effectiveness and efficiency of the resources deployed. It compares performance levels to the objectives and strategies that have been set out and questions whether key assumptions still hold true. Furthermore, it provides a learning forum which can then be used to formulate more effective strategies in the future. Essentially, if actual performance is below expectations, the role of monitoring and control systems is to determine whether under-performance is a result of poor execution, unrealistic budgets or unexpected events. Success can be measured in a number of ways, which include identifying the response rate to a campaign, tracking the number of resulting leads or sales on the database and tracking changes in purchasing patterns resulting from the campaign.

Monitoring is an ongoing process, which aims to provide management with information about the campaign. Monitoring occurs throughout the campaign, flags up unexpected results and is necessary to assist with the control of the execution process. Measurements taken during and after the campaign allow management to evaluate the whole campaign, and to feed this information into the next planning cycle. Monitoring involves:

- reviewing results on a regular basis (as laid out in the evaluation criteria);
- comparing actual with planned results;
- comparing actual spend with planned budgets;
- communicating with key personnel (orally or by report).

The database can assist in the monitoring process by:

- tracking responses generated, sales enquiries, sales;
- recording speed of fulfilment;
- tracking responses in different sectors;
- comparing conversion to response statistics;

- assessing which media were most effective in reaching the target audience;
- comparing response levels in different media;
- recording customer data capture through the campaign.

Thus, relational marketing managers need continually to monitor execution in order to ensure that all is going according to plan. However, the real world is far more dynamic than planners can accommodate, and thus it is most likely that changes will have to be made to ensure that campaign objectives can ultimately be met. Regular reports will assist in identifying whether targets are being met. The use of 'exceptional' reporting procedures (where extraordinary results are flagged up as a matter of course) provides particularly timely information. Where targets are not being met, management can make the required adjustments. Adjustments can vary from relatively minor issues like adapting action plans (increasing frequency of advertising, size of mailing, number of recalls etc.), to quite serious changes involving strategies. In deciding what changes are to be made, management will find that information from the database will be invaluable.

When the campaign is complete, it is usual to write a final report. This should include:

- statement of expectations (targets, objectives);
- statement of anticipated expenditure (budget allocations);
- statement of actual performance (response, conversion rates, sales, profitability, share);
- evaluation of actual versus expected performance;
- evaluation of actual versus expected expenditure;
- managerial justification (if there is a variation between actual and expected);
- recommendations.

The relational marketing manager should continually learn from his or her experiences. Thus, this report should be used as an input into the next planning cycle, and the whole process begins again.

Summary

- This chapter has provided a review of the relational planning process and this has been shown to be iterative. The process builds upon our previous coverage through this book and serves as an integrating framework for much of that earlier material.
- Our website is home to a great deal of additional material, including a fully worked relational marketing plan. The sequence of that plan is summarised below (Exhibit 14.11); the context was that of a loyalty programme for BMW.

EXHIBIT 14.11 BMW loyalty programme summary of components and report mission statement

Market definition
Situation analysis
Environmental analysis
Internal analysis
Market analysis
Customer analysis
SWOT
Identification and selection of target market
Key assumptions
Direct marketing objectives
Strategy
Action plan
BMW card positioning & benefits
BMW card technology
Direct marketing communications strategy
Database structure
Budget
Monitoring and control

Appendices
Appendix 1   Situation analysis
Appendix 2   BMW bank status
Appendix 3   Lifetime value calculations
Appendix 4   The BMW card range
Appendix 5   Loyalty card summary
Appendix 6   Credit card interest rate summary
Appendix 7   Smart card applications
Appendix 8   BMW card sample statement
Appendix 9   Database strategic applications
Appendix 10   Building loyalty & the BMW card
Appendix 11   A day in the life of a BMW card holder
Appendix 12   BMW customer profile data

- We would like to return you to our 'triangle' in the Preface and conclude the book by restating that data and research lead to the proposition that organisations can understand their customers to such an extent that relational interaction can not only be initiated but also maintained in mutually beneficial ways.

- At the same time, we now have a range of relational media that facilitate interaction and so marketers are increasingly turning to the relational paradigm. This paradigm also has its origins in services marketing, B2B, direct distribution, direct marketing, and in the way the marketing concept has itself evolved.

- But any resulting relational interaction can be undermined if its implementation is more rhetoric than reality. Indeed, the rather tarnished concept of CRM needs to be extended to include strategic sharing and use of knowledge across functions and partners in order to convert data into insight. We go a little further in these last few words of the book and suggest that the more usual interpretation of CRM (software-driven data mining) might do well to be renamed as customer data management (CDM) to screen out what can be rather mythical relational elements.

- Throughout the book we have drawn attention to potential areas of concern such as data protection and invasion of privacy. These are more important than ever before. Vance Packard was concerned about the manipulative effects of mass media advertising in 1957 but his concerns over mass media are, perhaps, minor compared with the nature of very personal data to which relational marketers have access.

- There is a potential mutual benefit from relational interaction but the balance of power needs to be even and there needs to be trust, commitment, cooperation and respect between all of the parties concerned.

Review questions

1 Identify the major components of a direct relational marketing plan and explain how they are interrelated.

2 In what way does a clear business mission aid direct relational planning?

3 Outline the process of environmental scanning. For what purpose is environmental scanning utilised?

4 What trends in the macroenvironment are likely to have the greatest impact on direct relational marketers?

5 Why is the existing customer base currently viewed as one of the organisation's most critical assets?

6 What are the characteristics of good objectives?

7 On what bases can we evaluate a strategy's applicability?

8 'The best plan is only a plan, that is, good intentions, unless it degenerates into work' (Drucker 1974). Discuss with reference to the process of plan execution.

Further reading

Bruhn, M. (2003) *Relationship Marketing: Management of Customer Relationships*, Harlow: FT Prentice Hall.

Day, G.S. (1984) *Strategic Marketing Planning: The Pursuit of Competitive Advantage*, St. Paul, MN: West Publishing Company.

Donaldson, B. and O'Toole, T. (2002) *Strategic Market Relationships: From Strategy to Implementation*, Chichester: John Wiley.

Egan, J. (2001) *Relationship Marketing: Exploring Relational Strategies in Marketing*, Harlow: Financial Times/Prentice Hall.

Gummesson, E. (1999) *Total Relationship Marketing*, Oxford: Butterworth Heinemann.

Little, E. and Marandi, E. (2003) *Relationship Marketing Management*, London: Thomson Learning.

Piercy, N. (1997) *Market-Led Strategic Change: Transforming the Process of Going To Market*, Oxford: Butterworth-Heinemann.

Stone, B. (1995) *Direct Marketing Success Stories and the Strategies that Built the Businesses*, Lincolnwood, IL: NTC Business Books.

References

Achrol, R.S. and Kotler, P. (1999) 'Marketing in the Network Economy', *Journal of Marketing*, 63, pp. 143–63.

Aguilar, F.J. (1967) *Scanning the Business Environment*, New York: Macmillan.

American Marketing Association (1960) Committee on Definitions, Chicago.

Anonymous (1997) 'Developing a New Bedside Technique', *Business World*, 22 May, p. 49.

BBC (2003) *Analysis*, Radio 4, April.

Berry, L.L. (1981) 'The Employee as Customer', *Journal of Retail Banking*, 3(March), pp. 33–40.

Bird, D. (1993) *Commonsense Direct Marketing*, 3rd edn, London: Kogan Page, p. 138.

Bloom, J. (1997) 'Digital Revolution?', *Marketing Direct*, June, pp. 46–8.

Brannon, T. (1993) 'The Profitable Power of the Response', *Marketing Business*, December–January, pp. 41–2.

Brownlie, D. (1987) 'Environmental Analysis', in M.J. Baker (ed.) *The Marketing Book*, London: Heinemann, p. 102.

Christopher, M. and McDonald, M.H.B. (1995) *Marketing: An Introductory Text*, London: Macmillan, p. 303.

Darby, I. (1997) 'Printing Gets All Creative', *Marketing Direct*, January, pp. 52–6.

Day, G.S. (1984) *Strategic Marketing Planning: The Pursuit of Competitive Advantage*, St. Paul, MN: West Publishing Company, p. 169.

Day, G.S. (1986) 'Tough Questions for Developing Strategies', *Journal of Business Strategy*, Winter, pp. 60–8.

Day, G.S. (1994) 'The Capabilities of Market-Driven Organizations', *Journal of Marketing*, 58 (October), pp. 37–52.

Deshpande, R. (1999) 'Foreseeing Marketing', *Journal of Marketing*, 63, pp. 164–7.

Drucker, P. (1974) *Management: Tasks, Responsibilities, Practices*, New York: Harper & Row.

Evans, M. (1988) 'Marketing Intelligence: Scanning the Marketing Environment', *Marketing Intelligence and Planning*, 6, pp. 21–9.

Evans, P. (2000) 'Strategy and the New Economics of Information', in D.A. Marchand, T.H. Davenport and T. Dickson (eds), *Mastering Information Management*, Harlow: FT/Prentice Hall.

Ghemawat, P. (1986) 'Sustainable Advantage', *Harvard Business Review*, September/October, pp. 53–8.

Hemsley, S. (1997) 'In the Line of Fire', *Marketing Week*, August, pp. 39–42.

Hofer, C.W. and Schendel, D. (1978) *Strategy Formulation: Analytical Concepts*, St. Paul, MN: West Publishing Company, p. 13.

Holder, D. (1993) 'Planning a Direct Marketing Strategy', *Direct Response*, May, pp. 24–6.

Jain, S.C. (1981) *Marketing Planning and Strategy*, Cincinnati, OH: South Western Publishing.

Jain, S.C. (1990) *Marketing Planning and Strategy*, 3rd edn, Cincinnati, OH: South-Western Publishing Co.

Johnson, G. and Scholes, K. (1984) *Exploring Corporate Strategy*, Englewood Cliffs, NJ: Prentice Hall.

Jones, T.O. (1996) 'Why Loyal Customers Defect', *KeyNote Presentation*, IDM Symposium, 6 June, London.

Jüttner, U. and Wehrli, H.P. (1994) 'Competitive Advantage: Merging Marketing and the Competence-based Perspective', *Journal of Business and Industrial Marketing*, 9(4), pp. 42–53.

Kruegar, J. (1996) 'Developing a Marketing Budget' *Target Marketing*, 19(10), pp. 118–22.

Linton, I. (1995) *Database Marketing: Know What Your Customer Wants*, London: Pitman.

Littler, D. and Leverick, F. (1994) 'Marketing Planning in New Technology Sectors', in J. Saunders (ed.), *The Marketing Initiative: Economic and Social Research Council Studies into British Marketing*, London: Prentice Hall, pp. 72–91.

McCorkell, G. (1997) *Direct and Database Marketing*, London: Kogan Page, p. 147.

McDonald, M.H.B. (1992) *Strategic Marketing Planning*, London, Kogan Page, p. 78.

McElhatton, N. (2001) 'Premier League', *Marketing Direct*, September, pp. 35–7.

Moutinho, L., Davies, F. and Hutcheson, G. (2002) 'Exploring Key Neo-Marketing Directions through the use of and Academic "Think Tank": A Methodological Framework', *European Journal of Marketing*, 36(4), pp. 417–32.

Nash, E.L. (1986) *Direct Marketing: Strategy, Planning, Execution*, 2nd edn, New York: McGraw Hill, p. 52.

Packard, V. (1957) *The Hidden Persuaders*, London: Longman.

Peattie, K. and Peattie, S. (2003) 'Sales Promotion', in M. Baker (ed.) *The Marketing Book*, Oxford: Butterworth Heinemann.

Piercy, N. (1990) 'Making Marketing Strategies Happen in the Real World', *Marketing Business*, February, pp. 20–1.

Piercy, N. (1997) *Market-Led Strategic Change: Transforming the Process of Going To Market*, Oxford: Butterworth-Heinemann.

Piercy, N. and Evans, M. (1999) 'Developing Marketing Information Capabilities', in M. Baker (ed.) *The Marketing Book*, London: Butterworth Heinemann.

Piercy, N. and Morgan, N. (1993) 'Internal Marketing – The Missing Half of the Marketing Programme', *Long-Range Planning*, 24(2), pp. 82–93.

Reed, D. (1998) 'Pointing the Finger at the Future of Printing', *Precision Marketing*, 9 November, pp. 23–6.

Roberts, M.L. and Berger, P.D. (1989) *Direct Marketing Management*, Englewood Cliffs, NJ: Prentice Hall, p. 52.

Schultz, D., Tannenaum, S.I. and Lauterborn, R.F. (1993) *The New Marketing Paradigm*, Lincolnwood, IL: NTC Books.

Stone, M., Davies, D. and Bond, A. (1995) *Direct Hit: Direct Marketing with a Winning Edge*, London: Pitman Publishing.

Teather, D. (1996) 'Recycled Paper: A Cause that's Gone to Waste?', *Marketing Direct*, October, pp. 47–53.

Unger, L. (1981) Consumer Marketing Trends in the 1980s When Growth Slows', *European Research*, April.

White, B. as reported in Teather, D. (1996) 'Recycled Paper: A Cause that's Gone to Waste?', *Marketing Direct*, October, pp. 47–53.

Yee, D.K. (1990) 'Pass or Fail? How to Grade Strategic Progress', *Journal of Business Strategy*, May/June, pp. 10–14.

Index

Painting
Watercolour Flowers
from Photographs

ROBIN BERRY

Search Press

A QUARTO BOOK

Published in 2010 by Search Press Ltd
Wellwood
North Farm Road
Tunbridge Wells
Kent TN2 3DR

ISBN: 978-1-84448-612-0

QUAR.MPWF

Conceived, designed, and produced by
Quarto Publishing plc
The Old Brewery
6 Blundell Street
London N7 9BH

Senior Editor **Katie Crous**
Designer **Louise Clements**
Design Assistant **Saffron Stocker**
Copy Editors **Diana Chambers and Liz Dalby**
Author's Photographer **Vicki Madsen**
Photographer **Phil Wilkins**
Proofreader **Claire Waite Brown**
Indexer **Ann Barrett**
Art Director **Caroline Guest**
Creative Director **Moira Clinch**
Publisher **Paul Carslake**

Colour separation by Modern Age
Printed in China by Toppan Leefung Printing Ltd

10 9 8 7 6 5 4 3 2 1

A3 306 724 X

Contents

Before You Begin

The core of this book is a series of 55 stunning photographs of flowers – a virtual library of flower photography. Each photograph occupies a whole page and is accompanied by a step-by-step demonstration of a watercolour treatment on the opposite page. Copy the watercolour demonstration or use it for reference, interpreting the subject in your own way.

How to Use This Book

Before rushing for your paints and brushes, take a look at the first section of this book to read about supplies, skills and techniques that will give flight to your imagination. If you are a beginner, this introductory information is indispensable; if you are an experienced painter, you will find new and exciting ways to enhance your approach to flower painting and reference materials that will help you throughout your painting experience.

THE FLOWERS

The flower photographs and their associated step-by-step paintings are divided into portrait and landscape formats. The portrait-format subjects are featured on pages 36–107 and include five steps to guide you through the painting; landscape-format subjects are featured on pages 108–145 and include six steps. Within these two formats, the flowers are loosely grouped into three categories: Single Specimens, Floral Still Life and Flowers Outdoors. Each open page, or spread, is one complete project.

ARTIST'S INTERPRETATION

All the demonstrations in this book have been specially commissioned from a team of professional watercolour artists, each of whom has an individual style and way of working. If you find you respond strongly to one artist's interpretation of a subject, you might want to try a mix-and-match approach, choosing a photograph that appeals to you and painting it first in the style of the associated artist and then in another. Trying out different methods is an important step toward finding your own style.

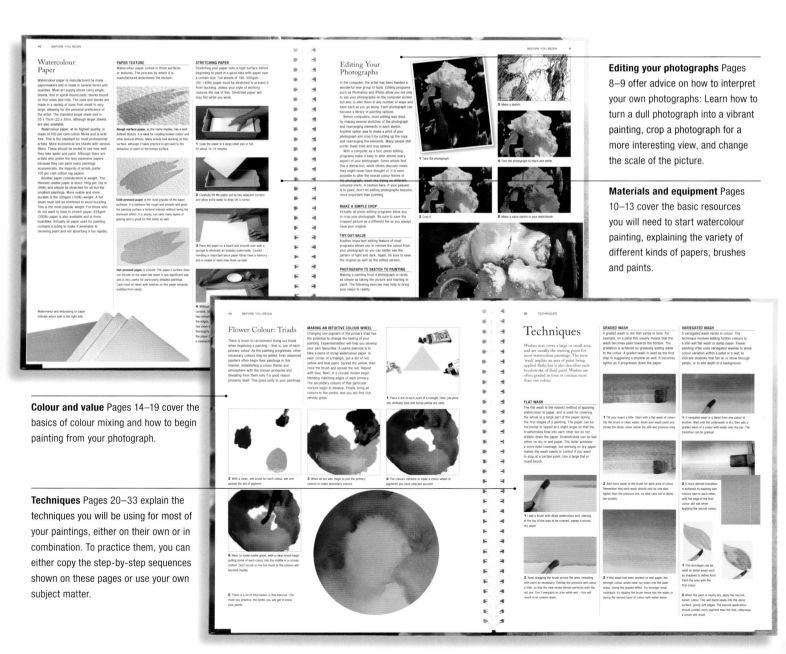

Editing your photographs Pages 8–9 offer advice on how to interpret your own photographs: Learn how to turn a dull photograph into a vibrant painting, crop a photograph for a more interesting view, and change the scale of the picture.

Materials and equipment Pages 10–13 cover the basic resources you will need to start watercolour painting, explaining the variety of different kinds of papers, brushes and paints.

Colour and value Pages 14–19 cover the basics of colour mixing and how to begin painting from your photograph.

Techniques Pages 20–33 explain the techniques you will be using for most of your paintings, either on their own or in combination. To practice them, you can either copy the step-by-step sequences shown on these pages or use your own subject matter.

The Projects

Look through all the projects before you decide on your first choice. There is an array of compositions, colours and styles to consider. Each painting project includes a list of the paints, tools and materials, and techniques you will need.

Techniques used The methods used by the artist are listed and cross-referenced to the Techniques pages at the front of this book so that you can refresh your memory if needed.

Details These additional images allow you to 'look over the artists' shoulders' as they use specific techniques.

Paints Colours are listed in alphabetical order. Note that names can vary according to the manufacturer.

Tools and materials The paper, brushes and other equipment used by the artist are listed in order of use.

Final painting The finished painting is shown in the final step.

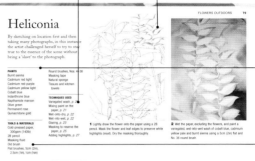

Heliconia

By sketching on location first and then taking many photographs, in this instance the artist challenged herself to try to stay true to the essence of the scene without being a 'slave' to the photograph.

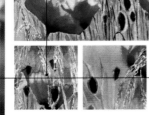

In Detail

Pages 146–157 feature selected projects on a larger scale and close up.

Poppies
Donna Jill Witty (see p. 140)

Crucial to the representation of light in watercolour is the protection of the white of the paper from washes. However, broad juicy washes are also fundamental to watercolour. To accomplish both of these in a single painting, Donna used two signature techniques – the precise masking of areas to remain white and an underpainting of saturated, wet washes.

Final painting Shown in a larger size, it is possible to see the full effect of the artist's work.

Details Certain techniques and elements of particular interest are shown close up.

Analysis The effect of specific techniques is explained.

Protea

The artist was concerned with capturing the detail of the numerous petals while keeping their overall shape and form. The background needed to be simplified to prevent a cluttered image.

The photograph The floral subject is shown in a large, high-quality image for you to use as a reference.

Step-by-step sequences Follow the steps to see how the artist builds up a painting from start to completion.

The 'Eye' of the Camera

With the coming of the digital age, almost everyone has the ability to take a picture – with a mobile phone, digital camera or more traditional equipment. And every artist who has done this has discovered that the resulting photograph, though it records the scene or the flower, rarely shows what was in the mind's eye. Therefore, try different views of the same thing or make a sketch with a few notes to go along with the shot.

In photographs, colour is not always true. It may be too blue, have a yellow cast or be washed out. Shadows are often opaque and detail is missing. You are the artist and can take away or add detail, lighten or darken, brighten or mute as you choose. The camera is another tool to help you bring your vision alive. It can help you to imagine or simply record what you see in the moment.

1 Choose your photograph (left).
2 Make a sketch (below). It will help you remember how you felt at the moment.

TRY DIFFERENT VIEWS

When approaching your subject, a quick way to begin focusing on a possible subject for painting is to turn your camera or even to turn yourself.

MAKE A SKETCH

When you find something that excites you, take a few minutes to make a sketch and make notes so you don't forget what went through your mind when you shot the photograph.

YOUR PHOTOGRAPH IS ONLY A GUIDE

Most flower painters take hundreds of photographs. Some may be works of art all by themselves but, more likely, they are only meant as a guide to the flower's form or some other aspect the artist noticed at the time.

The backlit aspect of this rose captured the artist's imagination, but the photograph is underexposed.

Horizontal format.

Vertical format.

The final painting, though dramatically different from the photograph, retains the backlighting and shadows.

Editing Your Photographs

In the computer, the artist has been handed a wonderful new group of tools. Editing programs such as Photoshop and iPhoto allow you not only to see your photographs on the computer screen but also to alter them in any number of ways and save each as you go along. Each photograph can become a library of painting options.

Before computers, most editing was done by making several sketches of the photograph and rearranging elements in each sketch. Another option was to make a print of your photograph and crop it by cutting up the copy and rearranging the elements. Many people still prefer these tried and true options.

With a computer as a tool, photo editing programs make it easy to alter almost every aspect of your photograph. Some artists find this a distraction, while others discover views they might never have thought of. It is even possible to alter the overall colour theme of the photograph, much like trying on different coloured shirts. A caution here: If your passion is to paint, don't let editing photographs become more important than painting.

MAKE A SIMPLE CROP

Virtually all photo editing programs allow you to crop your photograph. Be sure to save the cropped picture as a different file so you always have your original.

TRY OUT VALUE

Another important editing feature of most programs allows you to remove the colour from your photograph so you can better see the pattern of light and dark. Again, be sure to save the original as well as the edited version.

PHOTOGRAPH TO SKETCH TO PAINTING

Making a painting from a photograph is rarely as simple as taking the picture and starting to paint. The following exercise may help to bring your vision to reality.

1 Take the photograph.

2 Crop it.

3 Make a sketch.

4 Turn the photograph to black and white.

5 Make a value sketch in your sketchbook.

6 Make your full painting – by now you will know your subject well.

Watercolour Paper

Watercolour paper is manufactured by many papermakers and is made in several forms and qualities. Most art supply stores carry single sheets, end or spiral-bound pads, blocks bound on four sides and rolls. The pads and blocks are made in a variety of sizes from small to very large, allowing for the personal preference of the artist. The standard single sheet size is 55 x 75cm (22 x 30in), although larger sheets are also available.

Watercolour paper, at its highest quality, is made of 100 per cent cotton fibres and is acid free. This is the standard for most professional artists. More economical are sheets with various fillers. These should be tested to see how well they take water and paint. Although there are artists who prefer the less expensive papers because they can paint many paintings economically, the majority of artists prefer 100 per cent cotton rag papers.

Another paper consideration is weight. The thinnest usable paper is about 190g per 1sq m (90lb) and should be stretched for all but the smallest paintings. More usable and more durable is the 300gsm (140lb) weight. A full sheet must still be stretched to avoid buckling. This is the most popular weight. For those who do not want to have to stretch paper, 638gsm (300lb) paper is also available and is more boardlike. Virtually all paper used for painting contains a sizing to make it amenable to receiving paint and not absorbing it too rapidly.

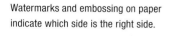

Watermarks and embossing on paper indicate which side is the right side.

PAPER TEXTURE

Watercolour paper comes in three surfaces or textures. The process by which it is manufactured determines the texture.

Rough surface paper, as the name implies, has a well-defined texture. It is ideal for creating broken-colour and other textural effects. Many artists love working on this surface, although it takes practice to get used to the behaviour of paint on the bumpy surface.

Cold-pressed paper is the most popular of the paper surfaces. It is between the rough and smooth and gives the painting surface a textural interest without being the dominant effect. It is sturdy, can take many layers of glazing and is great for fine detail as well.

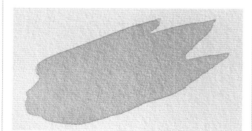

Hot-pressed paper is smooth. The paper's surface does not intrude on the wash laid down in any significant way and is very useful for particularly detailed paintings. Care must be taken with washes on this paper because puddles form easily.

STRETCHING PAPER

Stretching your paper onto a rigid surface before beginning to paint is a good idea with paper over a certain size. Full sheets of 190–300gsm (90–140lb) paper must be stretched to prevent it from buckling, unless your style of working reduces the risk of this. Stretched paper will stay flat while you work.

1 Soak the paper in a large clean pan or tub for about 10–15 minutes.

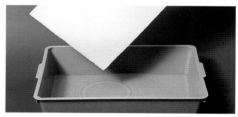

2 Carefully lift the paper out by two adjacent corners and allow extra water to drain off a corner.

3 Place the paper on a board and smooth over with a sponge to eliminate air bubbles underneath. Careful handling is important since paper fibres have a memory and a crease or bend may show up later.

4 Without overstretching, place a staple in two adjacent corners. Gently pull the unstapled end and staple the two remaining corners. Place wetted brown tape around the edges, overlapping the board and the paper. A few more staples will secure it well. Allow it to dry thoroughly. A border of white artist's tape that overlaps the paper by 1.25cm (½in) will surround your paper with a cleanable frame.

Brushes and Other Equipment

The world of brushes is a study in itself, and although this section is confined to the most common watercolour brushes, it is recommended that you spend time looking at various styles in an art shop or online. Brushes vary from the tiniest 000 sable brush to the giant 25cm (10in) wide hake brush, with hundreds in between.

The hairs of watercolour brushes range from sable to bristle to synthetic. The cost varies greatly and most shops stock a wide variety. Sable brushes are not essential, as there are excellent, less expensive alternatives.

The most common brushes for use with watercolour are round, sizes 6 to 24, and flat, sizes 1.25cm (½in) to 7.5cm (3in). (If you can afford only three, consider a No. 12 round with a good point, a 2.5cm (1in) flat and a rigger or liner – a longhair pointed brush for detail.)

Brushes (from left to right):
1 Rigger
2 Flat
3 Wash
4 & 5 Round
6 You will find an affordable tool in Chinese brushes. Far less expensive than most, they are very versatile, forming a fine point but with a full 'belly' to hold a great deal of paint.

ADDITIONAL EQUIPMENT

1 Kitchen towels Essential for cleaning up or dabbing the brush, or lifting clouds or highlights. Bathroom tissues work well, too, and you might want both.

2 Water containers Some artists keep one for the first rinse and a second with clean water.

3 Masking fluid For saving the white of the paper in watercolour. It is applied with a brush, but always use either a cheap or old brush, dipped in washing-up liquid and wiped off first. Always clean the brush immediately after use to prevent the masking fluid from drying in the bristles.

4 Masquepen A great asset to the flower artist, which enables you to 'paint' very accurately by reserving the fine veins or details on petals and leaves. Available in two nib widths of fine and super fine.

5 Masking tape or artist's white tape Most commonly used to tape down your paper or mask straight shapes. It may also be torn to form a jagged or rippled edge to save light on a flower.

6 Gummed brown paper tape For stretching paper.

7 Sponges Natural sponges are great for dabbing on foliage or lifting paint. Common kitchen sponges are useful to wipe off an overwet brush or an overly messy painting surface.

8 Drawing board, gator board or plywood For support or stretching your paper.

9 Pencils and erasers Use a B or HB pencil to draw on watercolour paper. A soft non-abrasive eraser, if used gently, will not harm the surface of the paper.

10 Palettes For tube paints there are many variations on a theme of the covered plastic palette, with wells for the paint and large mixing spaces. A cover is desirable to keep your paints clean and moist. That the palette is white is essential so you see your colours accurately.

You will find that, over time, your painting area will fill up with other useful equipment you have discovered. Such items as plastic plates, squirt bottles, scrapers, other media, towels and hair dryers are all useful.

Watercolour Choices

Some watercolour pigments are more expensive than others. Each pigment is derived from its own specific source, which may not have changed for centuries. For example, lamp black is made from soot. Its history can be traced back to cave paintings 35,000 years ago.

Watercolours are available in two qualities: student and artist grade. Student grade is less expensive but contains less pure pigment and more filler. It will not achieve the brilliance of colour that the pure artist pigments do.

Many companies manufacture watercolour. Most artists have favourites but often use more than one brand.

TUBES OR PANS?

Paint comes in dried blocks or pans and in tubes. The dried blocks fit into pans that close and are useful for travel. The tube paint is easier to use since it comes from the tube wet. Watercolour pigment is now available in sticks, crayons and pencils as well, all of which make paint when wet.

You will find varieties of watercolour that are pure and transparent; opaque, called gouache; mixed with a milk binder, called casein; and mixed with a plastic binder, called acrylic. All have the potential to spark your imagination and add brilliant colour to your flower paintings.

WHICH COLOURS?

Watercolour manufacturers produce such a large range of colours that the artist can always find a palette of colours to fit a particular style or subject. Below are suggestions for basic palettes and other colours you may like to add. The key is to have a balanced palette that will give you a good mixing range. The one pigment that most artists use is aureolin, a clear, cool transparent yellow. You would then choose a warmer yellow or gold, such as cadmium yellow, to give a good spectrum of yellows. A balanced palette also needs at least two reds, such as a warm cadmium red, and a cool alizarin crimson. Common blue pigments are cobalt blue and French ultramarine blue. Most colours can be mixed with these.

But flower painters, drawn to the endless variation in flower colours with their highlights and shadows, and preferring the relative purity of colour as it comes from the tube, will often have many more pigments with subtle changes in hue (colour). The important thing that these colours have in common is transparency, for unless one is drawn to a more opaque vision of flowers, it is the light – as it shines on and through the flower, as it penetrates upwards from the paper, as it brings the pigments to life – that gives watercolour flower painting its appeal.

Below you will find a typical flower painter's palette. With only a couple of exceptions, these are primary and secondary colours – a variety of yellows, reds and blues, as well as oranges, greens and violets.

As you work with a basic palette, you may find something missing and begin a search for new colours, adding an emerald green or a turquoise, a neutral tint (dark grey), or Payne's grey. The exploration of colour is half the fun for a flower painter. Useful tools in this search are art supplies catalogues, manufacturers' catalogues and books on colour.

A caution: Try adding only one or two pigments at a time. The temptation to add everything at once can be almost irresistible.

Cadmium red

Cadmium yellow

Alizarin crimson

Warm and cool primaries

Ultramarine

Lemon yellow

Winsor blue

Tube sizes vary from small finger-size tubes to more economical large tubes. As long as the tube is not left uncapped, the paint will stay moist for a long time.

How you organize your palette comes down to personal preference. One suggestion is to arrange the colours as the colour wheel, thereby limiting the effect of any one colour flowing over to the next.

Aureolin   Permanent lemon yellow   Cadmium yellow   Permanent orange   Quinacridone coral   Quinacridone red   Quinacridone magenta

Opera   Cobalt blue   French ultramarine blue   Cobalt turquoise light   Viridian   Phthalo green   Yellow-green

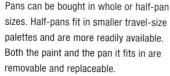

Pans can be bought in whole or half-pan sizes. Half-pans fit in smaller travel-size palettes and are more readily available. Both the paint and the pan it fits in are removable and replaceable.

You can buy boxes of pigments chosen by manufacturers that give a good starter palette and come with a built-in mixing area.

Understanding the Colour Wheel

The colour wheel will help you understand how to mix colours for your flower paintings. For example, it shows you how to achieve the brightest pinks and oranges or the best shadowy muted background colours. It is a good idea to paint swatches for your own wheel with your bought colours and add any subsequent purchases; in this way you can assess how warm or cool the colour is, and how it will mix with other colours.

A primary colour can't be mixed from any other colours. The three primaries are red, yellow and blue. You can see these, right, at the points of the solid triangle. When two primaries are mixed together, the result is a secondary colour – orange, green or violet (the grey dotted triangle). And when a secondary colour, such as orange, is mixed with a primary colour, such as red, the result is a tertiary colour – red-orange.

One of the things that makes colours so different from one another is 'temperature'. Some colours are perceived as 'warm' and others as 'cool', and red, yellow and blue have both warm and cool versions. When mixing secondary colours, it is important to choose the right primaries. For example, alizarin crimson and ultramarine blue are both warm and slightly purple in colour, so a mixture of these will make a bright purple, whereas a mix of cadmium red and Prussian or Winsor blue will result in a muddy brown – the result of cadmium red having an orange cast.

Cool colours – those with more blue or green – tend to recede, whilst warm colours – those with more red and yellow – come to the fore. Warm colours also appear larger and far more energetic. For this reason flower painters typically use cooler colours for the background of a painting – to produce a sense of depth – and warmer colours in the foreground.

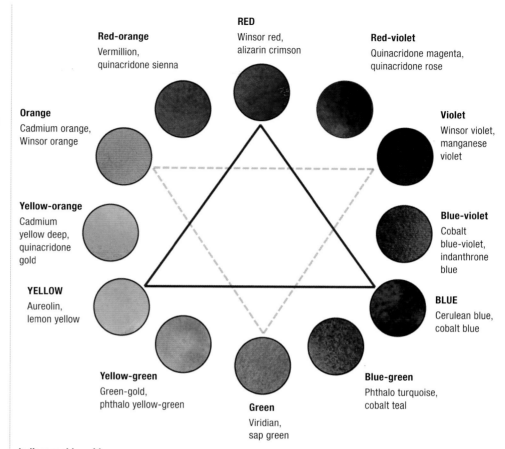

Red-orange
Vermillion, quinacridone sienna

RED
Winsor red, alizarin crimson

Red-violet
Quinacridone magenta, quinacridone rose

Orange
Cadmium orange, Winsor orange

Violet
Winsor violet, manganese violet

Yellow-orange
Cadmium yellow deep, quinacridone gold

Blue-violet
Cobalt blue-violet, indanthrone blue

YELLOW
Aureolin, lemon yellow

BLUE
Cerulean blue, cobalt blue

Yellow-green
Green-gold, phthalo yellow-green

Blue-green
Phthalo turquoise, cobalt teal

Green
Viridian, sap green

Indispensable guide
The colour wheel suggests possibilities for both experimentation and for individualizing your palette. Not only is it a guide to the colours you can mix to make another colour, it is a visual demonstration of analogous and complementary colours.

Mixing from one wheel
The same wheel as featured opposite is used here to show how to mix bright, intense secondaries with muted, subtle ones.

1 Cadmium red (yellow bias)
2 Alizarin crimson (blue bias)
3 Ultramarine blue (red bias)
4 Winsor blue (yellow bias)
5 Lemon yellow (blue bias)
6 Cadmium yellow (red bias)

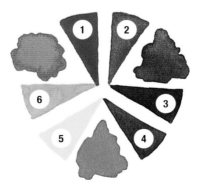

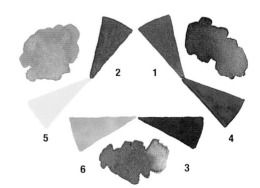

Intense secondaries
Here the colours closest together on the wheel have been mixed to produce intense secondaries. The blue-and-yellow mix, green, is cool, and the other two are warm.

Muted secondaries
The primary colours furthest apart create more muted mixtures, which could be useful for creating shadows.

Flower Colour: Triads

There is much to recommend trying out triads when beginning a painting – that is, one of each primary colour. As the painting progresses, other necessary colours may be added. Even advanced painters often begin their paintings in this manner, establishing a colour theme and atmosphere with the chosen primaries and deviating from them only if a good reason presents itself. This gives unity to your paintings.

MAKING AN INTUITIVE COLOUR WHEEL

Changing one pigment of the primary triad has the potential to change the feeling of your painting. Experimentation will help you develop your own favourites. A useful exercise is to take a piece of scrap watercolour paper. In each corner of a triangle, put a dot of red, yellow and blue paint. Spread the yellow, then rinse the brush and spread the red. Repeat with blue. Next, in a circular motion begin blending matching edges of each primary. The secondary colours of that particular mixture begin to develop. Finally, bring all colours to the centre, and you will find rich, velvety greys.

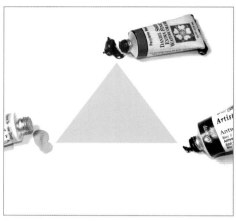

1 Place a dot at each point of a triangle. Here, perylene red, Antwerp blue and hansa yellow are used.

2 With a clean, wet brush for each colour, wet and spread the dot of pigment.

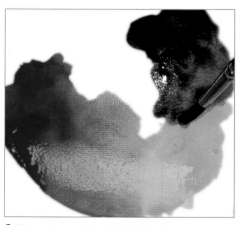

3 When all are wet, begin to join the primary colours to make secondary colours.

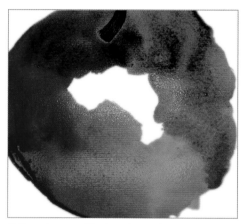

4 The colours combine to make a colour wheel of pigments you have selected yourself.

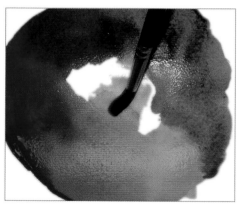

5 Next, to make subtle greys, with a clean brush begin pulling some of each colour into the middle in a circular motion. Don't scrub or mix too much or the colours will become muddy.

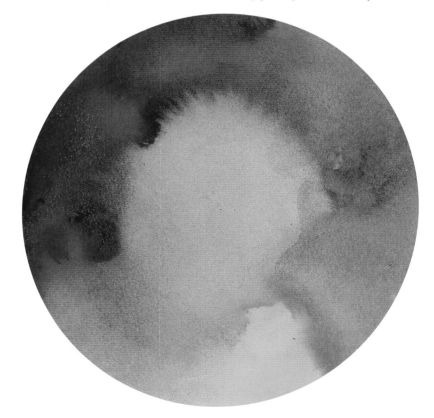

6 There is a lot of information in this exercise: The more you practice, the better you will get to know your paints.

GET TO KNOW THE TRIADS

Experiment with other triads to see the different secondary and tertiary mixes. For example, the cool triad makes the brightest greens, whereas the warm triad makes mossy greens; the best oranges come from the warm triad.

Quinacridone coral

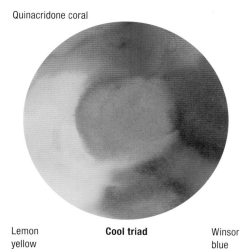

Lemon yellow   **Cool triad**   Winsor blue

Quinacridone red

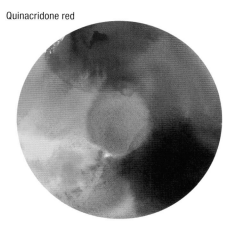

Aureolin   **Neutral triad**   French ultramarine blue

Quinacridone magenta

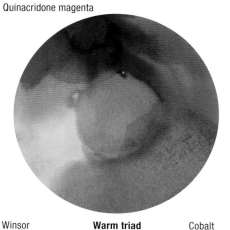

Winsor yellow deep   **Warm triad**   Cobalt blue

Warm and cool

These two poppy paintings demonstrate the benefit of understanding the principle of the triads. You can use them individually or, as here, mix them for different elements of your painting.

Cool bias poppy

Lemon yellow and quinacridone coral give these red petals a deep pink bias. The artist brought in some warmth to the shadow tones, using the warmer tones of cobalt blue. The green foliage and stem were similarly modified with cobalt blue (from the warm triad) and a touch of quinacridone coral, since the bright green that can be achieved using the cool triad seemed too artificial.

Colours used: Lemon yellow, quinacridone coral, cobalt blue.

Warm bias poppy

The warm tones of quinacridone magenta with Winsor yellow deep give flame-red petals, while the mix of the warm yellow – Winsor yellow deep, with French ultramarine blue (from the neutral triad) create a mossy mix for the stem and foliage colour.

Colours used: Winsor yellow deep, quinacridone magenta, French ultramarine blue.

Mixing greys from complementary colours

Colours opposite each other on the colour wheel are called 'complementary colours'. When complements are mixed, a soft grey colour is the result. A whole range of warm or cool colourful greys can be mixed in this way. The more the mixture uses equal parts of both colours, the closer it will get to neutral, but mixing more of one shade or another will push it to a warmer or cooler grey.

Colour Mixing

Watercolour dries lighter than the shade you see in your palettes because the white of the paper shows through the paint in transparent watercolour. Try out a colour on a scrap of the same paper until your results are reliable. It is always easier to darken a colour with another wash of paint if what you have laid down looks too light. At the same time, the more layers of paint you put down, the greater the risk of losing the translucence of light reflected upwards from the paper. Practice will help you find the desired colour in only one or two washes.

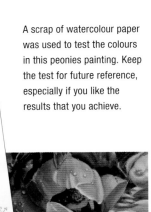

A scrap of watercolour paper was used to test the colours in this peonies painting. Keep the test for future reference, especially if you like the results that you achieve.

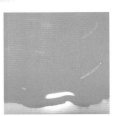

Winsor yellow deep puddle on the palette.

Single passage. Note how much lighter it is in the centre where it is dry.

Another glaze of the same colour resembles the colour in the puddle. It is closer because less of the white paper shows through.

STAINING AND NON-STAINING COLOURS

Some pigments sit on the surface of the paper and are easily removed even when dry. These are non-staining colours. They are transparent and ideal for glazing one layer upon another.

Other pigments stain the paper because they sink into its fibres. Unless freshly laid down, these are difficult to remove. Practice in using these brilliant hues is rewarding since the majority of paints stain the paper to some degree. Although they can be intimidating, persistence is rewarded with glowing results.

Staining   **Non-staining**

Left alizarin crimson
Right rose madder genuine

Left phthalo blue
Right cobalt blue

Left phthalo green
Right viridian

'MUD' VS. NEUTRAL

Not all brown or grey colour is mud. Here is an example of the difference.

When ultramarine blue, burnt sienna and cadmium yellow are mixed in the palette, the result is a dull, lifeless brown.

However, when the same pigments are laid down a layer at a time over a dried layer below, a lively colour is the result.

MULTIPLE MIXES

The freshest colour is the simplest colour. Try not to mix more than three colours, and use only two if possible; overmixing can produce muddy hues. Remember, you will continue to mix colours as you work.

In the palette these two mixtures look the same, but on paper the combination of three colours is darker and less translucent.

Cadmium red – the mix on the left of the picture above.

Quinacridone coral, cadmium orange and Winsor red – the mix on the right.

SEDIMENTARY OR GRANULATING COLOURS

Sedimentary colours are those denser pigments that have larger particles suspended in the paint that separate out when laid down on the paper. They add texture and interest to the wash. Many artists find these pigments preferable for the interest their texture adds.

Cobalt blue

Phthalo blue

Flower Mixing: Darks

Most watercolourists have no trouble painting the light and transparent washes necessary in flower painting. More challenging is creating the rich darks necessary to turn on the lights. There are plenty of dark colours that come in tubes and can be used directly, however, many artists prefer to mix their darks from some of the richer colours available. Some of these colours are alizarin crimson, quinacridone violet, burnt sienna, phthalo blue, Antwerp blue and phthalo green. A note of caution: Do not mix more than three transparent pigments together or a muddy colour may result. Two in a mixture is ideal.

Alizarin crimson (left) blended into phthalo green (centre). Phthalo green is blended into phthalo blue. These three pigments are so transparent that they can readily be mixed to form an almost-black colour.

Burnt sienna blended with Antwerp blue. In dense mixtures, together they appear greenish black. They also make an excellent natural deep green.

Quinacridone violet blended with phthalo green. The two together make a very deep navy. Quinacridone violet is not quite as transparent as alizarin crimson, so be careful not to make it thick or it will be chalky.

This painting makes use of a triad consisting of quinacridone rose, quinacridone gold and Antwerp blue, with spots of orange on the iris beards. You can see it would be a very different painting if the darks were washed out. The inset image has been edited in Photoshop to illustrate this.

The Value of Colour

Grey scale
This chart shows how some common pigments compare on the grey scale.

Tonal value refers to the continuum of white to black and all gradations of grey in between. In traditional transparent watercolour, tonal value is not only an element of design but also the critical element to the creation and maintaining of light in the design. In a flower painting, value can tell the time of day, the position of the sun, atmosphere and weather. A strong value design can bring a dramatic emphasis, leading the viewer's eyes to your focal point. Light in your painting is thus expressed in light values, and dark objects and shadows in dark values. It is the latter, the darkest values, that make the lightest values glow, and thus the designing of these lights and darks is crucial to the success of the painting.

Original photograph, as shot.

Make a black-and-white photocopy of your photograph.

GREY SCALE

In the chart above, you can see that although most pigments are in the middle, a few are almost black in value, and a few are near white. It is no accident that the yellows and golds are often used to indicate light and the blues to indicate shadow.

HOW TO SEE VALUE

There are several photographic ways to see value in a picture. In each example to the right, two values become immediately apparent. The light on the petals is clear and the darks are easy to see. Which of these methods you prefer may depend on where your paintings fall on the value scale above. Try them all. Each step you take to know your subject better will show in your final painting. When this is clear, move on to the next phase of getting to know your subject (see opposite).

On your computer's photo editing program (see p. 9) turn it to grey scale.

Squint at your photograph or blur it in a photo editing program. You will lose saturation, and the values will be clear.

Look at your photograph in dim light. It will lose saturation and the whites will pop out.

Use a red cellophane value viewer. Hold it to your eyes and view the photograph through it. This will show you the relative tones.

SKETCHING

Sketching brings your focus into the present and lets you get to know your subject intimately. Whether you are a beginner or an advanced artist, a sketchbook is your most important tool. Through it you can learn to see flowers in a new way.

3 Tone drawing: explores mass and surface. A tonal drawing avoids lines but uses light and shading to sculpt the three-dimensionality of the flower. Use the side of your pencil lead for this. Build up the darks gradually. To shade with a pen, use cross-hatching or stippling to build up your dark areas. This is a studied and slow procedure.

4 Wash: value sketch. Line and wash can put the entire form and attitude of the flower together. Begin with a light gesture, drawing to get all aspects of the flower correct. Use contour drawing to define the form and tones, created with paint or ink wash, to fill out the mass and value. This should also reflect how you would like to paint the flower in colour.

1 Original photograph: inspiration. A photograph of a beautiful flower. Ask what draws you to this particular flower. Explore the possibilities through drawing.

5 Final painting: interpretation. The finished painting should reflect a new vision that the drawing process has given you. More than just copying a photograph, you have the opportunity to emphasize the things you love most, eliminate extraneous detail and create a flower that moves not only you but all who see it.

2 Contour drawing: slow, careful exploration. Place your pencil on the paper but look at the flower. As your eyes follow the edges, not just the outline, your pencil moves as well. Don't watch your drawing.

Techniques

Washes may cover a large or small area, and are usually the starting point for most watercolour paintings. The term 'wash' implies an area of paint being applied flatly, but it also describes each brushstroke of fluid paint. Washes are often graded in tone or contain more than one colour.

FLAT WASH

The flat wash is the easiest method of applying watercolour to paper, and is used for covering the whole or a large part of the paper during the first stages of a painting. The paper can be horizontal or tipped at a slight angle so that the brushstrokes flow into each other but do not dribble down the paper. Brushstrokes can be laid either on dry or wet paper. The latter achieves a more even coverage, but working on dry paper makes the wash easier to control if you want to stop at a certain point. Use a large flat or round brush.

1 Load a brush with dilute watercolour and, starting at the top of the area to be covered, sweep it across dry paper.

2 Keep dragging the brush across the area, reloading with paint as necessary. Overlap the previous wet colour a little, so that the new stroke blends perfectly with the old one. Don't overpaint an area while wet – this will result in an uneven wash.

GRADED WASH

A graded wash is one that varies in tone. For example, on a petal this usually means that the wash becomes paler towards the bottom. The gradation is achieved by gradually adding water to the colour. A graded wash is used as the first step in suggesting a shadow as well. It becomes lighter as it progresses down the paper.

1 Tilt your board a little. Start with a flat wash of colour. Dip the brush in clean water, dilute your wash paint and stroke the dilute colour below the still-wet previous area.

2 Add more water to the brush for each area of colour. Remember that each wash should only be one step lighter than the previous one, so take care not to dilute too quickly.

3 If this wash had been worked on wet paper, the stronger colour would have run down into the paler areas, losing the graded effect. For stronger tonal contrasts, try dipping the brush twice into the water or laying the second band of colour with water alone.

VARIEGATED WASH

A variegated wash varies in colour. The technique involves adding further colours to a still-wet flat wash or damp paper. Flower painting often uses variegated washes to show colour variation within a petal or a leaf, to indicate shadows that fall on or show through petals, or to add depth to a background.

1 A varigated wash is a blend from one colour to another. Wait until the underwash is dry, then add a graded wash of a colour with water over the top. The transition can be gradual.

2 A more defined transition is achieved by washing two colours next to each other, with the edge of the first colour still wet when applying the second colour.

1 This technique can be used on detail areas such as shadows to define form. Paint the area with the first colour.

2 When the paint is nearly dry, apply the second, darker colour. This will blend easily into the damp surface, giving soft edges. The second application should contain more pigment than the first; otherwise, a bloom will result.

MIXING PAINT IN THE PALETTE

When mixing colours in the palette, make sure your wells of paint are moist and you are able to get a strong colour. Begin with the lightest colour. Once you have an adequate puddle of paint, rinse your brush well, wipe it on a towel or tissue and bring a little of the darker colour to your mix. Continue this process until the desired colour is achieved. Note: Don't start with a strong dark colour, such as phthalo blue, and attempt to mix a lighter colour, such as aureolin, into it. You could use a whole tube of the latter and still not achieve a spring green. Test your mix on a scrap of paper if you are unsure.

1 Use your brush to carry paint to be mixed to a clean area of the palette. Make a note of the individual character of both colours.

2 If mixed too thoroughly, you may achieve your desired colour, but you will also lose the individual colour personalities.

MIXING PAINT ON THE PAPER

Different colour mixing effects can be created by letting the colours blend on the paper surface, rather than mixing them in the palette. They do not mix as thoroughly, but each colour retains its identity. This is known as 'wet-into-wet' (see p. 22). Tipping the painting surface controls the direction of the flow in the blending pigments.

Colour mixing by glazing (see p. 23) a blue over a yellow. The yellow is still visible under the blue, a combination that forms green.

1 Colour mixing through working wet-into-wet (see p. 22). The still-wet paint allows the second colour to bleed into the first.

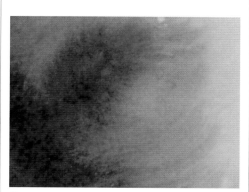

2 The blue and yellow merge magically to create green. As in the glazing method above, the integrity of the original is still obvious, which can create a more interesting and varied green than a palette mix or a green straight from the tube.

DROPPING IN COLOUR

You can drop a pure colour into a wet wash and, depending on the nature of each pigment and the wetness of the wash, exciting effects can be achieved. The colours retain their individual characteristics and blend as their nature determines. Other than to deliver the colour, you do little with the brush.

Quinacridone gold dropped into carbazole violet. A 'blast' of light appears.

Ultramarine blue dropped into carbazole violet. The colours blend and form a shadow effect.

To create the 'chaos' of a garden in full bloom, drop red into a green and gold mixture to indicate poppies and blue to indicate bachelor's buttons.

To form shadows of stamen in the centre of a flower (here, a hollyhock), drop in small amounts of phthalo green with the tip of a brush. Leave to dry before painting the centre.

WET-ONTO-DRY

The technique of applying watercolour to dry paper or over a layer of paint that has been left to dry is used in most paintings, and it allows you to take as much time as you need to consider your next step.

Poppies and bachelor's buttons applied on dry paper. The crisp edge is achieved as the paint dries almost immediately on the dry paper.

Linear marks for details or explaining shape can be painted with a small brush working wet-onto-dry. When painting veins on leaves or petals (above) work from the centre vein out towards the edge of the leaf, since the paint tends to thin out towards the end of the stroke, giving a natural effect. Stamen and markings on throats of flowers can also be painted using this technique (below).

WET-INTO-WET

Painting wet paint shapes onto wet paper or wet paint is the technique that gives watercolour its reputation as a soft, juicy medium. No other medium has the ability to flow like watercolour.

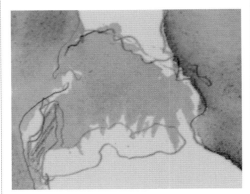

To apply paint to one area and save the white of the paper in another, wet the area to receive paint. Gently apply the colour(s) to the wet area and allow them to blend and run. They will stop at the dry edge.

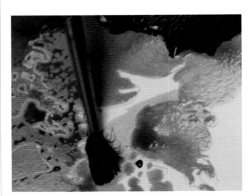

If you have masked the whites (see p. 25), wet as much of the paper as you need and freely apply colours, letting them blend together.

As you work wet-into-wet, some parts of the paper will begin to dry and give you contrasting soft and hard edges (see p. 24).

COMBINED WET-INTO-WET AND WET-ONTO-DRY

Most paintings use both wet-into-wet and wet-onto-dry passages to achieve the desired effect. Where wet-into-wet gives a feeling of mystery, wet-onto-dry gives the effect of clarity.

The combined techniques give this vase of flowers a realistic look, forming the rounded bunches of lilacs and the misty glass vase, set off by the harder-edged, dark leaves.

Contrast for emphasis: The hard edge of the background defines the edge of the petal, while the shapes within the petal are softer-edged to create texture.

PAINT LIGHT TO DARK

Traditionally, transparent watercolour is painted light to dark because light transparent colour has no density to cover a darker colour. You can gradually 'feel your way' into the shapes of the painting, using pale colours first. The technique is 'akin' to glazing (right) – in which the colour layers shine through each other to create transparent luminescent layers. By following this well-worn path, many problems can be avoided.

1 Establish the light tones of the painting with a wash of yellow, applied everywhere except where the white is to be saved. Most of this will be painted over with the subsequent transparent glazes.

3 Add the strong tones of the magenta petals. The petals represent what will be the mid-tones of the final painting.

2 Wash blue into the background areas and onto the shadow area of the petals. This starts to define the mid and dark areas and mixes with the yellow to create foliage colours.

4 Wash in mixes of blue and violet to create the dark tones. The basic light to dark tones of the painting are now established. All the final details and adjustments can now be painted (see below).

GLAZING

Glazing goes hand in hand with working wet-onto-dry and light to dark. It is a way of achieving maximum control while creating a transparent, glowing effect. This demonstration shows a test strip for a coral rosebud.

1 Paint a yellow base. Putting yellow under the other colours will add an upwards glow through the painting.

2 When the yellow is completely dry, apply a tea-strength glaze of quinacridone coral and, for the leaf colour, a mixture of aureolin and phthalo yellow-green. When dry, add quinacridone burnt sienna to the coral for the deeper colours of the flowers and paint another layer of the green mixture to deepen the green.

3 Mix a milk-strength puddle of quinacridone red and burnt sienna for the deepest corals and another layer of green for the deepest greens.

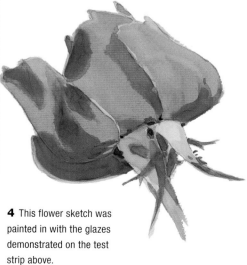

4 This flower sketch was painted in with the glazes demonstrated on the test strip above.

BLENDING

To avoid hard lines or edges with paint that has been laid down wet-onto-dry (see p. 20), try blending.

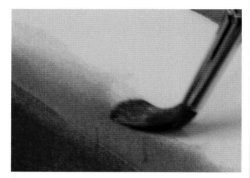

1 Place one colour next to another.

2 Blend the new colour into the old colour using rapid, light, back and forth movements with a dry or very thirsty brush.

3 A natural softness is the result.

LOST AND FOUND EDGES

Lost edges and found edges can be painted separately, but it is useful to paint them at the same time since one can define the other. Paint a wash with a defined edge on one side and a fade on the other. The technique is useful for defining the hard edge of a shape that then fades into the background. By blending both edges, soft transitions from one object to another, or into the background, can be achieved without any visible lines. Lost edges connect areas of light, shadow and colour.

1 To create a shape with hard and soft edges, paint a layer of clear water (no puddles) onto white paper. Wait until the water has sunk in but there is still a sheen.

3 Soft edges are also the way in which one colour meets another: They appear to blend. Use a natural sponge to intensify this effect.

2 Using a flat or large round brush, paint colour up to one of the edges of the wet area, allowing the other edge to bleed into the damp paper.

4 Soft edges give the sense of motion. In a garden, the breeze may stir the flowers, and it may be that feeling you want to capture. Hard edges are more fixed and defined.

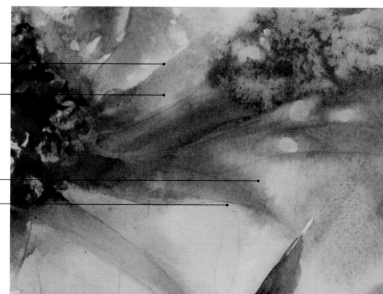

Hard found edge

Lost edge

Lost edge

Hard found edge

MASKING TO RESERVE THE PAPER

Masking fluids form a waterproof seal that protects the paper underneath, enabling washes to be painted over without having to carefully leave tiny areas white.

1 To apply masking fluid to all the white areas of a flower, such as this backlit magnolia, use an old synthetic fibre brush. Dipping it in washing-up liquid first and then wiping it will help you clean it after use.

2 You can now apply paint speedily and fluidly. Once the shadows have been painted and allowed to dry, rub or peel off the masking, revealing the white paper underneath.

3 You now have white areas you can work into. If the paper appears too white when the fluid is removed, lightly colour the area. In this case, the pure whites are ideal for the subject.

MASKING FOR DETAILS

The best method of reserving intricate highlights is to use masking fluid before painting.

1 To reserve stamens, such as these poppy stamens, paint with masking fluid using an old synthetic fibre brush. Wash the brush out immediately with warm, soapy water.

2 When the masking fluid is dry, you can paint freely over it because it acts as a block to the paint. Here new gamboge and permanent rose are used to complete the petal washes.

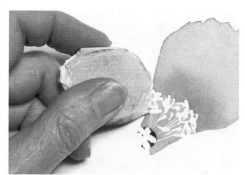

3 When the paint has dried, remove the masking by gently rubbing with a finger or a soft eraser to reveal clean, white paper. If the highlights are a pale colour rather than pure white, they can be tinted in the final stages.

SOFTENING MASKED EDGES

As useful as masking fluid is to the flower painter, when it is removed, the edges left are unnaturally hard and unpleasing.

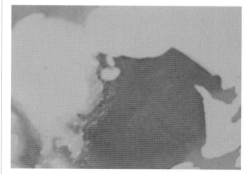

1 Remove the masking. The protected edge of the highlight will never be perfect and will require touching up. Evaluate which edges you would like hard and which you would like soft.

2 In the case of edges you want to leave almost as is, paint a thin line of water along the edge; dabbing with a tissue may be all that is needed to blend the colour into the white highlight area.

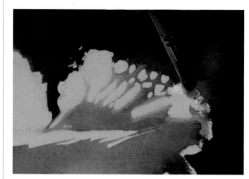

Alternative for small areas: Run a wet scrubber carefully along the edge to be softened. Dab with tissue.

MAKE SOFTENED EDGES GLOW

Once your masked edges are softened, you may want to add a glow to them. Notice that the edges of shadows in bright sunlight often have a golden edge. Recreating this can give warmth to your flower.

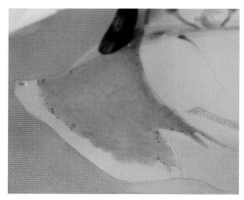

1 Before removing the masking, you may want to glaze around it with a deep yellow. Even if it fades into a darker background, there will be a glow.

3 Blend the yellow into the white and shadow colour (see p. 28). At the centre of interest, paint more golden colour and blend.

2 Once the masking is removed and the edges are softened, paint a yellow or golden almost-dry wash along the edge.

Softened masked edge

Masked edge

Glow

WHITE OF THE PAPER

In traditional transparent watercolour, it is the white of the paper that gives the painting its translucence and freshness. White paint is not usually used, although there are non-purist artists who find it useful at times.

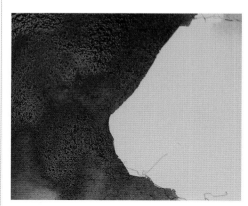

To reserve white highlight areas of paper, paint clear water washes on the areas to be coloured. When paint is applied to the wet area, it bleeds up to the edge of the dry area.

Hard-edge highlights on an open hollyhock. The technique detailed above can be applied to small areas as well as large.

Create a backlit situation once a background is painted by leaving a white edge as you paint the inside of the flower (here in soft ochre).

WHITE-ON-WHITE

There are many colours or tones of white. In bright light, white is simply white, but white objects in white surroundings will take on light shades or values of other colours due to the influence of the surrounding area.

1 A drawing of blue flags in a white vase, on a white mantle, against a white wall. Pale background washes establish the basic shape.

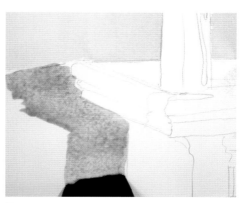

2 To establish the range of values in the painting, the mid-range values are painted first.

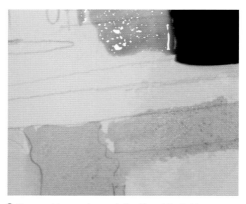

3 These mid-range tones define the white light even further. A cooler middle value has also been added to imply cast shadow.

4 With the surrounding whites in place, paint the vase and flowers. The light source is from the left and goes behind the vase as well.

5 With the vase painted and all the highlights preserved, there is a realistic look to this white-on-white painting.

ADDING HIGHLIGHTS

There are many ways to add highlights and glitter to a painting without using masking fluid or white paint.

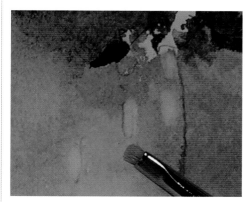

Scrubber: Use a firm synthetic brush, called a scrubber, to gently wipe away small spots of light. Take care not to overuse the scrubber and go through the paper.

Razor blade: Use a single-edge razor blade to recover dots of white by removing tiny 'divots' of painted paper.

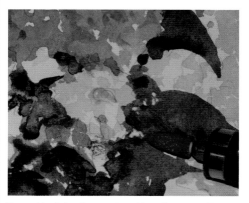

Dremel tool: Another way to achieve the same effect – but use extreme caution – is with a light touch from a Dremel tool with a sanding bit.

SHADOWS

Nothing brings out the light in a flower painting more than the presence of deep darks and shadows. These shadows 'turn on the lights'.

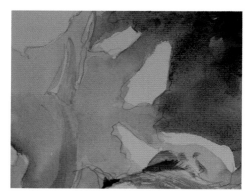

1 Paint a blue-and-white iris against a warm medium background, which emphasizes the predominantly cool colours of the flower. It will look a little washed out.

2 Add some very dark colour along the edge to make that part of the flower stand out.

3 Continue to paint the dark outwards, producing an even stronger effect.

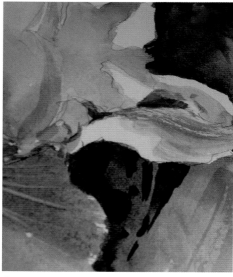

4 This application of dark leads into the negative painting of the flower's background. Glaze the violet above to a deeper value as well.

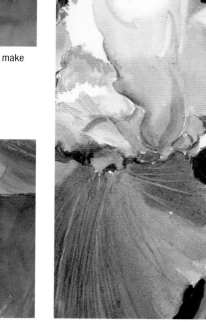

5 The iris stands out from the background due to the colourful shadows in the white of the flower and the rich dark that surrounds the flower.

NEGATIVE PAINTING

Negative painting is a way of painting into a shape to create the illusion of depth and the feeling that something is happening back there. Look carefully at the background in your photographs and you will find a jumble of abstract shapes that, from a distance, forms garden foliage.

1 First paint the positive shapes of the leaves, leaving (or reserving) the white of the paper for the pale flowers and the background areas.

2 Paint the negative shapes of the background in a cool recessive wash.

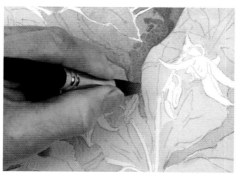

3 Pursue the tangle of shapes and shadows in the background, adding a glaze of orange to create interesting colours in the shadowy background.

POURING PAINT

Paint is often poured onto a painting, especially in the early stages, and also as an underpainting. This bottom layer will affect everything on top of it and can provide a warm or cool base from which to start. It gives unity to the whole painting. Generally a technique used for large paintings, you will need to stretch your paper to board first because this will give you better control.

4 Add a darker blue to define the negative background area. Also add cast shadows on the leaves using the same blue.

1 In a cup or the corner of a butcher tray, add clean water, with the tray tilted to keep it in the corner. Mix the first colour – usually yellow – into a creamy mixture.

4 Tilt the board in all directions, letting the paint run until you are pleased with the look. Place the board on a flat surface and allow to dry. You can repeat this process. The result is a luminous, rich layer of colour.

5 Every layer you paint into the negative space around the flower and leaves adds depth and interest to the entire painting. Notice these marks are simply abstract shapes.

2 Paint the areas of highlights with masking fluid, allow to dry, then wet the paper with water. Pour the mixture onto the desired area. The paint will bleed into the wet paper – drag it into areas requiring the base.

3 Repeat the process with red and blue.

5 Remove the masking fluid to reveal the final effect of the pouring. (See p. 26 for the final painting.) See how the red has dominated the purple.

SALT

Use of fine and coarse salt is one of the most common ways to create texture in a painting. Because it is used so often, it is wise to combine it with other techniques to avoid looking clichéd.

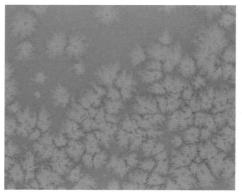

Coarse salt applied to a wet wash. Note how the paint is absorbed and repelled by the salt.

Salt applied to a mixture of two colours, at least one of which is a staining pigment, will allow the staining colour to remain in the paper.

Lightly spritzing with water (see right) will also avoid the 'salt only' look.

SPRITZ

Spritzing is a light spray of water from a pump or trigger spray bottle. A pump bottle is easier to control. The distance from which you spray determines the texture; spritzing close to the painting will create large water drops.

Spraying the background from 45–60cm (18–24in) produces a condensed texture.

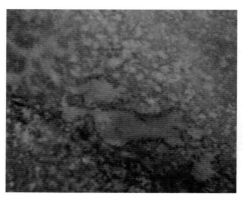

Spritzing with a pump bottle from 30cm (12in) or so gives a varied pattern.

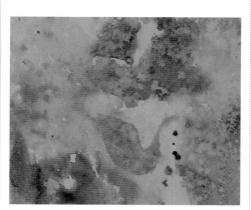

Spritzing combined with salt can give an interesting texture and is ideal for making lilacs.

THROWING PAINT

Throwing paint is a controlled way to mimic foliage and branches. It works best with an oriental brush. Note: This is messy. Put up barriers, such as cardboard, to keep your area clean when you are 'throwing'.

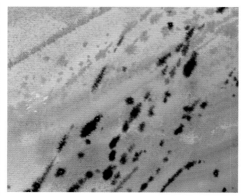

1 First, spritz the paper in the area to be covered. Then, protecting the uninvolved parts of the painting with kitchen towels, gently flick the brush at the angle you want the paint to land. This takes practice.

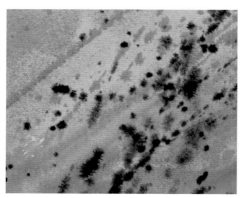

2 It may take several throws to produce the required effect.

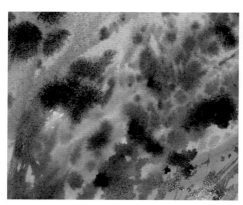

3 Here you can see that the thrown paint has blended and bachelor's buttons have been dropped in as well.

PENCIL AND WASH

For an artist wanting to sketch outdoors and carry only a sketchbook and pencil, this technique combines pencil drawing, done on site in detail, with a watercolour wash applied at a later time.

PEN AND WASH

Similar to pencil and wash, and generally employed for the same reasons, pen and wash also offers slightly different attributes. You can use permanent ink that will not run later when the wash is applied (below left), or you can use an ink pen that will run and join in the complete effect (below right).

1 Draw a complete tonal drawing. The single hatched lines radiating from the flower provide detail of the shape and angle of the petals.

Permanent ink

1 Draw your flower with permanent ink and in as much detail as you would like. To include shading, use hatching or cross-hatching.

Non-permanent ink

1 Draw your flowers with a regular, non-permanent ink pen.

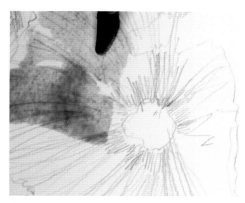

2 Keep washes fairly thin so the texture of the pencil shows through. Begin to lay in the colour.

2 Paint in the colour. You can see there is a slight 'cartoon' look.

2 When the ink is dry, use a brush wet with only water to rewet the ink and shade the drawing with the dissolving ink.

3 Maintaining transparency, move through the flower, dropping colour into wet washes. Let the pigments flow into each other and outside the lines.

3 In the end, when the darkest values are applied, some or all of the cartoon look can disappear by use of dark washes.

3 When the tonal drawing is dry, apply a watercolour wash, producing a subtle sketch of the flowers.

WATERCOLOUR AND PASTEL

Pastel is pure pigment compressed to chalk-like sticks. When pastel is used with watercolour, it has the effect of intensifying those areas by bringing pure and undiluted pigment to them. Breathing pastel dust is hazardous, so wear a protective mask and gloves.

WATERCOLOUR AND GOUACHE

Gouache is opaque watercolour; the same pigment as its transparent version with an opacifier added. It means that light colours can be painted over dark. It can be used for tiny details or highlights. Some artists use the opaque nature of gouache to produce body colour mixes (a colour mixed with white gouache), which can be laid over areas of the painting in flat or semi-opaque washes to produce a chalky effect.

1 Use pastel as a simple stroke.

Gouache for details
1 Paint the petal with yellow and, when nearly dry, paint the petal markings with a darker red.

Gouache for highlights
1 Glaze washes of aureolin yellow, phthalo blue and indigo over each other to create a dark background.

2 Use it to indicate tiny flowers that would get lost in a diluted wash.

2 If tinting white gouache, avoid diluting the gouache too much; otherwise, it will not cover the earlier colours – you need only enough dilution to produce a painting consistency.

2 In a palette, mix watercolours with white gouache to create two colours, for the leaves and petals. The colours need to be much lighter than required because they will sink into the wash background once applied.

3 Use pastel's intensity to draw the viewer's eye to certain spots in the painting.

3 Paint in the stamen stalks with a small brush, using the body colour sparingly, because gouache has a matte surface that can look dull and out of place beside a watercolour wash.

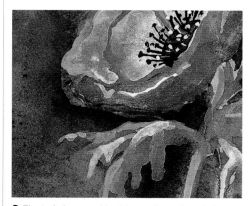

3 The technique would not be used over the whole painting. Here, the chalky highlights on the petals and leaves fade into the background, giving a sense of form.

WATERCOLOUR PENCIL

Watercolour pigment also comes in pencil form, either as traditional pencils or as solid sticks of hardened pigment. In either form, pencils are great for drawing or painting while travelling or outdoors. The drawing can be wet at any time later, and a painting will result.

WATERCOLOUR CRAYON

Although similar to watercolour pencils, watercolour crayons look and feel like those coloured sticks you used as a child. They have a waxy feel when applied but are water-soluble and can be used in the same way as the watercolour pencils.

1 Choose a selection of pencils and then make a tonal drawing.

1 Call out all the elements to be drawn with a quick pencil sketch. Cover the drawing in scribbled crayon.

4 Finish the sketch. All of this can be drawn dry and painted later.

2 When the drawing is complete, use a brush with plain water to turn the drawing into a painting.

2 Use a wet brush to turn the scribble into rich colour.

3 A second layer of pencil on the dry painting deepens the value in some areas.

3 While the yellow is wet, draw right into it with a red crayon. An intense colour will result.

A painting with washes of transparent watercolour and lines of gouache. When these lines were almost dry, watercolour crayon was used to heighten the colour and gouache to heighten the detail.

Projects

The flower photographs and their associated step-by-step paintings are
divided into portrait and landscape formats. Within these two formats,
the flowers are loosely grouped into three categories – Single Specimens,
Floral Still Life and Flowers Outdoors – so that you can find quickly
and easily the right subject for your painting.

Indian Reed Lily

A high-key painting dominated by light values presents a challenge, incorporating interesting dark values without creating harsh contrasts.

PAINTS
Aureolin
Hansa yellow medium
New gamboge
Organic vermilion
Perylene red
Phthalo blue
Phthalo green
Quinacridone rose
Sap green

TOOLS & MATERIALS
Cold-pressed paper,
  300gsm (140lb)
HB drawing pencil
Masquepen
Round brushes,
  Nos. 6, 8, 10
Tissues
1cm (½in) flat chisel
  brush

Soft-bristled scrubber
Rigger

TECHNIQUES USED
Variegated wash, *p. 20*
Mixing paint in the palette,
  p. 21
Mixing paint on the paper,
  p. 21
Dropping in colour, *p. 21*
Wet-onto-dry, *p. 22*
Wet-into-wet, *p. 22*
Glazing, *p. 23*
Masking for details, *p. 25*
Softening masked edges,
  p. 25
Adding highlights, *p. 27*
Shadows, *p. 28*

1 Make an accurate drawing of the flower. Sketched lines should be faint or easily lightened with an eraser before painting over them. Use a Masquepen to draw a thin line of masking fluid along the lightest edge of each bud and petal (inset). Let the masking fluid dry completely before beginning to paint.

2 When using yellow pigments, maximum value contrast can be achieved with multiple thin glazes of colour. To avoid lifting the initial layers when applying subsequent glazes, paint wet-into-wet. With a No. 10 brush, apply water to a petal. When the sheen has disappeared, brush on another thin wash of water. For a variegated wash, drop in aureolin for the cool, light value areas, and Hansa yellow medium and new gamboge for darker values.

3 Remove the masking fluid. Soften the masked edges by stroking a wet No. 6 round brush over the edge and blotting with a tissue. Similarly, ease out and lift any paint buildup along the edges. With a No. 8 brush, use wet-into-wet with only one glaze of water to lay in two to three thin washes of colour. Add a touch of cool phthalo green to the light side of the buds and warm sap green to the shadowed side. Introduce organic vermilion on the shadowed petals and between the buds.

4 Mix phthalo blue and quinacridone rose for the upper background and drop wet-into-wet with a No. 10 brush. Use a watery sap green and new gamboge mix for a subtle shadow colour. Paint the bold red lines and splashes with organic vermilion and perylene red with a No. 6 brush (inset). When dry, apply a second glaze. Deepen the shadows between the buds using sap green and vermilion.

5 Use a 1cm (½in) damp chisel brush and scrubber to lift paint from the light edges. Create fine striations on the buds with varying mixes of sap green, new gamboge and organic vermilion. Using a rigger, lightly paint the lines wet-on-dry with sweeping strokes. Apply a second layer to the lines in shadowed area.

Lisa Hill

Foxglove

The artist was drawn to the startling complementary play between the multiple greens and the rose-magenta coloured flowers. Very little artistic alteration was made to the photograph.

PAINTS
Cobalt blue
French ultramarine blue
Phthalo green
Quinacridone burnt scarlet
Quinacridone coral
Quinacridone gold
Quinacridone magenta
Quinacridone pink
Quinacridone red
Quinacridone rose
Quinacridone violet

TOOLS & MATERIALS
Cold-pressed paper,
    300gsm (140lb)
Mechanical pencil
Masking fluid
Old brush
Masking film
7.5cm (3in) wash brush
2.5cm (1in) flat brush

Round brushes,
    Nos. 6, 10, 14
Liner
Fritch scrubber, No. 2
Tissues and kitchen towels
Sharp tool, such as a
    seam ripper

TECHNIQUES USED
Graded wash, *p. 20*
Mixing paint in the palette,
    p. 21
Dropping in colour, *p. 21*
Wet-onto-dry, *p. 22*
Wet-into-wet, *p. 22*
Glazing, *p. 23*
Blending, *p. 24*
Lost and found edges,
    p. 24
Masking to reserve the
    paper, *p. 25*
Shadows, *p. 28*

1 Do a detailed drawing from the photograph. Mask over the entire area of flowers including the 'holes' in the stem area where the background can be seen. Cut out from masking film an approximate form, leaving 1cm (½in) around the edge. Apply masking fluid to seal the film (inset). Extend it out to the edge of the stem and flowers. When dry, apply a second coat to avoid any seepage.

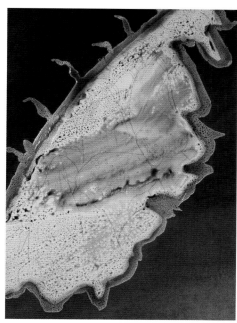

2 With a 7.5cm (3in) wash brush, lay down several layers of graded wash, drying between applications. Begin with a strong yellow. If the first layer dries too light, dry, apply again, and dry. Follow the yellow with a medium-value red. Then mix a natural-looking green to glaze several layers until you achieve the desired depth. Remove masking, mix a green to match the background and fill in the 'holes' with this colour.

3 Study the photograph to understand the complex layers of stems and leaves that top each flower. Use a green with some cobalt blue to cool it for the deeper layers (the blue makes the stems and leaves recede), and a warmer green with some red and yellow added to it to bring the rest forwards (inset). Green and red will make grey if mixed, so when you paint the red variegation in the green areas be sure the green is dry. Choose the appropriate brush size for the size of the area you are painting.

4 Mix puddles of the pink, rose and magenta quinacridone colours to the consistency of cream. Paint each hanging flower with your 2.5cm (1in) flat brush. Dab in highlights with tissue paper where the light hits the flower. Use violet and cobalt blue for the shadows. Leave the paper white where the bell meets the stem. When dry, use a diluted, warm yellow to warm up the white.

5 Paint around the inside white spots with a deeper mixture of the outside colour (by adding blue or quinacridone violet), using a small round brush. When dry, with a damp 2.5cm (1in) flat brush, stroke across the white spots to bring some colour across the white. Dry and apply the darker spots with a liner and using quinacridone violet. When the painting is dry, use a sharp tool to scratch the furry edge of the bell.

Orchids

The artist's challenge was to find the right combination of pigments that would express the delicate simplicity of the flowers with their brilliant pink colour, and that would behave wet-into-wet with just the right amount of movement and blending.

PAINTS
Cobalt blue
French ultramarine blue
New gamboge
Permanent sap green
Purple madder
Quinacridone magenta
Scarlet lake

TECHNIQUES USED
Mixing paint in the palette, *p. 21*
Mixing paint on the paper, *p. 21*
Wet-onto-dry, *p. 22*
Wet-into-wet, *p. 22*
Lost and found edges, *p. 24*

TOOLS & MATERIALS
Cold-pressed paper, 300gsm (140lb)
HB pencil
Small pointed round brush
Round brush, No. 5
Tissues

1 Draw the large shapes of the composition on watercolour paper using a soft HB pencil with a light touch. Paint the veins of the petals with a small pointed round brush using a watery mix of purple madder. Paint the veins first so that the next layer of paint will soften them.

2 Generously wet one background petal so that the surface glistens. Mix cobalt blue and quinacridone magenta each to the consistency of semi-skimmed milk. Apply a line of cobalt blue just inside the perimeter of the petal. Then drop quinacridone magenta into the centre of the petal (inset). Tilt the board in different directions to mingle the colours. Repeat for each petal.

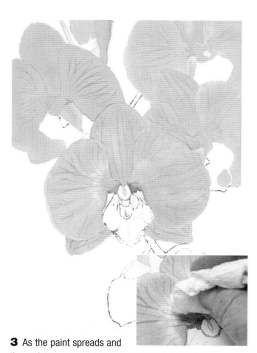

3 As the paint spreads and the moisture evaporates, you may want to lighten some areas. Use a 'thirsty' (wiped dry) brush or a tissue to lift some of the paint from those areas (inset). If some areas appear too light, wait until the petal is dry, gently wet the petal again and drop in a little more paint where needed. Again, dab with a tissue to bring out the highlights.

4 Paint the yellow and red centres of each blossom, using quinacridone magenta beside scarlet lake for the reds and new gamboge for the yellows. In the background flowers allow the colours to mingle. For the foreground flower, let the red dry before painting the yellow. Mix a nearly black colour from purple madder, sap green and scarlet lake. With the tip of a small round brush, paint in the lines and dots in the centre.

5 Paint the stems and buds directly, wet-onto-dry but allowing the colours to touch and blend for the first layer, using sap green with new gamboge for the yellower areas; sap green with French ultramarine blue for the darker areas; quinacridone magenta for the pinker areas, and all the above mixed together for the browner areas.

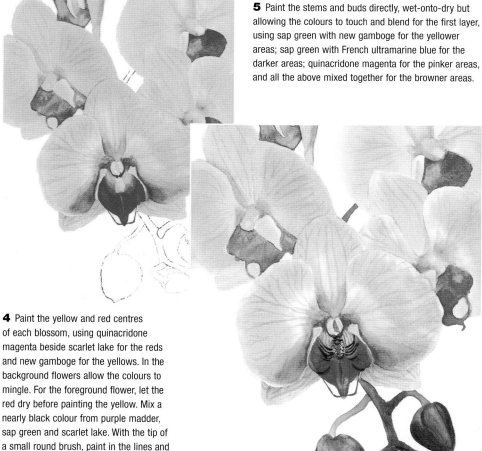

Rose

The artist saw this photograph of a rose as a challenge – to see it in a fresh way and to insert an air of mystery by having the beauty of the image emerge from the deep tones of the background.

PAINTS
Alizarin crimson
Antwerp blue
Aureolin
Cadmium orange
Cadmium yellow light
Cobalt blue
French ultramarine blue
Rose madder genuine

TECHNIQUES USED
Graded wash, *p. 20*
Mixing paint in the palette, *p. 21*
Dropping in colour, *p. 21*
Wet-into-wet, *p. 22*
Negative painting, *p. 27*
Pouring paint, *p. 29*
Spritz, *p. 30*

TOOLS & MATERIALS
Cold-pressed paper, 300gsm (140lb)
Clear acetate
HB pencil or pen
7.5cm (3in) hake brush
Large soft mop brush
Natural sponge
Spray bottle
Round brushes, Nos. 4, 8, 10
6mm (¼in) flat brush
12mm (½in) flat brush

1 On a piece of clear acetate laid on the image, draw a grid dividing the photograph into thirds in each direction, resulting in nine squares. Lightly repeat this grid on your watercolour paper. Methodically transfer the lines in each square in the photograph to the same square on the watercolour paper. The completed drawing should show all necessary detail with lines that are light enough to be erased.

2 With a hake brush, wet the paper and let it relax. Brush using a large mop brush or pour aureolin in areas of light and cobalt blue in areas of shadow. Tilt the paper and let the colours roll. Use transparent pigments to make a soft underpainting. Lift out areas with a damp sponge (inset) or brush to preserve a light value.

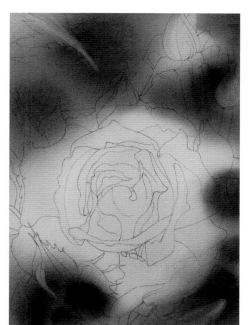

3 This stage is similar to step 2, but this time uses a mixture of opaque and granulating pigments (see p. 16). For this, the mixture should be a dark blue-green placed in the darkest areas of the negative space. Carefully control the mixture by spritzing and rolling. It should have soft graded edges with lots of open space.

4 Begin to carve the image by painting the dark values behind the back petals with a No. 10 round brush. Next, using a No. 4 and 8 round brushes, paint the dark areas in the rose centre to model the image (inset). Play warm yellows against cool ones with the deepest colour in the crevice areas. The underpainting intrudes into the petal area in places and softens the image.

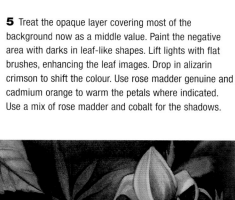

5 Treat the opaque layer covering most of the background now as a middle value. Paint the negative area with darks in leaf-like shapes. Lift lights with flat brushes, enhancing the leaf images. Drop in alizarin crimson to shift the colour. Use rose madder genuine and cadmium orange to warm the petals where indicated. Use a mix of rose madder and cobalt for the shadows.

Mallows

The artist found that the veined petals were almost impossible to replicate and were best represented by suggestion only. The subtle colour changes in the flower petals and buds were managed carefully to avoid hard contrasts.

PAINTS
Alizarin crimson
Burnt umber
French ultramarine blue
Lemon yellow
Permanent sap green
Prussian blue
Raw sienna

TOOLS & MATERIALS
Cold-pressed paper,
   300gsm (140lb)
HB pencil
Round brushes,
   Nos. 5 or 8 and 10 or 12
Masking fluid
Old brush

TECHNIQUES USED
Mixing paint in the palette,
   p. 21
Dropping in colour, p. 21
Wet-into-wet, p. 22
Paint light to dark, p. 23
Lost and found edges,
   p. 24
Masking to reserve the
   paper, p. 25
Masking for details,
   p. 25

1 Make a detailed drawing of the image. Mix a small puddle of raw sienna and, using a No. 5 or No. 8 round brush, paint each pistil and husk. When dry, use a stronger mixture of the same colour and dot a random pattern of tiny spots on each pistil. Dry. Apply a coating of masking fluid with irregular edges. Also apply dots of masking fluid to indicate the smattering of small specks around the base of each pistil.

2 Using a No. 10 or No. 12 round brush, wet the centre of the first flower with water half the distance to the edge of the petals. Introduce lemon yellow, drawing the brush from the centre outwards, allowing the colour to fade towards the edge. When dry, repeat the wetting process over a smaller centre and introduce a thin wash of sap green, not completely covering the first yellow wash.

3 Create a weak mixture of alizarin crimson and Prussian blue to add texture and shadows to the white petals (inset). An alternative to replicating the network of veins is to paint fine, sweeping strokes that are irregular in thickness. Be sure to preserve sufficient white between these strokes to indicate the veins. When dry, remove the masking fluid and touch up the colour of the pistils.

4 Using a thin mixture of sap green, paint the flower buds and stems. Work on small segments at a time and, while still wet, introduce a strong mix of sap green along the shadow side of the stem, allowing it to bleed towards the light side (inset).

5 Mix a large puddle of burnt umber and French ultramarine blue for the background. While the background paint is still wet on the paper, drop in colours such as ultramarine blue, alizarin crimson or sap green, adding interest. Paint short strokes out from the stems to create the furry look.

Sunflowers

To create a centre of interest in the sunflowers, the artist created a path of light to break up some of the yellow in the petals and to add luminosity to the already radiant flowers.

PAINTS
Aureolin
French ultramarine blue
Hooker's green
Permanent orange
Quinacridone
  burnt scarlet
Quinacridone
  burnt sienna
Quinacridone coral
Quinacrindone
  magenta
Quinacridone violet
Winsor yellow deep

Metal scraper
Masking film or tissue
  paper
Mouth atomizer
1-in. (2.5-cm) flat brush
Mat knife
Fritch scrubbers,
  Nos. 2, 12, 16

TOOLS & MATERIALS
Cold-pressed paper,
  300gsm (140lb)
HB pencil
Round brushes,
  Nos. 3, 6, 10
Coarse salt

TECHNIQUES USED
Mixing paint in the palette,
  p. 21
Mixing paint on the paper,
  p. 21
Dropping in colour, *p. 21*
Wet-onto-dry, *p. 22*
Wet-into-wet, *p. 22*
Adding highlights, *p. 27*
Salt, *p. 30*

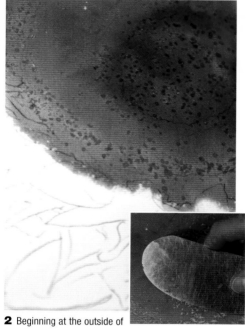

1 Make a detailed drawing with light HB pencil lines, since dark lines will show through the transparent yellow pigments of the petals. (Note that for the purposes of the photograph above, the lines are darker than you should make them.) Working with one flower centre at a time, wet the paper in that area with a No. 10 round brush, moving in a circular motion, allowing the wet to extend into the petal area.

2 Beginning at the outside of the circle, still using the No. 10 round brush, paint a medium value of quinacridone burnt sienna. Then switch to quinacridone burnt scarlet, and, in the centre of the flower, mix that with a little quinacridone magenta. Sprinkle coarse salt in the centre and in the outer ring. Dry thoroughly and scrape any salt away with a metal scraper (inset).

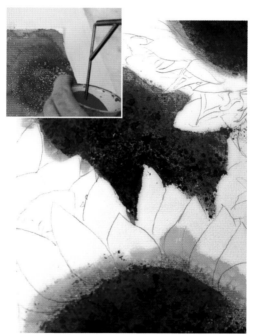

5 To create the illusion of a soft light hitting the flowers, use scrubbers appropriate to the size of area being worked on to remove some of the yellow paint on selected petal tips and edges. In this painting the artist used this method to remove the dark pencil lines as well.

3 Cover all remaining white areas with masking film cut around the petals or with tissue paper. Make a creamy mixture of quinacridone burnt scarlet and water, and a similar mixture of the burnt scarlet mixed with quinacridone violet and Hooker's green. Spatter the flower seed in the centre with a mouth atomizer (inset), working first with the red and then with the dark. Do not let any paint pool; otherwise, the texture will be lost. Dry and repeat if necessary.

4 Using a No. 6 brush in the larger areas and a No. 3 in the tighter crevices, wet the petals. Drop or paint in aureolin and, at the juncture with the central pod, Winsor yellow deep. Paint the leaves with a mixture of quinacridone gold and French ultramarine blue, using a knife to scrape in veins and highlights.

Crocuses

The large scale of this view results in large, even shapes that require variation in colour and form. It is important that the veining does not appear too busy.

PAINTS
Antwerp blue
Brilliant purple
Brilliant red-violet
Cadmium scarlet
Cadmium yellow light
French ultramarine blue
New gamboge
Orange lake
Permanent rose
Purple-magenta

TECHNIQUES
Mixing paint in the palette,
  p. 21
Wet-into-wet, p. 22
Glazing, p. 23
Adding highlights, p. 27

TOOLS & MATERIALS
Cold-pressed paper,
  300gsm (140lb)
Transfer paper
Pencil
7.5cm (3in) hake brush
Soft mop brush
Round brushes,
  Nos. 4, 8, 10
6mm (¼in) flat brush

1 On a piece of transfer paper taped to the photograph, make a drawing of the flower, shading in the dark areas and noting where you will save the light. Next, tape the transfer paper to the watercolour paper so that your hand can slide underneath it. With your pencil, follow the lines that you can see through the transparency of the paper (inset). Draw in the major shapes, adding details later.

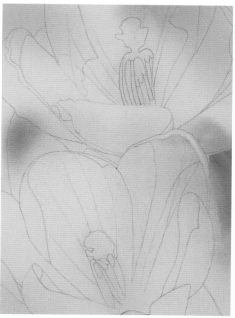

2 Use a hake brush to wet the paper on both sides until limp. With a soft mop brush, add new gamboge to the stamens of the flowers, keeping it away from most areas that will be purple. Brush Antwerp blue into the background area with a No. 10 round brush and let it expand into some of the petal shapes to soften the edges.

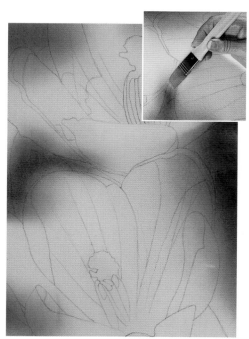

3 Make a mixture of transparent and opaque colours (French ultramarine blue, Antwerp blue and new gamboge). Use the hake brush to paint the mixture sparingly into areas of the background, intruding into petal areas (inset). Leave some of the previous wash open.

4 Glaze over the petals with the blues already used, permanent rose, purple-magenta, brilliant red-violet and brilliant purple to produce cool and warm violets. Keep the washes wet and vary the colour and value. Dry between glazes. While the washes are damp, use a 6mm (¼in) flat brush to lift out light lines in the direction of the veins. Repeat the process to get the desired colours and values.

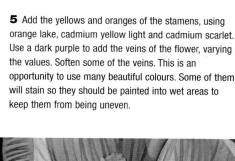

5 Add the yellows and oranges of the stamens, using orange lake, cadmium yellow light and cadmium scarlet. Use a dark purple to add the veins of the flower, varying the values. Soften some of the veins. This is an opportunity to use many beautiful colours. Some of them will stain so they should be painted into wet areas to keep them from being uneven.

Chrysanthemums

This photograph is all pink! The challenge is to use a variety of tone and the value of a single colour. Separating the forms of the foreground, middle ground and background make it less confusing as an image and more pleasing as a painting.

PAINTS
Cobalt violet
Dioxazine purple
Opera
Permanent alizarin
  crimson
Permanent rose
Quinacridone rose
Ultramarine blue

TECHNIQUES USED
Mixing paint in the palette,
  p. 21
Wet-into-wet, *p. 22*
Masking to reserve the
  paper, *p. 25*
Softening masked edges,
  p. 25
Adding highlights, *p. 27*
Spritz, *p. 30*

TOOLS & MATERIALS
Cold-pressed paper,
  300gsm (140lb)
H pencil
Masquepen
Stiff-bristled brush, No. 5
Masking fluid
Spray bottle
Round brushes,
  Nos. 5, 12, 16
Fritch scrubber, No. 3

1 As you begin the drawing, pay attention to the placement of form on the paper. Consider the large flower to be the foreground and place its top edge above the centre. The area above it will encompass the middle ground and background. Draw the petal shapes with careful positioning of all highlights.

2 Using a Masquepen, apply masking to each shape of light on the petals of the flowers. This pattern of light will define the placement of individual petals. Next, using a stiff-bristled brush, dip the tip into a small pool of masking fluid and, flicking your thumb against the bristles, spritz tiny flecks of mask all around the main flower (inset). Let it dry.

3 Squeeze onto your palette quinacridone rose, permanent rose, cobalt violet, opera and dioxazine purple. With a spray bottle, thoroughly spritz the entire sheet. Working wet-into-wet with a No. 16 sable brush, flow mixtures of colour and value. Pay attention to the reference photograph. Be aware of lights and darks, pinks and purples as you add colour. Leave the painting to dry before removing the masking (inset).

4 Use water, a No. 3 Fritch scrubber and a stiff bristle brush to define shapes and soften edges. 'Draw' the outline of petal shapes with a No. 5 round brush by softly lifting the pigment. Soften the edges on the highlights with the Fritch scrubber, since leaving the harsh edges would be too distracting.

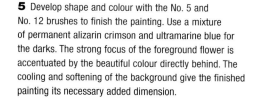

5 Develop shape and colour with the No. 5 and No. 12 brushes to finish the painting. Use a mixture of permanent alizarin crimson and ultramarine blue for the darks. The strong focus of the foreground flower is accentuated by the beautiful colour directly behind. The cooling and softening of the background give the finished painting its necessary added dimension.

Honeysuckle

The honeysuckle's beauty lies in its delicate curving shapes and warm glowing colours. This was a major consideration when choosing a palette – to create a strong, vibrant painting while retaining the flower's softness.

PAINTS
Aureolin
Indigo
New gamboge
Permanent rose
Perylene maroon
Quinacridone gold
Winsor green

TOOLS & MATERIALS
Hot-pressed paper,
    425gsm (200lb)
HB pencil
Masking fluid
Old brush
Round brushes,
    Nos. 00, 3, 7, 12
Filbert brush

TECHNIQUES
Flat wash, *p. 20*
Mixing paint in the palette,
    p. 21
Mixing paint on the paper,
    p. 21
Dropping in colour, *p. 21*
Lost and found edges,
    p. 24
Masking to reserve the
    paper, *p. 25*
Softening masked edges,
    p. 25

1 Draw the flower lightly onto the watercolour paper with an HB pencil. Put in just the basic shapes, emphasizing curves to strengthen the design. To retain white paper for highlights on the petals, apply masking fluid to those areas with an old brush.

2 Using a No. 12 brush and clean water, wet the background areas, leaving the stamens dry. Apply a dilute wash of new gamboge to the wet areas and let dry. Repeat for the buds and remaining yellow petals. Wet the pink petals and charge lightly with permanent rose, blending to give tonal value and shape.

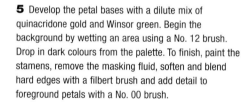

5 Develop the petal bases with a dilute mix of quinacridone gold and Winsor green. Begin the background by wetting an area using a No. 12 brush. Drop in dark colours from the palette. To finish, paint the stamens, remove the masking fluid, soften and blend hard edges with a filbert brush and add detail to foreground petals with a No. 00 brush.

3 For the darker petals, charge with permanent rose and new gamboge, adding more pigment and a touch of perylene maroon for deeper tones (inset). Apply aureolin and Winsor green lightly to the basal areas. With a No. 7 brush continue to build the petals, adding wet-into-wet layers of new gamboge, quinacridone gold and permanent rose.

4 Paint the central area with a dilute underpainting of Winsor green and aureolin, dropping in perylene maroon and indigo for the darker areas. Wet the central buds with a No. 3 brush and flood with permanent rose, adding perylene maroon for darker areas. Lift colour to preserve highlights.

Amaryllis

The artist's initial task was to eliminate some background detail, by adding white areas, in order to improve the overall layout. Overlaying shades of blue and yellow keep the abundant green areas of the painting visually stimulating.

PAINTS
Black
Brilliant cadmium red
Cobalt violet
Gamboge
Phthalo green
Quinacridone magenta
Sap green
Turquoise blue

TOOLS & MATERIALS
Cold-pressed paper,
   300gsm (140lb)
2B pencil
Invisible tape
Plastic putty knife
Exacto knife
Incredible Nib
Round brushes,
   Nos. 3–8
Hair dryer
Rubber cement pick-up

TECHNIQUES USED
Mixing paint in the palette,
   p. 21
Wet-onto-dry, p. 22
Wet-into-wet, p. 22
Blending, p. 24
Lost and found edges,
   p. 24
Softening masked
   edges, p. 25
Adding highlights, p. 27
Shadows, p. 28
Glazing, p. 31

1 Make a drawing of the photograph. Before applying any paint, tape the perimeter of the painting with invisible tape, securing its adhesion by pressing it with a plastic putty knife. (When the painting is completed, the tape releases easily and allows for a crisp, clean edge.) Pre-plan any small areas that will remain white and apply masking fluid with an Incredible Nib (inset).

2 To attain definition of the colour breakdown and prevent possible colour misplacement later, begin painting an overall light wash of sap green mixed with some phthalo green wet-into-wet, using a No. 8 brush for the leaf and stem areas. Dry with a hair dryer in order to proceed more quickly. Apply a mixture of quinacridone magenta and brilliant cadmium red wet-into-wet for the floral area.

3 Layer the submerged area of the flower stems wet-onto-dry. Use light layers of pigment to avoid overworking. Apply turquoise blue to the stems and vase reflections. Use a light gamboge yellow wet-into-wet for the flower centres and lighter stems. After completing an area, use a rubber cement pick-up to pull up the masking fluid (inset). Refine the white areas by softening the edges, allowing a few harsh white areas for impact.

4 Begin detailing the flowers with a wet-into-wet method for more intense colour, adding cobalt violet for the shadowed areas. Follow up with a wet-onto-dry technique for detail then wet-into-wet again for finer detail and softening the edges (inset). Complete the taller stemmed flowers in the same layering method described in step 3.

5 Use an Exacto knife to gently scrape the surface of the paper to achieve subtle white highlights on the flowers, leaves and vase. Add a few out-of-focus leaves by applying light wet-into-wet washes to the background. Mix cobalt violet and quinacridone magenta, and apply light washes to some of the petals.

Sunny Bouquet

The artist was drawn to the colourful impressionistic flowers in the centre of the photograph, and chose to make a painting that was both literal and looser than the original image.

PAINTS
Aureolin
Cadmium orange
Cadmium red
French ultramarine blue
French ultramarine
  blue-violet
Hooker's green
Naples yellow
Quinacridone coral
Quinacridone rose
Winsor blue
Winsor yellow deep

TOOLS & MATERIALS
Hot-pressed paper,
  300gsm (140lb)
HB pencil
Eraser
7.5cm (3in) wash brush
2.5cm (1in) flat brush
Round brushes,
  Nos. 6, 10, 14

TECHNIQUES USED
Mixing paint in the palette,
  p. 21
Dropping in colour, p. 21
Wet-onto-dry, p. 22
Wet-into-wet, p. 22
Glazing, p. 23
Blending, p. 24
Lost and found edges,
  p. 24

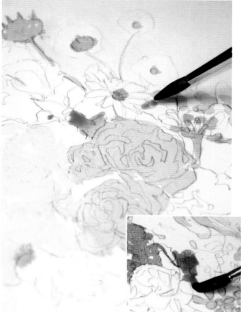

1 Mix a small, cream-like puddle of each of your colours. Use these freely in the following steps, to match the colour of the flowers and shadows. Draw the bouquet in more detail than you may need in the final painting, so that you will be able to select as you progress. Keep your lines light, especially in the centre of the large white rose on the left. Wet both sides of the paper thoroughly with a 7.5cm (3in) wash brush. This will help the paper to buckle less during painting.

2 With the surface still shiny, but no pooled water, use a 7.5cm (3in) wash brush to apply the background blue (leave the white areas). Take care to paint around the sun-washed daisies. When the paper is dry, if the colour is too light, rewet with a light, clean water wash and repeat. Next begin applying blocks of colour to the flowers (inset). Work one colour at a time all around the painting.

5 Finally, once again work around the flowers, particularly the ones in front. Paint in your darkest darks as shadows behind the flowers or under the petals. Take care not to get the values in the flower itself too dark because it will look unnatural. These darkest colours will fall in a green to purple range.

3 When painting the white rose in front left, keep the first petal shadows light (watery) and warm, using a deep gold or greyed orange. Several glazes will bring these shadows to the correct value as the painting progresses. When the shadow is put down, immediately blend the soft end with a thirsty brush where the shadow merges into the light.

4 Begin to deepen the values of the flower shadows by painting in a darker mixture of the same colour you used at first. In the large white rose, glaze in the deepest shadows only in the deepest crevices. Remember to step back from the painting for a perspective on your work.

Hyacinths

This painting focuses on colour, light and pattern, with the texture of the flowers contrasting with the softer washes in the bowl.

PAINTS
Cerulean blue
Manganese blue hue
Quinacridone coral
Quinacridone magenta
Quinacridone rose
Winsor yellow

TECHNIQUES
Flat wash, *p. 20*
Wet-onto-dry, *p. 22*
Wet-into-wet, *p. 22*
Dropping in colour, *p. 21*
Glazing, *p. 23*
Lost and found edges, *p. 24*
Adding highlights, *p. 27*
Negative painting, *p. 28*

TOOLS & MATERIALS
Cold-pressed paper, 300gsm (140lb)
HB pencil
2cm (¾in) oval brush
Round brush, No. 6
2.5cm (1in) flat brush

1 Draw the flower arrangement onto the watercolour paper using an HB pencil.

2 Wet the entire surface of the paper and wash in an underpainting of manganese blue hue and Winsor yellow using a 2cm (¾in) oval brush (inset). Let the colours flow together, establishing a strong under-structure where the grey to dark values will be placed. The brush has a point but is also plump and allows a lot of water and pigment to be carried to the paper. The point allows for easy cutting-in where necessary.

3 When the underpainting has dried, paint the local colour of each object. Wash cerulean blue into the background, creating negative spaces around the flowers. Next, with a No. 6 round brush, begin to apply light washes of quinacridone coral and rose. Drop Winsor yellow into the coral wash to produce a glow.

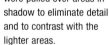

4 Glaze more local colour over dry areas and darker values over the flowers using stronger washes of quinacridone coral, rose and magenta. Dry well between each layer of glazed colour. A pattern of light and dark begins to form that helps to carry the viewer's eye through the painting. Using the flat brush, lift back to light values that add detail and dimension to the flowers (inset).

5 Establish soft washes and lost edges using the colour lifting technique to contrast with the hard edges and patterns of the flowers. Here, large unifying glazes were pulled over areas in shadow to eliminate detail and to contrast with the lighter areas.

Pansies

Intense, complementary colours and a full range of values from white to deepest green enhance the simple charm of violas. Soft, low-angled light falling on fading blossoms creates unusual shadows.

PAINTS
Aureolin
Hansa yellow medium
Hooker's green
New gamboge
Phthalo blue
Purple magenta
Sap green
Translucent orange

TOOLS & MATERIALS
Cold-pressed paper,
  300gsm (140lb)
HB pencil
Masquepen
Round brushes,
  Nos. 4, 6, 8
Rigger
White watercolour pencil

TECHNIQUES USED
Graded wash, *p. 20*
Mixing paint in the palette,
  p. 21
Wet-onto-dry, *p. 22*
Wet-into-wet, *p. 22*
Glazing, *p. 23*
Masking to reserve the
  paper, *p. 25*
Masking for details, *p. 25*
Shadows, *p. 28*
Watercolour pencil, *p. 35*

1 Make a detailed line drawing from the photograph. With the Masquepen, apply a thin line of masking fluid along the edges of the purple petals, edges of the brightest leaves and the flower centres.

2 Using a wet-into-wet technique and a No. 8 round brush, apply a wash of aureolin and Hansa yellow medium to yellow portions of the petals and the leaves. Using a No. 6 round brush, paint a graded wash of phthalo blue on the brightest leaf tips, which reflect the blue sky.

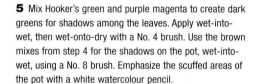

5 Mix Hooker's green and purple magenta to create dark greens for shadows among the leaves. Apply wet-into-wet, then wet-onto-dry with a No. 4 brush. Use the brown mixes from step 4 for the shadows on the pot, wet-into-wet, using a No. 8 brush. Emphasize the scuffed areas of the pot with a white watercolour pencil.

3 Establish the underlying pink glow of the purple petals with two to three graded, wet-into-wet washes of purple magenta applied with a No. 6 brush (inset). With the same technique and brush, lay in graded washes of sap green to the darkest areas of the leaves, stems and sepals.

4 Mix translucent orange and phthalo blue to create a variety of browns. Use these mixes in graded washes, wet-into-wet with a No. 8 brush, to define the pot. Apply the first of four to five glazes of a purple magenta and phthalo blue mix to the purple petals. Remove the masking. Lay in the veins of the petals, wet-onto-dry, with the purple mix and a rigger.

Calla Lilies

The artist was drawn to the extreme value range from white to black, and to the many-hued greens and rose colours in the flowers and leaves.

PAINTS

Aureolin
Cobalt blue
French ultramarine blue
Neutral tint
Phthalo green
Quinacridone burnt scarlet
Quinacridone coral
Quinacridone gold
Quinacridone magenta
Quinacridone rose
Quinacridone violet

TOOLS & MATERIALS

Cold-pressed paper,
   300gsm (140lb)
HB pencil
Masking fluid
Old brush
7.5cm (3in) wash brush
2.5cm (1in) flat brush

Round brushes,
   Nos. 10 and 14
Fritch scrubber, No. 2
Tissues and kitchen towels

TECHNIQUES USED

Flat wash, *p. 20*
Mixing paint in the palette,
   p. 21
Dropping in colour, *p. 21*
Wet-onto-dry, *p. 22*
Wet-into-wet, *p. 22*
Glazing, *p. 23*
Blending, *p. 24*
Lost and found edges,
   p. 24
Masking to reserve the
   paper, *p. 25*
Masking for details, *p. 25*
Softening masked edges,
   p. 25
Shadows, *p. 28*

1 Complete a detailed drawing of the calla lilies using the photograph as your reference. Take special care with the veins in the flower and the leaves. Because they are prominent, the accuracy of your drawing is important. Mask the light and white areas. If you choose to mask the veins, make those lines as thin as possible (inset). Dry thoroughly.

2 Begin glazing the dark background using a mixture of phthalo green and neutral tint using a No. 10 or a No. 14 brush. Keep this mixture on the green side for the first flat wash. To achieve an even wash, turn your painting 180 degrees and tilt it about 45 degrees. This will allow the paint to run down and not jeopardize the flowers with dripping paint. Fill in those spaces between the flowers and leaves where the background shows through.

5 When the painting is dry, remove the masking. Soften the highlights where the sun hits the flowers and leaves. Mix fresh quinacridone puddles, more diluted than before. With a 2.5cm (1in) flat brush, glaze a brighter colour where there are veins, but covering the whole shape to avoid paint lines. Dry and repeat until the veins fade into the body of the flower.

3 In your palette, make creamy puddles of aureolin, cobalt blue, French ultramarine blue, phthalo green, quinacridone gold, magenta and violet, and neutral tint. With these you should be able to mix all the greens you see in the photograph. As you paint the leaves, bear in mind that the leaves in the background will be cooler in temperature (add cobalt blue) and those in the foreground will be warmer (add yellow). In addition, shaded parts of the leaves will be a darker shade of the green you used in the leaf itself (inset).

4 To begin painting the flowers, mix creamy puddles of all the quinacridone colours as well as French ultramarine and cobalt blues. With a thirsty 2.5cm (1in) flat brush, blend the greyed underside of the two left calla lilies with the green of the stem. Paint one flower at a time. Once dry, glaze each of the flowers. Continue with successive glazes until the colours look realistic.

Ranunculus

The artist was drawn to the impact of dark against light, the rich colours and the complementary colour scheme of reds against greens, and yellow against violet.

PAINTS
Alizarin crimson
Burnt sienna
Cadmium orange
Cadmium yellow light
Cerulean blue
New gamboge
Permanent rose
Sap green
Ultramarine blue
Winsor green
Winsor violet

TECHNIQUES USED
Mixing paint in the palette, *p. 21*
Wet-onto-dry, *p. 22*
Wet-into-wet, *p. 22*
Paint light to dark, *p. 23*
Masking to reserve the paper, *p. 25*
Negative painting, *p. 28*

TOOLS & MATERIALS
Cold-pressed paper, 300gsm (140lb)
Transfer paper
Invisible tape
Ballpoint pen
Masking fluid
Old brush
Round brushes, Nos. 3, 7, 10

1 Place a sheet of transfer paper on top of your watercolour paper and lay the enlarged print on top. Tape them together at the top of the block to make sure it stays in place. Using a ballpoint pen, trace over the shapes of the flowers, leaves, stems and shadows to transfer graphite lines from the transfer paper onto the watercolour paper.

2 Use an old brush dipped in masking fluid to mask around the pitcher. When dry, paint the pitcher with ultramarine blue, permanent rose, alizarin crimson, cadmium orange and sap green wet-into-wet so that the colours blend. When the paint is dry, remove the dried masking. Then paint the wooden slatted table with burnt sienna (mixed with violet for the shadows).

3 Outline the petals and centres of the three large flowers with cadmium yellow light. Apply mixtures of cadmium orange, permanent rose and new gamboge to each petal (inset), letting it dry before going on to the next. Paint the other yellow and orange flowers, then paint the flowers' middle sections yellow, adding a dark mixture of burnt sienna and violet to the centre. Paint the first layer of the yellow-green flowers with cadmium yellow light mixed with a touch of cerulean blue.

4 Paint the leaves, stems, buds and little yellow-green flowers using a variety of greens mixed from yellows, blues and sap green. On the first layers of leaves, add a little burnt sienna to neutralize the colour for the greyer greens. Also use a green mixture to add details to the yellow-green flowers you painted in step 3.

5 Make several puddles of the following dark mixtures: Winsor green and alizarin crimson, ultramarine blue and burnt sienna, Winsor green and violet. Load your brush with one and start painting the empty area behind the flowers, switching to another dark puddle as the background colours change. Stay within the dark shapes and paint negatively around lighter shapes.

Peonies and Poppies

The artist was intrigued not only by the beautiful lights against the strong darks, but also by the ruffled shapes and the delicacy of the flower petals against the rough textures of the pots and the wall.

PAINTS

Bismuth yellow
Burnt orange
Cadmium scarlet
Cobalt blue
French ultramarine blue
Opera
Permanent rose
Viridian
Winsor green (blue shade)
Winsor red

TOOLS & MATERIALS

Rough paper,
    300gsm (140lb)
H pencil
Masking fluid
Old brush
Round brushes,
    Nos. 2, 4, 12
7.5cm (3in) hake brush
Coarse salt

TECHNIQUES

Flat wash, *p. 20*
Wet-onto-dry, *p. 22*
Wet-into-wet, *p. 22*
Masking to reserve the
    paper, *p. 25*
Shadows, *p. 28*
Salt, *p. 30*

1 Draw out the flowers in pencil on the watercolour paper. Pay attention to the details – include the ruffles in the peonies, the vines and their buds, as well as the stones and texture in the wall. Indicate the shape of the sundial. Use masking fluid and an old brush to carefully mask only the shapes that fall across the flowers.

2 When the mask is dry, use a No. 12 brush to run a light pink wash over the flowers and indicate their placement around the painting. Once the wash has dried, begin painting the individual flower shapes, using a No. 4 brush and a variety of pinks and reds (inset). When these are dry, turn your attention to the pots. Use burnt orange and French ultramarine blue to produce granulation and a textured effect.

3 Mask the flower shapes and the remaining vines and leaves to protect them from the background wash. Also mask the light parts of the sundial. With a hake brush, run water behind the flowers and around the pots. Paint in the darks with the No. 12 brush then sprinkle with coarse salt for texture (inset). As the dark wash begins to dry, paint shadows to indicate the shapes of the rocks. Make sure all of your shadows are dark enough.

4 When everything is totally dry, remove the mask. Using the No. 4 brush, begin to paint the vines, buds and leaves into the background, using greens and yellows.

5 Move down the painting as you work into the rest of the vines and stems. Adjust the colour and value of the flowers as well. Don't forget to paint in the light areas of the sundial. Use a No. 2 brush to make all of these final adjustments.

Primroses

These primroses form a very complex image – the greatest challenge lies perhaps in replicating the tin pails to give life to the reflections.

PAINTS
Bright pink
Burnt umber
French ultramarine blue
Hooker's green
New gamboge
Rose madder

TECHNIQUES
Mixing paint in the palette, *p. 21*
Dropping in colour, *p. 21*
Wet-into-wet, *p. 22*
Lost and found edges, *p. 24*
Masking for details, *p. 25*

TOOLS & MATERIALS
Cold-pressed paper, 300gsm (140lb)
Mechanical pencil with 5mm HB lead
Masking fluid
Old brush
Round brushes, Nos. 5 or 8 and 10 or 12
Natural sponge

1 Make a detailed pencil drawing on the watercolour paper of the flower to define the light and dark areas. Using masking fluid and an old brush, mask the white edges of the flower petals and the brightest highlights in the metal pails, edges, seams and ridges.

2 Paint the petals of the upper flower in bright pink with a No. 5 or 8 brush. Use the colour in varying intensities to differentiate the petals. Mix a second puddle of rose madder for the left-hand flowers, and a mixture of bright pink and rose madder for the right-hand flowers. Add French ultramarine blue and new gamboge to the last puddle. Apply to the darkest edge of a shadow and draw it towards the lighter area, using water in your brush to blend the outer edge.

5 To the background pots, apply a thin grey mix of burnt umber and French ultramarine blue with a sponge. Paint an uneven wash of burnt umber, rose madder and French ultramarine blue. For the shadows, add French ultramarine blue to the terracotta mixture, applying wet-into-wet and blending to achieve roundness. When dry, remove all masking.

3 Paint the leaves and stems as a single mass in a light shade of Hooker's green. To the Hooker's green, add French ultramarine blue and new gamboge. Use the mix and a No. 5 brush to paint the leaf wrinkles and various shadows that denote the stems and deep shade areas. When dry, apply masking fluid to the outer edge of all painted areas. For the upper pail, using a No. 10 brush, paint a watery mix of French ultramarine blue then, wet-into-wet, add the previous mixtures.

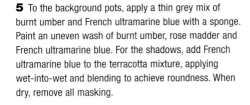

4 Paint the dirt in the pails with burnt umber and French ultramarine blue using a No. 5 brush. For the lower pails, mix French ultramarine blue, rose madder and new gamboge. Using a No. 10 brush, work in sections, wet-into-wet, blending edges as necessary. Add burnt umber for the reflections. Paint the planks with a mixture of the slate colour and then drop in burnt umber, adding detail with a darker shade once dry.

Tulips

This beautiful photograph of wet tulips begs to be painted. Re-creating the water drops is both challenging and fun.

PAINTS
Aureolin
Cobalt blue
Neutral tint
Permanent orange
Phthalo green
Quinacridone coral
Quinacridone magenta
Quinacridone red
Quinacridone rose
Quinacridone violet

TOOLS & MATERIALS
Cold-pressed paper,
  300gsm (140lb)
Mechanical pencil
Masking fluid
Old brush
7.5cm (3in) wash brush
Round brushes,
  Nos. 6 and 10
Fritch scrubber
2.5cm (1in) flat brush
Tissues and kitchen towels
Dremel tool

TECHNIQUES USED
Flat wash, *p. 20*
Mixing paint in the palette,
  p. 21
Dropping in colour, *p. 21*
Wet-onto-dry, *p. 22*
Wet-into-wet, *p. 22*
Glazing, *p. 23*
Lost and found edges,
  p. 24
Masking to reserve the
  paper, *p. 25*
Masking for details, *p. 25*
Softening masked edges,
  p. 25
Shadows, *p. 28*

1 Make a careful drawing from the photograph. Use caution when putting in the water drops. Do not make them too large and do not try to put in all of them. Mask the white edges and the water drops (inset). A tiny dot of masking fluid will suffice for the drops. Practice these on a separate sheet of paper before you mask the drawing.

2 Mix a large cream-consistency puddle each of phthalo green, neutral tint and the quinacridone colours. Begin in the upper left of the painting by wetting the first area to be painted with a No. 10 round brush. Paint in a very dark green (mixing phthalo green and neutral tint), going around the tulips and stems. While the green is wet, paint the flower colour right up against the green. Allow them to touch and blend lightly.

3 Paint the foreground tulips with relatively hard edges using warmer quinacridone mixtures as you move forwards in the picture plane (inset). Also paint the stems with a No. 6 brush and with various green and gold mixtures, brushing cobalt blue in shadows across them. Each time you dip your brush, use a different colour related to the previous one. This adds more dimension to each object in the painting.

4 When all the tulips are completed and dry, remove the masking, using caution not to smear the green into the protected white area. Using a Fritch scrubber, soften all lines left by the masking but not the water drops. Go deeper into some of the petals, dabbing with tissue to avoid unwanted water lines.

5 Make a weak mixture of quinacridone coral and permanent orange. Using a 2.5cm (1in) flat brush, stroke over the droplet areas until they are less spotty. Dry. Under each dot, make a fine shadow with a light blue-grey mixed from the leftover colours in your palette. When dry, use a sharp point or a Dremel tool to put a bright spot of white light in the centre of each droplet.

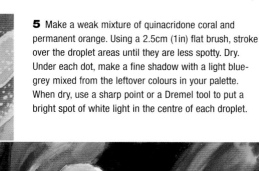

Tiger Lilies

The artistic challenge laid down by this photograph is to make the tiger lilies stand out from the flat green background. The artist added a cleverly chosen colour to do this.

PAINTS
Black
Brilliant cadmium red
Chrome yellow
Cobalt violet
French ultramarine blue
Gamboge
Hansa yellow medium
Quinacridone magenta
Sap green
Turquoise blue

TECHNIQUES
Mixing paint in the palette, *p. 21*
Wet-onto-dry, *p. 22*
Wet-into-wet, *p. 22*
Masking to reserve the paper, *p. 25*

TOOLS & MATERIALS
Cold-pressed paper, 300gsm (140lb)
2B pencil
Masking fluid
Incredible Nib
Round brushes, Nos. 3, 5, 12

1 Draw the flower in pencil on the watercolour paper. Apply masking fluid with the Incredible Nib to any area of the painting that will remain very light or white. For larger areas of white, don't bother applying masking – work around them.

2 Mix sap green, gamboge and turquoise blue in the palette – enough to complete five layers of the green background. Use a No. 12 brush to paint the larger areas and a No. 5 for smaller areas. Keep the paint moving to achieve an even colour. Near the bottom of the painting, apply the turquoise wet-into-wet. Layering wet-onto-dry will ensure an overall balanced colour. Paint the larger areas quickly; make at least four layers of background.

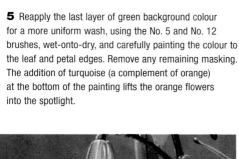

5 Reapply the last layer of green background colour for a more uniform wash, using the No. 5 and No. 12 brushes, wet-onto-dry, and carefully painting the colour to the leaf and petal edges. Remove any remaining masking. The addition of turquoise (a complement of orange) at the bottom of the painting lifts the orange flowers into the spotlight.

3 With the No. 5 brush, paint all the leaves with a combination of sap green and chrome yellow, using both wet-into-wet and wet-onto-dry techniques. Wet-into-wet, apply a mixture of brilliant cadmium red and chrome yellow to areas of the lily petals. Also apply quinacridone magenta where necessary, for deeper colour in the petals. Paint the stems using black and French ultramarine blue. Soften some of the edges of the stems by applying the same paint with a No. 3 brush wet-into-wet.

4 Remove the masking with a pick-up (inset). Reapply the masking fluid only to areas that are to remain white. Paint over the unmasked areas in the stem using a mixture of sap green, turquoise and a small amount of black to create the texture on the stems. Starting in the upper right-hand corner, paint one petal and one leaf at a time with a No. 3 brush, focusing on subtle colour variations within that area.

Fuchsia

It is important that the subject stands away from the background with a three-dimensional effect, and to emphasize the fluorescence of the main flower.

PAINTS
Bright violet
Dioxazine violet
French ultramarine blue
Madder lake
Opera
Orange lake
Permanent rose
Rich green-gold
Sap green
Viridian
Zinc white designers'
  gouache

TOOLS & MATERIALS
Cold-pressed paper,
  300gsm (140lb)
Pencil
Masking fluid
Taper point firm colour
  shaper, No. 0
Flat chisel soft colour
  shaper, No. 2
Natural sponge

Round brushes,
  Nos. 0, 2, 5, 12
Coarse salt

TECHNIQUES
Variegated wash, *p. 20*
Mixing paint on the paper,
  p. 21
Dropping in colour, *p. 21*
Wet-onto-dry, *p. 22*
Wet-into-wet, *p. 22*
Paint light to dark, *p. 23*
Glazing, *p. 23*
Blending, *p. 24*
Lost and found edges,
  p. 24
Masking to reserve the
  paper, *p. 25*
Softening masked edges,
  p. 25
Salt, *p. 30*
Watercolour and gouache,
  p. 32

1 After drawing the image on the watercolour paper with a pencil, mask the flower and leaves with the masking fluid, using the colour shapers (inset). Dry thoroughly.

2 For the variegated wash, apply water to the background with a natural sponge. Using a No. 12 round brush, drop and spread blobs of these colours, fully saturated: sap green, viridian, rich green-gold and dioxazine violet. Take care not to overwork the spreading; you don't want the background to get muddy. Sprinkle coarse salt onto portions of the wet background. When dry, brush all the salt off of the paper, being careful not to disturb the masked areas.

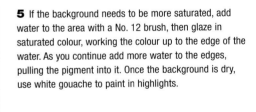

5 If the background needs to be more saturated, add water to the area with a No. 12 brush, then glaze in saturated colour, working the colour up to the edge of the water. As you continue add more water to the edges, pulling the pigment into it. Once the background is dry, use white gouache to paint in highlights.

3 Remove the masking fluid. With a No. 5 brush, moisten each area separately, wet-into-wet. Build colour depth with several glazings, letting each application dry. Lay in the colour, spreading the pigment to the edges. For the top petals, use permanent rose and glaze in madder lake and orange lake. For the bottom petals and sepals, glaze in permanent rose and opera (inset). Use bright violet and French ultramarine blue for shadows. Follow these techniques for the leaves, using the greens, purple and blue.

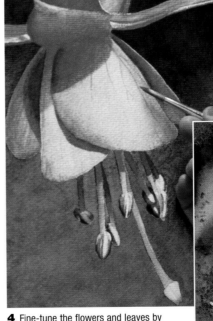

4 Fine-tune the flowers and leaves by glazing using different percentages of saturated colour. For the flowers, glaze many layers of the same colours to build the saturation. To paint in the veins, use a No. 2 or a No. 0 round brush.

Bluebells

Bluebells generally grow in woodlands, so it is important to capture the dappled light found in these shady environments. To achieve this, a palette of cool colours was selected.

PAINTS
Aureolin
Cobalt blue deep
French ultramarine blue
Indigo
Quinacridone gold
Quinacridone magenta
Winsor green

TOOLS & MATERIALS
Hot-pressed paper,
   300gsm (140lb)
HB pencil
Masking fluid
Old brush
Round brushes,
   Nos. 00, 3, 7, 10
Filbert brush

TECHNIQUES
Flat wash, *p. 20*
Mixing paint in the palette,
   p. 21
Mixing paint on the
   paper, *p. 21*
Dropping in colour, *p. 21*
Wet-onto-dry, *p. 22*
Wet-into-wet, *p. 22*
Blending, *p. 24*
Masking to reserve the
   paper, *p. 25*
Softening masked edges,
   p. 25
Adding highlights, *p. 27*
Negative painting, *p. 28*

1 Draw the bluebells and leaves lightly onto the watercolour paper with an HB pencil. They are complex flowers, so put in the basic shapes only. To retain white paper for highlights on some of the leaves and petals, apply masking fluid with an old brush.

2 Using a No. 10 brush and clean water, wet the background area, moving carefully around the flowers. Flood diluted washes of aureolin and Winsor green into the wet areas and move the paper, allowing paint to run between the petals. Section the background into smaller areas if necessary. Let dry.

3 Having set the lightest tonal value, continue painting the negative areas of the background by wetting background areas and dropping in stronger mixes of Winsor green, quinacridone gold, aureolin and indigo for the leaves, adding very light touches of quinacridone magenta with a No. 10 round brush. Use indigo, Winsor green and quinacridone gold to build up the strong darks for the shadiest areas (inset). Use a smaller brush (No. 7) for smaller spaces.

4 Add paint wet-into-wet to the background and soften hard edges. Drop French ultramarine blue into the darks above the lower leaves. Work on the longer leaves and ensure wet areas are not adjacent to one another. With a No. 3 brush, wet individual flowers, charging with cobalt blue deep for the midtones. Dilute quinacridone magenta for the light tones and French ultramarine blue for the darkest.

5 Lift colour with a filbert brush to preserve highlights. Remove masking fluid and soften some of the hard edges with the filbert brush. Using French ultramarine blue and a No. 00 brush, add detail to the petals. Increase the contrast by darkening the flowers and stems that are not growing in dappled light. Blend masked highlights on leaves and add dilute aureolin.

Heliconia

By sketching on location first and then taking many photographs, in this instance the artist challenged herself to try to stay true to the essence of the scene without being a 'slave' to the photograph.

PAINTS
Burnt sienna
Cadmium red light
Cadmium red-purple
Cadmium yellow light
Cobalt blue
Indanthrone blue
Napthamide maroon
Olive green
Permanent rose
Quinacridone gold

Round brushes, Nos. 4–36
Masking tape
Natural sponge
Tissues and kitchen
  towels

TECHNIQUES USED
Variegated wash, *p. 20*
Mixing paint on the
  paper, *p. 21*
Wet-onto-dry, *p. 22*
Wet-into-wet, *p. 22*
Glazing, *p. 23*
Masking to reserve the
  paper, *p. 25*
Adding highlights, *p. 27*

TOOLS & MATERIALS
Cold-pressed paper,
  300gsm (140lb)
2B pencil
Masking fluid
Old brush
Flat brushes, 5cm (2in),
  2.5cm (1in), 1cm (½in)

1 Lightly draw the flower onto the paper using a 2B pencil. Mask the flower and leaf edges to preserve white highlights (inset). Dry the masking thoroughly.

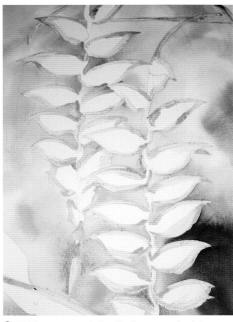

2 Wet the paper, excluding the flowers, and paint a variegated, wet-into-wet wash of cobalt blue, cadmium yellow pale and burnt sienna using a 5cm (2in) flat and No. 36 round brush.

3 When the wash is dry, remove the masking. Paint a wet-into-wet wash in each of the heliconia flowers with a No. 12 and No. 6 round brush. Wet the entire flower and then brush on the cadmium yellow light. Add permanent rose followed by cadmium red light and, in some flowers, cadmium red-purple. Let these mix on the paper (inset). The permanent rose helps the cadmiums to keep their brightness after drying.

4 Paint the leaves and stems using a combination of wet-into-wet and wet-onto-dry techniques. To achieve the sunlit effect, lift the highlights on the blossoms by isolating the shapes with masking tape and removing the colour first by wetting within the shape and then gently rubbing the area lightly with a sponge or tissue. Remove the tape and blot the area with kitchen towels.

5 Use olive green, napthamide maroon and indanthrone blue to create the deep colour on the bottom right. To achieve a glow here, use glazing, highlighting and charging with quinacridone gold and other pigments already found in the painting. Glaze the leaf patterns in the upper left and deepen some of the greens in the stalks. Smooth the petal edges with the 1cm (½in) flat brush and a small amount of water.

Columbines

The artist made few changes to the photograph in this painting, other than to warm up the entire scene by adding more glowing light.

PAINTS
Aureolin
French ultramarine blue
Quinacridone coral
Quinacridone gold
Quinacridone magenta
Quinacridone pink
Quinacridone red
Quinacridone rose
Quinacridone violet

TOOLS & MATERIALS
Cold-pressed paper,
  300gsm (140lb)
HB pencil
Masking fluid
7.5cm (3in) wash brush
Old brush
Coarse salt
2.5cm (1in) flat brush
Round brushes,
  Nos. 6, 10, 14
Tissues

TECHNIQUES USED
Mixing paint in the palette,
  p. 21
Mixing paint on the paper,
  p. 21
Dropping in colour, p. 21
Wet-into-wet, p. 22
Lost and found edges,
  p. 24
Masking to reserve the
  paper, p. 25
Softening masked edges,
  p. 25
Make softened edges
  glow, p. 26
Shadows, p. 28
Pouring paint, p. 29
Salt, p. 30

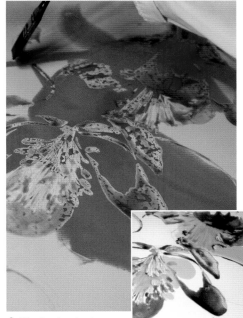

1 After the drawing is completed using an HB pencil, mask all whites, yellows and areas of light. Dry thoroughly. Pour an aureolin cream-like mixture onto the pre-wet sheet of watercolour paper (inset), spreading it around the focal area by tilting the board or brushing lightly with a 7.5cm (3in) wash brush. Repeat with quinacridone red and rose, followed by French ultramarine blue.

2 Sprinkle coarse salt into the still-wet poured washes of the background area for textural interest. Dry the painting on a flat surface. Remove the salt. Pour a second round of colours to intensify selected areas. Do not pour yellow over any area that is already dark; it will not show and could look muddy. Dry again, preferably overnight.

3 Remove the masking and soften the edges. One by one, wet the petals up to the white tip and drop in quinacridone red, coral and pink (inset). Let the photograph be your guide. Separate the overlapping layers of the flower parts, keeping those in the foreground warm and those in the background cool. In case of shadows, use a darker, cooler colour.

4 Paint the stamens in aureolin and quinacridone gold. Add shadows to the yellow with an orange mix of aureolin and quinacridone red. To show the glow coming down behind the flowers from above, paint a golden yellow-orange at the edge of the lowest petals.

5 Once the painting is thoroughly dry, tilt it to a 30-degree angle and paint a wash of clear water down the bottom third of the painting, making soft and lost edges of the lowest petals and anchoring them into their background. Take care to preserve whites by dabbing with tissue.

Snowdrops

These small flowers always appear in a cluster; pay attention to the design of negative shapes as well as the positive ones.

PAINTS
Antwerp blue
Burnt sienna
Cadmium scarlet
Cadmium yellow medium
Cerulean blue
Cobalt blue
French ultramarine blue
New gamboge
Perylene maroon
Rich green-gold
Rose madder genuine

TECHNIQUES
Mixing paint in the palette, *p. 21*
Dropping in colour, *p. 21*
Wet-into-wet, *p. 22*

TOOLS & MATERIALS
Cold-pressed paper,
 300gsm (140lb)
Pencil
7.5cm (3in) hake brush
Soft mop brush
Round brushes,
 Nos. 4, 8, 10
Natural sponge
6mm (¼in) flat brush

1 Make a careful pencil drawing of the photograph on watercolour paper. Block in the major shapes. As you prefer, details can be added now or later.

2 Use a hake brush to wet the paper on both sides until limp. With a soft mop brush, add new gamboge to the stamen areas of the flowers, keeping it away from most areas of purple. Brush Antwerp blue into the background area and let it expand into some of the petal shapes to soften the edges.

3 Make a mixture of transparent and opaque colours (French ultramarine blue, Antwerp blue and new gamboge). With a No. 10 round brush, paint into areas where the green leaves will be, keeping the edges soft and diffused. With a damp sponge, keep the white petals wiped out (inset). The edges will be soft.

4 Begin to add in the warm background with French ultramarine blue, dropping in burnt sienna. Keep the edges soft. Use the blues and yellows to mix a variety of greens, paying close attention to values. Use the dark colours to set off the white petals.

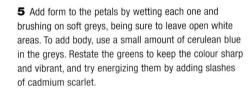

5 Add form to the petals by wetting each one and brushing on soft greys, being sure to leave open white areas. To add body, use a small amount of cerulean blue in the greys. Restate the greens to keep the colour sharp and vibrant, and try energizing them by adding slashes of cadmium scarlet.

Hollyhocks

In designing the painting of hollyhocks, the artist chose to simplify and abstract the background as well as backlight the flowers. A warm palette with fewer blues and greens was used to create a glow about the flowers, and reduce the pull between the red and green complementary colours.

PAINTS
Aureolin
Carbazole violet
Cobalt blue
Hooker's green
Permanent orange
Quinacridone coral
Quinacridone magenta
Quinacridone pink
Quinacridone red
Viridian
Winsor yellow deep

TOOLS & MATERIALS
Cold-pressed paper,
  300gsm (140lb)
HB pencil
Masking fluid
Ruling pen
7.5cm (3in) wash brush

Round brushes,
  Nos. 3, 6, 10
2.5cm (1in) flat brush
Fan brush

TECHNIQUES USED
Mixing paint in the palette,
  p. 21
Dropping in colour, p. 21
Wet-into-wet, p. 22
Glazing, p. 23
Lost and found edges,
  p. 24
Masking for details, p. 25
Shadows, p. 28
Pouring paint, p. 29

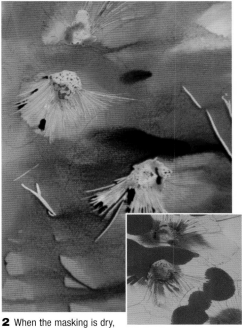

1 Draw the hollyhocks on the paper. Keep the HB pencil lines dark enough to see through several layers of poured pigment. Mask the centre area of each flower. A ruling pen – a traditional graphic design tool for making thin, straight lines with ink – was used to apply the masking to the veins in the petals (inset). A very fine brush or sharpened stick could also be used.

2 When the masking is dry, pour aureolin onto the paper, directing the movement of paint with a 7.5cm (3in) wash brush. While the yellow is wet, pour in red (inset), such as quinacridone coral, quinacridone red and quinacridone magenta. Tip and tilt your board to blend. Pour cobalt blue in selected areas. Continue tilting and tipping the board until the colours look natural. Let the board dry on a flat surface.

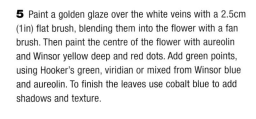

5 Paint a golden glaze over the white veins with a 2.5cm (1in) flat brush, blending them into the flower with a fan brush. Then paint the centre of the flower with aureolin and Winsor yellow deep and red dots. Add green points, using Hooker's green, viridian or mixed from Winsor blue and aureolin. To finish the leaves use cobalt blue to add shadows and texture.

3 Reinforce the glow around the centre of each flower by painting around the centre with Winsor yellow deep and permanent orange. Use a No. 10 round brush to define the petals and whole flowers, keeping in mind that a value difference can be used to separate the front flower from the one behind it. After each colour glaze, allow the paint to dry.

4 Before removing the masking, begin to define the dark areas and shadows of the flower using carbazole violet and working wet-into-wet. As a violet passage is laid down, place a deep quinacridone magenta passage next to it, leaving some lighter red on the petals where the sun comes through. Dry thoroughly and remove the masking.

Crown Imperial

This flower is floating on a turquoise background wash. The juxtaposing colours of cool turquoise and hot orange create a wonderful tension.

PAINTS
Aureolin
Burnt sienna
Cadmium orange
Cobalt teal
Green-gold
Mars yellow
Sepia
Winsor green

TOOLS & MATERIALS
Cold-pressed paper,
   300gsm (140lb)
Pencil
Masking tape
Masking fluid
Small old brush
Round brushes,
   Nos. 2, 8, 12
5cm (2in) wash brush
Craft knife

TECHNIQUES
Graded wash, *p. 20*
Mixing paint in the palette,
   p. 21
Wet-onto-dry, *p. 22*
Wet-into-wet, *p. 22*
Blending, *p. 24*
Masking to reserve the
   paper, *p. 25*
Adding highlights, *p. 27*

1 Draw the flower onto watercolour paper. Tape the edges of the paper with masking tape for a clean border. Mask the flower with masking fluid, applied with a small old brush and masking tape. Seal the masking tape with masking fluid (inset).

2 Wet the paper with clear water. Using the 5cm (2in) wash brush, paint the background with a graded wash beginning with dark cobalt teal at the top and graduating to a lighter blue. When the background is dry, remove all masking. Begin painting the background petals, keeping colours cool towards the back. Paint wet-into-wet using cadmium orange as the base.

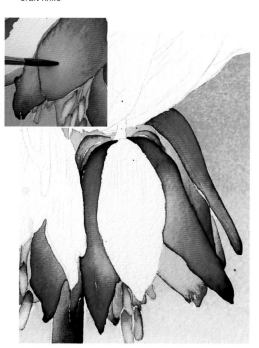

5 Using a craft knife, scratch out small white highlights. Use sepia at the tips of a few leaves to make some more prominent. Outline the leaves to ensure crisp edges.

3 Wet each petal shape and float in aureolin and cadmium orange leaving the centre of the petal light in value to create luminosity (inset). Use light layers of pigment to avoid overworking. Dry between layers. Using a small brush, outline the petals with burnt sienna and sepia.

4 When the petals are complete, paint the leaves one by one with a No. 2 brush. Gradate the wash from a soft yellow near the flower to dark green at the tip using mixtures of yellows, green-gold, Winsor green and sepia. This will keep the values light at the base and retain the glow in the centre of the flower.

Iris

The artist decided to crop the image and focus on the pattern and intensity of colour in the flower head. She created a textured background using the salt spatter technique.

PAINTS
Dioxazine violet
New gamboge
Sap green
Venetian red

TOOLS & MATERIALS
Watercolour board
B or HB pencil
Masking fluid
Old brush
Round brushes,
   Nos. 6 and 10
Dip pen
Tissues
Scrubber
Coarse salt

TECHNIQUES USED
Flat wash, *p. 20*
Mixing paint in the palette,
   p. 21
Dropping in colour, *p. 21*
Wet-onto-dry, *p. 22*
Wet-into-wet, *p. 22*
Masking to reserve the
   paper, *p. 25*
Shadows, *p. 28*
Salt, *p. 30*

1 Draw the flower on the board, then mask out all the highlights with masking fluid and an old brush.

2 Make up a strong mix of dioxazine violet and Venetian red for the dark petals and a more diluted version of the same colours for the lighter ones. Using a No. 10 round brush, work wet-into-wet within the outlines of the petals, dropping touches of the darker mix into the light petals and letting the colours blend.

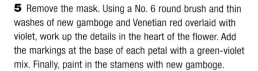

3 Dip a pen into the dark wash and draw in the fine veins of the upper petals (inset). When dry, use a No. 10 round brush to apply further washes of colour to each petal, dabbing with a scrunched-up tissue to give a papery texture. Build up with further washes of the light violet-red mix. For the shadow of the opposite petal, apply a warmer wash with a touch more red and new gamboge. Soften the edges with a scrubber.

4 Wet the background areas, leaving the petals dry, and apply a dark wash of sap green and dioxazine violet. While wet, sprinkle coarse salt into some areas and leave to dry before brushing off. Paint the papery-textured sepals wet-into-wet with all the colours used previously. When dry, dip the pen into the dark green-violet wash used for the background and draw in some linear detail.

5 Remove the mask. Using a No. 6 round brush and thin washes of new gamboge and Venetian red overlaid with violet, work up the details in the heart of the flower. Add the markings at the base of each petal with a green-violet mix. Finally, paint in the stamens with new gamboge.

Hibiscus

The way the light passes through the fragile petals and the translucency of the flower attracted the artist to this image. The flower is darker than the background, which allows the light to appear as if it is streaming through.

PAINTS
Alizarin crimson
Aureolin
Bismuth yellow
Cobalt blue
French ultramarine blue
Opera
Permanent rose
Quinacridone gold
Spring green
Winsor green-blue shade

TOOLS & MATERIALS
Cold-pressed paper,
   300gsm (140lb)
H pencil
Masquepen
Round brushes,
   Nos. 4, 10, 12
7.5cm (3in) hake brush

Stiff-bristled brush, No. 5
Masking fluid
Old brush

TECHNIQUES USED
Wet-onto-dry, *p. 22*
Wet-into-wet, *p. 22*
Masking to reserve the
   paper, *p. 25*
Softening masked edges,
   p. 25

1 Draw the image in H pencil, noticing that the placement of the image causes the form of the flower to touch the edges of the paper on three sides. The top-right petal creates an unusual line.

2 Identify the highlights and lightest parts of the image. Carefully apply the mask to protect these light elements. Initially, masking the raindrops allows for the option to retain them or paint them out at a later stage.

5 Using a 7.5cm (3in) hake brush, apply water over the entire sheet. Add colour on the background using a No. 10 sable brush. Echo the colours of the flower. While still wet, take the stiff-bristled brush and spritz some flecks of permanent rose. When all is dry, remove the mask from the flower. Use a No. 4 brush for fine details and to add the stamen in the centre.

3 Apply initial washes of aureolin onto dry paper with a No. 12 round brush. Switching to a No. 10 brush, drop in light mixtures of cobalt blue and French ultramarine blue to the petal shadows. On sunlit petal tips, paint some light quinacridone gold. Use opera and permanent rose to paint the pink centre, gently drawing colours out into the petal veins (inset).

4 Once the painting is completely dry, remove the mask and soften the edges with a stiff-bristled brush and a little water. Let it dry completely and then, using an old brush, mask the entire shape of the flower. White masking fluid allows the image to show through while protecting it from the paint you will apply around it.

Passion Flowers

A composition featuring two main subjects is a challenge. The artist decided to crop the photograph and alter the background to emphasize a diagonal composition with light coming from the upper left.

PAINTS
Aureolin
Cobalt blue
Indanthrone blue
Nickel azo
Perylene scarlet
Quinacridone magenta
Quinacridone sienna
Ultramarine turquoise

TECHNIQUES
Flat wash, *p. 20*
Mixing paint in the palette,
    p. 21
Wet-onto-dry, *p. 22*
Wet-into-wet, *p. 22*
Glazing, *p. 23*

TOOLS & MATERIALS
Cold-pressed paper,
    300gsm (140lb)
H pencil
Large wash brush
2.5cm (1in) flat brush
Round brush, No. 6

1 Make a careful drawing of the photograph onto the watercolour paper using an H pencil. There is a great deal of detail at the centre of this flower that should be addressed in the drawing if the painting is to reflect it accurately.

2 Wet the paper with a large wash brush. Use the same brush to paint a wash of aureolin to cover the entire painting, letting it dry completely before proceeding. This will give the painting a general warmth, even under the cooler background colours.

3 Paint in the main coloured shapes, still using the wash brush and using nickel azo as an underlayer. (This area will later be glazed with blues to achieve greens.) Next, with various reds and blues, paint the petals, sepals and radial filaments. Emphasize the colour variations formed by the light and shadows. Stay loosely controlled by using a 2.5cm (1in) flat brush. Mix a pale lavender from cobalt blue and quinacridone magenta for the gestured filaments, and paint with a No. 6 round brush.

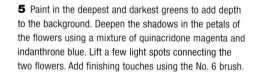

4 Using mostly cobalt blue, glaze over the underlying nickel azo passages in the background. Leave some unpainted areas to connect to the lights throughout the painting. When dry, add some darker mixed greens of ultramarine turquoise and quinacridone sienna. Using quinacridone magenta in varying mixes with indanthrone blue and cobalt blue, paint the filaments with the No. 6 brush (inset).

5 Paint in the deepest and darkest greens to add depth to the background. Deepen the shadows in the petals of the flowers using a mixture of quinacridone magenta and indanthrone blue. Lift a few light spots connecting the two flowers. Add finishing touches using the No. 6 brush.

Blue Thistles

The artist chose to follow the photograph closely, adding more light only in the centre to increase the backlighting effect.

PAINTS
Carbazole violet
Cobalt blue
Cobalt green
Cobalt turquoise
Cobalt turquoise light
Indanthrone blue
Mineral violet
Phthalo turquoise
Phthalo yellow-green
Ultramarine turquoise

TOOLS & MATERIALS
Hot-pressed paper,
　638gsm (300lb)
Pencil
Masking fluid
Old brush
7.5cm (3in) wash brush
Coarse salt
Fritch scrubber, No. 2
Tissues
2.5cm (1in) flat brush

Large round mop brush
Round brushes,
　Nos. 6, 10, 14

TECHNIQUES USED
Dropping in colour, *p. 21*
Wet-onto-dry, *p. 22*
Lost and found edges,
　p. 24
Masking to reserve the
　paper, *p. 25*
Masking for details, *p. 25*
Softening masked edges,
　p. 25
Salt, *p. 30*
Throwing paint, *p. 30*

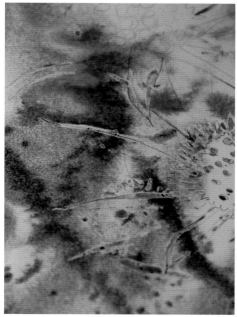

1 Make a detailed drawing from the photograph, being sure to mark a spot of light for masking. Using masking fluid and an old brush, mask any areas of white you would like to preserve, including light flower details, light flares in the photograph and sunlit edges of the petals. Leave to dry completely.

2 Wet the paper on both sides with a 7.5cm (3in) wash brush, so it buckles less during painting. With the surface still shiny, use the wash brush to apply large swatches of cobalt green and turquoise, avoiding the centre light area and the backlit area behind the thistles. Spatter or throw mineral violet, cobalt blue and cobalt turquoise for further textural effects.

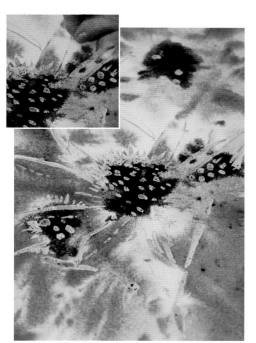

5 Finish the flowers by painting the centres and petals wet-into-wet using cobalt and indanthrone blues (inset). Let the paint blend. Dab on mineral violet at the top of the flower centre, and carbazole violet and indanthrone blue in the shadow. For the in-focus flower use harder edges.

3 While the paper is still wet, paint the centre of the flowers with mineral violet and carbazole violet. When the colour no longer pools but is still wet, drop grains of coarse salt into the violet at the centre of each flower (inset). Dry overnight.

4 Remove all masking and gently scrape away any salt grains. Using a No. 2 Fritch scrubber, soften all edges. This paper is soft, so do not scrub too hard but use plenty of water, dabbing with tissue as you go along.

Rhododendron

The velvety surface of hot-pressed paper is perfect for delicately blended shadows and the detailed edges of petals. The ruffles and frills of the flowers are a counterpoint to the thick, smooth-edged leaves.

PAINTS
Hooker's green
New gamboge
Phthalo blue
Purple magenta
Pyrrole orange
Sap green
Translucent orange

TOOLS & MATERIALS
Hot-pressed paper,
    300gsm (140lb)
HB pencil
Masking fluid
Old brush
Round brushes,
    Nos. 4, 6, 8, 10
Scrubber
Tissues

TECHNIQUES
Flat wash, *p. 20*
Mixing paint in the palette,
    p. 21
Wet-onto-dry, *p. 22*
Wet-into-wet, *p. 22*
Glazing, *p. 23*
Blending, *p. 24*
Masking to reserve the
    paper, *p. 25*
Shadows, *p. 28*

1 Make a detailed drawing of the photograph on the watercolour paper in pencil. Apply a thin line of masking fluid with an old brush along the outside edges of all the petals of the main flower heads and the stamens. Let dry completely before applying paint.

2 Mix phthalo blue and purple magenta and apply in light washes, wet-into-wet, with No. 6 and No. 8 brushes. Make several mixes ranging from cool blue to warm purple to establish the shadow patterns on the petals and the main leaves. Soften all edges with a damp scrubber and blot with a tissue.

5 Apply new gamboge, purple magenta and pyrrole orange wet-into-wet to the background with a No. 8 brush. Use the green mixes from step 4 and a muted mix of purple magenta and Hooker's green to deepen the background wet-onto-dry. Use pyrrole orange wet-into-wet with a No. 6 brush in the flower centres. Mix translucent orange and phthalo blue and apply to the flower centres in a dotted pattern with a No. 4 brush.

3 Using a wet-into-wet technique, establish the underlying pink in the flower centres with purple magenta and a No. 8 brush (inset). Glaze several layers, allowing the paint to dry between each. Soften and feather all the edges, especially along the lines of masking fluid.

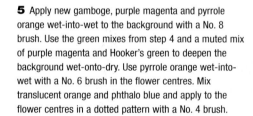

4 Use new gamboge in a wet-into-wet wash with a No. 8 brush as an underlay on the leaves (inset). A glow will result when sap green and Hooker's green, mixed with a touch of purple magenta, are glazed over the top. Apply the greens with No. 6 and No. 8 brushes. Remove the masking.

Snapdragon

The artist was drawn to the swirling, brilliant red shapes of each individual snapdragon flower. The opportunity to use beautiful and active reds against a complementary background of variegated greens is always exciting.

PAINTS

Alizarin crimson
Bismuth yellow
Cadmium scarlet
Cadmium yellow
Cobalt blue
French ultramarine blue
Permanent rose
Winsor green (blue shade)
Winsor red

TECHNIQUES

Mixing paint in the palette, *p. 21*
Mixing paint on the paper, *p. 21*
Dropping in colour, *p. 21*
Wet-onto-dry, *p. 22*
Wet-into-wet, *p. 22*
Masking to reserve the paper, *p. 25*
Masking for details, *p. 25*

TOOLS & MATERIALS

Rough watercolour paper, 300gsm (140lb)
H pencil
Masking fluid
Old brush
7.5cm (3in) hake brush
Round brushes, Nos. 4 and 12

1 Make a careful drawing, with pencil on watercolour paper, of the primary snapdragon stalk. Add an additional flower shape at the bottom left to improve the design. (Without the addition of this flower, the stalk would appear top-heavy and wobbly.) The bottom edge should feel solid to avoid creating tension that would draw the eye out of the painting. Lightly sketch in the background image on the left.

2 Precisely mask off the primary snapdragon stalk. Pay attention to the 'holes' that separate the individual blossoms and mask around them. Dry the masking before beginning to paint.

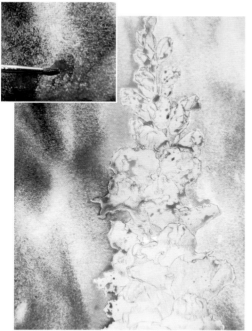

3 With a 7.5cm (3in) hake brush, apply water over the entire painting. Paint strokes of colour with a No. 12 round brush, using bismuth yellow, cadmium yellow, cobalt blue and French ultramarine blue, allowing the colours to mix on the paper to create greens. When all is dry, remove the mask. Lightly re-wet the area of the background image and, using a No. 12 brush, drop in a mixture of Winsor green and alizarin crimson for the rich darks and permanent rose to 'cool' the background buds (inset).

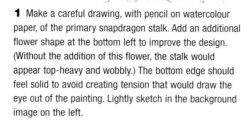

4 Paint the main flowers one by one (inset). Using a No. 4 round brush, build your image with a variety of reds: Winsor red, cadmium scarlet and alizarin crimson. Use bismuth yellow and cadmium yellow for the centres. A mixture of alizarin crimson and French ultramarine blue will give you a nice dark where required.

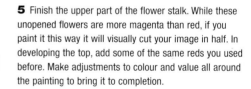

5 Finish the upper part of the flower stalk. While these unopened flowers are more magenta than red, if you paint it this way it will visually cut your image in half. In developing the top, add some of the same reds you used before. Make adjustments to colour and value all around the painting to bring it to completion.

Blue Poppies

The subject here stands away from the background with a three-dimensional effect, with the blue colours emphasized in the main flowers.

PAINTS
Aureolin
Cerulean blue
Cinereous blue
Indigo
Peacock blue
Phthalo blue
Prussian blue
Rich green-gold
Sap green
Viridian
Zinc white designers' gouache

Round brushes,
    Nos. 2, 4, 5, 12
Coarse salt

TECHNIQUES
Mixing paint on the paper,
    p. 21
Dropping in colour, p. 21
Wet-onto-dry, p. 22
Wet-into-wet, p. 22
Paint light to dark, p. 23
Glazing, p. 23
Blending, p. 24
Lost and found edges,
    p. 24
Masking to reserve the
    paper, p. 25
Softening masked edges,
    p. 25
Shadows, p. 28
Salt, p. 30
Watercolour and gouache,
    p. 32

TOOLS & MATERIALS
Cold-pressed paper,
    300gsm (140lb)
2H or HB pencil
Masking fluid
Taper point firm colour
    shaper, No. 0
Flat chisel soft colour
    shaper, No. 2
Natural sponge

1 Draw the image out on watercolour paper in pencil, and mask the flower and leaves with the masking fluid (inset), using the colour shapers. Apply water to the background with a natural sponge.

2 Using a No. 12 round brush, drop in phthalo blue, Prussian blue, indigo, cinereous blue, sap green, rich green-gold and aureolin. Do not overwork, otherwise the paint will get muddy. Sprinkle coarse salt onto portions of the wet background along with drops of water over already saturated areas to produce 'blooms' in the colour. When dry, brush all the salt off the paper, taking care not to disturb the masked areas.

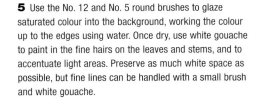

5 Use the No. 12 and No. 5 round brushes to glaze saturated colour into the background, working the colour up to the edges using water. Once dry, use white gouache to paint in the fine hairs on the leaves and stems, and to accentuate light areas. Preserve as much white space as possible, but fine lines can be handled with a small brush and white gouache.

3 Using a No. 5 brush, moisten each petal with water and add colour wet-into-wet. With the No. 4 and No. 2 brushes, spread the pigment to the edges. Build the saturation with several glazes, letting each application dry before applying the next. For the petals, use phthalo blue, cinereous blue and indigo, the last colour on the petals for the deepest shadows (inset).

4 Moisten each leaf area and add sap green, rich green-gold, viridian, aureolin and indigo wet-into-wet with a No. 4 brush. Build the saturation with several glazes, letting each application dry. Fine-tune the flowers and leaves by glazing with different percentages of saturated colour. The flowers need to be highly saturated.

Magnolia Blossom

The artist was drawn to the soft, pillow-like quality of these blossoms.

PAINTS
Aureolin
Cobalt blue
French ultramarine blue
Phthalo blue
Quinacridone coral
Quinacridone magenta
Quinacridone pink
Quinacridone red
Quinacridone rose
Quinacridone violet

TECHNIQUES USED
Flat wash, *p. 20*
Mixing paint in the palette, *p. 21*
Dropping in colour, *p. 21*
Wet-onto-dry, *p. 22*
Wet-into-wet, *p. 22*
Glazing, *p. 23*
Lost and found edges, *p. 24*
Masking to reserve the paper, *p. 25*
Softening masked edges, *p. 25*

TOOLS & MATERIALS
Cold-pressed paper, 300gms (140lb)
Mechanical pencil
Masquepen
Tissues and kitchen towels
7.5cm (3in) wash brush
1.5cm (1in) flat brush
Round brushes, Nos. 6, 10, 14
Liner
Fritch scrubber

1 Draw a detailed sketch from the photograph. Mask all the in-focus white flower tips (inset). Wet your paper on both sides and then blot away any standing water so the paper is damp.

2 With a wide wash brush, paint on cobalt blue diluted to the strength of tea – dark enough to look blue but very transparent. Repeat if the blue is too weak. While the blue is still wet, drop in a slightly stronger mixture of quinacridone pink. Let the colours mingle. Leave some blue areas. You should have a soft background when the paper is dry.

3 To paint the branches, mix a warm grey from aureolin, quinacridone rose and French ultramarine blue. With a No. 10 brush, wet a line of branch and drop this mixture into the wet stream. Move along the branches and twigs until all are painted and dried. Indicate colour irregularities and shadows in the branches with a slightly darker mixture (inset). Dry the branches. From mixtures of aureolin, phthalo blue (very little) and a drop of quinacridone red, mix two or three greens and paint the small leaves.

4 Mix three or four cream-consistency puddles of the quinacridone colours. Work your way through the blossoms, noting that the colours become more intense towards the foreground. Each time you dip your brush for a particular blossom, dip it in a different mixture of red so you have variety. Note where the shadows are and touch in cobalt blue. Dry.

5 Remove all the masking. Using a Fritch scrubber, wet the line between the rose and white, and move and blend the paint, filling out the volume and depth of each blossom (inset). Dab with tissue where necessary to recover the white.

Lilies of the Nile

The artist was challenged by the need to simplify the complex flower pattern while staying true to the form of these sunny agapanthus.

PAINTS

Alizarin crimson
Bismuth yellow
Burnt orange
Cobalt blue
French ultramarine blue
Permanent rose
Winsor green (blue shade)

TECHNIQUES

Mixing paint in the palette, *p. 21*
Mixing paint on the paper, *p. 21*
Wet-onto-dry, *p. 22*
Wet-into-wet, *p. 22*
Masking, *p. 25*

TOOLS & MATERIALS

Cold-pressed paper,
    300gsm (140lb)
H pencil
Round brushes,
    Nos. 4 and 12
Masquepen
7.5cm (3in) hake brush

1 With a pencil, draw the general shapes of the flowers and leaves onto the watercolour paper. Draw the individual flower shapes as best you can. There is an area of confusion in the upper right portion of the top flower. Don't worry about this yet.

2 Take a No. 4 round brush and begin to paint the individual flowers using mixtures of alizarin crimson, permanent rose, cobalt blue and French ultramarine blue. When you get to the upper right area on the top flower, pick out complete flower shapes one by one as you work your way around. Don't try to paint everything that is there — edit! Work at making sense of the area.

3 When dry, use a Masquepen to mask to the entire area of the foreground flowers. Once this has dried completely you will see how well the design sits on the paper. If you want to add a flower or two, simply 'paint' these new shapes using the Masquepen (inset).

4 Using a hake brush, wet the entire painting with clean water. Begin to paint in the darks with a No. 12 brush. When painting this background wash, the idea is to vary the colour across the paper. Create bands of dark blue, alizarin crimson and dark greens, allowing them to mix and blend slightly (inset). Work to produce a granulating texture.

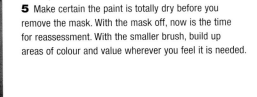

5 Make certain the paint is totally dry before you remove the mask. With the mask off, now is the time for reassessment. With the smaller brush, build up areas of colour and value wherever you feel it is needed.

Cyclamen

It is challenging to unify several busy elements into a good composition. Defining the leaf shapes and surface patterns with negative painting is like working a puzzle.

PAINTS

Hansa yellow medium
Hooker's green
Phthalo blue
Purple magenta
Quinacridone red

TOOLS & MATERIALS

Cold-pressed paper,
   300gsm (140lb)
HB pencil
Masking fluid
Old brush
Round brushes,
   Nos. 4, 6, 8
Scrubber
Tissues

TECHNIQUES

Mixing paint in the palette,
   p. 21
Wet-onto-dry, *p. 22*
Wet-into-wet, *p. 22*
Glazing, *p. 23*
Blending, *p. 24*
Masking to reserve the
   paper, *p. 25*
Softening masked edges,
   p. 25
Shadows, *p. 28*
Negative painting, *p. 28*

1 Draw the design in pencil on the watercolour paper. Apply a thin line of masking fluid using an old brush along the outside edge of each petal and the leaves in the foreground. Let dry completely before applying paint.

2 With a No. 8 brush, apply phthalo blue wet-into-wet to the background leaves and most of the foreground leaves. Use Hansa yellow medium in the bright, warm areas of the foreground leaves. Apply a mix of phthalo blue and purple magenta with a No. 6 brush to the shadowed petal areas.

3 Mix Hooker's green and purple magenta, and apply wet-into-wet with a No. 8 brush to the shadowed leaf areas. For the darkest shadows, use two or three glazes with a negative painting technique. Soften edges with a damp scrubber, especially where paint builds up along the lines of masking fluid. Blot with tissue.

4 With a No. 6 brush and the previous green mix, use negative painting to define the leaf splotches and veins (inset). Working wet-into-wet, use purple magenta alone and with phthalo blue on the petals. Remove the masking and soften the edges with a damp scrubber. Dry-brush quinacridone red with a No. 6 brush on the foreground petals.

5 Mix quinacridone red and Hooker's green, and apply wet-onto-dry to the stems. Enhance bright leaf areas with a thin glaze of Hansa yellow medium. Create loose, blurry background flowers, wet-into-wet with a No. 6 brush. Bring pink to the foreground with glazes of purple magenta along the edges of a few leaves. Push the value range of the shadows with wet-onto-dry glazes of the previously mixed dark greens and reds.

Peonies

The artist made several alterations to the photograph, the most significant of which was to sharpen the focus on the right-hand white peony and lighten the background in that area, giving weight and balance to the composition.

PAINTS

Aureolin
Cobalt blue
Phthalo blue
Quinacridone coral
Quinacridone
 magenta
Quinacridone pink
Quinacridone red
Quinacridone rose
Quinacridone violet
Winsor yellow deep

TOOLS & MATERIALS

Cold-pressed paper,
 300gsm (140lb)
HB pencil
Masking fluid
Old brush
7.5cm (3in)
 wash brush
Spray bottle
Fritch scrubber
Tissues
Round brushes,
 Nos. 6, 10, 14
2.5cm (1in)
 flat brush
Dremel tool

TECHNIQUES USED

Mixing paint in the
 palette, p. 21
Dropping in colour,
 p. 21
Wet-into-wet, p. 22
Lost and found
 edges, p. 24
Masking to reserve
 the paper, p. 25
Softening masked
 edges, p. 25
Adding highlights,
 p. 27
Shadows, p. 28
Pouring paint, p. 29
Spritz, p. 30

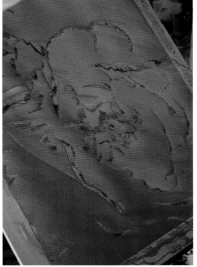

1 Draw the flower with an HB pencil, so that the lines can be rubbed out. Mask all whites, yellows and spots of light (above). Mix aureolin yellow, quinacridone red and phthalo blue each to the consistency of cream, ready for pouring. Wet the paper but leave no standing water.

2 Pour the yellow in the centre of the flowers. Spread with a 7.5cm (3in) wash brush. Repeat with quinacridone red and phthalo blue. After each pouring, tilt and spritz the painting so the paint runs freely. Keep taped edges wiped to prevent backruns. Dry the painting on a flat surface. If the colours are too weak, repeat this process.

3 Remove the masking and soften all the edges where paint meets white paper with a Fritch scrubber (inset). Use plenty of water and dab with tissue. This is a critical step in pouring colour over masking because of the hard lines left when you remove the masking. When softening the lines, use the paint you remove to blend colour into the white area, creating a soft transition.

4 Looking at the photograph, place shadows in the deep attachments of the petals as well as the background. The colour of the shadows should change slightly with the location of the petal. The deepest shadow colours are quinacridone violet mixed with a little phthalo blue. In the brighter areas, eliminate the blue and use only the deeper-coloured quinacridone colours. Wet the area close to the white edge, dip your brush in paint, and paint from the centre of the flower into the wet. Let it blend then dry.

5 Using a No. 10 or 14 round brush dipped in puddles of cobalt blue, Winsor yellow deep and quinacridone coral, paint the shadows in the white peony. Begin your stroke at the deepest area and pull the paint outwards into the light. Blend with clear water in a damp 2.5cm (1in) flat brush. In the tighter areas use a No. 6 round. Using phthalo blue and quinacridone violet, deepen the darkest areas on the left side of the background.

6 When all the darks have dried, carefully and lightly run a Dremel tool along the edge of the petal, making a clean, white, uneven line. Carefully pick away some highlights along the sunlit edges. Due to the yellow under-wash, the finished painting has a warm, sunlit feeling.

Protea

The artist was concerned with capturing the detail of the numerous petals while keeping their overall shape and form. The background needed to be simplified to prevent a cluttered image.

PAINTS

Alizarin crimson
  permanent
Antwerp blue
Aureolin
Cadmium scarlet
Cobalt blue
French ultramarine
  blue
New gamboge
Quinacridone gold
Quinacridone
  magenta
Rose madder
  genuine
Vermilion

TOOLS & MATERIALS

Cold-pressed paper,
  300gsm (140lb)
Transfer paper
Pencil
7.5cm (3in) hake
  brush
Large soft mop
  brush
Round brushes,
  Nos. 4, 8, 10
6mm (¼in) flat
  brush
Natural sponge
Aquacover natural
  white liquid
  watercolour paper

TECHNIQUES USED

Mixing paint in the
  palette, p. 21
Wet-into-wet, p. 22
Glazing, p. 23
Adding highlights,
  p. 27
Negative painting,
  p. 28
Pouring paint, p. 29

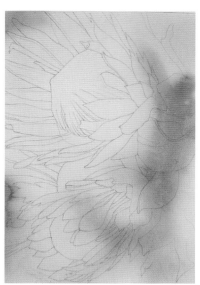

1 On a piece of transfer paper taped over the photograph, draw a grid in pencil. Make a duplicate, proportional grid on a piece of transfer paper taped to the watercolour paper. On each square of the watercolour tracing, draw the detail in the corresponding square of the photograph. Tape the transfer paper to the watercolour paper so that your hand can slide underneath it (inset). With your pencil, follow the lines that you can see through the transparency of the paper.

2 Wet the paper thoroughly with a hake brush. With a large mop brush, add new gamboge to the light areas and Antwerp blue to shadow areas, leaving some areas open. Gently roll the paint on the damp paper to diffuse the colours, still leaving open areas that should be white or very light. Dry.

3 Prepare a mixture of opaque and transparent red pigments, such as cadmium scarlet and vermilion. Pour or brush the mixture into areas that will be warm red. Avoid the cool red/white areas but use some of the mixture in parts of the background for balance. Gently tilt the paper to guide the mixture and diffuse the colours. Most of the paper should be left open. Use a damp sea sponge to wipe out any of the colour that gets into unwanted places.

4 Define the image by painting the negative spaces around it (inset). Use some of your darkest values. Use a variety of reds in the petals of the left flower. The underpainting will preserve the warmth. Use rose tones for the flower on the right. Modify the colour of both flowers with colour of the other for unity.

5 Continue working throughout the image. Complete the background last, keeping it simple and the edges of the shapes diffused. Use a 6mm (¼in) flat brush to lift out the white edges of the petals. If necessary, use Aquacover sparingly in some places if the value of the edges are still too close to the background.

6 The finished painting shows the tropical richness of the protea through the variation of warm and cool reds. The orange underpainting created a path through the painting, unifying the various small shapes of the petals with the background.

Love in the Mist

The beauty of this flower is heightened by the juxtaposition of the delicate petals and the finely cut leaves (bracts).

PAINTS
Aureolin
Cobalt teal
French ultramarine blue
Green (yellow shade)
Green-gold
Quinacridone burnt orange
Quinacridone magenta
Scheveningen blue light
Sepia
Turquoise blue deep
Winsor green

TOOLS & MATERIALS
Cold-pressed paper, 300gsm (140lb)
Pencil
Masking fluid
Old brush
Round brushes, Nos. 1, 8, 14
Craft knife
Ruby cellophane value screen

TECHNIQUES USED
Variegated wash, *p. 20*
Mixing paint in the palette, *p. 21*
Dropping in colour, *p. 21*
Wet-onto-dry, *p. 22*
Wet-into-wet, *p. 22*
Glazing, *p. 23*
Masking for details, *p. 25*
Adding highlights, *p. 27*

1 Make a detailed drawing of the photograph. The stamens form a very complex cluster – some simplification may be necessary to avoid a cluttered look. However, stay true to the design of the flower. Carefully cover the fine leaves and stamens with masking fluid. Dry the masking fluid completely before starting your washes.

2 Mix puddles of aureolin, quinacridone burnt orange, green (yellow shade) and sepia. Wet the background of the painting surrounding the blossom with clear water. Using a No. 14 round brush, drop in colour from the puddles, keeping the lighter areas above the flower (inset). Dry thoroughly. Remove the mask from the fine leaves and paint with lighter value washes of the background colours.

3 With either a No. 14 or No. 8 round brush, paint the petals of the flower from background to foreground using French ultramarine blue, turquoise blue deep, cobalt teal and Scheveningen blue light. Then with a No.1 brush, paint French ultramarine blue around the outside of the petals to make a crisp edge. Vary the line or make it wet-into-wet to avoid an outlined look.

4 Remove the mask from the stamens and paint them with Winsor green, quinacridone magenta, French ultramarine blue and aureolin. Next, use a small craft knife to scratch out and clarify the whites around the centre of the flower – small points of light and the light between the stamens. These crisp whites add more sparkle and life to the flower.

5 Check the values of the painting with a ruby cellophane value screen (inset). This screen shuts out colour and allows you to view only the grey-scale value of the work. Compare it with the value of the photograph to check that the darks are dark enough. If not, you can change the value by adding transparent glazes to the area to be darkened. Be sure to dry the area between glazes.

6 You have now called out the most compelling aspects of the photograph for attention: composition and detail. By adding backlight and using only the fringe colours of the petals, the flower is set apart from its background and made to glow, without losing the integrity of the photograph itself.

Gerbera Daisy

The petals of this flower are a mix of well-defined and very unstructured shapes that are difficult to replicate and can best be represented by suggestion only.

PAINTS

Brilliant pink
Crimson lake
French ultramarine blue
Quinacridone rose
Sap green

TOOLS & MATERIALS

Cold-pressed paper, 300gsm (140lb)
Mechanical pencil, 5 mm HB lead
Round brushes, Nos. 5 or 6 and 10 or 12

TECHNIQUES USED

Dropping in colour, p. 21
Mixing paint in the palette, p. 21
Wet-into-wet, p. 22
Paint light to dark, p. 23
Lost and found edges, p. 24

1 Make a detailed drawing of the flower to define the light and dark areas. Don't concern yourself with the background since it will be painted last.

2 Wet the upper half of the flower with clear water. Using brilliant pink, slightly thinned, drop the colour onto the paper and coax it around with a No. 10 or 12 round brush to approximate the amorphous shapes of the upper petals. As the paper dries, the colour will begin to form hard edges. Stop adding the colour. If you are not done, you can wait until the paper is totally dry, then rewet it and finish adding the colour. Once dry, you may wish to erase the pencil lines in the painted area to lighten them.

3 Still using brilliant pink, paint all the lower petals with strokes emanating at the centre of the flower and drawing out towards the tip of each petal. When dry, reduce pencil lines by erasing. With a No. 5 or 6 round brush and using quinacridone rose, begin working into the areas of shadow and use stronger colour in the upper petals, gently outlining the shapes. Then, with a brush moderately wet with clear water, draw away the edge of the wet paint to form a soft edge (inset).

4 With a strong mix of quinacridone rose, begin shading each of the large power petals, starting at the centre of the flower and drawing out towards the tip. Where the strong colour is to end (based on your drawing), use a clean, moderately wet brush and draw the edge of the quinacridone gently to fade out over the previously painted brilliant pink. Using crimson lake and a small round brush, apply similar techniques to deepen the shadow areas, primarily in the centre portion of the flower and the lower petals.

5 The background is a formless, indistinct swirl of colours. In your palette, mix puddles of sap green and French ultramarine blue and the three 'pink' colours. Wet the top half of the background with clear water, being careful to outline the flower petals. Drop the colours in wet-into-wet, allowing them to blend and merge on the paper. Work from the lightest colours to the darkest.

6 The lower background is executed similarly with more emphasis on the darker shades. When dry, paint the stem loosely. The final painting draws the viewer by the subtle flow from the front detail of the flower petals to the swirling background.

Parrot Tulips

The first glazes, used as an underwash, establish the patterns of dark values in the petals. The rich red hues retain a vivid glow when brushed over the shadows.

PAINTS

Aureolin
Permanent alizarin
  crimson
Phthalo blue
Phthalo green
Pyrrole orange
Sap green
Scarlet red

TOOLS & MATERIALS

Cold-pressed paper,
  300gsm (140lb)
HB pencil
Masking fluid
Old brush
Round brushes,
  Nos. 4, 6, 8
Scrubber
Tissues

TECHNIQUES

Graded wash, p. 20
Variegated wash,
  p. 20
Mixing paint in the
  palette, p. 21
Wet-onto-dry, p. 22
Wet-into-wet, p. 22
Glazing, p. 23
Blending, p. 24
Masking to reserve
  the paper, p. 25
Softening masked
  edges, p. 25
Shadows, p. 28

1 Draw the design onto the watercolour paper in pencil. Apply a thin line of masking fluid over the pencil lines along the outside edges of all the petals, stems and the vase. The pencil lines can be erased later when the masking fluid is removed. Let dry before applying any paint.

2 Mix phthalo green and scarlet red to make warm greys with a reddish tinge. Using a wet-into-wet technique and a No. 6 brush, apply graded washes of grey in all the shadowed areas of the petals. Let dry between washes. Develop the stems wet-into-wet with sap green.

3 With scarlet red and a No. 6 brush, apply graded washes wet-into-wet in the solid red areas. Use a wet-onto-dry technique and scarlet red to define the streaks and toothed edges of the petals (inset). Soften the edges of the dry-brushed paint with a damp brush.

4 Mix phthalo blue and phthalo green and apply wet-into-wet with a No. 8 brush to lay in the first variegated background wash (inset). Strengthen the red in the petals with additional glazes of scarlet red and permanent alizarin crimson.

5 Remove the masking fluid. Soften the hard edges with a damp scrubber and blot with tissue. Mix a touch of phthalo blue and phthalo green to permanent alizarin crimson, and apply wet-onto-dry with a No. 6 brush for deep reds in the petals.

6 Use pyrrole orange wet-onto-dry with a No. 6 brush over the brightest reds in the foreground petals. Build rich colour throughout the painting with additional glazes. Paint a dab of aureolin, then mix phthalo green and permanent alizarin crimson for a rich black, and define the tulip centres with a No. 4 brush.

Spring Bouquet

The artist chose to simplify the photograph to fit with a looser, interpretive style. By eliminating some of the detail, more movement is achieved in the painting.

PAINTS

Burnt sienna
Cadmium red light
Cadmium yellow
    light
Cobalt blue
Cobalt violet
Olive green
Permanent rose
Phthalo green
Ultramarine blue

TOOLS & MATERIALS

Cold-pressed paper,
    300gsm (140lb)
HB pencil
2.5cm (1in) flat
    brush
Mop brushes,
    Nos. 5 and 8
Round brush, No. 12
Small stiff-bristled
    brush
Natural sponge

TECHNIQUES USED

Flat wash, p. 20
Wet-into-wet, p. 22
Paint light to dark,
    p. 23
Lost and found
    edges, p. 24
Adding highlights,
    p. 27
Negative painting,
    p. 28

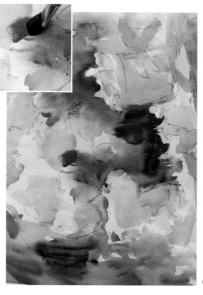

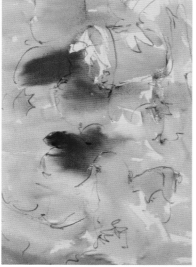

1 Begin with a very loose line drawing using an HB pencil to get the approximate placement of the major shapes. This sketch should take only a few minutes. It is not a blueprint but a guide.

2 Fully charge a 2.5cm (1in) flat brush with water and pigment. Painting wet-into-wet and light to dark, lay down the initial washes using permanent rose, cadmium red, cadmium yellow, cobalt blue, cobalt violet and olive green to represent the light pattern of the shapes. Even though the washes run together, the colour harmonies are established. Also, paint some of the mid-tones and darker values of the deep red flowers. Be careful not to overmix the colours at any point.

3 Block in the large shadow shapes of the flowers using the No. 8 mop and 2.5cm (1in) flat brush (inset). Begin to introduce some of the darker patterns seen in the lower centre. Having a dark pattern introduced early in the painting allows you to judge lights and mid-tones more easily. Introduce both soft and hard edges at this point. For darker colours, use mixtures of permanent rose, ultramarine blue, phthalo green and burnt sienna.

6 Add any final detail to the centre of interest with a No. 12 brush. Lift out a few highlights with a stiff-bristled brush and/or sponge.

4 Give the flowers definition by positive and negative painting. Begin adding detail within the flowers by breaking down the larger shapes into small ones, and using deeper values to bring out the detail and harder edges.

5 Using a No. 5 mop, reinforce the crispest edges in the centre of interest near the pot. Grey-out colours that need to be subordinated outside the area of dominance. Continue to break down the negative shapes into smaller pieces. Introduce calligraphic strokes to indicate leaves and stems.

Peruvian Lilies

The artist was compelled to retain the contrast between the actual flowers and the intense dark background. Keeping that sense of drama between the foreground and background meant careful realistic interpretation of the photograph.

PAINTS
Black
Crimson lake
Gamboge
Phthalo green
Quinacridone
    magenta
Raw umber
Sap green
Ultramarine blue
Venetian brown

TOOLS & MATERIALS
Cold-pressed paper,
    300gsm (140lb)
2B pencil
Masking fluid
Incredible Nib
Round brushes,
    Nos. 1, 4, 8
Old toothbrush
Craft knife

TECHNIQUES USED
Mixing paint in the
    palette, p. 21
Mixing paint on the
    paper, p. 21
Dropping in colour,
    p. 21
Wet-onto-dry, p. 22
Wet-into-wet, p. 22
Glazing, p. 23
Softening masked
    edges, p. 25
Blending, p. 27
Shadows, p. 28

1 Draw the picture with a 2B pencil. Apply masking fluid with an Incredible Nib to any small areas that remain white, such as the edges of the flower or any other highlights. In a palette, mix ultramarine blue, black and Venetian brown.

2 Apply the mix wet-onto-dry for the dark background, using a No. 8 round brush. After drying, repeat the wet-onto-dry background colour to achieve a rich, dark colour. Working quickly from side to side or top to bottom will create even colour, avoiding puddling. On the paper, mix Venetian brown, dropping in phthalo green and crimson lake for the bright reflection of the flower on the surface of the table.

3 Mix sap green and black, and paint the leaves in the darker green area wet-onto-dry, dropping in a mixture of gamboge and sap green to the brighter areas of the leaves and stem wet-into-wet. Soften the edges of the dark background by applying paint with a small brush and pulling the colour with a 'water only' brush. Add ultramarine blue to the background leaves in the shadowed areas. To achieve the table's texture, protect white areas and spatter with a toothbrush (inset).

6 Remove the masking. Detail the previously masked areas by using a No. 1 round brush for paint and a No. 4 round brush for water only. Soften any white areas by scraping carefully with a craft knife.

4 Using a No. 1 brush, paint the linear strokes on the inside of the petals using magenta mixed with a little black. Soften edges with a damp No. 4 brush. Keep the brush clean so that the colour does not spread. Begin painting gamboge onto the tips of the stamens (inset).

5 Using a No. 1 brush, intensify the magenta on the petal areas as needed and paint the stamens the same colour. Glaze a light yellow inside the flowers with a No. 4 brush and, once dry, follow with an ultramarine shadow colour. While this is still wet, touch in various reds and gamboge for reflected colour.

Clematis

The artist liked the soft and sharp areas of focus in the painting. They allowed for working wet-into-wet and blending techniques for the soft-focus areas, contrasting with the hard-edged linear details.

PAINTS

Cadmium yellow
Cobalt blue
Dioxazine violet
French ultramarine blue
Indian red
Quinacridone violet
Raw sienna
Ultramarine violet

TOOLS & MATERIALS

Cold-pressed paper, 300gsm (140lb)
HB pencil
Masking fluid
Old brush
Round brushes, Nos. 5 and 12
Flat brush, No. 10
Rigger

TECHNIQUES USED

Flat wash, p. 20
Mixing paint in the palette, p. 21
Dropping in colour, p. 21
Wet-onto-dry, p. 22
Wet-into-wet, p. 22
Glazing, p. 23
Lost and found edges, p. 24
Masking to reserve the paper, p. 25
Softening masked edges, p. 25
Shadows, p. 28
Negative painting, p. 28

1 Using an HB pencil on watercolour paper, lightly draw in the basic shapes of the flowers and stamens, then mask the stamen shapes with masking fluid and an old brush. Let dry. In the palette, mix cadmium yellow and cobalt blue to make a green. Wet the background foliage area with clean water. With a No. 12 brush, drop the green mixture into the wet areas. Add a touch of raw sienna for variety.

2 Next, still with the No. 12 brush, paint the petals using pale violet washes (inset). Let some areas bleed into the background where the focus is soft. Paint the soft-focus plant stems in Indian red into a just-damp background. Prepare two mixes in the palette using the two violets: Mix more of the quinacridone violet to make a warmer mix and more of the dioxazine violet for a cooler mix. Using a No. 5 brush, wet the petals with clean water.

3 Working on the clematis on the left, drop in the warmer mix to the central area and the cooler mix on the outer petal sides; let dry. Using ultramarine violet, loosely paint in the veins of this flower. It is soft-focus so this can be done on damp paper. Using a No. 10 flat brush, rub out the two ridges in the centre of each petal. Make a shadow mix of French ultramarine blue and raw sienna to paint the closed buds with successive pale, fading glazes to define form.

4 For the clematis on the right, using the warm violet mix with the No. 5 brush, paint the central area wet-onto-dry. Then, using a rigger, pull the veins out from the central areas. Drop some clear water onto the edge of some petals and let the vein colour bleed into it.

5 For extra detail, use the rigger and paint a criss-cross of clear water following the directions of the veins. Then drop ultramarine violet into the wet strands. Define the shadows and the central ridge areas on both flowers with soft blends of French ultramarine blue. Remove the masking from the stamens, and paint with a pale wash of cadmium yellow and the shadow mix from step 3.

6 Define the stems using the lost-and-found-edges technique with the shadow mix. Paint the veins on the leaves with the negative painting technique using the green mixture. Adjust dark tones with French ultramarine blue; work with soft edges in the soft-focus areas and with hard edges on the sharp-focus details.

Water Lily

The water here should be depicted strongly to make the image of the flower stand out, but requires that it be painted in one fluid effort to achieve a relatively even appearance.

PAINTS

Alizarin crimson
Indigo
New gamboge

TOOLS & MATERIALS

Cold-pressed paper, 300gsm (140lb)
Masking fluid
Old brush
Round brushes, Nos. 5 or 8 and 10 or 12

TECHNIQUES USED

Flat wash, p. 20
Variegated wash, p. 20
Mixing paint in the palette, p. 21
Dropping in colour, p. 21
Wet-into-wet, p. 22
Masking to reserve the paper, p. 25
Shadows, p. 28

1 Make a detailed drawing of the lily, pads and reflection (above), and apply masking fluid to the inside edge of the drawing where the image meets the water. Don't forget to mask the reflection. In a palette, mix a large puddle of rich indigo blue. Into the indigo, gradually add alizarin crimson to develop the warm hue of the water.

2 Lie the piece flat and, using a No. 10 or No. 12 round brush, apply the colour quickly as a flood to the entire water surface in one attempt, keeping it uniformly wet and even. Because these two pigments are sedimentary, they will not lend themselves well to a wash. Dry completely. Remove the masking fluid and reapply to those small areas of highlight and sparkle that you wish to preserve.

3 The shadow areas of the flower are created with a watered-down version of the same indigo/alizarin mix as the water, adding more indigo or alizarin, as you prefer. While the shadows are still wet, you can drop more indigo or alizarin into the wet and allow it to flow and bleed to add interest to the shadows. Using the same mixture with added alizarin, paint a wash over the reflection of the flower.

4 Still using indigo and alizarin in varying proportions, paint the shadows in the reflection (inset). Be mindful of the intensity and tone, a reflected image tends to be cooler and darker than the object reflected. Mix a small amount of new gamboge and, using the same brush, paint the pistils. Using the indigo/alizarin mixture, define the pistils by adding shadows. When dry, remove all the remaining masking fluid from the flower and reflection.

5 Mix a good quantity of new gamboge and indigo to create a rich green for the lily pads. Keeping the work flat, paint the pad surface quickly, leaving it evenly wet. Drop in extra indigo or new gamboge to add texture and variation. Remove the remaining masked highlights.

6 Using the original indigo/alizarin mix, add the shadows on the pads cast by the petals of the lily. When the shadows are still wet, drop in pure alizarin near the flower to warm the shadows with the reflected pink of the flower.

Bird of Paradise

The drama and colour of the bird of paradise almost demands that it is the centre of attention in the painting. The challenge was to integrate it with other elements in the background.

PAINTS

Alizarin crimson
Brilliant violet
Cadmium scarlet
Cadmium yellow
  light
Cobalt blue
French ultramarine
  blue
New gamboge
Permanent rose
Quinacridone gold
Rose madder
  genuine

TOOLS & MATERIALS

4-ply plate-finish
  Bristol board
6mm (¼in) plywood
Brown paper tape
Pencil
Staples
Round brush, No. 8
Filbert brush, No. 3

TECHNIQUES USED

Mixing paint in the
  palette, p. 21
Mixing paint on the
  paper, p. 21
Wet-into-wet, p. 22

1 Place the Bristol board on a 6mm (¼in) piece of plywood that has been sealed on both sides. Wet the edges of the board paper and plywood. Quickly apply 5cm (2in) brown tape around the edge of the paper and press to seal. Staple in a few places. Don't wet the full sheet of board to avoid stretching the paper. Let the tape dry before working. With a pencil, draw the image outline onto the board.

2 With a No. 8 brush, begin painting shapes in the farthest plane with mixtures of cadmium yellow light and French ultramarine blue, as well as brilliant violet and French ultramarine blue, working your way forwards. Put the darkest values in early so you can key other values to that. Colours will mix on the surface. Use a lot of paint in each shape for dark colours. Lift out excess paint to lighten areas and to avoid unwanted puddles.

3 Clean any rough edges of paint using a thin filbert brush to lift and blot any extra paint. Continue to paint the leaves in the background, using the same mixtures as in step 2. Think 'variety in unity' by keeping the negative space unified but varied in colour and value. Leave the partial flowers of the background to paint last, so that you can key them to the main flower to avoid having them too strong.

6 Plate-finish Bristol board produces a painting with energy and vibrant colour. The oranges, reds and purples are strong but the direction of the leaves, and the texture and touches of related colours, successfully pull the eye around the painting.

4 Use various reds and yellows in your palette to create the flower colour. The petals should be painted smoothly, contrasting with the texture of the leaves (inset). With this paper, it is hard to know how the paint will 'lay' when it dries. If you don't like it, you can rewet the area, blot it, or just mix up the colour inside the shape and brush it out again until you have something more pleasing.

5 Adjust values surrounding the main flower if needed to make it stand out. Next, paint the final flower segments in the background. Slightly grey the colours of those flowers so they won't overpower the main one, yet will still help to move the eye around the painting. Soften the edges of the most distant leaves and petals by using the tip of the wet brush. Colour can be added to small areas that are too light or open with the brush tip, as in pointillism.

Frangipani

The artist was drawn to the crisp-edged flowers and the value range from white to black. The challenge was to make a very dark background lively without distracting from the simple foreground flowers.

PAINTS

Antwerp blue
Aureolin
Brown madder
Cadmium orange
Cadmium yellow
Cobalt blue
French ultramarine
 blue
Neutral tint
Phthalo green
Quinacridone coral
Winsor yellow deep

TOOLS & MATERIALS

Cold-pressed paper,
 300gsm (140lb)
Mechanical pencil
Eraser
7.5cm (3in) wash
 brush
Round brushes,
 Nos. 3, 6, 10
Hair dryer
Tissues

TECHNIQUES USED

Variegated wash,
 p. 20
Mixing paint in the
 palette, p. 21
Dropping in colour,
 p. 21
Wet-onto-dry, p. 22
Wet-into-wet, p. 22
Glazing, p. 23
Blending, p. 24
Lost and found
 edges, p. 24
White of the paper,
 p. 26
Shadows, p. 28

1 Make a detailed drawing of the photograph. Keep your pencil lines fairly light around the flowers and in the centre. These will not be rubbed out after the paint is applied. They look darker here for demonstration purposes.

2 Wet some of the area of the upper background using the wash brush, leaving a few dry spots. With a No. 10 round brush, paint around the flowers and any leaves you have drawn in. Then drop in Winsor yellow deep, quinacridone coral, brown madder and cobalt blue. Let the paints spread. With a creamy mixture of phthalo green and neutral tint, paint wet-into-wet around the same area. This strong colour will bleed into the other colours. To stop the bleeding, dry with a hair dryer.

3 Move on to the leaves, using a variegated wash of the yellows and blues from your palette. Observe the many colours of green in the photograph. Some are more yellow, some are more blue, but all have a drop or two of red. Painting a coat of yellow first, then paint the blue or green mixture inside the leaf veins with a No. 6 or No. 3 brush (inset). The leaves can fade (wet-into-wet) in and out of the background dark.

6 Add reds, corals, blues and yellows to the background to create further depth. The finished painting shows the strong contrast between the dark background and the white and yellow flowers.

5 Mix a puddle of shadow colour using quinacridone coral, brown madder and Antwerp blue, so that it leans towards violet to set off the yellow flower colour. For all areas where the shadow is soft, wet the edge and let the colour blend into the wet. You will achieve a smoother shadow if the entire shadow area is damp. You may want to add a dot more brown madder to intensify the centre of the flower.

4 Moving through the cluster of flowers one by one and petal by petal, paint water at the top of the yellow area. Working inside the wet area and with a No. 6 round brush, paint aureolin, then cadmium yellow near the centre of the flower, and a dot of quinacridone coral at the centre (inset). When dry, add a dot of brown madder at the centre. With each layer of paint, work in ever-smaller circles into the centre of the flower. Paint around the curl in the petal unless indicated otherwise by the photograph.

Begonias

The artist was attracted to this image because of the variety of colour and interesting details in the flowers and leaves. It was decided that the light should come from upper right and that effect was kept throughout the painting.

PAINTS

Alizarin crimson
Cadmium lemon
Cadmium orange
Naples yellow
New gamboge
Permanent rose
Ultramarine blue
Viridian
Winsor green
Winsor violet

TOOLS & MATERIALS

Cold-pressed paper, 300gsm (140lb)
Transfer paper
Masking tape
Ballpoint pen
Round brushes, Nos. 3 and 5

TECHNIQUES USED

Mixing paint in the palette, p. 21
Dropping in colour, p. 21
Wet-onto-dry, p. 22
Wet-into-wet, p. 22
Paint light to dark, p. 23
Glazing, p. 23
Lost and found edges, p. 24
White of the paper, p. 26
Shadows, p. 28
Negative painting, p. 28

1 To trace the photograph onto the watercolour paper, place a sheet of transfer paper on top of the watercolour paper and lay the photograph on top of the transfer, taping them together at the top to prevent slipping. Using a ballpoint pen, trace over the shapes of the flowers and leaves (inset) to transfer the lines from the transfer paper onto the watercolour paper.

2 With a No. 5 round brush, paint the yellow, pink and orange flowers, letting each dry before painting the one beside it. Put darker and lighter colours beside each other and let them intermix wet-into-wet on petals that have variegated colour or shadows. Be careful to leave the white of the paper on the jagged edges of the flowers and on some turning edges by painting up to the edge. Permanent rose in combination with cadmium orange, Naples yellow, and alizarin crimson are good mixtures for these petals.

3 Next paint the greens and blues of the leaves. Glaze a layer of cadmium lemon on the leaves that have prominent yellow vein patterns. Dry. Work with negative painting to paint the shapes of the spaces between the veins, using blues and/or greens (inset). Paint less prominent leaves one at a time. Let colours mingle on some, and on others wait until the sheen has gone and then paint darker shapes or lines on top, which will have soft edges as the two colours merge. Experiment with hard and soft edges.

6 Finally, using a No. 3 round brush and a mixture of cadmium lemon, cadmium orange and permanent rose, paint the lines on the petals that indicate veins, ridges and shadows. To add a sunny highlight, use new gamboge for a few of the lines that would be in the sun.

5 Use viridian to glaze over the leaves with bright yellow veins to simplify and subdue them. Use a mixture of viridian and ultramarine blue to glaze shadows on the leaves, being careful to negative paint around the sharp edges of the leaves that are casting the shadow. With a damp brush, feather the edge of the shadow as it moves away from its source.

4 Paint the darks between the flowers and leaves, and glaze over leaves as needed to simplify and unify them. Mix dark variations of ultramarine blue, Winsor green and Winsor violet, and paint the dark shapes between the flowers and leaves. Vary the colours to make the darks more interesting and imply shapes in the shadows.

Lenten Rose

The artist was drawn to the way the light shines through the petals of the main flower. The upper half of the rose is warm from the light and the lower half is cool, in shadow.

PAINTS

Alizarin crimson
Bismuth yellow
Burnt sienna
Cobalt blue
French ultramarine blue
Manganese violet
Permanent rose
Quinacridone gold
Winsor blue (red shade)
Winsor green (blue shade)

TOOLS & MATERIALS

Rough paper, 300gsm (140lb)
H pencil
Masquepen
Round brushes, Nos. 4 and 12
Small stiff-bristled brush or scrubber

TECHNIQUES

Dropping in colour, p. 21
Wet-onto-dry, p. 22
Wet-into-wet, p. 22
Masking to reserve the paper, p. 25
Masking for details, p. 25
Softening masked edges, p. 25

1 Make a drawing using the pencil on watercolour paper; add interest by paying attention to the wonderful variety of shapes within the photograph. Place the main flower slightly above and to the right of centre. Don't forget to indicate the shadows showing through the petals of the centre rose. With a Masquepen, mask out the highlights, light on stems and edges, and lightest lights of the foreground shapes. Be precise (inset).

2 With the No. 4 brush, add bismuth yellow and quinacridone gold, and various blues and greens (cobalt blue, Winsor blue – red shade – French ultramarine blue, and Winsor green – blue shade) within the main flower. Put warm yellows on the top where sunlight shows through, and cool blues below, where it doesn't. Green should show at the centre. Edge the petals using purples and browns (burnt sienna, alizarin crimson, permanent rose and manganese violet).

3 Continue painting into the other flower and leaf shapes across the painting. Try not to make everything 'green' and the same value. Push some shapes towards yellow and others towards blues and purples. Keep in mind where the light is, and be aware of lighter and darker values. When dry, move on to the background.

6 Bismuth yellow, burnt sienna, manganese violet and permanent rose depict the light as well as keeping things from being too green. The placement of strong shadows in the petals of the lead flower makes it read as light showing through from behind.

5 Once the paint is dry, remove the mask. With a small, stiff-bristled brush or scrubber, soften some of the edges and paint into others (inset). Try to retain the light. Adjust your colour around the painting. To avoid the pitfall of 'isolated colour', use colours from the main flower in other areas of the painting. Your aim is unity – all of your elements should 'play' with one another.

4 Paint into the background with a No. 12 brush using darks. Winsor green, French ultramarine blue and alizarin crimson in various strengths and combinations will mix and separate into interesting textures and shapes. Load your brush with yellow to drop some leaf shapes here and there into the wet paint.

Lily of the Valley

The artist was drawn to the delicate flowers against the simple background. Unifying the white dots into larger shapes was the main challenge.

PAINTS

Aureolin
Cerulean blue
Dioxazine purple
Indigo
Peacock blue
Phthalo blue
Prussian blue
Quinacridone gold
Rich green-gold
Sap green
Viridian

TOOLS & MATERIALS

Cold-pressed paper,
300gsm (140lb)
HB pencil
Invisible tape
Masking fluid
Colour shaper,
size 0
Round brushes,
Nos. 2, 4, 5, 10
Kitchen towels

TECHNIQUES

Variegated wash,
p. 20
Mixing paint in the
palette, p. 21
Wet-onto-dry, p. 22
Wet-into-wet, p. 22
Lost and found
edges, p. 24
Masking to reserve
the paper, p. 25
Softening masked
edges, p. 25
White-on-white,
p. 27

1 Draw the image using a sharp pencil on watercolour paper, taking care not to press too hard to avoid indenting the paper. Tape off the edges of the painting to allow you to paint freely up to and over the edges. When the tape is removed, you will be left with crisp edges.

2 After drawing the image, mask the flowers and stems using masking fluid and a colour shaper. The white of the flowers is now protected.

3 Mix several yellow, blue, and green puddles of paint in your palette. With a No. 10 round brush, paint a variegated wash, keeping the foreground leaves lighter by using more aureolin, rich green-gold and sap green in the mixtures.

4 Some of the leaves are part of the background, so it is not necessary to call too much attention to them. Keep them soft-edged and let them fade. Paint the middle-ground leaves in more detail, using aureolin, rich green-gold and sap green. Reserve the dioxazine purple, indigo, and Prussian and phthalo blue for the background darks. When your painting is completely dry, remove the masking (inset).

5 Handle the flowers with a gentle touch, since they are small and delicate in nature. Shade the white flowers with various mixtures of cerulean blue, dioxazine purple and greens – but remember, they are white flowers.

6 Make any last touch-ups. When you assess the final image, if the flowers do not stand out, give the background a very dark green wet-into-wet wash by wetting only the areas to be painted and taking care not to get water on the white flowers. This helps to bring the flowers forwards.

Ipomoea

The artist liked the tangle of flowers and foliage. She used the negative painting method and worked from light to dark to define the leaf shapes and deep rich shadows; this also made the mauve flowers stand out from the background.

PAINTS

Aureolin
Cadmium yellow
Cerulean blue
Cobalt blue
Cobalt violet
French ultramarine blue
Indian red
Phthalo blue
Quinacridone pink
Raw sienna

TOOLS & MATERIALS

Cold-pressed paper, 300gsm (140lb)
HB pencil
Masking fluid
Old brush
Round brushes, Nos. 1, 5, 12
Tissues
2.5cm (1in) flat scrubber

TECHNIQUES

Variegated wash, p. 20
Mixing paint in the palette, p. 21
Dropping in colour, p. 21
Wet-onto-dry, p. 22
Wet-into-wet, p. 22
Paint light to dark, p. 23
Lost and found edges, p. 24
Masking for details, p. 25
Softening masked edges, p. 25
Adding highlights, p. 27
Negative painting, p. 28

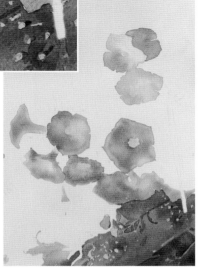

1 Lightly draw in the shapes of flowers on the watercolour paper in pencil. Mask the flower centres and the little white seeds with masking fluid and an old brush. Let dry. Wet the background area with clean water. With a No. 12 brush, paint a pale, variegated wash of aureolin. Leave the flower area white. In preparation for painting the flowers, mix two pale washes – one of cobalt violet and another of quinacridone pink.

2 When the background is dry, with a No. 5 brush randomly paint the flower mixes into the petal areas. Lift out paint with a tissue to make the soft white blends. Next mix a few different combinations of greens in the palette using blues and yellows. Using a No. 5 brush, paint the yellow-green mix for the seed-head foliage with Indian red and touches of cobalt blue around them (inset).

3 Use a No. 12 brush to add a variegated wash of cobalt and cerulean blue to the background. Drop in, wet-into-wet, some of the green mixes in your palette. Let dry. Draw the leaf shapes in pencil. Behind the leaves, paint negative dark shapes of the deep shadows with a variegated wash of phthalo blue, French ultramarine blue and Indian red. This will give you the positive shapes of the leaves.

4 Using the same colours, continue to paint the negative shapes, working into the background and painting successively darker washes. Paint hard edges to indicate the crisp fore edge of the leaves and allow the receding edges to blend into the background. Use the same technique to create the veins on the leaves.

5 Using the No. 5 brush, paint the petal shapes. Use cobalt violet for the main petals, leaving the star shapes. Let dry. Next paint the star shape with the quinacridone pink, allowing the edges of the two colours to overlap. With a flat scrubber, scrub out the highlight lines in the points of the star (inset). Remove the masking fluid.

6 Using a No. 1 brush, paint aureolin around the stamens in the centres of the flowers. Paint cobalt blue thin washes on the petals to describe the form. Tidy up the seed heads and their fine stems with body-colour mixes.

African Daisies

This is a complex image that offers challenges in replicating the details of the flower and the water droplets.

PAINTS

Burnt sienna
Burnt umber
French ultramarine blue
New gamboge
Sap green
Winsor violet

TOOLS & MATERIALS

Cold-pressed paper, 300gsm (140lb)
Mechanical pencil, 5 mm HB lead
Eraser
Round brushes, Nos. 5 and 8 and 10 or 12
Masking fluid
Old brush

TECHNIQUES USED

Mixing paint in the palette, *p. 21*
Dropping in colour, *p. 21*
Wet-into-wet, *p. 22*
Paint light to dark, *p. 23*
Lost and found edges, *p. 24*
Masking for details, *p. 25*

1 Make a detailed drawing of the flower to define the light and dark areas. Don't concern yourself with the background since it will be painted last.

2 Using a small, old round brush, apply masking fluid to each of the water droplets, keeping the edges as smooth as possible. Note that some of the droplets have refracted light spots outside the drop itself, and these must be masked as well. At this time you should also mask the yellow and white points in the flowers' compound centres. These will have more irregular edges.

3 Paint the shadows in the flower petals. Mix new gamboge on your palette with Winsor violet to create a fairly large puddle of a tertiary colour tending to the violet end. Identify the shadows and crease in the petals and, using a thin mix of this colour, paint the markings, petal by petal. If desired, you may soften the edges with a brush wetted with clear water.

4 Mix a strong puddle of burnt sienna and dab it into the centres of each of the flowers. While still wet, drop in strong French ultramarine blue (inset) and let it spread and flow in irregular patterns. Using the new gamboge and Winsor violet mixture, paint the shadows on the petals that are cast by the centres.

5 Using a rich mixture of new gamboge, draw the yellow from the tips of the petals towards the centre. Then, using a brush wetted with water, draw the yellow closer to the centre, allowing the colour to lighten and fade as you pass the middle of the petal. Remove the masking when dry. Using new gamboge, paint in the yellow stamens in the centres. Reapply masking fluid to the tiny points of light on a few of the water droplets.

6 With a bluish mixture of French ultramarine and burnt umber, paint a crescent and leave a spot of white on the lighter side of the droplet (inset). Apply sap green, French ultramarine blue, yellow and violet colours to the wet background, painting light to dark. Remove the masking fluid.

Poppies

The artist was drawn to the wonderful colour of the poppies, the quality of light created by the backlighting and the fuzzy haloes around the seedpods. Careful, precise masking controls the lights, and keeps the background paint layer fresh and colourful.

PAINTS
Azo green
Bismuth yellow
Cerulean blue
Cobalt blue
Permanent alizarin
  crimson
Prussian blue
Pyrrole red
Sap green
Ultramarine blue
Yellow ochre

TOOLS & MATERIALS
Cold-pressed paper,
  300gsm (140lb)
HB pencil
Masquepen
Round brushes,
  Nos. 4, 8,12
Spray bottle
Fritch scrubber,
  No. 4

TECHNIQUES USED
Variegated wash,
  p. 20
Mixing paint in the
  palette, p. 21
Dropping in colour,
  p. 21
Wet-onto-dry, p. 22
Wet-into-wet, p. 22
Masking for details,
  p. 25
Softening masked
  edges, p. 25
Adding highlights,
  p. 27

1 Begin with a rough drawing in HB pencil. A pattern of light as well as the major shapes of the poppies and grasses must be given consideration in the design. The drawing needs to portray a natural rhythm as the shapes dance across the paper.

2 The Masquepen (inset) is extremely precise and simple to use. Its blue colour is also easy to see against the white of the paper. Mask the shapes of light on the flowers and the shapes of the grasses, stems, and the 'fuzzies' on the pods and stalks.

3 With a No. 8 round brush, begin to paint the brilliant red of the poppies (inset). The backlight in each flower is already masked. Use pyrrole red, permanent alizarin crimson and touches of bismuth yellow to create variety within each shape. Use ultramarine blue and alizarin to create the darks.

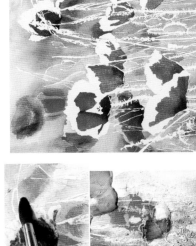

4 Once all is dry, apply more masking over the red flower shapes so that you are able to freely paint 'behind' the flowers (inset). When the mask is dry, create a variegated wash by wetting the entire sheet of paper with a spray bottle and, with a No. 12 brush, drop in areas of yellow ochre, pyrrole red, bismuth yellow and cerulean blue.

5 After the first background wash has totally dried, go over it once again, re-wetting the paper with the spray bottle and reinforcing the colour pattern using the No. 12 brush with yellows, oranges, blues and greens. When dry, remove the masking and begin painting into the shapes with a No. 4 round brush.

6 Continue refining the shapes using a No. 4 sable brush. Use a No. 4 Fritch scrubber to soften the edges and lift lights where needed. Add colour and value to the poppies with the two reds. Finally, paint the stems and buds using cobalt blue, Prussian blue, sap green and azo green.

Bachelor's Buttons

The cobalt blue summer-sky-coloured bachelor's buttons peep out from the rich textured grasses. The challenge here is to describe the grass shapes in the background without letting them overpower the delicate frilly petals of the flowers.

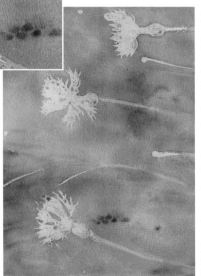

PAINTS

Aureolin
Burnt sienna
Cadmium yellow
Cerulean blue
Cobalt blue
Indian red
Indigo
Quinacridone pink
Yellow ochre
Zinc white
designers' gouache

MATERIALS

Cold-pressed paper, 300gsm (140lb)
HB pencil
Masking fluid
Old brush
Round brushes, Nos. 1, 5, 12
Masking tape
Rigger, No. 0

TECHNIQUES

Variegated wash, p. 20
Mixing paint in the palette, p. 21
Dropping in colour, p. 21
Wet-onto-dry, p. 22
Wet-into-wet, p. 22
Masking to reserve the paper, p. 25
Watercolour and gouache, p. 32

---

1 Using an HB pencil, lightly sketch positions and shapes onto the watercolour paper. Use the masking fluid and an old brush to mask flowers, hairs and highlights on the stems. Let dry. Wet the whole area with clean water. With a No. 12 brush, randomly apply a wash of aureolin. Let dry and then wash in a pale variegated wash of cerulean blue and cobalt blue, allowing the paint to create backruns and lively textures. Let dry.

2 Wet the surface again with clean water. Use a No. 5 brush to paint pale washes of cerulean blue, indigo, Indian red and burnt sienna. Drop in wet-into-wet blots and marks to represent the grass seed heads and background shapes (inset). Avoid painting the stems, which will now start to emerge from the background.

3 Continue to paint the background shapes, using stronger, darker mixes of the different blues and yellows. Paint the more defined shapes with crisp grass-blade edges. Wash in deeper shadow areas using indigo. Let the paint granulate for texture. Lay washes of yellow ochre over the grass area to soften into the background as required.

4 To paint foreground grasses, mix a body colour of zinc white designers' gouache with yellow ochre. Lay masking tape along the bottom edge of the painting and turn through 90 degrees. Using the rigger, support your wrist and make sweeping strokes from right to left – lift the rigger at the top end of the stroke to mimic the tip of the grass (inset). When dry, add Indian red to the tip. Remove the masking tape and fluid. With the No. 5 brush, start to paint the buds with quinacridone pink.

5 Using the No. 5 brush, paint the petal shapes in successive layers of cobalt blue, letting the paint dry between each. Paint the round base shape of the flower with mixes of pink and cobalt blue. Paint the bracts with a yellow-green mix.

6 With a No. 1 brush, paint the filaments with indigo. Drop white gouache on the tip for the anthers. On the bracts, leave touches of the green from step 5. Paint the detail with mixes of pink and indigo.

Fritillaria

The pink and magenta colours of the nodding flowers are beautifully complemented by vibrant green hues. Soft-focus leaves and grasses in the background give a strong sense of depth.

PAINTS

Hansa yellow medium
Hooker's green
Phthalo blue
Purple magenta
Quinacridone red

TOOLS & MATERIALS

Cold-pressed paper, 300gsm (140lb)
HB pencil
Masking fluid
Old brush
Round brushes, Nos. 4, 6, 8, 10
1.2cm (½in) angled shader
Scrubber

TECHNIQUES

Graded wash, p. 20
Variegated wash, p. 20
Mixing paint in the palette, p. 21
Wet-onto-dry, p. 22
Wet-into-wet, p. 22
Glazing, p. 23
Blending, p. 24
Masking to reserve the paper, p. 25
Softening masked edges, p. 25
Shadows, p. 28
Negative painting, p. 28

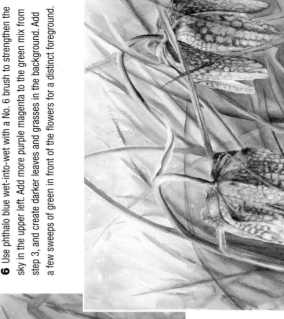

1 Draw the flower in detail in pencil onto the watercolour paper. Next, apply a thin line of masking fluid along the outside edges of all the petals and stems, and a few leaves. Let dry completely before applying paint.

2 To begin the background, apply Hansa yellow medium wet-into-wet with a No. 10 brush. Create random, overlapping stems, leaves and blades of grass. Define a few leaves and stems with a very thin glaze of Hooker's green applied to slightly damp paper with a No. 8 brush.

3 Wet sections of the background and drop in a mix of Hooker's green toned down with a touch of purple magenta. When the sheen has disappeared, lift out overlapping leaf and stem patterns with a damp shader. Create darker leaves and stems with the green mix.

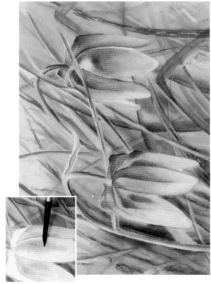

4 Working wet-into-wet, apply Hansa yellow medium, purple magenta and quinacridone red to the flowers in separate graded washes with a No. 6 brush (inset). Allow the paper to dry thoroughly between glazes. Create flower stems with variegated washes of purple magenta, quinacridone red and phthalo blue. Remove the masking and soften the edges.

5 Wet each petal individually. When the sheen has disappeared, lightly paint the checkered patterns with purple magenta, quinacridone red and phthalo blue with a No. 4 brush. When dry, build up rich colour in the shadowed areas with several wet-into-wet glazes. Soften hard edges with a damp scrubber.

6 Use phthalo blue wet-into-wet with a No. 6 brush to strengthen the sky in the upper left. Add more purple magenta to the green mix from step 3, and create darker leaves and grasses in the background. Add a few sweeps of green in front of the flowers for a distinct foreground.

In Detail

In this section, you can view some of the preceding paintings at a larger size, enabling you to examine in detail the effect of the techniques the artists decided to use and how they contributed to the overall exuberance of the finished piece. Smaller images zoom in to the most intriguing parts of the painting, with a professional appraisal of the artist's use of colour, light and technique.

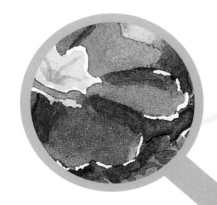

Blue Poppies
Katrina Small (see p. 100)

Katrina achieved this sunny painting of Himalayan blue poppies by using both traditional and non-traditional transparent watercolour techniques. The technique of dropping large blobs of pure colour into a wet, variegated wash created the perfect background against which to show the delicate leaf and stem details, painted in white gouache.

IN DETAIL To make the best possible use of the technique of dropping colour into a wet wash, the balance of paint to water had to be just right. The dropped-in colour had to have a higher ratio of pigment to water than the colour already on the paper, or accidental blooms would have been the result. Katrina showed complete control over this tricky technique.

The viscous nature of most masking fluid can make it difficult to achieve a very fine line, not to mention many fine lines. Also, in the process of painting the complex and very wet background, white could have been lost. In this painting, the artist used a delicate application of white gouache to solve these two problems. The result is a painting in which the fine detail glows against an intense background.

Primroses

Tom Love (see p. 68)

In Tom's tactile painting of primroses, in which there is little doubt the
pots are hard or that the petals are soft, two watercolour techniques serve
to completely support the main focus – the flowers – and emphasize their
softness by convincing the viewer that the pots and buckets are hard. These
two techniques were wet-into-wet painting and blending.

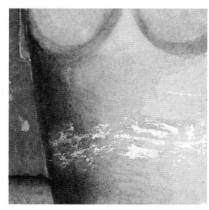

IN DETAIL To paint wet-into-wet, the artist
must apply paint to a surface that is already wet.
To paint convincing, reflective imagery of pail
handles, board slats and flowers onto that wet
surface, the artist here had to have absolute
control over a process, which, by design, is not
controllable. And he had to understand the exact
moment to apply the paint so that it didn't run
uncontrollably.

Blending is pulling wet colour with a damp
brush from an area where it is darker or more
intense to an area where it is less intense,
creating a seamless transition and a sense of
roundness. It is necessary to have the paper wet
at the light end of the pull so the colour fades
into the water.

Heliconia
Connie J. Adams (see p. 78)

Connie's heliconia is an example of two major techniques used together to produce a dramatic effect. Variegated washes – usually used for the background – were here used within the flower petals. In conjunction with this, lifting sharp highlights from some of the petals created areas of focus, since the edges are lost against the light.

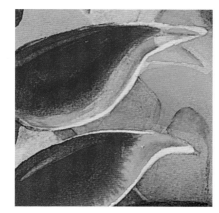

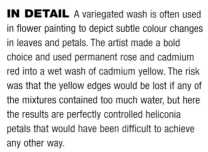

IN DETAIL A variegated wash is often used in flower painting to depict subtle colour changes in leaves and petals. The artist made a bold choice and used permanent rose and cadmium red into a wet wash of cadmium yellow. The risk was that the yellow edges would be lost if any of the mixtures contained too much water, but here the results are perfectly controlled heliconia petals that would have been difficult to achieve any other way.

Lifting colour is a technique that can be done in several ways. In this case, the artist chose to mask the area to be lifted with masking tape so that when the colour was lifted (by rubbing with a soft sponge or tissue) the result was a hard-edged 'shine' on the heliconia petal.

Love in the Mist

Carol Carter (see p. 112)

Carol chose to use two techniques that fit together perfectly – painting wet-into-wet and masking. Covering a paper with flowing water and paint is useful only if the detail to be dealt with at a later stage is protected from the paint. Masking has thus become the tool many artists choose to enable the use of one of watercolour's most cherished techniques.

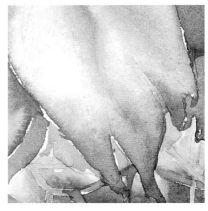

IN DETAIL Painting wet-into-wet can involve the whole sheet of paper or just a small area. In this case, the artist chose to paint one petal at a time using the technique. By wetting the entire petal first, she was able to flow in the subtle, shifting shades of a soft and curving petal; also outlining it at the end to set it apart from the other petals. In this petal you can see how four separate blues flow together seamlessly.

When the rest of the painting was finished, the artist removed the masking and, again, used a wet-into-wet technique to give subtle light and colour shifts to the stamens and spines. Using this technique also enabled her to reuse some of the blues from the flower and the greens from the background.

Bluebells
Heather Maunders (see p. 76)

In this beautiful woodland scene, Heather demonstrates the importance of the techniques working together to achieve a unified painting. The two techniques used here achieve the illusion of great depth on a flat surface. The viewer perceives some of these objects as being very close and others as being far away.

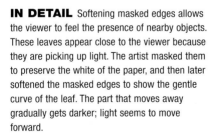

IN DETAIL Softening masked edges allows the viewer to feel the presence of nearby objects. These leaves appear close to the viewer because they are picking up light. The artist masked them to preserve the white of the paper, and then later softened the masked edges to show the gentle curve of the leaf. The part that moves away gradually gets darker; light seems to move forward.

In this intimate scene, the near and the distant are only inches apart on the paper. By employing the technique of charging colour into deep, glowing darks, the artist has given the impression that the viewer could reach into the space. Deep, barely discernible shapes and colour shifts are perceptible. Into the wet deep green, she charged aureolin, cobalt blue and ultramarine blue, making the space even deeper and darker.

Poppies
Donna Jill Witty (see p. 140)

Crucial to the representation of light in watercolour is the protection of the white of the paper from washes. However, broad juicy washes are also fundamental to watercolour. To accomplish both of these in a single painting, Donna used two signature techniques – the precise masking of areas to remain white and an underpainting of saturated, wet washes.

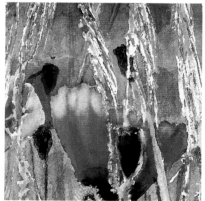

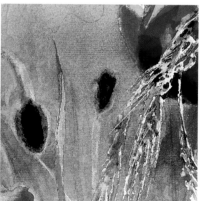

IN DETAIL Masking small and detailed areas in this painting necessitated the use of a special tool – a masking pen. Application of the masking required great patience and thorough drying. This was also the technique that allowed the other critical step to happen easily.

With all the whites protected, the artist freely applied large, juicy washes all over the paper using several colours. The more intense reds of the poppies were also painted at this stage. The pigments were allowed to mix, mingle and granulate. A unifying underpainting was the result. When the masking was removed, the painting was nearly done.

Calla Lilies

Robin Berry (see p. 62)

Robin chose two complementary techniques to add both glow and dimension to this painting of calla lilies. The use of several layers of transparent washes allowed the colour to build whilst retaining the luminosity of the flower. This set the flower off from the deep background of equally luminous, glowing dark.

IN DETAIL There are no less than six layers of paint in these flowers, built up light to dark and allowed to dry thoroughly between each layer. It is not always necessary to glaze the whole flower. Shadows showing the rounding of the form or shading by another object can be laid down in certain areas using a different colour – in this case, blue.

Had this flower – with its sunlit white edge – been set against a light colour, it would not have stood out. And had the background been painted with black paint, it would have been dull and chalky. A glowing dark, like this one, is composed of several transparent colours – in this case, red and deep green, laid down in a single passage, with other colours, such as a deep blue, dropped in. The paper glows through this transparent single layer of dark paint.

Protea
Nancy Taylor (see p. 110)

This was a difficult flower to paint because the photo presented a strong red presence (the closed protea) with a ball of white (the open flower). The issue is balance, since the two flowers lean away from each other. The techniques of dropping in colour, especially during the first underpainting, and lifting colour at the end helped to create an exciting, balanced painting.

IN DETAIL Underlying the ring of red petals surrounding the white flower is an underpainting of scarlet orange that was dropped in with a wide brush when the paper was first wet, and before any detail was added. Although you cannot see it in the finished painting, your eyes can feel its overall unifying power.

A factor in the beautiful balance achieved in Protea was the subtle lifting of red from the tip of each of the petals in the left flower, continuing around the open flower. Although you probably don't notice this as you look at the painting, your eye subconsciously picks it up and this also contributes to the unifying effect.

Parrot Tulips
Lisa Hill (see p.116)

In Lisa's painting, the two techniques that contributed most to the startling beauty of dancing reds across the painting are glazing and the use of rich shadows. The use of glazing unified the painting, while the incorporation of rich shadows both balanced the strong reds (by the use of complementary green) and anchored the vase in space.

IN DETAIL Glazing is the application of thin layers of colour to build up a more intense hue, while still remaining transparent. Each layer affects the one above it. Making sure the paint is completely dry between layers is essential. In Parrot Tulips, the luscious reds you see in the flowers are a result of glazing. Trying to achieve this in a single passage could have resulted in a chalky appearance, while glazing left the colours soft, translucent and intense.

The tulips are bathed in light and seem about to take flight. The rich shadows at the base of the vase are what give clarity and definition to the light. The choice of the colour green was important here, since it is not only the complementary of red – and so sets off the flowers – but provides a dark value in contrast to the white of the paper (the light) of the vase.

Ranunculus
Jana Bouc (see p. 64)

To create this beautiful burst of colour and bring to life a complex photograph, Jana used several techniques. Painting wet-into-wet retained the softness of the flowers and leaves, which contrast with strong colours and defining edges. The vase illustrates the use of reflected colour both to connect it to the flowers and to show the shiny nature of the surface.

IN DETAIL Wet-into-wet painting is accomplished by first wetting the paper then touching a paint-laden brush to the surface, letting the colour blend softly with the paper or other colours. This technique can be used throughout a painting to give it the cherished juicy look watercolourists love.

Wet-into-wet was also used in the vase to show the reflected colour. Here the vase was wetted and painted blue, and the colours of the leaves and flowers touched into the surface.

Peruvian Lilies
Denny Bond (see p. 120)

This painting works so well due to Denny's accuracy in replicating the petals of the flowers, both in colour and in softness. This was accomplished by glazing, which allows both the colours and the shadows to be applied in a most natural way. To make the liner strokes inside of the flower appear natural, the artist used the technique of blending.

IN DETAIL Glazing is accomplished by applying thin layers of paint over one another, letting the paint dry between applications. The end effect is transparent and allows the white of the paper to reflect light.

To blend the stripes inside the flower, a damp brush was carefully drawn over each stripe, with great care taken not to smear the paint. Blending softens edges and here embedded the stripe deeper into the paper, creating an attractive depth.

About the Artists

Connie J. Adams

www.conniejadams.com

Heliconia **79**

A resident of and teacher in Maui in the Hawaiian Islands, Connie Adams has always been fascinated by the exotic botanical image – a fascination that led her to travel the Caribbean, Bali and Costa Rica. In 2001 she graduated from the Maryland Institute, College of Art, with an MFA in Painting. Connie has won numerous awards.

Robin Berry

Foxglove **39**
Sunflowers **47**
Sunny Bouquet **57**
Calla Lilies **63**
Tulips **71**
Columbines **81**
Hollyhocks **85**
Blue Thistles **95**
Magnolia Blossoms **103**
Peonies **109**
Frangipani **129**

Author Robin Berry has been a professional artist for 35 years. After 20 years as a nationally recognized porcelain artist, Robin changed direction to painting, focusing exclusively on transparent watercolour. Today, her flower paintings regularly win awards in national shows. Robin lives and works in Minneapolis, Minnesota.

Denny Bond

Amaryllis **55**
Tiger Lilies **73**
Peruvian Lilies **121**

Denny Bond is an award-winning watercolourist and illustrator residing in East Petersburg, Pennsylvania. Using permanent liquid watercolours, Denny combines several elements in a painting to define the composition. His subject matter ranges from figurative to landscape and nature.

Jana Bouc

Orchids **41**
Ranunculus **65**
Begonias **131**

For over 25 years, Jana Bouc has used watercolour as her primary medium. Flowers are a favourite subject of hers, along with people, still lifes, animals and landscapes. She carries her sketchbook and watercolours everywhere, and can often be found sketching and painting around the San Francisco Bay Area or in her home studio where she teaches watercolour.

Carol Carter

www.carol-carter.com

Crown Imperial **87**
Love in the Mist **113**

Carol Carter received her MFA from Washington University, St Louis. She was voted Best St Louis Artist by The Riverfront Times in 2000. The US Embassy sponsored a solo exhibition of Carol's work at the Teatro del Centro de Arte, in Guayaquil, Ecuador in 2003, and she is the Artist-in-Residence for the Everglades National Park.

Moira Clinch

Clematis **123**
Ipomoea **137**
Bachelor's Buttons **143**

Moira Clinch trained at Central Saint Martins School of Art in London and has exhibited at the Royal Academy's Summer Exhibition in London. She is author of *The Watercolour Artist's Pocket Palette*.

Jan Hart

www.janhart.com

Passion Flowers **93**

Jan Hart, a watercolour artist with a background in science and architecture, has been painting and teaching for over 30 years. Now living in Costa Rica, she is author of *The Watercolour Artist's Guide to Exceptional Colour*, and her passion is colour and light in all she sees and paints.

Lisa Hill

www.lisahillwatercolourist.com

Indian Reed Lily **37**
Pansies **61**
Rhododendron **97**
Cyclamen **107**
Parrot Tulips **117**
Fritillaria **145**

Lisa Hill lives in Richland, Washington. The only medium she has worked with is watercolour, which she has been studying for four years. Realistic depictions of flowers and foliage are her preferred subjects, and she has a growing portfolio of bird, animal and butterfly paintings.

Tom Love

www.artincanada.com/thomaslove

Mallows **45**
Primroses **69**
Gerbera Daisy **115**
Water Lily **125**
African Daisies **139**

Tom Love lives in Western Canada and paints, exclusively in watercolour, a broad spectrum of subject matter, primarily the human form. His paintings hang in collections across Canada and in the United States, Europe and Australia. Tom is a senior member and past president of the Society of Western Canadian Artists in Edmonton.

Heather Maunders

Honeysuckle **53**
Bluebells **77**

After a career in scientific research, Heather Maunders now paints full time from her studio in Cambridgeshire, UK. Her preferred medium is watercolour, with its inspiring versatility in allowing the delicate transparency and bold layers of colour necessary to paint flowers.

Katrina Small

Fuchsia **75**
Blue Poppies **101**
Lily of the Valley **135**

Katirna Small is a fine art instructor and demonstrator, as well as a web and graphic designer. She enjoys working in watercolour, losing herself in moving pigment in water, saturating, blending and glazing. She also paints in pastel, oil and acrylic.

Nancy Meadows Taylor

www.nancymeadowstaylor.com

Rose **43**
Crocuses **49**
Snowdrops **83**
Protea **111**
Bird of Paradise **127**

Nancy Taylor studied interior design in college, developing skills she has used in 30 years of painting with watercolour and recently oil. She has memberships in the American Watercolour Society, the National Watercolour Society and the Rocky Mountain National Watermedia Society. She paints images from nature and has a studio in Raleigh, North Carolina.

Naomi Tydeman

Iris **88**

Naomi Tydeman runs her own gallery and studio in Tenby, Wales, where she produces delicate and realistic watercolour paintings. Self-taught, she is a member of the Royal Institute of Painters in Watercolour and the Welsh Watercolour Society.

Karen Vernon

www.karenvernon.com

Hyacinths **59**

Karen Vernon's paintings hang in museum and corporate collections in Europe, the United States and throughout the rest of the world. She is the founder of ACT (Artists Changing Tomorrow), and is one of only three watercolourists whose works were chosen to tour as part of the national museum exhibition, Sea to Shining Sea.

Eric Wiegardt

Spring Bouquet **119**

Eric Wiegardt has been painting for 25 years, displaying his watercolours at Wiegardt Studio Gallery in Ocean Park, Washington. He is an award-winning watercolourist, author and juror. Eric has influenced countless artists – who have attended his workshops throughout the United States and Europe – with his loose painting style.

Donna Jill Witty

Chrysanthemums **51**
Peonies and Poppies **67**
Hibiscus **91**
Snapdragon **99**
Lilies of the Nile **105**
Lenten Rose **133**
Poppies **140**

A professional artist for over 30 years, Donna Jill Witty holds signature status in the American Watercolour Society, National Watercolour Society and Transparent Watercolour Society of America. Her subject matter ranges from landscapes and street scenes, to still life and figures. She runs a studio in Woodstock, Illinois.

Index

Credits

Quarto would like to thank the following agencies for supplying images for inclusion in this book:

Photolibrary: p. 36, 38, 40, 42, 46, 52, 56, 58, 60, 64, 66, 68, 70, 72, 76, 84, 86, 92, 98, 101, 110, 112, 118, 122, 124, 126, 130, 132, 136, 138, 140, 142

Getty Images: p. 50, 88, 90, 116

Clive Nichols: p. 54, 94

All step-by-step and other images are the copyright of Quarto Publishing plc. Whilst every effort has been made to credit contributors, Quarto would like to apologize should there have been any omissions or errors, and would be pleased to make the appropriate correction for future editions of the book.